Poetry
for Students

Poetry for *Students*

Presenting Analysis, Context and Criticism on Commonly Studied Poetry

Volume 6

Mary K. Ruby, Editor

Foreword by David Kelly, College of Lake County

GALE GROUP

Detroit
San Francisco
London
Boston
Woodbridge, CT

Poetry for Students

Staff

Series Editor: Mary Ruby.

Contributing Editor: Lynn Koch.

Managing Editor: Drew Kalasky.

Research: Victoria B. Cariappa, *Research Team Manager.* Andy Malonis, *Research Specialist.* Tamara C. Nott, Tracie A. Richardson, and Cheryl L. Warnock, *Research Associates.*

Permissions: Maria Franklin, *Permissions Manager.* Kimberly F. Smilay, *Permissions Specialist.*

Production: Mary Beth Trimper, *Production Director.* Evi Seoud, *Assistant Production Manager.* Cindy Range, *Production Assistant.*

Graphic Services: Randy Bassett, *Image Database Supervisor.* Robert Duncan and Michael Logusz, *Imaging Specialists.* Pamela A. Reed, *Photography Coordinator.* Gary Leach, *Macintosh Artist.*

Product Design: Cynthia Baldwin, *Product Design Manager.* Cover Design: Michelle DiMercurio, *Art Director.* Page Design: Pamela A. E. Galbreath, *Senior Art Director.*

Copyright Notice

ISBN 0-7876-3567-7
ISSN 1094-7019
Printed in the United States of America.

10 9 8 7 6 5 4 3 2 1

National Advisory Board

Table of Contents

Just a Few Lines on a Page

I have often thought that poets have the easiest job in the world. A poem, after all, is just a few lines on a page, usually not even extending margin to margin—how long would that take to write, about five minutes? Maybe ten at the most, if you wanted it to rhyme or have a repeating meter. Why, I could start in the morning and produce a book of poetry by dinnertime. But we all know that it isn't that easy. Anyone can come up with enough words, but the poet's job is about writing the *right* ones. The right words will change lives, making people see the world somewhat differently than they saw it just a few minutes earlier. The right words can make a reader who relies on the dictionary for meanings take a greater responsibility for his or her own personal understanding. A poem that is put on the page correctly can bear any amount of analysis, probing, defining, explaining, and interrogating, and something about it will still feel new the next time you read it.

It would be fine with me if I could talk about poetry without using the word "magical," because that word is overused these days to imply "a really good time," often with a certain sweetness about it, and a lot of poetry is neither of these. But if you stop and think about magic—whether it brings to mind sorcery, witchcraft, or bunnies pulled from top hats—it always seems to involve stretching reality to produce a result greater than the sum of its parts and pulling unexpected results out of thin air. This book provides ample cases where a few simple words conjure up whole worlds. We do not ac-

tually travel to different times and different cultures, but the poems get into our minds, they find what little we know about the places they are talking about, and then they make that little bit blossom into a bouquet of someone else's life. Poets make us think we are following simple, specific events, but then they leave ideas in our heads that cannot be found on the printed page. Abracadabra.

Sometimes when you finish a poem it doesn't feel as if it has left any supernatural effect on you, like it did not have any more to say beyond the actual words that it used. This happens to everybody, but most often to inexperienced readers: regardless of what is often said about young people's infinite capacity to be amazed, you have to understand what usually does happen, and what could have happened instead, if you are going to be moved by what someone has accomplished. In those cases in which you finish a poem with a "So what?" attitude, the information provided in *Poetry for Students* comes in handy. Readers can feel assured that the poems included here actually are potent magic, not just because a few (or a hundred or ten thousand) professors of literature say they are: they're significant because they can withstand close inspection and still amaze the very same people who have just finished taking them apart and seeing how they work. Turn them inside out, and they will still be able to come alive, again and again. *Poetry for Students* gives readers of any age good practice in feeling the ways poems relate to both the reality of the time and place the poet lived in and the reality of our emotions. Practice is just another word for being a student. The information given here helps you understand the way to read poetry; what to look for, what to expect.

With all of this in mind, I really don't think I would actually like to have a poet's job at all. There are too many skills involved, including precision, honesty, taste, courage, linguistics, passion, compassion, and the ability to keep all sorts of people entertained at once. And that is just what they do with one hand, while the other hand pulls some sort of trick that most of us will never fully understand. I can't even pack all that I need for a weekend into one suitcase, so what would be my chances of stuffing so much life into a few lines? With all that *Poetry for Students* tells us about each poem, I am impressed that any poet can finish three or four poems a year. Read the inside stories of these poems, and you won't be able to approach any poem in the same way you did before.

David J. Kelly
College of Lake County

Introduction

Purpose of the Book

The purpose of *Poetry for Students* (*PfS*) is to provide readers with a guide to understanding, enjoying, and studying poems by giving them easy access to information about the work. Part of Gale's "For Students" Literature line, *PfS* is specifically designed to meet the curricular needs of high school and undergraduate college students and their teachers, as well as the interests of general readers and researchers considering specific poems. While each volume contains entries on "classic" poems frequently studied in classrooms, there are also entries containing hard-to-find information on contemporary poems, including works by multicultural, international, and women poets.

The information covered in each entry includes an introduction to the poem and the poem's author; the actual poem text; a poem summary, to help readers unravel and understand the meaning of the poem; analysis of important themes in the poem; and an explanation of important literary techniques and movements as they are demonstrated in the poem.

In addition to this material, which helps the readers analyze the poem itself, students are also provided with important information on the literary and historical background informing each work. This includes a historical context essay, a box comparing the time or place the poem was written to modern Western culture, a critical overview essay, and excerpts from critical essays on the poem, when available. A unique feature of *PfS* is a specially commissioned overview essay on each poem by an academic expert, targeted toward the student reader.

To further aid the student in studying and enjoying each poem, information on media adaptations is provided when available, as well as reading suggestions for works of fiction and nonfiction on similar themes and topics. Classroom aids include ideas for research papers and lists of critical sources that provide additional material on the poem.

Selection Criteria

The titles for each volume of *PfS* were selected by surveying numerous sources on teaching literature and analyzing course curricula for various school districts. Some of the sources surveyed included: literature anthologies; *Reading Lists for College-Bound Students: The Books Most Recommended by America's Top Colleges;* textbooks on teaching the poem; a College Board survey of poems commonly studied in high schools; and a National Council of Teachers of English (NCTE) survey of poems commonly studied in high schools.

Input was also solicited from our expert advisory board, as well as educators from various areas. From these discussions, it was determined that each volume should have a mix of "classic" poems (those works commonly taught in literature classes) and contemporary poems for which information is often hard to find. Because of the interest in expanding the canon of literature, an emphasis was also placed on including works by international, multicultural, and women authors. Our advisory board members—current high school and college teachers—helped pare down the list for each volume. If a work was not selected for the present volume, it was often noted as a possibility for a future volume. As always, the editor welcomes suggestions for titles to be included in future volumes.

How Each Entry Is Organized

Each entry, or chapter, in *PfS* focuses on one poem. Each entry heading lists the full name of the poem, the author's name, and the date of the poem's publication. The following elements are contained in each entry:

- **Introduction:** a brief overview of the poem which provides information about its first appearance, its literary standing, any controversies surrounding the work, and major conflicts or themes within the work.

- **Author Biography:** this section includes basic facts about the poet's life, and focuses on events and times in the author's life that inspired the poem in question.

- **Poem Text:** when permission has been granted, the poem is reprinted, allowing for quick reference when reading the explication of the following section.

- **Poem Summary:** a description of the major events in the poem, with interpretation of how these events help articulate the poem's themes. Summaries are broken down with subheads that indicate the lines being discussed.

- **Themes:** a thorough overview of how the major topics, themes, and issues are addressed within the poem. Each theme discussed appears in a separate subhead and is easily accessed through the boldface entries in the Subject/ Theme Index.

- **Style:** this section addresses important style elements of the poem, such as form, meter, and rhyme scheme; important literary devices used, such as imagery, foreshadowing, and symbolism; and, if applicable, genres to which the work might have belonged, such as Gothicism or Romanticism. Literary terms are explained within the entry, but can also be found in the Glossary.

- **Historical and Cultural Context:** This section outlines the social, political, and cultural climate *in which the author lived and the poem was created.* This section may include descriptions of related historical events, pertinent aspects of daily life in the culture, and the artistic and literary sensibilities of the time in which the work was written. If the poem is a historical work, information regarding the time in which the poem is set is also included. Each section is broken down with helpful subheads. (Works written after the late 1970s may not have this section.)

- **Critical Overview:** this section provides background on the critical reputation of the poem, including bannings or any other public controversies surrounding the work. For older works, this section includes a history of how poem was first received and how perceptions of it may have changed over the years; for more recent poems, direct quotes from early reviews may also be included.

- **Sources:** an alphabetical list of critical material quoted in the entry, with full bibliographical information.

- **For Further Study:** an alphabetical list of other critical sources which may prove useful for the student. Includes full bibliographical information and a brief annotation.

- **Criticism:** at least one essay commissioned by *PfS* which specifically deals with the poem and is written specifically for the student audience, as well as excerpts from previously published criticism on the work, when available.

In addition, most entries contains the following highlighted sections, set separately from the main text:

- **Media Adaptations:** a list of audio recordings as well as any film or television adaptations of the poem, including source information.

- **Compare and Contrast Box:** an "at-a-glance" comparison of the cultural and historical differences between the author's time and culture and late twentieth-century Western culture. This box includes pertinent parallels between the major scientific, political, and cultural movements of the time or place the poem was written, the time or place the poem was set (if a historical work), and modern Western culture. Works written after the mid-1970s may not have this box.

- **What Do I Read Next?:** a list of works that might complement the featured poem or serve as a contrast to it. This includes works by the same author and others, works of fiction and nonfiction, and works from various genres, cultures, and eras.

- **Study Questions:** a list of potential study questions or research topics dealing with the poem. This section includes questions related to other disciplines the student may be studying, such as American history, world history, science, math, government, business, geography, economics, psychology, etc.

Other Features

PfS includes a foreword by David J. Kelly, an instructor and cofounder of the creative writing periodical of Oakton Community College. This essay provides a straightforward, unpretentious explanation of why poetry should be marveled at and how *Poetry for Students* can help teachers show students how to enrich their own reading experiences.

A Cumulative Author/Title Index lists the authors and titles covered in each volume of the *PfS* series.

A Cumulative Nationality/Ethnicity Index breaks down the authors and titles covered in each volume of the *PfS* series by nationality and ethnicity.

A Subject/Theme Index, specific to each volume, provides easy reference for users who may be studying a particular subject or theme rather than a single work. Significant subjects from events to broad themes are included, and the entries pointing to the specific theme discussions in each entry are indicated in **boldface.**

Illustrations are included with entries when available, including photos of the author and other graphics related to the poem.

Citing Poetry for Students

When writing papers, students who quote directly from any volume of *Poetry for Students* may use the following general forms. These examples are based on MLA style; teachers may request that students adhere to a different style, so the following examples may be adapted as needed.

When citing text from *PfS* that is not attributed to a particular author (i.e., the Themes, Style,

Historical Context sections, etc.), the following format should be used in the bibliography section:

"Angle of Geese." *Poetry for Students.* Eds. Marie Napierkowski and Mary Ruby. Vol. 1. Detroit: Gale, 1997. 8–9.

When quoting the specially commissioned essay from *PfS* (usually the first piece under the "Criticism" subhead), the following format should be used:

Velie, Alan. Essay on "Angle of Geese."*Poetry for Students.* Eds. Marie Napierkowski and Mary Ruby. Vol. 1. Detroit: Gale, 1997. 8–9.

When quoting a journal or newspaper essay that is reprinted in a volume of *PfS,* the following form may be used:

Luscher, Robert M. "An Emersonian Context of Dickinson's 'The Soul Selects Her Own Society.'" *ESQ: A Journal of American Renaissance* 30, No. 2 (Second Quarterl, 1984), 111–16; excerpted and reprinted in *Poetry for Students,* Vol. 2, eds. Marie Napierkowski and Mary Ruby (Detroit: Gale, 1997), pp. 120–34.

When quoting material reprinted from a book that appears in a volume of *PfS,* the following form may be used:

Mootry, Maria K. "'Tell It Slant': Disguise and Discovery as Revisionist Poetic Discourse in 'The Bean Eaters,'" in *A Life Distilled: Gwendolyn Brroks, Her Poetry and Fiction,* edited by Maria K. Mootry and Gary Smith (University of Illinois Press, 1987, 177–80; excerpted and reprinted in *Poetry for Students,* Vol. 1, Eds. Marie Napierkowski and Mary Ruby (Detroit: Gale, 1997), pp. 59–61.

We Welcome Your Suggestions

The editors of *Poetry for Students* welcome your comments and ideas. Readers who wish to suggest poems to appear in future volumes, or who have other suggestions, are cordially invited to contact the editor. You may write to the editor at:

Editor, *Poetry for Students*
The Gale Group
27500 Drake Rd.
Farmington Hills, MI 48331–3535

Literary Chronology

700: *Beowulf* is composed at about this time.

1300–1699: Humanism as a philosophical view of the world is prevalent in this period.

1300–1699: The Renaissance begins in the 14th century and continues for the next 300 years.

1558–1603: The Elizabethan Age begins with the coronation in 1558 of Elizabeth I as Queen of England and continues until her death in 1603. Elizabethan literature is recognized as some of the finest in the English language.

1564: William Shakespeare is born in Stratford-upon-Avon.

1575–1799: The literary style known as Baroque arises in the late 16th century and remains influential until the early 18th century.

1600–1625: The Tribe of Ben, followers of Ben Jonson, were active in the early part of the 17th century.

1600–1799: The Enlightenment period in European social and cultural history begins in the 17th century and continues into the 18th century.

1600–1650: Metaphysical poetry becomes a prominent style of verse in the first half of the 17th century.

1603–1625: The Jacobean Age begins with the coronation in 1603 of James I of England and continues until his death in 1625.

1612: Anne Bradstreet is born in England.

1616: William Shakespeare dies in Stratford and is buried in the chancel of Trinity Church.

1625–1649: The Cavalier Poets, a group of writers that includes Robert Herrick, Richard Lovelace, and John Suckling , are active during the reign of Charles I of England (1625–1649).

1641: Anne Bradstreet's poem "To My Dear and Loving Husband" is written around this time.

1660–1688: The Restoration Period begins when Charles II regains the throne of England, and it continues through the reign of his successor, James II (1685–1688). Restoration literature includes the first well-developed English-language works in several forms of writing that would become widespread in the modern world, including the novel, biography, and travel literature.

1672: Anne Bradstreet dies.

1675–1799: Neoclassicism as the prevailing approach to literature begins late in the 17th century and continues through much of the 18th century.

1678: Anne Bradstreet's poem "To My Dear and Loving Husband" is published in the volume *Several Poems Compiled with Great Variety of Wit and Learning, Full of Delight.*

1700–1799: The English Augustan Age (the name is borrowed from a brilliant period of literary creativity in ancient Rome) flourishes throughout much of the 18th century.

1700–1725: The Scottish Enlightenment, a period of great literary and philosophical activity, occurs in the early part of the 18th century.

1740–1775: Pre-Romanticism, a transitional literary movement between Neoclassicism and Romanticism, takes place in the middle part of the 18th century.

1740–1750: The Graveyard School, referring to poetry that focuses on death and grieving, emerges as a significant genre in the middle of the 18th century.

1750–1899: The Welsh Literary Renaissance, an effort to revive interest in Welsh language and literature, begins in the middle of the 18th century and continues into the following century.

1775–1850: Romanticism as a literary movement arises in the latter part of the 18th century and continues until the middle of the 19th century.

1800–1899: The Gaelic Revival, a renewal of interest in Irish literature and language, takes place throughout much of the 19th century.

1809–1865: The Knickerbocker School, a group of American writers determined to establish New York as a literary center, flourishes between 1809 and 1865.

1830–1860: The flowering of American literature known as the American Renaissance begins in the 1830s and continues through the Civil War period.

1830–1855: Transcendentalism, an American philosophical and literary movement, is at its height during this period.

1830: Emily Dickinson is born on December 10 in Amherst, Massachusetts.

1837–1901: The Victorian Age begins with the coronation of Victoria as Queen of England, and continues until her death in 1901. Victorian literature is recognized for its magnificent achievements in a variety of genres.

1848–1858: The Pre-Raphaelites, an influential group of English painters, forms in 1848 and remains together for about ten years, during which time it has a significant impact on literature as well as the visual arts.

1850: The poets of the so-called Spasmodic School are active in the 1850s.

1861: Emily Dickinson's poem "There's a Certain Slant of Light" is written.

1874: Robert Frost is born in San Francisco, California.

1875–1899: Aestheticism becomes a significant artistic and literary philosophy in the latter part of the 19th century.

1875–1899: Decadence becomes an important poetic force late in the 19th century.

1875–1925: Expressionism is a significant artistic and literary influence through the late 19th century and the early 20th century.

1875–1925: The Irish Literary Renaissance begins late in the 19th century and continues for the next several decades.

1875–1925: The Symbolist Movement flourishes in the closing decades of the 19th century and the opening years of the 20th century.

1875–1950: Realism as an approach to literature gains importance in the 19th century and remains influential well into the 20th century.

1878: Carl Sandburg is born on January 6 in Galesburg, Illinois.

1883: William Carlos Williams is born on September 17 in Rutherford, New Jersey.

1885: D. H. Lawrence is born in Eastwood, Nottinghamshire, England.

1886: Emily Dickinson dies of Bright's Disease.

1886: Hilda Doolittle is born in Bethlehem, Pennsylvania

1888: The anonymous Scottish ballad "Lord Randal" is published in Francis James Child's *English and Scottish Popular Ballads.*

1890–1899: The decade of the 1890s, noted for the mood of weariness and pessimism in its art and literature, is known as the Fin de Siècle ("end of the century") period.

1900–1999: The philosophy of Existentialism and the literature it inspires are highly influential throughout much of the 20th century.

1900–1950: Modernism remains a dominant literary force from the early part to the middle years of the 20th century.

1902: Langston Hughes is born in Joplin, Missouri.

1907–1930 The Bloomsbury Group, a circle of English writers and artists, gathers regularly in the period from 1907 to around 1930.

1910–1920: Georgian poetry becomes a popular style of lyric verse during the reign of King George V of England.

1910–1930: New Humanism, a philosophy of literature, is influential for several decades, beginning around 1910.

1911: Elizabeth Bishop is born on February 8 in Worcester, Massachusetts

1912–1925: The Chicago Literary Renaissance, a time of great literary activity, takes place from about 1912 to 1925.

1912–1922: Imagism as a philosophy of poetry is defined in 1912 and remains influential for the next decade.

1913: D. H. Lawrence's poem "Piano" is published in his first collection of verse, *Love Poems and Others*.

1914: Robert Frost's poem "The Wood-Pile" is published in his collection *North of Boston*.

1916: Eve Merriam is born on July 19 in Philadelphia, Pennsylvania.

1917: Robert Lowell is born March 1.

1917: Gwendolyn Brooks is born in Topeka, Kansas.

1918: Carl Sandburg's poem "Cool Tombs" is published in his second collection of poetry, *Cornhuskers*.

1919–1960: The Scottish Renaissance in literature begins around 1919 and continues for about forty years.

1920: The Harlem Renaissance, a flowering of African American literary activity, takes place.

1920–1930: The label Lost Generation is applied to a generation of American writers working in the decades following World War I.

1920–1930: The Montreal Group, a circle of Canadian poets interested in dealing with complex metaphysical issues, begins in the late 1920s and flourishes for the next decade.

1920–1970: New Criticism as a philosophy of literature arises in the 1920s and continues to be a significant approach to writing for over fifty years.

1920–1960: Surrealism, an artistic and literary technique, arises in the 1920s and remains influential for the next half century.

1921: William Carlos Williams's poem "Queen-Ann's-Lace" is published in his fourth collection of poems, *Sour Grapes*.

1923: James Dickey is born in Atlanta, Georgia.

1923: Anthony Hecht is born on January 16 in New York City.

1924: Robert Frost is awarded the Pulitzer Prize in poetry for his collection *New Hampshire*.

1924: H.D.'s poem "Helen" is published in *Heliodora and Other Poems*.

1926: Robert Bly is born on December 23.

1930–1965: Negritude emerges as a literary movement in the 1930s and continues until the early 1960s.

1930–1970: The New York Intellectuals, a group of literary critics, are active from the 1930s to the 1970s.

1930: D. H. Lawrence dies of tuberculosis on March 2.

1931: Robert Frost is awarded the Pulitzer Prize in poetry for his *Collected Poems*.

1930: Derek Walcott is born on January 23 in Castries, on the island of St. Lucia.

1935–1943: The Works Progress Administration (WPA) Federal Writers' Project provides federally funded jobs for unemployed writers during the Great Depression.

1937: Robert Frost is awarded the Pulitzer Prize in poetry for his collection *A Further Range*.

1938: Ishmael Reed is born on February 22 in Chattanooga, Tennessee.

1940: The New Apocalypse Movement, founded by J. F. Hendry and Henry Treece, takes place in England in the 1940s.

1940: Postmodernism, referring to the various philosophies and practices of literature that challenge the dominance of Modernism, begins in the 1940s.

1943: Robert Frost is awarded the Pulitzer Prize in poetry for his collection *A Witness Tree*.

1946: Robert Lowell's "The Quaker Graveyard in Nantucket" is published in *Lord Weary's Castle*.

1950: The so-called Beat Movement writers begin publishing their work in the 1950s.

1950: The Black Mountain Poets, emphasizing the creative process, become an influential force in American literature in the 1950s.

1975: Structuralism emerges as an important movement in literary criticism in the middle of the 20th century.

1950: Gwendolyn Brooks is awarded the Pulitzer Prize in poetry for her collection *Annie Allen*.

1951: Carl Sandburg is awarded the Pulitzer Prize in poetry for his *Collected Poems*.

1951: Langston Hughes's "Theme for English B" is published in *Montage of a Dream Deferred*.

1956: Elizabeth Bishop wins a Pulitzer Prize in poetry for her volume *Poems: North and South— A Cold Spring.*

1958–1959: Robert Frost serves as Consultant in Poetry to the Library of Congress.

1960–1970: The Black Aesthetic Movement, also known as the Black Arts Movement, takes place from the 1960s into the 1970s.

1960–1999: Poststructuralism arises as a theory of literary criticism in the 1960s.

1960: Gwendolyn Brooks's "We Real Cool" is published in her fourth volume of poetry, *The Bean Eaters.*

1961: Hilda Doolittle dies of a heart attack in September in Zurich, Switzerland.

1962: Derek Walcott's poem "A Far Cry from Africa" appears in his volume *In a Green Night: Poems.*

1962: James Dickey's "The Heaven of Animals" is published in the collection *Drowning With Others.*

1963: William Carlos Williams dies in Rutherford, New Jersey.

1963: Robert Frost dies in Boston.

1964: Eve Merriam's "Onomatopoeia" is published in her book *It Doesn't Always Have to Rhyme*

1965: Elizabeth Bishop's poem "Brazil, January 1, 1502" is published in her volume *Questions of Travel.*

1967: "More Light! More Light!'" is published in Anthony Hecht's *The Hard Hours.*

1967: Carl Sandburg dies at the age of 89.

1967: Robert Bly's "Come with Me" is published in his volume *The Light Around the Body.*

1967: Langston Hughes dies on May 22 of congestive heart failure in New York City.

1968: Anthony Hecht wins the Pulitzer Prize in poetry for his collection *The Hard Hours.*

1968: Robert Bly's volume *The Light Around the Body* wins a National Book Award.

1970–1999: New Historicism, a school of literary analysis, originates in the 1970s.

1970: Ishmael Reed's "Beware: Do Not Read This Poem" is published in *Catechism of d neoamerican hoodoo church: Poems.*

1977: Robert Lowell dies in New York City.

1979: Elizabeth Bishop dies in Boston of a cerebral aneurysm.

1992: In April, Eve Merriam dies of cancer in Manhattan, New York.

1996: Jorie Graham is awarded the Pulitzer Prize in poetry for the collection *The Dream of the Unified Field.*

1997: James Dickey dies.

1997: Lisel Mueller is awarded the Pulitzer Prize in poetry for her collection *Alive Together: New and Selected Poems.*

1997: Robert Pinsky serves as Poet Laureate of the United States.

1998: Charles Wright is awarded the Pulitzer Prize in poetry for his collection *Black Zodiac.*

Acknowledgments

The editors wish to thank the copyright holders of the excerpted criticism included in this volume and the permissions managers of many book and magazine publishing companies for assisting us in securing reproduction rights. We are also grateful to the staffs of the Detroit Public Library, the Library of Congress, the University of Detroit Mercy Library, Wayne State University Purdy/Kresge Library Complex, and the University of Michigan Libraries for making their resources available to us. Following is a list of the copyright holders who have granted us permission to reproduce material in this volume of *Poetry for Students (PFS)*. Every effort has been made to trace copyright, but if omissions have been made, please let us know.

COPYRIGHTED EXCERPTS IN *PFS*, VOLUME 6, WERE REPRODUCED FROM THE FOLLOWING PERIODICALS:

American Transcendental Quarterly, v. 14, Spring, 1972. Copyright © 1972 by Kenneth Walter Cameron. Reproduced by permission.—*Ariel: A Review of International English Literature,* v. 23, October, 1992. Copyright © 1992 The Board of Governors, The University of Calgary. Reproduced by permission of the publisher and the author.—*The Explicator,* v. 31, October, 1972; v. 40, Fall, 1981. Copyright © 1972, 1981 by Helen Dwight Reid Educational Foundation. Both reproduced with permission of the Helen Dwight Reid Educational Foundation, published by Heldref Publications, 1319 18th Street, NW, Washington, DC 20036-1802.—*Concerning Poetry,* v. 18, 1985. Copyright © 1985, Western Washington University. Reproduced by permission.—*Poetry,* for "Come With Me" by Robert Bly. Copyright © by the Modern Poetry Association. Reproduced by permission of the Editor of *Poetry* and the author.—*South Atlantic Review,* v. 56, November, 1991. Copyright © 1991 by the South Atlantic Modern Language Association. Reproduced by permission.

COPYRIGHTED EXCERPTS IN *PFS*, VOLUME 6, WERE REPRODUCED FROM THE FOLLOWING BOOKS:

Bishop, Elizabeth. From "Brazil, January 1, 1502" in *The Complete Poems 1927-1979.* Farrar, Straus, and Giroux, 1979. Copyright © 1979, 1983 by Alice Helen Methfessel. Reproduced by permission of Farrar, Straus & Giroux, Inc.— Davis, William V. From *Understanding Robert Bly.* University of South Carolina Press, 1988. Copyright © University of South Carolina 1988. Reproduced by permission.—Hecht, Anthony. From "More Light! More Light!" in *Collected Earlier Poems.* Copyright © 1990 by Anthony E. Hecht. Reproduced by permission of the author. In North America by Alfred A. Knopf. Inc.—Housman, John E. From the introduction to *British Popular Ballads.* Edited by John E. Housman. George G. Harrap & Co. Ltd. 1952. Copyright © 1952. All rights reserved. Reproduced by permission.—Hughes, Langston. For "Theme for English B" in *The Collected Poems of Langston Hughes.* Edited by Arnold Rampersad.

Alfred A. Knopf, 1995. Copyright © 1994 by the Estate of Langston Hughes. All rights reserved. Reprinted by permission of the author's agents, Harold Ober Associates Incorporated. In North American by Random House, Inc.—Lowell, Robert. From *Lord Weary's Castle.* Harcourt, Brace and Company, 1946. Copyright © 1946, renewed 1973 by Robert Lowell. Reproduced by permission of Harcourt Brace & Company.—Merriam, Eve. From *It Doesn't Always Have to Rhyme.* Atheneum, 1967. Copyright © 1964, 1992 by Eve Merriam. Used by permission of Marian Reiner for the author.—Randall, Dudley. From *Cities Burning.* Broadside Press, 1968. Copyright © 1966 by Dudley Randall. Reproduced by permission.—Reed, Ishmael. From *Mumbo Jumbo.* Doubleday, 1972. Reproduced by permission of the author.—Stanford, Ann. From a preface to *Anne Bradstreet: The Worldly Puritan.* Burt Franklin, 1974. Copyright © 1974 Burt Franklin & Co., Inc. All rights reserved. Reproduced by permission of the Literary Estate of Ann Stanford.—Stanford, Ann. From *Anne Bradstreet: The Worldly Puritan.* Burt Franklin, 1974. Copyright © 1974 Burt Franklin & Co., Inc. All rights reserved. Reproduced by permission of the Literary Estate of Ann Stanford.—Walcott, Derek. From *In A Green Night: Poems.* Jonathan Cape, 1969. Reproduced by permission of the author.

PHOTOGRAPHS AND ILLUSTRATIONS APPEARING IN *PFS,* VOLUME 6, WERE RECEIVED FROM THE FOLLOWING SOURCES:

Bishop, Elizabeth, 1951, photograph. AP/Wide World Photos. Reproduced by permission.

Bly, Robert, photograph by Christopher Felver. Archive Photos, Inc. Reproduced by permission.

Bradstreet, Anne, photograph of stained glass. Vicar and church wardens of St. Botolph's Church, Boston, Lincolnshire. Reproduced by permission.

Brooks, Gwendolyn, photograph. AP/Wide World Photos, Inc. Reproduced by permission.

Dickey, James, photograph by Jerry Bauer. Jerry Bauer. Reproduced by permission.

Dickinson, Emily, photograph of a painting. The Library of Congress.

Doolittle, Hilda, 1949, photograph. AP/Wide World Photos. Reproduced by permission.

Frost, Robert, photograph. The Library of Congress.

Hecht, Anthony, photograph. UPI/Bettmann. Reproduced by permission.

Hughes, Langston, photograph. The Bettmann Archive/Newsphotos, Inc./Corbis-Bettmann. Reproduced by permission.

Lawrence, D. H., photograph. AP/Wide World Photos. Reproduced by permission.

Lowell, Robert, photograph. The Library of Congress.

Merriman, Eve, photograph by Layle Silbert copyright 1987. Reproduced by permission.

Reed, Ishmael, photograph. AP/Wide World Photos. Reproduced with permission.

Sandburg, Carl, 1962, photograph. AP/Wide World Photos. Reproduced by permission.

Williams, William Carlos, photograph. Archive Photos, Inc. Reproduced by permission.

Walcott, Derek, photograph by Jerry Bauer. Jerry Bauer. Reproduced by permission.

Contributors

Emily Archer: Emily Archer holds a Ph.D. in English from Georgia State University, has taught literature and poetry at several colleges, and has published essays, reviews, interviews, and poetry in numerous literary journals. Entry on *Queen-Ann's-Lace.*

David Caplan: David Caplan is a doctoral candidate at the University of Virginia. Original essay on *"More Light! More Light!"*

Lynn Davidson: Lynn Davidson has a master's degree in English literature and writes poetry and fiction. Original essay on *Beware: Do Not Read This Poem.*

David Donnell: David Donnell, who teaches at the University of Toronto, has published seven books of poetry. His work is included in the *Norton Anthology of Modern Poetry* and his volume *Settlement* received Canada's prestigious Governor General's Award. Original essays on *Cool Tombs* and *A Far Cry from Africa.*

Jhan Hochman: Jhan Hochman holds a Ph.D. in English and an M.A. in Cinema Studies. His articles have appeared in *Democracy and Nature, Genre, ISLE,* and *Mosaic.* Entries and original essays on *Beware: Do Not Read This Poem; Brazil, January 1, 1502; A Far Cry from Africa; Helen; "More Light! More Light!"; The Quaker Graveyard in Nantucket;* and *We Real Cool.*

Jeannine Johnson: Jeannine Johnson received her Ph.D. from Yale University and is currently visiting assistant professor of English at Wake Forest University. Original essays on *Helen* and *Theme for English B.*

David Kelly: David Kelly is an instructor of creative writing at several community colleges in Illinois, as well as a fiction writer and playwright. Entries and original essays on *The Heaven of Animals, Onomatopoeia, To My Dear and Loving Husband,* and *The Wood-Pile.* Original essay on *Helen.*

Aviya Kushner: Aviya Kushner, who is the poetry editor for *Neworld Renaissance* Magazine, earned an M.A. in creative writing from Boston University. Original essay on *A Far Cry from Africa.*

Michael Lake: Michael Lake earned an M.A. in English from Eastern Illinois University and is a published poet who has also taught composition and literature courses at the collegiate level. Entry and original essay on *There's a Certain Slant of Light.*

Mary Mahony: Mary Mahony earned an M.A. in English from the University of Detroit and a M.L.S. from Wayne State University. She is an instructor of English at Wayne County Community College in Detroit, Michigan. Entry on *Cool Tombs.* Original essay on *The Quaker Graveyard in Nantucket.*

Bruce Meyer: Bruce Meyer is director of the creative writing program at the University of

Toronto's School of Continuing Studies. He is the author of 14 books, including the poetry collections *The Open Room, Radio Silence,* and *The Presence.* Original essays on *Brazil, January 1, 1502; "More Light! More Light!"; The Quaker Graveyard in Nantucket;* and *The Wood-Pile.*

Carolyn Meyer: Carolyn Meyer holds a Ph.D. in modern British and Irish literature and has taught contemporary literature at McMaster University, Mt. Allison University, and, most recently, the University of Toronto. She has presented papers internationally on the poetry of Seamus Heaney and John Montague. Her article "Orthodoxy, Independence, and Influence in Seamus Heaney's Station Island" has been reprinted in *Critical Essays on Seamus Heaney,* edited by Robert F. Garratt (1995). She is the coeditor of *Separate Islands: Contemporary Irish and British Poetry* and of a forthcoming college reader. Original essay on *Lord Randal.*

Marisa Anne Pagnattaro: Marisa Anne Pagnattaro is a writer and teaching assistant at the University of Georgia in Athens. She is the book review editor and editorial board member of the *Georgia Bar Journal.* Pagnattaro is currently writing a dissertation on women, justice, and American literature. Original essay on *Brazil, January 1, 1502.*

Sean K. Robisch: Sean K. Robisch teaches composition and literature at Purdue University and holds a Ph.D. in American literature. His fiction has appeared in *Hopewell Review* and *Puerto del Sol.* Original essay on *Onomatopoeia.*

Joe Sarnowski: Joe Sarnowski is a doctoral candidate in the department of English at the University of Toledo. He has written articles for *The Kentucky Review* and the *Encyclopedia of American War Literature.* Original essay on *We Real Cool.*

Cliff Saunders: Cliff Saunders teaches writing and literature in the Myrtle Beach, South Carolina, area and has published six chapbooks of verse. Original essays on *Come with Me* and *Piano.*

Chris Semansky: Chris Semansky holds a Ph.D. in English from Stony Brook University and teaches writing and literature at Portland Community College in Portland, Oregon. His collection of poems *Death, But at a Good Price* received the Nicholas Roerich Poetry Prize for 1991 and was published by Story Line Press and the Nicholas Roerich Museum. Semansky's most recent collection, *Blindsided,* has been published by 26 Books of Portland, Oregon. Entries and original essays on *Come with Me, Piano,* and *Theme for English B.*

Alice Van Wart: Alice Van Wart is a writer and teaches literature and writing in the Department of Continuing Education at the University of Toronto. She has published two books of poetry and written articles on modern and contemporary literature. Original essays on *Beware: Do Not Read This Poem* and *Piano.*

Kristina Zarlengo: Kristina Zarlengo earned both an M.A. and Ph.D. in English and comparative literature from Columbia University. She taught writing and literature at Columbia University and has most recently worked as a freelance book reviewer and feature writer. Original essays on *Cool Tombs, Queen-Ann's-Lace* and *Theme for English B.*

Beware: Do Not Read This Poem

Ishmael Reed
1970

"Beware: Do Not Read This Poem" was included in Ishmael Reed's first volume of poetry, *Catechism of d neoamerican hoodoo church: Poems,* written by the end of 1968 but first published in 1970. The poem was then reprinted in Reed's second volume of poetry, *Conjure: Selected Poems, 1963-1970* (1972), which was nominated for a National Book Award for poetry in 1973, the same year his novel *Mumbo Jumbo* (1972) was nominated for the National Book Award for fiction. What one critic has said about Reed applies exceedingly well to "Beware: Do Not Read This Poem": "Ishmael Reed's importance to contemporary literary studies stems in part from his ability to channel his encyclopedic historical, political, and cultural knowledge into syncretic poetry and prose that resonate with the voices of diverse ethnicities, locations, and eras."

Reed was a key figure in the Black Arts Movement; as a poet, he rejected established forms and introduced a new black poetry. "Beware: Do Not Read This Poem" employs colloquial language, nontraditional spelling, innovative typography, and unexpected rhythms. The poem is a cautionary tale whose title is a warning. It begins by describing a vain "ol woman" whose obsession with mirrors leads to her disappearance. In the next section, the scene changes to the most present of moments, the time during which the reader is reading the poem. The concept presented here is that a poem is an entity able to engulf and devour the reader—another kind of disappearance. Finally, in the last lines,

Reed offers grim statistics concerning the number of people who disappeared during just one year in the United States. The form of the poem ties the various story lines together; with unexplained spaces around punctuation and between words, Reed reinforces a theme of isolation and loss.

Author Biography

Eminent scholar Henry Louis Gates called Ishmael Reed "the enfant terrible of black letters [who] may represent the culmination of the postmodern moment in American culture." Reed was born in Chattanooga, Tennessee, on February 22, 1938. His father was a fund-raiser for the YMCA and his mother, a homemaker, also held various jobs. His stepfather, from whom he gets his last name, was an autoworker. When Reed was four years old, his family relocated to Buffalo, New York. At age fifteen, Reed began a job delivering copies of *The Empire Star Weekly,* an independent newspaper. After a year, the editor of the *Star* allowed the teenager to write his first columns and jazz articles, which were characterized by what Reed called "a pungent writing style." He enrolled in night school at the State University of New York in 1956 and here wrote his first piece of fiction, "Something Pure," a piece of existentialist fantasy. His English instructor raved about the piece and initiated a petition, signed by members of the English department, that allowed Reed admittance into day school, where he noted he was "quite a celebrity" in English classes. In 1960, however, Reed dropped out of school because, he explained, "I became bored with the university and found that I did some of my best work outside it." He returned to a job at the *The Empire Star Weekly,* writing on assorted topics, and married his first wife, with whom he had one daughter. During this time Reed also conducted interviews on a radio show called "Buffalo Community Roundtable." The show was canceled after Reed interviewed controversial Nation of Islam spokesman Malcolm X. Reed subsequently left his job and wife in Buffalo and moved to New York City to nurture his career.

In New York, Reed met writer/intellectual Amiri Baraka at the Umbra Workshop, where Reed said he became acquainted with the techniques of "the Afro-American literary style." In 1965, Reed launched a newspaper, *Advance,* in Newark, New Jersey, but it folded after only ten weeks. The short-lived paper inspired the *East Village Other,* one of New York's first important underground newspa-

Ishmael Reed

pers. In 1967, Reed published his first novel, *The Free Lance Pallbearers;* soon afterward, he moved to Berkeley, California, and began teaching. In 1970, he divorced his first wife and married his second, Carla Blank, a modern dancer with whom he would have his second daughter in 1977. That same year, Reed also published his first volume of poetry, *Catechism of d neoamerican hoodoo church,* which included "Beware: Do Not Read This Poem."

Reed has written nine novels, five volumes of poetry, and four collections of essays. He co-founded Yardbird Publishing; founded Reed, Cannon, and Johnson Publishing; started the Before Columbus Foundation devoted to the production and distribution of works by unknown "ethnic" writers; and, later, began the publishing company I Reed Books. Reed has taught at America's most prestigious universities, including Yale, Dartmouth, Columbia, Harvard, the University of California, Santa Barbara, and the University of Arkansas. His awards include the John Simon Guggenheim Memorial Foundation Award for fiction, three New York state and three National Endowment for the Arts publishing grants for merit, and the Pushcart Prize in 1979 for his essay "American Poetry: Is There a Center?" Reed has continued his multifaceted literary work, writing plays and a libretto set to Bobby McFerrin's music for the San Francisco Opera Company and editing two Before Columbus Foundation collections of fiction and poetry. In 1995, Reed earned an honorary doctorate from his alma mater, the State University of New York, Buffalo.

Poem Text

tonite, *thriller* was
abt an ol woman, so vain she
surrounded her self w /
many mirrors

it got so bad that finally she   5
locked herself indoors & her
whole life became the
    mirrors

one day the villagers broke
into her house , but she was too   10
swift for them . she disappeared
    into a mirror
each tenant who bought the house
after that, lost a loved one to
    the ol woman in the mirror :   15
    first a little girl
    then a young woman
    then the young woman /s husband

the hunger of this poem is legendary
it has taken in many victims   20
    back off from this poem
    it has drawn in yr feet
    back off from this poem
    it has drawn in yr legs
    back off from this poem   25
    it is a greedy mirror
you are into this poem . from
the waist down
nobody can hear you can they ?
this poem has had you up to here   30
    belch
this poem aint got no manners
you cant call out frm this poem
relax now & go w/ this poem
move & roll on to this poem   35

do not resist this poem
this poem has yr eyes
this poem has his head
this poem has his arms
this poem has his fingers   40
this poem has his fingertips

this poem is the reader & the
reader this poem

statistic: the us bureau of missing persons reports
    that in 1968 over 100,000 people disappeared   45
    leaving no solid clues
    nor trace   only
    a space   in the lives of their friends

Poem Summary

Lines 1-4

Thriller is the name of a television program that ran from 1960 to 1962; it was similar to the more well-known *Twilight Zone* series and usually focused on ordinary people in extraordinary circumstances. These first lines summarize the plot of one particular program, which, in the second part of the poem, will become the basis of a comparison between looking into mirrors and reading poetry.

Lines 5-8:

The woman gets more and more involved with looking at herself, never leaving her house of mirrors.

Lines 9-12:

Reed does not say why the villagers broke into the house nor how the woman actually disappeared into a mirror—probably because such explanations do not impact the point he will be making. The reader must simply regard the fantasy as ground for what follows.

Lines 13-18:

The recounting of the *Thriller* episode ends with new tenants losing loved ones to the old woman in the mirror. Again, we do not know why, but we might guess that the old woman is desirous of company. One thing is common to all of the people whom the old lady grabs: they are young.

Lines 19-28:

The scene now shifts to the terrain of the poem itself—the actual words that the reader is contemplating. The poem is compared to a "greedy mirror," as if the poem—like the mirror—had an old woman inside of it who desperately wanted company. In these lines, the reader is taken feet first and swallowed up to the waist. Interesting here is how Reed comments on the poem he is writing; he makes one poem into two by saying that the poem has existed long enough for its hunger to be "legendary." The reason might be that as the mirrors stand for mirrors in general, this poem also stands for poems in general. In other words, this poem is meant as an example of the species, poetry, more than an individual piece of writing that just happens to be a poem. Poems absorb readers and, specifically, engross them bodily and viscerally. They have always done this, and that is why their power is "legendary."

Media Adaptations

- A cassette titled *Ishmael Reed Reading His Poetry* is available from Temple at Zeus at Cornell University, 1976.

- A film titled *Ishmael Reed and Michael Harper Reading in the University of California, San Diego New Poetry Series* was released by the university in 1977.

- Reed appears on a phonograph record, *New Jazz Poets* on AR Records.

Lines 29-33:

Though the reader reads, he or she makes no sound. It is the poem that "makes" the sound and unreels the words, or, in this case, belches as it takes the reader in, perhaps too quickly. The poem has no manners not just because it belches, but because it does not ask permission to swallow the reader and, in fact, attempts to steal him or her. The greedy individual inside of the poem will be even more gratified to snatch the reader if, at first, the reader is opposed to being overwhelmed.

Lines 34-41:

At this point, the poem is attempting to hypnotize the reader to not resist any longer and, instead, "go with the flow." Whereas before the reader was swallowed feet first, this time it is head first.

Lines 42-43:

Now the swallowing is complete, and the reader merges with the poem. Such a sentiment harkens back to Wallace Steven's "The House Was Quiet and the World Was Calm" (1946), where "the reader became the book." Notice that Reed does not say that the reader becomes the poet, but only the poem. This distinction was also made earlier, when the people absorbed into the mirror did not become the old woman, but just disappeared as themselves inside the mirror.

Lines 44-48:

These lines, as if outside the poem, caution the reader not to become too involved in poetry because the engrossed reader is a person not engaging with society. The statistic regarding missing persons ends the poem on a serious aftertaste. While the statistic exaggerates the absorption of the reader by comparing him or her to a missing person, the poem seriously addresses the power of words and literature to so engage readers that they become bookworms and exhibit antisocial behavior. Reed seems to council: "Read, but don't lose touch. Read, but resist becoming the poem or letting the poem possess you." The lesson is similar when it comes to looking in mirrors; looking too much might encourage you to see only what you want or to desire yourself as did Narcissus. This highly unique, perhaps even paradoxical sentiment comes from a poem we are in the process of reading.

Themes

Isolation

The old woman introduced in the first stanza gets caught up in the mirrors and isolates herself from others. The mind-set of the villagers who break into her house is not explained; they could merely be checking up on her out of concern for her well-being, or her strange behavior may have provoked them into a confrontation. The old woman is so interested in avoiding the villagers that she escapes into a mirror. We cannot be certain whether the mirrors caused the old woman's isolation or simply contributed to it, but, whatever the case, the woman, once in the mirror world, appears to have found that she is alone there—that she no longer has her reflection to keep her company. In the mirror world, the woman is probably alone and that could be the reason she steals people from the other side—to keep her company. Poems are similar to the woman's mirrors in that they attempt to absorb readers. A reader who immerses him- or herself in poetry can become withdrawn from others and, in that isolation, look desperately for some connection in the words of others. Solipsism, the theory that the self is the whole of reality, can be an easy way out of dealing with more difficult friendships, relationships, and ideas. Reed cautions us to beware of privately indulging ourselves, of constant reinforcement with our own image. Because no matter how much we multiply our image in the mirror or read poetry that speaks back to us our feelings and thoughts, we remain within our own little world—a world lacking the dimensions of criticism, praise, or feedback from others.

Perception

The old woman who disappeared into the mirror world snatches only young people from the real world. Alone and unreflected inside the mirror, she now desires the companionship of younger people. Or perhaps it is less a need for companionship than a selfish desire to surround herself with youth and deceive herself into thinking that she, herself, is young. She may even have deluded herself about her age before she disappeared into the mirror, based on her isolation and her obsession with her reflection. Forever looking into mirrors allows one to forget how much one is changing and getting older, because one is not able to assimilate all the small changes. When you have not seen someone for a long time, they look much older, whereas viewing your own image in the mirror everyday, you appear to almost stay the same age.

This looking into the mirror that makes us forget our age, then, is a way to slow time and thwart knowledge of death by keeping us perpetually preoccupied with a present that looks like the past. Such preoccupation leaves us unprepared for not only the shock of realizing one's age, but that one is going to die. This is why Michel de Montaigne (1533-92), in his essay "That to Philosophize is to Learn to Die," councils staring into the face of death:

> Let us have nothing on our minds as often as death. At every moment let us picture it in our imagination in all its aspects.... Amid feasting and gaiety let us ever keep in mind this refrain, the memory of our condition; and let us never allow ourselves to be so carried away by pleasure that we do not sometimes remember in how many ways the happiness of ours is a prey to death, and how death's clutches threaten it.... He who has learned how to die has unlearned how to be a slave. Knowing how to die frees us from all subjection and constraint. There is nothing evil in life for the man who has thoroughly grasped the fact that to be deprived of life is not an evil.

If Montaigne's philosophy of confronting aging and death was shared by both the old woman and readers, then we would not need to retreat to—and get lost in—reassuring images in mirrors and books.

Topics for Further Study

- Write a poem or short essay using a television show as the subject.

- Discuss and then write about the differences between watching television and reading, or more specifically, between watching a television soap opera or miniseries and reading a novel.

- Discuss and then write about how reading is not only like dying, but also like resurrection.

Style

"Beware: Do Not Read This Poem" is written in free verse, which means there is no established pattern of rhyme and it is devoid of regular stanzas and meter. Perhaps the most striking thing about the poem, however, is its nontraditional spelling and punctuation, a trait common to many of Reed's early poems. In an interview with Lee Bartlett, Reed explained, "Well, I was living in New York when my early poems were written, and the thing then was to be experimental. We thought that using slashes and 'wd' instead of 'would' was experimental writing." "Beware: Do Not Read This Poem" also is characterized by unshackled punctuation; commas, periods, question marks, and colons are set with a space on either side, which frees the punctuation marks from the phrase, clause, or sentence to which they are usually thought to belong. The typographical elements are unexpected and unfamiliar, which contribute to the unease created by the poem. The spaces scattered throughout the text also serve to reinforce the idea of loss and disappearance that the poem examines.

Historical Context

America's post-World War II years, the 1940s and 1950s, prepared the ground for 1960s unrest with increasing comfort levels that were the result of a boom in production and a new high in private

Compare & Contrast

- **1970:** In northern Peru, a massive earthquake, which included the Mount Huascarán avalanche, kills between 50,000 and 70,000 people.

  1970: In one of the worst disasters of the century, a cyclone and accompanying massive sea wave kills 150,000 to 200,000 people in eastern Pakistan (later Bangladesh).

  1998: Honduras and Nicaragua are hit by massive earthquakes that kill an estimated 10,000 people.

- **1970:** Black Panther Party leaders Fred Hampton and Mark Clark are killed by Chicago police.

  1999: A fence separating buried blacks from buried whites in a cemetery in Jasper, Texas, is torn down in memory of James Byrd, Jr., an African American killed in the summer of 1998. Three white supremacists, two of them former prison inmates, are held and accused of beating, stripping, and chaining Byrd to the back of a truck, then dragging him for three miles.

- **1970:** In his work *Infallible? An Inquiry,* Swiss theologian Hans Küng becomes the first modern major Roman Catholic figure to reject the idea of the pope's infallibility. He was later disciplined by the Vatican and forbidden to teach theology under Catholic auspices.

  1999: Pope John Paul II visits St. Louis, Missouri, and speaks out against the death penalty. In private, he pleads with the governor of Missouri to spare the life of a prisoner sentenced for execution. The governor grants the pope his request and stops the execution.

---

wealth. The result was two generations: those born in the 1920s and educated in the prosperous war and postwar years, and those born during or just after the war, the baby-boom generation, a generation born into the practice of mass and massive consumption. These two generations were lucky enough to have both leisure time and education enough to think about things other than economic security. Even African Americans, who were disadvantaged in comparison with their white counterparts, benefited from the war years; this period saw an increase in the number of educated, non-impoverished black youth. Martin Luther King, Jr., for example, was born into relative economic security, received a college education in the late 1940s and early 1950s, and did his work with civil rights in the late 1950s and early 1960s.

The first and most important result of the rising tide of economic prosperity was the Civil Rights Movement, which spanned the period of 1954 to 1965 and is credited with sparking all other American movements of this period: the antinuclear, antiwar, feminist, gay and lesbian, Native American, and environmental movements. The Civil Rights Movement also inspired struggles for freedom in other parts of the world. In 1965, three years before the publication of "Beware: Do Not Read This Poem," the last major piece of federal legislation, the Voting Rights Act, was signed into law; it was the latest in a series of federal acts aimed to stop state-sanctioned discrimination against black Americans. This was also the year that the pacifism of the Civil Rights Movement is said to have withered: Malcolm X was assassinated, some think by his own colleagues in the Nation of Islam; the Watts Rebellion and other uprisings exploded across the nation; the Congress of Racial Equality (CORE) and the Student Non-violent Coordinating Committee (SNCC) became equated with the Black Power movement; and the confrontational Black Panther Party was born. African Americans seemed through with keeping their anger bottled up. While on the one hand, the Civil Rights Movement produced a whole series of splits in the body politic—among blacks, among whites, and between blacks and whites—it also forced many to heal the split, to take a stand on race as they had never done before.

While whites and blacks fought at home, the U.S. government engaged the Vietnamese abroad. The covert war ended in 1964, and in 1965 America overtly carried on its first extended and extensive bombing attack of Vietnam (Operation Rolling Thunder) and sent in its first regular combat troops, which, by the end of 1965, totaled 185,000. Between 1965 and 1966, the CIA estimated 36,000 casualties in North Vietnam, 29,000 of which were civilians. Reports of civilian casualties ignited the burgeoning antiwar movement, which came together nonviolently in its first march on Washington in 1965—a march put together by Students for a Democratic Society (SDS). In the same year, at the University of Michigan, the first teach-ins against the Vietnam War were held, and at the University of California at Berkeley, the Vietnam Day Committee sponsored a thirty-six hour event presenting both sides of the war. Shortly thereafter, in 1966, the offices of the Vietnam Day Committee were bombed. In 1967, Reed began teaching at Berkeley. In an interview where he talks about being denied tenure there in 1977, he said that a reason cited by a faculty member was that Reed had canceled classes at Berkeley. Reed responded this way in a 1977 interview: " ... during the bombing of the campus, with tear gas and antipersonnel weapons, as well as three gases outlawed by the Geneva Convention, I wrote a letter to James Hart, then head of the English department. I said when I signed up to teach a course, I wasn't volunteering to fight in a war ... so I cancelled one summer course." The gassing of Berkeley is reported to have taken place in the summer of 1969 at the culmination of a struggle over People's Park, a University of California parking lot seized by students and then cooperatively turned into a public park in April of 1969. On May 15, after the park was already constructed, the University retook it. When a violent confrontation between students and police occurred a week or so later, then-governor Ronald Reagan sent in the National Guard. A rally on the university campus protesting the continuing presence of the National Guard turned violent; helicopters dropped tear and nausea gas, and an estimated 100 students were wounded by shotgun blasts. One youth, James Rector, was killed.

Critical Overview

"Beware: Do Not Read This Poem" appeared in Reed's first poetry collection, *catechism of d*

neoamerican hoodoo church: Poems, and was reprinted in *Conjure: Selected Poems, 1963-1970.* While *Conjure* was nominated for a National Book Award, the book did not receive substantial critical attention. Most critics choose to focus on Reed's prose and his attempt to create a black aesthetic called Neo-HooDoo rather than his poetry. Though Reed discussed other poems in his foreword to *Conjure,* "Beware: Do Not Read This Poem" is passed over in silence. The poem was included, however, in Dudley Randall's influential anthology *The Black Poets* in 1971. In a survey of Reed's work for *Dictionary of Literary Biography,* Caroline G. Bokinsky noted that *Conjure* "contains ... poems that echo the musical and rhythmical quality of the black dialect," but added that "Although the poems attain lyrical excellence, Reed's anger permeates the poetry."

Criticism

Lynn Davidson

Lynn Davidson has a master's degree in English literature and writes poetry and fiction. In the following essay, Davidson investigates how "Beware: Do Not Read This Poem" challenges the canon of Western literature.

American poet and activist Ishmael Reed is one of America's preeminent African-American writers and certainly one of its most controversial. His outspoken judgment of individuals—both black and white—and his denunciation in novels, essays, and poetry of racial divisions in America have attracted both awards and harsh criticism from literary critics and the popular press.

Reed's body of work is almost entirely satiric in nature. He uses parody, irony, and jokes to challenge American political, religious, and literary repression. Reed believes that the pen truly is mightier than the sword, and the device he most often reaches for to carry his message is irony. In "Beware: Do Not Read This Poem," the irony is part of the structure of the poem and creates the double meaning that runs through it. Irony is a double-edged sword and, as such, a powerful way of opening up interaction, or debate, with the reader. Reed is very aware that there is a person on each side of the poem (the poet and the reader), and he acknowledges the often comical or bewildering complexity of human interaction in "Beware: Do Not

What Do I Read Next?

- The anthology *The Sixties Papers,* edited by Judith and Stewart Albert, consists of documents and essays by the leading lights of the 1960s (C. Wright Mills, Allen Ginsberg, Malcolm X, etc.,) and on the leading struggles (antiwar, counterculture, feminist). The volume is introduced by an overview of the 1960s.

- Erich Auerbach's *Mimesis* (1953), is one of the most important books of literary criticism. The subject of the book is the attempt at realism through a history of literary representation or imitation.

- George Bataille's *The Literature of Evil* (1985) is a study of Emily Bronte, Baudelaire, Michelet, William Blake, Sade, Proust, Kafka, and Genet. Bataille, one of the major theorists of the twentieth century, writes that, "To reproduce oneself is to disappear."

- Plato's *Collected Dialogues* (1961), is an indispensable reference book for the humanities student. Included here is the complete *Republic,* in which Socrates discusses whether poets should be banished from his ideal state.

Read This Poem": "back off from this poem / it has drawn in yr feet." The title reads like a warning sign one sees on a building site or factory: "Beware: Dangerous Chemicals" or "Beware: Do Not Enter Site Without a Hard Hat." Reed is probably aware of the very human temptation to challenge such a bald directive. He may be suggesting that there is something in the poem that will disturb the reader. The irony here is that this is "just" a poem. How could words on paper present a danger? Is this a joke? Of course it is, isn't it? Already, the reader is in "two minds" about the experience of the poem—just as Reed intended. Reed knows that it takes more than one "mind," or one entrenched viewpoint, to debate an issue. He refers to the sparring of dual viewpoints in his writing as "boxing on paper." In juxtaposing opposing forces or ideas

on the page, Reed creates a tension in the poem so that ideas can move around, test their muscle—effectively "box it out." Reed has said, "Regardless of the criticisms I receive from the left, the right and the middle, I think it's important to maintain a prolific writing jab, as long as my literary legs hold up."

The first four stanzas of "Beware: Do Not Read This Poem" involve the retelling of a story—a thriller. Perhaps this thriller is a movie the narrator has seen on television. In reading the first two stanzas, one has the impression that the narrator is sitting down with a group of friends in a relaxed situation, retelling a story that has captured his imagination. However, he is speaking in the present tense: "tonite, thriller was." There is immediacy and instant contact with the reader, which comes as a surprise after the warning tone of the title. The story's colloquial language, with its missing words and word contractions ("abt an ol woman"), evokes the African-American oral storytelling tradition. In the *Dictionary of Literary Biography,* Robert S. Friedman recounted how, in 1985, Reed asserted that his aesthetic "owes more to the Afro-American oral tradition and to folk art than to any literary tradition. The oral tradition includes techniques like satire, hyperbole, invective and bawdiness…. It's a comic tradition in the same way that the Native American tradition is comic…. I use a lot of techniques that are Western and many that are Afro-American." His syncretism serves as the base of a satiric wit that spares no one. "It's a way of subverting the wishes of the people in power," he maintains.

In stanzas three and four, this very colloquial language changes pace a little into more general storytelling terminology: "one day" and "but she was too / swift for them." This change in tone shifts the story toward the weightier concept of mythology and lesson learning, the work of myths and legends being to explain ourselves to ourselves. In this context, the vain old woman has been consumed by her own reflection—her own mythology—to the exclusion of the rest of the world: "her / whole life became the / mirrors." This poem is about mythology, culture, and reflections of self. Locked inside her house, this vain old woman symbolizes the ethnocentric belief that the whole world is like her, or, if it differs from her, it is somehow wrong or "less" than she is. The old woman loses her connection with the rest of her life, and she becomes cut off from her roots. The "villagers" who represent a healthy diversity and community life are too late to save her from herself; they have become "outsiders." The villagers are "different," and the old woman escapes them by disappearing into the mirror. The mirror is a sterile country within which nothing can flourish naturally except illusion. The mirror is hungry. The mirror is an institution that only knows self-love. One could see the analogy here between the vain old woman and Western civilization's long history of believing itself to be the only "real" civilization. With this in mind, it is interesting to consider another story that is retold in this poem—the ancient Greek myth of Narcissus.

Narcissus was a beautiful young man who was much desired by youths and maidens in his community. However, Narcissus was so proud that no one dared to touch him. One day Narcissus lay down at a spring to quench his thirst and, in the spring's clear water, saw his own reflection. He gazed in wonder at his beauty, and soon fell deeply in love with his reflection. Eventually, reaching into the water to try and embrace his own image, he fell into the spring and drowned. In *Classical Mythology* by Mark Morford and Robert J. Lenardon, a section of the Narcissus myth in Ovid's *Metamorphoses* is reproduced: He marveled at all of the things that others had marveled at in him. Unwise and unheeding, he desired his very self, one and the same person approving and being approved, seeking and being sought, inflaming and being inflamed He did not understand what he was looking at but was inflamed by what he saw, and the same illusion that deceived his eyes aroused his passion.

This tragic story of self-love and self-destruction is one that has been retold in many forms throughout literary history. Why did Reed use this story, given that Greek mythology is at the center of Western European civilization? Why did he allow this powerful story to cast its spell over a poem about racism and exclusion? The answer, I think, is to be aware that this poem is not saying black culture is good and white culture is bad. In including the mythology of Narcissus, Reed is acknowledging both the richness of Western culture and the tragedy that it fell in love with itself, thus entering a relationship of deception, sterility, and exclusivity.

In stanza five, there is an abrupt shift of point of view, from telling the story of the hungry mirror into the immediate, dangerous hunger of the poem. This hunger is "legendary." Reed might be warning that this poem also has a long tradition that may or may not be reflecting an emptiness into which the reader could disappear. The narrator entreats the reader to "back off from this poem," as though it were a bomb about to explode or a gun

> *By literally drawing the reader into the poem, Reed demonstrates how poems can also be mirrors within which we can be lost if the experience of the poem negates our culture or presence on the earth."*

about to fire. However, in line 3 of the fifth stanza, the reader is in the poem. The narrator's point of view has shifted again—from warning the reader against the poem, to telling the reader how far he or she is already "lost" in the poem: "you are in this poem. from / the waist down."

The way the poem changes shape and point of view, its metamorphosis into which the reader is drawn, is an example of the colorful mixture and magic of Reed's writing. Reed believes that the black artist should function as a conjuror. To this end, he devised the concept of Neo-HooDoo, a modern version of the old idea of Voodoo, or "Black magic." In *Contemporary Poets*, Charles L. James wrote: "Reed's poetry is committed to no style, save *'The Neo-HooDoo Aesthetic,'* the title of one of his poems." A passage from *"Neo-HooDoo Manifesto"* iterates the point. "Neo-HooDoo believes that every man is an artist and every artist a priest. You can bring your own creative ideas to Neo-HooDoo.... Reed has developed the view that the black artist should function as a 'conjuror' who employs Neo-HooDoo as a means of freeing his fellow victims from the psychic attack of their oppressors."

"Beware: Do Not Read This Poem" parallels the magic in western mythology with the more ancient and non-Western source of "black magic." The black poet is a "conjurer"; the poem is a shape changer. The familiar becomes unfamiliar; the poet shakes us up just as we get a foothold on the poem. We, the readers, are made to see through different eyes and different points of view.

In stanza six, the line "nobody can hear you can they ?" is a sinister high point in the poem. The "you" in the poem is silenced and isolated. The tone of the narrator is knowing, as though this entrapment was planned. The poem belches rudely; it is not well-mannered or pleasing ("this poem aint got no manners"). In a total shift from the warnings of stanza five and the first two lines of stanza six, the narrator begins to champion the poem. Stanza six reads almost like a rape scene, in that the reader is trapped, silenced and told not to "resist": "you cant call out frm this poem / relax now & go w/ this poem / move & roll on to this poem // do not resist this poem."

It moves from the personal "yr" in "this poem has yr eyes" to the impersonal pronoun "his" in "this poem has his head." The poem has moved into an area of extreme discomfort. This is not the experience one expects when reading a poem; one does not expect trickery, muteness, and rape. A question rises out of this discomfort: is this negation of self in the poem what black students experience when they read through the canon of (white) English Literature? Is this why Ishmael Reed—in the foreword to his *Conjure: Selected Poems,* 1963-1970—said: "I wrote my second poem at the age of 14 (1952) while serving time at Buffalo Technical High School…. I didn't write another poem until dropping out of college in 1960."

It's important at this point to be aware of the irony that Reed employs in the poem. The message in the poem is to *resist* stepping into the mirror. By literally drawing the reader into the poem, Reed demonstrates how poems can also be mirrors within which we can be lost if the experience of the poem negates our culture or presence on the earth. The dense and sinister stanza six is underscored by the simple, two-line stanza seven: "this poem is the reader & the / reader this poem." If the reader is the poem and the poem the reader, there is no debate; there is only acquiescence. This is the infertile ground on which nothing will flourish. There will be no real criticism or extension of mind.

In this poem, we are encouraged, or goaded, into an awareness of a variety of viewpoints, unlike Narcissus or the vain "ol woman" who only see themselves. It is this awareness of a common and diverse humanity that will prevent societies from moving in ever-diminishing circles and creating spaces where there once were lives. The warning tone of the title echoes the grim statistics at the end of the poem. Set out in formal, dry language, the first three lines of the final stanza give figures on missing persons. The horrible finality of these statistics is redeemed by the last two lines that acknowledge—in understated, poignant simplicity—the sadness that occupies the spaces where people have been lost: "leaving no solid clues / nor trace only / a space in the lives of their friends." These human spaces are symbolized in the poem by typographical spaces and floating punctuation.

The story in "Beware: Do Not Read This Poem" drifts down the page until the "list" in the last lines of stanza four lead into the drawn-in, threatening tone of stanzas five and six. The language of these two stanzas becomes more and more oppressive as the shape of the poem becomes denser and more orderly. The final lines of stanza nine start to drift again when the language of the poem finds its heart and acknowledges a sadness for those lost loved ones. The final word of the poem is "friends." This word strikes a note similar to the beginning of the poem, when the relaxed and slightly vulnerable narrator begins to tell his story, as if to a group of friends. This circular structure is used in mythology, folk tales, and fairy tales. After an important journey, the main character or characters return to where they were in the beginning, but they are wiser and better people for having been out in the world. I believe this poem argues for a new mythology, one that includes cultural diversity and difference, providing a fertile ground for the growth of a truly representative literature.

Source: Lynn Davidson, in an essay for *Poetry for Students,* The Gale Group, 1999.

Alice Van Wart

Alice Van Wart is a writer and teaches literature and writing in the Department of Continuing Education at the University of Toronto. She has published two books of poetry and written articles on modern and contemporary literature. In the following essay, Van Wart shows how Reed uses voice and technical skill in "Beware: Do Not Read This Poem" to create a poem that works through wit and political nuance.

Tell a person not to do something and there is a good chance it will be done. So Ishmael Reed cleverly entices the reader with the title of his poem "Beware: Do Not Read This Poem." Not only is the imperative provocative, but so is the use of the word "beware," which suggests danger in the poem. Who wouldn't want to read it?

As a prolific writer of novels, poetry, essays, plays, as well as having worked as a publisher and an editor, Ishmael Reed knows the power of language. His writing is imbued with political and social intentions, often satirizing American culture and white social values and white society's perceptions of black people. Growing up in the working class of Buffalo and Harlem, Reed saw first-hand the disadvantages of being poor, uneducated, and black in America. As a young man during the years of the Black Power and Civil Rights movements, he became associated with a group of artists concerned with fostering innovative, authentic artistic expression by African Americans that would be meaningful to black people. Alienation from white society and its values, along with its art forms, led these artists to initiate the Black Aesthetic Movement. (In his first novel, *Mumbo Jumbo* [1972], Reed provides an autobiographical depiction of the movement, showing it to be an extension of two earlier periods of black creativity, most notably the Harlem Renaissance of the 1920s.)

Along with other poets of the movement, most notably Amiri Baraka (formerly LeRoi Jones), Reed rejected the poetic forms imposed by a white culture to create a new black poetry. For their material, they turned back to the earlier folk songs and stories of black people, adopting the colloquial language of the street, innovative typography, and the rhythms of jazz for its expression.

Critics have praised Reed's poetry for its power and versatility, but they have also condemned it for its stridency. In his poetry, Reed fights for and celebrates black achievement. It is often politically motivated by issues of race, class, and gender. The best of Reed's poetry is graced with power, simplicity, and rhythm, exemplified in his poem "Beware: Do Not Read This Poem." Using colloquial language, stanzas of varying length and line, voice, rhetorical device, and typography, Reed creates an organic form of theme and technique imbued with political nuance.

The poem begins casually when the poet announces he has just finished watching a thriller on television "abt an ol woman, so vain she / surrounded herself w / / many mirrors." He summarizes the plot, telling us the woman ended up locking herself in the house with her mirrors. One day the villagers (presumably afraid of her strange habits) broke into her house, but "she was too swift for them. she disappeared / into a mirror." Thereafter any person who bought the house "lost a loved one to / the ol woman in the mirror." After listing the people who disappeared into mirror—"a little girl," "a young woman," "the young woman /s husband,"—the poet abruptly shifts away from the subject of the movie to what appears to be a non sequitur, "the hunger of this poem," in the fifth stanza. The poet announces that the poem "has

> *Using colloquial language, stanzas of varying length and line, voice, rhetorical device, and typography, Reed creates an organic form of theme and technique imbued with political nuance."*

taken in many victims." He warns the reader "to back off from this poem," but, in fact, it is too late. The poet tells the reader, "you are into this poem." In the final part of the poem, the subject shifts to a "us bureau of missing persons," which reports the disappearance of people never heard from again. All they leave behind is "a space in the lives of their friends."

The poem's surface simplicity—with its use of colloquial language and prosaic free verse—is deceptive, betraying a complex intent. The story of the woman who disappears into the mirror prepares the reader for a series of associations played out in the second part of the poem. The old woman who disappears into the mirror recalls the story of Narcissus, who drowned while gazing at his own reflection in water. Narcissus symbolizes the dangers of introverted self-contemplation. The mirror is an instrument for self-contemplation. The image of the mirror suggests the danger of drowning in the image of the self, and in the film, the danger becomes reality. The horror in the film rests in the fact that each person who later lives in the woman's house loses "a loved one … to the mirror."

The abrupt shift in subject matter in the fifth stanza is accompanied by a change in tone and voice. The colloquial speech patterns and casual voice of the first four stanzas give way to the consistent use of phrasal repetition that creates a rhetorical effect quite different from the previous stanzas. The casual tone of the poet's voice becomes oracular. Despite the shift in subject, voice, and tone, the story of the woman in the mirror is intricately connected to the poem and its hunger.

The poet's announcement that "the hunger of this poem is legendary" connects to the legend of the woman who disappeared into the mirror and thereafter claimed victims. The poem, like the mirror, "has taken in many victims." To reinforce the association with victims, along with the suggestion of danger in the poem, the poet tells the reader to "back off from this poem." In other words, reading the poem holds a similar danger to staring at oneself in the mirror; the reader could disappear into the poem. The poet's pronouncement that the mirror is "greedy" confirms the connection. The parallel repetition of "back off" and "it has taken" points to the warning in the title and underlines the danger of reading the poem.

The poet, however, is crafty. He tells the reader, who has (obviously) come this far in reading the poem, that it is too late. "It has drawn in yr feet ... yr legs." In fact it has you from "the waist down," so there is no running away. Like the mirror into which people noiselessly disappear, the poem silently consumes. Like the mirror, it is totally undiscriminating in who it takes. The association with consumption in "this poem has had you up to here" is wittily confirmed in the poem's "belch." The rude belch shows the poem's lack of concern for polite behavior when it comes to its appetite. In fact, the poet tell us, "this poem ain't got no manners."

Having taken the reader in—literally and figuratively—the poet has established the poem's intention and now advises the reader to relax and go with the flow ("relax now & go w / this poem"). The sexual innuendo in "move & roll on to this poem" suggests a union of sorts, confirmed in the coming together of "Yr eyes" with "his head," "his arms," "his fingers," and "his fingertips." The use of synecdoche connects the words written by the poet's fingers onto the page with the eyes of the reader. The reader and the poem become one. The phrasal repetitions of "this poem has," concluding with "this poem is the reader & the / reader this poem," lends powerful effect to the confirmation that the reader colludes in silence with what is written in the poem.

The shift again in the subject, voice, and tone in the poem's concluding stanza further enhances the poem's purpose and its effect. The mention by "the us bureau of missing persons" of the disappearance of more than 100,000 people (in 1968) who have left "no solid clues / nor trace" suggests they have disappeared either into the mirror or into the poem. If the person who disappears into the poem is a "victim" as the poet says ("it has taken in many victims"), and the poem and the reader are one, then there must be an identification between victim and victimizer. However, if the danger of looking in the mirror is one of self-absorption and the inability to see beyond the self, the danger in reading a poem is the power of the poet's words to shape and form.

Reed suggests the differences between self-contemplation and the act of writing and reading is that one limits and narrows and the other expands. Where one only absorbs and reflects, the other has the power to bring about change. In this final implication, Reed illustrates the truth of the saying, the pen is mightier than the sword. Watch out for this poem: It might change the way you think.

Source: Alice Van Wart, in an essay for *Poetry for Students,* The Gale Group, 1999.

Sources

Bokinsky, Caroline G., "Ishmael Reed," *Dictionary of Literary Biography,* Volume 5: *American Poets Since World War I, First Series,* edited by Donald J. Greiner, Gale Research, 1980, pp. 180-84.

Dick, Bruce, and Amritjit Singh, eds., *Conversations with Ishmael Reed,* Jackson: University Press of Mississippi, 1995.

James, Charles L., "Reed, Ishmael (Scott)," *Contemporary Poets,* 6th edition, New York: St James Press, 1996, p. 904.

Montaigne, Michel de, *The Complete Essays of Montaigne,* Stanford, California: Stanford University Press, 1965.

Morford, Mark, P. O., and Robert J. Lenardon, *Classical Mythology,* New York: Longman, 1985.

Preminger, Alex, ed., *Princeton Encyclopedia of Poetry and Poetics,* Princeton, NJ: Princeton University Press, 1974.

Reed, Ishmael, *Conjure: Selected Poems, 1963-1970,* Amherst, MA: University of Massachusetts Press, 1972.

Reed, Ishmael, *New and Collected Poems,* New York: Atheneum, 1988.

Reed, Ishmael, *Writin' is Fightin': Thirty-Seven Years of Boxing on Paper,* New York: Atheneum, 1988.

Russell, D.A., and M. Winterbottom, eds., *Classical Literary Criticism,* New York: Oxford University Press, 1989.

For Further Study

Fox, Robert Elliot, *Conscientious Sorcerers: The Black Postmodernist Fiction of LeRoi Jones/Amiri Baraka, Ishmael Reed, and Samuel R. Delaney,* New York: Greenwood Press, 1987.
    These three fiction writers are brought together in order to examine their revolutionary and iconoclastic styles.

Randall, Dudley, ed., *The Black Poets,* New York: Bantam, 1988.

Randall's anthology begins with anonymous "folk poetry," continues with "literary poetry," and then concludes with poetry from the 1960s. The book was first published in 1971 and includes "Beware: Do Not Read This Poem."

Reed, Ishmael, *The Free-Lance Pallbearers,* Garden City, New York: Doubleday, 1967.

Reed's first novel is narrated by Bukka Doopeyduk, an incredible naïf who is disillusioned and crucified at the novel's end.

Reed, Ishmael, *Reckless Eyeballing,* New York: St. Martin's, 1986.

This novel continues Reed's critique of the irrational blend of faith, fascism, and racism rampant in modern society.

Brazil, January 1, 1502

Elizabeth Bishop

1960

Elizabeth Bishop's "Brazil, January 1, 1502" appeared in a 1960 volume of *New Yorker* magazine. The poem would also appear five years later in Bishop's verse collection titled *Questions of Travel*. A U.S. citizen, Bishop spent fifteen years in Brazil. She was enamored with the nation and its landscape, but she also questioned her place—as an outsider—in the country. "Brazil, January 1, 1502" explores that idea from an historical perspective. The poem's title refers to the day that the Portuguese anchored at Guanabara Bay, Brazil, and claimed the country as part of their empire. (In 1494, Spain and Portugal had signed the Treaty of Tordesillas, dividing the non-Christian world between them.) Bishop begins her poem with a quote from Sir Kenneth Clark's *Landscape Into Art* and goes on to examines the European perception of nature in this poem about colonial conquest.

Author Biography

Elizabeth Bishop was born on February 8, 1911, in Worcester, Massachusetts, to a well-off family. She was an only child whose father died when she was eight months old. Four years later, her mother suffered a nervous breakdown and was hospitalized. (After the age of five, Bishop would never see her mother—who was diagnosed as permanently insane—again.) Young Elizabeth was sent to Nova Scotia to live with her maternal grand-

Elizabeth Bishop

mother until she was six, then she moved in with her father's parents, and, finally, she settled in her aunt's home in Massachusetts. Although her formal education was spotty, Bishop did attend high school until 1930. She then spent four years at Vassar College, during which time she developed as a poet because of her education, the influence of her classmates (several of whom, including Muriel Rukeyser, Mary McCarthy, and Eleanor Clark, would also become noted writers), and through her friendship with the already well-known poet Marianne Moore, whom she met through a librarian. It was Moore who helped convince Bishop to renounce her plans to become a doctor and instead focus on poetry.

After graduating from Vassar College in 1934, the same year her mother died, Bishop moved to New York City, where she continued living comfortably off her father's estate. In 1935, Bishop had a poem published in Moore's anthology titled *Trial Balances.* For the next three years, Bishop traveled to Europe and north Africa; she also bought a house in Key West. From 1945 to 1951, Bishop lived in New York, and she published her first book, *North and South,* in 1946. Her personal life was not happy, however; she suffered from asthma, depression, and alcoholism and was alienated by her status as an orphan, woman poet, and lesbian. At

the advice of her doctor, Bishop set off on a cruise around the world in 1951. One of her first stops was in Rio de Janeiro, Brazil, where she visited Lota de Macedo Soares, a friend she had met at a party in New York. The two began a relationship, and Bishop stayed in Brazil until 1966.

Bishop returned to the United States to take a job at the University of Washington in Seattle in 1966. After her longtime friend Robert Lowell retired in 1969, Bishop assumed his post as poet-in-residence at Harvard University. By the time Bishop died in 1979 in Boston of a cerebral aneurysm, she had won the Pulitzer Prize for *Poems: North and South—A Cold Spring* (1955), a National Book Award for *Complete Poems* (1969), and a National Book Critics Circle Award for *Geography III* (1976).

Poem Text

. . . embroidered nature . . . tapestried landscape
—*Landscape Into Art,* by Sir Kenneth Clark

Januaries, Nature greets our eyes
exactly as she must have greeted theirs:
every square inch filling in with foliage—
big leaves, little leaves, and giant leaves,
blue, blue-green, and olive,   5
with occasional lighter veins and edges,
or a satin underleaf turned over;
monster ferns
in silver-gray relief,
and flowers, too, like giant water lilies   10
up in the air—up, rather, in the leaves—
purple, yellow, two yellows, pink
rust read and greenish white;
solid but airy; fresh as if just finished
and taken off the frame.   15

A blue-white sky, a simple web,
backing for feathery detail:
brief arcs, a pale-green broken wheel,
a few palms, swarth, squat, but delicate;
and perching there in profile, beaks agape,   20
the big symbolic birds keep quiet,
each showing only half his pugged and padded,
pure-colored or spotted breast
Still in the foreground there is Sin:
five sooty dragons near some massy rocks.   25
The rocks are worked with lichens, gray
       moonbursts
splattered and overlapping,
threatened from underneath by moss
in lovely hell-green flames,
attacked above   30
by scaling-ladder vines, oblique and neat
"one leaf yes and one leaf no" (in Portuguese).
The lizards scarcely breathe; all eyes

are on the smaller, female one, back-to,
her wicked tail straight up and over,   35
red as a red-hot wire.

Just so the Christians, hard as nails,
tiny as nails, and glinting,
in creaking armor, came and found it all,
not unfamiliar: 40
no lovers' walks, no bowers,
no cherries to be picked, no lute music,
but corresponding, nevertheless,
to an old dream of wealth and luxury
already out of style when they left home—   45
wealth, plus a brand-new pleasure.
Directly after mass, humming perhaps
L'Homme armé or some such tune,
they ripped away into the hanging fabric,
each out to catch an Indian for himself—   50
those maddening little women who kept calling,
calling to each other (or had the birds waked up?)
and retreating, always retreating, behind it.

Poem Summary

Lines 1-13:

The poem's title situates the poem in place and time: January 1, 1502, marked the day of the Portuguese sighting of and landing at Rio de Janeiro (River of January); it was the first time European eyes saw this place. According to the first two lines, nature has not changed much from the days of "theirs" (Portuguese invaders) to the present day of "our eyes" (readers of the poem). In other words, every January is pretty much the same, with the Brazilian, summer landscape dense with foliage and flowers. Bishop's description lets readers know that the most remarkable things a person not from the tropics might notice about Rio's nature is its size ("giant leaves," "monster ferns," and "flowers like giant water lilies"), its density (indicated by "every square inch filling in with foliage"), and its variety (the palette of colors, gradations of sizes, contrasts, and, even, textures—as in "satin underleaf").

Lines 14-15:

These two lines are crucial in that they compare nature, for the first time in the poem, to an artwork. Notice that Bishop states this obliquely (poetry being the art of stating indirectly): she does not use the word "tapestry" but instead refers to the "frame" from which the tapestry is removed; we know this artwork is not a painting, because paintings are most often displayed with the frame. This reference to tapestry refers us back to the epigraph, words from Kenneth Clark's book, which we can assume sparked some of the ideas for this poem.

Media Adaptation

- *Elizabeth Bishop, One Art* can be found in the PBS Voices and Visions series, New York: Center for Visual History Productions

Lines 16-23:

Lines 16 and 17 describe the upper portion of the landscape tapestry: sky, foliage ("simple web"), and the birds ("feathery detail"). "Brief arcs, a pale-green broken wheel" might indicate the arching palm branches with limp-hanging fronds, looking like a spoked wheel without hub or lower half. In the palms are birds, most likely macaws (a kind of parrot); these birds are not only identified with South America, but with a rich symbolic heritage—most generally as a solar symbol, as an avatar of heavenly fire—among the tribes of Brazil. These birds, Bishop seems to notice, are usually depicted in profile, perhaps to show off their magnificent beaks. They are likely quiet because asleep. As in a still life or tapestry, a general stillness pervades these lines.

Lines 24-32:

The word "foreground" calls further attention to this scene as a tapestry. Line 24 is important for the word "Sin," capitalized to link it with the idea in Christianity. What will be important for the following lines is nature seen in terms of Christian symbolism. For example, sin is figured as "five sooty dragons near some massy rocks." Dragons, often linked to serpents, are paradigmatic symbols of original sin. "Sooty" might be linking dragons to the fires of hell (described later as "hell-green" to link nature with fallen nature, nature as sinful). The rocks appear to symbolize earth attacked from below by hellish forces and from above by heavenly forces—earth is depicted as a battleground in the war between God and Satan. For example, the spreading "moonbursts" of lichens overtaking the rocks link the scene to a pagan and feminine, not a Christian, scene: the moon—a body that changes earth's tides, glows with indirect light, and proceeds through phases—is linked with earth, woman, and sin. With line 32, we are assured that the aforementioned lines have been a Portuguese, not a Brazilian Indian, conception of landscape, since the vine, attacking from above, is described in Portuguese. The "yes and no" alternating ladder pattern is the vine as a Christian symbol of passage to heaven, a conduit from earth to paradise.

Lines 33-36:

These four lines describe the "sooty dragons." They turn out to be five lizards—four males, one female. The lizards are sinful because they are depicted as ready for sex (earthly and sinful in strict Christian terms). The female lizard, like Eve and woman generally, is shown to be even more sinful—at least in the older Christian worldview—because females are supposedly changing creatures (their bodies change with pregnancy and with menses, and they are said to be fickle) and they lure men to their demise—in this case, with an alluring, yet "red-hot," "wire" in their tail.

Lines 37-46:

The "Just so" identifies the Christians with the lizards above, probably in separate areas of the tapestry. The Christians are depicted as nails, because they are dressed in armor and are violent, but there is also phallic symbolism attached to the description. The Portuguese Christians find Brazilian nature somewhat familiar because they had some experience with gardens back home. Kenneth Clark reports that gardens were the model for Paradise, a nature made altogether friendly to humans. True, the Brazilian rain forest did not have "lovers' walks" and the other amenities once part of the gardens of a flourishing aristocracy (persecuted in the late 1400s by the Portuguese king, John II), but the jungle was beautiful. And it even contained "a brand new pleasure" that was not part of Portuguese gardens: Brazilian women.

Lines 47-53:

Upon landing at what would become Rio de Janeiro, the Portuguese invaders hold a Mass on the beach where they sing, perhaps *L'Homme armé*, a Mass telling the basic story of Jesus and asking Him for mercy. Immediately afterward, the Christians walk into the jungle, tearing their way through with their swords (slashing at the fabric of the "tapestry" of nature) to chase the Indian women who hide behind the foliage. While the real Portuguese who ripped away the "hanging fabric" were outside of the tapestry, the Portuguese of Bishop's poem are also made part of the textile tapestry through Bishop's textual tapestry. This is only to say that the Portuguese were both of and not of nature. On the other hand, the Brazilian women are embedded so deep into the tapestry as to almost disappear behind it. They, like nature, are treated by the Portuguese as part of the scene—at one with the jungle's flora and fauna, as susceptible to capture and overpowering as macaws chased for their feathers.

Themes

American Dream

Bishop's poem commemorates a particular New Year's Day in 1502, when the crew, Captain Gonçalo Coelho, and the pilot major/scribe, Amerigo Vespucci, sailed for the first time (for Europeans) into what would eventually become the city of Rio de Janeiro on a continent eventually named for Vespucci, "America." The Portuguese had what is now known as the American Dream—in this case an early and somewhat different version of that dream. It was a dream of wealth gained by exploiting the people and nature of new lands. In the Portuguese version, the wealth consisted largely of logs of Brazil wood, a red wood processed for its crimson dye, and the wealth of birds and bird feathers. Both of these items were acquired from Brazilian natives in exchange for iron axes, used partially to cut down the trees for Portuguese manufacturers who would process the logs, sell the dye, and give part of their proceeds to the crown. This was the American dream in its original character—a dream to get rich, to get ahead by exploitation. This early version of the American dream would eventually become the dream of individuals all over the world who were willing to work hard and honestly to move from poverty to wealth, or at least to prosperity.

Nature and Its Meaning

In Bishop's poem, the Portuguese view nature as feminized, with native Brazilian women being part of that nature. Woman has long been considered more a part of nature than man; woman is associated with "mother earth," while man is associated with father sky. But many people still believe that it was dark skin that really led to white domination of native peoples. Hannah Arendt, in speaking of the colonization of Africa in *Imperialism* (1968), casts doubt upon this conception: "What made [Africans] different from other human beings was not at all the color of their skin but the fact

Topics for Further Study

- Research the flora and fauna native to Brazil. Then find out what has happened to the rain forest in the last several decades.

- Do a comparative study between the letters of Amerigo Vespucci on the Brazilian Indians and studies done in the twentieth century, such as those by Claude Levi-Strauss. How do the writings differ or remain the same?

- Research Christian conceptions of nature. An excellent beginning would be the book *Traces on the Rhodian Shore* by Clarence Glacken.

that they behaved like a part of nature, that they treated nature as their undisputed master, that they had not created a human world, a human reality, and that therefore nature had remained, in all its majesty, the only overwhelming reality—compared to which they appeared to be phantoms, unreal and ghostlike. They were, as it were, 'natural' human beings who lacked the specifically human character, the specifically human reality, so that when European men massacred them they somehow were not aware that they had committed murder." Elizabeth Bishop, herself, in her book, *Brazil* (1962) makes clear that it was not dark skin that led the Portuguese to degrade the Brazilian Indians, nor, particularly, the women: "The Portuguese had always been romantically drawn to women of darker races; they had long taken Moorish wives and Negro concubines, and there were already many Negro slaves in Portugal. In Brazil it was only natural for them to become eager miscegenationists almost immediately." Thus, the Brazilian woman becomes prey for the Portuguese not because she is dark, but because she seems so much part of the tapestry of nature, even more so than the Brazilian man. The Christian meaning, then, of woman was nature, and the meaning of nature (in its vulnerability, changeability, its ability to give birth to plants) was woman. The naturalization of women and the feminization of nature has led, as Bishop indicates, to rape, rapine, murder, and the obliteration of nature.

Art and Experience

The Portuguese explorers were perhaps familiar with the art that depicted nature as filled with Christian symbology. Kenneth Clark, in *Landscape Into Art*, theorizes why nature was made into a hollow shell inserted with Christian symbols of human construction: "If ideas are Godlike and sensations debased, then our rendering of appearances must as far as possible be symbolic, and nature, which we perceive through our senses, becomes positively sinful." With the Christian worldview as put forth by Clark, the experience of art becomes more important than the experience of nature, since art is what reveals the true meaning within or behind nature. Art, therefore, is not separate from experience, but is experience. On the other hand, nature becomes a kind of false or fallen experience. The Portuguese conception of nature as a tapestry then, is more akin to Christian truth than nature as itself truth—the latter a blasphemy that would diminish the importance of God, who is believed to have created nature. To the Christian, artistic experience, not experience in nature, is the way to God.

Style

"Brazil, January 1, 1502" is a modernist poem in free verse, or verse without established meter that may or may not employ rhyme. Bishop's poem seems to be the freest of free verse, without rhyme or metrics. Close to prose, every line is like a phrase between punctuation marks, the whole punctuated just like prose. There are, however, three stanzas, but without pattern in their number of lines. Why did she create such an unpoetic poem? Perhaps because its subject is so unpoetic, so antiromantic: these Portuguese Christians, neither chivalrous nor heroic, are uncritical plunderers, destructive of both nature and native peoples. Bishop might have used stanzas because the subject matter breaks up into parts: the first, describing nature in nonsymbolic fashion; the second, showing nature in terms of Christian symbols, and the third, positioning humanity's complex connection to nature as both insider and outsider. There is occasional alliteration in the poem (such as "puffed and padded") and occasional repetition of sound (such as the "f" sound in "fresh as if just finished / and taken off the frame"), but a prose writer might just as much seek such repetition. Perhaps what most characterizes "Brazil, January 1, 1502" is its mimicking of the way the explorers approached Rio. In other words, readers come to this poem as explorers, hardly

Compare & Contrast

- **1960:** The population of Brazil stands at over 70,000,000.

  1995: The population more than doubles to 156,000,000, almost all of which claims Christianity as their religion.

- **1960:** Brazilian coffee production totals 3,576,000 metric tons.

1996: Production decreases to 1,290,000 metric tons.

- **1960:** Brazilian passenger car production amounts to 133,000,000 metric tons.

  1995: Production increases to 357,000,000 metric tons.

knowing at all where they are going as they move slowly through its lines, only coming to "conquer" the poem with repeated readings and study. Though this poem may be as difficult to initially move through as a Brazilian rain forest, it should be stated that Bishop objected "rather violently" to other people's footnotes, perhaps because they seemed to her a kind of colonizing by literary critics, an easing of exploration of a place better left intact and without amenities—better left in its original state.

Historical Context

Brazil was the only Latin-American country to be colonized by Portugal, and Pedro Alvares Cabral was the first European to see Brazil. At this time, Spain and Portugal, the first imperial powers, ruled what had been discovered of the world. After the first explorations of Brazil in the early days of the 1500s, the Portuguese crown sent an expedition to establish fifteen captaincies to be administered by hereditary rulers. The rulers enjoyed a great deal of autonomy from the Portuguese crown until 1808. In that year, Napoleon invaded Portugal and forced King Joao VI to flee to Brazil. As a result of the king's residency, Brazil's economic life became consolidated and centralized. In 1821, Joao returned to Portugal; the next year, the king's son, Pedro, had himself crowned emperor of an independent Brazil. Pedro I had to contend with regular conflicts with the aristocracy over the degree of centralization, including a clash over slavery. The slave trade had begun in the mid-sixteenth century but was outlawed in 1850. In 1888, ownership of

slaves was abolished, but the landed elite expressed their discontent over this and other issues by getting the military to depose Pedro in a bloodless coup. This was the beginning of Brazil's first attempt at a republican style of government, referred to as "the Old Republic." Oligarchies henceforth ruled individual states and were bound together in a kind of federalism—called a polity of governors—not ruled by a central government, but more, dominated by the prominence of two states, Minas Gerais and Sao Paulo. Rights and freedoms were scarce, especially for immigrants. In 1930, the oligarchies of Sao Paulo and Minas Gerais could not agree on who they would make president. Amidst the confusion, Getúlio Vargas seized power, made himself president, and dissolved the Old Republic. Vargas ruled like a dictator, even dissolving the constitution when he saw fit. His *Estado Novo,* or New State, not only abolished all political parties, but consolidated the labor movement under Vargas's control. Vargas ruled as a dictator for another six years, until increasing pressure for a return to democracy led him to call an election. When it seemed as though he would again act the dictator and tamper with the results, the military stepped in and removed him from office. Getúlio Vargas, however, would remain a profound influence in his old government: there would continue to be a strong central government, weak oppositional parties, a co-optation of labor and class-based movements, and the consolidation of government with business interests. After the dissolution of the *Estado Novo,* the military played a larger and larger part in the governing of Brazil. They ran candidates in every election, and though they won only the first, the military finally took power in a coup in 1964, the beginning of two decades of military rule.

Elizabeth Bishop had this to say about the government of Juscelino Kubitschek (1956-60), the period in which she wrote "Brazil, January 1, 1502": "Under Kubitschek industrialization began in earnest: iron ore exports were doubled and a Brazilian automobile industry was started. He began an ambitious highway program and undertook the construction of great dams in order to increase the country's supply of electrical power. But the Kubitschek government was susceptible to corruption and graft.... Control of the country remained in the hands of a few powerful political and economic groups. While the south remained rich and prosperous, the northeast was still abysmally poor." The same kinds of divisions between rich and poor, dominators and dominated had continued for four hundred years. The only difference was that the Brazilian Indians were all but wiped out through miscegenation, slavery, disease, and murder.

Critical Overview

"Brazil, January 1, 1502" has been much written about, mostly late in Bishop's career or after she died. Likely, this is due to the poem being slightly ahead of its time, at one with a growing demand (at least in the West) for greater feminist, anticolonial and multicultural awareness. In a 1977 assessment, David Kalston remarked on Bishop's view of the tapestry of nature: "The tapestry—initially it seemed like a device to domesticate the landscape—instead excludes invaders from it.... Nature's tapestry endures, renews itself. After our initial glimpse of order, we shrink like Alice or Gulliver—toy intruders, marvelling." In *The Unbeliever: The Poetry of Elizabeth Bishop*, Robert Parker follows with a virtuoso examination of the poem—which he calls "grandly historical"—over the course of eight pages. He says that Bishop's conquistadors regard nature as symbol, seeing, for example, lizards as dragons as "Sin." But when the poet identifies the conquistadors themselves as lizards, it is they who become sinful and entrapped by their own symbol-making. As Parker says, the conquistadors "sin against the common creed of nature" and thereby become degraded by it. And true to Bishop's point, history has increasingly condemned these early "explorers."

In an article titled "Bishop's Sexual Politics," Joanne Feit Diehl comments, "The torn tapestry becomes the violated body of nature itself." But it is not simply the conquistadors who tear the tapestry and "tear after" the rain-forest women, but anyone who understands nature as a cultural artifact or an empty structure containing within it the more important germ, or essence, of what is symbolized. Diehl believes this implicates the reader in the very first lines; "Januaries, Nature greets our eyes / exactly as she must have greeted theirs." Thus, the poem becomes a cautionary tale for those in the business or habit of turning nature to symbolic ends (especially theologians, writers, painters, filmmakers, etc). In *Elizabeth Bishop: Her Poetics of Loss*, Susan McCabe writes that Bishop composed her "exquisite" poem on New Year's Day. In a comparison between a passage from F. Scott Fitzgerald's *The Great Gatsby* and "Brazil, January 1, 1502," McCabe indicates an historical progress in the general perception of these explorers: while Fitzgerald imagines these explorers as vessels overflowing with wonder, Bishop fills them with lust. Marilyn May Lombardi, writing in *The Body and the Song*, points out the link between the activity of conquering and that of translation that she believes Bishop, a translator of Brazilian poetry, was likely to have seen: "The conquering imagination of the translator has supreme power over the inert, obedient body of the original poem, just as the conquistador imposes his own values on the landscape that greets his eyes." Finally, Anne Colwell, in *Inscrutable Houses: Metaphors of the Body in the Poems of Elizabeth Bishop*, makes a comparison between tourists/travelers and conquistadors, both of whom enter into a foreign landscape only to be swallowed up by it. Colwell asserts that "Brazil, January 1, 1502," is "about the soldiers, the tourist, all of us, being drawn into what we draw in."

Criticism

Marisa Anne Pagnattaro

Marisa Anne Pagnattaro, J.D., Ph.D. in English, is a freelance writer and a Robert E. West teaching fellow in the English Department at the University of Georgia. In the following essay, Pagnattaro explores Bishop's depiction of the colonial conquest of Brazil.

In 1951, Elizabeth Bishop boarded a ship for Tierra del Fuego and the Straits of Magellan, eventually headed to Europe. Along the way, she planned to stop in Brazil and visit friends. At the age of 40, Bishop left behind New York, having yet to come to terms with a troubled childhood and her sexuality. Her biographer, Brett C. Millier, speculated in *Elizabeth Bishop: Life and the Memory of It* that Bishop "left the United States for South America contemplating ... questions of lifestyle and identity, specifically of a lesbian lifestyle as it might relate to her public and private identity." Courageously she set out to contemplate her life far removed from the northeastern United States where she had grown to adulthood.

After her arrival at Santos, Brazil, a port just south of Rio de Janeiro, Bishop boarded a train and was captivated by the landscape she saw. Millier incorporates Bishop's observations in her biography:

> Brilliant scenery suddenly appeared, in sunlight ... A *feathery* quality to the landscape—the grass has that bright but sparse look of Mexican grass—the lush banana trees, etc.,—but against the sky the bamboos & flamboyants & all the Lent trees—rather pale & lacy, slightly Chinese—& this effect appears in all the old engravings, I think.

Amazed by the Brazilian landscape, Bishop captured her fascination in her 1965 collection of poems, *Questions of Travel*. Dedicated to her long-time companion, Lota de Macedo Soares, many of the poems have personal resonances. For example, the title poem, "Questions of Travel," describes the speaker's process of trying to find herself in a distant place. Unlike this poem, "Brazil, January 1, 1502" is much less obviously personal. While in Brazil, Bishop spent time reading about the country's history; Bishop is inspired by this history in this poem. Originally appearing in the *New Yorker* on January 2, 1960, "Brazil, January 1, 1502" confronts headlong issues of the colonial conquest.

The title, "Brazil, January 1, 1502," commemorates the arrival of the Portuguese conquistadors who thought that they "discovered" the country when they landed at Guanabara Bay. The epigram of the poem is from *Landscape into Art* by Sir Kenneth Clark: " ... embroidered nature ... tapestried landscape." In *Stein, Bishop, and Rich: Lyrics of Love, War, and Place,* Margaret Dickie suggests that, by using these phrases, "Bishop draws on Clark's view that conceiving landscape as a tapestry is a medieval construction of nature as symbolic." Bishop was not wholly thrilled with this analogy, yet it seemed to her apt. Millier quotes from a March 23, 1956, letter to friends Ilse and Kit Barker, in which Bishop apologetically remarked that the mountains looked like a tapestry: "Sorry to be so unoriginal but they do,—a brand

What Do I Read Next?

- Elizabeth Bishop's *Brazil,* published in 1962, is full of illustrations and includes a history and cultural exploration of Brazil in the 1950s and 1960s.

- *Traces on the Rhodian Shore: Nature and Culture in Western Thought from Ancient Times to the End of the Eighteenth Century* (1967) by Clarence Glacken, is perhaps the most important volume of history on the perception of nature through time.

- *Woman and Nature: The Roaring Inside Her* (1978) is Susan Griffin's unusual extended prose poem against patriarchal culture, a text that catalogues different associations made between woman and nature.

- Bill McKibben's *The End of Nature* (1989) works hard at combating the persistent notion of the inexhaustibility of nature.

new tapestry, maybe." Later, in an exchange of correspondence with poet Robert Lowell, Bishop laments—in a February 15, 1960, letter—that the image is "a bit artificial but I finally had to do something with the cliché about the landscape looking like a tapestry" (quoted in Dickie's *Stein, Bishop, and Rich: Lyrics of Love, War, and Place*). The reference, however, is more than a mere platitude. The very image of embroidery suggests the imposition of European craft onto the indigenous landscape and the inherent tension between the Portuguese who set out to exploit this land.

The opening lines of the first stanza suggest that, like the colonists, Bishop approached Brazil as an outsider: "Januaries, Nature greets our eyes / exactly as she must have greeted theirs." The month of January has multiple resonances: the literal "January" in the name of Rio de Janeiro (misnamed as a river by the Portuguese); the month in which Bishop mailed the poem to Robert Lowell in 1959; and the Janus of Roman mythology, the guardian of the doors and gates who presided over begin-

> *The very image of embroidery [in 'Brazil, January 1, 1502'] suggests the imposition of European craft onto the indigenous landscape ...."*

nings with dual faces able to look backward and forward. Here, Bishop looks to the past exploitation, yet also implicitly tries to come to terms with her own relationship with Brazil. This exploration is inseparable from the lush, exotic landscape. The next twelve lines of this stanza describe the natural scene in detailed artistic terms. As if consciously trying to weave a tapestry into her reader's mind, Bishop details the varied size, hue and texture of the leaves:

> big leaves, little leaves, giant leaves,
> blue, blue-green, and olive,
> with occasional lighter veins and edges,
> or a satin underleaf turned over;
> monster ferns
> in silver-gray relief,
> and flowers, too, like giant water lilies
> up in the air—up, rather, in the leaves—
> purple, yellow, two yellows, pink,
> rust red and greenish white;
> solid but airy; ....

Bishop celebrates the fecundity of the landscape. Significantly, however, this dense array of images is depicted as if the artist has "just finished / and taken off the frame." The fertile natural world is more than a carefully constructed artifice; even though there is an overt absence of human intruders, the tapestry metaphor suggests their presence. Literary critic Roger Gilbert comments that this stanza "reads at first like one of Bishop's typically wry, elegant landscape poems, full of painterly touches and metaphorically resonant details," yet "the language of tapestry here figures the forcible imposition of a Christian ideology on the native culture."

The second stanza further develops the colonial violence and the introduction of the concept of "sin." The religious law of the Portuguese is imposed on the landscape: "Still in the foreground there is Sin" in the form of "five sooty dragons near some massy rocks." As Dickie notes, it is "as if the first colonizers' view of nature had permanently planted sin on the landscape along with or as their flag." The lusty image is predatory and riddled with tension:

> The lizards scarcely breathe; all eyes
> are on the smaller, female one, back-to,
> her wicked tail straight up and over,
> red as a red-hot wire.

Curiously enough, this sexually charged scene has its roots in one of Bishop's innocuous observations of nature. While writing the poem, Bishop described the same scene in a letter to her Aunt Grace Bowers (quoted in Miller's *Elizabeth Bishop: Life and the Memory of It*) in rather playfully innocent terms:

> Watching the lizards' love-making is one of our quiet sports here!—the male chases the female, bobbing his head up and down and puffing his throat in and out like a balloon—he is usually much larger and much uglier. The female runs ahead and if she is feeling friendly raises her tail up over her back like a wire—it is bright red, almost neon-red, underneath. He hardly ever seems to catch up with her though—

Bishop further reflects on how the Christian dogma of the Portuguese—ostensibly a mere reflection of the natural world—created a skewed perception of a natural event. Moreover, as Millier suggests, the much darker version in the poem equates the female lizard with "the female Indians and the female land as objects both exploited and somehow inviting that exploitation." This troubling image—Brazil and its people encouraging the Portuguese to take advantage of them—is presumably meant to be viewed from the conquistador's perspective.

Lest there be any doubt about Bishop's animosity toward the European visitors 450 years earlier, the final stanza is much more direct and hard hitting. The opening line plays on an old cliché: "Just so the Christians, hard as nails." While they may have set out to dominate, Bishop remakes them as small and almost ridiculous. In her verse, they are "tiny as nails, and glinting, / in creaking armor." What these conquers found was not a romanticized vision. On the contrary, there were "no lovers' walks, no bowers, / no cherries to be picked, no lute music." All of this corresponded "to an old dream of wealth and luxury" that was "already out of style when they left home." Nevertheless, they were able to accrue "wealth, plus a brand-new pleasure."

That pleasure was, apparently, the Indian women they colonized. Depicted as humming a little tune as they leave Mass, these men went about the business of "ripping away at the hanging fabric, / each out to catch an Indian for himself—" ravaging the landscape and its the female inhabitants. The closing lines are riddled with ambiguity. The women are described as "maddening" and "little"—seemingly both confounding and easily overtaken. They "call to each other" and retreat, "always retreating behind it." What is it? The tapestry of the landscape? Or of the overlay of European values? Even though Bishop, in Adrienne Rich's words (in *Boston Review*), grasp's "the presence of colonization and enslavement," Bishop's concluding image is not clear.

This vagueness was probably deliberate. Bishop's own relationship with Brazil and its people was fraught with conflict. Bishop may have just planned to stop in Brazil as part of a trip around the world on her way to Europe, but she stayed for more than fifteen years. In her memoir of Bishop that appeared in *Partisan Review,* Pearl Bell describes how the poet was persuaded by her friend Lota de Macedo Soares to abandon her voyage and remain in Brazil. Bell also notes an important point of reflection for Bishop: "Lota came from a wealthy family that traced its Brazilian roots back to the Portuguese settlers of the sixteenth century."

"Brazil, January 1, 1502" is, as Dickie asserts, "read often for its political insights into colonization," yet it "may also indicate how thoroughly Bishop herself had colonized Brazil, ransacked the landscape for her poetry, found pleasure in her sexual encounters there." In fact, in a letter to Lowell contained in the collection of letters titled *One Art,* Bishop expressed her anxiety: "I worry a great deal about what to do with all this accumulation of exotic or picturesque or charming detail, and I don't want to become a poet who can only write about South America. It is one of my greatest worries now—how to use everything and keep on living here, most of the time, probably—and yet be a New Englander herring-choker bluenoser at the same time." Bishop may have set sail for South America in search is greater self definition, but many questions of place and belonging were left unresolved. Indeed, they may even have been further complicated.

Source: Marisa Anne Pagnattaro, in an essay for *Poetry for Students,* The Gale Group, 1999.

Jhan Hochman

Jhan Hochman, who holds a Ph.D in English and an M.A. in cinema studies, is the author of Green Cultural Studies: Nature in Film, Novel, and Theory (1998). In the following essay, Hochman seeks to lend precision to Bishop's poem and implicates the reader in the acts of the Christian Portuguese conquerors.

Elizabeth Bishop's "Brazil, January 1, 1502" is about the disappearance of nature in the world and the concurrent appearance of nature in art and idea. Kenneth Clark, in *Landscape Into Art,* had already charted the increasing presence of nature in art from the Middle Ages to the nineteenth and twentieth centuries. It was Bishop who ran with Clark's theory: she noticed that as landscape proliferated, nature was decimated.

In the opening lines of "Brazil, January 1, 1502," Bishop tells readers the we must have seen nature much like the Portuguese of 1502 did. The first stanza shows us one way both we and they saw nature: in terms close to pure description filled with wonder, Brazilian nature at the height of variety and fecundity near the time of the summer solstice. Here, the purpose in describing nature is accuracy ("up in the air—up, rather, in the leaves—"). But at the end of the stanza, there is a turn: "fresh as if just finished / and taken off the frame." Bishop has shown us that though we seek accuracy in description we still do not get at the crux of nature. Instead we get color, size, depth ("in silver-gray relief"), and texture ("satin underleaf"). These are all issues important to the artist who must render mere appearance, but not to the observer of nature attempting to understand appearance, function, and behavior—or, in other words, that which makes each plant and animal particularly what it is as an individual, and a member of a group or species. Though the first stanza seems to portray nature as raw and fresh, the last two lines tell us that this is nature still heavily mediated by art.

By the second stanza, things change. Now landscape is described in both descriptive and symbolic terms: the sky is blue-white and a web; the detail feathery; the branches of palm are broken pale-green wheels; the birds (probably macaws) indicate Brazil, a kind of paradise on earth; the lizards are dragonlike and sinful; the lichens are moonbursts; moss is hell-green; the vines are described as attacking, as "scaling-ladder vines," and as "'one leaf yes and one leaf no' in Portuguese"; and the female lizard's tail is a "red-hot wire." In summary, the landscape of the second stanza is both descriptive and symbolic, more fully belonging to the realm of an earlier art when nature was depicted with painterly description and, further, injected with metaphors. This is not nature speaking for itself (the "birds keep quiet"), but nature spoken for—nature as still life, as *nature morte* (dead nature) filled up with "live" symbols and essences created from human imagination (though Christianity would call these essences products of revelation, not imagination).

The third stanza is less clear than the first two. I interpret the first four lines of stanza three as: This is just the way Christians (the Portuguese conquerors) saw nature—through eyes accustomed to nature in artwork; that is, nature in terms of color, shape, and symbol. Other critics have translated these lines as: These Christians (that pursue females in the last lines of the poem) are just like the lizards pursuing a female in the last lines of stanza two—in this way, the Portuguese are, like the lizards, implicated as sinful. While this latter reading functions to parallel features of the poem (soldiers with lizards), I believe it to be a strategy more of form than content—a kind of rhyme of imagery. My interpretation has Bishop saying that both we and the Portuguese see Brazil's nature as new because we have never seen it before; however, we are also familiar with it, since the idea of nature has already been "understood" or processed through artifice, or painting and tapestry yielding an "embroidered nature" suffused with symbol. One source for Portuguese knowledge of landscape is the garden depicted in tapestry and painting, several examples of which are shown in Kenneth Clark's *Landscape Into Art.* The garden represented "good" nature that is conducive to human existence and was the model for Eden and Paradise. Bishop describes this nature in the third stanza: "lovers' walks, … bowers … cherries to be picked … lute music." Clark's description of a garden refers to the painting called *Paradise Garden,* an anonymous work credited to the Cologne School: "It contains the elements of late mediaeval landscape in their most perfect form, and distills a world of delicate, sensuous perception, where flowers are there to please the senses of sight and smell, fruit to satisfy the taste and the sound of a zither, mingled with that of falling water, to delight the hearing." Paradisical nature is in marked contrast to "bad" nature, another nature with which both we and the Portuguese are somewhat familiar. Bad nature is that nature thought to have fallen with Adam and Eve and become resistant to humanity. This might even evolve into the forms of nature depicted in the hellish landscape of Hieronymous Bosch's *Garden of Delights* or the indifferent landscape of Pieter Breughel's *The Fall of Icarus.* Armed with both of these conceptions of good and bad nature, and nature seen in artistic terms of color and shape, we come to nature with preconceptions; we do not see it fresh, but, instead, "fresh, as if just finished / and taken off the frame."

Not only are plants, animals, land, and water seen in terms of previous conceptions of nature inherited or gained through texts and pictures, but so too anything lucky or unlucky enough to be associated with nature. This is what happens in the climax of the poem. Right after hearing songs (artworks)—not about landscape but about sin shouldered by Jesus Christ—the men go into the jungle, ready to understand it as a potential garden, to pluck from it what they desire and prune from it the sin they imagine hidden there. In the rain forest they saw not only plants and animals, but people thought to be ripe for the picking. Native Brazilians were not only naked but possessed and carried few material possessions. What they had was made of simply processed materials from the forest. Amerigo Vespucci's reported that though the Brazilian Indians were without clothes, they were decorated with bird feathers. Bishop even mentions in "Brazil, January 1, 1502" that the Portuguese confused the women's cries with those of the birds (in the second stanza). Such statements suggest that the Indians appeared to Westerners as belonging to nature even more than humanity—that they were closer to the world of animals than to the world of humans. The Indians then, like nature, become ripe for improving, plunder, salvation, or whatever rationalization suits the perpetrator.

While the jungle is large and the interlopers are referred to as "tiny," they are nonetheless hard as nails, because they are made of iron, a substance to which the jungle could offer little resistance. Like small nails invading a huge wall, the conquerors plunged their way into the rain forest. Bishop says they "ripped away into the hanging fabric," tearing the tapestry of nature. But Bishop employs two prepositions: "away" and "into." The Christians also "ripped into" the jungle and penetrated it like nails would.

As the Portuguese chased the "maddening little women" into a wild nature "domesticated" or "tamed" through tapestry (nature understood through art), the women—presumably decorated with bird feathers and calling to each other like birds—retreated behind it. If the Portuguese were so separated from nature that they could be thought outside and in front of it, contemplating it like an artwork, then the women—understood to be within nature—were so far into it as to seem able to hide behind it. With this kind of spatialization, the artwork stands in a space between conquerors and conquered, between Europeans and Indians as a kind of barricade. In addition, the idea of women as nature is reciprocally related to nature conceived of as feminine, mother nature, a nature Bishop refers to with the pronoun "she" in the poem's opening lines. Not only are natives and nature confounded, but so too are women and nature. What the Christians did was rape women and nature, both thought soft and penetrable.

Culture replaces nature not only in the mind but in practice. Nature becomes culture and keeps on becoming culture to such an extent that Brazilian natives have never ceased retreating behind an ever-disappearing nature (and being buried by an increase in representation); they have all but died out with the disappearance, not of a fabric, but of nature "herself." We may not be or act like these Portuguese invaders, but we are their offspring and manifest their deeds in a different fashion: "Nature greets our eyes exactly as she must have greeted theirs," says Bishop. The only difference between us and them is that most of us cause the suffering and disappearance of plants, animals, and elements not by direct, but by indirect action, not by outright invasion, but by a greed that fuels the machines of invasion.

Soure: Jhan Hochman, in an essay for *Poetry for Students,* The Gale Group, 1999.

Bruce Meyer

Bruce Meyer is the director of the creative writing program at the University of Toronto. He has taught at several Canadian universities and is the author of three collections of poetry. In the following essay, Meyer analyzes how "Brazil, January 1, 1502" supports the claim that "the surprise of seeing something for the first time ... is at the core of the artistic experience."

Elizabeth Bishop believed in the value of seeing things afresh. In one of her lesser-known poems, "The Prodigal," Bishop remarks that even a pigsty, when away from home, takes on a semblance of surprise because it is seen new for the first time. The surprise of seeing something for the first time, Bishop suggests in "Brazil, January 1, 1502," is at the core of the artistic experience. The poem, like much of her 1965 collection, *Questions*

of Travel, constantly reminds us not only of what we see but of how we see by taking us through a labyrinth of vegetation—a tapestry where web and weft are woven from threads of perception to form a much larger picture, "fresh as if just finished / and taken off the frame."

Bishop's "Brazil, January 1, 1502," examines the nature of beginnings—how they are perceived and the way that familiarity with something gradually changes our perceptions. For Bishop, the "tapestry" of the first impression can be deceiving; and like a tapestry, there is a reality behind the artifice (whether man's or nature's artifice) that is considerably different once the surface, its beauty, and its textures have been penetrated. To penetrate the surface, the mind's eye and the beholder must work their ways through a labyrinthine weave of images. And like a tapestry, where layers of stitching are overlaid, the life that underlies the immediate impressions is often different from the life that appears on the surface. For Bishop, "Brazil, January 1, 1502" is a poem that not only pays tribute to the conquest and discovery of a place but also to the process of finding life within the context of a place. She questions what that life beneath the surface is and how that vitality is perpetually fleeting, elusive, and unreadable. Like the very meaning at the heart of a poem, Bishop calls out to that which is "retreating, always retreating."

History, she claims, is full of surprises, and one need only imagine the beginnings of things—the moment of their discovery or their revelation—to see the value, the beauty, and the wonder in things. The historical moment Bishop records in the poem is the moment when the new country was first seen by Europeans. Pedro Alvares Cabral, the first European of record to visit Brazil, landed there in 1500 on his way to India. He claimed the portion of the South American continent under the Papal Bull of 1493 and the Treaty of Tordesillas in 1494. The line that Spain and Portugal drew down the center of the world to divide the rights to the eastern and the western hemispheres accidentally gave Brazil to Portugal. At the time, it seemed a workable "Christian" solution, and Pope Alexander IV was proud of the fact that he had avoided an armed conflict between the two Iberian powers. The discovery of Brazil, jutting out in the Atlantic, however, came as a surprise to both the Spanish and the Portuguese.

It is this element of surprise that underscores Bishop's use of the date in the title—and what a surprise it is. Like the "tapestried landscape" in the

> *If this New World is not quite the paradise it seems, Bishop warns us that part of the tapestry of seeing and perceptions is the spiritual and intellectual baggage that our civilized minds cannot leave at home."*

epigram from the aesthetic study of landscapes by art historian and critic Sir Kenneth Clark, the reader and the persona of the poem are meant to view the new world as a series of stories and textures that constantly give way to new beginnings and new interpretations. The fact that the poem opens on New Year's Day reminds us of fresh starts and that the distance between the moment of discovery and rediscovery of a landscape is not all that great. As Bishop sees it, each time we open our eyes to something new, we are in a state of "Januaries," where "Nature greets our eyes / exactly as she must have greeted" the first Europeans to set foot in Brazil.

What we are meant to experience is wonder, not only through the lushness of what is perceived in a new place, but of the overlaid layers that are supported by the tapestry's "simple web, / backing for feathery detail." What Bishop suggests is that underlying any natural or artificial structure or perception there is a broader design. Nothing in the world is mere happenstance and everything has meaning. The birds are "big symbolic birds" whose "beaks agape" suggest a startled nature that is inhabited by a spiritual presence. After all, the word "agape" not only means "wide open"; it also means "love of God." And it is this underlying web of mysticism and spirituality that Bishop recognizes in the second stanza of the poem. "Still," she notes, "in the foreground there is Sin: / five sooty dragons near some massy rocks." Like the paradise of The Bible, the potential for the New World to fall seems to be inherent in it very early on.

If this New World is not quite the paradise it seems, Bishop warns us that part of the tapestry of seeing and perceptions is the spiritual and intellectual baggage that our civilized minds cannot leave at home. Brazil, she suggests, was not discovered simply by explorers but by "Christians, hard as nails, / tiny as nails, and glinting, / in creaking armor." What they "came and found" was not "unfamiliar" to them. They carried with them a strong concept of paradise, albeit a paradise that was more a spiritual concept concerning possession and dispossession than a vegetative construct. The Biblical Eden in the "old dream of wealth and luxury" had become a positivist parable—that Man should be given dominion over all things and therefore claim and possess what is undiscovered. But strangely enough, the vision of the New World that was perceived by these "Christians" was not a morally rigorous one (like that of the Grail Chapel in Medieval romance) but rather a "Land of Cockaigne," a variation on the archetypal paradise of the Judeo-Christian mythos that presents a world where everything is provided without labor or law. This vision of the New World as a Land of Cockaigne is also found in Gonzalo's speech in Act II, Scene i of Shakespeare's *The Tempest* (lines 143-152). Gonzalo envisions a world without laws, government, possessions, labor, or hardship—a land that produces everything everyone needs and where everything is shared in a "commonwealth." The key lines from Gonzalo's musings that seem to be in the back of Bishop's mind in "Brazil, January 1, 1502" state that in such a perfect, lush, and wonderful, newfound land, "All things in common nature should produce / Without sweat or endeavor … but nature should bring forth, / Of its own kind, all foison, all abundance, / To feed my innocent people." The New World, whether imagined by Shakespeare or reinvented by Bishop to include a "brand-new pleasure," is a world that explodes with a bountifulness of growth and life as is suggested in the opening stanza of "Brazil, January 1, 1502."

But seeing something anew, says Bishop, is not enough. What seems to lie at the heart of perception is not simply artistic pleasure or even surprise, but curiosity and a drive to constantly see things new and to discover what lies beneath the surfaces and the textures. In the case of the early explorers who first encountered Brazil, that drive was a combination of religious zeal and simple greed that drove them to rip "away into the hanging fabric, / each out to catch an Indian for himself— / those maddening little women who kept calling, / calling to each other (or had the birds waked up?) / and retreating, always retreating, behind it." Paradise, it seems, is not a state of satisfaction but the process of pursuit, and that which is paradisal is always fleeting, always on the run from discovery.

The song that the Christians sing, *L'Homme armé,* suggests that the world of paradisal innocence inhabited by the bird-songed women of the penultimate line is the victim of this curiosity and this drive toward possession and "discovery." Man is literally "armed," and his spiritual values are constantly at odds with a nature that is unarmed. Yet, the women are "maddening," as if they are the solution to a puzzle or the satisfaction to a desire that is always one step beyond attainment. Here, Bishop is setting up a Blakean-type dichotomy between "innocence" and the world of "experience" or civilization, the religious-minded and "civilized" force of what Freud calls the "Superego." The suggestion on Bishop's part is that there is something innocent even in the Conquistadors, something primal in the self that identifies with the lush vegetation of the newfound Brazil of 1502—a world untouched and untainted by the experience of living and possessing.

The Bible's Book of Genesis tells us that man falls from paradise, and the Book of Revelations promises not a return to Eden but a reward at the end of time that replaces that lost, yet simple, place of innocence. The tension and the substance of history (as suggested by the historical intent of the poem's title) is not so much a question of how to get to the New Jerusalem but how to cope with the unquenchable desire for lost Eden and the proximity to God that Milton treats so comprehensively in *Paradise Lost.* And like Eden or the memory of it that is such a universal motif in what Carl Jung calls "the collective unconscious," the lost state of natural innocence that was Brazil can never quite be regained, even through the imagination.

In this context, Bishop is offering us a tropical elegy, a place where, as the Clark epigraph suggests, nature (innocence) and artifice (civilization) were once integrated in the kind of balance, where "loveliness" and "hell" are compatible and coexistent. Nature itself was a tapestry, a work of art that was complete. It is only civilization and all of its complex virtues that begs us to look behind it for whatever might be found. But the paradox is that the idea of the new paradise of "wealth and luxury" is somehow incongruous with the old. The New Jerusalem, which St. John of Patmos portrays as being a kind of holy Eldorado of gemology, is a far cry from the wild tapestry of "flowers," "monster ferns," and "giant water lilies" that are both the

substance and the motifs of man's original venue. Bishop cannot reconcile the two visions, yet it is that irreconcilability that is the substance and marvel of history. It is only through art, through the ability to imagine the relationship between the past of a January day in 1502 and the countless Januaries of the contemporary world, that we can reduce history to flash and find the connection between a paradise lost and a paradise regained.

Source: Bruce Meyer, in an essay for *Poetry for Students,* The Gale Group, 1999.

Sources

Bell, Pearl K., "Dona Elizabetchy: A Memoir of Elizabeth Bishop," *Partisan Review,* Vol. 58, No. 1, 1991, pp. 29-52.

Bishop, Elizabeth, *One Art: Letters Selected and Edited by Robert Giroux,* New York: Farrar, Straus, Giroux, 1994.

Colwell, Anne, *Inscrutable Houses: Metaphors of the Body in the Poems of Elizabeth Bishop,* Tuscaloosa: University of Alabama Press, 1997.

Dickie, Margaret, *Stein, Bishop, and Rich: Lyrics of Love, War, and Place,* Chapel Hill: University of North Carolina Press, 1997.

Diehl, Joanne Feit, "Bishop's Sexual Politics," *Elizabeth Bishop: The Geography of Gender,* edited by Marilyn May Lombardi, Charlottesville: University Press of Virginia, 1993, pp. 17-45.

Gilbert, Roger, "Framing Water: Historical Knowledge in Elizabeth Bishop and Adrienne Rich," *Twentieth Century Literature,* Vol. 43, No. 2, summer 1997, pp. 144-61.

Lombardi, Marilyn May, *The Body and the Song,* Carbondale: Southern Illinois University Press, 1995.

McCabe, Susan, *Elizabeth Bishop: Her Poetics of Loss,* University Park: The Pennsylvania State University Press, 1994.

Millier, Brett C., *Elizabeth Bishop: Life and the Memory of It,* Berkeley: University of California, 1993.

Parker, Robert Dale, *The Unbeliever: The Poetry of Elizabeth Bishop,* Urbana: University of Illinois Press, 1988.

Rich, Adrienne, "The Eye of the Outsider: Elizabeth Bishop's Complete Poems, 1927-1979," *Boston Review,* April 1983, pp. 15-17, reprinted in *Blood, Bread, and Poetry,* New York: Norton, 1986.

Schwartz, Lloyd, and Sybil P. Estess, *Elizabeth Bishop and Her Art,* Ann Arbor: University of Michigan Press, 1983.

For Further Study

Bishop, Elizabeth, *The Complete Poems,* New York: Farrar, Straus and Giroux, 1969.

This collection covers all but Bishop's last book of poems, *Geography III,* and includes several translations of poems from Portuguese.

Clark, Kenneth, *Landscape Into Art,* New York: Harper and Row, 1976.

Clark's volume traces the history of landscape art—both chronologically and thematically—and is a key text in thinking about the representation of nature.

Hemming, John, *Red Gold: The Conquest of the Brazilian Indians,* Cambridge: Harvard University Press, 1978.

One of the most fascinating themes of Hemming's history is that the discovery of Brazil and what would become the "noble savage" led to some of the ideas of Montaigne, Montesquieu, and Rousseau that would become important for the French Revolution.

Vespucci, Amerigo, *Letters From a New World: Amerigo Vespucci's Discovery of America,* New York: Marsilio, 1992.

Along with Vespucci's six letters back to Portugal from the New World are related materials. Especially relevant is Vespucci's fifth letter from the third voyage to South America, the one in which explorers landed in Rio de Janeiro for the first time.

Come with Me

Robert Bly

1967

"Come with Me" appeared in Robert Bly's collection of poems titled *The Light around the Body,* which was published in 1967 and received the National Book Award for Poetry in 1968. Many of the poems are expressions of protest—against the U.S. government's involvement in the Vietnam War, for example—and underscore the often destructive ways in which public events influence private lives and the ways that human beings seek, but do not always achieve, connection with one another and the natural world. The first poem in the book's section titled "The Various Arts of Poverty and Cruelty," "Come with Me" compares the emotional world of disillusioned and disappointed men to abandoned car parts. Bly's focus on the relationship between the external nonhuman world and the internal emotional human world would continue to inform all of his writing, and his description of the emotional complexion of men, in particular, foreshadows his later interest in men's issues.

The speaker of "Come with Me" acts as a guide, imploring the reader to follow him into the depths of things containing secret knowledge about human existence. He shows the reader how inanimate objects, such as abandoned car wheels, can evoke feelings of grief by describing them as if they had human properties. Bly relies on what has come to be labeled "deep imagery" to carry the emotional weight of the poem. This is a kind of imagery that makes intuitive, associative connections between disparate things—connections readers frequently have to take on faith. The speaker-guide piles up

Robert Bly

these comparisons to evoke the feelings of desperation and futility men often feel about their lives. Bly intends the poem to be a description of the American unconscious, and it is his role as poet to provide that description.

Author Biography

Like the Greek shape-shifting god, Proteus, Robert Bly has consistently managed to change his own identity, making a career out of his own spiritual and political preoccupations. Born on December 23, 1926 to farmer Jacob Thomas and his wife, Alice Bly, Robert Bly attended a one-room schoolhouse in Lac Qui Parle county, Minnesota. Upon graduating from Madison High School in 1944, Bly enlisted in the navy, where he met Marcus Eisenstein and Warren Ramshaw, who encouraged Bly's budding literary interests. Bly studied writing at St. Olaf College in Northfield, Minnesota, before transfering to Harvard, where he met many people who would be influential to his career and life, including poet Donald Hall and Bly's future wife, Carolyn McLean. In 1954 Bly enrolled at the University of Iowa, where he studied literature and writing. Before returning to Minnesota, he traveled to Norway on a Fulbright grant to translate Norwegian poetry. Though he has eschewed making a

career out of university teaching, Bly has continued to translate literature, earning a good part of his income from this activity. In addition to translating, Bly has been a prolific editor and publisher. In 1958 he published the first issue of his literary magazine, *The Fifties* (later to be renamed *The Sixties, The Seventies, The Eighties,* and *The Nineties*). Bly has been largely responsible for reinvigorating interest in Latin American and Eastern European poets such as Pablo Neruda, Cesar Vallejo, Antonio Machado, Georg Trakl, and Tomas Transtroemer—writers who were influential in the development of Bly's own aesthetic and attitudes towards poetry.

In 1966 Bly began organizing anti-Vietnam war poetry readings at various campuses. With David Ray, he founded the organization American Writers Against the Vietnam War. This was the time to be a poet in America, when so much of one's own political convictions could be expressed in work and action. Not only did Bly win the National Book Award in 1968 for *The Light around the Body,* but he also took the opportunity during his acceptance speech to attack American publishers for not actively opposing the war. During that speech at Lincoln Center, he presented his check for the award to a draft resister on the stage. It was also during this time that Bly's obsession with Jungian psychology and myth burgeoned, as he began to vigorously delve into the ways that certain images expressed largely unconscious and frequently irrational human desires. This kind of image, which he wrote about extensively in his book of poetics, *Leaping Poetry: An Idea with Poems and Translations,* Robert Kelly had named the "deep image," for it made connections between the human mind/brain and the external world that could be intuited but not explained. Exploring the ways in which imagery, both verbal and iconic, forms a bridge between these two worlds has remained a thematic constant in Bly's work as a writer. Sixteenth-century German mystic Jakob Boehme's writing heavily influenced Bly and appears frequently in the poet's work as both epigraph and inspiration. The following Boehme quotation, which appears in *The Light around the Body,* can serve as a central idea from which much of Bly's poetry is generated: "For according to the outward man, we are in this world, and according to the inward man, we are in the inward world.... Since then we are generated out of both worlds, we speak in two languages, and we must be understood also by two languages."

Bly's latest incarnation has been as unofficial spokesman for the Men's movement, which he helped popularize first with his seminars, then with his 1990 book, *Iron John: A Book about Men.* In *Iron John* Bly explores relationships between myth and society's definitions of and expectations for masculine behavior. As is the case with his poetry, critics and admirers abound. Never one to follow either popular or academic currents of thinking, Robert Bly remains an iconoclast, a poet of human consciousness, thinking and tinkering in the human imagination in Moose Lake, Minnesota, where he lives with his second wife, Ruth Counsell.

Poem Text

> Come with me into those things that have felt his
>   despair for so long—
> Those removed Chevrolet wheels that howl with a
>   terrible loneliness,
> Lying on their backs in the cindery dirt, like men
>   drunk, and naked,
> Staggering off down a hill at night to drown at last
>   in the pond.
> Those shredded inner tubes abandoned on the   5
>   shoulders of thruways,
> Black and collapsed bodies, that tried and burst,
> And were left behind;
> And the curly steel shavings, scattered about on
>   garage benches,
> Sometimes still warm, gritty when we hold them,
> Who have given up, and blame everything on the   10
>   government,
> And those roads in South Dakota that feel around
>   in the darkness …

Poem Summary

Line 1:

The title of this poem immediately programs our expectations as to its processes and positions the reader as a follower. We expect to be led somewhere, to be given secret knowledge. The narrator implores the reader to follow him, positioning himself as a guide of sorts—like Virgil is in Dante's *Inferno*—to the uninitiated. We are intrigued because he wants us to come with him "into those things" rather than into a place, and we want to know what he means by this statement. "This despair" is also cryptic, but we infer that the speaker has somehow experienced it as well, or else he would not urge us to follow and trust him.

Lines 2-4:

"One of those things" is named. The speaker wants us to enter the world of discarded car wheels. He compares these wheels to drunken naked men who "howl with a terrible loneliness." This makes sense if you have ever heard the noise of wind whistling through a freestanding tire. But these tires/men are also suicidal, or at least prone to accidents, as they "stagger" to their death. The words "at last" underscore the sheer exhaustion of these things, the hopelessness they feel about their existence. By personifying the tires, Bly is stating that some men lament their existence and are like the discarded wheels of Chevrolets. Their writhing about on the ground, drunk and naked, suggests a kind of bacchanalian ritual—yet this ritual seems more akin to a last meal, with their drunkenness being a confession of their pain and suffering. We can see the emergence of Bly's ultimate philosophy in these lines, as his focus on the deterioration of the inner man foreshadows his assertions that late-twentieth-century males have lost touch with what it means to be a man.

Lines 5-7:

The speaker continues his description of the tires and the implicit comparison to the men named earlier. The inner tubes of the tires suggest the inner lives of the men, which have been battered by their travel through life. That the tubes "tried and burst" makes them tragic. Like the tires, these men have been "abandoned" even though they made effort. The images Bly uses to evoke the emptiness and feeling of waste that human beings sometimes feel is appropriate if we think of these things as commodities—as human-made objects that are bought and sold. Increasingly, Western societies have made the dollar the criteria for human value. No longer are we valued for our ability to create and develop communities based on mutual interest, but, rather, we are judged by our capacity to compete and win in the marketplace. Human beings have become just one more item in that marketplace, Bly seems to suggest. And what better commodity to compare our inner lives to than the automobile, the symbol of mobility, prosperity, and progress in twentieth-century America? The automobile is also a central image of maleness. Men have long been characterized as being obsessed with machines, and in America, getting one's driver's license, especially for males, marks an initiation of sorts—an entry into adulthood.

Lines 8-11:

This last image appears out of place. Bly seems to have given up on the worn tire as symbol of human desperation and now uses "curly steel shavings" to evoke the once vital inner lives of the men their inscrutability—and the puzzle of the poem's associations. Now it is not the tires or the men who embody loneliness but the "roads in South Dakota." At the end of the poem, we are left with an unresolved mystery. The speaker (as guide) has not explained the meaning of these things or their interior lives; rather, he has shown us their exhaustion, their inability to revitalize themselves.

Media Adaptations

- An audio cassette of Bly reading his poems has been produced by Everett/Edwards. It is titled *Contemporary American Poets Read Their Work: Robert Bly.*

- Bly appears on the recordings *Today's Poets 5,* by Folkways, and *For the Stomach: Selected Poems,* by Watershed.

- Bly's positions on the men's movement can be found on the videos *A Gathering of Men* (1990) and *Bly and Woodman on Men and Women* (1992).

- Brockport Writers Forum and the State University of New York at Brockport's English Department produced a videotape titled *Robert Bly: Interviews and Readings*

- *A Man Writes to a Part of Himself,* a videotape of Bly reading and lecturing, is available from University Community Video of Minneapolis.

to whom he initially compared the Chevrolet wheels. The image fits because it too is related to automobiles—or at least the setting in which we often think of automobiles, the garage. The shavings are "sometimes still warm, gritty," because the men, though exhausted, remain alive though resigned to the used-up bodies that they inhabit. We are thrown off once more by the penultimate line of the poem because of its ungrammaticality. The only antecedent for "Who" is the steel shavings. But then we understand that the speaker must be writing about the men by association when he says they "have given up, and blame everything on the government." To what have these men succumbed? The poet never tells us specifically. We can only infer—from the landscape of discarded things that Bly describes—that the men feel depleted and useless, and instead of attempting to renew themselves, they have chosen to blame the government for the failures in their lives. The last image leaves us with both a sense of the mystery of these men's lives—

Themes

Alienation and Loneliness

"Come with Me" utilizes images of inanimate objects to suggest the alienation and loneliness of men at a time when self-worth was increasingly measured in terms of usefulness. Employing the prototypical symbol of American culture—the automobile—Bly compiles a list of its parts, now used up, to describe how the inner lives of human beings get depleted as well. When human beings' emotional (or physical) lives crash, they fall apart, or are taken apart, Bly suggests, similar to the way that automobile wheels are removed or left behind once they can no longer function. By focusing on parts of the car, a Chevrolet, without ever again mentioning the car to which the shavings, wheels, and inner tubes belong, the speaker suggests that as soon as humans beings become removed from the context of their larger lives, they, too, become despairing and may "howl with a terrible loneliness." Such emotional pain might also lead to self-destructive behavior, to a desire to escape from the source of the pain—the body—by such means as indulging in alcohol or, more ominously, by committing suicide—here implied by the words "to drown at last in the pond." (Note also that a common euphemism for getting drunk is "drowning one's sorrows.") Bly's writing style also underscores the theme of alienation, as we are never given information about how the shavings on the garage benches, the inner tubes, and the wheels are related. As readers, then, we are alienated from any kind of explicit meaning of the poem. Instead, we must make intuitive leaps of understanding based on the images in the poem.

Human Condition

In "Come with Me," Bly attempts to describe the relationship between human beings' inner and outer lives by exploring the connections between them. The inner life of a human being is instinct and feeling, while the outer life is, or should be,

Topics for Further Study

- Keep a diary of images from your dreams for one week, then attempt to find the sources of those images. How many of them can you trace to public events (e.g., news stories)? How many to private events? Write an essay exploring what these images tell you about your own identity.

- Many scientists today claim that despair is a result of genetic disposition. Conduct a survey asking people what makes them sad and why, then create a chart categorizing their answers. Compose a microtheme, explaining what the chart tells you. Provide examples.

- Bly contended that human beings have at least two selves—the spiritual, internal self, and the political, external self. Make a list of features describing your two selves, then write a short dialogue exploring how they would converse with each other.

---

connected to the natural world. Modern man, however, has lost touch with both worlds. People have become detached from the outer world because human consciousness has compromised it; we have become aware of ourselves as separate from nature and, hence, different. In the poem, such isolation is signified by the wheels that have been removed from their larger body, the car. To offset the resulting sense of detachment, we look elsewhere—to our inner lives—for a connection, and when that is also found lacking, alienation evolves into despair. Though we are still human, as suggested by the "warm, gritty" steel shavings, we are exhausted and bewildered about how to find our way back to our original selves. That we give up and blame our predicament on a manmade institution, "the government," serves to underscore the cyclical nature of the human condition.

Consciousness

Bly's images of defeat, despair, and resignation describe the consciousness of American society by evoking its purported unconscious. It is a consciousness of self-disgust, as suggested by the images of "cindery dirt" and drunken men. In the poems following "Come with Me" in *The Light around the Body,* Bly suggests reasons—historical and embedded in the national psyche—for that self-disgust. Bly implies that Americans are aware of their country's past use of slaves, its continuing poverty, and its capitalist exploitation of labor. However, Americans have been unable or unwilling to deal with such an awareness and the responsibility that comes with it; they feel powerless. As a result, the quality of their lives has diminished.

Style

"Come with Me" is a descriptive free-verse poem meant to induce feelings of despair through its use of surreal or "deep" imagery. Surrealism juxtaposes disparate objects in the same space in order to highlight a connection between them. That connection, however, is often intuitive and associative and not necessarily accessible to all readers. The "deep image," of which Bly has been a leading practitioner, is also meant to evoke a reality beyond that which we see, and it too relies on association and intuition to elicit meaning and emotion. The term "deep image" itself was coined by poet-critic Robert Kelley in 1961 to name the type of image that could fuse the experience of the poet's inner self and his outer world. Its predecessor was the image of Ezra Pound and William Carlos Williams, which attempted to cleanly describe the empirical world. Bly's image extends the kind of image used by early-twentieth-century writers such as French surrealists André Breton and Robert Desnos as well as Chilean writer Pablo Neruda. Bly uses the image in "Come with Me" to explore the region of the mind that could not be accessed by conventionally ratiocinative verse. The succession of images implies the movement from inner to outer reality and must carry the weight of the poem. Other well-known contemporary poets of the deep image include James Wright, W. S. Merwin, Galway Kinnell, William Stafford, and Diane Wakowski.

Historical Context

"Come with Me" appeared in *The Light around the Body,* an award-winning collection of poems that attempted to dramatically illustrate the connections

Compare & Contrast

- **1967:** More than 100,000 people demonstrate against the Vietnam War at the Lincoln Memorial, and Martin Luther King Jr. leads an anti-war march in New York.

  1992: The National Organization for Women (NOW) sponsored a march in Washington, D.C., that was attended by 750,000 people.

  1995: The Million Man March, organized by controversial National of Islam leader Louis Farrakhan, saw hundreds of thousands of black men demonstrate in Washington, D.C.

- **1967:** Heavyweight boxing champion Muham-mad Ali refuses to be inducted into the U.S. Army, claiming conscientious objector status due his religion of Islam. He is indicted by a federal grand jury in Houston, Texas, for draft evasion and is convicted. For the next three years, until the ruling is overturned, Ali is un-able to fight in the United States.

  1999: Heavyweight boxer Mike Tyson is sen-tenced to a one-year jail term for assault. Tyson, who at age 20 became the youngest heavyweight champion in history, had previ-ously had his boxing license revoked for a year after he bit Evander Holyfield during a bout in June of 1997.

---

between the personal and the political self. The Vietnam War was at its height in 1967, when the collection appeared. Demonstrations against the U.S. government swept the country. Hundreds of thousands of protestors descended upon the Lin-coln Memorial in Washington D.C., and in New York City, Martin Luther King led an anti-Vietnam War march. As President Lyndon Johnson's ad-ministration stepped up its attempts to garner do-mestic support for its Vietnam policy, protests in-creased. The privacy of people associated with Leftist organizations was violated by government intelligence organizations such as the Central In-telligence Agency (CIA) and the Federal Bureau of Investigation (FBI), which had been charged with compiling files on those peoples' activities. Histo-rians claim that by 1968 more than 100,000 dossiers had been put together on antiwar activists.

Many celebrities were influential in antiwar demonstrations. Actress Jane Fonda, dubbed "Hanoi Jane" and characterized as a traitor for her support of North Vietnam, spoke out against U.S. involvement in the war, while singers such as Phil Ochs, Joan Baez, and Bob Dylan led antiwar ral-lies. Norman Mailer's novel *Armies of the Night* chronicled the arrest and detention of more than 600 antiwar protestors (including Mailer himself), and poets such as Bly and Ted Berrigan organized readings to express public opposition. Expression of dissent did not always take the form of con-demnation, however. In addition to his more ex-plicit criticisms of the American government, Bly also attempted to detail the ways in which the chaos in America affected the emotional and moral land-scape of the country. "The poet's main job is to penetrate the husk around the American psyche, and since that husk is inside *him* too, the writing of political poetry is like the writing of personal poetry, a sudden drive by the poet inward," Bly said. Bly's own drive inward mirrored America's, as the country continued to wrestle with its legacy of racial and ethnic oppression. Not only did nu-merous Americans increasingly voice their dissat-isfaction with U.S. foreign policy, but many also began to more strongly denounce its domestic poli-cies as well. Inspired by Malcolm X, who had been assassinated in 1965, black leaders Bobby Seale and Huey Newton formed the Black Panther Party, which actively resisted what it viewed as white oc-cupation of black communities. Racial conflict came to a head in 1968 when rioting engulfed many of America's major cities. The 1960s also wit-nessed a reinvigorated interest in feminism. In 1964 Title VII of the Civil Rights Act banned gender dis-crimination in employment, and in 1966 the Na-tional Organization for Women (NOW) was founded with the help of author and activist Betty Friedan. NOW pushed for maternity leaves, legalized abortion, and an Equal Rights Amendment to the Constitution. The rapidness and intensity of these social changes left their mark on the American consciousness, as the impossibility of maintaining a coherent national identity also affected the possibility for keeping or cultivating a stable personal identity.

Critical Overview

The Light around the Body, the collection of poems in which "Come with Me" appears, has been widely reviewed. Most of those reviews have been favorable. Paul Zweig wrote that "the sadness in *The Light around the Body* is a sadness for America. The book quietly, but firmly, translates the inward mystery and melancholy ... into an expansive public language." Louis Simpson, another practitioner of the "deep image" and a friend of Bly's, deemed that "Bly is one of the few poets in America from whom greatness can be expected. He has original talent, and what is more rare, integrity." William Taylor summed up the opinions of those who reviewed the book unfavorably: "*The Light around the Body* is, at its worst, a document in the triumph of a kind of psuedo-poetry which Robert Bly has been importantly instrumental in fostering since the 1950s: a Cult of Goodness. This is a poetry in which the poet sounds rather like a hairy All-American Pen Woman. I believe someone should say something against it, and what needs saying is that it leads to just another kind of sentimentality, another kind of shrill melodramatic posturing, and worse, another kind of arrogance." One of the few people to write explicitly about "Come with Me" was critic Howard Nelson, who claimed that Bly succeeded in the poem by using images rather than circumstances to get at the emotional lives of human beings. Nelson noted that "'Come with Me' expresses grief through objects—images of metal shavings on work benches, shredded tires along thruways .... There is a marvelous depth and poignancy to these images."

Criticism

Chris Semansky

A widely published poet and fiction writer, Chris Semansky teaches literature at Portland Community College. In the following essay Se-

What Do I Read Next?

- Irwin Unger's 1974 study, *The Movement: A History of the American New Left,* provides a useful, if sketchy, outline of the protest movement against the Vietnam War. Bly was instrumental in the crusade, and "Come with Me" grew directly out of his frustration with the U.S. government's involvement in Vietnam.

- Bly's national bestseller, *Iron John: A Book about Men,* details the poet's thoughts about and experiences with the emotional lives of men.

- For those interested in Bly's poetic theories— many based on evolutionary psychology, physical anthropology, and the structure of the human brain—read *Leaping Poetry: An Idea with Poems and Translations,* published in 1975 by Beacon Press.

- James Mersmann's 1974 anthology, *Out of the Vietnam Vortex,* provides a sustained examination of the diverse group of poets who wrote about their opposition to the Vietnam War.

- Paul Zweig's 1968 essay for *The Nation,* "A Sadness for America," attempts to describe the loneliness and confusion Americans felt during the late 1960s and notes how well Bly's collection of poems *The Light around the Body* illustrates that sadness.

---

mansky argues that "Come with Me" fails as a statement about the human condition because it universalizes personal experience.

Robert Bly's "Come with Me" is part of his award-winning collection titled *The Light around the Body.* While many critics have praised the poem, I believe it exemplifies some of the poorest poetry that Bly has to offer. Critic Howard Nelson has written that "Come with Me" is "symptomatically, one of the most moving poems" in the book. To be moved by this poem, however, means to be moved by a cheap and stereotypical rendering of human experience. "Come with Me" resorts to cliched imagery and does not fulfill the promise—

> *Bly is ... a poet of the upper midwest, well-versed in the emotional landscape and physical details of that part of the country."*

implicit in the opening line—that readers will be provided with new insight.

The opening line of the poem asks readers to trust the speaker as someone who will, and can, show them something they have not seen before, but what we are shown is "removed Chevrolet wheels that howl with a terrible loneliness." By attributing human characteristics to an inanimate thing, Bly is personifying the wheels. Personification can be effective when it provides a way of seeing that is fresh and novel—when it allows us insight into an idea or emotion. Using car wheels to evoke human despair, rather than providing a distinctive way of understanding or feeling that despair, trivializes it. That trivialization turns to sheer silliness in the next lines when the speaker describes the removed wheels as "Lying on their backs in the cindery dirt, like men drunk, and naked." Because Bly uses the progression of the images themselves to elicit feeling in his readers, rather than, for instance, storytelling, readers must buy into his descriptions as apt. But the only readers who might actually feel the despair that Bly attempts to evoke are drivers who have recently experienced a blowout on the interstate.

Bly's personification of the wheels comes close to what critic John Ruskin, in 1856, named the pathetic fallacy. Ruskin coined the term to designate the way that poets and writers frequently assign human attributes to inanimate nature. Ruskin used the lines from William Coleridge's poem, "Christabel," as an example:

> The one red leaf, the last of its clan,
> That dances as often as dance it can.

Human beings dance, not leaves. Pathetic fallacies work only in the rarest of instances, Ruskin claimed, when no other means of description are available to reveal the truth. Though Bly makes automobile wheels—synthetic, not natural things—

into agents of human emotion, he is still guilty of falsification. This falsification is more apparent and more egregious for two reasons: the first is because as human beings we have little real rapport with automobile wheels (as opposed to the sun, for example, which we experience every day); the second is because we cannot visualize the way that Bly's speaker describes the wheels. He says that they lie on their backs. But wheels have no part that corresponds to a "back" per se, unless we think of the hubcapped side as the front, which would indeed be a stretch of the imagination. And though we can (if we picture the tires that litter so many of this country's lakes and rivers), envision the way that wheels might "stagger off down a hill at night to drown at last in the pond," the image progresses no further. What we are offered next is "shredded inner tubes abandoned on the shoulder of thruways," and after that, "curly steel shavings, scattered about on garage benches." Instead of a progression of images, we are presented with an array of seemingly arbitrary images. As readers, we are expected to emotionally respond to these images as though they touch an unconscious place inside of us, our collective, or species, memory. But these twentieth-century manufactured items do not resonate at that level. The only archetypal resonance they have is their shape. The circle has long been a symbol of eternity and wholeness across cultures and time; the Chevrolet wheel, on the other hand, is a twentieth-century Western object. It cannot and does not have the heft, symbolically speaking, to signify human despair.

Because the speaker relies solely on the poem's images to deliver his promised knowledge, and because those images are not poetically up to snuff, readers may feel disappointed and duped. This, in large part, is because the authority that Bly invests his speaker with is the authority of wisdom gained through experience. The poet's role, according to Bly, is to pierce the unconscious to root around in the depths of ancestral memory, the storehouse of meaning and symbol, and bring images from that place to the surface—to show what has been found. Before we can accept what is presented to us, though, we must believe the speaker. The speaker of "Come With Me" is unbelievable because he does not show us anything we have not seen before. Simply naming oneself a poet, or having others name you a poet, is not reason enough for readers to trust you. Bly's own public persona as a performer, self-anointed shaman, and, more recently, as a New-Age guru for the men's movement does not add to our inclination to trust him.

His poetics, the theory out of which he generates much of his writing, forms such a large umbrella that just about anything can fit under it. Here is a passage on "poethood" from one of his most cited essays, "On Political Poetry":

> In order for the poet to write a true political poem, he has to be able to have such a grasp of his own concerns that he can leave them for awhile, and then leap up, like a grasshopper, into this other psyche. In that sphere he finds strange plants and curious many-eyed creatures which he brings back with him. This half-visible psychic life he entangles with his language.

Some poets try to write political poems impelled upward by hatred or fear. But those emotions are stiff-jointed, rock-like, and are seldom able to escape from the gravity of the body. What the poet needs to get up that far and bring back something are great leaps of the imagination.

Reading his poem (written at around the same time as the essay) in the context of these remarks, we can glean a better understanding of his methods. Focus on the imagination is the stuff of Romantic theories about art and literature, and poets from John Keats to André Breton have trumpeted the powers of the imagination to tap the unconscious. The problem, of course, is that these "things" are both conceptual and highly personal. Even "this other psyche" that Bly speaks of, the psyche of the outward man, is personal. Hence, the "many-eyed creatures" that he brings back from that world and makes poems out of might not have any significance to other people at all. This is where "Come with Me" fails. Rather than resonating in the readers' psyche, images of the wheels, the inner tubes, the drunken men, and the South Dakota roads fall flat. They seem more like images a writer of local color would use to describe a place with which he was intimately familiar. Maybe that's what, finally, Bly is: a poet of the upper midwest, well-versed in the emotional landscape and physical details of that part of the country.

Lastly, "Come with Me" fails because, in critic William Taylor's words, it participates in a kind of poetry that can only be described as belonging to a "Cult of Goodness." That is, in simplified terms, Bly uses poems to make pronouncements about how bad things are because we do not know ourselves and about how "we" (sometimes Americans, sometimes men, sometimes humanity in general) need to get in touch with a part of ourselves that has been buried or ignored. The only person who can make these pronouncements, of course, is someone who has done that reconnecting himself,

someone who has "been there, done that." But such a person would not speak from that place, because he would be aware of the arrogance of such a gesture. Bly, apparently, is not aware of that. He continues to speak and write because there are those who listen to him. Shame on you, I say; get a life.

Source: Chris Semansky, in an essay for *Poetry for Students,* The Gale Group, 1999.

Cliff Saunders

Cliff Saunders teaches writing and literature in the Myrtle Beach, South Carolina, area and has published six chapbooks of verse. In the following essay, Saunders maintains that even though "Come with Me" is a political poem connected very much with the time and social conditions of the late 1960s, its message about the destructive nature of despair is as relevant now as it was then.

When *The Light around the Body,* the book in which "Come with Me" appears, first came out, much of the critical response to it was decidedly negative. Writing in the *New Statesman,* Alan Brownjohn complained that Bly's "generalized despair about the brutalities of politics gets lost in a haze of vague, over-reaching fantasy." Michael Goldman remarked in the *New York Times Book Review* that many of the volume's "poems are being superficial in the name of inwardness" and that "many of the images in these poems are surprisingly banal." Even Louis Simpson, who praised Bly for his "original talent" and "rare integrity" in his review of the book in *Harper's,* recommended that Bly "forget about images for a while and concentrate on music, the way things move together." Despite the harsh tone of these criticisms, *The Light around the Body* won the prestigious National Book Award for Poetry for 1967, and the book remains impressive for its passion and urgency. As Richard P. Sugg noted in his critical study titled *Robert Bly,* "Of all the literature to come out of the Vietnam War, Bly's award-winning book of poetry stands as the best example of the dangers and possibilities inherent in the artist's attempt to create political art."

One of the dangers of political poetry surely is its tendency to become trapped in a particular era, to be timely rather than timeless. Indeed, some of the poems in the volume that deal directly with the Vietnam War seem quite dated now, such as "Asian Peace Offers Rejected without Publication," which mentions a man named Rusk (i.e., Dean Rusk, U.S. secretary of state from 1961 to 1969), a reference few young readers encountering Bly's poetry for

> *In a political sense, 'Come with Me' describes a nation (the United States) whose spirit is collapsing under the weight of an immense despair...."*

the first time would be likely to catch. Shortly after the release of *The Light around the Body,* the book's Vietnam War poems became its most notorious and—for those standing in opposition to the war—most important poems. By that time, Bly had already become, as cofounder of American Writers against the Vietnam War, a key national figure in the war resistance movement. As poet David Ignatow noted in his essay "Reflections upon the Past with Robert Bly," Bly caused quite a stir when, during his acceptance speech for the National Book Award, he denounced the war, as well as those poets in the audience sitting idly by without a word of protest, and handed over his prize-money check on the spot to a representative of the War Resister's League. Even more shocking, Bly urged the representative to refuse to register for the draft, even though openly encouraging such a refusal was tantamount to a violation of a law that Congress had recently passed. With Bly gaining a national reputation as an antiwar leader, his poems against the war became ideological rites of passage for many young people. Unfortunately, a number of these poems no longer convey the power they once did, simply because their context was a war that has long since ended. Fortunately, though, "Come with Me" does not fall into this category. It is as relevant today as it was in 1968, and it will likely always be relevant.

In a political sense, "Come with Me" describes a nation (the United States) whose spirit is collapsing under the weight of an immense despair, a despair so enormous that even manufactured material objects (e.g., "removed Chevrolet wheels" and "shredded inner tubes") are being crushed by it. Bly is describing a nation whose political system is causing great suffering and helplessness. Presumably, the Vietnam War—which was in full swing in 1967, when *The Light around the Body*

was published—is the cause of much of this despair. The sense of despondency is so vast that it encompasses empty roads in South Dakota, a place geographically far removed from the jungles of Vietman but psychically as war-torn as that country in southeast Asia. To Bly's credit, he makes this despair so palpable that a reader can't help but see it, feel it, and be consumed by it. Making the reader aware of this all-consuming feeling is the poem's primary mission, and it clearly succeeds. As Sugg points out, Bly's poetry at this time "sought to establish a basis for universality it its analysis of social problems as emanating from 'inward,' psychic problems whose only cure could be increased awareness."

The important thing to understand, however, is that while this despair was tied into the social and political conditions of the 1960s, the poem is not locked into that time frame in the way that "Asian Peace Offers" is. The dismay that Bly describes in "Come with Me" knows no such restrictions. We can see this same despair today in places such as Kosovo, Somalia, Honduras—places where the disenfranchised and those discarded along the road of "progress" (like so many pieces of blown-apart truck tires) suffer in vulnerability and helplessness. Bly feels deeply for these people, the poor and exploited who "tried and burst / And were left behind," and passion for their cause transmits powerfully to the reader.

"Come with Me" is a fine example not only of political poetry but also of what Bly termed "leaping" poetry. According to Bly, leaping poetry is that which makes a jump from the conscious to the unconscious mind and back again; it connotes an ability to make associations quickly, and the presumption is that the quicker the associations are made, the more exciting the poetry. Often, the leaps are made back and forth between an external world of objects (the conscious) and the internal world of psychic energy (the unconscious). Writing about Pablo Neruda, the Nobel Prize-winning Chilean poet whom Bly translated and who had such a monumental impact on his poetry, Bly noted in his essay "Looking for Dragon Smoke" that readers frequently feel elation when encountering Neruda's poems "because he follows some arc of association which corresponds to the inner life of the objects; so that anyone sensitive to the inner life of objects can ride with him."

This same arc of association is clearly at play in "Come with Me," where all of the objects under consideration—Chevrolet wheels, inner tubes, steel shavings, and roads in South Dakota—are endowed with an internal life that is decidedly human in nature. Through the power of figurative language (e.g., simile, metaphor, and personification), Bly brings these objects to life. The Chevrolet wheels "howl with a terrible loneliness" and lie on their backs "like men drunk, and naked"; the inner tubes are "Black and collapsed bodies, that tried and burst"; the steel shavings "have given up, and blame everything on the government"; and the roads in South Dakota "feel around in the darkness …" Commenting on "Come with Me" in his book *Robert Bly,* Richard P. Sugg astutely points out that the poem delves "not only into the wreckage of cars that have tried and failed, but into the despair of the very road itself," or the political direction America was taking during the mid-1960s. Thus, the road's failure "symbolizes modern man's psychic failure to have a destination, or even to "connect one thing to another." Sensing this failure deeply, Bly took it upon himself to "connect one thing to another," to graphically associate the pain, despair, and sense of abandonment that many people were feeling with the icons of wreckage around them, to image that despair all around them.

In his critique of *The Light around the Body* in the *New Statesman,* Alan Brownjohn argued that Bly's "groups of ironical metaphors don't always seem to *apply* very effectively to the things he intends them to comment upon," that the details in the poems seem "too often arbitrary." While this may be true of some poems in the volume, Brownjohn's criticism has no merit when applied to "Come with Me," because that poem's group of metaphors is carefully chosen to convey wasteful expenditure; is organically of a piece (i.e., all are connected in some way with automotive travel); and is perfectly suited to Bly's theme in the poem: America's despair at the time and the destruction it was causing. Today, as it was in the 1960s, the automobile is a powerful symbol of materialism, and one point Bly seems to be making in "Come with Me" is that America's fascination with material objects has led the country astray, pulling it in a direction away from spiritual growth and moral awareness and into the darkness of despair. Given that America has grown even more materialistic since the late 1960s, the poem's implications have as much relevance now (if not more) as they did in 1968.

Brownjohn and several other critics who have written on *The Light around the Body* have made a point of addressing the book's ironic tone. Indeed, in *Robert Bly,* Sugg calls "Come with Me" "a poem of ironic invitation." And so it is, inviting

us, as it does, to take an unfortunate tour of America's wounded psyche circa 1968, with all of its visible signs of wreckage and abandonment. The poem is ironic because invitations are normally given to people to experience something entertaining or enjoyable, whereas this one coaxes the reader right into the dark side of Vietnam-era America. This ironic tone—sometimes scathing, sometimes subtle—was very prevalent in the American poetry of the mid-to-late 1960s, a revolutionary time for poetry as well as for so many other aspects of American life, from fashion to sexuality. At that time (and perhaps for the first time in U.S. history), just as many poets were composing in free verse as were writing in form. Bly, who himself began as a formalist poets of sorts in the 1950s, had, by 1967, made the leap fully into free verse, and "Come with Me" is a good example of his stylistic considerations at the time: easy, conversational tone; surrealistic imagery; and prose-like rhythm. As Louis Simpson and other critics have noted, there wasn't much music in Bly's verse during the 1960s. But with the daily body counts mounting in Vietnam, with a growing number of U.S. cities aflame in violent protest, and with a crushing despair spreading across the land, who felt like singing?

Source: Cliff Saunders, in an essay for *Poetry for Students,* The Gale Group, 1999.

William V. Davis

In the following essay, Davis provides an overview of Bly's career and work.

No poet of his generation has been more influential or more controversial than Robert Bly. No poet has ranged more widely in his interests or had a greater reciprocal relationship with writers and thinkers in other disciplines than has Bly. No other poet has written more important poetry in the lyrical, political, social, psychological, or philosophical modes or covered more critical ground in his essays and reviews. Because Bly's work has been so wide-ranging, his activity so exhaustive, and his presence so pervasive, he has become, in less than twenty-five years, the most conspicuous poet of his generation. To follow his career closely is to trace the major tendencies of much of the most significant poetry written during the past several decades.

Because Bly goes in so many different directions and because he is so prolific and, often, so unsystematic, even seemingly self-contradictory, he is difficult to categorize. No one, not even Bly himself in his extensive, self-analytic criticism, has succeeded in arriving at a convincingly systematic position with respect to his thinking in total. The task is complicated, in part, because Bly has worked his poetry into the larger context of his other activities. Therefore, the individual books of poems tend to be yoked with the philosophic speculations of the same periods, and the philosophic apparatus both complements and in large measure defines the poetry contemporary with it. Thus, Bly is best understood in his various individual phases and each phase is best dealt with as a cluster of thematically and stylistically similar materials, separated from other clusters of a rather different sort which precede and follow them. Bly himself is sensitive to this approach to his poetry and to his work in general, and he often tends to group together like poems from different periods—many of his books are mini-anthologies. He also has the habit of returning to a few favorite thematic and stylistic modes again and again.

In 1980 Bly edited an anthology called *News of the Universe: Poems of Twofold Consciousness* in which he traced the progress of poetry from the eighteenth century, "the peak of human arrogance," to the present, poems of "twofold consciousness," and on into the suggestion of a "unity of consciousness that we haven't arrived at yet." In the poetry of the "Old Position" a "serious gap" exists between man and nature: "The body is exiled, the soul evaporated, the mind given executive power." The first significant attack on the Old Position was the Romanticism of Friedrich Hölderlin, Gérard de Nerval, Johann Wolfgang von Goethe, Novalis, and, in England, William Blake. "Insane for the light," like Goethe's butterfly, these writers wished "to die and so to grow" on the dark earth as the "troubled guests" they knew they were. Thus, by the beginning of the twentieth century, in a poet like Rilke, Bly finds "an area of psychic abundance" nourished by the German Romantics. This, he thinks, is the true source of major modern poetry and is quite separate from the Jules LaForgue, T. S. Eliot, W. H. Auden, Ezra Pound tradition. It is a tradition not of irony but of "swift association."

Bly has always been able to find corroboration for his literary theories in other disciplines. In *News of the Universe* he adopts Robert Ornstein's speculations in *The Psychology of Consciousness* (1972) to the history of recent poetry. Since "the two halves of the body respond to and embody the modes of the opposite brain lobe," the left side, which "favors feeling, music, motion, touch … the qualities in us that enable us to unite with objects and creatures," have been trapped by the "bent

over" body and crushed. The poetry of the last hundred years, then, "is an effort to unfold the left side of the body." But, since "war crushes the unfolding left side all over again," recent history has not been without throwbacks toward elements of the Old Position. Still, the poetry since 1945 has gradually increased the "unfolding of the left side" through several new "developments": the concept of the poet as shaman; the "transparent poem," similar to the poems of the ancient Chinese poets; the "massive movement of poetry toward recitation, toward words that float in the air"; finally, "the emergence of the prose poem," which is "the final stage of the unpretentious style" and of "the object poem, or thing poem," associated with the "seeing" poems of Rilke or the "object" poems of Francis Ponge.

There are two reasons for detailing Bly's survey of the poetry of the last several centuries. First, it is useful to know these stages of poetic development as Bly understands them in order to appreciate and evaluate his critical and poetic perspectives. More importantly, this survey is important to an understanding of Bly's own poetry because he here rather clearly defines the stages of his own poetic development and ends his survey of the history of poetry at precisely the point where his own published poetry begins.

Bly began to publish at about the same time as the movement known as the New Left, which Paul Breslin [in an article in *The American Scholar*] rightly calls "*psycho*-political," appeared. Both the psychological and the political sides of this dichotomy had direct and profound influences on Bly's early work and the psychological side, maintained with the fervor of its original impetus, has remained important throughout his career.

Donald Hall was one of the first to see how different from the other poetry of the time Bly's early poetry was. In 1962, the same year that Bly published *Silence in the Snowy Fields,* Hall edited the anthology *Contemporary American Poetry.* In his introduction Hall said:

"One thing is happening in American poetry … which is genuinely new. In lines like Robert Bly's:

In small towns the houses are built right on the ground; The lamplight falls on all fours in the grass.

… there is a kind of imagination new to American poetry….

The movement which seems to me *new* is subjective but not autobiographical. It reveals through images not particular pain, but general subjective life.... To read a poem of this sort, you must not try to translate the images into abstractions.... You must try to be open to them, to let them take you over and speak in their own language of feeling."

Hall is quite right in identifying Bly with a new kind of imagination and in suggesting that his poetry is not "autobiographical" but reveals "general subjective life." Indeed, Bly has always attempted to speak with a "profound subjectivity" and to make that subjectivity objective in his poems. As Bly says in an important early essay [titled "A Wrong Turning in American Poetry"], "A poem is something that penetrates for an instant into the unconsious." Later he added [in "Leaping up into Political Poetry"], "What is needed to write good poems about the outward world is inwardness."

This obsession with inwardness has been present in Bly from the beginning, and it has taken various forms—some of them quite "outward." First there was the personalized private mysticism of his poetic beginnings in *Silence in the Snowy Fields.* Then there was the outward, public protest poems of his middle period, best seen in *The Light Around the Body.* Next, there was the attempt to plumb universal mythic consciousness in *Sleepers Joining Hands.* And, most recently, in *The Man in the Black Coat Turns* and *Loving a Woman in Two Worlds,* Bly searches out the "ancestors," both literal and psychological, which haunt his past, inhabit his memories, and continue to people his present world.

Bly's notions of "leaps" in poetry and of "leaping poetry" are important both as creative principles and as critical tools. He describes "a leap from the conscious to the unconscious and back again, a leap from the known part of the mind to the unknown part" as one of the necessities of leaping poems, which give off "constantly flashing light" as they shift from "light psyche to dark psyche." Until recently such poems have come from Europe and the South Americans. American poets, Bly believes, need to relearn the poetic traditions which have come down from the "ancient times," the "'time of inspiration,'" and from other cultures, even in our own time. This notion of the necessity for a "leap" in strong or authentic poetry is the basic tenet of Bly's poetic philosophy and the crucial test he applies to his own poems and to the poems of other poets.

Bly began his poetic career in the early 1950s when, in New York, he began to read seriously and in depth the poems of Virgil and Horace, Pindar and Rilke, the *Tao Te Ching,* Rudolf Steiner and,

especially, the seventeenth-century German mystic, Jacob Boehme. Boehme, an obscure, difficult writer, borrowed his terminology from a wide variety of diverse sources and lived his life in a state of religious exaltation bordering on frenzy. His insight flashed back and forth between divine text and human contexts, and he saw himself as a vehicle for divine illumination in the common life of man on earth. In Boehme there are immediate parallels to the life and intellectual interests of Robert Bly. One need only think of Bly's essay, "Being a Lutheran Boy-God in Minnesota" [in Chester G. Anderson's *Growing up in Minnesota*] or remember his historical analyses of poetic tradition, his criticism of his own contemporaries, or his unique literary theories to find obvious associations between the dichotomies of inner and outer, body and spirit, conscious and unconscious, light and dark, life and death, male and female which are also in Boehme. Indeed, it is surely the case that Boehme, Bly's first major influence (quotations from Boehme serve as epigraphs to *Silence in the Snowy Fields* and to the four of five sections of *The Light Around the Body* which have epigraphs) has remained one of the most abiding influences on his work and thought.

It is this Boehmean influence, along with Bly's interest in surrealism and South American poets, which causes him to be associated with the tradition of the "deep image" or "inwardness." These influences, Bly himself acknowledges, make his "a poetry that goes deep into the human being, much deeper than the ego and at the same time is aware of many other beings."

But Bly never seems to stop to take any stand for a very long time. Instead, he has constantly moved out into new territory to find new buttresses and new models for his philosophy and his poetry. In poets as diverse as Pablo Neruda, Cesar Vallejo, Federico Garcia Lorca, Juan Ramón Jiménez, Harry Martinson, Gunnar Ekelöf, Tomas Tranströmer, Kabir, Mirabai, Rolf Jacobsen, Rainer Maria Rilke, and Georg Trakl, Bly finds themes and voices which echo his own, or which he echoes. But it is in the work of the psychologist C. G. Jung that Bly finds perhaps his most useful and abiding sounding board. Jung had already defined and focused, from the psychological side, some of the issues and concerns Bly was interested in exploring in his poetry and thought and, as he had with Boehme, and as he would with other thinkers later, Bly was quick to make use of Jung's work for his own purposes. Indeed, Jung has been the most significant buttress for much of Bly's work in the last fifteen years, even though the clearest example of Jung's influence on Bly remains *Sleepers Joining Hands.*

The most overt use of Jungian sources can be seen in Bly's treatment of Jung's notion of the "shadow." For Jung, the shadow is the negative side of the psyche, containing "the contents of the personal unconscious." It is this "dark side of the human personality" that is "the door into the unconscious and ... from which those two twilight figures, the shadow and the anima, step" out into dreams and waking awareness. According to Bly "all literature can be thought of as creations by the 'dark side,'" and "literature describes efforts the shadow makes to rise." These are notions which permeate Bly's work.

In recent years, Bly has circled back upon himself with an even greater intensity. He continues to give readings and make public appearances and continually finds ways to make his work and the work of others relevant both to the literary and the non-literary world through, for example, the organization of Great Mother and New Father conferences and seminars (which in some ways parallel the poems of *The Man in the Black Coat Turns* and *Loving a Woman in Two Worlds* respectively). He has also further deepened and refined the forms and themes of his poems. In addition to his continuing interest in Blake, Jung, Boehme, and Freud, Bly has, more recently, been attracted to the work of Joseph Campbell, the "three brain" theories of Paul MacLean and the work of the psychologist James Hillman. As Bly has said, "I learned to trust my obsessions." Robert Bly is, if nothing else, a poet of obsessions, and any attempt to understand him and his work must account for these obsessions.

Bly's penchant for constantly revising his poems, and even his critical positions, suggests several things: first, he wants to remain open to a new, or more complete, vision of either poem or precept; second, and more importantly, he seems to be interested in documenting the final or more definitive versions of his visions, critical or poetic. Therefore Bly is exceedingly difficult to fix at any specific point in his career or with respect to any final vision, version, or revision because he is only seen fully in his final versions. In this respect, since he is still writing, and thus revising, one can never be certain that any critical comment will not need to be amended, or even contradicted, later on, just as Bly amends and even contradicts his earlier positions and poems. What this finally means is that Bly is interested in the developmental process itself and he recognizes that his work will not be fin-

ished until his life is. Although this philosophy and procedure may present problems for readers and critics along the way, it makes for reading and writing that seems constantly to be living and growing—the way readers are, the way Robert Bly is.

Source: William V. Davis, "Overview," *Understanding Robert Bly,* Columbia, SC: University of South Carolina Press, 1988, pp. 6–15.

Sources

Bly, Robert, "On Political Poetry," *The Nation,* April 24, 1967.

Brownjohn, Alan, *New Statesman,* August 2, 1968.

Davis, William Virgil, *Robert Bly: The Poet and His Critics,* Columbia, SC: Camden House, 1994.

Davis, William V., *Understanding Robert Bly,* Clemson, SC: University of South Carolina Press, 1989.

Goldman, Michael, *New York Times Book Review,* August 18, 1968.

Malkoff, Karl, *Escape from the Self: A Study in Contemporary American Poetry and Poetics,* New York: Columbia University Press, 1977.

Mersmann, James F., *Out of the Vietnam Vortex: A Study of Poets and Poetry against the War,* Lawrence, KS: University Press of Kansas, 1974.

Mills, Ralph J., *Contemporary American Poetry,* New York: Random House, 1965.

Molesworth, Charles, *The Fierce Embrace: A Study of Contemporary American Poetry,* Columbia, MO: University of Missouri Press, 1979.

Peseroff, Joyce, ed., *Robert Bly: When Sleepers Awake,* Ann Arbor: University of Michigan Press, 1984.

Roberson, William H., *Robert Bly: A Primary and Secondary Bibliography,* Lanhau, MD: Scarecrow Press, 1986.

Simpson, Louis, in a review of *The Light around the Body, Harper's,* August 1968.

Stepanchev, Stephen, *American Poetry Since 1945: A Critical Survey,* New York: Harper, 1965.

Sugg, Richard P., *Robert Bly,* Boston: Twayne, 1986.

For Further Study

Daniels, Kate, and Richard Jones, eds., *On Solitude and Silence: Writings on Robert Bly,* Boston: Beacon Press, 1982.
    A generous selection of essays from both poets and critics seeking to articulate the often inexpressible experience of reading Bly's poetry.

Howard, Richard, *Alone with America: Essays on the Art of Poetry in the United States since 1950,* New York: Atheneum, 1969, revised edition, 1980.

> A collection of essays on post-World War II American poetry by one of the preeminent poetry critics in the United States. This volume is useful for those who want to locate Bly's work among his contemporaries.

Lensing, George S., and Ronald Moran, *Four Poets and the Emotive Imagination: Robert Bly, James Wright, Louis Simpson, and William Stafford,* Baton Rouge: Louisiana State University Press, 1976.

> These authors define the term "emotive imagination" and attempt to provide an explanation of this poetic tradition. They examine Bly's career historically and in relation to three other American poets of the emotive imagination.

Nelson, Howard, *Robert Bly: An Introduction to the Poetry,* New York: Columbia University Press, 1984.

> A straightforward and solid sourcebook for information on Bly's life and career.

Cool Tombs

Carl Sandburg
1918

At the time of his death in 1967, Carl Sandburg was a popular icon, portrayed in *Time* and *Newsweek* magazines as a troubadour of the common man. When his poetry was first published, however, both his style and choice of subject matter were highly controversial. He was criticized for his use of free verse, as well as for incorporating the language of everyday speech into his poems. His subjects, drawn from the rich panorama of American life, were considered vulgar and inappropriate for poetry. His admirers, on the other hand, praised these same qualities, comparing him to Walt Whitman, an earlier poet who aroused similar artistic controversy when his first volume of poetry, *Leaves of Grass,* was published in 1855.

"Cool Tombs" appeared in Carl Sandburg's second collection of poetry, *Cornhuskers,* published in 1918. His first book, called *Chicago Poems,* had focused on city life and the people who worked there. This second volume portrayed different aspects of midwestern America: the land, the people, their values, and their dreams. This poem is part of a section called "Haunts," an appropriate designation, for the lines have the lyrical, haunting quality of a requiem.

Like many of Sandburg's poems, "Cool Tombs" combines details of history with events in the lives of the common man. The poem describes the equalizing role of death, where both the famous and infamous, the powerful and the ordinary individual, come to rest "in the cool tombs." In the absence of an eternal system of reward and punish-

ment, Sandburg requests that the reader examine the value of existence and reflect on the qualities that make life meaningful.

Author Biography

Carl Sandburg was born January 6, 1878, in Galesburg, Illinois. His father, an immigrant who could read the Bible in Swedish but was unable to sign his name in English, worked as a blacksmith for the Chicago, Burlington, & Quincy Railroad. Growing up in Galesburg, Sandburg was very much aware of the importance of the Civil War, which had ended just thirteen years before he was born. His first history lessons came from the lives of the adults around him. Many of the men in town had fought in the war, and Sandburg was fascinated by their conversations that vividly recreated the recent past for him.

Although Sandburg liked geography, history, and reading, he left school in 1891 after eighth grade in order to help support his family. During the depression of 1894, the family's economic struggles increased when his father's hours were cut back from ten to four a day. By 1897, the economy had recovered and Sandburg headed out West, supporting himself by working odd jobs in many different towns. During his travels, he became fascinated with the songs and folktales of the people he encountered. Both the stories and the rhythms of midwestern American song and speech would become a key influence on his subsequent prose and poetry.

Upon hearing the news that the battleship *Maine* had been sunk in Havana Harbor on February 15, 1898, Sandburg returned to Galesburg and enlisted in the army. His troop was sent to Washington D.C., where he first saw Ford's Theater, the site of Abraham Lincoln's assassination. They then traveled on to Cuba. After his company returned to the United States in September of 1898, he was offered a trial at West Point. Unfortunately, he was unable to pass some exams since he had never gone to high school. However, Sandburg enrolled in Lombard College in Galesburg. One professor, Philip Green Wright, recognized Sandburg's talent and encouraged his early attempts at writing. During his college years, Sandburg was active in sports, drama, and college publications, but he left school in the spring of 1902, shortly before he was due to graduate. Again, he took to the road, this time as a hobo, actually spending ten days in a Pittsburgh jail.

Carl Sandburg

Sandburg joined the Socialist-Democratic Party. In 1908, he was working in Milwaukee as a party organizer, campaigning for their candidate, Eugene V. Debs. That same year, he met and married Lillian Steichen. In 1914, Harriet Monroe published some of Sandburg's early poetry, which garnered the Levinson Prize. His first book of poetry, *Chicago Poems,* was published in 1916, and a number of other volumes followed. Sandburg spent the next several years producing children's books, collections of folk songs, biography, and fiction, as well as poetry. He was awarded two Pulitzer Prizes: one for prose in 1940 for *Abraham Lincoln: The War Years* and one for poetry in 1950 for his *Collected Poems.* Sandburg continued actively working as a writer, singer, entertainer, and social commentator until his death at the age of 89.

Poem Text

When Abraham Lincoln was shoveled into the
    tombs, he forgot the copperheads and the
    assassin ... in the dust, in the cool tombs.

And Ulysses Grant lost all thought of con men and
    Wall street, cash and collateral turned ashes
    ... in the dust, in the cool tombs.

Pocahontas' body, lovely as a poplar, sweet as a
red haw in November or a pawpaw in May,
did she wonder? does she remember? ... in
the dust, in the cool tombs?

Take any streetful of people buying clothes and
groceries, cheering a hero or throwing
confetti and blowing tin horns ... tell me if
the lovers are losers ... tell me if any get
more than the lovers ... in the dust ... in the
cool tombs.

Poem Summary

Line 1:

The free-verse lines of this poem are organized
using prose techniques, rather than the conventional line breaks of a more standard poetic stanza.
Thus, the individual sections of the lines are referred to as phrases.

Using a device Sandburg frequently employed,
the opening phrase combines the language of
everyday life with persons, ideas, or words that are
usually presented in a loftier, more formal, or more
idealistic way. The purpose, as in this line, is to
shock the reader to attention. For Carl Sandburg
and many northerners, Abraham Lincoln was considered one of the nation's best presidents, a true
hero who preserved the country while righting an
injustice by freeing the slaves. In addition, Sandburg was well aware of the dignity and importance
most Americans attach to funerals, particularly
those of beloved figures. One of his earliest memories was of his entire town turning out for a silent
ceremonial parade to mark the death of another
Civil War leader, Ulysses Grant. Thus, the words
"shoveled into the tomb," spoken in connection
with Lincoln, seem inappropriate; the word is more
frequently associated with getting rid of the trash
than with burying heroes.

This introduces one of the poem's major
themes: after death, there is nothingness. The body
is, in fact, an empty shell. The person no longer remains. Sandburg is totally detached about death.
The shell may be shoveled into the earth and be re-
cycled to dust without sentiment or ceremony.

The next phrase introduces two concerns Lincoln faced before death. The copperheads were
northern Democrats who opposed Lincoln and the
war. Some supported slavery or believed that the
federal government had no right to dictate what the
states should do. Many, however, opposed the mon-

etary policies Lincoln used to finance the war. In
1862, Congress passed the Legal Tender Act, creating greenbacks or paper money. The copperheads
were bitterly opposed to this, believing that coins
should be the only form of money. Their name was
derived from the habit many had of identifying
themselves by wearing a copper penny around their
necks.

The assassin was a Shakespearean actor, John
Wilkes Booth, a Confederate sympathizer. He shot
Lincoln on April 14, 1865, just five days after the
Southern Army surrendered. According to the
poem, after his death Lincoln no longer cared about
his enemies.

The refrain follows. It reminds us that human
worries have no place "... in the dust, in the cool
tombs." The first part of the refrain carries connotations of the Biblical injunction from chapter three
of *Genesis,* in which God reminds man that since
he has been cast out of Eden, death is his destiny:
"Dust thou art and to dust shalt thou return." Sandburg uses this to emphasize the idea of the body
fading away and rejoining the earth. He does not,
however, describe a spirit that carries on; death provides eternal peace. This sense of peace and calm
is enhanced by the final phrase of the refrain. The
use of the word "cool," rather than "cold," contributes to an impression of the tomb as a soothing, restful spot. No earthly burdens remain to disturb the peace of the grave.

Sandburg's free verse uses various types of internal rhyme to help the lines achieve a sense of
flow and rhythm. This becomes more pronounced
in each line. Here, "to" and "tomb" reinforce each
other. The assonance, or use of similar vowel
sounds, of "got" from "forgot" is repeated in "cop"
of "copperhead." Even the words "cool tombs"
themselves demonstrate assonance. In addition,
Sandburg utilizes parallel structure in the refrain to
help provide rhythm.

Line 2:

In this line, Sandburg follows the pattern of organization that he established in the first line. A
historical figure is named, the conflicts he faced are
presented, and the refrain follows. Notice that each
subsequent line builds slightly, adding increased
details and using more parallel items. Thus, instead
of the two conflicts Lincoln faced, four are presented for Ulysses S. Grant, another Civil War hero
and president, the historical personage in line two.

Grant's presidency was marred by corruption
and scandal. The conflicts Sandburg mentions de-

stroyed the credibility of Grant's administration, sending the country into a serious depression. The western railroads were being built at this time, and stockholders in the companies created a phony business in order to cheat the government out of millions of dollars. The "con men and Wall Street" refer to those financiers who deceived Grant. "Cash and collateral turned ashes" is a metaphor that refers to unsecured loans made to railroad companies. Because these loans had no collateral or backing, several banks failed. All of the money these banks were supposed to keep for their customers disappeared, just as effectively as if it had been turned to ashes in a bonfire. In his personal life, Grant was forced to declare bankruptcy because he invested in a corrupt bank. In spite of this, however, Grant's problems ceased in death, just as Lincoln's had.

Once again Sandburg uses several poetic techniques to give the line rhythm. Grant's problems are presented in two parallel phrases. Several forms of rhyme contribute to the even flow of Sandburg's words. He uses alliteration in "con," "cash," and "collateral." "Cash" and "ash" provide internal rhyme. The refrain sums up both subject and sentence, providing a smooth lyrical conclusion to the line.

Line 3:

The third line shows some variations in the pattern. Although Sandburg introduces a historical person, he does not speak directly of any conflicts Pocahontas faced. Instead, he describes her body, using several similes from nature. She is as "lovely as a poplar," a species of tree that flourishes in the northern hemisphere. They are tall, graceful trees; even slight breezes make them appear to shimmer—almost to dance in the wind. "Haw" and "pawpaw" refer both to types of trees and the fruits they bear. The haw is the fruit of the hawthorn; it is often called red haw, because its leaves turn scarlet in autumn. The fruit resembles a small apple. Pawpaw, a tree that grows in the southern and central United States, is a member of the custard apple family.

Pocahontas, described by these North-American plants, becomes a representative of the country—of the land itself. Sandburg follows these similes with a parallel set of questions. Notice that they are unspecific and incomplete. The reader must speculate about the wonder or memories of Pocahontas. Does she remember her youth, before she left this country to die in England? Does the land

Media Adaptations

- Carl Sandburg recites "Cool Tombs," along with other poems in *Carl Sandburg Reads,* a two-cassette set released by Caedmon-Harper in 1992.

- Additional songs and stories are included in *More Carl Sandburg Reads,* released by Caedmon-Harper in 1993.

- Poems by Carl Sandburg are included in the video *America in Portrait,* which was released by Monterey Video in 1989.

remember its youth, when forests stretched from coast to coast?

Once again, parallelism and internal rhyme create the rhythm. Alliteration appears in "poplar" and "pawpaw." Sandburg rhymes "haw" and "paw," "November" and "remember."

Line 4:

The final line turns to the ordinary individual. The first phrase describes everyday activities, the second joyous celebrations. Sandburg does not connect these people with tragedy as he did with Lincoln and Grant. Instead, he portrays them enjoying daily life.

In the next phrase, Sandburg asks two questions as he did in line three. While the questions are not answered directly in the poem, a comparison between any set of lovers and the historical figures of the previous lines makes it clear that the lovers have proved much more fortunate. For all of their fame, Lincoln and Grant represent loss on both a public and personal level. This suggests an answer to the second question: No one gets more than the lovers. It is love that provides humans with joy and consolation before they rejoin "the dust ... in the cool tombs."

The fourth line is the longest line. Sandburg continues to use parallel structures and internal rhyme. "Clothes," "cheer," and "confetti," as well as "lovers" and "losers," are alliterative. "Clothes" and "groceries" repeat the same vowel sound, an example of assonance. "Throwing" and "blowing" are complete rhymes, while "cheering" and "hero" involve half-rhyme. As fits a line dealing with "any streetful of people," Sandburg uses the idiom of everyday life. The opening word, "take," is used in its informal or idiomatic meaning. The last phrase before the refrain, "tell me if any get more than the lovers," is a type of slang.

Themes

Death

Sandburg's view of death in "Cool Tombs" is harsh and unequivocal. He does not present it as an entrance into a new life; there are no religious overtones to this poem. Instead, death is the end. It brings stillness, nothingness. Obviously this lends a sense of irony to the poem; all of the struggles of life prove to be futile in the face of this conclusion. However, the irony is blended with an acknowledgment that, in death, man has finally achieved his ultimate goal. He has acquired peace. At last, he has conquered all enemies and countered any fears that plagued him. Troubles are forgotten, betrayals erased. The ultimate peace is the silence of death.

Death is also presented as the great equalizer. The fame or wealth that one achieves during this life no longer matters. Those who watch parades for heroes and throw ticker tape to honor them are no less or more important than the heroes themselves. Death remains unimpressed by wealth, power, or even virtue. This is why Sandburg can speak so casually, almost unfeelingly, of his hero Lincoln being shoveled into the tomb. (Sandburg reinforces this theme in another of the poems in *Cornhuskers*, "Southern Pacific," in which he declares that in death both Huntington, the railroad owner, and Blithery, the railroad worker, now sleep the same, six feet under.)

Value of Life

Since death is the end, an essential issue in "Cool Tombs" centers on the value an individual places on life. Sandburg questions what is truly worthwhile in our daily existence. "Cool Tombs" stresses that personal experiences and simple activities provide more satisfaction and reward than the public or political ventures of the prominent and powerful. This becomes clear when the lines focusing on Lincoln and Grant are compared with the lines describing Pocahontas and the common man.

Topics for Further Study

- Carl Sandburg believed that poetry should express the feelings and concerns of ordinary individuals in the language they use daily. Choose a song that you believe accurately and poetically expresses your emotions. Explain the song's message, what kind of poetic techniques or language it uses, and why it is representative of many people's concerns.

- Carl Sandburg preferred to write in free verse, because he felt best able to convey meaning when not confined by a rhyme or meter pattern. Choose an ordinary object or place, such as a bridge, a favorite picture, a room in your house, or a park. Write a prose description of it, making sure you include specific and concrete details that will give your reader a clear picture. Next choose a meter and rhyme scheme, such as rhyming every other line and making each line ten syllables long. Describe the same object, this time using your poetic pattern. What difficulties did you encounter turning prose into poetry?

- In "Cool Tombs," all differences are settled by death. Imagine an afterlife where two historic or political antagonists meet. Write a dialogue recording what they might say to each other after death.

- Sandburg was a strong supporter of workers and unions. When labor groups first organized, violence frequently accompanied labor disputes. What are some of the problems faced by labor unions today?

It is important to remember that the Civil War was the most influential event in the lives of the people Sandburg knew when he was growing up in Galesburg. Many of the adults he admired had fought in the war. Therefore, the war and its heroes became representatives of honor and integrity. Lincoln and, to a lesser extent, Grant were foremost among these heroes: Lincoln is credited with freeing the slaves; Grant led the North to victory.

Yet, in the poem, Sandburg ignores these achievements. Instead, he chooses conflict and murder for Lincoln, scandal and disgrace for Grant. The opponents Sandburg describes for both men are those who chose violence, greed, or dishonor as a way of life. While seeking wealth, power, or fame for themselves, their false values created havoc for the nation.

Both tone and atmosphere change when Sandburg turns to Pocahontas. She is described as youthful, lovely, and sweet. Her body is mentioned, not her achievements or personal characteristics. She represents the richness and beauty of nature—of America as it was when the Europeans first arrived. In many ways, she seems to represent the land itself, glowing and alive. Then Sandburg poses two questions. Did she wonder? Does she remember? The questions are deliberately unspecific. In choosing to support the English, to marry John Rolfe and venture with him to England, she selected separation from the land. Did she wonder about the wisdom of the choices that she made? Did she speculate about the value of the world she had forsaken? Was her sacrifice worthwhile or did it cost too much?

In contrast, the ordinary people in line four seem more fulfilled than their more famous counterparts. They buy clothes and groceries, enjoy meals, and feel warmth. These simple activities provide a counterbalance to Grant, who threw away his money to men with false promises and allowed his entire administration to be tainted by those who honored money above all else.

Thus, in "Cool Tombs," ordinary human activity provides more satisfaction than the actions of heroes. After all, only through the individual can leaders achieve their successes. Lincoln's *Emancipation Proclamation* announced that the slaves were free, but the individual soldiers fought to make the words a reality. Sandburg believed in the importance of the common man. The first theme of the poem emphasizes that we are all equal in death. Sandburg wishes to remind us that in terms of kindness and virtue, as well as evil and vice, both rich and poor are equals in life itself. He sees the ordinary individual as truly heroic. Sandburg portrays the nobility of lives that are seldom honored; he speaks loudly for those who are seldom given a voice.

Love

Sandburg's final theme, dealing with the importance of love, is introduced with the questions in line four. Although the line begins with descriptions of ordinary people enjoying ordinary activities, Sandburg then asks the reader to make a decision. Are the lovers of the world losers? Of all the individuals in the poem, who is happiest? It is certainly not Grant or Lincoln. When a comparison is made, the answer becomes clear. No one has more satisfaction than the lovers. Love, rather than fame, power, or money provides the solace we need. "Cool Tombs" celebrates the love that elevates our ordinary lives to the extraordinary.

Style

"Cool Tombs" is divided into four lines, or sections. These lines are punctuated using conventional prose techniques, rather than the line breaks of a formal stanza. Each is composed of a long, free-verse sentence, which means that the poem has no specific rhyme scheme or rhythm. This is one reason why some critics have stated that Sandburg does not really write poetry.

Sandburg preferred writing free verse. In fact, he was very critical about the constraints of formal poetry. In his "Notes for a Preface" to *Collected Poems*, Sandburg compared searching for the exact rhyme and correct number of syllables with the type of skill needed to complete a crossword puzzle. He believed that poetry in which form is more important that the subject is simply an unpleasant and unnecessary exercise in word play. "Rhythm alone is a tether, and not a very long one. But rhymes are iron fetters."

Every line in "Cool Tombs" presents a separate vignette, or simple story. This is another technique Sandburg favors; he develops pictures taken from history or events in the lives of ordinary individuals. Each separate picture in these series helps to reinforce the overall themes of his poetry. Here each line makes a separate comment on the meaning of death and life.

The four lines are organized using parallel structure and repetition. The first two follow the same pattern. Both open with the name of a historical figure; next, they mention prominent concerns facing this person; and, finally, each line concludes with the refrain "in the dust ... in the cool tombs." The third line, introducing Pocahontas, shifts slightly from actual historical events. Although Pocahontas is real, the line describes her appearance and then speculates about her feelings; it does not mention any actual events that occurred. The poetic line also becomes longer, breaking the pattern slightly. The last line, featuring the lives of ordinary individuals, is the longest and most varied of all. Sandburg uses the refrain, however, at the end of each line to clearly relate each vignette to his theme.

Although Sandburg is often accused of being unpoetic because of his rejection of common verse forms, he frequently uses internal rhymes and rhythms to make his poetic lines flow smoothly. Examples of assonance and alliteration appear in every line. Notice the use of consecutively stressed words and syllables in the questions in line three, "did she wonder? does she remember?" In addition, parallel structure also helps to create poetic rhythm.

This rhythm employs the cadence of midwestern songs and speech. In her introduction to Sandburg's 1926 collection, *Selected Poems,* British critic and reviewer Rebecca West described the musicality of his style. "Much of his poetry is based on the technique of the banjo." She went on to say that his rhythms can best be heard when the lines are spoken with a midwestern accent.

A final technique Sandburg employs is the use of vernacular or the idiom of everyday speech. "Tell me if any get more than the lovers" is a typical example. Many critics feel such slang phrases have no place in poetry.

Historical Context

It is impossible to understand Sandburg without some knowledge of the political and historical events that helped shape his perspective. Like Walt Whitman, Sandburg was an intensely American writer, and both his prose and poetry reflect the American experience. The titles of his collections of poetry reflect his interests: *Chicago Poems, Cornhuskers, Smoke and Steel, Good Morning America, The People Yes.* The American people were both his subject and his inspiration.

Sandburg grew up in the period of economic and social turmoil that resulted from the growth of industry during the nineteenth century. During that time, the northern United States, in particular, saw an enormous shift from an agricultural to a manufacturing economy. Working conditions in the factories were harsh, and laborers grew dissatisfied. After the end of the Civil War, the trade union movement began to grow. In 1869, the Knights of Labor was formed, and soon they were joined by several other labor organizations.

Government corruption accompanied by ruthless business practices led to a serious depression in 1875, providing increased incentives for workers to unite. Strikes became a common method of protest. Unfortunately, a violent response to labor unrest became even more widespread. Police, called in to support management positions, were ruthless in their effort to break strikes.

One of the most violent labor demonstrations occurred in 1886. Many workers had gathered in Haymarket Square in Chicago to support the striking workers at McCormak Reaper. When the police arrived, a bomb was thrown, killing eleven officers. Although there was no firm evidence demonstrating who threw the bomb, the police arrested eight anarchists. These men were quickly tried and four were promptly executed. Conservative Republicans—such as Sandburg's father—applauded the government's response. However, the incident also produced a counter wave of antigovernment, antibusiness feeling among workers and progressives.

During the 1880s and 1890s, the progressive forces began to gain a following throughout the Midwest. They formed a third political party, the Populists, also known as the People's Party. It was loosely made up of farmer's associations (agrarians), labor unions, single taxers, greenbackers, and progressive reformers. Its philosophy expressed a desire to unite disparate classes and races in order to fight a common enemy, big business and big government. Interest in the party grew even stronger after the depression in 1893.

By 1894, one in five persons was unemployed. Many populists firmly believed that the government didn't care about their plight, but only about major corporations and trusts. Jacob Coxey, a wealthy businessman from Ohio and a populist, organized a protest march in Washington, D.C. Leading his supporters from mid-Ohio to the capital, he arrived with five hundred men, women, and children. Coxey was arrested and the police attacked his supporters. Although his protest did not meet with success, seventeen other groups followed his lead. Government and business leaders again reacted with violence and massive firings.

In 1896, the Democratic National Convention was held in Chicago. Many factions of the Populist Party became absorbed into the Democratic Party at that time. John Peter Altgeld, the governor of

Compare & Contrast

- **1918:** World War I ends when Germany and the Central Powers surrender to the Allied Powers on November 11, thus terminating the conflict idealistically called "The War to End All Wars."

  1939: World War II begins when Germany invades Poland on September 1.

  1964: The United States openly engages in military action in Vietnam to prevent Southeast Asia from turning communist. The conflict lasts until 1975.

  1991: George Bush launches Operation Desert Storm to force Saddam Hussein and Iraq out of Kuwait.

  1998: In the midst of a political impeachment scandal, Bill Clinton initiates Operation Desert Fox, an offensive aimed, once again, at Iraqi President Saddam Hussein.

  1999: NATO forces engage in a bombing campaign of Serbia and parts of Kosovo after Serbian leader Slobodan Milosevic rejects diplomatic solutions to an ownership dispute over the Kosovo region and steps up a program of "ethnic cleansing," which entails genocide and forced relocation of ethnic Albanian Kosovars.

- **1918:** A worldwide influenza epidemic kills almost 22 million people, approximately one percent of the world's population.

1929: Alexander Flemming makes the first clinical use of penicillin, definitely proving that it inhibits bacterial growth. By the 1940s, penicillin, antibiotics, and sulfa drugs will begin to eradicate infectious diseases.

1981: The Center for Disease Control reports five cases of Acquired Immune Deficiency Syndrome (AIDS) and begins tracking the disease.

1996: AIDS is the leading cause of death among young people. In addition, the Institute of Medicine of the National Academy of Sciences warns that certain viruses have mutated so that they now may be resistant to penicillin and other drugs.

- **1918:** The Bolsheviks execute the former czar of Russia and his entire family.

  1977: Boris Yeltsin, the Communist Party boss of Yekaterinburg, orders the destruction of the house where the former royal family was executed in order to prevent supporters of the Romanovs from viewing it as a shrine.

  1998: Eighty years after their execution, the remains of the last czar and his family are buried. Hundreds of members of the former aristocracy return to Russia to honor them. Russian President Boris Yeltsin also attends.

Illinois who aroused much public anger when he pardoned the remaining Haymarket anarchists, helped sway the platform to a populist stance. The Democrats nominated William Jennings Bryant from Nebraska who represented the Western farmers. Reformers rallied behind the Democrats, but the Republican corporations fought back. Mark Hanna, the businessman who ran the Republican campaign of William McKinley, raised more than $3.5 million from the banks, railroads, and trusts. Having only $300,000 at his disposal, Bryant was unable to compete; McKinley became the twenty-fifth president of the United States. (McKinley was assassinated shortly after his second term in office had begun.)

When the depression ended in 1897, business boomed. Slums grew and working conditions became even more inhumane. A multitude of activist reform movements gathered together under the progressive label, seeking justice for women, workers, children, and minorities. The Socialist Party also gained a large following, particularly in the cities. Many authors supported the idea of protest through their literature: Theodore Dreiser, Frank Norris, Upton Sinclair, and Lincoln Steffens all wrote graphic and brutal accounts of the plight of the lower classes.

Between 1900 and 1915, progressive reform gradually came to both state and federal governments. During his presidency, from 1901 to 1908,

Theodore Roosevelt brought labor and management together for discussions for the first time. He refused to provide federal troops to support business, and he challenged the railroads, meat packers, tobacco, and oil industries under the conditions of the 1890 Sherman Anti-Trust Act, which was designed to limit corporate power. Roosevelt proved to be popular with reformers. Although several corporations opposed his policies, today he is frequently credited with saving big business in America by forcing it to act more responsibly.

William Howard Taft, who followed Roosevelt, was a weak leader who antagonized both reform and business groups. He served only one term and was succeeded by Woodrow Wilson, a progressive Democrat. During Wilson's term, the United States entered World War I. The cycle of economic growth followed by depression continued with the stock market crash of 1929. The devastating consequences of the crash eventually resulted in the liberal reform policies of Franklin Delano Roosevelt.

Influenced by his childhood poverty and his sympathy for the working man, Sandburg became an ardent supporter of reform parties in the United States. His writing, both prose and poetry, reflects this political stance.

Critical Overview

Throughout his career, Carl Sandburg received widely varying critical reviews. His admirers praised the rough, vulgar power of his first collection, *Chicago Poems,* describing it as original, alive, and a true statement of the American people. Reviewers who preferred more conventional rhyme and rhythms attacked his lack of poetic style. *Cornhuskers,* Sandburg's second volume of poetry (which contains "Cool Tombs"), received more positive reviews. It is still considered by both his advocates and detractors as containing some of the most effective and evocative of his poems.

In *Carl Sandburg, Lincoln of Our Literature: A Biography,* North Callahan expressed his admiration for this volume, calling the poems more restrained in both style and subject. He felt that Sandburg abandoned the "harsh cacophony" of his city poems for a more pastoral tone. He praised the volume for showing "more lyrical quality, better imagery, and more contrast." He particularly lauded the mystic quality of "Cool Tombs." In his *Carl Sandburg,* Gay Wilson Allen hailed the irony of "Cool Tombs," finding it beautiful but "devastating." Daniel G. Hoffman, in an article for the *Explicator,* provides a line-by-line analysis of the poem, explaining that it "celebrates love as the greatest joy in life."

A major concern of many reviewers was Sandburg's partisan political and social context. In her assessment of *Cornhuskers* in the *New York Times Book Review,* poet Amy Lowell warned Sandburg that he had to choose whether he wished to be a poet or a propagandist. Sandburg, however, did not believe such a choice was possible. In his "Notes for a Preface" to his *Collected Poems,* he wrote that "a writer's silence on living issues can in itself constitute a propaganda of conduct leading toward the deterioration or death of freedom." In his opinion, the poet's duty is not to avoid political or social issues, but instead to fight for the rights of the common man.

Throughout his life, Sandburg was a popular figure, widely admired by the ordinary individuals he praised in his poetry. However, his literary reputation was frequently under critical attack. After his death, that reputation has been undermined even further. In the introduction to *Carl Sandburg: A Reference Guide,* Dale Salwak summed up several reasons for this. First, Sandburg had always been out of the academic mainstream, having little in common with figures such as Ezra Pound or T. S. Eliot. He was considered to be too blunt, having few "interesting ambiguities." In other words, he was much too easy to understand. Second, although Sandburg was called the poet of the people, he was frequently too optimistic, particularly in his later poetry, for many modern critics. His views were not considered radical enough. Finally, his popularity was often held against him. Accusations charged that he wrote for "the lowest common denominator."

Criticism

David Donnell

David Donnell, who teaches at the University of Toronto, has published seven books of poetry. His work is included in the Norton Anthology of Modern Poetry *and his volume* Settlement *received Canada's prestigious Governor General's Award. In the following essay, Donnell provides a glowing assessment of Sandburg's "Cool Tombs."*

What Do I Read Next?

- *Leaves of Grass* by Walt Whitman, first published in 1855 at the author's expense, is one of the most influential works of American poetry. Sandburg has often been called heir to Whitman's free-verse style, use of vernacular, and love for the common man. Many reprinted editions of *Leaves of Grass* are available, including a 1969 facsimile edition of the 1860 text.

- Sandburg's autobiography, *Always the Young Strangers,* published in 1953, focuses on his formative years in the Midwest. It provides a compelling view of the region and the period, revealing the influences that shaped his life and poetry.

- Upton Sinclair, like Sandburg, was concerned with the lives of workers and immigrants. *The Jungle,* first published in 1905, presents a graphic and disturbing account of the slaughterhouses in Chicago. Sinclair's descriptions led to such public outrage that Congress was forced to pass laws regulating the handling of meat, food, and drugs.

- *Top Drawer: American High Society from the Gilded Age to the Roaring Twenties* by Mary Cable, published in 1984, presents the glitter and ostentation of the wealthiest Americans. It provides an interesting contrast to the lives of the workers described in works by Sandburg and Upton Sinclair.

- *Abraham Lincoln: The Prairie Years* is a 1926 biography by Carl Sandburg that follows Lincoln from his youth through the period prior to his presidency. It provides a touching, insightful portrait, recreating history with a lyric grace.

- *The People Yes* (1936) is an interesting collection of folk wisdom and sayings gathered by Sandburg during his travels. In it, he hopes to present the true voice of the American people.

Carl Sandburg is certainly one of the most distinctive, and distinctively American, poets of the twentieth century. He began his writing career around the turn of the century, some time before the death of Vachel Lindsay, and received significant publication—*Chicago Poems* (1916)—before the careers of Wallace Stevens or Robert Frost began to soar and attract attention. We don't know if poetry was really Sandburg's first love as a young man or not. He was a labor organizer, a newspaperman, a poet, a biographer, and, of course, he somehow found time to write that delightful book of stories for children, *Rutabaga Tales.* Sandburg seems to have been able to bring a great deal of energy and fresh insight to everything he did, and he also brought a great deal of American sensibility and love for the American people and their various traditions.

It's difficult to think of the 1920s in the United States without thinking of Sandburg, and of poems such as "Cool Tombs" or "Chicago," or of stories about his concerts where he would appear with a banjo and read poems, sing ballads (sometimes the ballads were labor ballads), and tell stories. He wrote a four-volume biography of Abraham Lincoln, who was one of his great passions, and a separate biography of Lincoln's wife. He was an organizer for the Social Democratic Party for a period of time and campaigned with Eugene Debs, who was a socialist candidate for the presidency.

Sometimes with a career as colorful as Carl Sandburg's, a change of mood takes place. The critics or the reviewers suddenly started putting his writing in the background. By the 1930s, Wallace Stevens certainly seemed to have become a more graceful poet with a wider and more colorful vocabulary, and Robert Frost had honed his uniquely personal and dazzlingly clear individual philosophical voice. But this shouldn't prevent students from realizing how important Sandburg was to the overall development of American poetry, or, for that matter, just how plain good some of his early

> ['Cool Tombs'] is an absolutely lovely poem, written with a burst of natural enthusiasm and spontaneity that takes the reader like a summer storm."

poems are—how much they moved people and how well they read today.

"Cool Tombs" is one of Carl Sandburg's most famous poems. Although this work is not about Chicago, it certainly belongs to the "Chicago Poems" period of his early writing. He has obviously been thinking about the turbulence of American capitalism, which is something he did quite a lot. He has been thinking about money, and about how much things—commodities—cost and how hard we work to make enough money to pay for them. And he was probably thinking a bit about age and death. When "Cool Tombs" was published, Sandburg was forty years old.

The poem begins with Abraham Lincoln simply because Sandburg did so much work on Lincoln. "When Abraham Lincoln was shoveled into the tombs, he forgot the copperheads and the assassin … in the dust, in the cool tombs." Sandburg may have just paid a visit to a cemetery in Chicago or somewhere else in America, he may have just lost a close friend or finished reading an obituary in one of the Chicago papers of the day. It's interesting to note how, after reading the title, the subject "Cool Tombs" almost immediately becomes the central protagonist of the poem, despite all of the famous people that get mentioned.

Abraham Lincoln was the most talked about man of his day. He wasn't simply the President of the United States of America; more than that, he was the guardian of the Constitution, and of northern desire for a unified America, and a unified America without slavery. So during his lifetime, Lincoln was in every newspaper of the day.

But according to Sandburg's lovely poem (which is really more about our lives and time, or about Time and Being, perhaps, as the philosophers might put it), when Lincoln is "shoveled into the tombs," he forgets all of his earthly problems and negative attitudes. Sandburg's attitude at this point is almost Eastern or Christian. There is a giving up—the body simply relinquishes its drive to argue with the inexorable nature of time. Lincoln could, after all, have died of natural causes, and he might still appear in this starring role at the beginning of a famous poem. Sandburg doesn't dwell on the word "assassin"; he doesn't even mention the name "Booth" let alone the Latin motto that Booth called out after shooting Lincoln in the Ford Theater. He isn't interested in details.

In a sense, Sandburg himself is in charge of the shovel in this poem. It's rather interesting to look at just how neatly, and how naturally and spontaneously, Sandburg shovels Abraham Lincoln, the "copperheads," and the "assassin" into the "tombs." There is actually a whole period of American history here, ending with Lincoln, and a new period, starting off with increased northern prosperity and a lot of new money in places such as New York and Chicago. Sandburg has steeped himself in this history, writing a four-volume biography of the dead president, for example. And here, in the opening sentence of this great—rather classical in many ways, but also quite personal and quite unique—poem, Sandburg shovels the whole fiasco of Lincoln's tragic death into "the cool tombs."

The opening sentence of "Cool Tombs" is very simple. Sandburg was extremely good at doing that—taking the reader by surprise with a sentence so simple that a working person might almost, but not quite, use it himself in a conversation on a bus in Los Angeles or in a subway in crowded New York City. But being a master poet (on the basis of his best work), Sandburg picks just the right sentence, and then he uses it to his devastatingly successful advantage. In this poem, his genius lies in his having quite successfully put a temporal opening word, "When," together with the name of the most famous U.S. President of the previous century, the idea of a shovel, the suggestion of men shovelling, the idea of forgetting, "copperheads" and the "assassin," and also, of course, "dust," the idea of "tombs," and the notion that tombs are "cool."

So Sandburg has given us a whole vignette, even more, in just one fairly simple but very classical line. Wallace Stevens or Robert Frost might find it very difficult to do anything like this and make it work even half as successfully.

In the next line, Sandburg immediately makes reference to Ulysses Grant. Sandburg is the American poet who—among other jobs with newspapers and magazines—had worked as an organizer for the Social Democratic Party and campaigned for Eugene Debs as a presidential candidate. So when Carl Sandburg tells us about Ulysses Grant, we don't question why he chooses Grant, who is, after all, also a president and from the same period as Lincoln. Instead, we listen almost as hypnotically as if we were listening to a compelling national ballad in the form of a poem.

"Cool Tombs" is one of Sandburg's simplest and most accomplished poems. Everything in this poem seems to be perfectly chosen and everything moves perfectly, with a calm deliberation that is—despite the calm—always full of feeling. In the second line, Sandburg tells us, "And Ulysses Grant lost all thought of con men and Wall Street, cash and collateral turned ashes ... in the dust, in the cool tombs." The poem continues its inexorable logic and becomes more compelling and also more complete by including "con men," "Wall Street," and that simple beguiling word "collateral," along with "copperheads" and the "assassin" Booth from the first line.

The Civil War, because of his long and studious reading of Lincoln's life, and Chicago, where he spent so much of his time, both seem to be very much on Sandburg's mind. In "Cool Tombs," Sandburg not only manages to write an absolutely gorgeous poem but, at the same time, drawing quite naturally on his emotions of the moment, he seems to bury a great deal of his concern and dismay with the Civil War period, and he does so in a very classical, stoic, and graceful way. But of course this poem, which begins as something of a Lincoln poem, and which reaches out to encompass the Civil War period and the poet's apparent sense that the era saw a lot of extremely different men—such as "Abraham Lincoln," "con men," carpetbaggers, and men from "Wall Street"—is a poem in which Sandburg wants to touch on death, time, and the great mystery. And he wants to make a completely American event out of this piece of writing.

"Pocahontas' body, lovely as a poplar, sweet as a red haw in November or a pawpaw in May ..." is a truly lovely way of beginning the next part of his poem. It is really very unexpected; Wallace Stevens probably wouldn't do it, or if he had thought of doing it, Stevens might have been less direct. Of course that's where part of the unexpectedness comes from—the extraordinary direct-ness with which Sandburg begins the first of these two irregular final lines. When Sandburg brings "Pocahontas' body" into the poem, he immediately opens up our entire concept of the America he seemed, previously, to be talking about. Pocahontas was the famous Native-American princess of the early seventeenth century who was romantically linked with Captain John Smith, a British explorer who came to America very early in the colonial period. Pocahontas intervened with her father, chief Powhatan, to save Smith's life.

Pocahontas, beautiful, young, is in obvious contrast with Abraham Lincoln, bearded like a prophet, or with Ulysses Grant. Pocahontas is not only beautiful and young (and, of course, there is a suggestion of sexuality here, and certainly no suggestion of "con men" or "Wall Street"), she is also indigenous. "[L]ovely as a poplar," she has an American authenticity that perhaps Sandburg finds lacking in some of the developments he had been reading about in the newspapers of the day.

With unbelievable speed, Sandburg moves the big telescope that he seems to have set up to look at American life in "Cool Tombs." He has barely introduced Pocahontas and told us that her body is as "lovely as a popular"; almost immediately, he compounds this already distinct image with "sweet as a red haw in November." A "red haw" is simply Sandburg's colloquial expression for an American red hawthorn tree. This is wonderful writing. It's wonderfully direct, but, also, it never fails to be unexpectedly imaginative. "[S]weet as a red haw in November," Sandburg says, and then, the master writer totally in control of what he's putting together, he just adds a bit more, and goes on in the same line to say "or a pawpaw in May, ..."

Of course he's not finished yet. This is an absolutely lovely poem, written with a burst of natural enthusiasm and spontaneity that takes the reader like a summer storm. A "pawpaw," in May or otherwise, is a colloquialism, possibly from Chicago in the war years, for those big, luscious, pale-green papaya fruit. But having put that colorful image out in front of the reader, Sandburg has one thought to add within the same sentence. He continues," ... did she wonder? does she remember? ... in the dust, in the cool tombs?" This is nothing short of dazzling. Now Sandburg has developed his concept of time as something that happens to everybody. It is a universal, a classic universal, just as this is a very classical poem, despite Sandburg's easy, natural way of expressing himself in one brilliant colorful image after another.

Time is a dazzling and perhaps slightly amorphous stream of brilliant moments; Sandburg sees our experience of time as an experience where, during our lives and at the end, we forget, or lose all "thought," or "wonder," or "remember." Abraham Lincoln does these things; he forgets the "copperheads" and the "assassin." And Pocahontas, possibly the lover of Captain John Smith as far back as 1616 or 1617, was doing these things before the great Abraham Lincoln or George Washington were even young men.

But the great poet needs one more line to bring this remarkable poem into full balance—to bring our minds, so to speak, back into the immediacy of the twentieth century. Sandburg brings us back to the present after this lesson in American history in as simple and spontaneous a way as he started this poem. "Take any streetful of people buying clothes and groceries," he writes, "cheering a hero or throwing confetti and blowing tin horns …" Immediately, we seem to be back in Chicago, the great windy city, walking along a street or "throwing confetti and blowing tin horns" ourselves. Life is everything, Sandburg says at the end of this poem, and this is a bit of subtle philosophical populist upbeat at the end. We shouldn't spoil our lives while we have them, we should live fully; we should learn something from history, we should be calm. "… [T]ell me if the lovers are losers … tell me if any get more than the lovers … in the dust … in the cool tombs." Sandburg he has taken us from Abraham Lincoln to Ulysses Grant, and from Pocahontas to Chicago, to people blowing tin horns and to "the lovers." "Cool Tombs" is a profoundly twentieth-century American poem about time, and it's also an extremely brilliant poem about time, history, memory, and life. Life itself is the final subject of this poem. "Take any streetful of people buying clothes and groceries, cheering a hero or throwing confetti and blowing tin horns …" That's such a perfect and distinct ending for this great poem.

Source: David Donnell, in an essay for *Poetry for Students,* The Gale Group, 1999.

Kristina Zarlengo

Kristina Zarlengo, who received her doctorate in English from Columbia University in 1997, taught literature and writing for five years at Columbia University. A scholar of modern American literature, her articles have appeared in academic journals and various periodicals. In the following essay, Zarlengo points out how Sandburg trumpeted democracy, even when discussing death in his poem "Cool Tombs."

During the early decades of the twentieth century, poets writing in English took new liberties. Rather than organizing the sound of their poems around rhyme schemes, many of them ignored rhyme, preferring to find, for the end of their lines, the perfect word for their topic rather than a word selected for its rhyme. Many of them also rejected traditional poetic metrical forms—they did not constrain their sentiments to a fixed number of beats per line; in Ezra Pound's phrasing, revolutionary poets threw away the metronome, preferring the musical phrase. Not everyone writing verse in those years agreed it was a good idea to abandon formal conventions—a practice that came to be known as free verse. American poet Robert Frost famously declared that writing in free verse was like playing tennis without a net. For many others, however, free verse was the appropriate form for a new century that seemed to unfold in the midst of fewer conventions of all kinds. In a new century in which science, rather than God, could explain the stars, where the human constructs of the industrial age—from the wristwatch to the factory to the metropolis—seemed as important in their way as mountains, oceans and seasons, a free verse that paid closer attention to speech rhythms and vivid description of the world's prolific novelties than to traditions of any stripe seemed pertinent and proper.

"Cool Tombs" is typical Carl Sandburg poetry: a brief, free-verse composition. Dedicated to his chosen home, Chicago, which he described as a reporter before he wrote poetic tributes to what he called "City of the Big Shoulders," Sandburg was very much a man of the modern city. He was a man familiar with industry and with many pockets of urban life, having worked as a potter's assistant, a firehouse call man, a mail-order businessman, a milkman, a handbill distributor, a hobo, and a socialist organizer, among other occupations. But Sandburg chose free verse, and stuck with it after other practitioners of the form had abandoned it, not because of its novelty, but because of what he saw as its antiquity:

We have heard much in our time about free verse being modern, as though it is a new-found style for men to use in speaking and writing, rising out of the machine age, skyscrapers, high speed and jazz. Now, if free verse is a form of writing poetry without rhyme, without regular meters, without established or formal rules governing it, we can easily go back to the earliest styles of poetry known to the human family—and the style is strictly free verse. Before men invented the alphabet, so that poems could be put down in writing, they spoke their poems. When one man spoke to another in a certain beat and rhythm, if it happened that his words conveyed certain impressions and moods to his listeners, he was delivering poetry to his listeners, he was delivering poetry to them, whether he knew it or they knew it, and whether he or they had a name for an art which the poet was practicing on himself and on them.

It is perhaps this conviction that poetry is primal and natural, happening unself-consciously whenever words manage to convey some impression or mood, and happening chiefly with the spoken rather than the printed word, that kept Sandburg so committed to free verse. He was often labeled artless for his casual form. In a review of his *Collected Poems,* William Carlos Williams wrote, "Sandburg may not have known what he was doing, it may never have entered his mind that there was anything significant to do with the structure of the verse itself."

In the tradition of nineteenth-century American poet Walt Whitman—who also adhered to free verse—Sandburg does, however, consistently sing a sweet and charmed song of the common man, capturing the depths of everyday experience in a way that earned him a large and devoted following, and had even Williams conditioning his disapproval: "But the best of [Sandburg] was touched with fire."

We better understand the casual fire of Sandburg's death poem "Cool Tombs" by comparing it to another poem that digs in its thematic turf. A portion of the strictly metered, rhyming "Elegy Written In A Country Churchyard," by eighteenth century poet Thomas Gray, reads:

> The boast of heraldry, the pomp of power,
> And all that beauty, all that wealth e'er gave,
> Awaits alike th' inevitable hour.
> The paths of glory lead but to the grave.

Echoing this message, "Cool Tombs" also insists that no matter the grand fears and immortal stature of the powerful, they will be annulled "in the dust, in the cool tombs." But Sandburg forms this message not with neatly ordered syllables and sounds, whose words are sometimes forced to change to fit metric structure (e'er, rather than ever; th' rather than the), but in a language similar to American speech. Sandburg's poem is immediately accessible and comprehensible on a first read, even to those unfamiliar with poetic conventions. That "Cool Tombs" was composed in free verse does not mean, however, that the poem is free of any structure. Rather, its structure is generated by the subject, on the spot. Consider the poem's refrain: ellipses that suggest a pause, followed by "in the

> *Sandburg …*
> *consistently sing[s] a sweet*
> *and charmed song of the*
> *common man, capturing the*
> *depths of everyday*
> *experience in a way that*
> *earned him a large and*
> *devoted following …."*

dust, in the cool tombs." That these words complete each line hammers home the notion that all will end in dust and tombs. Each of the four stanza-like sections takes on a wholly new topic, but each ends in the same place—as indeed all human life will end in death. Further, each section of "Cool Tombs" reads like a complete thought, a notion that finishes with the idea of someone's death.

The first section, on Lincoln, establishes a pattern not only of word, but of insight. When Lincoln was buried, we are told, he had no more care for his political opponents (the copperheads) and no worry even about his ultimate threat: the assassin John Wilkes Booth. He has forgotten them; they are erased by the tombs. Moving on to another, parallel life (that of another president), Sandburg assures us of thematic pattern—the grand, powerful Grant also lost all care in the tomb. Of Pocahontas's memory or thought beyond life, Sandburg poses questions—yet they are questions already implicitly answered. The reader has learned, as Thomas Gray previously asserted, that "The paths of glory lead but to the grave."

The fourth section of "Cool Tombs" shifts the theme of the poem. That those with worldly power are as powerless over death as the lowly, the humiliated, and the common, is ironic. Nothing we can accomplish, no memory or thought—we learn from Gray and Sandburg alike—will secure us against death. Yet Sandburg adds another irony to this. In section four, we are delivered a vision of people on the street. These are common people with everyday worries such as buying groceries and clothes. They are so ordinary that they celebrate heroes (rather than become heroes themselves) with cheap tin horns and confetti. Yet it seems that among these people are lovers—perhaps couples in love, perhaps those lovers of heroes. Thus, when we are asked, twice, "if the lovers are losers ... If any get more than the lovers," we want to answer, "no, all will go to dust." If we respond so in this context, we also place loving on the same plane as governing America—we are flattening the hierarchy of power seen as social class, or fame, and admitting a power generated by one's capacity to feel. To the irony that death humbles the powerful, Sandburg adds the irony that death ennobles anyone with a capacity to feel deeply. Death deals its hand democratically.

In delivering this message, Sandburg evokes historical figures who we remember, though they themselves can remember no longer from within their tombs. But in the final section, we are brought to the present; the poem seems to demand of us a commitment to fullness of life and feeling, since we, too, will end in the tombs. Morbid as this poem most obviously is, its message remains cheering. It is a reminder that we are alive and that merely by feeling that life, we are accomplishing the most that we will have, when finally all tallies are evened in the dust.

It is unsurprising that Sandburg launches "Cool Tombs" with a reference to Lincoln, about whom he wrote a vast and detailed biography, and of whom he said, in a 1959 address to the United States Congress, "He stands for decency, honest dealing, plain talk, and funny stories." But the power Lincoln commanded, as hailed by Sandburg, was not his command of armies or his capacity to conduct war. "Perhaps we may say that the well-assured and most enduring memorial to Lincoln is invisibly there, to day, tomorrow and for a long time yet to come. It is there in the hearts of the lovers of liberty, men and women who understand that wherever there is freedom there have been those who fought, toiled and sacrificed for it." Concerned with poetry that freely tells a history of the now, Sandburg worked in the name of heartfelt freedoms and common loves.

Source: Kristina Zarlengo, in an essay for *Poetry for Students,* The Gale Group, 1999.

Sources

Allen, Gay Wilson, *Carl Sandburg,* Minneapolis: University of Minnesota Press, 1972.

Callahan, North, *Carl Sandburg, Lincoln of Our Literature: A Biography,* New York: New York University Press, 1970.

Hoffman, Daniel G., "Sandburg's 'Cool Tombs,'" *Explicator,* Vol. 9, May 1951.

Lowell, Amy, "Poetry and Propaganda," *New York Times Book Review,* October 24, 1920, p. 7.

Salwak, Dale, *Carl Sandburg: A Reference Guide,* Boston: G. K. Hall & Co., 1988.

Sandburg, Carl, "Notes for a Preface," *Collected Poems,* New York: Harcourt Brace Jovanovich, 1950, pp. xxiii-xxxi.

Sandburg, Carl, *Selected Poems,* edited and with an introduction by George and Willene Hendrick, New York: Harcourt Brace & Co., 1966.

Steichen, Edward, *Sandburg,* New York: Harcourt Brace & World, Inc., 1966.

West, Rebecca, preface to *Selected Poems of Carl Sandburg,* New York: Harcourt Brace Jovanovich, 1926, pp. 15-28.

Williams, William Carlos, "Carl Sandburg's Complete Poems," *Poetry: A Magazine of Verse,* 1951.

For Further Study

Blum, Louis, et. al., *The National Experience: A History of the United States,* 6th ed., New York: Harcourt Brace Jovanovich, 1985.

The section of this book that covers the period from the Gilded Age to the 1930s is very informative. It presents factual detail in a clear, readable format. Since Sandburg's writing has strong political and social overtones, this is a source that helps to place his subjects into perspective.

Crowder, Richard H., *Carl Sandburg,* New York: Twayne, 1964.

This biography includes a good critical evaluation of Sandburg's writing, covering both his strengths and weaknesses.

Durnell, Hazel, *The America of Carl Sandburg,* Washington D.C.: University Press of Washington D.C., 1965.

Durnell discusses Sandburg's immigrant heritage, evaluating both the influences of his personal background and of the period on his writing. She praises him for his social conscious and for his role as the voice of the people.

Untermeyer, Louis, *The New Era in American Poetry,* New York: Henry Holt, 1919.

Untermeyer was an early admirer of Sandburg's poetry who praised his writing throughout Sandburg's career. This book provides an interesting historical perspective.

Yatron, Michael, *America's Literary Revolt,* Freeport, New York: Books for Libraries Press, 1959.

This volume provides a clear, concise historical background for Sandburg's work, discussing the influence of the Populist movement on his philosophy.

A Far Cry from Africa

Derek Walcott
1962

Derek Walcott's "A Far Cry from Africa," published in 1962, is a painful and jarring depiction of ethnic conflict and divided loyalties. The opening images of the poem are drawn from accounts of the Mau Mau Uprising, an extended and bloody battle during the 1950s between European settlers and the native Kikuyu tribe in what is now the republic of Kenya. In the early twentieth century, the first white settlers arrived in the region, forcing the Kikuyu people off of their tribal lands. Europeans took control of farmland and the government, relegating the Kikuyu to a subservient position. One faction of the Kikuyu people formed Mau Mau, a terrorist organization intent on purging all European influence from the country, but less strident Kikuyus attempted to either remain neutral or help the British defeat Mau Mau.

The ongoings in Kenya magnified an internal strife within the poet concerning his own mixed heritage. Walcott has both African and European roots; his grandmothers were both black, and both grandfathers were white. In addition, at the time the poem was written, the poet's country of birth, the island of St. Lucia, was still a colony of Great Britain. While Walcott opposes colonialism and would therefore seem to be sympathetic to a revolution with an anticolonial cause, he has passionate reservations about Mau Mau: they are, or are reported to be, extremely violent—to animals, whites, and Kikuyu perceived as traitors to the Mau Mau cause.

As Walcott is divided in two, so too is the poem. The first two stanzas refer to the Kenyan conflict, while the second two address the war within the poet-as-outsider/insider, between his roles as blood insider but geographical outsider to the Mau Mau Uprising. The Mau Mau Uprising, which began in 1952, was put down—some say in 1953, 1956, or 1960—without a treaty, yet the British did leave Kenya in 1963. Just as the uprising was never cleanly resolved, Walcott, at least within the poem, never resolves his conflict about whose side to take.

Author Biography

Derek Walcott was born January 23, 1930, in the capital city of Castries on the eastern Caribbean island of St. Lucia, a territory at that time under the dominance of Britain. While the official language of St. Lucia was English, Walcott grew up also speaking a French-English patois. Both of his grandfathers were white and both grandmothers were black. From the beginning, Walcott was, in terms of St. Lucia, a bit of an outsider. In a poor, Catholic country, his parents were middle class and Protestant: his mother was a teacher at a Methodist grammar school who worked in local theater, and his father was a civil servant by vocation and a fine artist and poet by avocation. Walcott's father died shortly after Derek and his twin brother were born. The Walcott home was filled with books, paintings, and recorded music. Derek studied painting and published, at age fourteen, his first poem. At eighteen, Walcott borrowed two hundred dollars from his mother to publish his first book, *25 Poems*. To pay back his mother, he sold copies of the book to his friends.

In his early years, Walcott was schooled on St. Lucia, but in 1950, he attended the University of the West Indies in Jamaica, getting his degree in 1953 but staying on one more year to study education. From 1954 to 1957, Walcott taught in Grenada, St. Lucia, and Jamaica, and wrote and produced plays along with his brother, Roderick. In 1954, Walcott married. Since then he has been married three times and has had three children. In 1958, his play *Drums and Colours* earned him a Rockefeller grant to study theater in New York City. Alienated in the United States, Walcott re-

Derek Walcott

turned to Trinidad in 1959 to found, with his brother, The Trinidad Theater Workshop, a project that lasted until 1976. From 1960 to 1968, Walcott also wrote for the local newspaper, the *Trinidad Guardian.*

Walcott has taught in both America and the West Indies and has earned numerous awards. He has taught at New York University, Yale, Columbia, Harvard, and, since 1981, at Boston University. Walcott has won numerous awards: in 1965 he received the Royal Society of Literature Heinemann Award for *The Castaway and Other Poems;* his play *Dream on Monkey Mountain* earned the 1971 Obie for the most distinguished off-Broadway play; in 1977 he was awarded a Guggenheim and in 1981 a MacArthur Foundation Award. In 1992, however, Walcott received literature's highest honor, the Nobel Prize. The author of more than twenty books, Walcott continues to write, paint, and direct.

Poem Text

A wind is ruffling the tawny pelt
Of Africa. Kikuyu, quick as flies
Batten upon the bloodstreams of the veldt.
Corpses are scattered through a paradise.

Only the worm, colonel of carrion, cries: 5
'Waste no compassion on these separate dead!'
Statistics justify and scholars seize
The salients of colonial policy,
What is that to the white child hacked in bed?
To savages, expendable as Jews?   10

Threshed out by beaters, the long rushes break
In a white dust of ibises whose cries
Have wheeled since civilization's dawn
From the parched river or beast-teeming plain.
The violence of beast on beast is read   15
As natural law, but upright man
Seeks his divinity by inflicting pain.
Delirious as these worried beasts, his wars
Dance to the tightened carcass of a drum,
While he calls courage still that native dread   20
Of the white peace contracted by the dead.

Again brutish necessity wipes its hands
Upon the napkins of a dirty cause, again
A waste of our compassion, as with Spain,
The gorilla wrestles with the superman.   25

I who am poisoned with the blood of both,
Where shall I turn, divided to the vein?
I who have cursed
The drunken officer of British rule, how choose
Between this Africa and the English tongue I love?   30
Betray them both, or give back what they give?
How can I face such slaughter and be cool?
How can I turn from Africa and live?

Poem Summary

Lines 1-3:

The first three lines depict the poem's setting on the African plain, or veldt. The nation itself is compared to an animal (perhaps a lion) with a "tawny pelt." Tawny is a color described as light brown to brownish orange that is common color in the African landscape. The word "Kikuyu" serves as the name of a native tribe in Kenya. What seems an idyllic portrayal of the African plain quickly shifts; the Kikuyu are compared to flies (buzzing around the "animal" of Africa) who are feeding on blood, which is present in large enough amounts to create streams.

Lines 4-6:

Walcott shatters the image of a paradise that many associate with Africa by describing a landscape littered with corpses. He adds a sickening detail by referring to a worm, or maggot, that reigns in this setting of decaying human flesh. The worm's admonishment to "Waste no compassion on these separate dead!" is puzzling in that it implies that the victims somehow got what they deserved.

Lines 7-10:

The mention of the words "justify" and "colonial policy," when taken in context with the preceding six lines, finally clarifies the exact event that Walcott is describing—the Mau Mau Uprising against British colonists in Kenya during the 1950s. Where earlier the speaker seemed to blame the victims, he now blames those who forced the colonial system onto Kenya and polarized the population. They cannot justify their actions, because their reasons will never matter to the "white child" who has been murdered—merely because of his color—in retaliation by Mau Mau fighters or to the "savages," who—in as racist an attitude as was taken by Nazis against Jews—are deemed worthless, or expendable. ("Savages" is a controversial term that derives from the French word *sauvage* meaning wild, and is now wholly derogatory in English. Walcott's use of "savage" functions to present a British colonialist's racist point of view.)

Lines 11-14:

Walcott shifts gears in these lines and returns to images of Africa's wildlife, in a reminder that the ibises (long-billed wading birds) and other beasts ruled this land long before African or European civilization existed. The poet also describes a centuries-old hunting custom of natives walking in a line through the long grass and beating it to flush out prey. Such killing for sustenance is set against the senseless and random death that native Africans and European settlers perpetrate upon each other.

Lines 15-21:

These lines are simultaneously pro-nature and anticulture. Animals kill merely for food and survival, but humans, having perfected the skill of hunting for food, extend that violent act to other areas, using force to exert control—and prove superiority over—other people; they seek divinity by deciding who lives and who dies. Ironically, wars between people are described as following the beat of a drum—an instrument made of an animal hide stretched over a cylinder. Walcott also points out that for whites, historically, peace has not been the result a compromise with an opponent, but a situation arrived at because the opposition has been crushed and cannot resist anymore.

Media Adaptations

- Bill Moyers interviewed Walcott, primarily on the subject of empire, for his *A World of Ideas,* released by PBS videos in 1987.

- A cassette titled *Derek Walcott Reads* (1994) is available from Harper Collins.

Lines 22-25:

These lines are difficult to interpret, but they appear to be aimed at those judging the Mau Mau uprising from a distance—observers who could somehow accept brutality as necessary and who are aware of a dire situation but wipe their hands, or refuse to become involved, in it. The poet appears to condemn such an attitude by comparing the Mau Mau Uprising to the Spanish Civil War (1936-39). Leaders of France and Great Britain wanted to avoid another war that would engulf all of Europe, so they introduced a nonintervention pact that was signed by twenty-seven nations. Nonetheless, the Insurgents, or Nationalists, (under the leadership of General Francisco Franco) were aided by and received military aid from Germany and Italy. The Loyalists, or Republicans, had no such backing; they fought valiantly but were outmanned, lost territory, and were eventually defeated in March of 1939. Line 25 presents a cynical view of the Mau Mau Uprising as just another colonial conflict where gorillas—negatively animalized Africans— fight with superman—a negative characterization of Europe.

Lines 26-33:

This stanza is a change of scene from primarily that of Africa, to that of the poet. Walcott, being a product of both African and English heritage, is torn, because he does not know how to feel about the Mau Mau struggle. He certainly is not satisfied with the stock response of those from the outside. Walcott is sickened by the behavior of Mau Mau just as he has been disgusted by the British. By the end, the poet's dilemma is not reconciled, but one gets the sense that Walcott will abandon neither Africa nor Britain.

Themes

Violence and Cruelty

The wind "ruffling the tawny pelt of Africa" refers to the Mau Mau Uprising that occurred in what is now independent Kenya, roughly from October 20, 1952, to January of 1960. During this span, the white government called an emergency against a secret Kikuyu society that came to be known as Mau Mau and was dedicated to overthrowing the white regime. Against the backdrop of a cruel, long-lasting British colonialism erupted the more short-term cruelty of Mau Mau insurrection. While some versions have it that Mau Mau was put down by 1953 and others by 1956, the government kept the state of emergency in place until the beginning of 1960. It is the violence of Mau Mau that most disturbs Walcott, apparently because it makes Africans look even worse than their British oppressors. There were many stories of Mau Mau violence directed at whites, the animals owned by whites, and at other Kikuyus who refused to join Mau Mau. The violence was especially grisly since many of the Kikuyus used a machete-like agricultural implement, the *panga,* to kill or mutilate victims after killing them. One such murder—one that Walcott could be describing in "A Far Cry from Africa"—was reported of a four-and-a-half-year-old white child. And on March 26, 1953, in the Lari Massacre, Mau Maus killed ninety-seven Kikuyu men, women, and children, apparently for collaborating with the British. But it was not only the violence of insurrection that terrorized animals, whites, and Kikuyus, but also the reportedly gruesome Mau Mau oathing ceremonies in which initiates pledged allegiance to the Mau Mau cause. A Kikuyu schoolmaster gave this account of a ceremony initiating seven members: "We were … bound together by goats' small intestines on our shoulders and feet…. Then Githinji pricked our right hand middle finger with a needle until it bled. He then brought the chest of a billy goat and its heart still attached to the lungs and smeared them with our blood. He then took a Kikuyu gourd containing blood and with it made a cross on our foreheads and on all important joints saying, 'May this blood mark the faithful and brave members of the Gikuyu and Mumbi [analogues of Adam and Eve] Unity; may this same blood warn you that if you betray secrets or violate the oath, our members will come and cut you into pieces at the joints marked by this blood.'" Before Mau Mau, one gets the impression that Walcott was not so torn between Africa and Britain; he may have viewed British

Topics for Further Study

- The phrase "far cry" from the title of Walcott's poem has several possible meanings. Try to identify them all.

- Research the history of various countries in Africa, focusing on colonial rule and the quest for independence. Discuss how circumstances have changed for these countries in the post-colonial era.

- Have a discussion about the cultural heritage of class members. If possible, make family trees.

colonialism as arrogant, ignorant, and cruel, and Africa as victimized. But then, when Africans themselves turned violent, Walcott was torn and could not so easily side with Africans against the British.

Culture Clash

There are many clashes in this poem. The first image signalling conflict is the hint of a storm brewing in the opening lines where Kikuyu flies feed upon the land and maggots upon dead Mau Mau. Here is the first of several culture clashes: pro-Mau Mau pitted against anti-Mau Mau Kikuyu. And within this, a subconflict also exists between those Kikuyu believing that the rights of the individual ("these separate dead") do not necessarily violate those of the group and those convinced that individual rights do violate group rights (the Mau Mau philosophy). In lines six through ten, there is also the clash between the culture of those outside the uprising and those killed by it, outsiders ("scholars") with the luxury of judging the conflict, and insiders (victims) for whom no explanation is sufficient. There are also the outsiders of stanza three, surmising that the conflict is not worth their compassion or involvement, a position against which victims would vehemently argue.

Within the poet, all of these exterior clashes also rage. Walcott is pro-African and pro-Kikuyu but anti-Mau Mau, is pro-English (as in culture and language) but anti-British (as in colonialism), an

outsider to the conflict, but an insider in the sense that within his body exist both English and African blood. These conflicts yield up the main confrontation of the poem, that between Mau Mau and the British, and the conflict within the poet about which side to take. Walcott is, then, completely conflicted: while both an outsider and insider he is ultimately unable to be either. While both British and African, he is unable to sympathize with either. While both pro-revolutionary and anti-violent, he cannot defend the uprising or completely condemn it. Still, he feels he must face these clashes, rather than wish or rationalize them away. From the cultural clash on the continent of Africa, the poem moves to the battlefield within the poet—a place less violent but more complex, since Walcott is, at the same time, on both sides and neither side.

Style

"A Far Cry from Africa" contains four stanzas of mostly iambic tetrameter. Actually, the poem starts off in iambic pentameter, the prevalent form of poetry written in English, but it soon veers off course metrically—a change that reflects the changing scene and perspective in the poem—with lines of varying length and number of stresses. A point of consistency is Walcott's use of masculine endings (lines ending with accented syllables) and masculine rhymes (one syllable rhymes). Rhyme is as irregular as meter. The rhyme scheme of the first stanza might be rendered *ababbcdecd* or *ababbaccad*. On the other hand, both of these schemes leave out the related sounds in "Jews," "flies," "seize," and "policy" that give this stanza two basic end sounds upon which lesser or greater variation occurs. The second stanza has its fourth and seventh lines rhyming and also lines five, ten, and eleven. In stanza three, the scheme is *abba,* but in stanza four there is only the rhyme of its sixth and eighth lines. In sum, then, a loose rhyme scheme for two stanzas is present, but none for the other two. Fluctuation between rhyme and non-rhyme, rhyme and near-rhyme, between iambic tetrameter and iambic pentameter lends itself, though loosely, to the poet's own unresolved schism between Africa and Britain.

Historical Context

Most of the area of contemporary Kenya was made a suzerain by the Imperial British East African

Compare & Contrast

- **1958-64:** This period of civil war in Africa's largest country, Sudan, comes to an end in the October, 1964 revolution when a student is shot and killed. A general strike and protests bring down the military junta.

  1999: CBS News reports that slavery is "alive and well in Sudan." Islamic groups, taking only women and children of the Dinka tribe in raids, use them as sexual servants, housekeepers, and farmhands. Dinka slaves are sold for about $50, the price of a goat.

- **1962:** The long, immensely expensive Ethiopian-Eritrean War (1962-1991) begins after Ethiopia cancels Eritrean autonomy within the Ethiopian-Eritrean federation, in effect since 1952.

  January, 1999: Eritrean news reports that 243 Eritreans are rounded up, jailed, and deported from Ethiopia. To date 49,500 Eritreans have been deported from Ethiopia.

- **1962:** Civil war begins in Rwanda (1962-63), as Tutsi military forces try to gain control of the new country after the majority Hutus had won control in free elections.

  1998: In Rwanda, during the course of the year, 864 people are tried for the 1994 genocide in which between five hundred thousand and one million are slaughtered in the Hutu government's attempt to wipe out the Tutsi minority. Civil war follows the 1994 genocide, and the Tutsi Rwandan Patriotic Front defeat the Rwandan military, which, with an estimated two million Hutus, flee Rwanda into neighboring countries.

Company in 1888. The British government then took over administration in 1895, calling the area a "protectorate." White settlers started moving in, cutting down trees, and amassing estates (some of the largest were over 100,000 acres). The migration of both whites and Indians continued, unabated. The settler built roads and a railroad, and, over time, dispossessed a great many Kenyans—mostly Kikuyus—of their land. Once dispossessed, Kikuyus were forced, through tax, work, and identity-paper schemes—and by outright force—into employment, primarily as servants on white estates. To gain back self-government and their land, the Kikuyu Central Association sent representative Jomo Kenyatta to England in 1929. During the next sixteen years, Kenyatta tried unsuccessfully to convince England to alter its method of government in Kenya; he returned to his home country in September of 1946.

In 1947, Kenyatta became president of the Kenya African Union (KAU), a nationalist party demanding an end to the numerous injustices of white rule. These demands were met with British resistance or excuses. While Kikuyus at large were becoming increasingly angry at white rule, a militaristic wing emerged, The Kenya Land Freedom Army, from which the organization Mau Mau grew (origins of this term are unknown but most agree it began as a derogatory label of settlers). On August 4, 1950, Mau Mau was declared illegal, even though the government knew little about it except that militant Kikuyus were winning over, coercing, or forcing other Kikuyus to take an oath against foreign rule. Then, on October 20, 1952, after Mau Mau killings of European cattle and the execution of a Kikuyu chief loyal to the British, a state of emergency was declared and an order sent out for the arrest of 183 people. Kenyatta was one of those arrested and, after a trial, was incarcerated for masterminding Mau Mau. Though this charge was never confirmed, he was imprisoned for seven years.

While fearful whites collected guns to protect their lives and property, the first Kikuyu murder of a white settler occurred a week after the emergency: the settler was hacked to death with a machete-like tool, a *panga*. Some thirteen thousand people and untold animals were to be killed in the Mau Mau anticolonial struggle, most of them Kikuyus. By 1953, the guerilla fighting force of Mau Mau had largely been defeated, and by 1956, the fighting had mostly stopped; the unequal political, economic, and social conditions leading to Mau Mau's rise, however, were still in place. While the state of emergency continued, governmental reforms between 1953 and 1960 did attempt to appease further threats from Mau Mau. The state of emergency finally ended end in 1960, likely well after Walcott finished writing "A Far Cry from Africa." Kenyatta was released from prison in 1961, Kenya gained its independence in 1963, and Kenyatta assumed the presidency in 1964, the same year Martin Luther King received the Nobel Peace Prize.

Walcott was most likely in the English-speaking Caribbean when he wrote "A Far Cry from Africa," an area, like Kenya, under the domination of the British. It was not until the 1930s, at a time of Caribbean social unrest, that even political parties were allowed and universal suffrage introduced. The growth of nationalism and the effects of World War II led to increasing pressure from West Indians for Britain to loosen its grip. So, in 1958, a federation including most of the English-speaking Caribbean islands was formed to prepare for eventual independence. Increasing friction between the archipelago and Britain led to Trinidad and Tobago, as well as Jamaica, withdrawing from the federation and becoming independent in 1962. Walcott's home island, St. Lucia, would not gain its independence until 1979, sixteen years after Kenya attained hers. During the period of greatest Mau Mau activity, Walcott was attending university in Jamaica. Until 1960, he spent most of his time teaching in West Indian schools and working in theater with his brother. It is likely that Walcott's West Indian origins, linked back to part of his family's original homeland in Africa, and the domination of both his country and Kenya by Britain spurred him to take special note of events in Kenya—events that at the time could have been a specter of a similar future for England's Caribbean colonies.

Critical Overview

When analyzing "A Far Cry from Africa," most critics comment on the poem's message and what it reveals about the poet, rather than the technical aspects of its creation. In an article titled "West Indies II: Walcott, Brathwaite, and Authenticity," Bruce King remarks, "The poem is remarkable for its complexity of emotions" and that it "treats of the Mau Mau uprising in terms that mock the usual justifications for and criticisms of colonialism." King notes that the narrator is stricken with "confused, irreconcilably opposed feelings: identification with black Africa, disgust with the killing of both white and black innocents, distrust of motives, love of the English language, and dislike of those who remain emotionally uninvolved." In his article "Ambiguity Without a Crisis? Twin Traditions, The Individual and Community in Derek Walcott's Essays," Fred D'Aguiar also deals with the division at the heart of the poem: "Already there is the ambivalence which hints at synthesis at the heart of the proclaimed division, a wish to artificially expose long buried oppositions between ancestries in need of reconciliation if the artist—and his community—are to grow." Though the poet seeks reconciliation, he does not appear to achieve it, which only accentuates his dilemma, a point Rei Terada makes in his *Derek Walcott's Poetry:* "His often anthololgized early poem 'A Far Cry from Africa' (1962), for example, places the poet 'Between this Africa and the English tongue I love.' Even in this poem, however, betweenness is not a solution, but an arduous problem. Even here, betweenness cannot adequately conceptualize the poet's position, since betweenness doesn't necessarily question the authenticity of the oppositions supposedly surrounding the poet."

Criticism

David Donnell

David Donnell, who teaches at the University of Toronto, has published seven books of poetry. His work is included in the Norton Anthology of Modern Poetry *and his volume* Settlement *received Canada's prestigious Governor General's Award. In the following essay, Donnell analyzes "A Far Cry from Africa" as the poet's personal credo.*

A Credo in Isolation

Even the title itself of Derek Walcott's lovely poem "A Far Cry from Africa" suggests that the author is writing about an African subject and doing so from a distance. It's an apt title, to be sure; Walcott is of African descent but was born and raised in what we might call the southeast corner of the American sphere without in any way encroaching on West Indies' independence. Writing from the beautiful island of St. Lucia, Walcott feels, as a well-educated and totally independent black West Indian, that he is indeed at some distance from Africa and the brutal atrocities of whites against blacks and blacks against whites that he has been reading about in Kenya, a large African state famous for its Veldt and for its extraordinary wildlife—giraffes, antelope, even rhinoceros.

The title "A Far Cry from Africa" may have a second meaning in addition to the obvious geographic and personal sense the author feels. The title also seems to say, "well, look, this is a far cry from the Africa that I have been reading about in descriptions of gorgeous fauna and flora and interesting village customs." And a third level of meaning to the title (without pressing this point too much) is the idea of Walcott hearing the poem as a far cry coming all the way across thousands of miles of ocean—the same routes, perhaps, as the Dutch ships of the late seventeenth century—to land in his accepting ear on the island of St. Lucia. He hears the cry coming to him on the wind. He writes, in the first line of his poem, "A wind is ruffling the tawny pelt / Of Africa." He has seen photographs of Kenya. He knows that light brown and yellow, of various shades, are two of the most prominent colors of this large African state; they are veldt colors, and there are lions out on the veldt.

"Kikuyu," in the second line, is the only African word in the poem. The Kikuyu were a Kenya tribe who became Mau Mau fighters in a grass-roots effort to oust the British colonial administration of Kenya. Walcott, as if mesmerized, describes the Mau Mau fighters as moving with extraordinary speed—they know the geography of their country and they "Batten upon the bloodstreams of the veldt." The use of the word batten is interesting; it generally means to fasten or secure a hatch on a ship. The upsurge of violence is justified in some ways perhaps, but what rivets Walcott's attention, because he's a well-educated man and a humanist, is given very simply in the following image, still from the powerful opening stanza: "Corpses are scattered through a paradise." Walcott, born on St. Lucia, a lovely island with a fairly low economy, would like to believe that Africa is just as paradisial and peaceful as the West Indies.

Most of Walcott's poems since the early 1960s have been written in very open but quite controlled language. "A Far Cry from Africa" is such a com-

pressed and tightly structured poem that the author tends to cover the ground he wants to talk about point by point and sometimes with what we might call caricatures, or images verging on caricature. "Only the worm, colonel of carrion cries: / Waste no compassion on these separate dead!" He follows this surprising image with two very sharp lines about the foolishness of statistics and alleged political scholars who want to discuss fine points. And then he ends his powerful opening stanza by saying, "What is that to the white child hacked in bed?" Or to Kenyans, he says, who are being treated as if they were "expendable." What appears to horrify Walcott partly in the case of Kenya is that the conflict and savagery taking place are happening on the basis of color; his reaction is almost Biblical in its unusually compressed and angry personal credo. At no time in this poem does he waste his time referring to any particular historical agreement. He sees the tragedy as essentially human tragedy, and the violence on both sides as essentially inhuman.

Walcott's dilemma seems to be very much in synch with some of the participants in this poem. "Threshed out by beaters," he says at the beginning of the second stanza. The poet has dealt with his initial horror at these events in Kenya and has outlined his initial focus on the general area of comment. He seems to see in this second stanza what he regards as the acceptable violence of nature or "natural law" as having been turned into a nightmare of unacceptable human violence based on color. "Beaters" on big game safaris in Africa are the men who beat the brush, sometimes singing or chanting as they do so, and flush out birds and animals for the hunt. Of course, in a lot of cases, beaters will flush out a variety of animals they hadn't expected.

"A Far Cry from Africa" continues this meditation on the landscape of the Kenyan veldt by saying, "the long rushes break / In a white dust of ibises whose cries / Have wheeled since civilization's dawn / From the parched river or beast-teeming plain." Walcott's image of Africa may strike some readers as a bit innocent, but it doesn't seem to be in any way affected or insincere as he expresses himself in this personal credo. Quite the contrary; it seems idealistic and uplifting, although it does leave the reader—and perhaps Walcott as well—in the position of saying, "How can we prevent these outbreaks of violence?" Or, perhaps more specifically, "How can we be fair?" Should the United Nations have intervened on behalf of the Kenyans? This is a very intense and bitter poem—a lashing out at injustice and an attempt to formulate both some distance for the writer as well as a sense of his own eventual or fundamental juxtaposition to the uncomfortable and agonizing subject.

Anthropologists, both American and European, have published an enormous amount of material in the twentieth century on different questions of social personality, physicality, and to what degree many of our fundamental social responses—for example, defensiveness, lust, comfort, and pride—seem to have an animal basis. Walcott lashes out at both sides of the Kenyan situation from a position in which he strongly and intensely believes that human and animal are not only different but should be regarded at least as absolute opposites. He seems to know and be aware of the fact that they are not truly absolute opposites. But a large portion of the middle of this poem is Walcott's expression of his coming to terms with human nature and the mixed good and bad, up and down, nature of history.

"A Far Cry from Africa" is such an agonizing and didactic personal poem, and such a tightly structured poem in which Walcott never relaxes and explains to the reader in casual asides that he himself is of African descent, that some readers may at first feel that the poem is more a comment on news of the day than it is a personal response, and a credo, and to some extent a partial deconstruction of his own credo. There is a weighing of different examples from the Kenyan upsurge in this poem, and the writer obviously wants to come out on top of his own material; he wants to see the argument in a perspective that makes some kind of sense, and he doesn't want to get swallowed by his own feelings of anger and outrage at these events.

And so we have the "Kikuyu" and violence in Kenya, violence in a "paradise," and we have "Statistics" that don't mean anything and "scholars" who tend to throw their weight behind colonial policy. Walcott's outrage is very just and even, perhaps by the standards of the late 1960s, restrained. And his sense of amazement and awe, and his desire to love the Africa he describes, surges at one point when he notes what is probably a fairly salient and typical detail of Kenya, how "the long rushes break / In a white dust of ibises whose cries / Have wheeled since civilization's dawn ...."

Of course the African continent is nothing if not enormous. The range of geography and of fauna and flora seem to be extraordinary. Different cultures are in different kinds of motion in various parts of the continent. The north of Africa contains some of the old Arabic civilizations of the eastern

What Do I Read Next?

- The anthology *Modern African Poetry* (1984), edited by Gerald Moore and Ulli Beier, includes poems by 64 poets from twenty-four African nations, including three poets from Kenya of the same generation as Walcott.

- *Orientalism* (1979) by Edward Said is a pioneering work in postcolonial studies. Although it mostly centers on the Muslim world (including north Africa), the book is a must for the student wanting to understand the roots of Western imperialism as its ideas were disseminated through intellectual practice.

- Ella Shohat and Robert Stam's *Unthinking Eurocentrism* (1994), a text of multicultural media studies, links the often separated studies of race and identity politics on the one hand, and on the other, third-world nationalism and (post)colonial discourses.

- Gayatry Chakravorty Spivak's *The Post-Colonial Critic: Interviews, Strategies, and Dialogues* (1990) speaks to questions of representation and self-representation, the situations of postcolonial critics, pedagogical responsibility, and political strategies.

half of our world, including Libya, which is across the Mediterranean from Italy, and Egypt, where historical records show at least one or more black African Pharaohs before the period of time described in the Bible's New Testament. Walcott may or may not be interested in these ideas; he may or may not have visited Africa at some time. We have to concentrate on the poem and on what happens in the poem. How does he develop his sense of weighing these different negative facts of violence in a paradise of ibises and different cultures?

Walcott could be a little more informative in this poem. For example, he could allude to some of the newspaper reports that he's been reading; he could mention a particular town in Kenya, or a local hero. Even though he identifies Kenya and the

> *What appears to horrify Walcott partly in the case of Kenya is that the conflict and savagery taking place are happening on the basis of color; his reaction is almost Biblical in its unusually compressed and angry personal credo."*

great veldt and begins with a powerful opening line that sets the tone and motion for the whole poem ("A wind is ruffling the tawny pelt / Of Africa"), he still wants this poem to be timeless and to apply to other situations in different parts of the world. Near the end of the poem, however, having accomplished his first objective, the charting of the Kenya upsurge and his own humanistic denunciation of brutality, Walcott does come into "A Far Cry from Africa"—and he does so very dramatically.

Perhaps the most brutal and categorical movement in the whole poem occurs after that lovely image of the "ibises" wheeling in historical patterns since "civilization's dawn." Frustrated with every aspect of this brutal color war in Kenya, Walcott comes up with an image that more or less generalizes the history of English, European, and African wars: "his wars / Dance to the tightened carcass of a drum, / While he calls courage still that native dread / Of the white peace contracted by the dead." In this powerful image, coming to the penultimate point of the poem, Walcott says basically that everybody dances, everybody gets emotionally intoxicated with the egoism of taking sides, everybody in that kind of situation is listening to a drumbeat of some kind or another. "Brutish necessity," he calls it, comparing the Kenyan fighters to the revolutionaries in Spain: "A waste of our compassion, as with Spain / The gorilla wrestles with the superman." At this point, Walcott seems to have spoken out on the issue, identified the problem, and to some degree disposed of the whole subject.

But there is more to "A Far Cry from Africa" than what we have read so far. There is, as a mat-

ter of fact, the very fulcrum of his being so involved and so intense about the subject in the first place: not just humanistic anger, but also a very personal outrage. "I who am poisoned with the blood of both, / Where shall I turn, divided to the vein?" he says as a beginning to the last stanza. Born and raised in St. Lucia, educated in the British system, and an omnivorous reader by the time he was in high school, Walcott is very much a citizen of the world. Quite a well-known poet by the time he was in his twenties, Walcott had, by the time he wrote "A Far Cry from Africa," spent considerable time in Trinidad, working on different theater projects, and he had also been exhibited as a talented painter.

One of the most moving aspects of this poem, once the reader accepts the very terse, basic, logical arguments regarding the struggle in Kenya, is the general image of the poet/author at the end of the poem. He has no choice but to watch both sides rather sadly continue their violence against each other. But he ends this powerful polemic with six devastating lines: "I who have cursed / The drunken officer of British rule, how choose / Between this Africa and the English tongue I love? / Betray them both, or give back what they give? / How can I face such slaughter and be cool? / How can I turn from Africa and live?" And of course, Walcott has never turned from Africa or gone to live there. He has continued writing and publishing and has, since the 1980s, become famous all over again for an enormous book-long Homeric poem about the islands, the Caribbean, the Mediterranean, and the coming together of a multiple of cultural convergences.

Source: David Donnell, in an essay for *Poetry for Students,* The Gale Group, 1999.

Jhan Hochman

Jhan Hochman, who holds a Ph.D in English and an M.A. in cinema studies, is the author of Green Cultural Studies: Nature in Film, Novel, and Theory *(1998). In the following essay Hochman examines the role of animality in "A Far from Africa."*

When most of us think of Africa, one of the first things that comes to mind are the animals— lions, elephants, zebras, giraffes, rhinos, hyenas, etc. And although the issues of Walcott's "A Far Cry from Africa" are cultural—are concerned with people—animals materialize throughout the poem in generally two ways. As kinds, such as flies and ibises, animals are compared similarly to particular groups of people. But as a kingdom, as in "animal kingdom," animals are largely contrasted to humankind, even though Walcott does acknowledge a shared animality.

The opening image of "A Far Cry from Africa" is "A wind … ruffling the tawny pelt / Of Africa." A pelt, in this case, most likely refers to the furry or hairy skin of an animal, such as a wild cat, dog, or antelope. Not only is the continent of Africa associated with animals in Walcott's poem, but it is represented as an animal. The specific topography referred to is the "veldt," a Dutch Afrikaans word meaning field or a flat grassland or prairie with few or no trees. Within this landscape are (as one might expect to find around large animals) insects, specifically flies. The flies Walcott mentions, however, are not really flies, but metaphors for the Kikuyu, a tribal people of Kenya living in the region long before Europeans arrived. This is a controversial metaphor, indeed: likening African tribal people to pesty insects sucking the blood out of Africa.

The metaphor of the Kikuyu as flies is developed further. As flies lay eggs that turn into maggots (Walcott's "worms"), the Kikuyu also brought forth something considered unappealing by Walcott: Mau Mau, a secret terrorist organization. The Kikuyu were an influential people whose economy revolved around agriculture. Their land was increasingly taken by white "settlers" when Britain, in 1895, turned what is now The Republic of Kenya into the East African Protectorate. The Kikuyu were forced off their land and into servitude. Kikuyu anger over this predicament increased and reached its peak with the Mau Mau Uprising against the British regime. Mau Mau began as a militant faction of the Kikuyu, the Kenya Land Freedom Army, and became a secret society bent on expelling the British from Kenya. From 1952 to 1956, it engaged in a bloody terrorist campaign; Mau Mau was infamous for its hackings and mutilations of whites, animals owned by whites, and Kikuyus who refused to join Mau Mau or who collaborated with the British. (Though the British defeated Mau Mau, the country of Kenya earned its independence in 1963 from colonial rule.)

It was reports of this violence that reached other parts of the world and must have appalled Walcott to the extent that he compared Mau Mau to maggots eating away at a field of corpses. One might infer here that Walcott is not just appalled, but ashamed at Mau Mau because he is, himself, part African. His problem is that Mau Mau might synecdochically (in a substitution of part for whole) become all Africans, even all black peoples. Mau Mau became so infamous that it was used as a verb

in American slang; "to Mau Mau," meant to threaten or terrorize. In comparing Mau Mau to maggots, Walcott is distancing himself from Mau Mau and against the synecdoche, Mau Mau equals all black peoples.

The second stanza begins with ibises, large birds related to herons and storks. The ibis was a favorite animal of the ancient Egyptians, becoming not only the incarnation of the god Thoth—patron of astronomers, scribes, magicians, healers, and enchanters—but a bird whose appearance heralded the flooding Nile, the season of fertility. In this stanza, (white) ibises are apparently being hunted by black Africans, which could be read as a metaphor of black Mau Maus "hunting" white estate owners and farmers. Some reading this poem are apt to synecdochically understand the white ibis, intuitively or intellectually, as a good symbol. Once the association is made, whites hunted by Mau Mau can seem blameless, guiltless, and good. Further, calling white ibises inhabitants of Africa since "civilization's dawn," makes it seem as if whites resided in Africa even before the Kikuyu. While the metaphor of "ibis equals white person" may work with the thrust of the poem, it is far too positive an image to represent the whites who took Kenya away from Kenyans.

The third stanza may be read as two comments made by an outsider to the Kenyan conflict that justify complacency. The word "brutish" comes from the Latin *brutus,* meaning heavy, inert, and stupid; it most commonly refers to beasts. Walcott's outsiders to the uprising complacently remark that nothing is to be done since Africans are possessed by "brutish necessity" to wipe their bloody hands upon "napkins of a dirty cause." "Napkins" indicate a civilized nicety, and the "dirty cause" of the British is known as the "white man's burden"—the purported altruistic duty of white people to "civilize" black people. The other comment in this same stanza made by outsiders about the Mau Mau Uprising is: "The gorilla wrestles with the superman." The "gorilla" represents black Africans and the "superman," white Brits. Walcott's outsider considers both sides of the conflict reprehensible: that Africans, like gorillas, are not civilized, and that Brits, like Nietzsche's overweening superman, are too civilized—so arrogant as to think it their destiny to rule the nonwhite world. The speaker of this section apparently wants nothing to do with Africans, Mau Mau, or imperialism. Walcott is disgusted by both views put forth in this stanza, not only because they are distasteful, but because he cannot so easily remove himself from the conflict since he is "poisoned with the blood of both."

Walcott, or the persona of the outsider, has compared people to animals, but, in the second stanza, animals are contrasted with people:

> The violence of beast on beast is read
> As natural law, but upright man
> Seeks his divinity by inflicting pain

The "is read" makes the speaker seem just barely willing to go along with the thrust of the first statement. He does seem, however, in agreement with the second idea—that man does indeed seek "his divinity by inflicting pain." With these two thoughts, beasts come out better than "upright man" since animals do what they must do, and do not seek divinity through inflicting pain.

Although Walcott never solves—within the poem—his problem of loyalty, one thing does look clear-cut: Walcott believes that humans, unlike animals, have no excuse, no attractive rationale, for murdering noncombatants in the Kenyan conflict. While we cannot be sure if Walcott, at this point in his life, was a pacifist, he does make plain in "A Far Cry from Africa" that whatever the rightness of the Mau Mau cause, its mode of operation was shameful. We geographical outsiders might be apt to agree. Still, Mau Mau's swift, rude terror would better represented if juxtaposed against the knawing, polite oppression of British imperialism. Unfortunately, Walcott only briefly mentions the vivid extremity of British practice ("The drunken officer of British rule" and "dirty cause" do not do justice to the extent of British injustice), making it far easier to condemn Mau Mau. Walcott's dilemma (and ours) might have been more righteously difficult had the poem added a few stanzas condemning the British. Instead, Walcott displaces a political situation in which large numbers of people suffered and died to the "action" inside himself—personal shame and confusion. In the process of shaming Mau Mau by claiming its members do not even measure up to animals, both Mau Mau and animals are demeaned. At the end of "A Far Cry from Africa," Walcott appears as torn about his identity as both animal and human as his identity as both African and European.

Source: Jhan Hochman, in an essay for *Poetry for Students,* The Gale Group, 1999.

Aviya Kushner

Aviya Kushner, who is the poetry editor for Neworld Renaissance *Magazine, earned an M.A. in creative writing from Boston University, where she studied under Derek Walcott, among others. In the following essay, Kushner analyzes "A Far Cry from Africa" as the speaker's quest self-description.*

Island boy. That's how Nobel Prize-winning poet Derek Walcott often describes himself, in both his poems and his conversation. However, that simple self-portrait can be misleading. At best, it's only part of the story of a man whose wanderings have produced rich, skillful, multilayered poems that draw on the poetic tradition of many nations, ranging from modern England, Russia, and Spain to ancient Greece.

Of course, the island bit has some truth to it. Walcott is a major English-language writer who was born—and still lives, for part of the year—in the multilingual Caribbean. His accent and warm manners are from the tiny, tourist-attracting island of St. Lucia, but his heroes in both his reading and writing have taken him far past the sunny, postcard blue-and-green Caribbean landscape. Walcott's historical conscience also extends far past the island's borders, and his readers live all over the world.

Walcott is so admired in England that he was mentioned in leading newspapers as a possible candidate for the position of Poet Laureate when Ted Hughes died. For a son of the colonies, being named England's chief poet would certainly be an impressive turn of events. But that irony of personal success amid his native country's history as a conquered land has not been lost on Walcott. His precarious perch between two cultures has become a key subject for him.

In fact, this lifelong conflict between his tiny native island and the wider world, between his love of English and his knowledge that it is the colonizer's tongue and the oppressor's language—and thus part of its power—is a factor in the depth and strength of Walcott's poems.

Many poems are built on ambivalence, and "A Far Cry from Africa" is an example of how a masterful poet can mold ambivalence into art. In this poem, Walcott extends his ambivalence about the English language and the heritage it bears to everything meter, subject matter, and even the choice of English as a language to write in. While the poem starts off in the iambic pentameter Walcott has mastered—the bread and butter of poetry in English—the poem soon veers course metrically, just as it changes place, perspective, and point of view. Like ownership of countries and empires, everything here is subject to change.

Much of the poem can be read in more than one way, starting with the title. At first glance, if "a far cry" is read as "a subject far removed from daily reality," "A Far Cry from Africa" is a title that might apply to most of Walcott's work. With a few exceptions, he is not influenced by the sound or tradition of Africa, but rather the titans of Western poetry. Personally close to Russian-born Joseph Brodsky and Canadian-born Mark Strand, a deep admirer of Britons Edward Thomas and W. H. Auden and Russian poet Marina Tsvetaeva, Walcott frequently writes homages to his favorite writers. African writers, however, rarely figure among Walcott's models.

But the "far cry" of the title can also be taken literally, as simply a cry from a far place. This is supported by the poem's opening lines, which detail human misery and the cries that must come with it. The phrase then leads into a questioning of colonization and the pain it has brought. The poem subsequently details a deep, personal division that is paralleled by the double meanings of the title and much of the poem. As the poem progresses, it questions itself, and it ends in a series of questions.

This division mirrors the speaker's feelings about Britain's colonization of so many countries. Despite the violence, Walcott the poet cannot fully condemn the colonizers because he has taken so much from them. His vocation—English—comes from the colonizer, and yet, as a moral human being, he feels he must condemn colonization.

Naturally, this produces an inner division. By the final passages, the rumbling references to a divided self have reached a shriek. This division is the heart of the poem, but it is only clear at the end. Therefore, all of the stanzas fall more easily into place if they are read as steps to the crucial line in the last stanza: "I who am poisoned with the blood of both / Where should I turn, divided to the vein?"

Now it makes sense to return to the beginning. Every word in the poem is part of the step-by-step march to that deafening moment of self-division at the end. The poem starts with a personification of the entire continent, and this speaker-Africa parallel continues to some extent throughout. For a poem that moves to the grandiose, its first step looks modest: "A wind is ruffling the tawny pelt / Of Africa." But like Walcott's characterization of himself as merely "a man who loved islands," this first line is misleadingly simple. A trip to the dictionary is one way to uncover the layers of the poem.

> " … '*A Far Cry from Africa*' is an example of how a masterful poet can mold ambivalence into art."

The word "pelt" is normally defined as the skin of an animal (with fur or hair still on it), and so the opening line compares the continent to an animal, with "tawny pelt" possibly evoking the color of the African desert. But there's more. "Pelt" can also be human skin, and here, the wind is ruffling the pelt of a person. What seems modest is actually horribly frightening. Finally, "pelt" as a verb means "to strike," an image that begins a few lines later.

In the second line, the pace quickens. "Kikuyu, quick as flies, / Batten upon the bloodstreams of the veldt." After the confident iambics of the first line and a half (trademark Walcott), the poem draws on alliteration, forsaking meter as primary device for other poetic tools. The alliteration of "Kikuyu/quick" and "batten/bloodstreams" physically speeds up the poem; the action parallels the sound. Kikuyu are indigenous African people, and here they are rushing to feed upon the streams of blood in the level grassland of the continent. In this landscape, people feed off people. This is a ghastly paradise, populated with scattered corpses.

Amid all of the hubbub, the smallest of creatures—the worm—wily and slinky, loudly warns those who would be compassionate. Walcott injects some humor into the gruesome scene, with the characterization "colonel of carrion" depicting the worm as king of those who prey on flesh. Suddenly, Walcott takes us out of this frightening, jumbled-up world and anchors it in "statistics" and "scholars" who try to justify colonial policy. Once again using alliteration to point to a turn in the poem, the speaker puts the spotlight on those who write and think but don't really look at a hacked child or a dead savage rotting in the desert.

The reference to "statistics" and "scholars" borrows from W. H. Auden's famous poem "The Fall of Rome," in which an "unimportant clerk" writes "I DO NOT LIKE MY WORK" on a pink official form. Here, too, Walcott mixes the fall of an empire with a humorous jab at bureaucrats and their statistics.

Apart from that slight tangent for some humor, stanza one sticks to its mission—to set a scene. It also shows off some poetic gymnastics, pushing alliteration and rhyme as far as they can go. Slant rhymes such as "pelt/veldt" and "flies/paradise" share space with conventional rhymes such as "bed/dead." Most important in its role of scene-setting, the first stanza ends with questions, which are integral to this poem. Just as the title proclaims "A Far Cry from Africa" and then the first line proceeds to set a scene in Africa, the questions announce that the poem will offer a far cry from answers. This is a poem about far cries, about divisions of the self, a gulf as wide as a continent—all contained within one man.

While the first two lines of stanza one were all iambs, for a lulling, ta-tum sound, the second stanza begins quite differently. Instead of a light ruffling, there is the loud "Threshed by beaters, the long rushes break." The plants that are used for mats or furniture bottoms are literally broken by beaters, which are revolving cylinders that chop up stalks or brush. "Beaters" also recalls "to beat" or "to conquer," a major theme of the poem. This technique of a noun that also resonates as a verb was seen earlier with the word "pelt."

Once again, as in the first stanza, sound is king. "Threshed" is a single, forceful syllable, placing a clear stress on the stanza's first word. "Rush" and "break" reinforce the sensation of power and violence. The speaker is getting ready to roll out some grand ideas, with that kind of drumbeat sound. And so "have wheeled since civilization's dawn" does not come as a huge surprise. The phrase "civilization's dawn" lets the poem shift from a scene in Africa to a rumination on the world itself—to the history of man.

"Civilization's dawn" also recalls the Bible's book of Genesis, which is why the poem's quiet opening followed by loud, active rumbling seems so familiar. In the next few lines, Walcott takes that opening image of paradise marred by violence coupled with a personal conflict and expands it into a tale of humanity—a sorry story repeated throughout human history:

> The violence of beast upon beast is read
> As natural law, but upright man
> Seeks his divinity by inflicting pain

While English naturalist Charles Darwin may have proclaimed survival of the fittest as natural law, and while in the creation story God may have granted animals to men to eat, the speaker here sees man as a conqueror attempting to mimic God. According to the Biblical story, God has power over all things, including, of course, the power to give life. Man can be God-like by literally lording power over his fellow man. The speaker here questions the wisdom of having mere people possess so much power over their fellow men.

The next stanza begins with another shake to the reader and another powerhouse image—"brutish necessity" wiping its hands "upon the napkin of a dirty cause." The word "Again" signals the stanza will continue what the other stanzas have done. As we have seen, each stanza's first few words are crucial to the poem's overall structure, and this stanza is no exception.

"Again" means that this story has happened many times over, and the repetitive questions at the end reinforce the feeling of a cycle. These are questions the speaker has asked himself many times before. This is a story of conquest and divided loyalties that snakes back to the Bible, and later, to the great empires that rose and fell and figure so prominently in Walcott's work. Here, for example, Walcott deliberately alludes to the Bible and mentions Spain. ("A waste of our compassion, as with Spain …") Finally, like the earliest Greek epic poets, Walcott is fascinated by senseless brutality of man over man and how even great humans are tripped up by their simple human nature.

These grand ideas should not distract from the tools of poetry that are used here, since they point to meaning. The careful rhyme throughout the poem is especially important as the ending nears. The "flies/paradise" lines that came early on have already focused a spotlight on line endings, and the last few create an interesting juxtaposition of "live" and "love." The speaker seems to be realizing that how he lives and what he loves are not compatible. Though his elegant, Westernized lines that draw on the classical epic and lyric traditions are indeed "a far cry from Africa," Walcott nevertheless realizes that his life—what makes him live—is wider than the Western canon. He must address those close to him who are struggling to live. He cannot turn from Africa, despite all the years, the accolades, and the devotion to its oppressors' tongue.

And so, in this poem that evokes a continent, a world, and an entire history of the world in four stanzas, the speaker faces Africa and uses its desert and its violence as a means of looking at himself. The only conclusions he reaches, though, are a series of questions. All of the violence and self-division reach an intense pitch with those final questions:

> I who am poisoned with the blood of both,
> Where shall I turn, divided to the vein?
> I who have cursed
> The drunken officer of British rule, how choose
> Between this Africa and the English tongue I love?
> Betray them both, or give back what they give?
> How can I face such slaughter and be cool?
> How can I turn from Africa and live?

Fittingly, the poem ends in the word "live." For this speaker, questioning and living are one and the same. Forming questions into art—in perfectly controlled lines, displaying all of poetry's power—is how this poet approaches a crisis of identity. Somehow, a speaker nearly ripped apart by inner conflict produces a poem that races up and down but, in the end, seems overwhelmingly whole. Despite the questions, the mission of self-description within the context of history is accomplished.

Source: Aviya Kushner, in an essay for *Poetry for Students,* The Gale Group, 1999.

Sources

Brown, Stewart, ed., *The Art of Derek Walcott,* Mid Glamorgan, Wales: Seren Books, 1991.

D'Aguiar, Fred, "Ambiguity Without a Crisis? Twin Traditions, The Individual and Community in Derek Walcott's Essays," *The Art of Derek Walcott,* edited by Stewart Brown, Mid Glamorgan, Wales: Seren Books, 1991, pp.157-70.

Delf, George, *Jomo Kenyatta: Towards the Light of Truth,* Garden City, New York: Doubleday, 1961.

Hamner, Robert D., *Derek Walcott,* New York: Twayne, 1993.

Hamner, Robert, D., ed., *Critical Perspectives on Derek Walcott,* Washington, D.C.: Three Continents, 1993.

King, Bruce, "West Indies II: Walcott, Brathwaite, and Authenticity," *The New English Literatures: Cultural Nationalism in a Changing World,* New York: St. Martins, 1980, pp. 118-39.

Terada, Rei, *Derek Walcott's Poetry,* Boston: Northeastern University Press, 1992.

For Further Study

Baer, William, ed., *Conversations with Derek Walcott,* Jackson: University Press of Mississippi, 1996.
> This text contains eighteen interviews spanning the period from 1966 to 1993. Also included is a good bio-chronology of Walcott's life.

Grant, Nellie, *Nellie's Story,* New York: William Morrow, 1981.
> For those wanting a firsthand account of what it was like to be a white farmer in Kenya during the period of 1933 to 1977, this is a valuable text.

Huxley, Elspeth, compiler, *Nine Faces of Kenya,* New York: Viking, 1991.
> For firsthand accounts by both blacks and whites who lived in Kenya during Mau Mau, this is an excellent source. The book is divided into themes: Exploration, Travel, Settlers, Wars, Environment, Wildlife, Hunting, Lifestyles, Legend, and Poetry.

Walcott, Derek, *Collected Poems: 1948-1984,* New York: Farrar, Straus and Giroux, 1986.
> This collection contains "A Far Cry from Africa" and 135 other poems, from Walcott's first major book, *In a Green Night,* to *Midsummer.*

The Heaven of Animals

James Dickey
1962

"The Heaven of Animals" was published in James Dickey's 1962 collection, *Drowning With Others,* and was later reprinted in the more widely distributed *Poems 1957-1967.* It is one of Dickey's most popular and anthologized poems. In the poem, the discrepancy between a violent life and a blissful afterlife is settled. Animals, which kill because it is their instinctive nature and not because of evil intentions, find that they are not only allowed to kill in heaven but that they are encouraged to do so, with "claws and teeth grown perfect." This poem is more than simply a justification of the place of violence in the natural order, although Dickey's sympathies with the predatory species are obvious. The tranquility of the heaven presented here stems from the way that the victimized animals are at peace with the role they are given to play in the social order. Most literary works in Western culture show death as something to be mourned and feared, but the animals in this poem accept death in peace, glad to know their place on the grand order and to be free of the burden of finding themselves. "The Heaven of Animals" is unique among James Dickey's poems because of the way that predators and prey are at harmony with each other. Dickey was a bow-and-arrow hunter who made a point of building up his macho image to the public, as well as to himself, and most of his poems reveal an underlying discomfort about the relationship between hunter and prey.

Author Biography

It is a mark of our culture that James Dickey's most notable achievements were in poetry, but that he received his greatest fame for his one novel, *Deliverance* (1970), and that the celebrity he gained from that book shaded the public's reaction to everything he did for the rest of his life. Even more ironic is the fact that he would not even be generally recognized for the novel had it not been for the successful 1972 film based on it, for which Dickey wrote the script. He was a versatile man who had interests and accomplishments in a number of fields. He was a novelist and critic, a movie and television writer; and a successful advertising writer who wrote copy for Coca-Cola® and Lay's® potato chips; he was a hunter and outdoorsman who could spin great yarns, and, after *Deliverance* made him famous, he was a frequent and welcomed guest on television talk shows; he tried his hand at acting, playing the Southern sheriff in the movie adaptation of his book; and he was an intellectual whose essays commanded the respect of his peers. At the center of all of this, though, he always saw himself as a poet.

Dickey, who was born in 1923 in Atlanta, Georgia, was a product of the South (but not of the rural South that has provided the rich literary tradition of writers such as William Faulkner and John Crowe Ransom). In high school he starred on the football field. He was a bomber pilot in World War II, from 1942 to 1946. It was during his time in the air force that he started reading poetry seriously, while waiting for the librarian he was dating to get off duty. He went back to college after the war, earning his master's degree in 1950 from Vanderbilt University, a school famous for the writers it produced—especially poets—from the 1920s through the 1950s. Dickey taught for a few months in Houston, then was recalled to the air force to fight in the Korean War. For a few years he wrote, won awards for his poetry, and taught at various schools. He quit trying to secure a full-time teaching appointment, however, after a scandal prompted him to leave the University of Florida in 1956: after reading the sexually explicit poem "The Father's Body," Dickey was asked to apologize to offended audience members; he refused. He then went to work for an advertising firm, but despite finding success there, he could not resign himself to writing solely for monetary gain. Dickey wrote the poem "The Heaven of Animals" while at his desk at the advertising agency, and it was published a few years later, in 1962. Throughout the 1960s,

James Dickey

Dickey and his family traveled, living off of money he earned from writing awards and a Guggenheim Fellowship. During this time, Dickey also served, for brief periods, as a poet-in-residence at several universities. After the publication of *Deliverance* in 1970, Dickey's output of poetry dwindled. He was a colorful, popular speaker on talk shows and on college campuses, where he actively promoted the image of himself as a hard-drinking outdoorsman and a ladies' man. He wrote a script for a television adaptation of Jack London's *The Call of the Wild* in 1975. In 1977 he was chosen to read his poem "The Strength of Fields" at the inaugural celebration for President Jimmy Carter. For the rest of his life Dickey published poems, essays, interviews, and opinion pieces. He was respected, but not considered a major influence when he died in 1997.

Poem Text

Here they are. The soft eyes open.
If they have lived in a wood
It is a wood.
If they have lived on plains
It is grass rolling   5
Under their feet forever.

Having no souls, they have come,
Anyway, beyond their knowing.
Their instincts wholly bloom
And they rise.   10
The soft eyes open.

To match them, the landscape flowers,
Outdoing, desperately
Outdoing what is required:
The richest wood,   15
The deepest field.

For some of these,
It could not be the place
It is, without blood.
These hunt, as they have done,   20
But with claws and teeth grown perfect,

More deadly than they can believe.
They stalk more silently,
And crouch on the limbs of trees,
And their descent   25
Upon the bright backs of their prey

May take years
In a sovereign floating of joy.
and those that are hunted
Know this as their life,   30
Their reward: to walk

Under such trees in full knowledge
Of what is in glory above them,
And to feel no fear,
But acceptance, compliance.   35
Fulfilling themselves without pain

At the cycle's center,
They tremble, they walk
Under the tree,
They fall, they are torn,   40
They rise, they walk again.

Poem Summary

Lines 1-6:

This poem opens with a quick, direct statement that introduces the animals of the title without any further explanation about who "they" are or where they are or why, leaving readers to understand all of this from the title. Critics have mentioned the fact that this vision of heaven is unusual because things change here, as opposed to visions where the situation in heaven is established and stays one way forever. This "changing" idea is more important in later stanzas, but it is introduced in the first line, with "The soft eyes open." Throughout the poem, the speaker avoids mentioning any specific types of animals, but here (and in line 11, when the phrase

is repeated) the poem focuses on particular, individual animals as they arrive in heaven. The poem itself is not specific enough, though, to give any details about the animals beyond the fact that their eyes are soft. Noteworthy in the structure of the first stanza is that the phrase in lines 2-3 is nearly, but not actually, repeated in lines 4-6. Each starts with the same first four words, but the second version rolls past the monosyllabic bluntness of "wood / It is wood" to a longer, more luxuriant phrase about eternity.

Lines 7-11:

The main function of the second stanza is to explain the poem's moral situation to readers. The situation is a paradox: if these animals have no souls, then what exactly is it that has gone to heaven upon their deaths? The statement that they have no souls does not quite fit with what the rest of the poem says. It is here to ridicule theological tradition, especially the writings of Saint Thomas Aquinas, who wrote much about the subject and was firm in his belief that animals lack souls. Dickey wrote that he was upset with Aquinas's position when he wrote this poem, but the poem uses that position, along with the claim that animals act on instinct alone. He also grants these animals a heaven, which would be useless if they have no soul. By repeating the phrase "The soft eyes open," the poem implies some level of awareness on the part of the animals, because "soft" implies a degree of kindness, and "eyes open" is usually associated with the broader sense of knowing, or understanding, where one is.

Lines 12-16:

The third stanza is the only stanza that is not directly about the situation of the animals, and instead is focused on letting readers know what their heaven is like. The key word in this stanza is, of course, "outdoing," and correspondingly the main idea is to take concepts that have already been presented and to stretch them to an extreme. The use of the word "flowers" in line 12 shows Dickey's nimble use of language in order to get as much meaning as he can from his words. Line 12 implies a field of flowers to the reader, but word "flowers" is actually used here as a verb, meaning that the landscape grows healthy and then opens up. The reason why the heaven of animals is so "desperate" to make itself an exaggerated version of their earthly habitat is unclear, other than the basic fact that it is, after all, heaven, and is therefore responsible to be great.

Lines 17-21:

With the beauty and opulence of the setting established, the fourth stanza introduces a new element: blood. While earlier parts of the poem, especially stanza 3, focused on establishing the positive concepts of heaven—the ways animal heaven would differ from earth and the ways it would be the same—the fourth stanza brings the main contradiction of this idea out into the open. As the poem points out, this "could not be the place / It is, without blood." If heaven is supposed to be a place where all of one's desires are fulfilled, leading to perfect happiness, then there would need to be blood, because some predatory animals have no desire other than to catch and kill their prey. Heaven, or the power that rules heaven, even shows approval for their blood lust by making their tools of killing, claws and teeth, better than ever. But while the common notion of heaven includes perfect happiness, it also assumes that there would be peace. In this case the two ideas clash with one another: a predatory animal could not be happy living in peace.

Lines 22-26:

This transitionary stanza starts in the middle of a statement about the predators and ends in the middle of a statement about the prey. Its main contribution is that it gives the mental state of the predators as one of surprise, as they discover their newfound heavenly skills. Here again is the concept of time passing in heaven. The animals that opened their eyes earlier in the poem discover new things about heaven here. They find themselves more deadly and more silent: this version of heaven involves taking the things of the earth and pushing them to unearthly extremes.

Lines 27-31:

The joy of the predatory animals and the complacency of their prey are examined here. Joy, for the hunter, is not just a matter of finding a prey and killing it immediately. Since it likes to hunt, its pleasure is extended when the hunt is extended, and so, with the physical rules of the heaven different than the ones we know, a pounce from a tree can take years, and not seconds, to complete. Up to this point, the poem has focused on what makes animals happy and has looked at the unusual case, the animals that live to kill, assuring readers that heaven will accommodate their desires. That leaves the problem of the ones who are killed and the issue of how this could be considered a heaven for them. This stanza mentions their awareness of what is happening to them, and it uses the phrase "their reward," but that

Media Adaptations

phrase, often used positively, is also often ironically. At this point in the poem, Dickey is unclear about whether the animals that are hunted are allowed to participate in all heavenly privileges, or if this is just a heaven for the strong and aggressive.

Lines 32-36:

By using the words "fulfilling themselves" in line 36, Dickey establishes the moral structure of this version of heaven: victimization is good for the victim, it is the thing that makes the victim's personality complete. "Fulfillment" clearly has a more positive meaning than the words used in line 35, "acceptance" and "compliance," which only explain how the victims behave without commenting on what is right. Saying that this is their fulfillment announces that this is right for them. Some of the misery associated with victimization is eliminated, because the negative elements of fear and pain are disavowed in this stanza. Although it still seems that the animals that are being preyed upon are not being treated to a very positive experience in heaven, the poem does imply one benefit for them: freedom from uncertainty. They may not be able to escape their fate, but, without pain or fear, that fate is not nearly as bad as it is in life. If uncertainty is taken to be one of life's greatest miseries, then this situation does appear to be at least somewhat like heavenly bliss.

Lines 37-41:

The poem's last stanza sounds mythic, with its reference to the cycle of life alluding to a grand scheme, but the real significance of stanza 8 is to clear up the logical inconsistency in the situation that has been posed. One of the central defining truths about heaven is that it is supposed to be eternal, but it could not be so for animals that have been ripped to shreds by others' "perfect" claws and teeth. The previous stanza explained how there could be a place in this heaven for animals that are traditionally preyed upon, and this stanza explains how they could remain there. The solution is simply that they rise up again after being "killed" and continue to rise up, over and over. If heaven for the killers would be to kill continuously, then heaven for the prey must be to be killed again and again.

Themes

Consciousness

One of the key contradictions in this poem is that it says directly that animals have no souls and no awareness of where they are when they are in heaven, but, in order for it to be heaven, the ones who are devoured are said to be aware of what is happening to them. The unevenness of their state of awareness is due to a central problem of heaven being a place of plurality, not harmony. A heaven for each individual creature would not be hard to think of. The heaven for a lion, for instance, would be a place where it could chase down and eat any antelope or zebra it wants. But how can that, at the same time, be heaven for the antelope? In the second stanza, the poem addresses this problem in the same way that philosophers and theologians have traditionally dealt with the problem of humans profiting from the deaths of other animals: by denying that animals have souls, that they know what they are doing or what is being done to them. The poem suggests, at this point, that they are unconscious—that they are acting only on instinct. The problem this raises is whether, logically, this would be heaven at all if all of its occupants were unaware of what was going on. After all, it would not be heaven if they were not happy there, and their contentment or complacency could not be called happiness if they were not conscious of it. The poem solves the problem by giving the prey the ability to rise up from the dead time after time, shaking off their death in order to fulfill their destiny. In this way, there is no cruelty in the fact that they are conscious of being hunted and they will be killed. The benefit of being aware of life is not offset by awareness of death, because death is, in this heaven, a temporary thing.

Topics for Further Study

- Research the abilities of the most deadly predatory species in the world and report, with pictures and graphs, on what their capacities are. Explain what particular changes they would undergo if their hunting abilities were perfected.

- Most of the world's major religions do not support the position that animals have souls or that they are bound for an afterlife. Choose one religion and study its policy on this issue.

- If you have a family pet or some other animal acquaintance, write a poem to it, explaining what heaven will be like for it.

- Draw a picture showing what the hell of animals would be like. Be prepared to explain your reasoning.

Cycle of Life and Search for Self

James Dickey said in his book *Self-Interviews* that the idea of the "cycle of nature" came into this poem from a Walt Disney Company nature film called *The African Lion*. He was impressed, he said, that, while the film showed a wildebeest being ripped limb from limb by a lion, the narration, to make the grisly scene acceptable material for young audiences, explained the on-screen violence as being part of the larger cycle of one thing's existence feeding another's. Dickey commented that he loved this film and went to the theater to see it often. He also explained that, while it may have comforted frightened children, the "cycle of nature" explanation probably would not have been much comfort to the wildebeest. In "The Heaven of Animals," this cycle is not followed because of biological need, as the film's narration suggested. The animals here do not kill and eat because they need to, or because of their part in some grand design. They do it because their instincts have programmed them to behave that way. The animals that are caught and killed tremble, instinctively, even though they really have nothing to fear. Dickey retains the "cycle" idea, but this cycle is not necessary to promote life. It is more of a "cycle of identity," with each animal playing its part in the grand scheme of things so that they can all continue being who they are. Unlike other philosophies that imagine heaven as a place where there would be no killing, or those that allow killing because it is necessary to spare lives, Dickey's heaven allows for killing so that animals can retain their individual selves. "[T]he lion would not really be a lion," he explains in *Self-Interviews,* "if, as the Bible says, the lion lies down with the lamb. It would be the form of the lion but not the spirit."

Good and Evil

Readers are often uncomfortable with this poem, because it presents a moral situation that would be unacceptable in the heaven of humans but that seems perfectly fitting for the animal heaven. The early mention of "the soft eyes" of the animals draws readers to sympathize with them, and they are presented, as animals often are, as being innocent. They are in fact innocent, in the sense that they have no souls and can therefore do no evil. The heaven that they are sent to confirms their innocence by "outdoing," making them more than comfortable in this new home, giving them "The richest wood, the deepest field." Evil creatures certainly would not be rewarded like this. Having seen these animals pampered like good beings, readers are then told that they regularly kill other animals. Among humans, killing is the most forbidden, taboo act, the worst evil: moral systems may find times when killing is acceptable, such as in self-defense or in times of war, but these are specific cases that humans approach cautiously. In the heaven of animals, killing is not even said to be necessary for food. By making readers sympathize with the animals and then taking away the usual moral arguments against killing, Dickey implies questions about human behavior. For instance, how much is human behavior instinctive, like animals'? Depending on one's beliefs about this issue (and scientists are always adding new evidence to make a clear-cut conclusion more difficult), the question of what behaviors are good and which are evil are more complicated than they might at first seem.

Style

The most interesting thing about the construction of this poem is that it follows no set pattern of poetry, while at the same time giving the feeling that there is a controlling hand organizing the words. It does this by using repetition, even though the repetition is erratic and follows no known pattern. The very nature of pattern is repetition. Many poems use some type of rhythmic pattern, with an arrangement of stressed and unstressed syllables appearing and reappearing; this pattern is called the poem's meter. Many also use some pattern of sound repetition, the most identifiable being rhymes that appear at the ends of lines. The poem is written in blank verse, which means that it follows no set rhyme scheme. In this poem, a few things happen more than once. The most obvious is the repetition of the phrase "The soft eyes open"—when it appears in the first line of the first stanza and then the last line of the second, the poem seems to be following the style called the rondeau, with this line being a refrain that will show up again throughout the poem. But it never appears in the poem again. Another pattern that seems to be on the brink of emerging can be seen in stanzas 2 and 3, which each end with two three-syllable lines: however, none of the other stanzas carry this pattern on. The last stanza uses the word "they" six times, which gives special weight to the subject, but this does not apply throughout the poem. There are some isolated pockets of sounds repeated throughout, such as the repetition of the "s" sound in stanza 5 and the "uh" sound in stanza 7, but these only hint at order without actually providing it. The most organized thing about this poem is that most of the stanza keep to a five-line limit, but even that general rule only develops after the first stanza, as if to assure the animals' freedom in heaven before showing how each, in her or his own way, is resigned to repetition.

Historical Context

The Organization Man

When James Dickey wrote this poem, he was working at an advertising firm—in fact, as he relates in his book *Self-Interviews,* he wrote it at his office and took it to his secretary to type. After typing it, she asked, "What is it?" What company does it go to?" and after he explained that it was a poem, she asked, "What are we going to sell with it?" "We're going to sell God," he explained. By the mid-1950s, Americans had become suspicious that the corporate structure, represented by the advertising industry in particular, was a soulless giant that sucked the creativity and morality from ordi-

Compare & Contrast

- **1957:** *The Cat in the Hat* and *How the Grinch Stole Christmas* were published by Dr. Seuss. Seuss is the pen name of author Theodore Geisel, who was not a doctor at all. He had been writing children's books since 1937, producing more than 40 books before his death in 1991.

  Today: These two books have never been out of print and are part of the childhood memories of several generations of children around the world. Both have been adapted to best-selling CD-ROM's, using Dr. Seuss' original characters.

- **1957:** In an effort to keep nine black students from attending Little Rock's all-white Central High School, the Governor of Arkansas, Orval Faubus, led jeering protestors. When the Arkansas National Guard did nothing to protect the children's safety from the governor and his mob, President Eisenhower sent in federal troops.

  Today: Many Americans express resentment and fear about federal laws without realizing the role that such laws played in promoting social equality.

- **1957:** Entrepreneur Berry Gordy invested $700 to start a new recording company, Motown Corp. The name "Motown" comes from "motor town," a reference to the fact that the company's home city, Detroit, was the center of automobile production in the United States.

  Today: Although not the pop music juggernaut that it was in the 1960s and 1970s, the distinctive sound that Motown developed is still easily recognizable due to continuous play on radio stations around the world.

- **1957:** The Frisbee was introduced.

  Today: The Frisbee is as popular as ever as a recreational toy, and it is also used in serious sporting competitions.

---

nary people and left them well-dressed, well-groomed and empty—slaves of the system. The country was enjoying greater prosperity than it had in a generation, since the stock market crash of 1929 had triggered the Great Depression. Poverty was common during the Depression, which hit a peak of unemployment in 1932 of 15 to 17 million people jobless, and another 34 million with no income, at a time when the U. S. population was only 124 million. When World War II broke out in 1939, the economy began to grow, as America produced goods and weapons that European factories could not, because the war was being fought in Europe, and that growth expanded while America was in the war, 1941-1945. After World War II, the countries of Europe and Asia had suffered great destruction, leaving America as the world's strongest economy. Postwar production and new management theories created a whole new level of non-producing bureaucrats—managers, vice-presidents, analysts, and efficiency experts. Through the late

1940s, the country was happy to see so many new jobs, but in the 1950s people began taking the healthy economy for granted, and a backlash developed against the office workers who held high incomes without getting dirty from work: white-collar workers, they were called, to distinguish them from the blue-collar workers who worked with their hands. Best-selling books of the 1950s examined the new class of professionals. Sloan Wilson's 1955 novel, *The Man In the Gray Flannel Suit,* about the discontents of the new middle-class, starts: "By the time they had lived seven years in the little house on Greentree Avenue in Westport, Connecticut, they both detested it." A 1956 sociological study by William H. Whyte Jr., called *The Organization Man,* pointed out ways in which society was becoming less humane and more efficient, describing its subject this way: "He honestly wants to believe the tenants he extols, and if he extols them so frequently it is, perhaps, to shut out the nagging suspicion that he, too, the last defender of the faith, is no longer pure." Vance Packard's *The Hidden Persuaders,* published the following year, exposed the psychological tricks advertising used to make everyone a part of the collective way of thought. These books had tremendous influence on the culture of their time, and their titles became familiar parts of the English language. The way of life they examined was the one that Dickey was living when he wrote this poem.

The Space Race

On October 4, 1957, radio and television receivers around the world picked up a strange, unidentified beep. When the source was finally traced, the knowledge it brought greatly changed America's perception of itself. The interference was caused by the first manmade satellite ever to be put into orbit around the earth: *Sputnik I.* The main significance was that *Sputnik* had been launched by the Soviet Union, and that it had been completely unexpected. During World War II, the Soviet Union had been America's ally, but almost immediately after the war ended in 1945, the U.S.S.R. (which stood for Union of Soviet Socialist Republics) became hostile and reclusive. British Prime Minister Winston Churchill coined the phrase "the Cold War" at a speech in Missouri in 1946 to describe the competition between the Communist countries of the world, led by the Soviets, and the Democratic countries. It was considered a "cold" war because there was never actually any battle between America and the Soviet Union, although military and economic strategies were constantly planned for a massive conflict. During the first decade of the Cold War, America was fairly confident. Not only was the United States the only country that had ever dropped an atomic bomb on an enemy, but it also had nuclear warheads ready in allied countries that could be fired on the Soviet Union, in the event of a war, and cause untold destruction. The Soviets had no such ability, and their technology was considered laughably behind. *Sputnik* changed this in a flash. It was the first achievement in which the Soviets had proven themselves technologically better than America. While dealing with their wounded pride, Americans also had a more practical matter to cope with: their new rocket superiority gave the Soviet Union the ability to fire Inter Continental Ballistic Missiles with nuclear warheads that could hit the United States. For the first time in the Cold War, Americans had to accept the fact that they might not be the predators, but the prey. The world, like Dickey's poem, was seen in terms of mortal competition.

Critical Overview

James Dickey's poetry was accepted with enthusiasm in the late 1950s and early 1960s, when he first started publishing. The admiration of his peers continued on to the end of his life in 1997, although general enthusiasm for his work fell off around the time his novel *Deliverance* made him an international celebrity in the early 1970s. Some feel that this gain of stature represented a sharp decline in his talent as a poet—that he became too immersed in the praise and money showered upon him and then spent too much time socializing and not enough time crafting his poems with the care he had taken before. Others felt that his work had stayed the same, but that the critics had changed their attitudes toward him; they had become merciless and unsympathetic once he was more popular than poets generally are.

Early in his career, critics approached Dickey's work with a sense of discovery, and they challenged themselves to understand him. In the *Sewanee Review* in 1963, poet Howard Nemerov summed up his critique of what made Dickey's poems work (and the few things that weakened them) in this way: "About all I shall say to the reader: If you believe you care for poetry you should read these poems with a deep attention." Three years later, in the same publication, H. L. Weatherby took an even more scientific approach to understanding Dickey. Weatherby's essay "The Way of Exchange in James Dickey's Poetry" looks at points in most of his poems where energy is exchanged, including in "The Heaven of Animals," where the landscape and the animals energize each other. Weatherby's essay on Dickey contains more theory than evaluation, although he does make a point of saying that he did not think much of the book that this poem comes from, *Drowning With Others.* During the mid-1960s, reviews in general followed this pattern, saying less and less about whether Dickeys poems were good and concentrating on how they accomplished what they did. Many mentioned "The Heaven of Animals" as representing the poet's tendency to join the living with the dead, as in David C. Berry's "Harmony With the Dead: James Dickey's Descent Into the Underworld." Other writers noted that this poem combines his recurring theme of life meeting death with another constant image, animals. Richard J. Calhoun and Robert W. Hill put a psychological spin on these obsessions in 1983: "Perhaps the fixed and predictable carnage of 'The Heaven of Animals' is one way of Dickey's handling metaphysically based fear." They went on to note that "as a poet, his fears in nature are most often when animals are present or are thought to be." Those who tired of Dickey after his novel made him famous pointed out, as Herbert Leibowitz did, that his earlier poems at least were willing to take chances, but the later poems only followed along with already established patterns, just pretending to be daring and coasting along on what Leibowitz termed "sheer bravado."

Criticism

Marion Hodge

In the following excerpt, Hodge analyzes Dickey's seemingly contradictory idea of a natural yet imperfect heaven.

James Dickey's message for the world may be, finally, that earth is all we have and all we will ever have of heaven. This is the meaning of "The Heaven of Animals," a text that acts as a nexus of concerns in *Poems 1957–1967.* Especially prominent themes in this collection are the status of predation in animal life and the relationship between nature and culture.

The heaven in "The Heaven of Animals" … is not an ultimate place, as are traditional human heavens; rather, it is a primal place. It is not the ultimate abode of the ultimate bodily form involved in ultimate activities; it is the earth, where natural beings kill to eat and struggle to reproduce their kind. "The Heaven of Animals" does not describe what will be in some higher realm; it describes what *is* in our own "natural heaven." The perfection shown in the poem is not perfection as we ordinarily think of it; it is the way instinctive beings live their lives right now in the natural world.

"The Heaven of Animals" is a metaphor for the timelessness of life on earth. It is not about the immortality of individuals but the immortality of species. If any genesis is suggested, it is the continuous "genesis" of life and generation. This is not a heaven of reverent joy, nor of potential come to fruition, nor of fulfillment after an existence of incompleteness, nor of unity after chaos, nor of wholeness after fragmentation, nor of security after threat. This heaven is not a place where negation of ego is rewarded. It is a place where the whole physical panorama of life on earth is condensed to its fundamental elements: killing and

birth. In fact, Dickey's own comments about "The Heaven of Animals" support the natural-heaven interpretation. In an interview reprinted in *Night Hurdling,* Dickey rejects a number of traditional ideas and says, finally, that the poem is indeed symbolic of physical life on earth.

Of initial concern to Dickey is the tendency of those who use the cycle-of-nature trope to rationalize—or ignore—the suffering of individual victims. "[A]ll this talk about the cycle of nature," Dickey says, "must be a tough thing to hear if you're the animal that's getting torn to pieces." Dickey's own trope in the poem, "the cycle's center," is perhaps used as a kind of moral bullseye to cause readers to zero in on individual suffering, for suffering is certainly suggested when the victims "tremble," "fall," and "are torn." Still, the matter of individual suffering is made problematical in the poem by the statements that the prey "feel no fear" and are "without pain." Why do they tremble if they feel no fear? Why do they feel no pain when they are torn apart?

Resolution of this paradox would seem to hinge upon the matter of individual identity, which is Dickey's subsequent concern in the interview reprinted in *Night Hurdling.* Dickey finds "grossly unfair" the belief that "animals have no souls, and therefore they're perishable, not like us wonderful human beings." Interpreting "soul" as essential identity, Dickey says that a heaven of animals "wouldn't really be a heaven if the animal was deprived of his nature. I mean the killer must still be able to kill, and the hunted should still be hunted." Finally, Dickey summarizes his understanding of the theme when he says the poem is "some kind of mystical vision of creation." If "creation" means "this world," then heaven, as the poem depicts it, must consist of the "knowledge" as well as the "acceptance" of our role as both death-dealer and mortal being.

Traditional heavens are perfect because they conceive of the individual as existing in a place where, as there is no necessity to eat and thus to kill, there is neither threat nor guilt and where, except for that modification, the individual ego is maintained throughout all no-time. Traditional heavens are places of peace because individuals, no longer prey to others, experience no fear and because, no longer predators, they experience no guilt.… In contrast to such metaphors, the images in Dickey's heaven of animals are full of action, and temporality is directly mentioned: the predators' descent upon the prey "May take years / In a sovereign floating of joy." Dickey's heaven, then, from just this perspective, would not seem to contain typical paradisaical bliss....

It is true that there is no question of good or evil in Dickey's heaven of animals; the animals are indeed incapable of evil, and they certainly feel no remorse, but the reason is not that they have been translated into a realm that perfects their identities. The reason is that animals are not encumbered with such matters as they go about their lives of surviving—eating and avoiding being eaten—right now on earth. Animals kill without remorse because they must eat, not because they find pleasure in it. Furthermore, the argument that Dickey is ignoring the entire cycle by omitting scavengers from his heaven fails to consider that the predation is the symbol of *all* animal killing and eating. The predator in the poem is all predators and the prey is all prey. In nature, and so in the "heaven" of animals, a predator is also prey and an animal that is prey is also a predator....

[T]here is no evidence that Dickey is suggesting that domination is the superior quality. The prey receive the final, emphatic attention, and in nearly half the poem, Dickey is entirely unconcerned with the predator and its prey, showing the reader animals in general and their heavenly environment:

> Here they are. The soft eyes open.
> If they have lived in a wood
> It is a wood.
> If they have lived on plains
> It is grass rolling
> Under their feet forever.
>
> Having no souls, they have come,
> Anyway, beyond their knowing.
> Their instincts wholly bloom
> And they rise.
> The soft eyes open.
>
> To match them, the landscape flowers,
> Outdoing, desperately
> Outdoing what is required:
> The richest wood,
> The deepest field....

This passage emphasizes clearly positive qualities: softness, blooming, rising, richness, depth—not domination. It also emphasizes the importance of individual identity rather than domination; *all* the animals, not just the predators, get in heaven the environment that has given them their identities on earth, or, to say it as we have been saying it, the natural environment is all the heaven there is. How could it be possible otherwise, for them and for us, to maintain identity except among the places and actions that created those identities in

What Do I Read Next?

- This poem was published in Dickey's book *Drowning With Others* and became widely available in the collection *Poems: 1957-1967,* published by Wesleyan University Press in 1967 and since republished by The MacMillan Co. It has been reprinted in countless anthologies since then, and Dickey's writings have been collected in various forms, but that volume, covering a ten-year span early in his career, provides a good look at the work Dickey was producing then.

- James Dickey wrote a great quantity of nonfiction. One of his best collections of essays is *Babel to Byzantium: Poets and Poetry Now,* published by Farrar Straus and Giroux in 1968. This volume contains short impressions and critical assessments of dozens of his contemporaries, from those now obscure (Josephine Miles) to those whose fame and importance lives on (such as W. S. Merwin). This book also includes his famous essay, "Barnstorming for Poetry," about life on the lecture tour circuit.

- The year after his death, in 1998, the poet's son Christopher Dickey published a memoir about what it was like growing up in the shadow of a famous man. His book, *Summer of Deliverance: Memoir of a Father and Son,* examines the public persona of hard-drinking ladies' man that Dickey worked hard to project and the toll it took on his family.

- Admirers of James Dickey's works will almost always end up reading his most famous publication, the novel *Deliverance.* The book, about a group of friends who go on a canoeing trip and have to fight for survival against a family of primitivistic mountain men, is similar to this poem in its mix of violence and philosophy about the human condition.

the first place? A setting can be heaven only if the animals can keep their instincts, which developed in a particular environment.

James Dickey may be *searching* for heaven on earth, as Peter Davison says [in his article "The Great Grassy World from both Sides: The Poetry of Robert Lowell and James Dickey" in *James Dickey: The Expansive Imagination*], but it is clear that in several moments he has found it. The purest discovery is told in "The Heaven of Animals," but there are many other poems in which the natural heaven is found and entered....

"For the Last Wolverine" (*Poems* 276–78) is Dickey's despairing, angry eulogy for the natural heaven and the poetry that is this heaven's voice as they are being destroyed by civilization. The poem ends with one of the most poignant pleas in the poetry of our time: *"Lord, let me die but not die / Out."* Our age is the first in which people have been able to watch—and have caused—the extinction of species. Dickey's poem is largely a dream of revenge for this murderousness; the poet imagines a terrible beast, a combined wolverine and eagle, attacking the fur trappers and road- and railroad-building crews who are threatening the environment, the implication being that the incursion of civilization into the wolverine's habitat is the animal's curse and doom. Furthermore, since the wolverine is made a symbol of the "wildness of poetry," civilization is seen as the imagination's curse and doom as well, eliminating what "the timid poem needs," and so what timid modern life needs: the "mindless explosion" of "rage." The wolverine's doom is the doom of the natural heaven: "Lord, we have come to the end / Of this kind of vision of heaven." The earth is no longer heaven but, instead, deadening, destructive civilization.

Before the wolverine-eagle takes its revenge, the speaker imagines the wolverine gaining knowledge, an "idea," by eating, as its "last red meal," the heart of an elk. The knowledge gained is that the wolverine, being the last of its kind, can afford to confront its enemies directly, come out of hiding and take on the insurgents, fight to the inevitable end. And as this predatory meal is the source of the wolverine's courage, we have come full circle, back again to the "horrid dream" of "The Heaven of Animals," the nightmare of the natural world we must accept if we are to live fully.

But Dickey cannot maintain such a vision any longer; the enemy is too strong. The fight is hopeless. The wolverine will die out. The eagle will die out. Civilization will kill them. And civilization will kill the poet, too. The earth is no longer raw heaven but, rather, cuisine—bloodless, cooked, and flavorless.

And that is the ultimate meaning of the natural-heaven theme in James Dickey's poems: to live successfully, intensely, we must accept the natural world as it is, bloody as it is, and fight to keep our place in the processes of earth, here and now. Eating, which, on earth, means also to be eaten, is the symbol of an active powerful love of life, and love of the earth that is life's source.

Our way to heaven, Dickey cries in "For the Last Wolverine," is "to eat / The world, and not to be driven off it." According to some readers, however, Dickey himself has driven humanity from the world of "The Heaven of Animals."...

The omission of people from Dickey's heaven does not, of itself, mean that the unity of existence is destroyed by humanity's consciousness. Omission does not necessarily mean exclusion; it means, possibly, that people are to be included in the natural processes as one with the animals, as predators even, without morally superior natures. We are not like animals, we are animals. It is not a matter of being psychologically unable to participate in a "remorseless" cycle of killing and eating; we do participate in the cycle. That we do not recognize our part in it, or that we try to make ourselves superior to it, proves the strength of our ancient fear and guilt. The point of the natural-heaven theme is to show us that we do indeed participate in the violent cycle and to suggest that the acceptance of our place in it would lead us to "heaven," a message that makes moot the question of humanity's corruption. Beatitude is what is; each being is a part of it.

In virtually every James Dickey poem, the sympathetic reader finds the poet's serious effort to say something fundamentally important. There is probably no less whimsical poet, yet there is no poet more joyful. This blend of seriousness and joy stems, at least in part, from Dickey's rejection of the traditional ideal realm built upon denial of life's physical realities, and from his own acceptance of those realities. But we should not think that joy easily achieved. As such poems as "Falling," "For the Last Wolverine," and even "The Heaven of Animals" demonstrate, much—the luxuries of civilization and the notion of an entirely free will—must be divested, and this divestiture sometimes happens only as a last resort. The woman in "Falling" becomes a goddess because there is nothing else she can do except fall to earth. The last wolverine achieves its ferocious nobility only because it is cornered. The predators and prey in "The Heaven of Animals" cannot choose any other course of action. Thus, an emotional-philosophical struggle pushing the poet toward visions of unity seems to underlie these poems. It is possible that Dickey's emotional-philosophical struggle arises from his knowledge that the creatures of nature, including humans, must kill and die but that he rejoices because he knows species exist far longer than the individuals that compose them ("forever" he might say in his expansive "heavenly" mood) and because he knows that individuals are species' particular loci of uniqueness. Perhaps such knowledge has given rise to the passionate regard for the dignity of each creature and of all creation—and for the union of the two—Dickey has shown in the natural-heaven images.

Source: Marion Hodge, "James Dickey's Natural Heaven," in *South Atlantic Review,* Vol. 56, No. 4, November 1991, pp. 57-61, 66-8.

David Kelly

David Kelly is an instructor of creative writing at several community colleges in Illinois, as well as a fiction writer and playwright. In the following essay, Kelly argues that a simplified vision of heaven, as a place of infinite space and time, weakens this poem's credibility and its message.

Writing about his poem "The Heaven of Animals," James Dickey once explained that he had a long-standing fascination with the concept of heaven, not because of all the wonders it might hold but because heaven is an eternal place. Think about those last few words, and you can see how the concept could linger in his mind—it's a fascinating, self-negating concept. It's harder to get an idea of an eternal place than it is to think of eternal life. We might be able to accept the idea that life goes on in some different bodiless form after death, because nobody really understands the mysteries involved there. The mysteries of the physical world are much fewer, though; its workings are better understood, and so the idea of an eternal place is much harder to swallow. Places as we know them cannot be eternal. For one thing, they decay: molecules reorganize, things fall apart.

And yet, the idea of a continuing soul is always linked to this idea of a place where the soul can go. As Dickey explained his interest once, "the fact that men have held the idea of heaven, or some kind of eternal life, for such a long time in so many different ways gives the concept a certain authenticity, I think." This takes the poet's interest beyond the scientific question of whether the existence of an eternal place is or isn't provable to the workings of the human mind that would be so interested in such a far-fetched idea. To a creative mind such as Dickey's, the concept of an eternal place is gold. It's pyrite, though: fools' gold, deceptively worthwhile, a thrilling discovery that turns out to be worthless.

The "twist" of "The Heaven of Animals"—the thing that makes it fresh and original and keeps it from being a stuffy old philosophical treatise—is that he applies the concept of eternity to animals. We don't like to think about animals having a place in eternity. We butcher and swat and trap and poison too many to reconcile our actions to the thought of their immortal souls. Worse, though, but seldom considered, is the fact that their presence in heaven would increase the population of the place many times over. It is hard enough to conceive of some area that could hold all of the people you ever met, and then adding to that everyone you ever heard of, then multiplying by a few million to account for the worthy people whose existence never touched your own; but add to that chipmunks, lemurs, musk-oxen, tapirs, gnats, crocodiles, finches, and the rest of the animals that have lived on earth since life began here, and whatever it is that you dream heaven to be eventually becomes inconceivable. This might not bother some, who accept the poem's "Outdoing, desperately / Outdoing what is required" to settle the problem of space. Heaven, being theoretical, can be thought to have ample elbow room, or else the problem can be washed away with some fancy theory about how heaven isn't a place but a different mode of existence. But how should we think of that different mode? If it's not physical, then what is it? I say that if we can't think of heaven in terms that we understand, then we can't think about it at all.

When we picture heaven, it has enough room for milling about with our friends, or, if you would like, to go and look up people you wish you had a chance to know, to have question-and-answer sessions with Socrates and James Weldon Johnson and Elvis. Dickey allows milling-about space to the heaven of animals, too, and this is what causes his worst problem. Once he has established his theoretical boundaries—actually, once he has waved boundaries away—he is left with the question of what these animals, with unlimited time and space, would do there.

Of course, since it is heaven, the first answer that comes to mind is that they will do whatever they feel like doing (and perhaps be reunited with their owners). As an old proverb put it, "Heaven is the place where the donkey at last catches up with the carrot." Good for the donkey, but not much of a heaven for the carrot. In "The Heaven of Animals," Dickey recognizes that some animals don't like to eat carrots, that they want to eat the donkey. He thinks they should be allowed to indulge the one thing that their instincts desire. This is their heaven, after all. Good for the carnivores, bad for the donkeys.

Richard J. Calhoun and Robert W. Hill, who explained Dickey well in their insightful book-length study of his career, raised an interesting point that might indicate conflicting emotions at the heart of this poem. Along with other poems they studied, they saw in "The Heaven of Animals" a fear of animals and their potential for mindless violence. Dickey was an avid hunter, more public about his fascination with the struggle against nature than any writer, perhaps, since Hemingway, and it is easy to believe that at the center of his struggle is an "eye-for-eye" philosophy; that we should get them before they get us, if it comes to that. The problem is that it does not come to that for us who live in developed areas, as Dickey did. There are very few places where one might, while going about one's business, happen across an animal that wants to kill. If Dickey felt uneasy about the fact that it is the nature of predatory animals to kill, as Calhoun and Hill tell us he was, he could avoid the situation by staying home. As a hunter, he sought out the mindlessly violent animals that disturbed him, and, as a poet, he had to explore how he felt about them.

And yet, he must not have felt complete adversity, because he allowed eternity. As a premise of this poem, he had to decide what the vicious creatures and, more important, what their helpless prey, would do with timeless time and endless space and the nature of good and evil. The poem touches on issues of power, identity, and the nature of good and evil. In some ways it resembles human actions, but too much of the way these animals behave is derived from the fact that the situation Dickey has made up for them can't support his light characterizations.

It does not matter how perfected the claws and teeth are: being torn apart by them just cannot be anyone's idea of a happy way to spend eternity. The only way Dickey can make this a convincing heaven and fill the gap in the situation he has postulated is to use the most basic, clunky sort of metaphysics—deciding that victims must be made for victimization, because, on earth, they keep going for it, time after time. The prey in this poem not only accept their fate, but they relish the chance to be attacked, reassembled, and attacked once more. The prey he imagines "feel no fear / But accep-

tance, compliance." Perhaps this is true of animals low on the food chain, whose neural systems are barely developed: they would see no difference between being devoured and winning a prize. In the course of things, they might not care one way or another about being another animal's prey, although a big hole is blown in Dickey's scheme by the existence of animals that are vegetarian but are also fleet of foot—clearly their nature is not to catch nor to be caught. But Dickey might be right—he has studied this whole hunter/prey relationship more than most. Prey might accept their lot, especially since, as the poem tells us, the pain and fear we associate with animal attacks just does not exist in the heaven of animals. They might not mind it, but that is a far cry from their finding a heaven in the constant cycle of dismemberment and reassembly.

In order to integrate the preyed-upon into the heaven of animals and to make it worth their sticking around for eternity, Dickey has to give them a higher purpose. Whether he does this to parody man's own inclination to offer up adversity to a higher cause or because he actually believed animals to be playing a necessary role in a big system is not clear from the poem. This heaven can apparently be worth experiencing to them, as long as they know what is going to happen next: as long as they walk in full knowledge. Killer or killed, both seem equally content as long as they don't have to struggle with uncertainty. The "heaven" part of their afterlife seems to be that they are allowed to shed their consciousness. But these are animals: it was the poet who projected consciousness on them to begin with. It might seem a nice idea to grant to animals the eternity that man always imagines for himself, but without granting them consciousness in order to know what to do with infinite space and time, they just become little eating machines matched with corresponding masochists. This might be meant as a reflection of humankind, but it would be hard to take a lesson seriously when it is doled out in such vague terms.

Source: David Kelly, in an essay for *Poetry for Students,* The Gale Group, 1999.

Nelson Hathcock

In the following excerpt, Hathcock discusses the importance of realizing that "The Heaven of Animals" entails human viewpoint and perspective.

James Dickey has been called a neo-Romantic primitive often enough for this appellation to have acquired the ring of truth, and the earlier poems in the volume *Poems 1957–1967* tend to bear it out. In the volume partially included there, called *Drowning With Others,* one of the concerns of a significant number of poems is with the kinship of human and animal, a phenomenon for which Dickey obviously has special feelings. For him the natural world is rarely a mere literary symbol of the "not me"; it is, rather, another chamber of the full life, one he is able to penetrate by means of the willful imaginative act. Essentially, it is in this all-embracing outlook that Dickey's particular Romanticism obtains.

Yet Dickey never fails to be contemporary, for all of his sanguinary urges to run with the beasts; as twentieth-century man he experiences the general dissolution and frustration that seem a portion of life in these times. I wish to point out how this feeling of separateness creeps in, and it will suggest a new meaning for one of Dickey's most discussed and most frequently anthologized poems, "The Heaven of Animals."...

"The Heaven of Animals" is an oddly quiet poem even though the scene described could be characterized as one of Darwinian ruthlessness. The lines are mostly short—three-stress measures—steadily paced, and there is never any doubt that the unseen speaker is in absolute control of his utterance.

The location is more specifically realized in the first line by the immediacy of present time and place—"Here they are"—than by specific evocations. As we read on, we see the reason. This heaven is amorphous, with the existence of the animals themselves dictating its features after they have awakened from some previous life "in a wood" or "on plains." This place, if we can call it that, does share something with the human conception of heaven, for it is permanent, with "grass rolling / Under their feet forever."

With the second stanza, such similarities end, and the heaven of animals is apparently distinguished from any human ideal:

> Having no souls, they have come,
> Anyway, beyond their knowing.
> Their instincts wholly bloom
> And they rise.
> The soft eyes open.

These animals seem to have qualified for their rewards by virtue of a deficit—"having no souls." But this lack is compensated for by something else—their instincts which "wholly bloom." Here is a heaven uncomplicated by any questions of good or evil. No words of judgment have made it avail-

able, for that human factor does not exist. The beasts have simply become, somehow, more fully animal, their instincts honed and heightened. Reflecting the presence of these beings, the natural surroundings alter:

> To match them, the landscape flowers,
> Outdoing, desperately
> Outdoing what is required:
> The richest wood,
> The deepest field.

This heaven is figured in superlatives, a place where all is the same, only better, fuller, richer.

Then the poem shifts its focus and the next four stanzas introduce the animals themselves, but not through any particularized description. Rather, they are divided into two groups—the hunters and the hunted—and any world in which the inhabitants can be divided into two classes is basically uncomplicated. The predators are shown only to "hunt, as they have done, / But with teeth and claws grown perfect, / More deadly than they can believe." These are generic beasts of prey descending upon the backs of generic prey. It might even be argued that they are not real animals, but that is not important. The point that the poem seems to make here is that it is the act—what Paul Carroll [in his *The Poem in Its Skin*] calls "the ecstasy of violence"—which is most arresting. The lines which depict the slaying tell much about how the beasts are perceived through a man's eyes:

> And their descent
> Upon the bright backs of their prey
> May take years
> In a sovereign floating of joy.

In this image we can see the Disney nature film which Dickey claims [in *Self Interviews*] provided a measure of inspiration for the poem, but we also are made aware of the timelessness of the vision. Like a film projected again and again, this same sacrifice in the jungle or on the veldt is a momentary stage in the natural cycle, certain to be relentlessly duplicated. Carroll explains the final word of the passage above in this way: "On earth, predatory beasts hunt only to find food; in heaven, they hunt only for the joy of it." This observation has some validity, as far as it goes, but I must disagree with Carroll's basic contention that we are seeing through the animals' eyes in this poem. The "joy" and "glory" of this heaven are imposed by the imagination of the man (or God, if you will) who has created this place. "Joy" and "glory" can only be perceived by the eye of the soul.

The second category of beast here, the hunted, reveals one more vital aspect of Dickey's creatures:

And those that are hunted
Know this as their life,
Their reward: to walk

Under such trees in full knowledge
Of what is in glory above them,
And to feel no fear,
But acceptance, compliance.

In this world one's "life" equals his "reward," a truly Edenic state. Certainly, the awareness of one's place and the acceptance of it in the ever-shifting cycle of nature and history is a kind of perfection. The final stanza is a capsule of the entire poem, the Heraclitean cycle reproduced in miniature, serving also to end the piece where it began. The poem's structure reflects the cycle that is its ostensible subject.

But I must now return to a point made earlier and elaborate on it. It is a mistake to believe that the poet has intended us to see this vision of heaven through the "soft eyes" of its beastly citizens. The poem is a human utterance, "a man speaking to other men," and therefore the question of perspective and viewpoint is crucial. In this case it is the key to the meaning.

The questions that arise are, "Why has Dickey chosen to show us this heaven?" and further, "What does the poem show us about him?" Of course, we do not read poetry to learn about the lives of its writers; poems are a singularly unreliable source for such information. But we do read it to find out something more about ourselves, about Man with capital "M." So, let us say that what we have here is an unlocated, unspecific landscape with unnamed creatures in it, presented to us by an unknown man, not necessarily by our neo Romantic-sportsman-warrior poet. What, then, is the consequence?...

We can assume ... in "The Heaven of Animals" that a man is telling us of the heaven, but ..., he is not *in* the scene which he describes, not strolling the "richest wood" or the "deepest field," but is somewhere else, excluded. (For a heaven of animals it is only appropriate that the sign above the gate reads—No Humans Allowed.) This exclusion creates the subliminal lament of the poem. Our speaker persists in observing, however, because he feels that something is here for him. In the chant-like cadence of his sentences and in the type of detail he dwells upon, there runs a current of wistful envy and longing. He envies the power of blood and claw—the elemental, instinctive act—a power made possible by the animals' curious lack of spirit.

Without souls, these beasts are spared necessarily the guilt, the desire, the fear, the frustrations that men know intimately each day. Each day we remark the mixed blessing of the soul, that complicating factor in our existence. The pure intellect would allow us to rationalize dispassionately, but the very nature of the soul makes that impossible; there is always more to consider. The events of our lives, if granted more than a passing glance, are never simple. At one time or another we have all envied the terrible bliss of a heaven like the one described, a submission to naturalistic urges. Dickey's choice of a preposition in his title is therefore significant. It is not "The Heaven *for* Animals" because the heaven is *for* the poet, for the man who considers it and creates it in his mind. It is made *of* animals living on the plane of instinctive motivation we humans have long since tried to bury or subdue. While this heaven is one into which the yaks and leopards and buffalo awaken, it is also a heaven from which we have awakened and found ourselves human.

At base a certain purity and simplicity are the attractions of this state, qualities which make possible the "glory" of the hunter and the "full knowledge" of the hunted with their "acceptance, compliance." These creatures are simple beings moving resistlessly toward simple fates "without pain," without fear. To live is their reward; they look no further and hope for no heaven. Not so for the man who stands by and watches. Dickey's demonstrated love for the primitive and elemental forces of the natural world qualifies him as one who would stand and watch. At the same time, his power as a poet guarantees us that only standing and watching would not be enough for him. "The Heaven of Animals" represents an instance of longing transfigured by creative power. This heaven is the poet's possession, a stay against the fear of death. In a strange way he has looked at the animals and, in so doing, confirmed his own fragile humanity as a man who cannot after all become a beast—in that respect he is like all of us—but he also realizes that there is a heaven there to be had, and in that sense he is like few of us indeed.

Source: Nelson Hathcock, "The Predator, the Prey, and the Poet in Dickey's 'Heaven of Animals,'" in *Concerning Poetry,* Vol. 18, Nos. 1 and 2, 1985, pp. 47, 52–5.

Sources

Calhoun, Richard J., and Robert W. Hill, *James Dickey,* Boston: Twayne Publishers, 1983.

Dickey, James, *Self-Interviews,* recorded and edited by Barbara and James Reiss, New York: Dell Publishing Co., 1970.

For Further Study

Dickey, James, "The Self As Agent," *Sorties,* Garden City, NY: Doubleday & Co., 1971. pp. 155-70.

In this essay, the author explains the ways that a poet is revealed through his works. This exploration is especially interesting when examining a poem like "The Heaven of Animals," which has no clear persona for the speaker.

Howard, Richard, "On James Dickey," *Partisan Review,* Vol. 33, summer 1966, pp. 111-28.

Howard examines themes and images that run throughout Dickey's works, drawing from a huge number of poems for examples.

Leiberman, Laurence, *The Achievement of James Dickey: A Comprehensive Selection of his Poems With a Critical Introduction,* Glenview, IL: Scott, Foresman Co., 1968.

Although this study was written relatively early in Dickey's career, almost thirty years before his death, it is a useful source because it covers the era of this poem and examines major poetic interest and concerns that ran throughout his works.

Oates, Joyce Carol, "Out of Stone, Into Flesh: The Imagination of James Dickey," in *The Imagination as Glory: The Poetry of James Dickey,* edited by Bruce Weigl and T. R. Hummer, Chicago: the University of Illinois Press, 1984, pp. 64-107.

Oates looks at Dickey's whole career with careful deliberation, finding "The Heaven of Animals" to be well structured but strangely, for Dickey, impersonal.

Ramsey, Paul, "James Dickey: Meter and Structure" in *James Dickey: The Expansive Imagination,* edited by Richard J. Calhoun, Deland, FL: Everett/Edwards, Inc., 1973, pp. 177-94.

Although "The Heaven of Animals" is written in free verse, it is interesting to compare it to Ramsey's observations about structural techniques used in other poems.

Vanetta, Dennis, "James Dickey: A Checklist of Secondary Sources" in *The Imagination as Glory: The Poetry of James Dickey,* edited by Bruce Weigl and T. R. Hummer, Chicago: The University of Illinois Press, 1984, pp. 174-95.

Because Dickey was a famous and popular poet at a time when English literature departments were tuning out a record number of theorists and intellectuals, there has been much written about him—too much, in fact, for the average reader to keep track of. This bibliography lists more than three hundred articles about Dickey and includes information about other, even more complete, check lists.

Helen

H.D.
1924

Helen of Troy was considered the most beautiful woman on earth, who was so desirable to men that they fought the twelfth-century B.C. Trojan War over her. For several reasons, poet H.D. found similarities between herself and Helen. In the realm of art, H.D. identified her efforts with her mother's, whose name was Helen. Helen was to become H.D.'s name for herself and for the Helen situation in all women throughout history. H.D. once remarked, "The mother is the Muse, the creator, and in my case especially, as my mother's name was Helen." Helen of Troy's daughter was named Hermione; this was what H.D. called herself as a child in the autobiographical novel of the same name. More and more, H.D. came to associate herself with Helen because so many of the men in her life—including Ezra Pound, D. H. Lawrence, Richard Aldington, and Cecil Gray—found her desirable. Poet William Carlos Williams wrote of her: "She fascinated me, not for her beauty, which was unquestioned if bizarre to my sense, but for a provocative indifference to rule and order which I liked." It is indifference that also characterizes the statue of Helen in H.D.'s "Helen"; her indifference to the convention of marriage angers the Greeks who look upon her. H.D.'s relationship to Helen went even further. She likened Pound, to whom she was once engaged, to Helen's first husband, Menelaus. She compared Richard Aldington, whom she married after she split with Pound, to Paris, the most handsome man on earth who stole Helen from Menelaus. Lawrence, who "made war" on H.D.'s marriage with Aldington, became identified with the warrior Achilles, Helen's lover after the Trojan War.

"Helen" is a picture poem, a verse in which the picture or image of a marble statue of Helen is conveyed in words. This statue of Helen, H.D. tells us, has been reviled by Greeks throughout history. The primary reason is that Helen is blamed for starting the ten-year Trojan War. The poem is a cautionary tale describing how a woman's beauty can be doubly tragic: deadly not only for the men risking all to possess it, but for the woman victimized by the beauty so coveted.

Author Biography

Hilda Doolittle, who wrote under the pen name H.D., was the inspiration for Imagist poetry, and, with Richard Aldington and Ezra Pound, she helped formulate the principles of the poetic form known as free verse. One could therefore argue that H.D. should rank as one of the most important poets of the twentieth century. Present-day critics, however, pay more attention to her varied prose offerings than to her poetry. One critic even suggested that H.D wrote no more than a dozen good poems, which were characterized by classical mythology and mysticism as well as interesting formal experiments with free verse.

Born in 1886 in Bethlehem, Pennsylvania, Hilda Doolittle was brought up by an artistic and musical mother who attended the local Moravian Church. The mystical rituals that young Hilda participated in at the Moravian seminary would have a profound and continuing effect on her. H.D.'s father, a Puritan, was the director of Sayre Observatory and a professor of astronomy and mathematics at Lehigh University before taking on similar positions at the University of Pennsylvania. After being educated at private schools, Hilda attended Bryn Mawr for one and a half years, dropping out because of ill health in 1906. At Bryn Mawr, she met poets Marianne Moore and William Carlos Williams, the first of many famous figures she would become involved with throughout her life. In 1907, she became engaged to Ezra Pound, a man she had known since 1901, when she was fifteen. In 1911 she joined Pound in England and there met William Butler Yeats, May Sinclair, D. H. Lawrence (with whom she would become closely involved), and her future husband, Richard Al-

H.D.

dington, whom she married in 1913. During that same year, H.D. published her first poems—the first Imagist poems according to Aldington—in *Poetry* magazine through the intermediary of Ezra Pound, who dubbed her "H.D., Imagiste." The three poems in *Poetry*—"Hermes of the Ways," "Priapus," and "Epigram"—incorporated elements from classical Greek lyrics, Japanese haiku, and French symbolism. At the time, the poems were deemed revolutionary. Her early verse came to epitomize Imagism: use of concrete and sensual images, common and concise speech, and new rhythms intended to produce "poetry that is hard and clear, never blurred nor indefinite."

While Aldington was off fighting in World War I, H.D. took over as literary editor of the *Egoist,* a forum for Imagist writers; she eventually gave up her position to T.S. Eliot. She was also a major contributor to *Des Imagistes: An Anthology* (1914), an anthology of Imagist poetry. In 1918, H.D. and Aldington separated, and in 1919, she gave birth to her first and only child, Perdita. The two most likely candidates as fathers were D. H. Lawrence and Cecil Gray. Right after the birth, H.D. began living with a woman, Winifred Ellerman, pseudonymously known as "Bryher." Supported by the wealthy Bryher, H.D. would later be able to travel through Europe, Egypt, and the United States, finally settling in Switzerland. H.D. joined with Bryher and Kenneth Macpherson to create photomontages, a film journal, and a film, *Borderline* (1930), in which H.D. starred with Paul Robeson. Throughout the 1920s, H.D. continued to write, using techniques of flashback and stream-of-consciousness monologues. In the 1930s and 1940s she began her psychoanalytic sessions, first with Sigmund Freud, whom she studied with for two years. Under Freud's supervision, she worked on such issues as writer's block and sexual identity. Psychoanalysis also prompted her to view herself as somehow linked to women throughout history, and she thought she could discover this connection through poetry. During the early 1940s, H.D. investigated matriarchal figures in esoteric religion and, during World War II, wrote about them in her poems while living in Britain. After the war, H.D. returned to live in Switzerland, where she wrote her fourth work of fiction, *Bid Me to Live (A Madrigal),* published in 1960. During that same year, she became the first woman to receive the Award of Merit medal from the American Academy of Arts and Letters. She died of a heart attack in September of 1961 in Zurich.

Poem Text

All Greece hates
the still eyes in the white face,
the lustre as of olives
where she stands,
and the white hands.   5

All Greece reviles
the wan face when she smiles,
hating it deeper still
when it grows wan and white,
remembering past enchantments   10
and past ills.

Greece sees unmoved,
God's daughter, born of love,
the beauty of cool feet
and slenderest knees,   15
could love indeed the maid
only if she were laid,
white ash amid funereal cypresses.

Poem Summary

Lines 1-2:

The poem has an unexpected beginning. Here Greek statuary engenders hate instead of awe or adoration; the still eyes and white face represents

Media Adaptation

- A recording titled *Readings from Helen in Egypt* (1982) is available from Watershed Tapes.

that which deserves hate, not the visage of otherworldly tranquility. Helen draws this hate because she is blamed for starting the Trojan War (c. 1200 B.C.), a war begun when she eloped to Troy with the handsome youth Paris. But the Greece H.D. is talking about is one in which Helen has long been dead, a place where Helen lives on only in myth and in a monument H.D. seems to have sculpted out of words for her.

Lines 3-5:

Helen's face has the luster of olives, a product of Greece and famously identified with it. The fact that it is not olive-colored skin, but skin as smooth as olives—skin showing like olives "where she stands"—indicates further that the subject of this poem is not a living Helen, but a classical statue of her. While Greek statues were once painted, almost all have come down to us with the color worn off by time. H.D. seems to understand this white as a purification of Helen's image through time, a purity that the Greeks, however, are all the more angered by.

Lines 6-7:

This is a smiling statue of Helen, an insult to the Greeks reviling her. Yet the face is sickly, or wan. Which is it? Can it be that Helen is simultaneously both happy and gloomy?

Lines 8-11:

Greece apparently hates the statue of Helen the more it ages, the purer it looks, because Greeks remember how so many died to have her or rescue her.

Lines 12-13:

The unmoving statue of Helen mimics what to Greeks (according to H.D.) was Helen's nature: cold and unmoved. Here Helen is a pure object, an object of desire that lacks desire. Helen was the daughter of Zeus and, thus, "God's daughter."

Lines 14-15:

From color (wan and white), H.D. moves to Helen's temperature, her coolness. Again, the statue of Helen is an object absent of the warmth of desire or emotion—a fitting representation of a woman thought to possess the wan, white coolness of the statue. Helen's feet and "slenderest knees" point to Helen's beauty, not only to the usual foci of female beauty, but to the unusual; Helen is so perfect that even her feet and knees provoke longing.

Lines 16-18:

The last three lines indicate that Greece cannot love Helen as a statue, for her beauty only galls. Even after death and in effigy, the beautiful statue of beautiful Helen provokes desire and anger among viewers. Are the viewers who want to see Helen's monument turned into a pile of ashes both men and women? Or do only men curse the beauty of the femme fatale who, they think, leads them to their doom? Perhaps women, as well as men, hate Helen for setting the standards of beauty too high— for being the object of so much desire. If so, the pure white beauty of Helen must be reduced to pure white ashes scattered among cypresses, symbols of life after death and, therefore, planted in graveyards. The paradox is that Helen cannot be loved in remembrance unless dead and gone from sight. But lost from sight, it would also be impossible to love her. Helen stands in an impossible position— the point where hate equals love, a position trembling with instability.

Themes

Objectification

H.D.'s "Helen" is a chain of objectifications, a near mise-en-abyme (a picture of a picture of a picture, etc., all the same) in words. The first picture is of Helen objectified in her time. She is a woman always described in terms of her appearance, her beauty; a woman desired and coveted by so many men; a woman with numerous suitors, three husbands, and two lovers. Ever since she was young, Helen had been an object of desire, first carried off by Theseus. This is Helen objectified, a complex person of flesh and blood reduced to appearance, at least during the Trojan War. The second Helen is Homer's, an object of beauty by way

Topics for Further Study

- Begin a class discussion about whether "Helen" is deserving of more critical attention, either praiseworthy, explicatory, or as the germ of a problem in feminist criticism: how woman as an object destined for the pedestal is thereby made to suffer the consequences of that praise.

- Discuss "the objectification of women." How precisely are women made into objects? By whom are they so made—only by men? To what extent are these objects good, bad, or ambivalent? Are men made into objects? How? By whom?

- Discuss or research other women in history who were desired and idolized, and who then suffered for it.

of words that, through time, has given birth— directly or indirectly—to numerous other images of Helen in picture and word. The next image containing the Helen of myth is the statue, or the painted or carved image of Helen in H.D.'s poem, an artwork that, if it exists, is not at all well-known. In its dubious existence, the artwork is an object flickering between insubstantiality and substance, an object seen through the imagination, then as an object in space and time. Next, there is the Helen of the poem titled "Helen" that depicts a real or imaginary artwork. Lastly, there is the image of Helen in the reader's mind. The point of noticing all of this is that the early objectification of Helen might have contributed to the further objectification of Helen—and even, perhaps, of women in general. While H.D.'s poem might simply be one more in this chain of Helens, it also attempts to break the chain whereby women are held to their status as objects judged by their appearance.

Guilt and Innocence

Why does H.D. write a poem in which Greeks stand around hating a statue of Helen? Is this poem more about Helen or about the Greeks reviling her? If we conclude it is the latter, what is H.D. attempting to convey through showing this hatred of Helen? It is probably safe to say that because the Greeks are shown in the process of hating, it is they who are being "reviled" by H.D. The chain of hatred would thus begin with Greeks hating Helen and end with H.D. "hating" the Greeks for hating Helen. H.D. probably finds these Greeks distasteful, because Helen seems much further from blame than do the Greeks, who would blame Helen for their own desire for the beauty Helen embodied. Was it Helen's fault she was born beautiful, a state of affairs over which she had no control? Not to mention that her abduction by Paris was foretold and almost fated by Aphrodite. Why do these Greeks hate Helen? For one thing, she might arouse in them overwhelming desire through her reputation as the most beautiful woman in the world. This kind of desire makes people lose control and makes them vulnerable to actions they themselves might disdain. Others find Helen guilty and hate her for all of the deaths during the ten years of trying to rescue her from the walled city of Troy. But this amounts to something similar in that she is hated, not for the desire the viewers themselves feel, but for the desire the Greeks and Trojans felt for Helen. Lastly, she might be seen as first cause or most prominent symbol of the political problems throughout history between Greece and Turkey. In all, Helen becomes the unfortunate marker at the crossing where genders and nationalities meet in mutual distrust and war.

Style

"Helen" is an early modernist poem in free verse. Ezra Pound, having deliberated with H.D. and Richard Aldington, wrote in 1912 that poetry, to be modern, must follow three principles: "1. Direct treatment of the 'thing' whether subjective or objective. 2. To use absolutely no word that does not contribute to the presentation." These two principles apply to modern verse and, more specifically, to Imagism, an image being defined by Pound as "that which presents an intellectual and emotional complex in an instant of time." Pound's third and last principle, however, describes only free verse: "3. As regarding rhythm: to compose in the sequence of the musical phrase, not in sequence of a metronome." A more recent definition of free verse is Laurence Perrine's (1956): "Free verse, by our definition, is not verse at all; that is, it is not metrical. It may be rimed or unrimed. The word *free*

means that it's free of metrical restrictions. The only difference between free verse and rhythmical prose is that free verse introduces one additional rhythmical unit, the line…. Beyond its line arrangement there are no necessary differences between it and rhythmical prose." What neither Pound or Perrine say here, however, is that free verse, while free of a metrical pattern, is also free to construct a pattern beyond rhyme, conforming to the contents or message(s) of the poem being crafted.

"Helen" is partially rhymed free verse. For example, the rhyme scheme in the first stanza is, loosely, *aabbb*. However, the *b* lines only partially rhyme by way of the plural "s" sound. Full and partial rhyme is used throughout the poem, as is occasional assonance. There are three stanzas, each reading as a single sentence. The second stanza is one line longer than the first, and the third stanza is one line longer than the second. The lines are mostly short and concise, conforming to Pound's first and second principles listed previously. The poem also adheres to Pound's third principle in that the poem's meter is not regular. Yet overall, "Helen" contains a ragged regularity. The first stanza wholly consists of lines of two accents in a variety of combinations of accented with unaccented syllables. The second stanza is irregular but does begin and end with lines of two accents. The last stanza consists of lines mostly of three accents, with the last line of the poem having as many as four or five accents, depending on how it is read. In this respect, as the stanzas accrete lines, the lines accrete accents. While the reader moves down the poem, an image of Helen is built up … mostly downward—from the face and hands of the first two stanzas to the knees and feet of the third.

Historical Context

Post-World War I Europe was the time and place in which H.D. wrote "Helen," and H.D.'s years just prior to 1920 were painful. Her marriage with Richard Aldington ended in 1917 when he began to live with another woman. In 1918, one of her brothers was killed in the war, and soon thereafter, her father died. In the summer of 1918, H.D. became pregnant and gave birth to a daughter, Perdita, in 1919, her only child (whose paternity was either uncertain or kept secret). At the time of the birth, H.D. almost died from double pneumonia and felt that all the men in her life—Aldington, Pound, Lawrence, and Cecil Gray—had deserted her. But

Compare & Contrast

- **1924:** Costantin Brancusi carves the first versions of his sculpture series *The Fish* (1924-30) and *The Cock* (1924-49)

  1998: The Bilbao Guggenheim Museum opens in Bilbao, Spain. Designed by architect Frank Gehry, the titanium structure may look like a gigantic sculpture, but it also functions as an art museum.

- **1924:** The gas chamber, which releases lethal gas in a closed box, was first used for an execution at Nevada State Prison in Carson City. It was developed by Major D.A. Turner of the U.S. Army Medical Corps as a more "humane" method of execution than hanging and the electric chair (used since 1890). During World War II, the Germans would use the gas chamber for exterminating Jews, Gypsies, and homosexuals.

  1998: Texas leads the U.S. in terms of the number of executions. The practice is now carried out by lethal injection.

---

a woman named Bryher, rich and adoring of H.D., stepped in to rescue her. In 1920, the two sailed to Greece, a setting that became the source of so much of H.D.'s writing, including "Helen." Bryher would furnish money and nurturance for H.D. and her child; this support would carry H.D. through the 1920s—those years of travel, writing, and relative peace in Switzerland, away from the turmoil in much of the rest of Europe.

The two major preludes to the first half of the 1920s in Europe were World War I (1914-18) and the events of the Russian Revolution (March 15, 1917), followed by the takeover of the provisional Russian government by the Bolsheviks (November 6-7, 1917). World War I began with a local conflict: the assassinations of the heir to the Austria-Hungary throne and his wife in Sarajevo. The killings touched off the first declaration of war: Austria-Hungary—allied with Germany—against Serbia, which was backed by Russia. Within three months of Germany's invasion of Belgium, France, allied with Britain, joined the proceedings. Japan subsequently allied itself with France and England and set about taking over German holdings in the Far East. The Ottoman Empire then joined the side of Germany and Austria-Hungary. The next year, Italy entered the war with Britain, France, and Japan. Later, Greece also entered on the side of Britain, and Romania on the side of Germany. In 1917, the United States entered the war, aligning itself with England and her allies. Fighting between powers with far-flung empires soon caused hostil-

ities to spread from Europe to Africa to Asia. Most of the battles of the war up until 1917 were either deadlocked, or long, hard, and heavy with casualties. The events in Russia, however, would have a profound effect on the war and the rest of twentieth-century history.

In March of 1917, Tzar Nicholas Romanov of Russia abdicated when the Russian Revolution deposed him. The revolution began as just another strike, one of 1,330 that occurred in the first two months of 1917. While the army had usually put down the strikes, this time it joined the one in Petrograd, turning the strike into a revolution. Leon Trotsky was perhaps most responsible for the revolution: he was president of the Petrograd Soviet (workers' council) and, according to an early statement by Stalin, convinced the army to join the side of the Soviet. It was also Trotsky who was most responsible for engineering the overthrow of the provisional government eight months later by the Bolsheviks under the guiding genius of Vladimir Ilyich Lenin. Lenin, unlike his counterparts in the opposition parties—the Mensheviks and the Social Revolutionaries—believed that land from the rich should be seized and broken up among the peasants—immediately, not later. The other parties feared that to redistribute land so fast would result in chaos, paralyzing Russia's ability to continue in World War I. Lenin, however, wanted out of the war effort. So, when two million Russian soldiers deserted, decimating the Russian army, Lenin believed the country—decaying at its core—was ripe for Bolshevism. But so did other factions in the government: in September of 1917, Kornilov, the Russian commander and chief, attempted to seize power. To stop him, the provisional government armed the Bolshevik Red Guards. In fear, Kornilov's army refused to march, and in the aftermath, the Bolsheviks claimed credit for saving Russia from Kornilov's military takeover. The Bolsheviks' good name led to even more Bolshevik recruits for the Soviets in Petrograd (now St. Petersburg) and Moscow. Lenin, having won his Soviet majorities, called for insurrection. To Marxists everywhere, the Bolshevik takeover would become the classic example of a successful workers' revolution. Once in power, Lenin called for an end to Russian involvement in the war. In December of 1917, nine months after the abdication of the Tzar, the Treaty of Brest-Litovsk was negotiated with Germany which demanded from Russia the cession of the Baltic provinces, White Russia, Ukraine, and the Caucasus. For several months, Lenin attempted to convince his unwilling Bolsheviks to accept this humiliating treaty with Germany. Lenin prevailed, and on March 3, 1918, the treaty was signed. In only one year, Russia had ended its monarchy, instituted a revolutionary form of government, and surrendered a large tract of its western territory.

Russia's surrender to Germany changed the course of the war. Germany was now able to shift soldiers on the Eastern Front (from the Baltic to the Black Seas), where it fought Russia, to the Western Front (from the North Sea to Switzerland), where it was fighting Britain, France, and the United States. But Germany and her allies would lose the war. The armistice, signed November 11, 1918, occurred eight months after Russia surrendered to Germany. Luckily for Russia, the Treaty of Brest-Litovsk was annulled. The Versailles Treaty ending World War I would take six months to negotiate, and the map of Europe needed year to be redrawn. The Baltic states of Finland, Estonia, Latvia, Lithuania, and Poland—all formerly parts of the Russian Empire—gained independence. The Austrian Empire was divided into Czechoslovakia, Austria, Hungary, Rumania, and Yugoslavia.

On August 14, 1919, Germany became a democracy. During the first four years of its existence, the Weimar Republic lived from crisis to crisis. Financial collapse and a weak government led to left-wing Bolshevik bids to institute communism. The government put the insurrections down, and a right-wing nationalist backlash occurred against Bolshevism. It was then that Adolph Hitler,

an anti-Bolshevist and nationalist/nativist, made his first, though unsuccessful, bid for power. Meanwhile, in Italy, workers' strikes amounted to—by August, 1920—half a million workers taking over factories and raising the Bolshevik flag. But when the time came to seize power, the workers, without a genius like Lenin's behind them, could only hand back the factories in exchange for higher wages and better working conditions. Now, Bolshevism was, as Benito Mussolini, the leader of the fascist party, said, "mortally wounded." Factory owners, estate owners, and their sympathizers, wanted vengeance on Bolshevism and thus supported Italian Fascism. Money poured into the Fascist Party when it promised to protect factory and estate owners, and the Italian government gave tacit approval to Mussolini. With this backing, Mussolini raided left-wing organizations, gaining fame for a brutality that was largely accepted as a necessary corrective for the spreading threat of Bolshevism. In 1921, when Mussolini threatened to take over the government, he was asked to become prime minister of a coalition. England's Winston Churchill, an anti-Bolshevist, called Mussolini "the saviour of his country." Fifteen years later, in World War II, Churchill would be fighting on the side of the Bolshevik Soviet Union against the right-wing nationalism and anti-Bolshevism he had supported. The extremity of the right proved itself even more fearful than that of the left.

Finally, and most directly relevant to H.D.'s poem, Greece, in its postwar struggle with Turkey (1919-22), lost its bid to take territory from its Aegean neighbor, being summarily defeated by the forces of Kemal Atatürk in 1923. Greece's loss to Turkey could have led to H.D.'s depiction of Greeks—in the early 1920s—hating Helen, a figure who reminded them of that war of long ago when Greeks lost so many people in the ten-year fight against Troy, now a ruined city in present-day Turkey.

Critical Overview

By the paucity of criticism on H.D.'s "Helen" (1924), one might guess that either the poem has not been received very well, or that it is too simple or obvious to pay it more than passing attention. Since the poem frequently appears in anthologies, the latter guess is likely the best. Those critics who do address the poem briefly praise it or quickly sum up the poem's form or content. In his book *Hilda Doolittle (H.D.)*, Vincent Quinn calls "Helen" "one of H.D.'s most admired lyrics." Quinn first sums up the theme of "Helen," writing that it "is concerned with man's fear of beauty because of the trouble it brings." In an article titled "H.D.: Poems That Matter and Dilutations," Bernard F. Engel notes that "The poem moves in a simple overall rhythm from beginning to end, each of the three stanzas being a single sentence. The end-rhyme is skillful enough to suggest that H.D. might well have used it more often." Writing in *Dictionary of Literary Biography*, Susan Stanford Friedman's provides this assessment of "Helen": "As an answer to the representations of Helen in Homer, Poe, and Yeats, H.D.'s "Helen" is an ominous poem about the paralyzing misogyny at the heart of male worship of woman's beauty." And in *Stealing the Language: The Emergence of Women's Poetry in America,* Alicia Ostriker comments, "Among her early lyric poems, 'Helen' implies that men and nations hate the woman-as-erotic-object they claim to love, until they can embalm her as art."

Criticism

David Kelly

David Kelly is an instructor of creative writing at several community colleges in Illinois, as well as a fiction writer and playwright. In the following essay, Kelly explores the connection that critics often make between H.D.'s life and her work, and he questions whether it is justified.

It is easy for a lover of poetry to love H.D. She was erratic and committed, obscure to the general public, practically embodying all of the great things about poetry in the first half of the twentieth century (which, it has turned out, is certainly better than embodying poetry in the century's rundown half). H.D. was present at the beginning of the century's defining artistic wave, Modernism. She witnessed the birth of the Imagist movement, one of the strongest forces in shoving stuffy old traditions aside to let poetry stand tall and free. Imagism redefined the relationship between words and reality; teachers of poetry stress the image so much nowadays that is hard to remember that someone had to "represent" the idea once. To people who have just peeked into Imagism briefly—usually lovers of poetry and fans of revolution, but not scholars—H.D. looms large over the movement, a distinction

What Do I Read Next?

- John Boardman's *Greek Art,* published in 1964, is full of illustrations and includes an index and bibliography. It makes an excellent introduction to the varied arts of ancient Greece.

- *The Greek Myths,* by Robert Graves (1955), not only recounts the basic myths with their variations but provides annotations and bibliographic sources for the earliest tellings of the myths. It is an extremely valuable reference book.

- *Hermione* (1981) is H.D.'s autobiographical novel, an interior self-portrait. The book covers a year in H.D.'s twenties, a particularly bad year in her personal life.

- Kate Millet's *Sexual Politics* (1970) was a watershed book for feminism. It includes a history of feminism, an overview of its history, and feminist criticism of male writers, including D. H. Lawrence, Henry Miller, Norman Mailer, and Jean Genet.

mostly caused by her having signed her first works "H.D., Imagiste." In the 1930s she underwent psychoanalysis, which, regardless of its value as a tool for mental health, was a trend among all of the avant-garde intellectuals for the next three decades. Even better for her legend, H.D.'s psychoanalysis was not with some ordinary couch pilot with a Park Avenue address, but with the kingpin of them all, Sigmund Freud. As a result, H.D.'s work became even more complex and symbolic as she passed through middle age, more twisted personally at a time of life when most writers tend to settle into some sort of literary ambassadorships. H.D.'s later works, such as her retelling of the Helen of Troy story some thirty years after the poem about Helen who "All Greece hates," reworks the ancient myths to fit the story of her own psychological profile. Readers, on first coming across H.D., tend to ask, "Why haven't I heard of her before?"

But then they read the poems. It's good poetry, to be sure, but it has a hard time keeping up with her biography. There can be no doubt about the

> *Look at a picture of H.D. and you see the Helen that is represented in the poem; read about H.D.'s life, and the haunted alienation that Helen feels is depicted."*

value of her work and of her life, but there also is no doubt about which one interests readers more. Why doesn't her poetry, on its own, thrill readers as much as her life does?

"Helen" was written too late to be swept up in the flow of Imagism or Vorticism, and too early to be dragged down to the depths of her journey of self-understanding; the poem stands a comfortable distance both from the social forces of the time and from its own author. It is careful with its words and smart regarding what makes the world go around. With all of that going for it, I, as a reader, would expect the poem to curl itself around me and take control of what I think and do—at least for the couple of minutes just after I've read it, if not longer. Instead, the poem just lays there, its pieces honed and fitted perfectly together. It doesn't come to life at all.

One reason that it stays cold is that coldness is its subject. Helen herself is sterile and untouchable in this poem, and the poem captures her exquisite essence. Therefore, it hardly seems fair to blame the poem when it is effective in its aim. Stillness, whiteness, coolness, and wanness results in something unloved by both Greeks and readers. One could reasonably argue that being unmoved equates with being held under the poem's spell. But the poem is not entirely without passion: only Helen's drained cheeks are. The poem is filled with the hatred belonging to the Greek people, which intensifies as they think about how Helen stands untouched, oblivious to all of the death and waste that has gone on in her name. Their hatred should mean more—it is expressed as the first verb in the poem, and it is the source of the blood lust that brings the last line to a fulfilling conclusion. It stands to reason that readers should be moved to some feeling—

if not hatred then pity or disgust that the mob gangs up on someone so frail as Helen.

Readers instead are suspended in some weird unfocused purgatory, identifying with neither Helen nor the Greeks. She is pictured as unapproachable and impenetrable—as a statue to be appreciated but not understood. The Greeks are not even pictured, just represented as pure emotion: hatred. They represent ugly emotions, the kind of perversity that finds its joy in someone's death—jealousy, grudge-bearing. It would not take much to make readers empathize, even with things they would rather not catch themselves feeling, but this poem does not try to turn its readers into angry Greeks. It talks about the Greeks, but it doesn't show them. And talking without showing is wrong in literature, not just because it violates the cardinal rule taught in creative writing classes everywhere, but also because it makes the poem ineffectual and unconvincing. Perhaps H.D. had a reason for wanting Helen to appear as an object in this poem, to transmogrify the woman from flesh into marble, as so many sculptors have throughout the ages, but there is no good reason for not making the Greeks the poem's subject. I suspect that she held back from identifying with them because they are, after all, a pack of louts, and she didn't want to associate herself with them.

But, there I go trying to think through her motives and use them as part of understanding what is on the page. Some poems stand by themselves, but a poem such as "Helen" recedes from the reader, runs away from being understood, so that readers taking more than a minute to look at it end up having their attention drawn to the hypnotic personality of H.D. There are different schools of literary criticism: some argue that a poem should speak for itself, regardless of who wrote it or where it came from; others find no reason to exclude the author in analysis of a poem. And, even when knowledge of the author is not required, it is usually interesting to examine the poet's creative process. In a case like this, exploring the author and her insecurities helps to fill in the gaps missing from the poem. We know that beauteous Helen was the cause of the Trojan war, and, as such, it would make sense that the Greeks would resent the damage she caused. However, literary sources, such as Homer and Euripides, don't emphasize the common people's feelings about her. Capturing the mood of a whole society wasn't important to them; such a quest is a fairly new and linked to poll-taking and political science. It is not unusual, then, that H.D. should give modern sensibilities to the citizens of Greece. The unusual thing—the "gap" in sensibility that the poem does not fill in itself— is why Helen is pictured the way she is here. Look at a picture of H.D. and you see the Helen that is represented in the poem; read about H.D.'s life, and the haunted alienation that Helen feels is depicted. Fiction and screenplay writers call this the back-story. It is a story not presented, but one that the author knows in order to flesh out a character.

"Helen" does not offer readers the point of view necessary for them to approach it, understand it, and take it in and make it real to themselves. Not enough is said about either of the parties portrayed to fully comprehend the significance of this poem. It is incomplete as it stands. Like many of H.D.'s works, "Helen" is like a mechanism that is ready to go but just sits still, waiting for something to make it work. Background about H.D.'s life provides the electrical current it needs to move into action.

Source: David Kelly, in an essay for *Poetry for Students,* The Gale Group, 1999.

Jhan Hochman

Jhan Hochman's articles appear in Democracy and Nature, Genre, ISLE, *and* Mosaic. *He is the author of* Green Cultural Studies: Nature in Film, Novel, and Theory *(1998), and he holds a Ph.D. in English and an M.A. in cinema studies. Hochman's essay examines "Helen" from the perspectives of H.D.'s biography, Helen's mythology, and the history of conflict between Greece and Asia Minor.*

H.D.'s poem "Helen" can be viewed through at least three filters: the Greek myths of Helen; H.D.'s life; and, finally, the history of conflicts between Greece and Turkey—or, more specifically, between Greece and inhabitants of the peninsula between the Black and Mediterranean seas in what is now Turkey and is also known as Asia Minor.

Before recounting the two most important stories regarding Helen, it is necessary to place her birth. Although there are several variations, the usual story is that Helen was the daughter of Zeus and Leda. Leda was the wife of Tyndareus, the King of Sparta, but she was pursued and raped by Zeus, who took the form of a swan. Leda laid eggs, from which were hatched Helen, Castor and Pollux (Dioscuri), and Clytaemnestra. (Whether the latter three children were all Zeus's is a matter of variation.) The swan and egg appear, at least partially, to be an impetus for H.D.'s repeated references in "Helen" to "white" and "wan."

The next story involving Helen takes place in Sparta, where the twelve-year-old (or younger) is worshipping an effigy of the Upright Artemis, a fertility goddess of the moon and hunt. As Helen makes her sacrificial offering, Theseus and Perithous ride up, abduct her, and gallop away. These two abductors decide by lots who will marry Helen. Theseus wins but, fearing Helen will be found and taken back by her brothers, the Dioscuri, hides her in the village of Aphidnae in the care of his mother. Several years pass before Helen is old enough to marry Theseus. Before that happens, Theseus must honor his promise to help Perithous—the loser in the drawing of the lots for Helen—find another daughter of Zeus to marry. While Theseus and Perithous are off on their adventure to Tartarus (the land of the dead) to find Persephone, the Dioscuri assemble an army and demand that Athens return their sister. After a war between Athens and the army of the Dioscuri, Helen's whereabouts are finally revealed. In retaliation, the Dioscuri's army razes Aphidnae. The conflict marks the first war between Peloponnesians and Athenians and the first of two wars fought over Helen.

When Helen is at the marrying age, she resides in Sparta with Tyndareus, her foster father. Because of Helen's renowned beauty, many suitors—an all-star cast of princes from all over Greece—are vying to marry her. So that none of the suitors attempts revenge on the winning suitor, Odysseus decrees that they all must take an oath to defend the winner in the case of a jealous attack. Upon the pieces of a sacrificed and dismembered horse sacred to Poseidon, the suitors swear allegiance to Helen's future husband—whoever he turns out to be. Menelaus ends up marrying Helen, and after Tyndareus's death, he also assumes the Spartan throne. There's only one problem: once before Tyndareus died, he committed the blunder of paying tribute to all of the gods except Aphrodite. In revenge, Aphrodite cursed his daughters— Clytaemnestra, Timandra, and Helen—and pledged to turn them into infamous adulterers. Helen would commit adultery by being abducted or eloping with the handsome Paris, also under the sway of Aphrodite. This abduction/elopement provoked Menelaus to call upon the losing suitors to honor their word to defend him from any attack. Thus, a large Greek Army sailed across the Aegean Sea to the walled town of Troy on the coast of Phrygia. The war to take back Helen of Troy lasted ten years, and by the end, Paris was dead and Helen was once again Menelaus's wife. This, then, is the recounting of the turmoil surrounding Helen, a woman with beauty no more her choice than the choice to accept or reject Aphrodite's curse that impelled Helen to become an adulterer and Paris an abductor. If anyone is to be blamed in this story, it is Tyndareus, a Spartan Greek, for forgetting to honor Aphrodite and starting a chain reaction that led to the Trojan War.

H.D. viewed the events surrounding the Trojan War as partially analogous to her private life. First, Helen was the name of H.D.'s mother. As a child, H.D. referred to herself as Hermione, Helen of Troy's child, and as an adult, H.D. would see herself as Helen, her mother, and also Helen of Troy. H.D. viewed her marriage to Richard Aldington as the Trojan War by way of the following associations: Aldington (Paris) wrested H.D. (Helen) away from Ezra Pound (Menelaus). The marriage (war) was tempestuous, with H.D. being torn between those men and an additional man, writer D. H. Lawrence (Achilles, the hero on the Greek side of the war). When the "war" ends, H.D. is rescued by Bryher, a woman comparable to the postwar Menelaus, who takes H.D. on a cruise to Egypt and Greece—just as Menelaus had once taken Helen back to Egypt then Greece.

The Trojan War (c. 1194-1184 B.C.) was only the first of many conflicts between Greece and the land called Asia Minor, which was inhabited, successively, by Phrygians, Persians, and Ottoman Turks. Although the Greeks won the Trojan War, they incurred significant casualties. But thereafter they would not always be so "lucky." In the sixth century B.C., the Persians (present-day Iranians) moved westward, first taking over the Ionian coast of Asia Minor and then penetrating into much of Greece. But the city-state of Athens held firm, repulsing the Persians in the first two decades of the fourth century and causing the slow retreat of Persians from what is present-day Greece. As most historians affirm, Greece gave birth to western civilization, especially Western-style democracy through the efforts of the ruler Solon. The next major historical period of the region saw the gradual takeover of the Ottoman Turks, a west Asian nomadic people said to be descended from Othman (or Osman). From an Anatolian border emirate, the Ottomans expanded through most of what is now Turkey and the Balkans and completely engulfed Greece. In the early sixteenth century the Ottoman Empire expanded its borders even more. The apex of its conquests was Constantinople, the former eastern capital of the Roman Empire, in 1453. The Ottomans had turned the eastern Christian empire—including Greece—into an Asian Empire.

One source of hostility between Greeks and Turks during Ottoman rule was the aftermath of a naval battle between Turks and Christians in which the Turks were defeated. To take advantage of Turkish naval losses, the commander of the European fleet encouraged the Greeks to revolt. But the Turkish infantry was still strong and slaughtered thousands of Greek revolutionaries on land. Catherine the Great of Russia instigated another abortive attempt at Greek revolt, but when it was put down, the Turkish grip intensified. But on March 25, 1821, (Greek independence day) an Arcadian archbishop raised the blue and white flag, inaugurating the fight for Greek independence, a conflict that did not end until 1829. The next major conflict between Greece and Turkey did not occur until World War I, during which the two countries fought on opposite sides. The famous yearlong battle at Gallipoli (1915), very near the ruins of Troy, ended with defeat and a terrible loss of life for the Allies, with whom the Greeks were aligned.

Even after Greece won independence and finished on the winning side of World War I (Turkey, of course, on the losing side), one out of five Greeks lived in Asia Minor under Turkish rule. To rectify the situation, an irredentist Greece sent forces across the Aegean to occupy Izmir (Smyrna), just south of Troy, in 1919. While Greece contemplated proceeding to Istanbul, Turkish commander Mustafa Kemal launched a fierce attack on August 26, 1922, in the region of Afyonkarahisar. The attack became a Greek rout, a retreat all the way back to Izmir. On September 8, the Greek soldiers evacuated the city and the Turks took it back the following day. To show the "infidel" city a lesson, the Muslim Turks began a massacre of Christians, with the Armenian, Greek, and Frankish quarters suffering the most heavy losses. Thirty thousand people were killed, and a quarter of a million fled to the sea to escape a Smyrna set ablaze. Within a few days, Greeks had completely fled Asia Minor, having suffered what they would thenceforth refer to as "the catastrophe." In Izmir there is a reverse analogue of what happened at Troy almost three thousand years prior. At Troy, Greeks finally invaded and decimated Troy and slaughtered Trojans. At Izmir, the Turks invaded and decimated Izmir, slaughtering Christians.

H.D., then, could have viewed Helen through these two lenses: that of her own life and that of the Greek mind. While H.D. recalled her suffering at the hands of male companions, H.D.'s Greeks gazing upon and reviling Helen might just have had in mind those long years of conflict with Asia Minor when they preposterously concluded that Helen was an accursed traitor, that an image of this most beautiful of women was unacceptable unless burned in effigy and reduced to "white ash amid funereal cypresses."

Source: Jhan Hochman, in an essay for *Poetry for Students*, The Gale Group, 1999.

Jeannine Johnson

Jeannine Johnson received her Ph.D. from Yale University and is currently a visiting assistant professor of English at Wake Forest University. In the following essay, Johnson argues that, though H.D. is sympathetic to Helen, the poet never fully absolves her complex heroine of her imperfections.

The legendary Helen is a recurrent figure in H.D.'s writing. She is, for instance, the central subject of H.D.'s final major work, *Helen in Egypt* (1961). This epic poem, published just after H.D.'s death, examines the character of Helen and attempts to reconcile the fact that she represents both the greatest properties of love and the worst elements of war. To some extent, H.D.'s feministic and pacifistic poem redeems Helen, but it does not do so naively or with complete success. The poet ultimately does not resolve either the ambiguity of Helen's ethical standing or the complexity of her identity, and H.D. proceeds in her poem with a mix of celebration and criticism.

An earlier poem by H.D., simply titled "Helen" and published in 1924, is a more compact but equally conflicted portrait of the woman who has always been associated with both love and war, with both beauty and destruction. Helen was world renowned for her unparalleled physical attractiveness, but she was also maligned as the cause of the ruinous Trojan War. Her father was Zeus, the king of the gods, and she herself was queen of Sparta in ancient Greece. Once, when her husband Menelaus was away from home, the Trojan prince Paris came to Sparta and kidnapped her, removing her to the city of Troy. In order to rescue her, Menelaus enlisted the help of other kings of Greek city-states, and for ten years they laid siege to Troy. The Greeks were ultimately victorious, but their losses were very heavy and Troy was demolished.

In "Helen," H.D. explores the depths of resentment that the Greeks feel toward the infamous title character after the war. She has safely returned home from Troy, but thousands of Greek soldiers have not, and it is clear that they blame her for this national injury. The poem focuses on their extreme position, a stance the poet suggests is all too eas-

> " *Though [H.D.] does not judge Helen as the Greeks do and tries to insulate her from the judgments of others, she does not thoroughly sever Helen from the enduring guilt that clings to her name.*"

ily adopted and one that she subtly condemns. Nevertheless, H.D. is unwilling to dismiss their contempt altogether. Though the poet does not judge Helen as the Greeks do and tries to insulate her from the judgments of others, she does not thoroughly sever Helen from the enduring guilt that clings to her name.

H.D.'s heroine is perhaps best known and most often referred to as "Helen of Troy," but she is also sometimes called "Helen of Sparta" or "Helen of Egypt." Such names contain an implied judgment of Helen and suggest a natural connection between her and the men who inhabit those sites. The title "Helen of Troy" signals that she belonged to that city and to Paris. It may further insinuate that she was content there and, therefore, partly responsible for her own kidnapping and for the Trojan War. The name "Helen of Sparta" emphasizes Helen's rightful place as wife of Menelaus and as daughter of Leda, the previous queen of that city. It affirms that her identity and her allegiances are fully Greek. To refer to her as "Helen of Egypt" recalls lesser-known stories about her and foregrounds the mysteriousness and the arbitrariness of the human condition. An alternative version of the incidents surrounding the Trojan War maintains that Paris carried a ghost double of Helen back to Troy while the real Helen was hidden by the gods in Egypt during the war. Some authorities say that after the war, the true Helen was reunited with Menelaus when, on his voyage back to Sparta, he inadvertently landed on Egypt's shores; other sources hold that she married a reborn Achilles there. H.D. chooses not to attach any place designation to her heroine's name, thereby underscoring her identity as an individual and minimizing her relationship with various powerful men and kingdoms. This suggests a belief that Helen was largely innocent of the trials that befell her and that she possessed a character with value independent of the many dramatic stories associated with her.

Nevertheless, H.D.'s poem centers on the fact that, to these Greeks, she is unalterably Helen of Troy. The citizens of her own country perceive her both as a foreigner and as a reminder of unnecessary suffering. They "revile" her even when she seems to acknowledge her own responsibility, and they hate her face all the more when it looks sad as Helen is "remembering past enchantments / and past ills." Christopher Marlowe, in his play *Doctor Faustus,* wrote that Helen's was "the face that launched a thousand ships." Contrary to the sense of universal admiration underlying Marlowe's famous assertion, H.D. reports that "All Greece hates / the still eyes in the white face...."

Although the poet would lean toward protecting Helen, she does not explicitly defend her, as if to do so would be to concede Helen's guilt and to admit that she requires defending. Neither does H.D. defend the Greeks, and her tone is that of a nearly neutral observer. Her dispassionate voice is at odds with the fierce feelings of animosity she describes, creating an extraordinary tension that conveys the extent of the strain between Helen and her countrymen. H.D. takes us inside the minds of the Greeks, and we watch as they contemplate their rage. She leads us through their meditations, which only feed their anger, and, over the course of the poem, they conduct Helen imaginatively to death, hatred's inevitable extreme. The poet declares that the Greeks despise Helen so much that they could love her only if she were dead: they "could love indeed the maid, / only if she were laid, / white ash amid funereal cypresses."

The light-colored features attributed to Helen are gruesomely preserved in her ashen death. From the beginning of the poem, H.D. stresses the fairness of Helen's beauty, repeating the word "white" in the first stanza in describing her face and hands. The poet again uses "white" in the second stanza and also twice employs the word "wan" in reference to Helen's face. H.D.'s word choice here is significant because "wan" indicates not only the color of her skin, but it also symbolizes an underlying sickness or affliction. If we read that word from Helen's perspective (that is, as if she were using it to characterize herself), then the drain of color in her face might suggest an internal conflict and perhaps remorse for the past. If we interpret her

paleness as the hostile Greeks would (or as they would apply the word to her), then "wan" may reflect their view that she is an unhealthy and alien figure and may reveal their hope that she will soon die.

Throughout the poem, the hatred belongs to the Greeks, but the language is the poet's. H.D. displays the Greeks' extremism without directly commenting on it; instead, she tries to soften their loathing with pleasing images. She mentions Helen's face with "the lustre as of olives" and her "beauty of cool feet / and slenderest knees" to remind us of her extraordinary loveliness. But the enduring presence of Helen's beauty is precisely what infuriates the Greeks: "Greece sees unmoved, / God's daughter, born of love." They are unimpressed by her attractiveness, and they are not inspired to stir because of it—in sharp contrast to the story of a thousand ships launched for her sake. The quality of stillness, further communicated by the final image of Helen's unmoving corpse, contrasts with the volatility of the Greeks' passionate scorn that builds over the course of the poem.

The poem's structure parallels the ideas being presented in it and mirrors the buildup of malice. As the poem develops, the stanzas lengthen—from five lines in the first stanza, to six in the second, to seven in the third. This structural expansion reveals H.D.'s need to enlarge her poem's framework in order to accommodate the Greeks' increasing hate for Helen. The poet repeats "All Greece" at the beginning of the first two stanzas, followed by "hates" and "reviles," to denote that their hostility is continuously renewed. She drops the "All" at the start of the third stanza and simply states "Greece sees...." Whereas the implied meaning of "All Greece" is "All the people of Greece," the single word "Greece" marks that culture's entire identity—its land, customs, history, and traditions—in addition to every Greek citizen. By eliminating one word, the poet demonstrates that profound spite pervades the whole of a civilization and does not simply distinguish a group of its inhabitants.

H.D.'s rhymes also help to reinforce the sense of ceaseless menace and tension in the poem. Several of the rhyming pairs contain one word related to the Greeks and their perspective and one affiliated with Helen and her qualities. The words "hates" and "face" create a slant rhyme in the first stanza. In the second, "reviles" and "smiles" are rhymed, and in the third "unmoved" is connected with "love," while "maid" is joined with "laid." The similar sounds link these opposing pairs, as if to signify that neither the Greeks' antipathy nor

Helen's stature could exist without the other. Certainly H.D.'s poem shows that to consider one in the absence of the other would be to oversimplify a complicated and enduring myth, even at the risk of leaving Helen vulnerable to further attacks on her character. It is perhaps because she does leave Helen unprotected, that H.D. can return again and again to this rich subject for poetic study, pursuing more radical revisions of the myth and rendering more clearly sympathetic visions of her controversial heroine.

Source: Jeannine Johnson, in an essay for *Poetry for Students,* The Gale Group, 1999.

Sources

Clogg, Richard, *A Short History of Modern Greece,* Cambridge: Cambridge University Press, 1986.

Doolittle, Hilda (H.D.), *Helen in Egypt,* New Directions, 1961.

Eliot, Alexander, *Greece,* New York: Time, 1963.

Engel, Bernard F., "H.D.: Poems That Matter and Dilutations," *Contemporary Literature,* Vol. 10, No. 4, autumn 1969, pp. 507-22.

Friedman, Susan Stanford, "H.D.," *Dictionary of Literary Biography,* Vol. 45: *American Poets, 1880–1945,* First Series, Detroit: Gale Research, 1986.

Healey, Claire, "H.D.," *American Women Writers,* Volume I, edited by Lima Mainiero, New York: Frederick Ungar, 1979.

Ostricker, Alicia, *Stealing the Language: The Emergence of Women's Poetry in America,* Boston: Beacon, 1986.

Quinn, Vincent, *Hilda Doolittle (H.D.),* New York: Twayne, 1967.

Robinson, Janice, *H.D.: The Life and Work of an American Poet,* Boston: Houghton Mifflin, 1982.

For Further Study

Coffman, Stanley K., Jr., *Imagism: A Chapter for the History of Modern Poetry,* New York: Octagon, 1972.
Coffman's study tackles Imagism as it changes through time and also focuses on major and minor figures of the movement.

Erskine, John, *The Private Life of Helen of Troy,* New York: Frederick Ungar, 1925.
Erskine's easygoing retelling of the story of Helen begins at the end of the Trojan War when Menelaus rescues her from Troy.

Gage, John T., *In the Arresting Eye: The Rhetoric of Imagism,* Baton Rouge: Louisiana State University Press, 1981.
Gage attempts to salvage Imagist poems from the failings of Imagist theory, a body of ideas Gage finds unconvincing.

H.D., *Helen in Egypt,* New York: Grove Press, 1961.
H.D.'s epic poem of numerous shorter poems rewrites the later portion of the Helen myth, taking up the Helen story when she falls in love with Achilles in Egypt after the Trojan War has ended.

Hughes, Glenn, *Imagism and the Imagists,* Stanford: Stanford University Press, 1931.
Hughes's study is interesting for its appearance at a time right after Imagism ceased to be a controversial body of work. It is more literary history than literary criticism.

White, Edward Lucas, *Helen,* New York: George H. Doran, 1925.
White's tale of Helen commences when Theseus and Peirithous abduct Helen (before her subsequent abduction by Paris) and then covers her history through her marriages to Menelaus, Paris, and Deiphobos, or up to the time of her rescue from Troy by Menelaus.

Lord Randal

Anonymous

1629

"Lord Randal" is a traditional Scottish ballad. Scholars believe its original source to be an Italian ballad, "L'Avvelenato." The earliest printing of this Italian version exists in a 1629 advertisement for a performance by a singer in Verona, in which excerpts of the ballad appear. The Scottish version is found in Francis James Child's famous collection of English and Scottish ballads, which was published in five volumes from 1882 to 1898. Along with the Italian source, Child recognizes versions of the "Lord Randal" story from Czechoslovakia, Hungary, Sweden, and Calabria. Like most ballads, it is difficult to date precisely, and it probably existed in oral tradition earlier than the seventeenth-century reference to it.

As are all traditional ballads, " Lord Randal" is a narrative song—a song that tells a story. Ballads tell their stories directly, with an emphasis on climactic incidents, by stripping away those details that are not essential to the plot. "Lord Randal" tells of a man who has been poisoned by his lover. It does not give any details about the background incident; in this case, the listener does not know why Lord Randal has been poisoned. The ballad refers to it merely as the event that triggers the action. The action itself consists of Lord Randal's revelation that he has been poisoned, a statement of his last will and testament, and his final curse on the lover who killed him.

Poem Text

"O where ha' you been, Lord Randal, my son?
And where ha you been, my handsome young
     man?"
"I hae been at the greenwood; mother, mak my bed
     soon,
For I'm wearied wi' huntin, and fain wad lie
     down."

"An wha met ye there, Lord Randal, my son?   5
An wha met you there, my handsome young man?"
"O I met wi' my true-love; mother, mak my bed
     soon,
For I'm wearied wi' huntin, and fain wad lie
     down."
"And what did she give you, Lord Randal, my son?
And what did she give you, my handsome young   10
     man?"
"Eels fried in a pan; mother, mak my bed soon,
For I'm wearied wi' huntin, and fain wad lie
     down."

"And wha gat your leavins, Lord Randal, my son?
And wha gat your leavins, my handsome young
     man?"
"My hawks and my hounds; mother, mak my bed   15
     soon,
For I'm wearied wi' huntin, and fain wad lie
     down."

"And what becam of them, Lord Randal, my son?
And what becam of them, my handsome young
     man?"
"They swelled and they died; mother, mak my bed
     soon,
For I'm wearied wi' huntin, and fain wad lie   20
     down."

"O I fear you are poisoned, Lord Randal, my son!
I fear you are poisoned, my handsome young
     man!"
"O yes, I am poisoned, mother, mak my bed soon,
For I'm sick at the heart, and I fain wad lie down."

"What d' ye leave to your mother, Lord Randal,   25
     my son?
What d' ye leave to your mother, my handsome
     young man?"
"Four and twenty milk kye; mother, mak my bed
     soon,
For I'm sick at the heart, and I fain wad lie down."

"What d' ye leave to your sister, Lord Randal, my
     son?
What d' ye to your sister my handsome young   30
     man?"
"My gold and my silver; mother, mak my bed
     soon,
For I'm sick at the heart, and I fain wad lie down."

"What d' ye leave to your brother, Lord Randal,
     my son?

What d' ye to your brother my handsome young
     man?"
"My houses and my lands; mother, mak my bed   35
     soon,
For I'm sick at the heart, and I fain wad lie down."

"What d' ye leave to your true-love, Lord Randal,
     my son?
What d' ye to your true-love my handsome young
     man?"
"I leave her hell and fire; mother, mak my bed
     soon,
For I'm sick at the heart, and I fain wad lie down."   40

Poem Summary

Lines 1-4:

The first stanza introduces the main character, the nobleman Lord Randal. The listener also learns that he is "handsome" and "young." His youth suggests that he is susceptible to danger, because he probably lacks worldly experience that would enable him to sense and thwart treachery. Lord Randal's mother asks him where he has been, and he answers that he has been hunting in the forest; he says he is tired, and he requests that she ready his bed for him because he would like to lie down. In this first stanza, there is no indication of anything out of the ordinary about Lord Randal's day, but the fact that he has been in the "greenwood," or forest, carries with it the connotation of adventure and danger.

Lines 5-8:

As if she suspects that her son has been doing something other than hunting, Lord Randal's mother asks him who he met in the forest. He answers that he met his "true love" there and repeats his complaint of tiredness and request that his bed be readied for him. The idea of meeting a sweetheart on a hunting trip raises the first suspicion that something out of the ordinary has happened to Lord Randal.

Lines 9-12:

The mother continues her questioning, asking Lord Randal what he received from his sweetheart. He answers that he ate fried eels that she gave him. Once again, Lord Randal concludes his answer with his complaint and request. At this third repetition, it seems more urgent that Lord Randal be given a place to rest.

Lines 13-16:

The mother now asks Lord Randal who got his leftover food. He answers her that he gave it to his hunting birds and hounds. (Trained hounds and hawks were used to chase prey and to retrieve it after it was shot.) Lord Randal again complains of his tiredness and asks for his bed to be made ready. At this point, the listener becomes curious about the mother's line of questioning and also anxious for Lord Randal.

Lines 17-20:

Lord Randal's mother asks him what happened to his hawks and his hounds. He tells her that they became bloated and died, and then, once again, he says that he is tired and wants to lie down. The pieces of the story begin to come together—Lord Randal's pets died with symptoms of poisoning after eating the same food that Lord Randal ate. His statement that the hunting tired him and his request for a bed, now repeated for the fifth time, suggest his own illness.

Lines 21-24:

The mother finally states her suspicion that Lord Randal has been poisoned. He confirms her belief, and the last line changes. Lord Randal no longer claims that he is tired from hunting; he now asserts that he is "sick at heart," implying that he has been hurt by his "true love."

Lines 25-28:

In this stanza the nuncupative testament begins. Lord Randal's mother asks him how he wants his belongings dispensed when he dies. She begins by asking what he will leave to her. He answers that she will receive twenty-four milk cows and repeats his request for his bed to be readied. The listener now knows the bed will be Lord Randal's deathbed. Lord Randal precedes his request with the new refrain, "For I'm sick at the heart," throughout the second half of the ballad. The association of the pain of a broken heart and the deathbed establish this ballad as one that speaks of the tragedy of love.

Lines 29-32:

Lord Randal's mother next asks what he will leave to his sister. The gift to his sister represents possessions of more value than the cows that Lord Randal willed to his mother. His sister will receive Lord Randal's "gold" and "silver." Repetition of the refrain causes the reader to pity and feel anxious for Lord Randal, whose complaint sounds more desperate each time he makes it.

Lines 33-36:

When asked what he will leave his brother, Lord Randal names the most valuable of his possessions, his houses and his lands. The increasing value of these bequests creates an excitement for the listener, a sort of priming in anticipation of the final stanza. In keeping with the pattern, this stanza closes with the refrain, and upon hearing it again, the listener should feel deeply moved by Lord Randal's suffering.

Lines 37-40:

The mother finally asks Lord Randal what he bequeaths to his true love. The listener may expect the greatest gift of all to be named in keeping with the pattern in which Lord Randal names increasingly valuable gifts. However, Lord Randal will not leave his true love anything; he curses her with "hell" and "fire," revealing at last the extent to which she has hurt him—not only physically, by the poisoning, but also emotionally, due to her lack of love. This last repetition of the refrain establishes the closing of the ballad with a final pitiable cry from the sad, dying lover.

Themes

Death

The first part of the conversation between the mother and son that comprises "Lord Randal" gradually reveals how Lord Randal comes to be dying prematurely and relates the emotional reaction of the mother to this situation. At the beginning of each stanza, Lord Randal's mother prompts him with a question, from which she gets a terse reply. The withholding of complete details in her son's answers prompts the mother to ask another question. The gradual way in which the mother learns of her son's condition creates a sense of tension in her words—from the very opening lines, "O where ha' you been, Lord Randal, my son? And where ha' you been, my handsome young man?" her sense of panic crescendoes until it reaches an apex in the sixth stanza when she exclaims, "O I fear you are poisoned, Lord Randal, my son! I fear you are poisoned, my handsome young man!" The use of exclamation points in this stanza relates to the reader the mother's sense of dread as she realizes that her son's death is imminent.

Likewise, Lord Randal's responses to his mother's questions reveal his own reaction to his impending death. His responses, however, are largely open to interpretation. One thing is for certain, though: Lord Randal's statements are much milder than those of his mother. His repetitive, matter-of-fact responses to his mother's questions are not what one expects from someone who is dying. It can argued, therefore, that Lord Randal is in shock and in denial of the situation, insofar as he states that he is merely "wearied wi' huntin." This implies that Lord Randal is dealing with his death by not acknowledging the fact that he is dying. Notice in the sixth stanza how mild his response is to his mother's exclamations: "O yes, I am poisoned, mother, mak my bed soon, / For I'm sick at the heart, and I fain wad lie down." It is as if he has just remembered that he was poisoned. He is of sound enough mind to state his last will and testament to his mother, and yet does not have a frenzied reaction to his own demise.

The common folk of the Middle Ages, especially the high Middle Ages, surrounded the death experience in religious ritual in order to find reassurance and comfort in a life after death. According to Frances and Joseph Gies in their work *Marriage and the Family in the Middle Ages,* "death was immured in ritual, the laments of daughters and daughters-in-law commencing before the stricken peasant expired and continuing until burial," and that "to the man or woman on the deathbed … two things were important: to be surrounded by one's family and, whatever the ritual, to achieve salvation." The ideal situation for a death in the Middle Ages was for an individual to anticipate his death, having suffered an illness or debilitating wound. In doing so, the person could ensure the two essential requirements were met. In Lord Randal's case, however, death has caught him unprepared. This certainly increased the already frightening experience of dying. Due to the lack of detail in the ballad, it is hard to ascertain whether or not Lord Randal was surrounded by any family members other than his mother. However, based on the two-sided conversation, it seems fair to surmise that his sister and brother were not present, and the father is never mentioned in the poem. It is also impossible to determine whether or not Lord Randal received the aid of a member of the clergy in his final moments. However, evidence would suggest that he did not participate in any salvation-producing ritual. Therefore, Lord Randal achieved neither of the desired elements of the ideal death experience. His was a worst-case scenario of dying: unprepared and unsaved. This is one of the key reasons why the ballad "Lord Randal" has remained in existence for so many centuries: it is unnerving, causing one to consider the possibilities of an extremely fearful death experience.

Media Adaptations

- A record titled *Edward Jabes Sings Songs of Old France and Old England* was released c. 1970 by Luminar Records in Berkeley, California.

- A record titled *Lord Randal: An Old Ballad of which there are Several Versions* was released c. 1926 by Galaxy Records of London.

- The recording of a version of "Lord Randal" is available online at http://www.deltablues.com/ midi/LORDRAND.mid.

Guilt and Innocence

While the themes of guilt and innocence in "Lord Randal" are not as readily apparent as the theme of death, they do exist outside the text of the ballad. These ideas are conjured in the reader's mind after the ballad has been read. The obvious perpetrator of the crime is the lover; she poisoned Lord Randal and is therefore guilty. The converse theme, coupled with the emotion surrounding his death, leads the reader to view Lord Randal as the victim and, therefore, as innocent. After the initial shock of the story fades, the reader begins to question the events leading to the action depicted in the ballad. However, because no detail is provided by the author, the reader is left to wonder: Why did she poison him? Did they quarrel? Was he unfaithful? The distinction between guilt and innocence begins to fade. If Lord Randal was unfaithful, or if they did argue, then he is not completely innocent; and, some may argue, if she had some cause to poison him, she would not be completely guilty. In crimes of passion, it is often difficult to adequately place blame. The author uses the themes of guilt and innocence in such a way as to create an unanswerable riddle that has persisted through the ages.

Style

Although most ballads use some dialogue as a technique in telling the story, "Lord Randal" differs in that it uses nothing else. The listener learns of the

Topics for Further Study

- Why did Lord Randal leave his possessions to his family in the manner he did? Does each possession match the family member to whom he left it? If yes, how does each item benefit the recipient?

- Examine the author's use of the phrase "sick at heart." What are the possible meanings of this phrase? Why do you think the author chose to use this particular phrase?

- Why do you think Lord Randal changed the description of his symptoms from "wearied wi' huntin'" to "sick at heart" only after his mother voices her fear that he has been poisoned?

- Given what you know about people who lived in medieval times, what is the significance of the word "greenwood" in stanza one? What impact does this word have on the tone of the ballad?

incident that will result in Lord Randal's death only through the conversation between Lord Randal and his mother. Since the ballad derives from oral, rather than written, verse, the structure of the poem relies on repetition to make it easy to memorize. Repetition of the words "Lord Randal, my son" and "my handsome young man" and the parallel formation of the first two lines of each stanza along with the repetition of the last line to form a refrain from stanza to stanza all serve this mnemonic purpose. This repetition also lends tension to the unraveling story; as Lord Randal asks repeatedly for a resting place, a sense of urgency develops. In the sixth stanza, the closing refrain changes from "wearied wi' hunting" to "sick at the heart," so that the listener now fully understands Lord Randal's predicament. At this point in the ballad, Lord Randal and his mother settle his estate. Again, repetition ties the ballad together and intensifies the drama. Each question follows the pattern, "What d' ye leave," and each answer varies. In each stanza Lord Randal bequeaths more valuable possessions than in the previous stanza. In the last stanza this

question-and-answer pattern allows Lord Randal to make a final judgment on his lover, leaving her a curse instead of any possessions. The device of listing the possessions and then culminating in a curse for the murderer appears as a structural technique in other ballads as well; this technique is called a nuncupative testament.

Historical Context

The first printed version of "Lord Randal" appeared in 1629, but the ballad had existed in Scotland long before—at least since the 1500s, a time of great turmoil in that country. Scotland's rivaling neighbors, England and France each vied for a degree of sovereignty over Scotland and each sought to establish Scotland as an ally with whom, as nations, they would hold common religious precepts—France remained a predominantly Catholic nation, while England, under the rule of Henry VIII, was converting to Protestantism. The royal families of the three nations during this century often negotiated peace by arranging marriages among themselves; a marriage between the prince of one nation and the princess of another was an act of diplomacy. Thus, several monarchs during this century were the rulers of two nations at the same time. One such monarch was Mary Stuart, who was, during a short period, both Queen of Scotland and Queen of France.

Mary was the daughter of Mary of Guise, a French noblewoman, and James V, who was king of Scotland from 1513 to 1542. James V died of illness shortly after a battle in which Scottish forces were defeated following an English invasion; Henry VIII had dispatched forces to Scotland after James refused Henry's expectation that James would take actions to suppress the powerful Catholic Church of Scotland. James V died, leaving his six-day-old daughter to become Queen of Scotland and his wife, Mary of Guise, to act as regent.

Just a year after Mary Stuart's birth, the Treaty of Greenwich was signed, which stipulated that the child-queen was to marry England's Prince Edward, the child of Henry VIII, and would be sent to live in England when she turned ten years old. When Scotland's leaders realized that England planned to instill control over the nation, however, Scotland's government broke the treaty and canceled the marriage. Invasions planned by Henry ensued, and Scotland enlisted the help of France, who

Compare & Contrast

- **1620:** The oral tradition is largely responsible for the transmission of stories and events throughout Europe.

  1990: Satellite television and the internet provide the world with up-to-the-minute news reports on current events.

- **1600s:** Europe was wracked by religious intolerance, and members of groups whose beliefs differed from official religions were often persecuted for their beliefs. The Protestant Huguenots were forced to leave Catholic France, Protestant sects such as the Puritans and Quakers, as well as Roman Catholics, were driven underground or forced to leave England. In Italy the Waldensian (Vaudois) sect was driven into the Alps and eventually murdered.

1990s: Religious persecution is often as bloody today as it was three hundred years ago. Christian Serbs have waged a war of extermination against Bosnian Muslims for most of the 1990s. The conflict between Hindus and Sikhs in India erupts regularly into violence. And although a settlement has been sought for nearly twenty years, the tensions between Palestinians and Israelis usually take the form of violent demonstrations, police beatings, and military action.

- **1620:** Ballads serve as entertainment for the common people.

  1990: Urban legends are shared around campfires as entertainment.

would send troops to fight off the English invaders. The nations' leaders decided that Mary would marry the French Dauphin, or the first son of the king, Francis.

As a five-year-old, Mary was sent to France to live among the young Francis's relatives and, over the next ten years, she received a solid classical education. In April of 1558, she married Francis in a grand Catholic ceremony in Paris's Notre Dame Cathedral. While she had a relatively uneventful childhood, the few years following her wedding were turbulent ones. Just a few months after the ceremony, Henry II, Francis's father, died after a jousting accident, and Francis and Mary ascended as France's ruling monarchs. Only sixteen years old, Mary was the queen of both Scotland of France. Her reign as the queen of two nations, however, was brief; Francis died of complications from an ear infection in late 1560, only several months after Mary's mother died. A few months after Francis died and his brother Charles IX claimed the throne, Mary returned to Scotland to take a more active role in her homeland's affairs.

When Mary arrived in the Palace of Holyrood in Edinburgh, the effects of the Reformation were prevalent in Scotland. Protestant reformers held positions of power in the Scottish government, to the extent that while Mary had Mass conducted in her own palace chapel, she publicly declared that she would not take any actions to interfere with the now widespread practice of Protestantism in Scotland. Actions such as these, along with her gracious and warm personality, made Mary a popular and admired Queen, even though she was devoutly Catholic at a time when Catholicism was persecuted and Scotland allied itself with England rather than France.

However, Mary's golden years as reigning queen were few. In 1565 she became enamored with and married her Catholic first cousin, Henry Stuart, Lord Darnley, to the dismay of many Scottish leaders. Mary had already expressed her desire to claim the English throne, upon which was Elizabeth I, the daughter of Henry VIII and his first wife, Anne Boleyn. Mary was the next heir to the English throne, while her new husband was heir to it after Mary. Scottish and English leaders feared the union of two powerful Catholic heirs on the Scottish throne. Though their fears were not unfounded—as would be evidenced by Mary's actions in the succeeding few years—the royal couple would gain notoriety for matters altogether different.

Although Mary had political motives for marrying Darnley, she also had been enchanted with him. This, however, soon changed, as Darnley, who was three years younger than Mary, revealed to Mary unsavory aspects of his personality. Mary had been taking the companionship and the counseling of David Rizzio, a musician, who became the Scottish secretary of French affairs. Their relationship aroused the suspicion of other Scottish nobles, including Darnley. In 1566 Darnley and a group of other nobles broke into the Queen's chambers and stabbed Rizzio to death in front of Mary. Because Mary was pregnant at the time, she hid her hatred of her husband and rejected divorce since it would likely cause her child to lose claim as the Scottish sovereign.

Mary, however, saw her child claim the throne much sooner than was to be expected. Around the time her son James was born, Mary began a romantic relationship with James Hepburn, Earl of Bothwell. The Queen, Bothwell, and other nobles who were enemies of Darnley met in secret and conspired against him. On February 10, 1567, Mary had convinced her husband that they would stay in Kirk o'Field, a lodge outside of Edinburgh. Mary made an excuse to leave him that evening, and hours later the building where Darnley sojourned exploded. Darnley was found strangled outside. Bothwell's stood trial but was acquitted. However, when Bothwell, after a quick divorce from his wife, and Mary got married, Mary's remaining loyal followers rebelled against her. In July of 1567, Mary was coerced into abdicating sovereignty to her infant son, who became King James VI.

After being dethroned, Mary was imprisoned at Lochleven castle. In May of 1568 she escaped and, later that month, she left Scotland for the last time to seek refuge in England. Elizabeth I welcomed her cousin, but because Mary had previously expressed her desire to be Queen of England and because she had the support of many English Catholics, she was not trusted. Mary spent the rest of her nineteen years in England under supervision. The English government's qualms proved well-founded. Mary repeatedly conspired to take the throne from Elizabeth. After already being investigated twice during her residence in England, another trial was held in 1587 in which Mary was implicated in an assassination plot against Elizabeth. Found guilty of high treason, Mary was sentenced to death, and Elizabeth reluctantly signed her death warrant. On February 8, 1587, Mary was beheaded in Fotheringhay Castle. She was eventually buried in Westminister, and her son, James VI, claimed what Mary could not—the thrones of both England and Scotland.

Critical Overview

In his collection of essays *The Ballad as Song,* Bertrand Harris Bronson lists "Lord Randal" as one of the seven most popular ballads in the world. As he puts it, the popularity of this ballad and many others stems from its presentation of "love as a disease from which no one recovers." Louise Pound discusses the transformation of "Lord Randal" into several American ballads. She points out that it has been sung in all regions of the country, going through transitions that fit it to the culture in which it reappears. For example, in the nineteenth century it was sung in Colorado as a railway camp song about the tragic poisoning of "Johnny Randal" by his sweetheart. Though it has been popular for centuries, the listener never knows why Lord Randal's "true love" poisons him. In explanation, MacEdward Leach discusses "the tendency in the ballad to pass quickly over the first half of the plot—the unstable situation—to come to the second—the solution." He feels that listeners traditionally accept this lack of background information because they are "the folk [who] are not concerned with why, for they are not introspective or analytical. Rather they are concerned with the drama of the moment and the character's reaction to it." Leach reminds the reader that ballads belong to common folk who have kept them alive through the centuries, and these people enjoy the dramatic tension of an immediate encounter, such as this one between Lord Randal and his mother at their last meeting before his death.

Criticism

Carolyn Meyer

Carolyn Meyer holds a Ph.D. in modern British and Irish literature and has taught contemporary literature at several Canadian universities, including the University of Toronto. In the following essay, Meyer gives a general overview of the ballad form and a specific analysis of "Lord Randal."

By turns scandalous and heart-wrenching, the popular folk ballad known as "Lord Randal" rivals any of today's tabloid tales in its swift and urgent encapsulation of youthful passion, maternal jealousy, bitter rejection, murderous betrayal, and scornful reproach. Though it speaks to us today because of what it shares with the familiar mainstays of the popular press and also because of its timeless themes of love and death, its origins can be traced back as far as the fourteenth century, with its clearest antecedent coming from seventeenth-century Italy, where the song "L'Avvelenato" ("The Poisoned Man") popularized the story of a young man murdered by his mistress, according to Alfred B. Friedman in his *The Viking Book of Folk Ballads of the English-Speaking World.* Later, this narrative poem, by way of translation, made its way to England and Scotland. From there, the poem's perennial appeal spawned countless variants worldwide, even as far afield as Europe and Canada, with the young huntsman of the title going under an array of aliases—from Duranty and Durango in Oklahoma to Johnny Randolph in Virginia and McDonald in South Carolina. What is common to most versions is the standard ballad motif of the nuncupative testament (or spoken will) voiced by the murder victim himself who, as he dies, vows undying hatred and bequeaths not wealth but eternal damnation to the true love who ultimately proves so false. Helping to sustain the ballad narrative in a memorable way is the dialogue between mother and son that serves as its vehicle as well as the insistent strains of incremental repetition that add to its sense of immediacy and intensity. These qualities, combined with its subtle shifts in mood, help to make "Lord Randal" distinct within balladry and explain why scholar Bertrand Bronson lists it as third in his "top seven" Child ballads—poems collected by Francis J. Child in his landmark compilation, *The English and Scottish Popular Ballads.*

"Vivid, impersonal, dramatic and rhythmically simple," "Lord Randal" fits critic Ian Bold's definition of a genuine ballad. For centuries, even as far back as the Middle Ages, folk ballads existed not as written texts but as performances—songs to be sung, committed to memory and given new life with each retelling over the span of generations. Only in the past two centuries, when they became the objects of antiquarian curiosity, have ballads been collected and printed. They survive as living artifacts of illiterate and preliterate cultures, having been not so much transmitted as transmuted by the enriching variations that occur over time. Their style incorporates necessary aids to memory, such as rhyme and refrain, while their substance reflects the tragic and stoical conception of life held by the unlettered peoples responsible for their creation. Not surprisingly, their tunes are most often in minor keys.

Women are now believed to have been the prime custodians of the popular ballad tradition, handing down the "vulgar" old-wives' tales through the distaff side, yet as anonymous compositions, the origins of these poems remain a mystery, according to K. K. Ruthven, in an article in *Feminist Literary Theory: A Reader.* Among scholars, speculation continues as to whether they are the creations of individual entertainers—minstrels, for example—or the collective efforts of entire communities. Whatever the case, the ballad-poet keeps himself out of the poem, and on the rare occasions the personal pronoun "I" intrudes, it expresses a communal rather than subjective viewpoint—one that is not prone to moralizing or analyzing the characters' motives. Visceral, simple, and decidedly unsubtle, ballads speak to the heart rather than to the head. Whether they concern domestic crimes (such as adultery, battery, or abandonment), supernatural encounters, or the exploits of revered heroes or outlaws, all attention is focused on a single explosive situation—often a single, dramatic scene—for which there is little preparation and a minimum of amplifying detail. Ballads have a tendency of plunging almost immediately into the middle of the action, so that the climactic event or catastrophe becomes the point from which the episode unfolds. With the utmost brevity and intensity, events are shown as they happen, rather than simply being reported, aided in large part by liberal exchanges of dialogue that imply more than they ever assert. Since stock figures, accepted conventions, and formulaic phrases (such as "lily-white") predominate, there is little need for lengthy description. The momentum that drives the ballad toward its hasty and unhappy conclusion comes, in large part, from the insistent rhythms and predictable rhymes of its characteristic stanza types. The most common of these stanzas features alternating lines of four and three stresses each that acquire unity through the rhyming of the second and fourth lines. Ballads tell their stories with a few bold strokes that retain their essential character through countless variations.

The story of Lord Randal's untimely demise emerges through a limited sequence of events: his hunting expedition to the "wild wood"; his rendezvous with his true love; the dinner of poisoned

What Do I Read Next?

- Considered the most famous play in the English language, William Shakespeare's *Hamlet* was written between 1598 and 1602 and also involves death by poison.

- "Edward," an anonymous, medieval ballad, is very similar to "Lord Randal," with some stanzas almost matching word for word. However, there are enough differences to justify a study of the contrasting elements of the two ballads. Like "Lord Randal," "Edward" has one or two unsolved riddles nestled in the text.

- Randall Wallace's novel *Braveheart* (1995) takes place in the fourteenth century, a time England tightened its hold on Scotland and stripped Scottish lords of many privileges. Commoner William Wallace unites the Scots in a battle against England's King Edward II.

---

eels she prepares for him; his recounting of his predicament to his mother; his portioning out of his worldly goods; and his deathbed condemnation of his fickle former lover. Yet the ambiguity that surrounds these events and the lack of clear motives for them make the pathos of Lord Randal's situation more profound. Only gradually is the reader, like the young man's mother, made aware of the fact that weighs heavily on Lord Randal's mind from the moment he arrives home complaining of his weariness—that he is dying, not simply from his poisonous dinner but from the equally incurable heartache stemming from betrayal. The delay in breaking this news deepens its emotional impact and heightens the contrast between the poem's initial cheerfulness, reinforced through the buoyancy of its interspersed triple meters, and the bitter anguish that consumes the young nobleman by the end of the poem.

Not only does dialogue "bulk large" here, as Alfred B. Friedman observed of balladry in general in his introduction to *The Viking Book of Folk Ballads of the English-Speaking World,* but the entire poem is cast in the form of a single dialogue in which the mother poses the questions and her stricken son dutifully answers them. The mother's line of enquiry may be simply polite or rhetorical (an expression of her concern for her son), but it may well be more akin to a cross-examination—an expression of her possessiveness, over-protectiveness and jealousy at being relegated to second place in her son's affections. In the first four stanzas, as her identically phrased questions meet with his identically phrased replies, she is able to determine where he has been, whom has he been with, what he has eaten, and what has become of the hunting hounds that consumed his leftovers. At the poem's pivotal middle stanza, she briefly switches to the declarative mood to voice the suspicion "I fear ye are poisoned," a fact her son duly corroborates. But as ballad critic E. Flatto points out in an article in *Southern Folklore Quarterly,* "her solicitous inquiries" prove "unnecessary and superfluous; he has long known what she discloses as a supposedly novel revelation." In the brutal and comfortless world of "Lord Randal," even traditional authority figures, such as mothers, are incapable of responding to suffering with compassion or wise words of advice. What the dialogue counterpoints are two distinct outlooks on life: one based on materialism and an appreciation for nothing more than cold, hard fact; the other founded on an emotional reality where to be "sick at heart" from betrayal is a fate worse than death itself. The symmetry of the catechismal exchanges between the mother and her dying son in the first four and final four stanzas gives added emphasis to the central stanza that not only breaks the pattern but sounds the death knell of the title character. "Lord Randal," in this way, gives structural prominence to a sense of inevitability and foreboding—the stark fatalism for which ballads the world over are well known.

The iteration present in the mother's incessant demands for answers and her son's equally insistent demands for a bed that turns out to be a deathbed creates an ever-increasing and, by the end, almost unbearable sense of urgency and suspense. This technique, known as incremental repetition, is the poem's sole structuring principle—one that assists memory but also makes "Lord Randal" memorable within the general context of ballad literature. Incremental repetition involves minor substitutions or revision to repeated lines and phrases. It is by establishing, then altering the pattern that the story is advanced and monotony is broken. In "Lord Randal" only the first halves of the first and third lines alter stanza by stanza, so that the rest of the poem serves as a still point against which the narrative unfolds, the repeated lines carrying what Samuel Taylor Coleridge called the weight of emotion that "cannot be discharged in one saying." The minor successive changes to the last line of each stanza are vital in showing the deepening of Lord Randal's tragic self-awareness, as his self-described weariness—the natural consequence of a day's exertions—changes to metaphysical complaint, "For I'm sick at heart and fain would lie down." The meaning of the latter expands every time it is heard. Moreover, the refrain's regular recurrence, like the ticking of a clock, measures out the passage of time and serves as a reminder of what little time Lord Randal has left, according to Alfred Corn in *The Poem's Heartbeat: A Manual of Prosody*.

There is nothing, at the beginning, that would help to account for the evil that befalls the title character or indicate the sinister nature of the world into which he unwittingly ventures. In keeping with the epithets and character types that abound in ballad literature, everything about Lord Randal is youthful, hopeful, and innocent. He is "handsome" and adventurous—a man of action in quest of love. His undoing is to stray from the security of his home into the "wild wood," a place long associated with primal fears and the unconscious, a place of danger in the realm of fairy tale and folk belief. According to some versions of the poem, Lord Randal's encounter with his true love takes place in the "greenwood," traditionally the scene of "madmerry marriages" or secret assignations unsanctioned by the church that capped off May Day festivities. Despite the amorous associations of their meeting place, the exact nature of Lord Randal's relationship with his true love remains as shadowy, enigmatic, and mysterious as the woman herself. Her crime, a crime of passion rather than a culinary mishap, is all the more reprehensible and horrifying because, as E. Flatto observes, the lethal meal "masks its aggressive intent behind the traditional trappings of love." At the hands of a fatal female, Lord Randal becomes the unsuspecting victim of his own besotted trust, and nothing epitomizes that trust more than the image of the young huntsman feeding the fatal morsels to his hawks and his hounds. Neither the irony of the epithet "true-love" nor the imminence of his own death, foretold in the death of his dogs, is lost on him. When he returns home, reeling from rejection as much as from the effects of poison, it is with the knowledge that his former faith and optimism had been entirely misplaced and out of keeping with the rest of the world. He is not merely tired from phys-

> *Visceral, simple, and decidedly unsubtle, ballads speak to the heart rather than to the head."*

ical exertion, but tired of the world where such wickedness is possible. Restating the obvious, his confirmation of his affliction comes with characteristic ballad understatement—"O yes, I am poisoned, mother"—but that very understatement reinforces the tragic conception of life on which ballad literature is founded.

The final half of the poem is sustained by a ballad motif known as the nuncupative testament. Lord Randal is asked to designate the heirs to his belongings. He leaves his livestock to his mother, his cache of precious metal to his sister, and his property to his brother. With a parting irony, he reserves only contempt and vitriolic condemnation—"hell and fire"—for his homicidal paramour, leaving her what Alan Bold, in *The Ballad: The Critical Idiom,* calls "a curse rather than a commodity." It would seem that Lord Randal's final response is a forgone conclusion, but for his mother, whose curiosity is not only insatiable but cruel, her son's utter disenchantment is perverse proof that her rival for his affections has been unseated once and for all.

The incantational, almost obsessive quality of "Lord Randal," combined with the poignancy of a hero who must explain the circumstances of his death and see to the settlement of his estate, lifts the ballad to the level of classical tragedy. Lord Randal is a victim of fate just as he is a helpless witness to its slow, inevitable workings. In its melancholy and despair, "Lord Randal" conveys what the ballad folk knew all too well—that life is short and happiness is fleeting. In its brief span, it manages to contrast themes as expansive as "innocence and experience, trust and betrayal, love and rejection," according to Flatto. There are few happy endings in the realm of balladry, and "Lord Randal," in its hard-edged narrative of love gone wrong, of shattered illusions, and life cut short, is clearly no exception.

Source: Carolyn Meyer, in an essay for *Poetry for Students,* The Gale Group, 1999.

John E. Housman

In the following excerpt, Housman provides general information about traditional British ballads and comments on the existence of multiple versions of the Lord Randal story.

The ballad seems to have come into existence throughout these islands and all over Europe during the late Middle Ages, probably from the late fourteenth century onward. Occasional references to short, popular narrative poems are found before that date, but in the absence of extant texts it is impossible to prove that these poems were ballads in any real sense.

After the introduction of printing in the late fifteenth century a new kind of popular ballad came into existence. This is the so-called 'broadside,' or 'stall' ballad, printed on one side of a sheet of paper and hawked in the streets or sold from stalls at the big fairs....

The traditional British ballad of the late Middle Ages developed from two main sources—dance songs and narrative poems. The dance songs (Low Latin, *ballare*—to dance) and carols of early medieval France gave the traditional ballad its lyrical characteristics, such as the form of its stanza, its natural imagery, its refrain, and, above all, its close connexion with musical accompaniment. A study of these early dance songs and carols shows a close relationship with the ballad. We know, also, that the Danish ballad, not dissimilar from English and Scottish ballads in stanza-form, natural imagery, and refrain, originated under the influence of the French carol. In medieval Denmark a singer, accompanied by a fiddler, would recite a ballad, and the dancers in a ring round them would sing the refrain in time with their dancing. While some of the form and imagery of these earlier dance poems was preserved in later lyrical poetry, developments in poetic and musical technique tended to separate lyrical poetry and music, from the latter half of the seventeenth century onward. The simpler traditional ballad, however, enjoyed by a less sophisticated public than the lyric, could retain its tune; and ballad text and ballad tune continued as a unit well into the nineteenth century. The relatively simple forms of the ballad stanza and the frequent occurrence of refrains helped to preserve this unity....

If medieval French dance songs and carols gave the ballad its lyrical characteristics, much of its earliest subject-matter, and even its general attitude to such problems as war, love, and the supernatural, were derived from older narratives, such as the Germanic epic, the French *chanson de geste,* and the medieval romance. Later ballads continued this tradition, even when their subjects were derived from other sources.

The ballad public was not found in the great courts, but in smaller feudal castles and manor houses, and in the village communities dependent on them. Entertainment was supplied by the travelling minstrel, who moulded the long narratives of epic and romance, suitable only for leisurely circles, into the crisper and more economic form of the ballad narrative. Sung in this fashion, stories were acceptable to the village community; they were easily remembered, and they survived through centuries on the lips of gifted singers. Many of the stories from which these ballads derive were lost. Frequently divergent forms of the ballad remained. When in the eighteenth and nineteenth centuries collectors recorded these ballads from men and women of no literary pretensions, sometimes not even literate, they were faced with a poetic form of uncertain age and authorship, yet clearly with considerable claims of an aesthetic kind. While many ballads did not derive from romances or similar long narratives, but related an event in history, a local feud or love story, they were composed by gifted individuals, working in the tradition of ballad-making and were then transmitted from one singer to another. In this way, such ballads survived on the lips of the people, and, though based on written sources, in course of time they became the property of the people who sang them, moving further and further away from their literary origins. In this sense the traditional ballad is oral literature, and as oral literature it should be sung and heard, not read silently.

If we are right in suggesting that ballads were originally composed for the entertainment of the baron and his company, or for the village community so closely linked with feudal society, and that many of our best ballads were collected from the lips of villagers, it seems clear that the ballad supplied musical and verbal entertainment for rural communities, especially valuable in the absence of instrumental music and written literature. In order to fulfil its function as entertainment the ballad had to deal with many possible emotions, and, in fact, its scope varied from the intensely tragic to the broadly humorous, from the sweetly delicate to the starkly terrible. Even if the events narrated were in many cases either timeless or of the past, their setting and the treatment accorded to them were not, on the whole, as unsuitable for the men and women of the village as are the setting and sophisticated treatment of urban literature. We shall find that the overwhelming majority of ballads are set in the country or in the castles of the lesser nobility, while the treatment of the story is fundamentally unreflective, with an absence of that philosophical and speculative generalization dependent on greater leisure than village life permits....

English and Scottish balladry is also particularly rich in tragic ballads, in the sense that, as in Scandinavian ballads, the terrible effects of passion and unbalanced emotion are faced without too frequent sentimental evasion. The result is sometimes a starkness which invites comparison with the greatest narrative poetry....

It is, perhaps, not surprising that tragic power is frequently found in ballads dealing with one or other aspect of love....

In assessing the value of the traditional ballad as poetry, it should be remembered that the ballad is a true and separate form of poetry, not a miniature epic or a lyric with narrative additions....

It has been shown that the ballad poet, with his gift for compression, ignores the antecedents of his characters. The vicissitudes of biographical development cannot be coerced into the limits of the ballad, where the climax of a sharp and sudden conflict between characters counts for everything, and the antecedents and motivations of such conflicts for infinitely less. We do not know precisely why the mistress of Lord Randal poisons her lover. We have no idea what lies behind the wonderful opening of *The Dowy Houms O Yarrow*....

But we willingly accept the facts because we move in a poetic form defined by the immediacy of story-telling. Ballad heroes and heroines are committed to action for good or ill. They act freely and spontaneously, and their action defines the quality of balladry. That such action involves them again and again in tragic situations has its cause in the essentially unsentimental temper of the ballad, in the deep realization of the ballad poet that strife and struggle in human relationships lead to irretrievable loss and sorrow....

Conflict between certain groups of individuals is taken for granted within the poetic form of the ballad. The world of the bride's or the bridegroom's family and the world of the lovers, in their sentiments of authority and love respectively, are contrasted in such ballads as *Earl Brand, Clerk Saunders,* and *The Cruel Brother,* and the hatred of the bride's brothers for the bridegroom, in the choice of whom they were not consulted, needs no motivation. It is an emotion accepted for poetic purposes by the ballad poet and his public. The psychological motive is nothing; the sudden clash brought about by the contrast between the world of authority and the world of love is everything. The same insistence on the clash of two attitudes appears in dramatic vividness in ballads of outlaws and reivers as the clash between the world of the outlaw, with his own moral codes, and the world of civic law and order.

The central importance of this clash of values is enhanced by the impersonal attitude to his story of the ballad poet, who commonly leaves the hearer to draw his own conclusions. Pity, compassion, and horror are rarely forced upon the reader by an explicit statement, even though at times one may sense where the poet's sympathies lie....

By being impersonal and objective the ballad gains enormously....

Closely related to this objectivity of the traditional ballad is its dramatic power, a natural basis for poetry dealing with conflicts of opposed interests. Some of our finest ballads, *Edward* and *Lord Randal* among them, consist entirely of highly dramatic dialogue employing conversation of a stylized character with consummate success....

On the formal side one of the most obvious features of the traditional ballad is its tendency towards repetition of phrases, so that verses and half-stanzas are repeated in the same ballad or even transferred to different ballads. This feature of repetition seems to fulfil two different purposes: within one and the same ballad it helps to knit the ballad together and serves as an obvious help to memory; secondly—and this applies particularly to repetition of epithets such as "bonnie," "fair," "sweet," and to the repetition of stock comparisons, "as green as any grass," "as white as morning milk"—it offered the ballad poet the continuity of a poetic tradition in which he could move conveniently....

With regard to the form of the ballad, there existed for the ballad poet certain accepted metres, dictated in the main by musical considerations, and developed from the metrical forms of the medieval French carols and dance lyrics. Ballad metres vary considerably, but they vary within certain limits of length of line and length of stanza; extremes are, on the whole, avoided. The four-line stanza, composed of alternating four- and three-beat lines, with or without refrain, gives us the traditional metre....

Usually only the second and fourth lines rhyme. This stanza-form is capable of great variation, in accordance with the tune of the ballad.

There is no strict rule of alternating an accented with an unaccented syllable or vice versa; half-accents and hypermetric syllables are constantly found; musical considerations override regularity; but, on the other hand, the four-line stanza remains a clearly recognizable form, eminently suitable for compressed narrative.

As might be suspected in a form of poetry with such strong lyrical tendencies, traditional ballads are rich in lines of high poetic quality, quite apart from the power of their refrain or the lyrical effect of the whole poem....

[A] considerable number of our traditional ballads enjoy international currency, in the sense that many Continental ballads resemble British ballads in plot, treatment, turn of phrase, and often in melody. Nor is such resemblance due to the simple descent of Continental versions from British ones or vice versa. The problem is more complex, ...

Lord Randal, the extraordinarily moving ballad in dialogue of the young man poisoned by his sweetheart, presents us with ... [A] fascinating problem. This fine ballad, which seems at first so typically Scottish, "has been found," to quote Professor Gerould, "as far East as CzechoSlovakia and Hungary, as far North as Scotland and Sweden and as far South as Calabria," and there are innumerable North American versions. We know that it was known in Italy over three hundred years ago, and it is worth while comparing in detail the Italian version, noted down in the middle of the nineteenth century, with the Scottish ballad. Not only does the Italian version agree with the Scottish ballad point for point in the dialogue treatment of the story and in the outline of the plot—the return of the poisoned youth to his mother, the questioning, the confessions of the visit to his sweetheart, the meal of eels or snakes and its effect on the dogs, the testament of the dying youth—but both versions show complete agreement as to the structural arrangement and the musical character of each stanza. To show this more clearly we give the Scottish and Italian versions ...

Scottish (2nd stanza)
"And wha met ye there
Lord Randal, my son?
And wha met you there
My handsome young man?"

Italian (1st stanza)
"Where have you been yesternight,
My son, dear, handsome and wise?
Where have you been yesternight?"

Scottish (2nd stanza)

"O I met wi my true-love
Mother, mak my bed soon;
For I am wearied wi hunting,
And fain wad lie down."

Italian (1st stanza)
"I have been at my lady's
Mother, I am sick at heart,
I have been at my lady's
Alas, I am dying, alas."

Structural agreement could scarcely go further, and the stylized and at the same time caressing address of the mother to her son in the Italian version is found with equal effect in another Scottish version, where the mother calls him tenderly "my jollie young man." That there may exist a close connexion between the English and Italian versions is indicated by the fact that the victim of the poisoning is called by the Italian-sounding names of Tiranti, Tyranty, and Teronto in certain North American versions, instead of Randal, or Roland. But quite apart from Italian, British, and American ballads, German, Scandinavian, and other versions show the same treatment of the ballad in plot, form, and essential structure; and, while the relation of poisoner, poisoned, and interrogator varies (sometimes a child is poisoned by his step-mother or grandmother, sometimes a husband, poisoned by a mistress, speaks to his wife) there can be no doubt that we deal with the same ballad, yet there is no clear way to tell where the ballad originated....

Where, as with many parallel ballads existing in different countries we deal with clear cases of borrowing and conscious imitation, the question of how ballads travelled from one country to the other is of special importance. Now it seems clear that in the past when ballad singing was a common accomplishment ... ballads must have spread from country to country in a great variety of ways: sailors bringing wine from Bordeaux to English ports, pilgrims visiting shrines in strange lands, apprentices seeking experience abroad, artisans fleeing from religious persecution, minstrels, international by their very profession—all these doubtless helped to spread a knowledge of ballads.

Source: John E. Housman, introduction to *British Popular Ballads,* Freeport, NY: Books for Libraries Press, 1969, pp. 13-40.

Sources

Bird, S. Elizabeth, "'Lord Randal' in Kent: The Meaning and Context of a Ballad Variant," *Folklore,* Vol. 96, No. 2, 1985, p. 248.

Bold, Alan, *The Ballad: The Critical Idiom,* London: Methuen, 1979, p. 27.

Bronson, Bertrand Harris, "About the Most Favorite British Ballads," in *The Ballad As Song,* University of California Press, 1969.

Cannon, John, and Ralph Griffiths, *The Oxford Illustrated History of the British Monarchy,* New York: Oxford University Press, pp. 299-345.

Child, Francis J., *The English and Scottish Popular Ballads,* 5 vols., Boston, 1882-1898, reprinted by Cooper Square, 1965.

Corn, Alfred, *The Poem's Heartbeat: A Manual of Prosody,* Brownsville, OR: Story Line Press, 1997, p. 104.

Flatto, E., "Lord Randal," *Southern Folklore Quarterly,* Vol. 34, 1970, p. 332.

Friedman, Alfred B., *The Viking Book of Folk Ballads of the English-Speaking World,* New York: Viking Press, 1966, pp. xix, xxi, 178.

Gies, Frances, and Joseph Gies, *Marriage and the Family in the Middle Ages,* New York: Harper & Row Publishers, 1987, pp. 13-14, 185.

Graves, Robert, *The White Goddess,* London: Faber, 1961, p. 398.

Harris, William H., and Judith S. Levey, eds., "Mary Queen of Scots," *The New Columbia Encyclopedia,* New York: Columbia University Press, 1975, pp. 1711-12.

Leach, MacEdward, *The Ballad Book,* Harper, 1955.

MacDiarmid, Hugh, ed., *The Golden Treasury of Scottish Poetry,* Miami: Granger Books, 1940, pp. 110-112.

Mackie, R. L., *A Short History of Scotland,* edited by Gordon Donaldson, New York: Frederick A. Praeger, Inc., 1962, pp. 100-47.

"Mary, Queen of Scotland," *DISCovering World History,* Gale, 1998.

Pound, Louise, *Poetic Origins and the Ballad,* Russell and Russell, 1962.

Power, Eileen, *Medieval People,* New York: HarperCollins Publishers, 1963, pp. 158-162.

Ruthven, K. K., "Feminist Literary Studies," *Feminist Literary Theory: A Reader,* edited by Mary Eagleton, Oxford: Blackwell, 1986, p. 93.

Shakespeare, William, "Othello," in *The Complete Works of Shakespeare,* New York: Dorset Press, 1988, pp. 818-57.

For Further Study

Gies, Frances, and Joseph Gies, *Marriage and the Family in the Middle Ages,* New York: Harper & Row Publishers, 1987.

> Frances and Joseph Gies provide an overview of the life of the family unit throughout the rise and decline of medieval Europe. This work discusses the lifestyles and struggles of the family within each social class, taking into account such events as the Black Death. This is a very insightful work that gives the reader a true sense of life during the Middle Ages.

Leach, MacEdward, ed., *The Ballad Book,* New York: A.S. Barnes and Company, Inc., 1955.

> In this anthology of American, Scottish, English, and Danish ballads, Leach presents as many variant forms of each poem as possible to promote comparative analysis. This work is full of historical information about each ballad.

MacDiarmid, Hugh, ed., *The Golden Treasury of Scottish Poetry,* Miami: Granger Books, 1940.

> This is a comprehensive anthology of Scottish poetry from the early Middle Ages to the 1900s. It is an excellent text for any student who wishes to become more familiar with reading and understanding the Scottish language.

Power, Eileen, *Medieval People,* New York: HarperCollins Publishers, 1963.

> This work provides one of the most insightful glimpses into the Middle Ages available. Focusing on six individuals from the Middle Ages, Power delves into the personal histories of actual people from different social classes in medieval Europe. This work provides answers to the questions regarding everyday life in the Middle Ages.

"More Light! More Light!"

Anthony Hecht

1967

Poet Anthony Hecht may be said to suffer from Weltschmerz, which the *American Heritage Dictionary* defines as "sadness over the evils of the world ...." Hecht served as a soldier during World War II and encountered painful evidence of the atrocities committed at the Nazi death camp at Buchenwald. This experience plays a role in "'More Light! More Light!" as well as several other poems in Hecht's Pulitzer Prize-winning volume, *The Hard Hours* (1967). From title and dedication to poem's conclusion, "'More Light! More Light!'" involves a dying man's plea, a reference to a woman who wrote about the "banality of evil," and the murders of four individuals whose only guilt was not sharing the same religious beliefs or ethnic backgrounds as their executioners. A central issue of this poem is why Hecht attempts to create poetry out of horrifying incidents. Indeed, cultural critic Theodor Adorno made a famous and oft-quoted statement: "After Auschwitz, no poetry." Hecht not only defies that directive, but his poetry broaches the subject, the Holocaust, that caused such a disheartened conclusion—that art should not survive atrocity. This disturbing poem may leave readers with the lingering question of why Hecht chose the topics he did. The poet, however, seems to imply that this focus is skewed. Why should the poem, because of its subject matter, be questioned when the actual incidents that prompted it appear to have been, albeit sadly, accepted? Why would anyone tolerate barbarity over art?

Author Biography

Anthony Hecht was born on January 16, 1923, in New York City. In 1944, he graduated from Bard College in New York. For the next three years—during World War II—he served as a rifleman with the U.S. Army, both in Europe and Japan. Later he served in the Counter-Intelligence Corps, in which capacity he bore witness, at the end of the war, to the mass graves outside of the Buchenwald death camp. This experience was to greatly influence what are arguably Hecht's most stunning poems. At war's end, Hecht taught at Kenyon College in Ohio, where he studied with the poet and new critic John Crowe Ransom. Hecht also tutored under members of a group of writers at Vanderbilt University known as the Fugitives, among whom were Allen Tate, Robert Penn Warren, and their teacher, Ransom. In 1950, Hecht earned his master's degree from Columbia University, and in 1954, his first volume of poetry, *The Summoning of Stones,* was published. In that same year he married, and eventually had two sons. Hecht married again in 1971 and had one more son.

Hecht's career includes a long line of teaching posts and awards. He has taught at Kenyon, the State University at Iowa, Smith College, Bard, and the University of Rochester, where he was the John H. Dean Professor of Poetry and Rhetoric from 1967 to 1982. In 1982 he was named poetry consultant to the Library of Congress, and in 1984, he took a teaching post at Georgetown University. His awards include a Pulitzer in 1968 for *The Hard Hours* (1967), the volume from which "More Light! More Light!" is taken; a Bollingen Prize (1983); the Eugenio Montale Award; the Academy of American Poets Award; and grants from the Guggenheim and Ford Foundations. He has also received numerous honorary doctorates. Perhaps the most important honor bestowed on Hecht was an invitation to present the A.W. Mellon Lectures in the Fine Arts at the National Gallery of Art in Washington D.C.; it was the first time such an invitation went to an American poet.

Poem Text

For Heinrich Blücher and Hannah Arendt

Composed in the Tower, before his execution
These moving verses, and being brought at that
time

Anthony Hecht

Painfully to the stake, submitted, declaring thus:
"I implore my God to witness that I have made no
    crime."

Nor was he forsaken of courage, but the death was   5
    horrible,
The sack of gunpowder failing to ignite.
His legs were blistered sticks on which the black
    sap
Bubbled and burst as he howled for the Kindly
    Light.

And that was but one, and by no means one of the
    worst;
Permitted at least his pitiful dignity;   10
And such as were by made prayers in the name of
    Christ,
That shall judge all men, for his soul's tranquility.

We now move to outside a German wood
Three men are there commanded to dig a hole
In which the two Jews are ordered to lie down   15
And be buried by the third, who is a Pole.

Not light from the shrine at Weimar beyond the
    hill
Nor light from heaven appeared. But he did refuse.
A Lüger settled back deeply in its glove.
He was ordered to change places with the Jews.   20

Much casual death had drained away their souls.
the thick dirt mounted toward the quivering chin.
When only the head was exposed the order came
To dig him out again and to get back in.

No light, no light in the blue Polish eye. 25
When he finished a riding boot packed down the
    earth
The Lüger hovered lightly in its glove.
He was shot in the belly and in three hours bled to
    death.

No prayers or incense rose up in those hours
Which grew to be years, and every day came mute 30
Ghosts from the ovens, sifting through crisp air,
And settled upon his eyes in a black soot.

Poem Summary

Title:

The quotation marks around the phrase "More Light! More Light!" signify that Hecht is borrowing it from another source. Indeed, we discover that celebrated German poet and dramatist Johann Wolfgang von Goethe allegedly uttered these words on his deathbed. Immediately, the poem's title—a dying man's plea—sets a somber mood for the poem.

Dedication:

Hecht inscribes his poem to Heinrich Blücher and Hannah Arendt, a couple who left Germany and immigrated to the United States in 1941. Arendt was a leading political philosopher, perhaps best known for her works *Origins of Totalitarianism* and *Eichmann in Jerusalem: A Report on the Banality of Evil.* A second reference to Germany before the poem even begins, as well the knowledge that Arendt wrote about Nazi ideology, leads the reader to believe that the poem will focus on this place and subject.

Lines 1-4:

Despite the setup of the title and dedication, the poem opens in sixteenth-century England. While the syntax of this stanza is confusing, the meaning is clear: a prisoner held in the Tower of London awaits execution by writing poetry. Then the unrepentant man is transported to a place where he will be burned at the stake. Hecht plays on the word "submitted"—in one sense it is related to the man submitting his verses to his executioners; the other referring to the man submitting to his executioners even as he protests his innocence.

Lines 5-8:

Despite his courage, the man suffers a horrible death. "The sack of gunpowder," according to Foxe's *Book of Martyrs,* was hung around the vic-

tim's neck to hasten death (the explosive powder would quickly cause the subject to be engulfed in flames). In this instance, however, the gunpowder fails to ignite and the victim slowly burns, his agony emphasized by the comparison of his legs to pieces of hot-burning, sap-filled wood. The "Kindly Light" likely refers to God's salvation; this phrase derives from a hymn titled "Lead, Kindly Light," which was composed in 1833 by John Henry Newman.

Lines 9-12:

After the gruesome imagery of the preceding stanza, the speaker provides the unsettling information that this was only one of numerous executions and that others were actually worse. One reason the victim's suffering is downplayed is because he was allowed a shred of purported dignity by speaking his peace before dying. Furthermore, the victim's soul was prayed for by onlookers.

Lines 13-16:

The scene now shifts to "a German wood." Based on the details of the task described ("dig[ing] a hole") and the designation "Jews," we realize that the events are taking place during World War II and that three men—two Jews and one Pole—are digging a grave. The Pole is then ordered to bury the Jews alive.

Lines 17-20:

The word "light" appears once again, but this time it refers to the illumination from "The shrine at Weimar," a museum dedicated to Johann Wolfgang von Goethe that is not far from the Buchenwald concentration camp. Goethe, a poet, novelist, and dramatist, was "widely recognized as the greatest writer of the German tradition," according to Jane K. Brown in *Dictionary of Literary Biography*. Weimar, the small town in which Goethe lived, was a cultural center during his lifetime and for decades afterward. More than a hundred years after Goethe's death, the Pole receives neither strength and inspiration from Goethe's shrine nor the light of heavenly salvation; however, he still refuses to kill the Jews. For this act of defiance, a German soldier, represented only by his Lüger—a German automatic pistol—and glove (a trope known as synecdoche), orders the Pole to switch places, lie down in the grave, and await being buried alive by the Jews.

Lines 21-24:

The Jews, already demoralized and stripped of any will to resist, follow orders and bury the Pole up to his "quivering" chin. His fear is evident, yet he stoically accepts his fate. But before the Jews finish, the soldier orders them to dig out the Pole and switch places with him.

Lines 25-28:

Line 25, "No light, no light in the blue Polish eye," echoes the poem's title, "'More Light! More Light!'" At the moment preceding death, Goethe shouted the plea that serves as the title, suggesting that the absence of light is tantamount to death. That light has extinguished from the Pole's eye implies that he is already dead—that the trauma he has just endured and the unspeakable act he is forced to commit have obliterated his spirit. As if out of respect and to avoid blaming the Pole, Hecht does not describe him burying the Jews alive; he only uses the words "when he finished." Afterward, the soldier shoots the Pole in the stomach so he will bleed to death, slowly and agonizingly.

Lines 29-32:

Unlike the sixteenth-century English martyr, the Pole and the Jews offer no last words nor are they prayed for—either verbally or in the form of incense lit as offering to God. The Pole is not even buried. The "mute / Ghosts from the ovens" are Jews who been cremated at Buchenwald and comprise the soot that descends to cover Pole's body. The image of soot settling upon the Pole could convey the smothering of decency and courage by the evils of Nazism. The detail that the corpse's eyes are covered is significant, because not only has the light extinguished from the eyes, but a "black soot" (that blocks light) is covering them.

Themes

Death

Death is the most obvious theme of "'More Light! More Light!'" The title, itself, comes from the last words of a dying man. The prisoner burned at the stake was a heretic, or someone who holds a religious opinion that is in opposition with church dogma. Hecht's own note to the poem verifies this: "The details [of the execution] are conflated from several executions, including Latimer and Ridley whose deaths at the stake are described by Foxe in *Actes and Monuments* (1563). But neither of them wrote poems just before their deaths, as others did." In Mary Tudor's attempt to turn England back to Catholicism, the state ruthlessly murdered those who did not go along; in the early 1550s, some 300 people were burned for their beliefs. During World War II, death was carried out by the Nazis on a massive scale. Six million Jews were killed in the Holocaust, a figure estimated as two thirds of the European Jewish population. Two million Poles and Slavs were also murdered by Nazis. (There were other victims, including Gypsies, Soviet prisoners of war, and a quarter of a million mentally and physically disabled people.)

Victims and Victimization

In the English execution, the victim is burned because his difference in belief matters (recall that Latimer and Ridley were bishops). The victim is granted last words and retains his courage even when the burning is protracted. The auto-da-fé (another word that means "the burning of a heretic) is carried out in public and with some ceremony. However, the victim retains some dignity, as prayers are said for him. The executions in Germany, however, are quite different. The victims are ordinary citizens who are not executed for their beliefs or official position, but for their identity. The Jews appear neither to proclaim their innocence or even to speak; they seem to have lost all courage and dignity. The Pole's last words are a courageous protest, but one not lasting long—he too is worn down by the fear of being buried alive. These executions seem completely private—almost secretive—and it seems amazing that the event was ever discovered. The incident is based on a real story told by Eugen Kogon, a survivor of Buchenwald, in his book *The Theory and Practice of Hell*. From Kogon, we find out that the murders took place at Buchenwald, the concentration camp near Goethe's former hometown of Weimar. Some critics believe

Topics for Further Study

- Discuss why a heretic would be afforded the right to speak before being executed. Then discuss the Nazi soldier's actions in regard to the Pole.

- Use synecdoche (in this case, the trope where parts stand for the whole and not vice versa) to describe a person or object and have others guess who or what is being described.

- Consult the poem "Tichborne's Elegy" (1586), written by Chidiock Tichborne who wrote the elegy for himself while in the Tower of London before he was hanged, drawn, and quartered for being implicated in the Babington Conspiracy to murder Queen Elizabeth. Try to find other poems written in the Tower before execution. A good place to begin is *The Actes and Monuments of John Foxe.* Why would someone write a poem before being executed?

that because of the difference between the executions, the burning at the stake is less tragic.

Dignity and Salvation

In the case of the English prisoner, he was afforded last words which took the form of a final protest. Did this soothe him in any way? Uttering the protest might have bestowed a small measure of dignity on the man; he was granted the opportunity to be heard. And did the prayers of those who witnessed the execution lead to the heretic's salvation? While the question cannot be answered, it could be argued that salvation resides less in assurances of salvation than in the hope of salvation. Some comfort therefore might have been afforded the Englishman. As for the Pole, he showed dignity by initially refusing the soldier's order. And the silent Jews? Their dignity, as Hecht says, was already "drained away." For all three individuals, it is possible that silence was the only tatter of dignity left them. As to prayer by witnesses, the fact there was none at the murder of the Jews and Pole is, for some, a problem for the salvation of Jewish

and Polish souls. This is a more Catholic than Protestant or Jewish view, Catholics believing their relationship to God is mediated by others—church officials or members. For religious Protestants and Jews, there is always a witness to killings—God. This condition, makes it quite difficult to say whether the publicly executed and vocal Englishman was afforded more dignity and salvation that the privately executed and silent Jews, or the privately executed and temporarily courageous Pole.

Style

Anthony Hecht's "'More Light! More Light!'" consists of eight quatrains of more or less regular iambic pentameter. In lines one and two, however, two feet are not iambic. They consist of two unstressed syllables followed by a stressed one: "in the **tow**er" and "at that **time**." This pattern is defined as an anapest. Other lines have other variations of feet, such as two stresses placed together—"**black sap**"—which is known as a "spondee." The rhyme scheme for every stanza is *abcb,* though there are the near-rhymes of "earth" and "death" (in stanza 7) and also "mute" and "soot" (in stanza 8). The endings of the rhymed lines are called "masculine," since the last syllable in each is accented (feminine endings are unaccented). In addition, masculine rhymes primarily involve one-syllable words, whereas feminine rhymes consist of two or more syllables (as in the rhyme of "dignity" and "tranquility") There are also instances of both assonance ("black sap") and alliteration ("Bubbled and burst"). One other technique of note is Hecht's use of synecdoche, a use of words whereby parts stand for the whole or vice versa. Hecht employs synecdoche when describing the Nazi soldier with the words "Lüger," "glove," and "boot."

Historical Context

Hecht's "'More Light! More Light!'" was published in 1967. In the United States, the late 1960s was one of the most dynamic and violent times the nation had seen since the end of the Civil War. The war in Vietnam drove millions of citizens, many of them young college students, into opposition against the federal government, and the frustration of urban blacks boiled over into race riots. Assas-

Compare & Contrast

- **1967:** Israeli forces mount successful, surprise air and ground attacks on Egypt, Jordan, Syria, and Iraq in the Six-Day War (the third Arab-Israeli War), destroying most of their opponent's air force and completely defeating their ground forces. Israelis take the Sinai Peninsula, the Jordanian-held portions of Jerusalem, the West Bank, and the Golan Heights, which they continued to occupy; no peace treaty ended the war.

  1999: The United States and Germany announce a tentative agreement to compensate 240 U.S. survivors of Nazi concentration camps. They stand to receive about $100,000 each.

- **1967:** Ché Guevara, one of the leaders of the Cuban Revolution (1959) who, with Fidel Castro, toppled dictator Fulgencio Batista, is executed after fighting the Bolivian military that had recently overthrown the government.

  1999: A right-wing death squad outlawed by the Columbian government guns down, execution-style, fourteen people, raising the death toll for three days to sixty.

- **1967:** Civil war begins in Nigeria (1967-70), as the Christian and animist Ibos of Biafra secede from Muslim-dominated Nigeria. The war would result in the loss of between 1.5 million and 2 million people, many of them children and most of them noncombatants who died of famine and famine-induced disease while government forces blocked international relief supplies.

  1998: In Rwanda, during the course of the year, 864 people are tried for the 1994 genocide in which 500,000 to one million are slaughtered in the Hutu government's attempt to wipe out the Tutsi minority. Civil war follows the 1994 genocide, and the Tutsi Rwandan Patriotic Front defeat the Rwandan military which, with an estimated two million Hutus, flee Rwanda into neighboring countries.

---

sinations of two major political figures, not two months apart, stunned the nation.

Dr. Martin Luther King, Jr., was murdered on April 4, 1968. King was one of the principal leaders of the civil rights movement in the United States, a staunch advocate of nonviolent protest who is remembered by a national holiday on the third Monday of every January. Dr. King rose to national attention in 1954, as the leader of the famous boycott against the bus system of Montgomery, Alabama, where black citizens had only been allowed to ride in the backs of buses. The following year, when the Southern Christian Leadership Conference was formed, he was named its president. He was a leader of nonviolent protests against segregation throughout the South, facing death threats and spending time in jail. In 1963, he was one of the organizers of the march on Washington and delivered his famous "I Have A Dream" speech before a crowd of 200,000. These public, peaceful displays of African-American determination for equal rights and the violent opposition of some whites to their reasonable demands helped President Lyndon Johnson gain support for the Civil Rights Act of 1964 and the Voting Rights Act of 1965. Near the end of his life, Dr. King did have opponents: black separatists, represented most visibly in 1968 by the formation of the Black Panthers, did not approve of King's nonviolent tactics or his willingness to work with whites on racial problems, and the director of the Federal Bureau of Investigation, J. Edgar Hoover, waged an almost fanatical crusade of spying on King and spreading propaganda against him, fearful that he might become a black "messiah" who would lead the overthrow of the white race. When Dr. King was shot in Memphis, riots broke out in most major cities in the country, including Baltimore, Boston, Chicago, Detroit, Kansas City, Newark and Washington D.C. Forty-six deaths resulted. In Chicago, Mayor Richard Daley issued orders for police to "shoot to kill" looters who broke store windows. National Guard troops were mobilized in many states, and 21,270 people were arrested.

On June 5, 1968, with the shock of the King assassination still fresh, the nation was stunned once again when presidential candidate Robert Kennedy was gunned down while campaigning in Los Angeles. He was the brother of former President John F. Kennedy and had been the attorney general in his administration. His assassination was a frightening reminder of the trauma the country had felt five years earlier, when President Kennedy was killed. At the time of his death, Robert Kennedy had been the leading candidate for the presidency: he was young (42) and opposed to the war in Vietnam, and was favored by young voters, who were politically active and vocal but alienated from the system. His death, so soon after Dr. King's and so closely paralleling his popular brother's, became a symbol of great disillusionment to a generation that had believed in making the world a better place.

Protests against the Vietnam war took place regularly on college campuses throughout the late 1960s, and in August of 1968, at the Democratic National Convention in Chicago, thousands of protestors gathered, setting off a confrontation between police and radicals that became the image of what "the Sixties" means to many Americans. The protest was originally the idea of Abbie Hoffman, a youth leader and self-proclaimed "prankster" who, the previous New Year's Eve, had suggested to friends that they stop calling themselves "hippies" (the generic name for rebellious youth at that time, much like "beatniks" before them and "gangstas" after) and instead represent themselves as the Youth International Party, or Yippies. In Hoffman's plan, the Yippies would go to the Democratic Convention and demand representation. By August, word had spread from one antiwar organization to the next. The members of the peace movement were widely varied: some were committed to peace through peaceful means, some supported violence to end the war, and some treated it all with a sense of fun, relishing the chance to annoy their stuffy elders. In Chicago, though, all were considered serious threats—Chicago Mayor Richard Daley looked on the youths as terrorists who wanted to start a revolution to overthrow the government. Sixteen thousand Chicago police, 4,000 state troopers and 4,000 National Guardsmen were equipped with riot gear and posted around the hotel where the convention was held to face what turned out to be between 5,000 and 10,000 demonstrators. The "Festival of Life" that the war protestors had assembled for included rock concerts, marijuana smoking, public lovemaking and draft card burning. When the protesters threw bricks and bottles, the police responded by firing tear gas and swinging nightsticks. Participants later said that the whole situation felt like being at war, but observers who watched it on television saw kids and news reporters and uninvolved bystanders being clubbed and sprayed with gas by police, despite a frequent chant by the protestors reminding them that, "The whole world is watching." An independent commission studying the event later referred to it as a "police riot." Throughout the 1960s, America's security had declined, as the war and the never-ending struggle for civil rights eroded faith in the government: with men of peace gunned down and the military fighting against unarmed citizens, strange, irrational violence was all too familiar.

Critical Overview

One point at which polarized readings of Anthony Hecht's "'More Light! More Light!'" are produced concerns the character of the Pole. In an article titled "Comedy and Hardship," Edward Hirsch writes of the Pole's "impossible purity of action," but Daniel Hoffman, in his essay "Our Common Lot," makes a more controversial statement when he conjectures, "In the absence of the light of either Goethe's humanism or the Word, the Pole's refusal may suggest that he, like their Nazi captor, is too scornful of Jews to kill them himself." Hoffman seems to be one of few, if not only, critics to hold out the possibility the Pole is an anti-Semite. Another focus of criticism fixes on the comparison between the death of the Christian heretic of the first three stanzas, and the death of the triad of two Jews and one Pole in the last five stanzas. One strand of this thread divides between those who think the situations comparable in gravity ("there is nothing new under the sun" writes Alicia Ostriker in an article titled "Millions of Strange Shadows: Anthony Hecht as Gentile and Jew") and those reasoning that Jews and Pole suffer a worse fate than the heretic. Writing in *The Explicator*, Ellen Miller Casey sums up the case this way: "Hecht condemns not merely the infliction of pain but the destruction of the person—both victim and executioner. It is that destruction that makes the deaths in the German wood so much worse than the fiery death in the Tower."

Criticism

Bruce Meyer

Bruce Meyer is the director of the creative writing program at the University of Toronto. He has taught at several Canadian universities and is the author of three collections of poetry. In the following essay, Meyer looks at how Hecht is able to respectfully contradict Adorno's declaration, "After Auschwitz, no poetry."

The twentieth century has been an epoch of horror in which the ability to seize the poetic in the unspeakable has become less and less a possibility. In a famous statement, critical theorist Theodor W. Adorno declared, "After Auschwitz, no poetry." Indeed, it is remarkable that Anthony Hecht has found a way to express the horrors of this century in his own poetic forms; he was present at the liberation of the Nazi concentration camps and witnessed the atrocities first hand. He once commented that "the cumulative sense of these experiences is grotesque beyond anything I could possibly write." In many ways, Hecht's poetry—its blunt and courageous vision—faces the horrors of the world head on. His poems are not grotesques as much as they are confrontations of the terrible inhumanity that is the nightmare of history. For Hecht, writing is an act of courage because, as World War I poet Wilfred Owen suggested, the purpose of poetry is to bear witness and "the poetry is in the pity." In an effort not to shock but to reveal, Hecht stretches the role of the observer and the chronicler to new extremes, because the observer/chronicler of poetry, a figure who could once muse upon pleasant prospects or great acts of achievement, must now testify to the realities of the world and convey those realities to the reader. In this aspect, "'More Light! More Light!'" is a plea for a redefinition of the role of the poet—an eye-opening experience that begs the reader for greater scope.

In terms of poetic form, "'More Light! More Light!'" is written in a stanza where only the second and fourth lines rhyme. This "delayed" rhyme and the extended meter of certain lines postpones the sense of lyric connection. Thus, the lyricism is still present, though strained and somehow twisted by the intervention of the delaying tactics of the irregular rhythms. Poetically, the form seems to suggest that the lyricism of poetry is still possible but that it is under an enormous pressure—that art itself is under an enormous pressure to contain and express the horrors of the poet's discourse.

As a rhetorical structure, the poem moves through a series of stories. The first, the story of the execution of the Protestant martyr Latimer during the reign of the Catholic Queen Mary I of England, borrows from Foxe's *Book of Martyrs* the horrific description of the bishop being burned at the stake in Oxford in 1555. Here we are meant to see the

What Do I Read Next?

- The anthology *The Sixties Papers,* edited by Judith and Stewart Albert, consists of documents and essays by the leading lights of the sixties (C. Wright Mills, Allen Ginsberg, Malcolm X, etc.) and on the leading struggles (antiwar, counterculture, feminist). The volume is introduced with an overview of the 1950s.

- Hannah Arendt's *The Origins of Totalitarianism* (1951) consists of three volumes: *Antisemitism, Imperialism,* and *Totalitarianism.* The volumes cannot be overpraised and are recognized as the definitive account of the philosophical origins of the totalitarian mind.

- *Discipline and Punish: The Birth of the Prison* (1979), by Michel Foucault, presents a provocative study of how penal institutions became a part of everyday life. The book opens with a famous and graphic passage recounting an execution.

- Max Horkheimer and Theodor Adorno, two of the major theorists of what became known as The Frankfurt School, wrote the group's defining text, *The Dialectic of Enlightenment,* which was first released in 1947. The text includes sections on mass media and on anti-Semitism.

- Elain Scarry's *The Body in Pain: The Making and Unmaking of the World* (1985) is divided into three major subject areas: first, the difficulty of expressing physical pain; second, the political and perceptual complications arising as a result of that difficulty; and third, the nature of human creation. It is a highly original book.

death of the bishop as an act of faith, a martyrdom in the cause of belief. The painful consequences ("legs were blistered sticks on which the black sap / Bubbled and burst") of being burned alive at the stake when the "sack of gunpowder" failed "to ignite" and lessen the Bishop's suffering are mitigated, albeit just slightly, by the piety with which he suffers his death, howling for "the Kindly Light."

> *From Hecht's point of view there must be poetry, for poetry is one of the few instruments humanity has at its disposal to respond to the horrors of meaninglessness and negation that have gripped the century."*

"Dignity" is something that is "pitiful," though it is still dignity, and there is the underlying premise that suffering and death at least meant something in the savagery of the English Reformation. Latimer's death is seen as a signal not only of courage but also of the power of belief to overcome "the worst," so that "prayers in the name of Christ / Shall judge all men, for his soul's tranquility." In the way he meets his death, Latimer becomes a symbol of courage, and his death has meaning.

Such is not the case in the second story Hecht tells. "We move now to outside a German wood," Hecht tells his reader, as if the persona is the narrator in a documentary who is setting a shift in scene for the viewer. He recounts the story of the deaths of three men at the hands of the Nazis in a clearing near the Buchenwald concentration camp. The problem Hecht confronts in telling this story is that death is no longer a matter of belief, but simply an act of uncontrollable tyranny and sadism. When the Pole defies his oppressors and is ordered to trade places with the two Jews who are being buried alive, there is no grand or eloquent meaning beneath the act—it is merely a matter of courage and defiance in the face of evil. "No prayers or incense," writes Hecht, "rose up in those hours / Which grew to be years ..." The horrors of the twentieth century, the poet implies, are so massive and so universal that they are blanketed by a kind of indifference, an unanswerability where "mute / Ghosts from the ovens, sifting through crisp air, / ... settled upon his eyes in a black soot." Not only is the light of dignity extinguished in this modern world—there is an absence of spiritual meaning, the vacuum of which is impossible to fill.

Hecht tries to grasp the thin straw of civilization, the frail and tormented shards of what Freud called the "superego," the cloak upon the minds of men and women that was created to protect us from our base instincts and our own destructiveness. He does so in the title of the poem, " 'More Light! More Light!'," presumably the last words of the great German poet Wolfgang von Goethe. In works such as *The Sorrows of Young Werther* and *Herman and Dorothea*, Goethe attempted to show the individual as he or she grappled with the weight and the complexities of civilization, the purpose of man in nature, and the role of the human spirit in relation to the universe. In German literature, Goethe was the high point, the cultural zenith that became misplaced beneath the evolving militaristic tyranny that reached its apex under the Nazis. Weimar, the city closest to Buchenwald, was Goethe's home. The irony in all of this is really Hecht's attempts to show the breakdown of the superego in the twentieth century—the failure of civilization to save us from ourselves. And it is irony that Hecht uses as his most effective means of opening his reader's eyes. He has commented that irony "provides a way of stating very powerful and positive emotions and of taking, as it were, the heaviest possible stance toward some catastrophe."

That "heaviest stance" of which he speaks is found in the comparison between Goethe's dying request for "more light" and the light that seems to disappear from "the blue Polish eye" in the moment when courage can no longer sustain the individual. In this world, death is not a signal to create icons or trigger "prayers," but rather an act of callous indifference; yet it is the same experience suffered by Latimer. There are still the murderers and the victims. What has changed is the meaning of the deaths. In this, Hecht sounds a stern warning. What can civilization do to stop the process of inhumanity and victimization as well as to give back the modicum of dignity in which such deaths reinforced our values and our determination by providing us with some meaning?

The answer seems to be the poem itself. The poem and its frank address of such "grotesque" and horrific subject matter, its blunt language and eye-witness-style imagery, is meant to answer Adorno. From Hecht's point of view there must be poetry, for poetry is one of the few instruments humanity has at its disposal to respond to the horrors of meaninglessness and negation that have gripped the century. Hecht fears that "Much casual death has drained away their souls," that the aesthetics of violence, as suggested by such critics as A. Alvarez in his famous essay "The New Poetry or Against the Gentility Principle," will either acclimatize us to horror or awaken in us a revulsion to it. The poet must believe the latter. Hecht, a poet whose craftsmanship and care with his verses belie a courageous belief in the power of civilization, offers the poem as one of the few valid responses to the twentieth century. What is amazing is that in this vision of inhumanity there is still the possibility of lyricism, there is still that rhyme in every second line that is neither trivial nor trite but which speaks of the last few straws we have to grasp in our arsenal of answers to the forces of negation. The title, Goethe's request for light in the face of interminable darkness, is actually a cry for poetry—a cry that Hecht answers with honesty, even courage, to confront that which is least poetic on its own harsh terms and to answer it with the faint hope of music in silence and light in darkness.

Source: Bruce Meyer, in an essay for *Poetry for Students,* The Gale Group, 1999.

David Caplan

David Caplan is a doctoral candidate at the University of Virginia. In the following essay, Caplan considers " 'More Light! More Light!' " in the context of other writing about the Holocaust.

"To write poetry after Auschwitz is barbaric," cultural critic Theodor Adorno declared. Indeed, the Holocaust caused many to wonder about the value of culture, as Germany, one of the West's most literate, well-educated countries, used its collective wisdom to murder large numbers of Jews, Gypsies, and other "undesirables." Did lessons learned from the arts make the Germans into better murderers, not people? If so, poetry bore some of the blame for the carnage. Does it follow then that, as Adorno believed, "it has become impossible to write poetry today"?

Of course poets are disinclined to agree. However, even those who continue to compose poetry after Auschwitz find the Holocaust to be an uncomfortable subject for their art. To write about an event as awful as the Holocaust is to risk trivializing it. After all, a poem gives pleasure to both its writer and its readers. Pleasure, though, is the last emotion that a genocide should inspire.

Yet poets do write about the Holocaust, at least partly because its very awfulness demands remembrance. Among the many poems written on this subject is W. D. Snodgrass's *The Fuehrer Bunker: The Complete Cycle,* a series of lyrics from the perspectives of Nazi leaders such as Adolph

Indeed, the setting of 'More Light! More Light!' is crucial, as the depicted action transpires at both a concentration camp and a scene of great cultural achievement."

Hitler, Heinrich Himmler, and Hermann Goering. In this sequence, Snodgrass, a contemporary American poet, attempts to understand Nazism by humanizing it—that is, by trying to imagine how people committed what seem to be such incomprehensibly evil acts.

Anthony's Hecht's " 'More Light! More Light!' " uses a different strategy. The poem's title and dedications quickly signal its intentions. The title quotes the last words of Johann Wolfgang von Goethe, Germany's greatest poet. This allusion suggests how Hecht's poem explores the close connections between German culture and the Holocaust. The dedication is to Henrich Blücher and Hannah Arendt, a couple who escaped the Nazi persecution by immigrating to America in 1941. The dedication to Arendt, a leading political philosopher, is particularly important. In addition to her 1951 study, *Origins of Totalitarianism,* she wrote *Eichmann in Jerusalem: A Report on the Banality of Evil.* In this book, Arendt describes Eichmann, one of the executioners of Hitler's "final solution," not as an extraordinary person but as a rather common one. What strikes Arendt is (in her famous phrase) "the banality of evil." Accordingly, Arendt argues against the very popular position that the Holocaust was unprecedented. Instead, she asserts the opposite, citing several examples of previous genocides.

Befitting its dedication, " 'More Light! More Light!' " clearly agrees with Arendt. The first three stanzas of the poem describe a sixteenth-century religious persecution whose horrors foreshadow the Holocaust's. In the first three stanzas, Hecht lingers over the details of the executions. As a consequence, the poem gives a sense of the execution's painfully slow progress, as the prisoner endures a prolonged death by fire. After a particularly grue-some image, "the black sap / Bubbled and burst as he howled for the Kindly Light," the poem's speaker calmly notes, "And that was but one, and by no means of the worst." Though the details might appall the reader, he or she should not for-get that innumerable, similarly gruesome murder-ers also have taken place.

The poem continues this seemingly dispas-sionate tone in its transition, "We move now to out-side a German wood." The first three stanzas es-tablish evil as a persistent theme in Western civilization; the poem's last six stanzas detail this theme's continued relevance. Indeed, despite the seeming casualness of this reference to "a German wood," the wood in question is notable. The poem refers to "the shrine at Weimar beyond the hill," indicating that the action takes place at Buchen-wald, near Goethe's home. As Eugen Kogon noted in *The Theory and Practice of Hell,* the book in which Hecht read of the incident that dominates this poem, "The location itself [of the camp] was symbolic. Weimar had long been regarded as the cultural heart of Germany, the one-time seat of the German classicists whose works lent the highest expression to the German mind. And here was Buchenwald, a piece of wilderness where the new German spirit culture was to unfold." Indeed, the setting of "'More Light! More Light!'" is crucial, as the depicted action transpires at both a concen-tration camp and a scene of great cultural achieve-ment. In Kogon's terms, here "the cultural heart of Germany" meets "the new German spirit." Allud-ing to both, the poem implicitly raises the question I began this essay with: did the lessons learned from the arts make the Germans into better murderers, not people?

If the poem answers this complex question, it does so only through the series of negative propo-sitions that dominate the second half of the poem. At the crucial moment when the Pole must decide whether or not to bury the Jews alive, the poem de-clares, "Not light from the shrine at Weimar be-yond the hill / Nor light from heaven appeared. But he did refuse." If this man enjoys moral illumina-tion, it does not arrive from outside him but from within. To put this idea a little more bluntly, the symbols of European culture and religion—"the shrine at Weimar" and "heaven"—clarify nothing. Instead, the prisoner makes the courageous, hon-orable moral choice without help from these guid-ing moralities.

Of course, the poem's bleak landscape pun-ishes anyone who dares to act humanely. The neg-

ative propositions continue: "No light, no light in the blue Polish eye" and "No prayers or incense rose up." The twin references to "no light, no light" ironically echo the poem's title. In Goethe's dying moments, he begged for "more light! more light!"; a little more than a century later, within a short walk from the poet's former home, a fellow coun-tryman displays an absolute lack of moral clarity. One might expect the expression of even slight re-morse to pass across any human's eyes as he kills another person. However, the poem explains that, "Much casual death had drained away their souls." Diminished by the murders he has already com-mitted and the others he has witnessed, the soldier mechanically performs his grim work.

The final stanzas are effective only if the reader anticipates a revelation. In other words, the poem works under the assumption that the reader longs for an insight to make sense of this apparently senseless waste of life. No such revelation occurs. In fact, the poem's final stanza adamantly opposes the notion that any truth can give meaning to the Holocaust.

The poem conveys this idea in its last, cine-matic movement. Like a camera panning from a close-up then back toward it, the poem broadens from the particular scene to the larger panorama of the soot-filled sky and then narrows to a final, haunting shot of the dead man's "eyes in a black soot." This last image offers no comfort. The corpse's blank expression registers neither solace that he acted courageously nor a sense that his soul has found what the poem earlier calls "tranquility."

Ultimately, this final image is so mysterious as to beg the question of what the poem ultimately believes about the issues it raises. In a sense, it re-sists simple answers to complicated questions. Or to put this idea into slightly more precise terms, the poem gives painful answers to painful ques-tions. Set near Goethe's home, "'More Light! More Light'" implies that art helped create a cli-mate fertile for Nazism. At the same time, the poem displays an impressive erudition, a vast his-torical knowledge, and an elegant command of lan-guage.

In the dark times "'More Light! More Light!'" depicts, the punishments only get worse. While the Christian martyr perishes with a "pitiful dignity," the Pole suffers his death without the consolations that a religious faith might offer. Literally, he dies without a prayer. It may be true that, as Adorno be-lieved, "it has become impossible to write poetry." Indeed, another of Hecht's poems seems to concede this point: "The contemplation of horror is not edifying. / Neither does it strengthen the soul." For precisely these reasons, though, "'More Light! More Light!'" aspires to the Polish prisoner's example. Like his faithless act of faith, the poem tries to edify and strengthen the soul while convinced that these goals are impossible.

Source: David Caplan, in an essay for *Poetry for Students,* The Gale Group, 1999.

Jhan Hochman

Jhan Hochman's articles appear in Democracy and Nature, Genre, ISLE, *and* Mosaic. *He is the author of* Green Cultural Studies: Nature in Film, Novel, and Theory *(1998), and he holds a Ph.D in English and an M.A. in cinema studies. Hochman's essay is a meditation on darkness and light—its different appearances and different meanings in the poem.*

Anthony Hecht's "'More Light! More Light!'" is a poem about darkness and light. The poem's first story involves a man (a heretic, according to Hecht) confined to the dark of the Tower of London who will be burned at the stake. As the prisoner writes his poetry, a kind of light is produced by the heat of thought and sense, perhaps even the fire of passion. The light of versification, even if dim, will lighten this man's load and tell him something about himself, tell us something about him, and tell both him and us something about the world. In other words, what might result is illumination if the poem approaches accuracy, or obfuscation (from the Latin *obfuscare,* to darken) if avoiding it. The verses are submitted to those officiating the execution—under the light of the public eye—so that officials are less able to deny that the verses were written and presented, and so there is better chance the heretic's words will reach the "light of day." The heretic also declares himself to be free of criminality, to not have darkened the word of God, whose first words, according to the Bible's book of Genesis, were "Let there be light." Now the heretic is to have his light put out by fire, the source of light. The fire is a reminder to those who would oppose the regime. The execution, while meant to look horrific, is not supposed to be too drawn out or look overly cruel. The victim was often, therefore, given a sack of gunpowder to wear around his neck to speed death. Hecht read about deaths like these in *The Actes and Monuments of John Foxe,* first published in English in 1563 and popularly known as *The Book of Martyrs.* This enormous multivolume work is a history of the Christian Church from the earliest times, but with special reference to the sufferings of the Christian martyrs, particularly those of Mary Tudor's Catholic reign (1553-58). It is estimated that some 300 heretics were executed in these years. Of the many deaths described, Hecht said he was thinking especially of Nicholas Ridley, Bishop of London, and Hugh Latimer, Bishop of Worcester. According to Foxe's work, Bishop Latimer died quickly, but Bishop Ridley did not, because the fire was badly built and did not rise high enough to ignite the sack of gunpowder around his neck. In his poem, Hecht writes that Ridley shouted for the "Kindly Light," words taken from an 1883 hymn by Cardinal Newman and referring to a light issuing from heaven, from God. Just before dying, Latimer had told Ridley: "Be of good comfort Master Ridley, and play the man: we shall this day light such a candle by God's grace in England as I trust shall never be put out."

Hecht now edits us through time and space: from Renaissance England to what some suppose to be the end of the Enlightenment—Nazi Germany. The end of the Enlightenment, then, is a moral darkness descending over Europe and over the mostly proud reputation humanity had bestown upon itself. While Hecht's German scene could have—for maximum effect or at the risk of overkill—taken place at night or in a cave to highlight the darkness, the scene does take place in the forest, a shaded place commonly associated with fear and intellectual/ moral darkness. This incident, Hecht says, came from Eugen Kogon's *The Theory and Practice of Hell: The German Concentration Camps and the System Behind Them.* The scene of this peculiarly sadistic proceeding is, we know from Kogon, outside the concentration camp of Buchenwald. Weimar was home to Johann Wolfgang von Goethe (1749-1832), whose legendary last words appear as the title of Hecht's poem. Goethe was a man of the Enlightenment, one of the great German figures, who now has a museum (the "shrine at Weimar") dedicated to him at Weimar. A writer of prose and verse, Goethe was a dilettante scientist who for many years studied light. About light, Goethe made a statement with the whole history of humankind behind it, a kind of cliché: "Light and darkness wage constant war with one another." In his research into light and color, his enemy was Sir Issac Newton (1642-1727) probably the most famous scientist prior to Einstein and author of the spectrum theory of color. Goethe, against Newton, argued that before color there is light and darkness, each of them unified and homogeneous like the undiluted light of

God and the unmitigated evil of Satan. Darkness, while opposed to light, is also its indispensable partner. For Goethe, color issued from light split or broken by a prism; light, however, was not composed of color. Goethe's theory of color as discussed in his *Farbenlehre* (1810) is arguably far more an issue of metaphysical ideologies than physics but what is crucial here is how important his research was to him:

> [Goethe] has gone to great pains. For this single work [the *Farbenlehre*] he has read, or thumbed through, more books and journals than in the whole of the rest of his life put together. He has made endless experiments, with the spiteful prism, with lenses and coloured pieces of glass, with plants, candles and mirrors. He has also cast his eyes about him, and to such observations we owe his most valuable results. For eighteen years he has worked on the book and now, under pressure of war and upheaval, it has to go to the printer, in two thick volumes of over thirteen hundred pages and a third volume of plates, the bulkiest work Goethe ever published. Even this was only a fragment, and was meant to be continued. He calls it *Zur Farbenlehre,* a contribution to the theory of colours, and he divides it into three parts: a didactic, a polemic, devoted to his battle against *Bal Isaak* [a devilish, false prophet conflated with Newton], and an historic.

Not only do we have Goethe's passion about light reported by a biographer, but by Goethe himself:

> "I do not pride myself in the least on any of my poetic achievements. There have been excellent poets in my time, there were still more excellent ones before me and there will be again after me. But that I am the only one in my century to know the true solution to the difficult science of the theory of colours—on this I do pride myself, and because of it I have a consciousness of superiority over many people."

The light the Pole did not see coming from Goethe's Weimar, nor issuing from heaven, is very similar because Goethe's undivided light is inspired by the light from God. The Pole can be said to have refused to kill the Jews because of an inner light—a light signifying moral resolve, passion, and hatred of the Nazi soldier. Yet out of the numerous concentration camp incidents reported by Kogon, why did Hecht select this one? One answer is that this incident involved live burial: an eradication of light, the absolute opposite to death by burning, which is an overpresence of light. After the Pole is subjected to partial live burial, the light flees his eyes. By reading Kogon's account, we know this meant the courage—the inner light—had disappeared from the Pole to such a point he could now inflict darkness on the Jews; after all, were they not willing to do the same to him? So the Pole buries the two Jews. Here we must refer back to Kogon since Hecht now alters the telling. In Kogon's work, the Pole disappears from the story once he has buried the Jews, and the implication is that he lives. On the other hand, the Jews are, after about five minutes, ordered dug up again by prisoners. One Jew, whose face is cut by a spade, is already dead; the other is barely alive. The Nazi detail leader sends them both to the crematory. Kogon's story seems darker than Hecht's, since the Pole survived by losing his courage and committing murder. But Hecht denies the Pole any redemption by having him killed for "letting" his inner light be snuffed: because the Pole killed (at gunpoint), Hecht has him executed. Hecht doles out severe justice, whereas, in Kogon, no justice is to be found. Recall the statue of blindfolded Justice, and the saying, "Justice is blind." Justice works without light to the extent that all people, Jew or Gentile, attain equal treatment. The Pole dies because he "murdered" the Jews, just as the Jews had to die for their willingness to kill the Pole. Some critics have said the Pole is a kind of Christ figure since he is buried, resurrected, and takes three hours to die like the three days it took Christ to come alive. Of course, if the Pole is comparable to Christ, it is for the sake of contrast, since the Pole, once resurrected, dies and saves no one. Symbolically then, Hecht has constructed a dark poem of ruthlessly cruel, blind justice.

Hecht is not through with darkness; he has one stanza left to make his final statement. Whereas the heretic had received the benefit of prayers and was burned in a type of sacrificial act, the Pole's death occurs without plea and is not perpetrated in the name of God. The Pole's death is utterly empty, without meaning. The smoke and soot from the ovens at nearby Buchenwald do not waft toward heaven—as some Nazi ideologues, thinking they were doing God's work, might have hoped—but instead settle on and fully extinguish whatever light the Pole once had. Thus, the descending smoke of the crematory hovers over the earth in a ghostly light. Hecht's poem is also a ghost—fleeting light composed of shadow haunting the lightness of prosperity and optimism. His black words on a white page light a candle, one illuminating religious doctrines based upon the (proper) light of God's word and racial beliefs based upon the purity of light skin, showing these ideologies for what they are: darkness posing as light.

Source: Jhan Hochman, in an essay for *Poetry for Students,* The Gale Group, 1999.

Sources

Adorno, Theodor, *Prisms,* translated by Samuel and Sherry Weber, Cambridge, MA: MIT Press, 1981, p. 34.

Arendt, Hannah, *Eichmann in Jerusalem: A Report on the Banality of Evil* (revised and enlarged edition), New York: Penguin Books, 1964.

Brown, Ashley, "The Poetry of Anthony Hecht," *Ploughshares,* Vol. 4, No. 3, 1978, pp. 9-24.

Brown, Jane, "Johann Wolfgang von Goethe," *Dictionary of Literary Biography,* Vol. 94: *German Writers in the Age of Goethe: Sturm und Drang to Classicism,* Detroit: Gale Research, 1990, pp. 46-67.

Casey, Ellen Miller, "Hecht's 'More Light! More Light!'" *The Explicator,* Vol. 54, No. 2, winter 1996, pp. 113-15.

German, Norman, *Anthony Hecht,* New York: Peter Lang, 1989.

Hecht, Anthony, *Collected Earlier Poems,* New York: Alfred A. Knopf, 1990, p. 43.

Hecht, Anthony, *The Hard Hours,* New York: Atheneum, 1967.

Hirsch, Edward, "Comedy and Hardship," *The Burdens of Formality: Essays on the Poetry of Anthony Hecht,* edited by Sydney Lea, Athens: University of Georgia Press, 1972.

Hoffman, Daniel, "Our Common Lot," *The Harvard Guide to Contemporary American Writing,* edited by Daniel Hoffman, Cambridge: Harvard University Press, 1979.

Kogon, Eugen, *The Theory and Practice of Hell: The German Concentration Camps and the System Behind Them,* translated by Heinz Norden, Farrar, Straus and Giroux, 1976, New York: Octagon Books, 1979.

Lea, Sydney, ed., *The Burdens of Formality: Essays on the Poetry of Anthony Hecht,* Athens: University of Georgia Press, 1989.

McClatchy, J.D., "The Art of Poetry XXXX: Anthony Hecht," *Paris Review,* Vol. 30, fall 1988, pp. 161-205.

Ostriker, Alicia, "Millions of Strange Shadows: Anthony Hecht as Gentile and Jew," *The Burdens of Formality: Essays on the Poetry of Anthony Hecht,* Athens: University of Georgia Press, 1989, pp. 97-105.

Snodgrass, W. D., *The Fuehrer Bunker: The Complete Cycle,* Brockport, NY: BOA Editions, Ltd., 1995.

For Further Study

Friedenthal, Richard, *Goethe: His Life and Times,* London: Weidenfeld and Nicolson, 1963.

> Freidenthal's 530-page biography of Johann Wolfgang von Goethe (1749-1832) includes a chronology and an excellent index. Although Freidlander discusses Goethe's research into light at length, he makes no account of Goethe's legendary dying words.

Hecht, Anthony, *Obbligati: Essays on Criticism,* New York: Atheneum, 1986.

> Hecht's book of essays include those on the pathetic fallacy, on a poem by W.H. Auden, *Othello,* Robert Lowell, Elizabeth Bishop, and Richard Wilbur.

Hecht, Anthony, *On the Laws of the Poetic Art,* Princeton: Princeton University Press, 1992.

> This is the publication (with very little change) of the A.W. Mellon Lectures at the National Gallery of Art in Washington D.C. The lectures include those about poetry's relation to painting and music, and art's relation to nature and morality.

Sayres, Sohnya, Anders Stephanson, et. al., eds., *The 60s Without Apology,* Minneapolis: University of Minnesota Press, 1984.

> This anthology is a leftist's guide to the period and includes essays by distinguished critics, such as Fredric Jameson, Stanley Aronowitz, and Cornel West.

Onomatopoeia

Eve Merriam

1964

Eve Merriam was a prolific and talented writer who produced a wide variety of types of literature. She wrote biographies, plays, and fiction for both adults and children. However, she is best known for her poetry. Even as a child, Merriam loved the sound of words and word play. She was taken with many Gilbert and Sullivan musicals and fell in love with their lilting rhythms and lyrics. She brings this love for word play into her own poetry. An excellent example of this occurs in "Onomatopoeia," a poem from her collection *It Doesn't Always Have to Rhyme* (1964), which is part of a trilogy including *There is No Rhyme for Silver* (1962) and *Catch a Little Rhyme* (1966). The titles of these books indicate Merriam's interest in teaching children about poetry in a lighthearted manner. While not all of the poems in her trilogy deal with a particular aspect of poetry, many do, including "Metaphor," "A Simile," "Quatrain," and "Leaning on a Limerick." The poem "Onomatopoeia," like the word itself, deals with words that imitate the sound that they define. Although the poem, and the collection in which it appears, is neatly labeled under children's poetry, it provides not only children but adults as well with a clear introduction to the terminology and the joy of poetry.

Author Biography

Merriam was born on July 19, 1916, in Philadelphia, Pennsylvania, to parents who had

Eve Merriam

Poem Text

The rusty spigot
sputters,
utters
a splutter,
spatters a smattering of drops,   5
gashes wider;
slash,
splatters,
scatters,
spurts,   10
finally stops sputtering
and plash!
gushes rushes splashes
clear water dashes.

Poem Summary

Line 1:

One of Merriam's strongest beliefs concerned the innate love that children have for the rhyme and rhythm of language. In fact, she once said that there were only two rules necessary to introduce a poem to a child: the first was to read it aloud for the idea in the poem; the second was to read it aloud again for the music in the words. This is an ideal way to begin looking at "Onomatopoeia." Since the whole poem deals with words that imitate sounds, listen to the poem. Throughout it, Merriam will try to re-create for the reader the sound of water coming out of an old, unused, rusty faucet. Spigot is another word for a faucet; Merriam chooses it instead of the more common term "faucet" or the less formal word "tap" because of its alliterative quality. Imagine the sound that the spigot will make when it has been turned on after a long period of not being used.

Line 2:

Merriam first introduces the concept of onomatopoeia in this line, describing the water as it "sputters" out of the faucet. The definition of sputter is to spit out in an explosive manner. When you say the word sputter aloud, the "sp" at the beginning of the word causes you to imitate the sound that an object makes when it sputters. Try saying the word out loud, forcefully. The "p" forces the lips to close fully before they open to complete the word; the sounds that follow the "sp" emerge in a burst of air. In linguistics, this sound is referred to as plosive.

Merriam develops the visual image of the water, as well. Notice how lines 2 through 4 are arranged to look like drops of the poem themselves,

both been born in Russia. Merriam showed an early interest in poetry, reading the verse column of the *Philadelphia Bulletin.* She began writing her own poems while she was in elementary school and later contributed poems to high school publications. After earning a bachelor's degree from the University of Pennsylvania in 1937, Merriam moved to New York to pursue graduate studies at Columbia University. She abruptly ended her studies and began working, first as a copywriter and later as a radio writer for Columbia Broadcasting System (CBS) and for other networks. She later worked as the fashion copy editor for *Glamour* magazine.

Merriam's first collection of poetry, *Family Circle,* won the 1946 Yale Younger Poets Prize. Several years later Merriam turned to writing full time. Sixteen years after her debut volume of verse, she published her first book of children's poetry; it is for this work that she became most recognized. In 1981 Merriam received the National Council of Teachers of English Award for excellence in children's poetry. Apart from her own literary endeavors, she also taught creative writing at City College of New York.

Merriam died of cancer in April of 1992 in Manhattan, New York.

Media Adaptations

- A filmstrip, and accompanying audio cassette, titled *Eve Merriam* is part of the "First Choice: Poets and Poetry" series and was released by Pied Piper Productions in 1979.

- Part of the "Profiles In Literature" series, the *Eve Merriam* video cassette is available from the Department of Educational Media.

- In 1961, the Library of Congress released an audio tape reel, *Eve Merriam Reading Her Poems With Comment in the Recording Laboratory, October 19, 1961,* as part of its Archives of Recorded Poetry and Literature.

- An audio cassette titled *Sharing Poetry With Children, by Eve Merriam* is part of the "Prelude Children's Book Council Mini-Seminars on Using Books Creatively, Series 7" and was released by the Children's Book Council in 1983.

with lines 2 and 3 only one word each, while line 4 is two words.

Line 3:

While this line rhymes with the lines before and after it, it is not an example of onomatopoeia. The explosive "p" sound is missing. Instead, this is a metaphor comparing the sound of the faucet to human speech. Since utter means to send forth using the voice, this line adds to the impression that the faucet is making sounds as the water drops struggle to emerge. It also is an example of personification, or giving human qualities to inanimate objects.

Line 4:

Merriam returns to her use of onomatopoeia, with this line, as a two-drop splutter comes out of the faucet.

Line 5:

When Merriam indicates that a number of drops come from the faucet, splashing down on the

surface below the tap, the words in this line also appear in a group. Spatter, of course, is still another example of onomatopoeia. In this line, however, Merriam adds assonance, using similar vowel sounds in words, as the "u" in the previous lines changes to an "a."

Use of rhyme is a very important pre-reading and reading skill for young children. Children learn the different phonetic pronunciations connected with both vowels and consonants. The change of sounds that occurs when "sp" is changed to "sm" helps children to learn skills such as blending consonants.

Lines 6-7:

With these lines, Merriam introduces another type of word that is often described as onomatopoetic. In the strictest sense of the word, gash and slash do not belong in this category, since they do not refer to a sound. However, there are groups of words that seem somehow to imitate the action that they describe. For example, many words ending in "ash" or "ush" are associated with hurried or even violent action (for example, dash, thrash, crash, rush, gush, and push). When these words are spoken, the terminal sound is issued forcefully through the teeth. Therefore, they are sometimes considered a type of onomatopoeia.

Lines 7-8:

Merriam appeals to children's fascination with tongue twisters as lines 7 through 10 provide a miniature example of this form.

Lines 9-10:

In the book *It Doesn't Always Have to Rhyme,* Merriam provides two versions of this poem. The words are exactly the same in each; the only difference is in the arrangement on the page. The second version is a concrete poem, so Merriam tries to fully involve the reader in picturing the drops falling from "the rusty spigot." "Scatters" and "spurts" each take up a single line in the first version of the poem, like individual drops of water. In the second version of the poem, Merriam has scattered the letters themselves across the page.

Line 11:

Stop is also a word that is often called onomatopoeic because of the "p" sound. The alliteration helps the line flow smoothly.

Line 12:

Merriam definitely creates a sound for us as we hear the water hit the sink (or ground) in full force now. The exclamation point dramatizes this. The reader, like the person who turned on the water, has been anxiously waiting for this moment.

Line 13:

The next two lines will be longer, visually demonstrating that the water is no longer trickling out in drops. Rhyme and assonance connect the words in this line. "Splashes" is a clear example of onomatopoeia, while "gushes" and "rushes" imitate actions, rather than sound.

Line 14:

The final two lines of the poem end Merriam's picture-poem as the reader sees and hears the water flow. These are the two most regular lines of the poem, in terms of both rhyme and meter. In many ways, they are very close in style to a final couplet, providing an ending to the poem as satisfying as the water that now runs freely from the spigot.

Themes

Language and Meaning

Poets try to use words that go beyond their obvious surface meaning in order to connect to people through as many meanings as possible. The words, of course, must have the appropriate definition for whatever the poem is trying to describe—if the poet has in mind a piece of footwear larger than a shoe, then it would be more accurate to call it a boot than a shoe. The accurate, officially recognized meaning of a word, as found in the dictionary, is its denotation. Poetry becomes challenging when poets and readers realize that each word also has several connotations: these are the meanings that are not part of the word's definition, the associations that it carries with it. For instance, the dictionary might give very similar definitions for "boots" and "galoshes" and "rubbers," but a poet would not dream of using one word where another belongs. There are several ways that words acquire their connotations. One is the way that the culture uses the word differently through the years. "Crazy," for instance, used to have a completely negative association when it was used to describe mental fitness, but now it just as often means "fun-loving"; on the other hand, "clever," which once was a high compliment, is seldom used now except sarcastically.

Another source of a word's connotation is its sound. To the careful ear of the poet, the sound of

Topics for Further Study

- Come up with onomatopoetic words to describe a process that you are familiar with: use the words in a poem to give your reader the fullest sense of what is going on.

- Try to compose the music that should accompany the reading of this poem, using ordinary household items at the musical instruments.

- Do you think "Onomatopoeia" is a good title for this poem? What does the poet gain from drawing attention to the poetic device she uses? What does she lose?

every word is onomatopoetic: that is, every word sounds something like what it represents. The most obvious examples of this are words like those used in the poem—such as "splutter" and "gushes"— which can, by themselves, bring their meanings to mind. A more subtle use of this principle comes into play when a poet has several similar words from which to choose. "Saunter," for instance, might be a more specific word that "walk," but a writer might decide that the less specific word is required, in certain circumstances, if the word's bluntness fits the tone of the poem better. A word like "galoshes" might not give away the meaning of the word by its sound, the way true onomatopoeia would, but it does have a sound, a silly sound that would skim some seriousness off of the context around it. Poets, and many linguists, believe that the names of actions and things are not just assigned to them or handed down from one generation to the next, but that the sounds the words we use are intrinsically related to what they are trying to say.

Absurdity

In twentieth-century literature and philosophy, absurdity has become an important concept, because it describes the lack of meaning that many modern thinkers consider exemplified in contemporary life. There is another sense of the word, though, that is not as large or grim as its relation to the meaning (or nonmeaning) of life. The prospects for humanity look bleak if life in general is meaningless, but the right amount of absurdity helps to break up the dull monotony of logic and order. Silliness occurs when absurdity is applied to rules. A fair amount of absurdity is used to create the humor in Marx Brothers or Jim Carrey movies, even though they could not be entirely absurd without being just tiresome and confusing. A healthy dose of absurdity is needed for fun, and "Onomatopoeia" is, at its root, silly and fun.

At first glance, the poem appears to be anything but absurd. Not only is the image it presents clear, but the very sounds of the words are harnessed to add to the meaning. The absurd element becomes apparent when the reader sits back and thinks about what is being presented here and what has gone into the presentation. The poem gives a virtuoso performance with words—a verbal ballet—just to describe a common, leaking faucet. The style of the poem is out of sync with the meaning of the words. Like using a three-page-long equation to describe how to make a peanut butter sandwich, like a full symphony orchestra applying decades of classical training to the song "Twinkle Twinkle Little Star," the absurdity of this poem lies in the idea that someone is expending talent where it is not needed. The author does not seem to have spent the extra, unneeded effort foolishly or unknowingly: there is a sense that the poet is in on the fun. Merriam has produced a verbal exercise far greater than is necessary to describe a faucet, a description that has no reason except for the sheer fun of its creation.

Style

Onomatopoeia is defined as words that imitate the sound or action they describe; "buzz" and "coo" are examples. In "Onomatopoeia," Merriam uses the poem itself to give both a clear auditory and visual illustration of this poetic term. The image and sound Merriam chooses is water coming out of a rusty faucet. The words in the poem will imitate the sounds the water makes, first as it slips out in drops and sputters, and then as it gushes forth in full force.

The key poetic elements in "Onomatopoeia" involve sound. Although there is no formal rhyme scheme, many of the words rhyme: "sputters," "utters"; "splash," "gash." The poem also uses alliteration, words that begin with similar letters, such as "spigot" and "sputters." Assonance, using similar vowel patterns, is another poetic element Merriam plays with in the poem, as in "water" and "dashes" where the vowels are located in the same places in the two words.

Including articles such as "the" and "a," the poem has only twenty-nine words. Twenty-four of these words are related by the one or more rhyming elements. One entire group of words begins with "sp": "sputter, splutter, spatter, splatter, splash, spurt," and "spigot." Using rhyme, Merriam changes "spatter" to "scatter" and "smatter," while "splash" brings "plash, dash" and "gash." By changing vowels, she turns "gash" to "gush"; changing consonants makes "rush" become "rusty." Some words are connected by half-rhyme, as in "clear, wider" and "water." Instead of meter or an established rhythm, Merriam uses shape to control her poem. She tries to create a visual impression of drops of water, as well as an aural one. When the reader looks at the poem, the words drip one by one down the page, occasionally becoming a splutter or scattering of drops.

Historical Context

"Onomatopoeia" was first published in 1964, when the last children of the Baby Boom were becoming old enough to read. The general term "baby boom" is used to describe a surge in the birthrate of a population. In the United States, the Baby Boom refers to the generation born between 1947 and 1961. The country had been experiencing a low birthrate for almost twenty years because of two of the most far-reaching events of the twentieth century: the Great Depression and World War II. Many economic causes converged to throw the country into the depression, but the main one—the one that we mark as the beginning of it all—was the stock market crash on October 29, 1929. On that day, investors lost faith in their stocks and started selling at low prices in order to make some money from them; the sell-off, however, created more panic and lower prices still in a vicious cycle throughout the day. Most American investments, tied to the stock market, plummeted in value. Banks that had invested went out of business, and people who had money in the banks lost their savings, leaving them unable to meet their debts. As a result, numerous businesses were forced to close and unemployment rates soared. The United States spent the 1930s trying to rebuild from the depression, particularly with

Compare & Contrast

- **1964:** The entire world was stunned by the callousness of citizens of Queens, New York, who watched from windows while Kitty Genovese was stabbed to death outside of her apartment building. In all, 38 people heard her cries for help, but no one called the policed because they did not want to "get involved."

  Today: Urban crime has decreased, thanks in part to citizens' watch groups that encourage neighborhood involvement.

- **1964:** The Vietnam War escalated after three North Vietnamese boats in the Gulf of Tonkin allegedly fired torpedoes on a U.S. ship in international waters. Congress passed the Tonkin Gulf Resolution, giving the president new military powers to fight aggression.

  Today: Because of the Tonkin Gulf Resolution, presidents have—and have taken advantage of—the power to commit troops without congressional approval.

- **1964:** The Warren Commission released the report of their investigation of the death of President John F. Kennedy, concluding that Lee Harvey Oswald acted alone in the shooting.

  Today: More than seventy percent of Americans think that the Warren Commission was covering up some sort of conspiracy.

---

the New Deal, which was the name given to the economic policies of President Franklin Roosevelt. Unfortunately, the event that really revitalized the American economy was the war in Europe, which had been building slowly but then broke out in full force when the Germans invaded Poland in 1939. Early in the war, the American economy prospered, manufacturing goods that the countries involved in the fighting could not make. This changed in December of 1941, when Japan bombed Pearl Harbor, Hawaii, and brought America into the war. The war lasted until 1945, with sixteen million U.S. men serving. They came home in 1946 to the first stable economy the country had seen in a generation, and, having seen the world and feeling financially secure, they married the girlfriends they had left behind. The Baby Boom began the next year.

The period stretching from the late 1940s to the 1960s are remembered as a time of stability in American society. There were certainly social crises, such as the Korean War from 1950 to 1953, the anti-Communist scare of the early 1950s, and the Civil Rights struggle in the 1950s and 1960s. There was also low unemployment and a healthy economy. The population rose by 18 percent during the 1950s, marking the sharpest increase since the first decade of the century, but there was one major difference: in 1910, 15 percent of Americans were foreign born, while in 1960 the immigrant population was only 5.5 percent. The swell in the population was due to the babies that were born in that time.

The Baby Boom dried up in the early 1960s for a number of reasons. Cultural changes, such as the youth movement that created the rise of rock and roll, made the stable family life that had encouraged child rearing seem boring. Birth control methods improved. The postwar economic expansion slowed, forcing couples to stop and think seriously about the added expense of children.

Critical Overview

In *Language Arts,* Gina Sloan provides an interesting examination of Merriam's writing, analyzing her views about children and poetry. Merriam's main message to children and teachers is that poetry is fun. She felt that it was important for adults to realize that children are fascinated by language. "Poetry's musical effects of rhyme, rhythm, and alliteration, extensions of children's own speech, naturally appeal to them." Her poems attempt to demonstrate the wonderful games that words can play. Merriam believed that poetry must be read aloud to children in order for them to learn to appreciate it. This is so important to Merriam that she wrote several pamphlets to help guide adults and children through the world of poetry.

Sloan traces three main thematic elements in Merriam's poetry. The first is the use of word play and puzzles, or "kidding around" with language. The second involves the social commentary that appears throughout her work. Merriam found poetry a very effective tool to comment on the problems that children face growing up in the latter part of the twentieth century, such as war, the corruption of the environment, poverty, and racism. The last element deals with her desire to convey to children the joy of life and nature.

In *Books for the Gifted Child,* Barbara Baskin and Karen Harris praise Merriam's use of language in *It Doesn't Always Have to Rhyme,* describing the collection as an "unrestrained and effervescent compendium of word games in poetic form." They particularly laud the subtle ways in which she managed to convey sound and imagery to children, noting her effectiveness in teaching both the techniques of poetry and phonics in her work.

Criticism

David Kelly

David Kelly is an instructor of creative writing at several community colleges in Illinois, as well as a fiction writer and playwright. In this essay, he explores the ways in which a poem such as "Onomatopoeia" is democratic, as opposed to "elitist" poems that sometimes seem to be purposely difficult.

As a poetic device, onomatopoeia has what it takes to hold the attention of a young, unskilled audience: it is self-sufficient. The beauty of the onomatopoetic word is that readers are spared the trouble of knowing the Latin root in order to appreciate its nuances. Words that give up their meaning through their very sound are great for those who would rather avoid the trouble of looking up the dictionary definition.

Merriam's "Onomatopoeia" is fun because it allows children to use words at their own level—to play and to rhyme and to make believe that words are sounds and sounds are words—and it does so without screaming for attention the way that some poems do, begging readers to find out what they

are hiding. I am sure that at the end of a long day of facing unfamiliar ideas, a child is not interested in poetry that raises questions. Most poets don't mean to be difficult; in fact, most don't know that they are being difficult, or they think that their difficulty is part of their own particular charm. Think of a painting or a poem or a musical piece that has left you scratching your head, that you just didn't "get," and the odds are that the artist feels that their work was accessible to all. He or she was probably just as confounded by the lack of enthusiasm as audiences are by this one person's artistic "vision." Artists always expect that the newly finished piece will delight everyone and affect them to the depths of their souls.

In general, poets want to be inclusive, but most readers feel that the obscurity of art means something has eluded them. This isn't a paranoid assumption; there are certainly things in this world that exist to let some people into the in crowd and to keep some people out. Schools have admissions requirements, employers have experience and education requirements, politicians are screened through the primary elections. It is not too far-fetched for readers to assume that language with multiple layers is somebody's way of separating "poetic" people from the nonpoetic. The thing that makes "Onomatopoeia" an effective children's poem is that it is nonexclusive. What is the point of this poem? What should a reader take away from the time spent with it? Nothing! That is the beauty of it. The pressure of trying to understand poetry is released, and readers are welcome to like what they find without feeling that they are missing something that almost everyone else knows. The emphasis is on what readers can do and on what they do know. This is bad for literary critics, who aren't needed to interpret a poem like "Onomatopoeia" because everyone gets it. If every poem contained its meaning within the sounds of the words themselves, there would be no need for analysis, but if every poem were that simple there would be a need for poets to dig deeper, to confront and make use of words with deceptive meanings instead of walking around them.

In its defiance of meaning, "Onomatopoeia" resembles Merriam's poem "Schenectady," which was written about the same time. That poem starts, "Although I've been to Kankakee / And Kalamazoo and Kokomo / The place I've always wanted to go, / The city I've always wanted to see / Is Schenectady." The cities mentioned are in, respectively, Illinois, Michigan, Indiana and New York, but it does not matter if the reader knows this. What is important is that the reader knows they are places—a fact that comes out of the context they are used in—and that they are musical, funny words, which anyone can see. The common link between a word like "Schenectady" and a word like "splatters" is that neither follows the dry old rules of verbal genealogy with which even children are too well familiar. Both words show up from somewhere outside the range of customary patterns: "Schenectady" from Native-American roots, which few words in English except place names come from; and "splatters" from "splat," the sound made in cartoons when something wet hits another object and explodes. Words chosen for their original sound might or might not refer to a hidden level of meaning (in this poem's case, they don't), but, in either instance, readers can appreciate them upon first contact.

The strength of "Schenectady," and the thing that makes it helpful for understanding "Onomatopoeia," is that it makes no pretense about wanting to accomplish anything more than saying a silly word as often as it can and to say words that rhyme with the silly word:

> Schenectady, Schenectady,
> Yes I want to connect with Schenectady.
> The town I select is Schenectady,
> I elect to go to Schenectady,
> I'll take any trek to Schenectady,
> Even wash my neck for Schenectady,
> So expect me next at Schenectady,
> Check and double check
> Schenectady!"

In contrast to this, "Onomatopoeia," based as it is on a literary device, represents high culture. Both poems celebrate the sounds of words, which draw children toward one of the functions of poetry, but "Schenectady" is freer to dance and sing without the encumbrance of meaning.

"Onomatopoeia," on the other hand, practically preaches in the way that it asks readers to think over the relationship between the physical world and the world of words. "Spatter" and "utter" and "splutter" and "splatter" might be words that mean just what they sound like, but the fact that we even have such words ... what does that mean? For children, who are used to understanding the meanings of words from rote memorization, this question can open up a different way of looking at things. It can make them wonder what words and reality have to do with each other, and that can lead to the entomology of the roots of common words and methods that will increase their verbal abilities a hundredfold. Or they may learn a civics

What Do I Read Next?

- The poems of nineteenth-century English poet Edward Lear are remembered for their sense of fun and delight in nonsense. Among his best-known collections are *A Book of Nonsense* (1846), *Nonsense Songs* (1871), and *Laughable Lyrics* (1877).

- Ogden Nash was a droll, witty writer who used clever rhymes and puns. Many of his works appeared in *The New Yorker* from the 1930s to the 1960s. A good representation of his work is the collection *I Wouldn't Have Missed It: Selected Poems of Ogden Nash,* selected by Linell Smith and Isabel Eberstadt and published in 1975.

- One of the most respected poets of the twentieth century was e. e. cummings, whose experimentation with style and syntax of verse resembles the spirit that Merriam tried to give her children's poetry. Most of his major works are available in *Collected Poems of e.e. cummings,* published the year after his death, in 1963.

- Eve Merriam is just one of the poets interviewed in Jeffrey S. Copeland's collection *Speaking of Poets: Interviews with Poets Who Write for Children and Young Adults,* which was published by the National Council of Teachers of English in 1993. Also included are Lillian Moore, Aileen Fisher, X. J. Kennedy and William Cole.

lesson: that words, like humans, are sometimes drawn from what ordinary people say and do, although most often their meanings come from a mash of tradition, expertise, and invisible forces that are even more mysterious. Ultimately, though, children do not have to make anything out of "Onomatopoeia": they can just have fun with the unusual sounds because it asks nothing more.

Anyone who has ever lifted a child up to work the buttons at an ATM terminal or has asked a preschooler, "Why do you suppose that is?" knows what it is to introduce the big, complex world to

> *In 'Onomatopoeia,' Eve Merriam has introduced a concept without forcing anyone to see its serious side, leaving the serious aspect of poetry to be reckoned with another day."*

someone both fascinated and frightened by it. Children will have to know how things, including poetry, work, to prepare for the day they are in charge, but they have plenty of time to learn. In "Onomatopoeia," Eve Merriam has introduced a concept without forcing anyone to see its serious side, leaving the serious aspect of poetry to be reckoned with another day. As a poetic device, onomatopoeia has few practical applications, and few accomplished poets could say that they thrill to the chance to use it, but its very uselessness accounts for why it is fun.

Source: David Kelly, in an essay for *Poetry for Students,* The Gale Group, 1999.

Sean Robisch

Sean Robisch teaches composition and literature at Purdue University and holds a Ph.D. in American literature. In the following essay, Robisch describes how Merriam was an advocate for poetry and, furthermore, language itself.

Eve Merriam might best be thought of as a poetic advocate. For four decades, she has been a voice for the rights and dignity of women. All of her life, she has been a voice for the pleasure that poetry can bring to children. She is, in a very important way, an advocate for the voice itself—a person interested in teaching students from preschool through college how to value words for their intrinsic power. Several years before writing *It Doesn't Always Have to Rhyme,* the collection in which "Onomatopoeia" appears, she had produced *After Nora Slammed the Door,* a substantial book on feminism in the 1950s and 1960s that used as its principal metaphor a character from Ibsen's *A Doll's House* and spoke for the rights of women to speak for themselves. Merriam

understood well how literature works on all age groups of readers, and this may be what made her one of the truly passionate writers working to better the human condition.

In the introduction to *Man and Woman: The Human Condition,* Sister Edwin Mary McBride writes, "After knowing Eve Merriam one is no longer surprised to know that the author of *After Nora Slammed the Door,* and *Catch a Little Rhyme,* poems for children, are one and the same." Merriam's children's poetry avoids gender bias as much as does her writing in social criticism. It is democratic in the best sense: accessible to all. She once said that she wrote for the person, rather than for the man or woman, boy or girl. Her writing reminds us that in the most fundamental ways, including an appreciation for the music of words, we humans are very much alike.

Merriam wrote "Onomatopoeia" in 1964, the year I was born. We—the poem and I—are the same age, and it seems worth thinking about that a poem and a person can grow up together. You might consider what poems were written the year you were born that have grown up with you, as a way of understanding that children's writing does not remain only for children. The stories our parents read to us when we are young will have great value to us in our adulthood. They will remind us that we were once very young and that we may think with childlike pleasure about the physical world as long as we do remember. Eve Merriam was aware of this, and she wrote poems that engage children, so that, as adults, they will continue to be drawn to poetry—partly because they remember fondly the day they first heard it.

Also in 1964, the year *It Doesn't Always Have to Rhyme* first appeared, one of the last publications by e. e. cummings reached the market. Merriam said that she was influenced by William Butler Yeats, Gerard Manly Hopkins, T. S. Eliot, and W. H. Auden. But her attention to sound, to the arrangement of the words on the page, seems very similar to cummings. The poems in many of Merriam's books are playful, made—almost required, for their full effect—to be read aloud. She also worked out of the tradition of such other modernists as William Carlos Williams and Amy Lowell, who concentrated on the simple image sparsely presented on the page. Just as Williams wrote about a red wheelbarrow, or cummings wrote about a grasshopper, Merriam wrote in "Onomatopoeia" about a rusty spigot—a simple item that produces sounds worth repeating in language and worth making into music.

So what's the point of reading about a rusty spigot? One anthology of poems, *Rhythm Road: Poems to Move To,* puts Merriam in the company of cummings, Marianne Moore, Lewis Carroll, Carl Sandburg, and many other great poets as writers who understood a kind of poetry that drew its importance from how an image was presented, as much as from the image itself. In fact, the anthology uses the line "The Rusty Spigot Sputters" as the title for its chapter on television and technology. Marshall McLuhan, a critic who was famous for his work concerning television and technology around the time "Onomatopoeia" appeared, once said that "the medium is the massage"—a play on words meaning that what we see and hear is more than just a message. We are affected by the means by which we see or hear, or even read, something— so much so that our emotions may be changed and our perceptions altered. Perhaps the only reliable way to experience this with "Onomatopoeia" is to read it aloud and let it do what it was designed to do, which is not to languish on a page in silence.

I sometimes give writers in my college classes an assignment they might have been given in the second or third grade: to write about their favorite colors. As a seven–year-old, you might write a certain kind of essay about the color blue; it would be honest, passionate, and based on your experience. You would have blue objects important to you that you could present as a show and tell. Now consider writing the same assignment late in high school or in college. Rather than thinking of it as juvenile and dismissing it, you would want to bring sophistication to the work. You would have the power to write about the color with the vocabulary and added experience of your age. Merriam is after just such a moment—when the adult you remembers what it was like to be the child you. Theologian and writer Frederick Buechner has written that children "are more likely to go around with their hands open than with their fists clenched," meaning that they are open to the world and all of the things it has to show them. You were once small enough to get close to a sputtering, rusty spigot without having to bend down. And you were probably more likely to pay attention to how it sounded.

In this way, Merriam's work—like cummings's or Williams's or A. A. Milne's—tempts us to read the poetry as though it is "only" for those who like their poems fun and musical. But perhaps it is also meant to remind us that our efforts at sophistication are still based on the same language that produces words at which small children laugh. Say "Schenectady" or "burghermeister." Say "per-

> *[Merriam] is, in a very important way, an advocate for the voice itself—a person interested in teaching students from preschool through college how to value words for their intrinsic power."*

spicacious" over and over until it no longer even sounds like a word. Merriam has said in an interview that she finds poetry criticism too often to be impersonal, clinical, and detached from the poem's voice. She wants poetry to reach children's ears and bodies before it is vivisected by their teachers. This way, they will grow up passionate about language and may work toward developing strength in their own voices. To act as an advocate for others ultimately means to empower them, and even (maybe especially) through the simplest of images and most humorous of sounds, Eve Merriam did this for her readers. She got at what she called, at the end of *It Doesn't Always Have to Rhyme,* "the quiddity of you and me."

Source: Sean Robisch, in an essay for *Poetry for Students,* The Gale Group, 1999.

Sources

Baskin, Barbara H., and Karen H. Harris, *Books for the Gifted Child,* Bowker, 1980, pp. 192-95.

Buechner, Frederick, *Wishful Thinking: A Theological ABC,* New York: Harper & Row, 1973.

Copeland, Jeffrey S., *Speaking of Poets: Interviews with Poets Who Write for Children and Young Adults,* Urbana, IL: National Council of Teachers of English, 1993.

McLuhan, Marshall, and Quentin Fiore, *The Medium Is the Massage,* New York: Random House, 1967.

Merriam, Eve, *After Nora Slammed the Door: American Women in the 1960s: The Unfinished Revolution,* Cleveland, OH: The World Publishing Co., 1958.

Merriam, Eve, *It Doesn't Always Have to Rhyme,* New York: Atheneum, 1965.

Merriam, Eve, *Man and Woman: The Human Condition,* Denver, CO: The Research Center on Woman, 1968.

Merriam, Eve, "Out Loud: Centering the Narrator in Sound," in *The Voice of the Narrator in Children's Literature,* edited by Charlotte F. Otten and Gary D. Schmidt, New York: Greenwood, 1989, pp. 231-51.

Morrison, Lillian, *Rhythm Road: Poems To Move To,* New York: Lothrop, Lee, and Shepard, 1988.

Sloan, Gina, "Profile: Eve Merriam," *Language Arts,* No. 58, November-December, 1981, pp. 957-64.

For Further Study

Bettelheim, Bruno, and Karen Zahn, *On Learning to Read: The Child's Fascination with Meaning,* New York: Alfred A. Knopf, 1982.
One of the most well-known and well-respected child psychologists of modern times, Bettelheim examines the urge to read as an almost magical fascination.

Goodman, Kenneth, *What's Whole in Whole Language?* Portsmouth, NH: Heinemann, 1986.
Goodman is one of the driving forces in the Whole Language movement and one of the leading supporters of the use of good literature in the teaching of reading.

Kennedy, X. J., and Dorothy M. Kennedy, *Talking Like the Rain,* Boston: Little, Brown and Co., 1992.
The sampling of poems in this anthology captures the spirit of Merriam's, with a slightly more contemporary twist.

Sloan, Gina, "Profile: Eve Merriam," *Language Arts,* No. 58, November-December 1981, pp. 957-64.
This is one of the few good background studies of the poet available.

Piano

D. H. Lawrence
1913

A lyric poem reflecting the speaker's struggle to ward off childhood memories that threaten to engulf him, "Piano" embodies many of the conflicts that would plague D. H. Lawrence throughout his life. The poem describes how a man is "transported" to the past while listening to a woman singing at a piano. Though he fights against what he sees as his sentimental response to the music, the speaker finally surrenders, giving himself over to his memories, until, finally, he is living in the past. Critics and biographers have written at length about Lawrence's relationships with women, and Lawrence himself has made the examination of man-woman relationships the thematic center of both his fiction and poetry. "Piano" has become widely anthologized not because it is necessarily a good poem but because editors consider it representative of Lawrence's ideas about mother-son relationships.

"Piano" exists in two versions. The first was written in 1906 and begins with the following stanza: Somewhere beneath that piano's superb sleek black / Must hide my mother's piano, little and brown, with the back / That stood close to the wall, and the front's faded silk, both torn, / And the keys with little hollows, that my mother's fingers had worn … " This stanza was dropped in the revised version, written in 1911, a year after Lawrence's mother had died. There are other changes as well, most of them serving to make the revised version of the poem less subtle, less about the piano per se. "Piano" appeared in Lawrence's first collection of verse, *Love Poems and Others,* published in 1913.

Author Biography

The son of coal miner Arthur Lawrence and schoolteacher Lydia Beardsall, David Herbert Richard Lawrence was born in Eastwood, Nottinghamshire, England in 1885. Although his later novels, stories, and poems would address the possibilities of living in harmony with both the opposite sex and the natural world, Lawrence experienced neither of these during his childhood. His parents bickered and quarreled regularly. Biographers maintain that Lydia Beardsall and her family believed she married below her and that her life as the wife of a coal miner never lived up to her expectations. Compounding her misery was her husband's drinking and carousing with his male friends. Eventually, Lydia turned the five children against their father, and the family lived in a tense atmosphere, with the children devoted to their mother but disdainful of their father. Lawrence had a close relationship to his mother; she had nursed him back to life after a childhood bout of double pneumonia, and he, in effect, became the person on whom she hung her hopes and dreams. When she died, Lawrence's sickness returned in full force and almost killed him. After recovering, he quit his teaching post, terminated his romantic relationships, and flung himself into his writing career.

More than most fiction writers, Lawrence drew upon his own experiences to inform his work. His modern attitude manifested itself in his depiction of his family life and in his relationships with men and women. *Sons and Lovers,* Lawrence's autobiographical novel about his relationships with both his mother and a love interest from his youth, illustrates what some critics refer to as Lawrence's conflicted desire for his mother. Lawrence's own theories about human behavior revolved around what he called "blood consciousness," which he opposed to "mental and nerve consciousness." Lawrence contended that "blood consciousness" was the seat of the will and was passed on "through the mother or through the sex." Modern society, however, had somehow come to be dominated by mental consciousness and was thus largely unconscious of its own desires. Lawrence wrote about his theories of human behavior in *Psychoanalysis and the Unconscious* (1921) and *Fantasia of the Unconscious* (1922). By explicitly depicting human

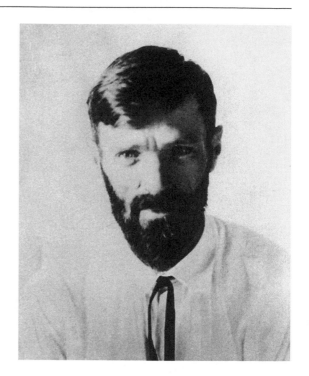

D. H. Lawrence

sexuality in his fiction, Lawrence flouted the moral conventions of the genre and of society, and his notoriety grew. His controversial novel *Lady Chatterly's Lover* (1928) was accused of being obscene and pornographic, and its publishers were taken to court. Lawrence also disregarded accepted mores in his personal life. In 1912 he eloped with Frieda von Richthofen Weekley, the (still-married) wife of a professor at the University of Nottingham, who left her three small children to be with Lawrence. Weekley divorced her husband two years later and married Lawrence.

Though a few of Lawrence's poems, such as "Snake" and "Piano," are often anthologized, he made his reputation as a novelist. Lawrence's own view of his poetry was that it was not only autobiographical, but that it documented a mind in process, rather than one already made up. He called his verse a "poetry of the present," distinguishing it from a "poetry of the beginning and poetry of the end," which attempted to create finished products that could be easily consumed. This process-oriented approach to writing marked his work as distinctly modern. Lawrence's own peripatetic existence—he and Frieda traveled constantly—was also a work in progress. That work came to an end on March 2, 1930, when he finally succumbed to tuberculosis, a sickness he had battled his entire life.

Poem Text

Softly, in the dusk, a woman is singing to me;
Taking me back down the vista of years, till I see
A child sitting under the piano, in the boom of the
  tingling strings
And pressing the small, poised feet of a mother
  who smiles as she sings.

In spite of myself, the insidious mastery of song   5
Betrays me back, till the heart of me weeps to
  belong
To the old Sunday evenings at home, with winter
  outside
And hymns in the cosy parlour, the tinkling piano
  our guide.

So now it is vain for the singer to burst into
  clamour
With the great black piano appassionato. The   10
  glamour
Of childish days is upon me, my manhood is cast
Down in the flood of remembrance, I weep like a
  child for the past.

Media Adaptations

- The Twayne Authors series has put out a video documentary about the life and work of Lawrence. Many libraries carry the video, but it can also be ordered at amazon.com.

- In 1983, Spoken Arts produced an audiobook titled *The Poems of D. H. Lawrence.*

- An audio cassette of Lawrence reading his *Women in Love* has been produced by the BBC and is available from Bantam Books.

- The D. H. Lawrence Collection at The University of Nottingham can be accessed through the World Wide Web at http://mss.library.nottingham.ac.uk/dhl_home.html.

Poem Summary

Lines 1–4:

From the opening line of "Piano" we are asked to see from the point of view of the speaker, who waxes nostalgic as he listens to a woman singing to him in the evening. Lyric poetry is defined by the expression of strong emotion from a first-person point of view, so we are given every indication of what to expect. The imagery of this first stanza sets the tone for a poem about memory. Because memory itself is a function of the relationship between past and present, it is significant that the poem takes place at dusk, a time somewhere between day and night. The image that sets up his memory, "the vista of years," is also apropos because it prepares us for a visual remembrance: the speaker literally sees a younger version of himself "sitting under the piano." The "boom of the tingling strings," an aural image, echoes the suddenness with which the memory hits the speaker, and, as readers, we are left in the same place as the speaker.

The scene embraces sentimentality because of its clichéd representation of a mother and her child: he is sitting at her feet, adoringly, pressing her "small, poised feet." Though we have come to expect this type of imagery in greeting cards, we usually do not expect it from poetry, especially modern poetry. It is significant that this image pits the interior world of the house against the exterior world of winter, as domesticity suggests safety and the innocence of childhood, whereas winter suggests the insecurity and experience of adulthood. The *aabb* rhyme scheme also adds to the clichéd nature of the image, as it underscores the conventional form of the poem.

Lines 5–8:

The second stanza takes us deeper into the speaker's memory, which he tells us he is fighting against. By using the word "insidious" to describe the woman's "mastery of song," the speaker suggests an almost adversarial relationship with her. That he is "betrayed" deeper into his memory, emphasizes the resistance he is putting up against the onslaught of the memory. The last two lines of the stanza participate again in image building. Now the speaker presents us with an idyllic picture of his childhood. Like the initial image of the speaker as a child with his mother, this representation is also stock; it conforms to all of the stereotypes of what a middle-class Sunday night with the family would be like in the late-nineteenth century. The image of the piano links the first and second stanza to highlight the relationship between music and memory. Music was the speaker's guide when he was a child, and it remains his guide as an adult.

Lines 9–12:

The third stanza signals the speaker's thorough capitulation to his memory. It is "vain" for the singer "to burst into clamour" because the speaker has already done that, giving himself over to the barrage of feeling and memory. But it is not to the singer that he gives his passion, but to the past. In this stanza, the speaker also makes a link between manhood and childhood. It is not only the adult world of the present that he is forsaking for the past, but also the adult world of manhood. By equating manhood with the ability to resist the temptation of sentimentality, Lawrence embodies yet another stereotype: that of the male whose identity rests upon his capacity not to feel. The image we are left with is the adult as child, uncontrollably weeping for his past.

Themes

Identity

"Piano" suggests, quite literally, that the child is the father of the son. The bond that the speaker formed with his mother in childhood follows him through life and makes him the adult he is. Lawrence's notions of both adulthood and manhood were configured during his childhood, and both of these concepts are represented in the way he writes about them. Making a woman singing to him the catalyst for memories about his childhood tells us that Lawrence sees one of the essential attributes of adulthood existing in the relationship between man and woman—more specifically, a romantic or sexual relationship between man and woman. That he is unable to pay attention to that relationship tells us that he believes he has lost, albeit temporarily, that adult part of himself. For Lawrence, adulthood is also tied up in notions of gender or, as he put it, "manhood." He is "betrayed" by "the insidious mastery of song"; hence, he has lost self-control, a feature of being an adult. But it is also the way that he has lost control that makes him say that "[his] manhood is cast / Down in the flood of remembrance ...." It is not only remembering his childhood days with his mother that makes Lawrence think he is less of a man, but it is the crying that accompanies such memory. Lawrence's conception of manhood, then, rests upon conventional, even stereotypical, ideas of what constitutes masculine behavior. Seen in this light, the emotional turmoil of the speaker is a turmoil caused, in large part, by the loss of identity.

Topics for Further Study

- For one month, keep a journal of all the times that a particular sight, sound, smell, touch, or taste causes you to think about an event from your childhood. Pay attention to the strength of the memory and to the amount of time it makes you think about the past. Write an essay examining your own relationship to the intrusion of these kinds of memories into your dail · life.

- Many sociologists and psychologists claim that human beings are only aware of their gender at certain times. That is, we don't go around thinking that "I am a woman" or "I am a man." For one week keep a record of the times when you are made aware of your gender. Then examine your notes and write a short essay exploring what it is about these times that make you aware that you are a male or a female.

- Provide your own definition of "regret," then argue for why you think it is a mostly positive or mostly negative human emotion. Use personal examples to back up your argument.

Such a loss, however, is ultimately ironic, for it is only through articulating what he has lost that the speaker can name what he is. However, sappy and sentimental the poem may be, as readers we can only be sympathetic to the emotions of the speaker.

Memory

In "Piano" Lawrence suggests that memory is so powerful it can prevent us from living in the present, effectively making life a haunted affair. The speaker ignores the singer in front of him and instead begins to fantasize about the past, imagining himself as a small child at the feet of his mother, who is also singing. It is the past that the speaker desires to live in; the present is only pretext. The speaker is sucked into an idea of his past, believing his childhood was a time of contentment and bliss. Without memory he wouldn't have even an idea of the past and, hence, an object for his longing. "It is vain for the singer to burst into clamour" because the speaker can no longer appreciate the passion of the singer, only of her song. It is song, Lawrence implies, that is like memory, starting small and building toward an emotional climax in which the listener/rememberer becomes lost in another world. By foregrounding memory in this poem, Lawrence pays homage to Mnemosyne, the Grecian goddess of memory and mother of the muses. If we consider the singer in "Piano" as being analogous to Mnemosyne, then the speaker's memory of his own mother becomes the muse.

Style

"Piano" is a lyric poem, written in quatrains and rhymed *aabb,* that juxtaposes the speaker's present experience to his childhood. Lyrics are short poems that reflect the feelings and thought of a single speaker. The term "lyric" derives from the Greek word for lyre, which is a type of musical instrument. "Lyric" was initially meant to name any poem that was sung accompanied by the lyre. Now it means short, first-person poems in which the focus is on subjective experience, imagination, and melodic tone. Today, the plural "lyrics" refers to the words of a song. The title "Piano" is significant because it foregrounds the poem's song-like qualities.

The central image of the poem is the childhood scene that the speaker remembers. This image evokes the myth of the ideal family, a myth at the heart of western-European, Christian capitalist societies. Many readers will be attracted to this image because it is so deeply ingrained in our psyches. Sunday evenings are the time when the entire family can be together after a week of work. As such, the image functions to evoke in us the same feelings the speaker experiences: nostalgia, security, and the desire for better days.

Tone signifies the relationship between the speaker and his subject matter. "This poem's tone is intimate and self-aware. Reading "Piano," we have the sense of watching someone falling. The reader's own awareness that the speaker is falling into the "trap" of sentimental nostalgia and his inability to stop it provide a sense of irony to the poem, as a child's perspective that everything is well with the world is undercut by the adult's knowledge that, in fact, everything is not.

Historical Context

A poem of personal experience and pain, "Piano" was perhaps most shaped by ideas of the human mind—particular those of Sigmund Freud—that circulated at the beginning of the twentieth century. Freud established his own practice in Vienna in 1886, espousing controversial views on the psychological causes of mental illness. In 1896 he named this field of study psychoanalysis. Freud introduced the technique of free association to explore his theories of repression and resistance, focusing on the patient's free flow of thoughts to uncover the mental processes at the root of the disturbance. Analyzing dreams enabled him to construct a theory of infantile sexuality, at the heart of which was the Oedipus Complex. This condition—representations of which are evident in much of Lawrence's work, including "Piano,"—involves a child's erotic attachment to the parent of the opposite sex and his or her hostility to the other parent. Lawrence's own preoccupation involved examining the ways this complex manifested itself in adults as well as children. After World War I, Freud began examining ways in which he could apply his theories not only to living patients but to art, mythology, and religion as well.

The popularization of Freud's theories accompanied the birth of what we now call "popular culture." The late-nineteenth and early-twentieth centuries witnessed the exponential rise of literacy, which meant an increase in newspapers and reading in general. Pulp fiction, cheaply produced paperbacks detailing lurid crime, was also born during this time. Providing an escape from the drudgery of increasingly routinized work, these books could be purchased at newsstands or taken out from a lending library. As more and more people moved to cities from the country, various entertainment industries also boomed. Theaters and music halls sprung up in London and other European capitals, and football (soccer) established itself as the first mass spectator sport. More than one hundred thousand people attended the Football Cup Final in England in 1901, for example.

Poets and novelists documented these rapid changes in culture. A group of British poets known as Georgians—because they wrote during the reign of King George V—attempted to yoke together nationalist sentiment with their love for the natural world. They published an annual anthology called *Georgian Poetry,* which included the work of poets such as Walter de la Mare, Robert Graves, Siegfried Sassoon, and Rupert Brooke. Lawrence himself was also occasionally included, but he later distanced himself from the Georgians, as he began to focus more and more on love and the relationship between men and women in his writing. But

Compare & Contrast

- **1912:** Sigmund Freud delivers a speech before the London Society of Psychical Research for the first time and details his theories on the unconscious as a repository of thoughts repressed by the conscious mind. Over the next few decades, psychoanalysis grows in popularity, with thousands of psychiatrists undergoing and then practicing Freudian psychoanalysis.

  Today: Though academic interest in Freud remains strong, very few practicing Freudian analysts remain.

- **1906:** Scottish anthropologist James Frazer publishes the twelve-volume version of *The Golden Bough,* a seminal work on religion, music, and folklore.

  Today: *The Golden Bough* is required reading in most anthropology, and many humanities, courses in higher education.

- **1910:** The first wireless telegraph message was transmitted between land and an airplane.

  Today: Satellite technology and the internet have made international communication almost instantaneous.

- **1913:** D.H. Lawrence publishes his first collection of poems, *Love Poems and Others.*

  Today: Lawrence's poetry is largely ignored, but he is widely considered one of the greatest novelists of the twentieth century.

- **1928:** The publisher of Lawrence's novel *Lady Chattererly's Lover* is taken to court on obscenity charges.

  Today: Sexual themes and content in books and movies have become commonplace. By today's standards *Lady Chattererly's Lover* would be considered tame.

---

like many of the modernists writing at the time, Lawrence, for the most part, wrote in free verse and put much of his energy into content rather than form, choosing to write direct, often confessional statements about his own experiences. The overt nostalgia and depiction of his love for his mother in "Piano" illustrates this technique.

Critical Overview

Critical reception to "Piano" has been mixed. In *Poetry and the Common Life,* M. L. Rosenthal praises the poem, calling the scene that Lawrence creates "romantic and evocative" and claiming that the poem "catches the rush of emotional surrender as the speaker's childhood self leaps from the darkness of forgotten life." In *Practical Criticism,* I. A. Richards had a group of readers respond to and evaluate "Piano." Although sixty-six percent of the readers gave the poem an "unfavorable" rating—many claiming that it was "grossly sentimental"—Richards largely

dismissed these readings as being uninformed, exemplifying an ignorance of critical principles.

On the other hand, critics such as Philip Hobsbaum have maintained that the poem does not deserve the praise it has been given, largely because Lawrence could not find the right form to harness its emotional intensity. Hobsbaum examines two versions of the poem, one written in 1906, and one (the published version) in 1911. He claims that the first draft was more "authentic" and that the second draft, written after Lawrence's mother had died, suffered because it had lost a degree of subtlety. Hobsbaum attributes this to what he claims was a sudden shift in Lawrence's personality brought on by his grieving, which manifested itself in "a period of hyperactivity and disturbance." W. D. Snodgrass thought the poem ironic in that Lawrence, known as a modern prophet of sexual emancipation, could not respond to the woman singing passionately in front of him. "Must our sexual emancipator present such an image of impotency?" Snodgrass asks.

Criticism

Alice Van Wart

*Alice Van Wart is a writer and teaches litera-
ture and writing in the Department of Continuing
Education at the University of Toronto. She has a
Ph.D. in Canadian literature, has published two
books of poetry, and has written articles on modern and contemporary literature. In the following
essay, Van Wart argues that Lawrence's mastery
of form is evidenced in "Piano," which expresses
a complex, emotional response to loss.*

D. H. Lawrence, a British writer of novels, poetry, drama, and travel pieces, and the son of a
miner in the industrial town of Nottingham, England, published his first poems at the age of nineteen. He began writing poetry as a way of expressing himself, and during his life he wrote more
than a thousand poems, which were collected in
two volumes. While attending Nottingham University for his teacher's certificate, he wrote his
first novel, *The White Peacock*. From its publication in 1911 to end of his life (with the exception
of a short period as a schoolmaster), Lawrence
lived entirely by his writing, leading a peripatetic
life, traveling extensively, living in Europe and
New Mexico, and, always, writing.

In his writing, Lawrence explored the tension
between passion and reason, nature and civilization. He also attempted to create new modes of expression that would better accommodate his own
acute perceptions and emotions. He broke with traditional structures in search of a form that would
express the rhythms of deeply felt emotion. In these
attempts, he was both praised as a major poet and
criticized for being egotistical and self-absorbed.

Lawrence's early poetry is largely autobiographical and traditional in form. The poems depict a young man of genius struggling with inadequate modes of expression. In his poem "Piano,"
however, he was able to use a traditional form to
successfully render unsentimental feelings of tenderness and loss about the death of his mother. In
three quatrains of rhyming couplets, Lawrence
moves beyond conceptual statement to express, in
form and language, his personal response to loss.

In "Piano," Lawrence recounts personal emotions awakened by hearing a woman singing. The
song stirs memories of childhood and his mother.
Remembering his mother makes him experience
again his loss, and he begins to weep. The emotions that Lawrence describes in the poem are more

What Do I Read Next?

- Harry T. Moore's 1974 biography, *The Priest of
  Love*, provides a detailed and highly entertain-
  ing account of the relationship between
  Lawrence's love life and his work.

- In *The Triumph of the Therapeutic: Uses of
  Faith after Freud*, Philip Reiff examines ways
  in which artists and writers manifest their secular belief systems in their work.

- Pelican's *Social History of Britain: British Society 1914-1945* documents the social history of
  Britain from the beginning to the middle of the
  twentieth century.

- Roger Ebbatson explores the role of sex, sur-
  vival, and self–interest in the works of three
  British novelists in *The Evolutionary Self:
  Hardy, Forster, Lawrence*.

- In *Culture and Society 1780-1950* Marxist critic
  and writer Raymond Williams looks at the how
  the material world has shaped ideology in Great
  Britain during the modern era. This is one of the
  most perceptive examinations of the inner life
  of a country ever written.

than those of sentimental nostalgia and loss, however. The poem demonstrates a complex interplay
of feeling behind the poet's experience, conveying
the sense of the presentness of a past experience
and the changing emotions of this awareness.

In the first stanza, the poet sits in the dusk listening to a woman singing. The singing takes the
poet "back down the vista of years." There is a suggestion of intimacy between the poet and singer
when he says, she is "singing to me." The song not
only wakens feelings from his childhood, but it also
provides the bridge between the present and past.
The past becomes a part of the present as the poet
sees "a child sitting under the piano" and hears "the
boom of tingling strings." In these lines, the use of
the progressive present tense conveys a sense of
immediacy. The poet hears the "boom" of the music and feels the sensation of the piano strings as

In three quatrains of rhyming couplets, Lawrence moves beyond conceptual statement to express, in form and language, his personal response to loss."

he watches "the small, poised feet" of his mother, "who smiles as she sings." Present time gives way to the past as the woman's singing becomes his mother's. The mother's smile and the child's awareness of her "poised feet" suggest a close bond between mother and child and the adult perception of her self-possession. The image prepares for the sharp jolt back to the present when the poet acknowledges that the song "betrays me back."

The use of the word "betrays" complicates the reader's perception of the poet's initial feelings. There is a darkness in the poet's admission that he is being pulled back in spite of himself. The description of the singer's "insidious mastery of song" shows that the poet is aware of the treachery behind the song; it entices him into remembering "the old Sunday evenings at home," where he sang hymns with his mother in "the cosy parlour." Though the song entices, it also betrays because the recollection makes him want to be there so badly that his heart "weeps to belong."

In the third stanza, the poet admits that since he has been tempted by the song into remembering another time, he now claims little interest in the song and notes—"It is vain for the singer to burst into clamour." The use of the word "vain" suggests both the singer's vanity in continuing to sing and the futility of her effort. The "burst into clamour" contrasts with the poet's recollection of the sounds of the "tinkling strings" in the second stanza. The mood evoked by the phrase "piano appassionato" also contrasts with the atmosphere of the "cosy parlour," in which hymns were sung. The implicit difference between the child's world and that of the adult's is made explicit in the enjambment of "appassianto" with "glamour." The line break clarifies that the glamour is not associated with passionate playing of the piano, but with "childish days." The play on the word "glamour"—in its association

both to alluring charm and to enchantment—points to the contrast between the poet's unconscious perceptions of childhood innocence and the unruly passions associated with adulthood. When the poet admits the "childish days" are "upon" him, "childish" suggests both the qualities of childhood and the poet's awareness of being childish—"the flood of remembrance" makes him weep "like a child."

The connection between childhood and adulthood creates a complex duality in the poem. In the third line of the last stanza, "childish days" are connected to the poet's "manhood" which, the poet says, "is cast." The word "cast" suggests something that is formed and cannot be altered. But the line break connects "cast" to the first word of the last line of the quatrain, so his "manhood is "cast, / Down." The play on the word "cast" shows the poet being over taken by remembrance and giving in to weeping "like a child. In the second stanza, the recollection of childhood made the poet "weep to belong." Having given in to "the flood of remembrance," the poet is in the past, or the past has become one with the present." The "childish days" of the past connect with the poet's weeping "like a child for the past." In the poet's unconscious, past and present time are one.

The paramount sense of "Piano" is of the dominating presentness of past experience. The poem subtly conveys the poet's awareness of inner experience that seems to live on beneath the level of ordinary waking consciousness and, at the same time, it shows the poet's awareness of what, in fact, is remembrance. "Piano" presents a complex awareness of inner being characterized by what Alfred Alvarez, in his essay "D. H. Lawrence: The Single State of Man," calls "a complete truth of feeling." The power of the poem lies in the seemingly effortless way that Lawrence's conveys—though the poem's language and form—the process of the poet's changing response to personal experience. By reading the poem, the reader shares in the process and watches the barriers between past and present collapse. Though, in his later poetry, Lawrence would abandon traditional forms in favor of a looser or "free" verse that would be shaped by the material, in "Piano," Lawrence achieves a perfect union between content and form.

Source: Alice Van Wart, in an essay for *Poetry for Students,* The Gale Group, 1999

Clifford Saunders

Clifford Saunders teaches writing and literature in the Myrtle Beach, South Carolina, area and has published six chapbooks of verse. In the following essay, Saunders contends that while "Piano" may come dangerously close to sentimental indulgence, it nevertheless captures—in memorable fashion—a universal experience.

Whoever said that "all great art borders on sentimentality" must have been thinking about D. H. Lawrence's "Piano." The poem conveys, quite simply and beautifully, an experience more common than many of us would like to admit: the headlong tumble into emotion-laden nostalgia brought on by "the insidious mastery of song." The experience happens to most people at one time or another. It could be a seventy-five-year-old concentration camp survivor who gets goose bumps at the opening chords of "Lili Marlene," a song made popular by actress Marlene Dietrich during World War II. It could be a forty-year-old baby boomer who becomes misty-eyed for a romantic past whenever Bruce Springsteen's "Born to Run" bursts forth from the car radio. It could even be an eighteen–year-old high–school student who fondly remembers a friend whenever he or she hears the song "Under the Sea" from Disney's *The Little Mermaid*. Music, for some reason, has the power to open the floodgates of remembrance in the human psyche, and it is this universal experience that Lawrence captures so memorably in "Piano."

Of course, Lawrence comes dangerously close to succumbing to sentimentality in the poem. In such phrases as "the heart of me weeps to belong / To the old Sunday evenings at home," he verges on the kind of fuzzy-warm, sentimental language that frequently characterizes greeting-card verse. Indeed, criticism of the poem's "sentimentality" goes back at least as far as I. A. Richards's *Practical Criticism* (1929), in which several of Richards's students express annoyance with what one of them termed the poem's "gross sentimentality." As Richards himself pointed out, however, sentimentality develops in such poems from the excessive response of readers, not solely from an author's expression. Richards also emphasized his judgment that "Piano" is actually a study in universal longing for the past, not an indulgence in nostalgia for nostalgia's sake. So, if this poem strikes the reader as a lapse into sentimentality, the reader should question whether the fault is Lawrence's or the reader's own.

It is also important to note that the speaker of the poem is characterized as someone who is not an easy mark for the sentimental impulse. "In spite of myself, the insidious mastery of song / Betrays

> *Music, for some reason, has the power to open the floodgates of remembrance in the human psyche, and it is this universal experience that Lawrence captures so memorably in 'Piano.'"*

me back," he says, clearly indicating that he is one not prone to slipping into tearful outbursts. In fact, he seems to be resisting the grief welling inside of him over his lost childhood, and he possibly would have succeeded if not for the "insidious" ability of music to strip away all intellectual defenses against the onrush of deeply felt emotion. Any thick-skinned moviegoer who has wept at the happy ending of a romance in spite of him- or herself knows how easily a well-placed crescendo of violins can melt the heart—even if that happy ending is forced, tacked on, or otherwise undeserving of such a response.

Perhaps it is the speaker's resistance to the emotional nostalgia building inside of him that saves the poem from "gross sentimentality." In less capable hands than Lawrence's, the poem could have easily slipped into self-indulgent mawkishness. The important point to remember is that Lawrence is totally aware of the poem's flirtation with sentimentality and doesn't allow it to go any further than that. A greeting-card versifier would have demonstrated no such resistance to the sentimental impulse; in fact, that impulse would likely have been milked for all it was worth.

Something else, though, is at work in the poem, preventing from wallowing in cheap sentiment: its very form. When sentiment becomes overbearing in a poem, it is often because the poem's form reinforces the sentiment with, say, a heavy-handed meter or a highly predictable choice of rhyme (e.g., moon-swoon-June). Such is not the case in "Piano," with its nonmetrical, almost prose-like rhythm and unobtrusive rhyme scheme. No greeting-card obviousness is evident here; in fact, Lawrence fought consistently against the "habits" of verse, prefer-

> *Curiously, the poem explores the muddy terrain of remembering in a rather conventional verse form.*

ring what he called a "poetry of imperfection" that stressed the ebb and lift of emotion to the "tyranny of the ear." And so it is with "Piano," where the poem's long, loping lines tend to obscure the *aabb* rhyme scheme and diffuse any emphasis on words that might go begging for an overly emotional response from the reader. It's interesting to note that at the place in the poem where the emotional current runs strongest ("my manhood is cast / Down in the flood of remembrance, I weep like a child for the past"), the rhyme scheme fairly vanishes into the page because Lawrence uses an enjambment—i.e., splitting the closely related words "cast down" so that they fall in different lines—in such a way that any emphasis on end words is undercut. By doing so, he allows the emotion—rather than the ear—to become, in a naturally organic way, the master of the poem.

This isn't to say that Lawrence doesn't have an ear for poetry. On the contrary, "Piano" is a textbook example of how sound patterning can greatly enhance a reader's enjoyment and understanding of a poem. For instance, Lawrence's use of assonance (i.e., resemblance of sound in words or syllables, especially vowel sounds), particularly in the first two stanzas of the poem, strikes a tone that corresponds with the highest notes on a piano's keyboard. Notice how often the soft "i" tone appears in the poem:

> Softly, in the dusk, a woman is singing to me;
> Taking me back down the vista of years, till I see
> A child sitting under the piano, in the boom of the
>   tingling strings,
> And pressing the small, poised feet of a mother
>   who smiles as she sings.
>
> In spite of myself, the insidious mastery of song
> Betrays me back, till the heart of me weeps to
>   belong
> To the old Sunday evenings at home, with winter
>   outside
> And hymns in the cosy parlour, the tinkling piano
>   our guide.

That soft "i" tone is subtle but dominant in the poem, and what makes it doubly effective is its corresponding intonation to the tinkling sound of a piano's upper register. Lawrence may not have even known consciously what he was doing; it may have all been intuitive. But Lawrence was an intuitive writer, and he trusted his ear enough that he could allow such "beautiful accidents" to occur in his poetry. Decades before poet Charles Olson made his famous declaration, "form is an extension of content," Lawrence was doing just that—allowing the content to dictate at least one aspect of the poem's form, its sound patterning.

Lawrence's repeated use of the sibilant "s" sound also contributes to the poem's subject matter and emotional context by reinforcing the tenderness that is at the heart of "Piano." Notice how many words start with "s" in the first stanza alone: "Softly, singing, see, sitting, strings, small, smiles, she," and "sings." The combination of the soft vowel "i" and the soft consonant "s" adds to the poem's musicality, producing an overall mood of softness and tenderness. And, ultimately, it is this tenderness, not "gross sentimentality," that one takes away from the poem. It is the tenderness of childhood, the kind of tenderness that can "cast down" someone's rugged manhood, the tenderness one feels when recalling a moment of pure innocence, the tenderness that is shared between family members singing hymns, the tenderness between mother and son.

While "Piano" is a very memorable poem, it is by no means a perfect one. Something falls apart in the writing during the third and final stanza. The emotional truth underlying the stanza is inviolable, but one gets the feeling that Lawrence hasn't expressed it as well as he could have. One reason may be that he was still caught up in the conventions of the day and wed to a rhyme scheme that leads him into some questionable choices of diction in that final stanza. The rhyme of "clamour" and "glamour," for example, seems heavy-handed and jarring, both rhythmically and contextually. The choice of "childish" in the stanza's third line also is an unfortunate one; the word has a negative connotation (i.e., "Stop being so childish!"), but Lawrence is, in fact, looking back at his childhood with fondness as well as loss. A better word there would have been "innocent." And, come to think of it, when is childhood ever "glamorous?"

Perhaps most bothersome of all, however, is the monotonous rhythm conveyed by the poem's final sentence: "The glamour / Of childish days is upon me, my manhood is cast / Down in the flood of remembrance, I weep like a child for the past." The poem's conclusion would have been much more effective if Lawrence had varied the syntax instead of allowing the rhyme scheme to coax him into such rhythmically plodding closure. One gets the feeling that if Lawrence had abandoned the rhyme scheme in the third stanza and switched to free verse instead, his expression might have more powerfully and aptly delivered the emotional catharsis at poem's end. Indeed, it wouldn't be long before free verse would become Lawrence's modus operandi. Then, and only then, did Lawrence start writing the kind of incantatory verse that he was born to compose.

Source: Clifford Saunders, in an essay for *Poetry for Students,* The Gale Group, 1999.

Chris Semansky

Chris Semansky's most recent collection of poems, Blindsided, *has been published by 26 Books of Portland, Oregon. In the following essay Semansky argues that, in "Piano," Lawrence uses form to hold the speaker's volatile emotions in check.*

A common-enough desire, nostalgia evokes a sentimental longing for the past. For the speaker of D. H. Lawrence's poem "Piano," however, nostalgia also evokes longing for the person he was as a child, before his own adult identity was solidified. Curiously, the poem explores the muddy terrain of remembering in a rather conventional verse form. The relationship between the restricted form and the theme of the poem makes for an intriguing reading of how the speaker of the poem implicitly, though not consciously, constructs an image of himself.

We can think of form as a container of sorts, the thing that holds the "stuff" of the poem (i.e., what it is about). If we think of a poem as a can of beer, the form would be the can and the beer would be the content. The poem's three quatrains, rhymed *aabb,* provide the container for the speaker's longing for and reminiscence of his childhood—the content. By relying on rhymed quatrains, the poem carries with it a certain set of expectations. In *Poetic Designs,* Stephen Adams claimed that "Rhyme has a powerful capacity for structuring the dynamic movement of the stanza. The first rhyme word sets up an anticipation and thus forward momentum; the second creates satisfaction and thus the possibility of closure; any further rhymes create a sense of insistence, saturation, or excess." After the first stanza, not only do we anticipate that the lines will contain end-rhymes, but we are also able to antic-

ipate, or flesh out, the scene being described after being given the initial image. Once we are told that "a child [is] sitting under the piano," being sung to by a woman, we can infer that the woman is the speaker's mother. The image of a child sitting at the feet of his mother is fairly common; no surprises there. However, we are surprised when the speaker's longing takes on a life of its own. In the second stanza, the speaker's nostalgia deepens, throwing him into emotional turmoil.

> In spite of myself, the insidious mastery of song
> Betrays me back, till the heart of me weeps to
>   belong
> To the old Sunday evenings at home, with winter
>   outside
> And hymns in the cosy parlour, the tinkling piano
>   our guide.

No longer are we in the realm of sentimental yearning for a more innocent time. Rather, we get the sense that the speaker has been hijacked by memories beyond his control. He has been "betrayed" by the very thing that initially brought on this nostalgia: it's not simply a woman singing softly to him, but the "insidious mastery of song" that works on his emotions.

That music triggers the speaker's daydream about the past is not unusual. Sensory stimuli often cause the human brain to call up past events. Novelist Marcel Proust's *Remembrance of Things Past,* in fact, is largely based on this very premise. That the speaker becomes overwhelmed by these memories is more unusual, though, as it suggests an almost pathological relationship to his past. The speaker is not merely seeing from a child's perspective, as some critics suggest; he is seeing from the perspective of an adult who has constructed an image of his younger self. This distinction is important when we examine the idealized way in which he has represented his younger self. Though we should never assume that the speaker of a poem is, indeed, the poet, Lawrence's work invites us to, as he has always woven autobiographical material into his writing. As his biographers tell us, Lawrence's own childhood was anything but ideal. His parents quarreled and bickered, and his mother frequently attempted to turn Lawrence and his siblings against his father, a heavy drinker and embittered man. Seen in this light, the conflict in the poem is not between the demands of adulthood and the security and comfort of childhood, but rather between a sentimentalized version of the past and his actual past.

It is unclear whether Lawrence is aware of this conflict. The first line in the second stanza suggests that he is. He claims that he is being drawn back into the past "In spite of myself." Reasonable readers might infer that by acknowledging that he is no longer in control of himself, Lawrence also opens the door for readers to think that whatever he says will be suspect because of his heightened emotional state. The last stanza provides evidence suggesting that he is not aware of his rose-colored view of the past:

> So now it is vain for the singer to burst into
>   clamour
> With the great black piano appassionato. The
>   glamour
> Of childish days is upon me, my manhood is cast
> Down in the flood of remembrance, I weep like a
>   child for the past.

After spelling out the futility of the singer's music to stave off his plunge into the past, he states, "The glamour / Of childish days is upon me ...." Our reading of the poem turns on the word "childish." If he uses it to designate the silliness of his present state of mind, we can assume that he is cognizant of his fantastic rendering of his family life. If, however, Lawrence uses it as a synonym for childhood, we can safely assume that he is not aware of his sentimentalized view of his past. The latter, I believe, is the correct way to read the poem. This is because he refers to "the glamour" of those days, which suggests a naivete, rather than an awareness, of his nostalgia. Why call childish days glamorous unless one is valorizing those days? Lawrence cements this reading of the poem by saying that his "manhood is cast / Down in the flood of remembrance." In his mind, he has become the child that he has been longing to be by the very act of his longing to be that child. And he has surrendered his adult identity as a man in the process. But it is not the child Lawrence was (a sickly child who endured a household full of parental discord), but the stereotype of a happy, well-adjusted child. What is ironic about this poem is that the speaker—in his almost maudlin dip into what might have been—becomes an adult version of what he was: a child deeply conflicted both about his loyalties to his parents and about the meaning of his own manhood. This is not only the manhood of adulthood or chronological age, but also the manhood of one who does not cry for his mother. Such a view of manhood itself further underscores the speaker's inability to choose between competing versions of reality. Not only can he not distinguish between his actual and his imagined past, but he cannot live up to the image of being a man that he equates with adulthood.

All of the psychological movement in this poem—the speaker's mind oscillating between past and present, between former and current conceptions of himself—takes place in the tight form of rhymed quatrains. Stanzas themselves, of which quatrains are one kind, have their origin in lyric poetry written for music, with each line fitting into one of the tune's musical phrases. Lawrence plays on our expectations for the regularity of rhymed stanzas in his poem, but he does so by writing about an emotionally chaotic experience. In this way, he uses the form of the poem to hold in check the volatile emotions of the speaker and provides the reader with the curious feeling of being pushed, then pulled.

Source: Chris Semansky, in an essay for *Poetry for Students,* The Gale Group, 1999.

Sources

Adams, Stephen, *Poetic Designs,* Ontario: Broadview Press, 1997.

Hobsbaum, Philip, *A Reader's Guide to D. H. Lawrence,* London: Thames and Hudson, 1981.

Langbaum, Robert, *Mysteries of Identity: A Theme in Modern Literature,* New York: Oxford University Press, 1977.

Leavis, F. R., *Thoughts, Words, and Creativity,* New York: Oxford University Press, 1976.

Moore, Harry T., ed., *A D. H. Lawrence Miscellany,* Carbondale: Southern Illinois University Press, 1959.

Richards, I. A., *Practical Criticism,* New York: Harcourt, Brace, and World, 1929.

Rosenthal, M. L., *Poetry and the Common Life,* New York: Oxford, 1974.

Ruderman, Judith, *D. H. Lawrence and the Devouring Mother: The Search for a Patriarchal Idea of Leadership,* Durham, NC: Duke University Press, 1984.

Snodgrass, W. D., "Against Your Beliefs," *Southern Review,* Vol. 26, No. 3, summer 1990, pp. 479-96.

Williams, Raymond, *Culture and Society,* New York: Columbia University Press, 1983.

Worthen, John, *D. H. Lawrence: The Early Years 1885-1912,* Cambridge: Cambridge University Press, 1991.

For Further Study

Bloom, Harold, ed., *D. H. Lawrence,* New York: Chelsea House Publishers, 1986.
    A hearty selection of twenty essays—most of which have been reprinted—on the poetry, fiction, and nonfiction of D. H. Lawrence, edited by one of the foremost literary critics of our time.

Lawrence, D. H., *Studies in Classic American Literature,* New York: Penguin, 1977.

Lawrence provides iconoclastic takes on some of America's best-known writers, including Nathaniel Hawthorne, James Fenimore Cooper, and Herman Melville. An entertaining as well as thoughtful study, this text tells us as much about Lawrence as a writer and utopian thinker as it does about the writers he evaluates.

Leavis, F. R., *D. H. Lawrence, Novelist,* London: Oxford University Press, 1955.

Leavis is an unabashed admirer of Lawrence. Focusing on Lawrence's major novels, Leavis praises the writer's courage and originality of thought. Leavis claimed that Lawrence was "the greatest kind of artist" and "one of the major novelists of the English tradition."

The Quaker Graveyard in Nantucket

Robert Lowell

1946

"The Quaker Graveyard in Nantucket," one of Robert Lowell's most anthologized and respected poems, was published in *Lord Weary's Castle* (1946) and serves as an elegy for Lowell's maternal cousin, Warren Winslow, who was killed in an explosion aboard a naval ship during World War II. The poem is unusual because, while it mourns the lost cousin, it also assigns him responsibility for his own death. By the time Winslow died in January of 1944, Lowell had already served approximately six months in jail for refusing to fight in World War II, having converted before that to Catholicism in 1941. Considering this history, Lowell appears to have used the occasion of his cousin's death to compile a poem of not only political and religious importance, but of immense referential scope—a poem assembling snippets of Melville, Thoreau, Milton, The Bible, and still other sources. "The Quaker Graveyard in Nantucket" uses the occasion of a relative's untimely death to cobble together a poem asserting that humanity's decimation of nature and humankind's self-destruction in war are affronts to a ever-present Judeo-Christian God, who may forgive, but cannot forget.

Author Biography

Robert Lowell—the so-called father of confessional poetry, which was inaugurated in his 1959 poem "Skunk Hour"—was born March 1, 1917, an only child in a wealthy and distinguished family. His father was a naval officer; his great-great-uncle was James Russell Lowell, a poet, educator, and editor; and his cousin was Amy Lowell, the poet whose name Ezra Pound used to sarcastically dub a degenerating Imagism ("Amygism"). Lowell attended Harvard University for two years. During his summer vacation in 1937, he and novelist Ford Madox Ford stayed at the home of poet Allen Tate. The following fall, Lowell transferred to Kenyon College to study with poet and critic John Crowe Ransom. At Kenyon, Lowell met poet Randall Jarrell and short–story writer Peter Taylor. Lowell graduated summa cum laude in Classics and, in 1940, married novelist Jean Stafford. Lowell then pursued graduate studies at Louisiana State University under critics Cleanth Brooks and Robert Penn Warren. In 1941, Lowell officially converted to Catholicism and married Stafford once again, in a Roman Catholic ceremony. Before finishing graduate school, Lowell and Stafford moved to New York, where he became an editor for a Catholic publishing house. In 1943, when Lowell refused to fight in World War II because he opposed the bombing of civilian targets, he was jailed as a conscientious objector; he served half of a year-long sentence in a federal prison in Danbury, Connecticut. In 1944, Lowell's first book, *The Land of Unlikeness* was published, followed by *Lord Weary's Castle* (the volume containing "The Quaker Graveyard in Nantucket") two years later. *Lord Weary's Castle* won what would be the first of Lowell's two Pulitzer Prizes; Lowell also won a Guggenheim Fellowship and the American Academy of Arts and Letters Prize. During 1947, Lowell was poetry consultant to the Library of Congress. The next year he divorced Stafford. During 1949 he served on the committee for the first Bollingen Prize. With Lowell's vote, the award went to Ezra Pound for the *Pisan Cantos.* In April of 1949, Lowell was teaching at Indiana University in Bloomington, where he was arrested for unspecified behavior. He was then put in a small private hospital near Georgetown, Massachusetts, for a short stay. There he was visited by writer Elizabeth Hardwick, whom he married shortly after being released. Lowell would continue to suffer from a bipolar disorder and be sporadically hospitalized.

During the 1950s, Lowell travelled in Europe and taught at Kenyon, the University of Iowa, Indiana University, the University of Cincinnati and Boston University. Among his many students were poets W.D. Snodgrass, Sylvia Plath, and Anne Sexton and critic Helen Vendler. Lowell also published

Robert Lowell

three books of verse, won two prestigious awards, and had his first child, Harriet Winslow. For the whole of the 1960s, Lowell lived in New York City, worked as a poet-librettist for the Metropolitan and New York City operas, published poetry and plays, received more awards and a lifelong appointment at Harvard, and taught at Yale University. From 1970 to 1976, Lowell lived in England and taught at Essex University for two years. In 1972, he was divorced from Elizabeth Hardwick and then married writer Caroline Blackwood, with whom he had already had a child in 1971. In 1973, Lowell's tenth volume of poetry, *The Dolphin,* won the Pulitzer Prize. Still more awards followed for books and lifetime achievement. Then, while in New York City in 1977, Lowell died suddenly in a taxi. By the time he died at the age of sixty, Lowell was considered one of the most important writers in English in the latter half of the twentieth century.

Poem Text

(For Warren Winslow, Dead at Sea)

Let man have dominion over the fishes of the sea
and the fowls of the air and the beasts and
the whole earth, and every creeping creature
that moveth upon the earth.

I

A brackish reach of shoal off Madaket,—
The sea was still breaking violently and night
Had steamed into our North Atlantic Fleet,
When the drowned sailor clutched the drag-net.
    Light
Flashed from his matted head and marble feet,   5
He grappled at the net
With the coiled, hurdling muscles of his thighs:
The corpse was bloodless, a botch of reds and
    whites,
Its open, staring eyes
Were lustreless dead-lights   10
Or cabin-windows on a stranded hulk
Heavy with sand. We weight the body, close
Its eyes and heave it seaward whence it came,
Where the heel-headed dogfish barks its nose
On Ahab's void and forehead; and the name   15
Is blocked in yellow chalk.
Sailors, who pitch this portent at the sea
Where dreadnaughts shall confess
Its hell-bent deity,
When you are powerless   20
To sand-bag this Atlantic bulwark, faced
By the earth-shaker, green, unwearied, chaste
In his steel scales: ask for no Orphean lute
To pluck life back. The guns of the steeled fleet
Recoil and then repeat   25
The hoarse salute.

II

Whenever winds are moving and their breath
Heaves at the roped-in bulwarks of this pier,
The terns and sea-gulls tremble at your death
In these home waters. Sailor, can you hear   30
The Pequod's sea wings, beating landward, fall
Headlong and break on our Atlantic wall
Off 'Sconset, where the yawing S-boats splash
The bellbuoy, with ballooning spinnakers,
As the entangled, screeching mainsheet clears   35
The blocks: off Madaket, where lubbers lash
The heavy surf and throw their long lead squids
For blue-fish? Seas-gulls blink their heavy lids
Seaward. The wind's wings beat upon the stones,
Cousin, and scream for you and the claws rush   40
At the sea's throat and wring it in the slush
Of this old Quaker graveyard where the bones
Cry out in the long night for the hurt beast
Bobbing by Ahab's whaleboats in the East.

III

All you recovered from Poseidon died   45
With you, my cousin, and the harrowed brine
Is fruitless on the blue beard of the god,
Stretching beyond us to the castles in Spain,
Nantucket's westward haven. To Cape Cod
Guns, cradled on the tide,   50
Blast the eelgrass about a waterclock
Of bilge and backwash, roil the salt and sand
Lashing earth's scaffold, rock
Our warships in the hand
Of the great God, where time's contrition blues   55
Whatever it was there Quaker sailors lost

In the mad scramble of their lives. They died
When time was open-eyed,
Wooden and childish; only bones abide
There, in the nowhere, where their boats were   60
    tossed
Sky-high, where mariners had fabled news
Of IS, the whited monster. What it cost
Them is their secret. In the sperm-whale's slick
I see the Quakers drown and hear their cry:
"If God himself had not been on our side,   65
If God himself had not been on our side,
When the Atlantic rose against us, why,
Then it had swallowed us up quick."

IV

This is the end of the whaleroad and the whale
Who spewed Nantucket bones on the thrashed   70
    swell
And stirred the troubled waters to whirlpools
To send the Pequod packing off to hell:
This is the end of them, three-quarters fools,
Snatching at straws to sail
Seaward and seaward on the turntail whale,   75
Spouting out blood and water as it rolls,
Sick as a dog to these Atlantic shoals:
Clamavimus, O depths. Let the sea-gulls wail

For water, for the deep where the high tide
Mutters to its hurt self, mutters and ebbs.   80
Waves wallow in their wash, go out and out,
Leave only the death-rattle of the crabs,
The beach increasing, its enormous snout
Sucking the ocean's side.
This is the end of running on the waves;   85
We are poured out like water. Who will dance
The mast-lashed master of Leviathans
Up from this field of Quakers in their unstoned
    graves?

V

When the whale's viscera go and the roll
Of its corruption overruns this world   90
Beyond tree-swept Nantucket and Wood's Hole
And Martha's Vineyard, Sailor, will your sword
Whistle and fall and sink into the fat?
In the great ash-pit of Jehoshaphat
The bones cry for the blood of the white whale,   95
The fat flukes arch and whack about its ears,
The death-lance churns into the sanctuary, tears
The gun-blue swingle, heaving like a flail,
And hacks the coiling life out: it works and drags
And rips the sperm-whale's midriff into rags,   100
Gobbets of blubber spill to wind and weather,
Sailor, and gulls go round the stoven timbers
Where the morning stars sing out together
And thunder shakes the white surf and dismembers
The red flag hammered in the mast-head. Hide,   105
Our steel, Jonas Messias, in Thy side.

VI

Our Lady of Walsingham

There once the penitents took off their shoes
And then walked barefoot the remaining mile;

And the small trees, a stream and hedgerows file
Slowly along the munching English lane,   110
Like cows to the old shrine, until you lose
Track of your dragging pain.
The stream flows down under the druid tree,
Shiloah's whirlpools gurgle and make glad
The castle of God. Sailor, you were glad   115
And whistled Sion by that stream. But see:

Our Lady, too small for her canopy,
Sits near the altar. There's no comeliness
At all or charm in that expressionless
Face with its heavy eyelids. As before,   120
This face, for centuries a memory,
Non est species, neque decor,
Expressionless, expresses God: it goes
Past castled Sion. She knows what God knows,
Not Calvary's Cross nor crib at Bethlehem   125
Now, and the world shall come to Walsingham.

VII

The empty winds are creaking and the oak
Splatters and splatters on the cenotaph,
The boughs are trembling and a gaff
Bobs on the untimely stroke   130
Of the greased wash exploding on a shoal-bell
In the old mouth of the Atlantic. It's well;
Atlantic, you are fouled with the blue sailors,
Sea-monsters, upward angel, downward fish:
Unmarried and corroding, spare of flesh   135
Mart once of supercilious, wing'd clippers,
Atlantic, where your bell-trap guts its spoil
You could cut the brackish winds with a knife
Here in Nantucket, and cast up the time
When the Lord God formed man from the sea's   140
       slime
And breathed into his face the breath of life,
And blue-lung'd combers lumbered to the kill.
The Lord survives the rainbow of His will.

Poem Summary

Title, Dedication, and Epigraph:

Nantucket Island lies off the coast of Massachusetts. Once a whaling capital, there is now a whaling museum in the main city, Nantucket. Warren Winslow was Lowell's maternal cousin who died along with his crew when his ship accidentally exploded in the Ambrose Channel of New York Harbor on January 3, 1944, during World War II. The epigraph comes from Genesis 1:26, in which God declares humanity superior to the rest of nature. This epigraph will be important, especially in respect to humanity's treatment of nature and, more specifically, the whale—the first-created animal and, in Islamic myth, the one holding the world on his back.

Lines 1-7:

Madaket is on the east side of Nantucket. A drowned sailor—an analogue for Winslow—is seen hanging from the dragnet of the narrator's naval vessel one stormy night.

Lines 8-12:

The following lines come from the early pages of Thoreau's *Cape Cod,* when Thoreau sees a wrecked ship on the beach. Cape Cod is just north of Nantucket. The drowned body is compared to a drowned ship, a shipwreck.

Lines 12-16:

The corpse is weighted down and buried at sea, making the "Graveyard" of the title applicable to both the ocean and to an actual graveyard on Nantucket. An association is made between the drowned sailor and Ahab, the whaling captain of Herman Melville's *Moby Dick* (1851); they share identities as both attackers and victims. The ocean is a place where the dogfish "barks" its nose—"barks" referring both to the sound a dog makes and to the verb form of the word, meaning "to break." "Ahab's void and forehead" is ambiguous but might be a variation of heart and head. The "name / … blocked in yellow chalk" possibly refers to the sailor's name (found on his dog tags) written in block letters (capitals) upon an empty coffin to be later placed in a cenotaph in a graveyard on land. Thoreau, in *Cape Cod,* says he saw coffins on the beach upon which the names of the bodies were written with red chalk. Lowell might have substituted the more-common yellow chalk for his description.

Lines 17-19:

The body that is pitched back into the sea from "whence it came" (a reference both to the place where the corpse was found and to the sea as the source of life) is a "portent," or sign, to other dreadnoughts (a kind of battleship) of what happens to those with too much pride, to those with a "hell-bent deity"—namely, military sailors and whalers.

Lines 20-24:

The narrator tells the sailors that they cannot protect their ship and themselves against the stormy Atlantic, deified as a "chaste" (punishing), "green" god—Poseidon or Neptune from Greek mythology—with fishlike "steel scales" and called "the earth-shaker" because of its ability to unleash powerful storms. Further, the sailors should not expect to be saved by the likes of Orpheus, who was con-

Media Adaptation

- *Robert Lowell: A Mania for Phrases* can be found in the PBS Voices and Visions series, New York: Center for Visual History Productions

sidered the greatest Greek poet before Homer and who was given the lyre (Lowell's "lute") by Apollo. Orpheus hoped that with his lyric power he would be able to rescue his dead wife, Eurydice, from the underworld. The lute's charm worked, allowing her to leave, under the condition that Orpheus would not turn to look at her as they escaped. When he did, she was swallowed up into the inferno.

Lines 24-26:

Once the body is tossed overboard, the naval vessel shoots its guns. "Recoil" refers both to the backward kick of the guns and a standard reaction to seeing something horrible, such as death. The salute for the dead has been repeated so many times that its sound has become "hoarse."

Lines 27-39:

The birds in these lines are able to sympathize with the sailor's death because they have experienced the peril of stormy seas. The narrator then asks the sailor if, in the land of the dead, he can hear the Pequod, Ahab's destroyed whaling ship, breaking apart on the shores of Siasconset on Nantucket and off Madacket where fishermen fish with artificial squid bait for blue-fish.

Lines 39-44:

In this stanza, the birds, Ahab's ship, and the wind itself are all described as having wings. All of nature, as well as the bones of the Quakers, keen and moan for both Winslow's death and the whale's.

Lines 45-49:

As at the end of the first stanza, death is final. There is no redemption either for Winslow or the tortured ("harrowed") ocean. Poseidon, as a blue beard (Bluebeard was a fictional personage who

killed his numerous wives), is unsympathetic to the sailors. The description of Spain as "Nantucket's westward haven" is mysterious, since Spain is east of Nantucket.

Lines 49-57:

In the twentieth century, warships carry out violence on what whalers long ago violated: nature. No lesson has been learned, and so time is contrite, "blue," sad. Time also "blues" these dead lessons—killed or forgot by people—because time must continually bury them in the blue ocean.

Lines 57-62:

Lowell uses metonymy when he states that time was young, since it was the sailors or humanity that was young and naive when they believed in sea monster gods—often whales—that Lowell goes on to equate with IS, or God, since God told Moses he was called "I AM THAT I AM" or simply "I AM" (Exodus 3:14). God, by the way, goes unnamed, because names contain or sum up, but God cannot be. The "whited monster" is a reference to Isaiah 23:27, where a "whited sepulchre" is mentioned, meaning a grave site that looks beautiful on the outside but contains bones and "uncleaness on the inside." Moby Dick was considered, likewise, a beautiful monster.

Lines 62-68:

It is likely that the secret cost to the death of the mariners was their salvation, since Lowell has already intimated that the sailors would not be reborn, especially since—even as they were drowning—they could not understand that what they were doing was an affront to God and nature. Lowell imagines that even when the sailors' ship was destroyed and they were drowning in the "sperm-whale's slick" (*slick* referring to a substance called ambergris that originates in the whale's intestines and is secreted into the water), they rationalized that God must have been "on their side" or else they would have died long ago. Lines 65 to 68 are slightly altered from Psalm 124.

Lines 69-72:

"This" refers to the Nantucket graveyard (death). "Whaleroad" is a variation of railroad, to make resonant that whales spew like trains, and in the case of Moby Dick, "spewed Nantucket bones" just as train engines once spewed smoke and whales spew water from their blowhole. "The end" is the literal end of the whaling expedition, the virtual end of whaling, the death of Moby Dick, and the death of the Pequod's whalers.

Lines 73-78:

Those who chased whales were fools, paying for it with their lives. They were "drowning men clutching at straws," a cliché meaning that they were desperate for money and adventure while living and desperate for life while drowning. "*Clamavimus*" is Latin for "We have cried." Compare this to Psalm 130:1—"Out of the depths have I cried unto thee, O Lord."

Lines 78-84:

The seagulls seem the most sympathetic of all of the entities in this poem. Where before birds sympathized with Winslow, now they mourn for the hurt sea, imagined as being sucked dry by the land at low tide.

Lines 85-88:

Again, this is the end of the whaling journey. "We are poured out like water" comes from Psalm 22:14, meaning to be exhausted with reference to sweating. The question beginning "Who will dance" will likely be answered "No one," since no one is able to bring back the dead "mast-lashed master." Odysseus was tied to the mast to resist the Sirens' call in *The Odyssey,* and Ahab was hoisted up the mast to look for Moby Dick in chapter 130 of *Moby Dick.* "Mast-lashed" indicates that these captains were victims of fatal desire.

Lines 89-93:

"Corruption" refers to the whale body corrupted by whalers' harpoons. Wood's Hole is the closest point to Martha's Vineyard on the mainland of Massachusetts. Here Lowell asks the crucial question of whether the military man of World War II is similar to the whaler of yesteryear.

Lines 94-102:

Jehoshaphat was said by Lowell to refer to "the valley of judgment. The world, according to some prophets and scientists, will end in fire." By way of comparison, see Joel 3:12—"Let the heathen be wakened and come unto the valley of Jehoshaphat; for there will I sit to judge all the heathen round about." The other lines depict the slaughter of the whale, with it twisting and turning in agony from having its "sanctuary" (body) violated by harpoons. The whale, however, is not wholly depicted as a victim, since, in its violent death throes, it can become a weapon, a "swingle"—the freely swinging part of a flail. The implication appears to be that if whales destroy ships, as Moby Dick sunk the Pequod, it is because they are treated savagely.

Lines 102-105:

These lines describe the ship destroyed. The singing stars come from Job 38:7, where God describes them singing at the time of the creation of the world. Why they are singing in Lowell's poem is puzzling, which just might be the point: humans, like Job, are too insignificant to understand the workings of the universe, such as why stars would sing as a ship sinks. The red flag comes from the last chapter of *Moby Dick,* where the Indian sailor, Tashtego—in a final human act of arrogance and foolishness—tries to nail a red flag to the mast even as the ship quickly sinks.

Lines 105-106:

The statement "Hide, / Our steel, Jonas Messias, in Thy side" is a plea for redemption from a syncretic god. Jesus was pierced in his side by centurions and crucified, then resurrected after three days; Jonah was vomited up from the belly of the whale after three days; and the whale was harpooned. The plea to hide the spear or harpoon is a plea for salvation from the very being who is crucified or killed. It appears that the plea will go unanswered without a confession of sin, something these sailors do not do. In Catholicism, one does not, without right action, get saved without confessing. These sailors are Quakers (characterized by their use of "Thy"), not Catholics.

Lines 106-112:

Walsingham is a famous shrine in Norfolk, England. For much of this stanza, Lowell relied upon E. I. Watkins's *Catholic Art and Culture,* where the author describes the lane leading to Mary as well as Mary's display and expression. There, Catholics walk barefoot along a lane to Mary in order to be healed. But Lowell is unhappy with this ritual as the penitents walk unthinkingly, like cows. The "munching English lane" is an instance of metaphor combined with metonymy: the penitents are seen as cows, who munch as they walk down the lane. Therefore, the lane is called "munching."

Lines 113-116:

Lowell's critique continues as the lane is described as lined with the druid tree (oak). Druids were pagans, and Lowell, by not capitalizing the word, shows his disapproval. The stream refers to the peaceful waters of Shiloah or Siloam in John 9:7 and Isaiah 8:6, also referenced in the opening lines of *Paradise Lost.* These peaceful whirlpools are in marked contrast to the turbulent ocean of previous stanzas, and in John they are also healing, as a blind man cures his blindness by splashing the waters of Siloam on his eyes. The Sailor in this poem once came to Walsingham and sung Sion, a reference to Isaiah 51:11, where Jews return to Zion, a hill in Jerusalem, singing. The Sailor (standing for a kind of everyman) was glad here.

Lines 116-120:

Mary is expressionless, even if somewhat sorrowful with her heavy eyelids. And the mention that she does not fit under the canopy indicates she belongs more to heaven than earth.

Lines 120-126:

Mary's expressionless face is without comeliness or charm ("*Non est species, neque decor*") because she knows what God knows. She is not just the Mary of Jesus's birth (crib) and death (Cross), but has assumed Heaven. When people learn to do without gladness and cease seeking selfish ends such as being healed, then, with deep meditation, the world will come to Mary and understand. A type of right Catholicism might then be achieved and God's creatures saved from humanity's war against itself and nature.

Lines 127-132:

The scene shits from a place of sanctuary to a cemetery. This is a graveyard scene out of a horror film: an "empty" wind blowing creaky oak trees against the gravestones of empty graves (cenotaphs). In the ocean, a "gaff" (both a weapon to land fish and a stout pole from a ship) is tossed into a shoal bell (a bell to warn ships of shallow water). This is not a chime marking living time ("untimely"), but a death knell in the "greased" wash, an ocean covered with a slick of ambergris.

Lines 132-135:

The death knell is apropos because the sea is filled with dead sailors either compared to, or accompanied by, the fallen angels mentioned in Book I of Milton's *Paradise Lost,* especially the Philistine sea-god, Dagon: "Dagon his name, sea-monster, upward man / And downward fish" (lines 462-3). These sea devils are unmarried and corroding and "spare of flash" (some versions print "spare of flesh") because they have lost the lustre and glory they possessed in heaven before their fall. Milton's reference for Dagon is I Samuel, 5, where Dagon is shown as a false god.

Lines 136-142:

The Atlantic is called a "mart," short for market because the ships shop the waves for sea life.

In the phrase, "wing'd clippers," sails are likened to wings of clippers, or swift sailboats. But the Atlantic also cuts; it is a butcher shop, gutting ships in its "bell-trap." After describing what the sea does, Lowell proceeds to suggest what it could do if it revenged itself upon humanity: the sea could rise up, cut the wind, and toss humanity off the ocean; the ocean gives life, but it could also take it away.

Line 143:

This line references Genesis 9:8-17, where God makes a covenant with humankind and all of nonhuman nature—for which the rainbow is a sign—never to flood the earth again or almost destroy the whole of life. The rainbow was, by some ancients, conceived as a weapon from which lightning bolts were shot. God's display of his bow is to be read as a sign of former hostility now abated. When Lowell writes, "The Lord survives the rainbow of His will," he likely means at least two things. First, that the Lord, despite man's wickedness, will keep his promise and not send down another flood. Thus God remains a trusted protector. Second, and closely related in meaning, the line indicates that despite humankind's attacks on nature, nature will endure and even be sympathetic to human death. In summation then, whether humanity perpetrates war on itself or on nature, ultimately both will survive, even if humanity does not learn the proper attitude as shown by Mary in section VI.

Themes

Violence and Cruelty

"The Quaker Graveyard in Nantucket" begins as an elegy for a dead cousin but swells into an elegy for all of creation. And in reciprocation, Lowell configures Nature grieving for drowned humans, an example of the pathetic fallacy. In section I, Warren Winslow is mourned by shipmates and honored with a salute by guns, as if to announce his passing to God and Nature. In section II it is Nature—sea birds and wind—that laments Winslow's death. But Nature is not one, since the wind attempts to strangle the sea where Winslow drowned. By the time section III rolls around, the person who was mourned is now blamed, a soldier representing soldiers in general who are responsible for violently blasting the ocean and lashing the shore. A link is forged between soldiers and the whalers who stab the ocean with harpoons. While these men are all held responsible for violence, the blame is mitigated by the poet's understanding that the men were like children who knew no better. Even as the whalers drown, their childlike minds do not understand why—the reason they cry out that God must have been on their side. There is no contrition, since they do not accept error or blame. There is only the sailors' self-justification. By section IV, the blame is intensified somewhat as the sailors are mostly called ("three quarters") fools. Moreover, the ocean is not here responsible for engulfing sailors; instead, it has become the victim. The final question of section IV would likely be answered by "No one," since the poet believes that no one would want to bring back the days of whaling. The violence reaches its height in section V as the whale is gruesomely harpooned and torn apart and, in its death thrashings, brings the ship down with it. The equation is now complete, summarized by many clichés: violence begets violence; he who lives by the sword dies by the sword; reap what you sow; etc. Still, in utter ignorance, the whalers pray for a redemption that Lowell has already remarked they will never receive ("ask for no Orphean lute …"). Skipping to the last section, readers are returned to a synthesis of earlier sentiments: it is right men die for they are devils, "hell-bent" deities, assaulting nature. And the ocean might also be thought of as a "hell-bent" deity, bent on taking down and out the people who cruelly use it. Still, the last line asserts that despite human cruelty and the ocean's defense of itself, God will never again overwhelm humanity in a flood because He honors his promise—He is not cruel, but fair.

Sin and Punishment

Lowell configures the practices of war and whaling as related because both are crimes of destruction—of murder—against creation, against nature. And because they are crimes against creation, they are sinful. The question, then, is how people pay for sin. Two possibilities are presented: humankind will, at the end of history, in an apocalypse, be washed away with the rest of terrestrial plant and animal life; or, people will pay on an individual basis for their sinful acts. The first answer, says Lowell, is not possible, because God, in Genesis, promised never to commit such a general housecleaning again. Perhaps God made such a promise for He realized that to punish all of terrestrial life for the sins of humanity was an overreaction. Lowell thus comes down on the side of individual punishment—along the lines of reaping what you sow—in a type of karmic retribution either in this life or the next: if you kill whales or fellow hu-

Topics for Further Study

- Discuss the reasons for and effects of using material—wholesale or altered—from other sources. The discussion might be continued with music that make a practice of using melodies and lyrics from other music.

- Research the history of whaling, especially the reasons for a worldwide effort to stop its practice.

- Discuss the function of Part VI in "The Quaker Graveyard in Nantucket." Why is it included? How does it affect the rest of the poem. How does this section work with the poem's end?

- Have a discussion comparing and contrasting what some critics think was the model for "The Quaker Graveyard in Nantucket": Milton's "Lycidas."

- Delineate the differences between Catholicism and Protestantism and how both religions underpin "Quaker Graveyard."

mans you will pay by violent death and/or in the fires of hell. So where does the atonement described in section VI fit in? By asking the following question: if one commits sin and is truly penitent, or more specifically, approaches Mary with the proper attitude, will God spare the rod? Because Lowell included this section, it can be assumed that penitence is a way out of the dilemma of fatally paying for one's mistakes. But for this solution to be effective, one must realize he has committed sin or made a mistake. This, unfortunately, happens only occasionally. Lowell must, therefore, end the poem more soberly: since God will not punish humankind in an apocalypse, humans pay on an individual basis for their devilishness—their attempt to usurp the superior position of God and, if you will, Nature. Their fall is as inevitable as Satan's fall for his impertinence before God.

God and Religion

"The Quaker Graveyard in Nantucket" is a Catholic, not Protestant, poem because it stresses salvation by one's actions, by "works." In other words, in order to be saved from hell or violent victimization, the Catholic must do good. This may include one or all of the following acts: penitence, confession, or right behavior. If Catholics commit sin, they are encouraged not just to confess and ask for forgiveness, but also to correct their action. Lowell's poem is a plea for the cessation of violence and for right action directed toward all creation. Quakers on Nantucket, on the other hand, are characterized as unrepentant whalers and—if we are to believe Melville in *Moby Dick*—the most zealous and bloodthirsty of whalers. Quakers, Lowell implies, do not reach salvation for two reasons: first, because they never acknowledge the sin of whaling. Second, Quakers cannot achieve salvation because a basic tenet of Protestantism is that salvation is not won by works, but by faith. Warren Winslow becomes connected with Quaker whalers by Lowell at least partially because Winslow comes from Pilgrim and Puritan stock, both similar to Quakers in that these sects were examples of early American Protestants. Edward Winslow, an ancestor of Warren Winslow's, came over on the *Mayflower,* the historic ship that landed just north of Nantucket on Cape Cod. There the religious sect, the Pilgrims, established a colony. Massachusetts, itself, began as a successful Puritan colony, or company, called the Massachusetts Bay Company.

Style

"The Quaker Graveyard in Nantucket" is a complex work both in message and style. In *Masterplots Poetry Series,* John M. Muste calls the poem "one of the noisiest poems in the English language. Robert Lowell employs a multitude of harsh sounds, broken rhythms, and recurring patterns of alliteration to reflect the poem's preoccupation with the violence and turbulence of the world it depicts." Lowell's poem uses not only what Muste mentions above, but also internal rhyme ("turntail whale") assonance ("Spouting out"), and a mixture of harsh and mellifluous sounds in the same phrase ("… ask for no Orphean lute / to pluck life back" or "… will your sword / Whistle and fall and sink into the fat?"). In addition to sound play, the poem employs a panoply of allusions to works by Milton, Thoreau, Melville, and to the Bible, Greek myth, etc. Throughout the poem, there are also numerous rhetorical and tropic (as in trope) devices, such as personification ("… the high tide / mutters to its hurt self"), simile (the penitents are "like cows"),

metonymy ("night had steamed into our North Atlantic Fleet"), metaphor ("its open, staring eyes / Were lustreless dead-lights / Or cabin windows on a stranded hulk / Heavy with sand."), double entendres ("Then it had swallowed us up quick," where "quick" means both fast and alive), and near homonyms coupled with double entendres ("whaleroad"). Lowell also writes sentences able to be read in two ways, for example: "Let the seagulls wail / For water, for the deep where the high tide / Mutters to its hurt self, mutters and ebbs." A search for other and different devices reveals the immense time and thought Lowell devoted to this poem.

While every stanza could be examined for its particular rhyme scheme and metrical patterns, close analysis of one portion, section IV, should suffice to instigate investigations of the rest of the poem. Section IV is composed of two ten-line stanzas with their respective rhyme schemes, *abcbcaac'c'a* and *abcbcadeed.* Both stanzas are, with few exceptions, composed of primarily ten-syllable lines. But the lines differ in accents per line and the kind of feet; while there are numerous trochees and anapests, most are iambs—iambic rhythm seeming fitting for a poem concerning the ocean's regular repetitions of waves and tides, and the repeated attacks (and the pauses between them) launched on nature and humanity. Perhaps the most incredible of Lowell's strokes in section IV is the final liquid or "l" sound of each line of the first stanza, culminating with the *rime riche* of "whale" and "wail"—homonyms said to rhyme. One would be hard put to find a more watery poem.

Historical Context

The event with the most singular impact on "The Quaker Graveyard in Nantucket" was World War II, a war in which Lowell refused to fight. For refusing to obey the Selective Service Act (and accept being drafted), Lowell served six months in a federal prison in Danbury, Connecticut in 1943. When his cousin, Warren Winslow died at sea with the rest of his crew in 1944, Lowell used the occasion of his elegy to rail against violence perpetrated against humanity and nature. Lowell's convictions would never leave him: in 1965, he turned down an invitation from President Johnson to appear at the White House, giving this statement: "We are in danger of imperceptibly becoming an explosive and suddenly chauvinistic nation, and we

Compare & Contrast

- **1945:** The American bomber *Enola Gay* drops the first atomic bomb used for purposes of war on Hiroshima, Japan, killing between 70,000 and 80,000 people. From 75,000 to 125,000 subsequently died from bomb-related causes. Hundreds of thousands of people were injured. A second atomic bomb was dropped by the United States on Nagasaki three days later killing between 40,000 and 70,000, with 50,000 to 100,000 dying from bomb-related causes.

  1952: In Operation Crossroads, the U.S. military explodes two atomic bombs in a lagoon off Bikini atoll in the Marshall Islands in the Pacific. These would be the first of some seventy atomic tests on Bikini and nearby Eniwetok, which heavily contaminated islands as far as 200 miles downwind.

  1995-96: France, against world protest, explodes a test series of underground nuclear bombs.

  1998: India and Pakistan exchange hostile displays of nuclear weaponry in repeated underground blasts near a shared and contested borderland.

- **1946:** The International Whaling Commission is established, reflecting increasing concern over the fate of the great whales; many species were already endangered. In its early days, the commission had little power.

  1982: The International Whaling Commission adopts a worldwide ban on whaling that becomes fully effective in 1986. While this ban sharply cut the world's whale kill, Japan and the Soviet Union continued their whaling practices.

  1985: Whaling around Antarctica is prohibited under an international moratorium, although Japan and the Soviet Union would continue hunting until the end of the decade.

  1993: The International Whaling Commission reaffirms its ban on commercial whaling. Norway openly defied the ban, killing 296 minke whales, some for what it said was research.

  Late 1990s: Keiko the killer whale, star of the movie *Free Willy,* becomes a household name as the continuing saga of Keiko's release back into the wild becomes of worldwide interest. As of January, 1999, Keiko resides in Iceland, and the plan to gradually introduce him back into the open seas is said to show promise.

---

may even be drifting on our way to the last nuclear ruin." Lowell would march on the Pentagon in 1967, protest the war at the 1968 Democratic National Convention, and, in 1968, campaign for antiwar candidate Eugene McCarthy.

Though Hitler previously invaded Austria and Czechoslovakia, his invasion of Poland in September, 1939 was the act that prompted other nations to declare war. The two sides squared off into what would be the Axis powers—primarily Germany, Japan, and Italy—and the Allies—Britain, France, the Soviet Union, and, eventually, the United States. By the time of full participation, fifty-seven nations were at war, forty-six on the side of the Allies, eleven on the side of the Axis. Only nine countries retained their neutrality through the whole of the war: Afghanistan, Saudi Arabia, Siam (now Thailand), Spain, Portugal, Sweden, Turkey, Switzerland, and Eire (now Ireland). While Hitler's and Japan's imperial actions were the immediate cause of the war, deeper causes might be summed up as destabilization arising from the decay of long-established empires in Central and Eastern Europe; the rise of a unified German nation; and the wide dissemination of nationalist, imperialist, and social Darwinist ideologies (domination by the strongest as natural and therefore morally correct). While Germany was successful at the outset of the war in absorbing Austria and Czechoslovakia, and in controlling Poland, Denmark, Norway the Netherlands, Belgium, and France, the tide began to turn because of two events: when America joined the war after the Japanese bombing of Pearl Harbor on December 7, 1941, and when Hitler's bid to take over the Soviet Union in Operation Barbarossa failed at the long battle of Stalingrad in February, 1943. The reason Hitler went so feverishly after the vast Soviet Union was due to a combination of factors, including that he was a fervent anticommunist, he associated the Russian regime with what he imagined as a Jewish conspiracy to take over the world, and he wanted Germany returned to the glory it held before World War I—before it was humiliated by the Treaty of Versailles (1919). With Germany fighting a war on two fronts—the Soviets to the east and the Americans and British to the west—Nazi successes could not be maintained against the superior populations and productive forces of the Allies. Nazi Germany finally began to collapse under heavy bombing, including the ignominious fire-bombing of Dresden in 1943 in which 100,000 civilians were killed by the Allies (this—the killing of civilians—being the primary reason Lowell gave for refusing to fight in the war). By May of 1945, Germany and Italy had surrendered. In August, 1945, Japan surrendered. By war's end, 400,000 Americans had died in battle and 670,000 were wounded. In Europe, an estimated twenty million Russians, five million Germans, 1.5 million Yugoslavs, and six million Jews died. World War II also presented the world with the largest killing fields in history: the Nazi concentration camps, where nine million were bureaucratically murdered; and the devastated cities of Hiroshima and Nagasaki, where approximately 150,000 lost their lives immediately and 250,000 in the aftermath (most of them civilians) after the nuclear-bomb attack by the United States in August of 1945.

The political changes in America set off by joining the war effort were immense. The population became uprooted by the drafting of young men and by relocation of civilians to work in factories for the war effort. Many of these civilians were women, who, for the first time in their lives, were encouraged to work and not depend upon a male for living expenses. This economic independence from a male partner is often credited with preparing the minds of both men and women for a more fully staged political and cultural feminism in the 1970s. While women were readied for independence, African Americans put many of their plans for civil rights on hold. Despite the war, A. Philip Randolph, "the Gandhi of the Negroes" threatened to lead a march on Washington of 100,000 blacks to protest blacks being shut out from high-paying

jobs in the defense industry. Franklin Roosevelt responded, in June of 1941, with Executive Order 8802, banning racial discrimination in industry and government. Meanwhile, racism raged to the extent that even black soldiers were subjected to insult, injury, and murder. Pre-Civil Rights era (1954-1965) uprisings also occurred. In Harlem, the shooting of a black military police officer by a white policeman prompted a riot in which five people were killed, 367 injured, and property damage amounted to more than $5 million. In addition to racism directed at African Americans, there was the bigotry aimed at the Japanese living in America. While official acts of harassment directed at Italian and German Americans—curfews, restrictions on entering strategic areas, on carrying cameras and shortwave receivers—were soon lifted, the violations of the rights of Japanese Americans were far more serious and ongoing. In the spring of 1942, several months after Pearl Harbor, the government rounded up and shipped off 112,000 Japanese Americans living in California, Oregon, and Washington to "inland concentration camps" in remote and barren regions of the western states. There, Japanese Americans had to live in one-room barracks after having their land and possessions confiscated, and their professional and private lives ruined. Last of those groups whose civil rights were violated were the conscientious objectors, Robert Lowell being one of them. Six thousand conscientious objectors were jailed during the war years. While America appears in many histories as hero of the "good fight" of World War II, other accounts point to massive civilian casualties in Dresden, Hiroshima, and Nagasaki, and the violation of the civil rights of African and Japanese Americans, and of conscientious objectors at home as a reason for America not deserving such a positive label.

Critical Overview

Randall Jarrell, a close associate of Lowell, wrote the earliest important criticism on "The Quaker Graveyard in Nantucket." The last line of Lowell's poem, said Jarrell, does not open out into liberation, but into "infinite and overwhelming possibility." The most seminal essay on "The Quaker Graveyard in Nantucket" is the extended and explicative one written by Hugh B. Staples in 1962. Staples sees in Lowell's last line a manifestation of Catholic mysticism, an attempt to unite with God rather than the world—a practice also suggested by Father Mapple in *Moby Dick.* In an article titled "The Growth of a Poet," Irwin Ehrenpreis sums up the poem as less mystical and more traditionally Catholic: "The world, [Lowell] keeps saying, exists as a moral order in which separate men are not masters but participants: both the sea slime from which we rose and the whale that we plunder lie beneath the same law that subsumes humanity. To sectarian arrogance he opposes the innocence of the humbler orders of creation, for whom cruelty is an accident of their nature. As the solvent of arrogance he offers the Catholic compassion of Christ embodied in Mary his mother." Philip Cooper, the author of *The Autobiographical Myth of Robert Lowell,* believes that Lowell does not choose between Catholicism and Protestantism but merely juxtaposes or counterpoints the two. But this multiplicity is seen negatively by Marjorie Perloff, who writes, in "Death by Water: The Winslow Elegies of Robert Lowell," that the poem has no coherent system. Similarly, Patrick Cosgrave says, in *The Public Poetry of Robert Lowell,* that the poem has all these meanings and is therefore a failure since to say everything is akin to saying nothing.

Criticism

Bruce Meyer

Bruce Meyer is the director of the creative writing program at the University of Toronto. He has taught at several Canadian universities and is the author of three collections of poetry. In the following essay, Meyer asserts that Lowell uses the elegiac form in "The Quaker Graveyard in Nantucket" as part of the process by which to understand "that the death of his cousin is a tragic though necessary step in the revelation of God's purpose."

Numerous critics have pointed out that Robert Lowell's "The Quaker Graveyard in Nantucket" is an elegy, based largely on Milton's "Lycidas." Anthony Hecht, for example, in his essay on Lowell in *Obligati,* goes so far as to suggest that the original draft version of Lowell's poem contained the same number of lines (193) as Milton's poem. Hecht suggests that this was a conscious attempt on Lowell's part to associate an elegy for a cousin lost at sea with Milton's remembrance of his drowned friend, Edward King. In both cases, the loss of the protagonist by drowning suggests an enormous fall in nature. But in the case of Lowell's poem, the fall is not only a fall of Nature but of an individual who is the embodiment of a culture. When Warren Winslow drowns in "The Quaker Graveyard in Nantucket," he takes with him the identity of New England—its historical concerns and its psychological structures. Yet his death is an essential element in the recognition of what that identity is about. In "Lycidas," Milton hopes that, through the poem, "some gentle Muse / With lucky words favor my destined urn" and create a reminder not only of what is lost in Nature with the death of the elegiac protagonist but of what remains. Elegy is, after all, as Lowell notes in "The Quaker Graveyard in Nantucket," about both loss and what remains after the loss—what is able to rise above and beyond Nature and endure.

The sense of "fallen" nature that is common to the elegy as a poetic conceit is driven home in the opening lines of the poem, where the scene is set in the "brackish reach" off the extreme tip of Nantucket. The world, or what is given to us by the poet, is all water and it is "breaking violently," a statement that suggests an enormous sense of disorder and chaos. Lowell presents the image of the drowned sailor. Winslow's body is hauled aboard a ship and retrieved momentarily from the sea that will eventually reclaim him in an act of Christian burial, as if the sacrament of burial and the grace that comes with it is incapable of allaying the power of destructiveness within nature. Such is the power of the sea that "you are powerless / To sandbag this Atlantic bulwark, faced / By the earth-shaker, green, unwearied, chaste / In his steel scales." Even poetry, it seems in the early going of the poem, is powerless against the destructiveness of nature, and the simple consolations of an "Orphean lute / To pluck life back" present an impenetrable and unanswerable silence.

Part of the enigma inherent in the elegiac form is the paradox that it attempts to answer the unanswerable, to offer life's reply to a Nature that cannot hear replies. The question, then, is what is the purpose of elegy? There are two answers. The first is that elegy laments. It recognizes what is lost in Nature when the shepherd or the drowned Lycidas-figure is dead and tries to rally what is left in Nature under the banner of stoicism and readjustment. But lamentation, as Milton points out in lines 55-62 of "Lycidas" is hollow and purposeless if all it accomplishes is just a reiteration of woe. The poetry of grief, without any kind of consolation, is empty. Lycidas, at the conclusion of Milton's poem is "sunk low, but mounted high." There is a pur-

> *Part of the enigma inherent in the elegiac form is the paradox that it attempts to answer the unanswerable, to offer life's reply to a Nature that cannot hear replies."*

pose in his death, and that purpose is to enable both the poet and the reader to see some sort of higher force at work in Nature and in human destiny. In the end, Lycidas, the drowned traveler, becomes a "genius," a spirit that inhabits the place of his death and a protector for all who venture upon the seas. Milton's solution is strangely pagan, Ovidian in its message and of little Christian recompense. What Milton offers us is the fall of the Arcadian world, where the remnants are protected as a result of the sacrifice or loss of the individual from Nature.

Lowell offers us a more Christian view that is both theologically complex yet true to the Miltonic concept that loss at least provides some sort of consolation. All of Nature, as Lowell suggests in the second part of the poem, must recognize and come to terms with the loss of young Warren Winslow that is being born not only by the poet but by the world so that all Nature "screams for you." This is the anticipated point of catharsis, the outpouring of grief at the realization of the tragedy that has taken place. It is a natural human reaction that is common both to elegy and to tragedy. But remember there are two purposes to elegy. The second purpose of elegy is to move beyond grief to a reconciled vision of Man's status in Nature, while still sounding the sober warning to the reader that the world is a fragile and unforgiving place, wracked by temporality, mortality, and inconstancy. For Lowell, there is a glimmer of resurrection that drives us to faith, hope, and belief.

Lowell opens the sixth part of the poem, "Our Lady of Walsingham," with a reference to the Slipper Chapel near the ancient pilgrimage shrine in Norfolk, England. The Slipper Chapel was so venerated during the Middle Ages that both kings and commoners were required to enter the chapel barefoot as an act of supplication and reverence. As

Lowell suggests, the place is holy not just to Medieval Christianity or even to Catholicism (to which Lowell converted) but to ancient pagan beliefs in the druidic tradition that perceived divinity not only through belief but in nature itself. The reference to the "druidic" traditions associated with the Slipper Chapel and the Walsingham pilgrimage is also a direct borrowing from "Lycidas," where Milton, in line 53, refers to the resting place of "the famous Druids." In what amounts to a mixture of Wordsworthian Romanticism and Boethian Providentiality, the same savage nature that kills Warren Winslow is invested with the power of forgiveness, grace, and love and is an expression of God himself. It is reminiscent of St. Augustine's moment in *The Confessions* when he asks "where is my God" and sees Him in the beauty, wonder, and power of all creation. Boethius, the fourth-century Roman philosopher, takes St. Augustine's view a few steps further when he declares that all fortune is ultimately good because it is an expression of a destiny that God (the ultimate goodness) has shaped for mankind. In the post-Boethian Christian world, there is no sense of classical tragedy because everything has a purpose. The struggle is to find what that purpose is. This concept of "Providentiality," when blended with William Wordsworth's nineteenth-century view that Nature has the power to restore (as Wordsworth suggests in "Lines Written a Few Miles Above Tintern Abbey"), is embodied in the statue of the Virgin at Walsingham Abbey. Her visage suggests that "She knows what God knows."

God, in Lowell's conclusion, "survives the rainbow of his will." Lowell refers to God's covenant with Noah after the flood as related in Genesis 9:13 when, as a promise that He will not again destroy the world by the force of water, he sets his "bow in the cloud." What Lowell seems to be saying here is that God, or at least our belief in Him, is stronger than either the destructiveness of Nature or the weakness that would have us break into lamentation and declare woe when the world appears to fall from its state of grace upon the death of a young man. In other words, faith is stronger than despair and belief is stronger than the fall of Arcadia. Lowell's elegy, therefore, which moves methodically through an examination of the New England, seafaring Quaker culture of the nineteenth century via numerous references to Melville and Thoreau, implies that belief, strength of faith, and the very power of "inspiration" (both poetic and natural) that "breathed" into Warren Winslow's "face the breath of life," is an element inherent in the culture itself. The courage of the Quaker forbearers is, in itself, an act of the imagination that can see beyond death into the promise of life after death.

For Lowell, in "The Quaker Graveyard in Nantucket," Man's battle with Nature is an expression of both faith and cultural identity. Those who dare to challenge Nature, the Ahabs of Melville's *Moby Dick,* are seekers of divinity and God's purpose who dare to discover God, in all His grace and ferocity, by challenging Nature itself in all of its beauty and extremity. Metaphorically, they seek to draw the Leviathan from the sea by engaging in whaling; yet the whaling story that is told by Melville and retold by Lowell is a dicey business. The seafarer knows the risks but takes the challenge anyway. The New England spirit and culture provides one with an identity that, historically, demands that individuals venture forth to seek the purpose behind Nature. The strength of spirit Lowell is chronicling is the strength that sees the fall of Man and the collapse of the Arcadian or pastoral balance of the world as a test of belief.

The fourth part of the poem, for example, examines the New England tradition of whaling in considerable detail. Lowell makes reference to Ahab's ship, the Pequod of *Moby Dick,* and in Melville-like fashion in the fifth part of the poem discusses how the whale, the symbolic Leviathan of *The Bible* or the devouring sea beast of the Book of Jonah, is harvested and, ultimately, tamed. The metaphor here is not simply a parable of whaling but of how Man symbolically tames Nature and turns it to his own use—a reminder of the first covenant of the Book of Genesis, where Man is given dominion over Nature, especially the "fish of the sea" (Genesis 1:28). When Man falls from Paradise in Genesis 3:22, he is given the power "to know good and evil." What Lowell is demonstrating in "The Quaker Graveyard in Nantucket" is the strange and powerful balance between good and evil, that eschatological teeter-totter manifested in a world that can both kill and redeem.

In the elegiac process, therefore, Lowell recognizes that the death of his cousin is a tragic though necessary step in the revelation of God's purpose. Our perception of God outlasts the force of His destructiveness in Nature ("The Lord survives the rainbow of His will"). The rainbow at the conclusion of the poem is simply a refrain on the Biblical postdiluvian agreement that God offers Noah that enables Man to see purpose in an otherwise purposeless world. The death of Warren

What Do I Read Next?

- Steve Baker's *Picturing the Beast,* published in 1993, argues that representations of animals shape our understanding of both animal and human identity. Baker's examples range from Disney to zoos to political cartoons.

- Clarence Glacken's *Traces on the Rhodian Shore: Nature and Culture in Western Thought from Ancient Times to the End of the Eighteenth Century* is one of the best and most important books published on the West's cultural history of nature. It is an invaluable reference book for anyone thinking about how the meaning of nature has changed through history.

- Stephen J. Gould's *Dinosaur in a Haystack: Reflections on Natural History* is a collection of thirty-four essays, originally published in the journal *Natural History,* that brings together different manifestations of culture and establishes their roots in nature.

- Bill McKibben's *The End of Nature* (1989) works hard at combatting the persistent notion of the inexhaustibility of nature.

Winslow, therefore, is a death that is a means, albeit a tragic one, of finding a way to see God's hand at work in the universe. Like the culture from which the elegiac protagonist springs, as Lowell points out, the poem is not only engaged in an observation of Nature but in a challenge to it. The 'tradition that the poem celebrates through the death and remembrance of Warren Winslow is the New England vision of self-reliance and self-sufficiency—the tradition of examining the world with a straightforward attitude that trusts in God and gives little sway to fear. This is the message of Thoreau's writings and it is one of the fundamental precepts at the root of the Quaker faith. "The Quaker Graveyard in Nantucket," therefore, is not merely an elegy or even a chronicle but a testament to faith, a marker that records and memorializes a culture and its ideals.

Ironically, the actual graveyard on Nantucket that is the subject of Lowell's poem met a fate that makes Lowell's poem all the more important as a cultural "marker." Until the early 1980s, there was a wooden fence surrounding the actual burial grounds, and the fence bore the names of many of those who were buried there as a way of marking the stoneless graves. However, the fence was destroyed in a fire set by vandals, and the names, unrecorded elsewhere, were lost. The plot of ground today resembles an open field, and there is nothing other than a small sign, with no mention of Lowell or his poem, to signify the importance of the place.

Source: Bruce Meyer, in an essay for *Poetry for Students,* The Gale Group, 1999.

Jhan Hochman

Jhan Hochman's articles appear in Democracy and Nature, Genre, ISLE, *and* Mosaic. *He is the author of* Green Cultural Studies: Nature in Film, Novel, and Theory *(1998), and he holds a Ph.D. in English and an M.A. in cinema studies. In the following essay, Hochman explains how the doubleness of Lowell's vision is fleshed out by examining the characters in "The Quaker Graveyard in Nantucket."*

Perhaps you feel the same way I do about Robert Lowell's "The Quaker Graveyard in Nantucket": I both like it and don't like it. On one hand I find the poem "forbidding and clotted" (as John Crowe Ransom said of Lowell's early poems); the poem tries to do so much that it becomes overwhelmed and overwhelming. On the other hand, I like the poem for this very reason, because it is so replete with imagery, reference, ingenuity of form, and complexity of message. I think my ambivalence issues from Lowell's conflicted listening to the creatures sitting atop his shoulders (neither of which is devilish or angelic). One creature is the muse of formalism (every section of the poem is an adventure into form), and the other, the muse of the message, of the content of the poem. In attempting to placate the urgent demands of both muses—demands that cannot be completely satisfied—Lowell produces a compromise. The result is that while neither the muse of form or content is completely satisfied, neither is it wholly disappointed. And it is not, necessarily, that Lowell seeks to be oblique in order to be impressive, but, more, that he wants to be so impressive in satisfying the demands of both form and content that he ends up being oblique. The dilemma of doubleness

does not stop here: the muse of content is actually itself two creatures, balanced by a tortured or tolerable ambivalence.

This ambivalence is inherent in certain characters throughout "The Quaker Graveyard in Nantucket, specifically, the ocean, whale, land, wind, birds, stars, rainbow, Winslow, God, and the Virgin Mary. Most of these entities are, under Lowell's scrutiny, bipolar—they are depicted in polarized ways, not at exactly the same time, but not at altogether different times, either. For instance, in section I, the sea is "breaking violently" and is deified as the "earth-shaker," Poseidon, who allows no rebirth from death. In section II, the ocean is not a threat, but a victim of "lubbers" who "lash" it, and a throat in the wind's grip. Section III is bipolar: the ocean is once again a victim ("the harrowed brine"), but this time of the onslaught by humanity. The Atlantic is also, as in section I, the drowner of humanity ("When the Atlantic rose against us"). Section IV depicts the ocean as victim of both whalers and land (from whence the whalers come). The sea is a "hurt self" and land is "Sucking the ocean's side." Parts VII and III are similar, since the sea is both victim ("fouled with the blue sailors") and killer of sailors and the wind that previously strangled it: "Atlantic, where your bell-trap guts its spoil / You could cut the brackish winds with a knife."

The whale first appears in the last two lines of section II, in the character of Moby Dick, as, most definitely, a victim ("hurt beast"). But Moby Dick, in part III, is a "whited monster," and the sailors drown in the sperm whale's bodily emissions of ambergris. The whale of section IV is also a killer, but only because it is hunted: "Spouting out blood and water as it rolls." In part V, the whale, though overwhelmingly savaged, becomes a weapon in its death throes: "The gun blue swingle, heaving like a flail." In section VII, the whale is only implied, the prey of "blue-lung'd combers." It must be said here that Lowell is least successful when depicting the whale ambivalently since it is more conspicuously a casualty of human rapacity. The land, in part II, is directly beaten by the wind or by ships blown by wind, but in section III, the land is lashed by warships. In contrast again, the land is shown in part IV, "Sucking the ocean's side." The wind is most prominent in section II as it "heaves at the roped-in bulwarks of this pier," blows the "yawing" boats, "screams," and "claws at the sea's throat." It makes one other appearance in the last section when it blows the oak and the sea but is also threatened with being cut by an all-powerful ocean: "Atlantic ... / You could cut the brackish winds with a knife." Even what seem to be sympathetic birds are double natured. In part II, "The terns and sea-gulls tremble" because of the death of Winslow, and the sea-gulls have "heavy" (sorrowful) eyelids. Likewise, in part III, sea birds are sympathetic creatures, but this time for ocean and, by implication, for the whale: "the sea-gulls wail / For water." In section V, however, the sea-gulls appear joyful at the destruction of the ship, for, as the birds "go round," the stars "sing out together" and the thunder finishes off the whaling vessel.

The rainbow appears in the poem's last line only, but even in this single instance, it seems an ambivalent symbol, both in Lowell's hands and in the place from where he took it—the Bible. A rainbow, of course, usually appears after a storm, and so it functions as a sign of calm. By extension, in some ancient cultures, a rainbow was imagined as a bow from which bolts of lightning were shot. When, in Genesis, God hangs up his rainbow in the sky, it is a sign that his anger at human evil has abated. In this way, the rainbow functions like a superannuated antique rifle hung over a fireplace, the sign of perhaps a former hunter, but now of no threat to anyone. Still, the rainbow is a displayed weapon, and, as such, threatens with being used again. And what is to be thought when a rainbow cannot be seen? That the day might again occur when God will destroy the earth with a flood? The rainbow, then, while a beautiful symbol of peace, was once construed as a weapon, quietly threatening in both appearance and absence. This brings us to the wielder of this weapon, God. God once destroyed the vast majority of life on earth with a flood according to *The Epic of Gilgamesh* and, later, Genesis. Afterward, in Genesis, He promised to both human and nonhuman animals that He would never do it again. Why? Because in Genesis 8:21, God states that "the imagination of man's heart is evil from his youth." In other words, it would do no good to create another flood and another ark, for humanity cannot learn and will always be evil, despite God's threats. So though the Old Testament God might like to eradicate life once again, he restrains Himself. God, it should be noticed here, is not One, but divided within Himself. In fact, it even appears He made a mistake by thinking the flood would cleanse the earth of iniquity. Realizing he made a mistake, he pledges to bow out of any further project for inundation. Indeed, He makes another mistake. Lowell refers, in his epigraph, to the passage in Genesis where God gives humanity dominion over the rest of life. Like

the rest of the characters in "The Quaker Graveyard in Nantucker," God is not One but (at least) Double, Two, or Ambivalent—sympathetic and protective toward, yet also disdainful of and threatening to, humanity. Going further, God is an ambivalent character because He is at one time the destroyer of individuals (in the guise of ocean, storm, etc.) who commit evil. At another time, God is the victim of human evil, for it is humanity who has ruined His good creation.

As Lowell says, "It's well." All there is to do now is figure out why this poem should swim in two directions. My proposition is that Lowell was uncomfortably conflicted—or comfortably ambivalent—about the death of his maternal cousin, Warren Winslow. On one hand, "The Quaker Graveyard in Nantucket," is an elegy to a dead Winslow. On the other, it is an indictment of a soldier who fought a war (World War II) that Lowell refused to fight, for whose conscientious objection he was jailed. Lowell, like most of us, maintains the usual respect and sorrow at death. But unusually, Lowell sees Winslow getting what he deserved for fighting a war Lowell was against (if Lowell was not against all wars). In this respect, Winslow bears comparison to whalers about whom Lowell also felt ambivalent. Lowell characterized the whalers as those who did not (or do not) know better since "They died / When time was open-eyed, / Wooden and childish" and suggest that they deserve sympathy for what they suffered by dying. Also plain is that Lowell felt that whalers, like soldiers, deserved to pay for their violence—that both were "Sea-monsters, upward angel, downward fish," devils deserving to fall for climbing too high.

Lowell's ambivalence in this poem—comfortable or conflicted—might have partially issued from his recurrent bipolar disorder (formerly called manic-depressive disorder) for which he was sporadically hospitalized and frequently medicated. Lowell, in an interview with Ian Hamilton in 1971, described his illness this way: "I have been through mania and depression.... Mania is extremity for one's friends, depression for one's self. Both are chemical. In depression, one wakes, is happy for about two minutes, probably less, and then fades into dread of the day. Nothing will happen, but you know twelve hours will pass before you are back in bed and sheltering your consciousness in dreams, or nothing.... [I think it] dust in the blood." Esther Brooks had this to say about the poet: "For those of us who loved him there never could have been a Jekyll so opposite to his Hyde, nor a figure who could have suffered more from being so inwardly at odds with himself." And this description from James Atlas: "Every few semesters he had to be confined to McLean's, the Boston-area mental hospital described in his poem, 'Waking in the Blue.' I had never witnessed one of these breakdowns, but I had heard about them in grim detail: Lowell showing up at William Alfred's house and declaring that he was the Virgin Mary ...."

Recall now, if you will, section VI, *Our Lady of Walsingham,* where Lowell describes Mary in order to show the proper attitude of the penitent Catholic: neither gladness nor grief. Mary's is the pose of heavy equanimity, an otherworldness that shows her knowledge of God. Wavering with mania for others and depression about himself, with grief and condemnation of the violent who are now dead, between the good Dr. Jekyll and the evil Hyde, and between the doubleness of phenomena and nature, it is no wonder the bipolar Lowell took temporary refuge (in poetry and episodes of mental illness) in Mary's image of equanimity. On the other hand, Lowell did not end the poem with Mary's equanimity, but with an angry God's fragile promise. Perhaps because Lowell felt closer to the God bursting with Old Testament rage at human violence, he displayed his poems for all to see, poems often being—like rainbows—a sign of anger subsided or sublimated.

Source: Jhan Hochman, in an essay for *Poetry for Students,* The Gale Group, 1999.

Mary Mahony

Mary Mahony is an instructor of English at Wayne County Community College in Detroit, Michigan. In the following essay, Mahony discusses Robert Lowell's use of language, allusion, and symbol.

In a 1964 *Book Week* review, Richard Poirier described Robert Lowell's literary status at that time, declaring him "by something like a critical consensus, the greatest American poet of the mid-century, probably the greatest poet now writing in English." An appraisal of Lowell's place in the literary pantheon at the end of the twentieth century, however, provides a somewhat less secure position. While it is impossible to doubt the power and influence of his work, several critics have challenged his role as the major poet of his generation. Much of this criticism revolves around his earlier poetry from the 1940s and early 1950s, the period that established his reputation. This is also the era during which he wrote "The Quaker Graveyard in Nantucket," one of the most famous and most analyzed of all of Lowell's poems.

Published first in two parts in the *Partisan Review* and then revised in the book *Lord Weary's Castle,* "The Quaker Graveyard in Nantucket" is considered by many critics to be one of Lowell's greatest works. It also illustrates some of his major weaknesses. Like many of the poems in his first volumes, "The Quaker Graveyard in Nantucket" is characterized by elaborate poetical structures, dense imagery, and complex symbolic and literary references. Irwin Ehrenpreis, in his article "The Growth of a Poet," believes it to be "Lowell's most commonly overpraised work," adding that the dense use of symbol makes it "more impressive for aspiration than for accomplishment." Ironically, in many ways, Lowell's strengths are also his weaknesses. Both those critics who admire and those who criticize the poem do so, in part, because of the complexity of its symbolism, the obscurity of its images, and the variety of its possible meanings.

On a first reading, "The Quaker Graveyard in Nantucket" is dazzling, a poetic tour de force. Phrases soar, almost attacking the reader. The sheer sensual power of the language is nearly overwhelming. Lines sound and resound as Lowell evokes images from history, classical mythology, the Bible, and literature that are designed to evoke an intense response. Lowell's words force the reader to visualize the power of the sea, to become sickened by the brutality of the whale hunt, and to ponder the current state of humanity's relationship with God. The violent power of his vocabulary can be felt in phrases such as this, where nature seemingly turns upon itself, ironically mimicking man's own mistreatment: "The winds' wings beat upon the stones, / Cousin, and scream for you and the claws rush / At the sea's throat." Here, Lowell masterfully uses vocabulary, rhythm, and multiple aspects of rhyme to emotionally engage the reader.

However, while the emotional effect of the poem is undeniable, a student who is attempting to assign theme and meaning to it may be overwhelmed because of more than just the power of the language. Like the night that Lowell portrays storming onto the fleet, the poem assaults the reader—not only with its harsh and powerful language, but with the complexity of its imagery and references. Many readers will agree with this statement from *Robert Lowell* by Richard Fein: "Has there ever existed a reader not puzzled or disturbed by *Lord Weary's Castle?* The reader weathers not only all that knowledge rammed into the poems, all those allusions, all that heavy historicity, and a prosody of wrenched anger, but also an insistence on attitudes that seem almost dictatorial on the part of the poet—dictatorial to history, to God, to the poet himself, and to his rhythms."

One of the major reasons for Lowell's use of such elaborate and ambiguous imagery in the poem is because his themes themselves are complex. In "The Quaker Graveyard in Nantucket," he explores abstract historic and religious truths that are not easily explained or revealed. This creates a distinct problem for both poet and reader, because such issues are not easy to conceptualize. His scope includes criticism not only of the religious, military, and economic history of New England and, later, of the United States, but also of the moral commitments and betrayals of humankind. One major focus of the poem is man's complex relationship with God: both the angry and vengeful God of the Old Testament who played such a prominent role in the sermons of his New England Puritan ancestors and the New Testament Messiah who saves the world through love and sacrifice. Lowell attempts to define the parameters of this relationship for twentieth-century America. Because, in his opinion, this society has long favored capitalism, secularism, and militarism over religion, any discussion requires complex symbolism, as well as a wide range of Biblical, mythological, and historical allusions. Metaphysical theory is not easily served up in simple, concrete terms.

An additional reason for the extraordinary complexity of many of Lowell's poems occurs because of the frequent ambiguity of his language. His phrases hint, or even hide meaning at times, often masking far more than they reveal. Lowell al-

> *Like the night that Lowell portrays storming onto the fleet, ['The Quaker Graveyard in Nantucket'] assaults the reader—not only with its harsh and powerful language, but with the complexity of its imagery and references."*

lows, or perhaps even demands, that his readers draw their own conclusions from his words.

Notice the multiplicity of possible meanings contained in this passage from Part III: "Where time's contrition blues / Whatever it was these Quaker sailors lost / in the mad scramble of their lives." These lines require the reader to make many decisions: Does time represent God? If so, is God remorseful? What other possible meanings are there for the words "time's contrition?" How is the word "blues" being used? Making it a verb is vivid, attention-getting, and unconventional; however, the verb has more than one meaning. Is Lowell using the term in the sense of cleansing, since bluing is a type of bleach? Or does the word mean to dye, to turn blue, and is it connected with the "blue sailors" who foul the Atlantic in Part VII?

By using the relative pronoun "whatever," which the *American Heritage Dictionary* defines as "everything and anything that," Lowell grants the reader an open-ended invitation to speculate on the dreams and motivations of these nineteenth-century whalers. A few lines later, he adds that "What it costs / Them is their secret." This is typical of much of Lowell's poetry. There is not and can not be one simple, single summary that provides readers with an explanation of Lowell's precise meaning. While this forces the reader to become an active participant in the poem, it can also be unsettling for students seeking to interpret lines. Jerome Mazzaro, in *The Poetic Themes of Robert Lowell,* notes that Lowell's "obscurity ... places a barrier of unconveyed information between the event, the poet, and the reader."

> *Metaphysical theory is not easily served up in simple, concrete terms."*

Still another reason for the poem's difficulty is because of Lowell's varied and continual use of adaptation and allusion, much of which may be unfamiliar to the average reader. Fortunately, "The Quaker Graveyard in Nantucket" has been analyzed frequently. In fact, it has become, in certain ways, a literary critic's version of the children's game, "Find the Hidden Picture." While many references are direct, others are obscure. Several critics have pointed out that the poem, an elegy, is similar in subject, death by drowning, and the number of lines to Milton's "Lycidas." The opening images have been borrowed from Henry David Thoreau's *Cape Cod*, and the section on Walsingham has been adapted from *Catholic Art and Culture* by E. I. Watkins. The debt to Herman Melville's *Moby Dick* is clear in the frequent references to Ahab and the Pequod. However, even critics disagree on whether "the mast-lashed master of Leviathans" is Ahab or another character from the novel, Tashtego. Several critics, in fact, find hints of a reference to Odysseus from the poem by Homer. In addition, allusions to classical and Christian mythology permeate the poem. Both Lowell's personal history and regional history play a role in the symbolism, as well. In spite of this personal connection, however, even the poem's source of inspiration is obscured from the reader. While it is dedicated to Warren Winslow, Lowell's cousin who died in World War II, his role in the elegy seems minimal. Even the manner of his death is never explained in the poem, although eventual research has shown that he died in an accidental explosion in New York harbor. Discovering the allusions may enrich the poem's meaning—and the reader's knowledge, as well. However, the excessive use of allusion may help to create the barrier that Mazzaro mentioned, since Lowell always seems to know more than the reader.

A final difficulty in interpreting "The Quaker Graveyard in Nantucket" lies in Lowell's use of symbol. The powerful imagery he chooses is often overwhelming, particularly since symbols often function in different, even diametrically opposed ways. One example is the sea, which, as both object and symbol, is central to the poem. It is, in fact, the graveyard for the Quakers as well as the sailors lost on torpedoed warships, all now buried in "unstoned graves." Throughout the poem, Lowell presents the sea in a variety of contexts. Alan Williamson, in his study of Lowell's vision titled *Pity the Monsters,* demonstrates that the last lines of the Part I present three different personifications of the sea. The first is Poseiden, the Greek god of the seas, who was also known as the "earth-shaker." In this guise, Lowell presents the sea as creator of the devastating storms that recur throughout the poem. The reference to the "steel scales" hints at the presence of a sea serpent or Leviathan, a destructive figure in Biblical and Judeo-Christian mythology. In Psalm 74, God crushes Leviathan, who symbolizes primeval chaos; Leviathan is frequently portrayed in the mythology as a giant whale. The words "green, unwearied, chaste" indicate the presence of Lowell's God, the God whom Mary represents at Walsingham. These three personifications demonstrate the type of contradictions that appear in Lowell's symbolism. The sea is both the life-giver and the destroyer throughout the poem. The final lines reinforce this concept, reminding the reader that the Atlantic is "fouled with blue sailors," descended from the time when "the Lord God formed man from the sea slime."

Another major symbol in "The Quaker Graveyard in Nantucket" is the white whale, a creature of fable whose literary forerunner is Melville's Moby Dick. Once again, Lowell allows multiple interpretations. The whale in Part III, "IS the whited monster," destroys the Quakers. He is clearly a destructive force, but is he also a punishing God whose revenge may be ultimately the fault of the violent and materialistic practices of the whalers? Critics have interpreted Lowell's religious symbolism here in many ways. Several believe that the whale in Parts III through V represents Christ, Jesus or Iesus Salvatore. They state that Part V's apocalyptic vision clearly demonstrates the identification of the whale with Christ. He is Christ the Messiah, taking man's sins upon himself. Other critics, however, believe IS to be a variation of the name that the harsher God of the Old Testament used to reveal himself to Moses in Exodus, "I Am That I Am." Many critics feel that both interpretations fit the poem's theme. Patrick Cosgrave, however, in *The Public Poetry of Robert Lowell,* believes that identifying the whale with Christ contradicts identifying the whale with the God of the Old Testament.

Lowell's symbolic use of the statue of Our Lady of Walsingham in Part VI also disconcerts the reader, perhaps more than it aids in clarifying the poem's theme. This section, with its quiet tone that provides a respite from the tortured violence of the previous sections, is often praised. Some critics, like Mazzaro, even feel that it provides the poem's resolution. Taken from E. I. Watkins's *Catholic Art and Culture,* it describes the pilgrim's route to Walsingham. However, the end result of this peaceful journey comes as a surprise. Lowell's statue of the Virgin, unlike the one described by Watkins, is neither warm nor welcoming. Instead, "There's no comeliness / At all or charm in that expressionless / Face." This unconventional portrayal contrasts uncomfortably with the pleasant, soothing descriptions of the English countryside. It is difficult to envision the Lady guiding supplicants to salvation. Although "she knows what God knows," the reader does not share in this knowledge. In *The Poetic Art of Robert Lowell,* Marjorie Perloff criticizes the entire section, saying that it "fails to cohere with the rest of the poem." She finds it hard to reconcile these two very separate settings, Nantucket and Walsingham. Although "the world shall come to Walsingham," what does this have to do with World War II American sailors or Quaker whalers?

Since critics disagree about so many aspects of Lowell's symbolism in "The Quaker Graveyard in Nantucket," it is not surprising they would also disagree about the poem's ultimate expression of the relationship between God and man. Lowell clearly conveys the fact that man has violated his part in the covenant with God. Nature itself—the sea, birds, beasts/whale—are personified in order to fully demonstrate this betrayal. However, it is possible to draw different conclusions about the future that Lowell envisions. One group of critics believe that the sixth and seventh parts of the poem provide a message of reconciliation, holding out the possibility of the restoration of the covenant, along with the hope of salvation. Others find that the poem presents a dire warning about the consequences of plundering nature, espousing violence, and repudiating God. They believe that the conflicts between man and nature, man and God are almost certainly irreconcilable. A final interpretation views the poem as a despairing vision of the imminent apocalypse that Lowell feels is hanging over twentieth-century humanity.

Despite its complexity and obscurity, "The Quaker Graveyard in Nantucket" is a poem of great power and vision. In ways, it resembles a kaleidoscope; each slight shift in perspective brings a dif-

ferent insight. And like the kaleidoscope, the separate pictures in the poem enhance rather than negate each other. This multiplicity of visions may be necessary to accomplish Lowell's extraordinary task. Mark Rudman, in *Robert Lowell: An Introduction to the Poetry,* noted that "The Quaker Graveyard in Nantucket" seemed almost an attempt to rewrite *Moby Dick* in 143 lines. However, Lowell's accomplishment is even more far reaching. The poem encapsulates human history from a Christian theological standpoint, ranging from God breathing life into man and forming a covenant in Genesis, moving through Exodus, Psalms, Job, Isaiah, the gospels, then reaching the apocalyptic devastation of Revelation. Finally, the poem's last line returns history to its beginning, to Genesis as "The Lord survives the rainbow of His will."

Source: Mary Mahony, in an essay for *Poetry for Students,* The Gale Group, 1999.

Sources

Bloom, Harold, ed., *Robert Lowell,* New York: Chelsea House, 1987.

Cooper, Philip, *The Autobiographical Myth of Robert Lowell,* Chapel Hill: University of North Carolina Press, 1970.

Cosgrave, Patrick, *The Public Poetry of Robert Lowell,* New York: Taplinger Publishing Company, 1972.

Diggins, John Patrick, *The Proud Decades: America in War and Peace 1941-1960,* New York: W.W. Norton, 1988.

Ehrenpreis, Irwin, "The Growth of a Poet," in *Critics on Robert Lowell,* University of Miami Press, 1972, pp. 15-36.

Fein, Richard J., *Robert Lowell,* second edition, Boston: Twayne, 1979.

Hobsbaum, Philip, *A Reader's Guide to Robert Lowell,* London: Thames and Hudson, 1988.

Mazzaro, Jerome, *The Poetic Themes of Robert Lowell,* Ann Arbor: University of Michigan Press, 1965, p. 5.

Muste, John M., "The Quaker Graveyard in Nantucket," *Masterplots Poetry Series,* Vol. 5, edited by Frank Magill, Pasadena: Salem Press, 1992, pp. 1757-59.

Parkinson, Thomas, ed., *Robert Lowell: A Collection of Critical Essays,* Englewood Cliffs, NJ: Prentice-Hall, 1968.

Perloff, Marjorie, "Death by Water: The Winslow Elegies of Robert Lowell," *English Literary History,* March, 1967 pp. 116-40.

Perloff, Marjorie, *The Poetic Art of Robert Lowell,* Cornell University Press, 1973, p. 144.

Poirier, Richard, "For the Union Dead," in *Critics on Robert Lowell,* University of Miami Press, 1972, pp. 92-6.

Procopiow, Norma, *Robert Lowell: The Poet and His Critics,* Chicago: American Library Association, 1984.

Rudman, Mark, *Robert Lowell, An Introduction to the Poetry,* Columbia University Press, 1983, p. 20.

The Whale, New York: Simon and Schuster, 1968.

Williamson, Alan, *Pity the Monsters: The Political Vision of Robert Lowell,* New Haven, CT: Yale University Press, 1974.

For Further Study

The Oxford Annotated Bible: Revised Standard Version Containing The Old and New Testaments, New York: Oxford University Press, 1962.
This Bible, because of its annotations, is an excellent reference tool for students of literature and history.

Melville, Herman, *Moby Dick,* London: Everyman, 1993.
A. Robert Lee's edition of the classic whaling tale contains scholarly material on Melville and the text, and contains criticism from the time the novel was released.

Meyers, Jeffrey, *Robert Lowell: Interviews and Memoirs,* Ann Arbor: University of Michigan Press, 1988.
In addition to intelligent interviews, this volume presents a wide range of essays by distinguished poets, novelists, and critics, including John Crowe Ransom, Norman Mailer, and V. S. Naipaul.

Milton, John, *Paradise Lost and Other Poems,* New York: Mentor, 1961.
This collection contains helpful annotations and "Lycidas," part of the inspiration for "The Quaker Graveyard in Nantucket."

Thoreau, Henry David, *Cape Cod,* New York: The Library of America, 1985.
Thoreau documents a walking trip he took along Cape Cod. The work furnished inspiration for a passage in the first section of Lowell's poem.

Queen-Ann's-Lace

William Carlos Williams
1921

"Queen-Ann's-Lace" appeared in William Carlos Williams's fourth published collection of poems, *Sour Grapes,* in 1921. With its keenly observed and passionate images of flowers and women, this poem constitutes—along with "Daisy," "Primrose," and "Great Mullen"—the book's well-known floral quartet, an example of Williams's Imagist style. "Queen-Ann's-Lace" is a love poem that shifts seamlessly between the image of a woman, imperfect and impassioned, and that of the beautiful weed also known as the wild carrot. The comparison of the beloved to a flower is nothing new: "My luve is like a red, red rose," wrote Robert Burns in the late-eighteenth century. Reading in this tradition, it is tempting to say that Williams's white field of wild carrot is simply a metaphor for the sexually aroused female body. But it is not as simple as that. Like many Williams poems, this one resists easy one-to-one correspondences and challenges the traditional uses of metaphor. On the other hand, the poem also contradicts what Williams himself said of it: "Straight observation is used in four poems about flowers ... I thought of them as still-lifes. I looked at the actual flowers as they grew." No one reading "Queen-Ann's-Lace," the famous "The Red Wheelbarrow," or the epic poem *Paterson* would doubt that Williams knew how to *look* at things. But there is little "still" and little about the life of flower, woman, or even poetry itself, in "Queen-Ann's-Lace." Williams's "straight" looking broke ground as a new way to handle the poetic line and image. But there is much more than "straight observation" at work here, as this poem's last words tell us. Beyond what can be seen is the mystery of whiteness, silence, "or nothing."

Author Biography

William Carlos Williams was born in Rutherford, New Jersey, on September 17, 1883. He died in the same city at age 79, on March 4, 1963, having married, raised two sons, and maintained a respected pediatrics practice, all the while living the intense life of a poet at the cutting edge of a new aesthetic. Few poets have been as committed to the "local" as Williams. Rutherford, the Passaic River, and his home at 9 Ridge Road have become synonyms for William Carlos Williams's devotion to the here and now. Many other major writers of his day— including Ezra Pound, T. S. Eliot, Ernest Hemingway, and Gertrude Stein—left the United States in the 1920s for the fertile artistic life of Paris and London. Upon returning from his own visit with his wife to Europe in 1924, Williams confessed that even though "Paris has gotten violently into our blood in one way or another" it was not enough to keep him there. So he and Florence returned to Rutherford, their children, his medical practice, and to a clearer sense of the direction he wanted his own art to take.

Williams Carlos Williams was born to William George Williams, a British perfume merchant who, according to his poet son, "never got over being an Englishman." His mother, Raquel Hélène Rose Hoheb Williams, known as "Elena," was a temperamental woman of French, Dutch, Spanish, and Jewish descent who showed little interest in speaking fluent English. Elena's passion for the arts and Europe provided her sons an exposure to painting and music that was lacking, in her view, in the daily life of Rutherford. When William and his brother Edgar were young teenagers, Elena insisted on returning to Europe for a while and sent the boys to various schools in Geneva and Paris, hoping they would become fluent in French. Instead, the boys floundered, and they returned to New Jersey to attend Horace Mann High School, one of the best public schools on the East Coast.

Another important feminine influence on William Carlos's young life was his grandmother, Emily Dickinson Wellcome. While Elena Williams appeared aristocratic, exotic, and somewhat aloof

William Carlos Williams

as a mother, Emily Wellcome practically raised William and Edgar herself and was a source of stability, fierce practicality, and, not least, a colloquial English that would help "tune" Williams's ear to American speech. Elena and Emily thoroughly disliked each other, but their counterpointed influences gave profound dimension to the feminine presence and images in Williams's poetry, no less in the five-book poem *Paterson* than in the short lyric "Queen-Ann's-Lace." Later, Florence "Floss" Herman, Williams's wife, became yet another source of inspiration for the feminine idea in his work, as well as a steady source of support for her husband's literary life in the midst of disapproval from family and from Rutherford itself, where, she said, "he was misunderstood and parodied."

At Horace Mann High School, Williams began preparing for a "scientific" career that eventually led to his practice of obstetrics and pediatrics. But under the encouraging teaching of "Uncle Billy" Abbott, Williams also began to enjoy reading the classics, especially the poetry of Milton, Coleridge, and Keats. And "out of the blue, with no past," as he described it, came the "thrill" and "discovery" of his first poem: "A black, black cloud / flew over the sun, / driven by fierce, flying / rain." His passion for literature and the arts grew at the University of Pennsylvania, where he was enrolled in the medical school. There, Williams met Ezra Pound and the literary circle that helped him transform his first serious poetic efforts—imitative, "bad Keats," as he put it—into an art that depended on close attention to the drama of common things and ordinary people, the rhythms and sounds of the immediate. Meeting Pound "was like B.C. and A.D.," said Williams. Out of Pound's "Imagist" insistence on clear, exact, concrete language, and natural rhythm, Williams forged his own aesthetic, summed up in his famous dictum, "No ideas, but in things."

In the busy decade between 1910 and 1920, Williams established his practice, married, moved to 9 Ridge Road, had children, and published his first three volumes: *The Tempers, Al Que Quiere!,* and *Kora in Hell: Improvisations. Sour Grapes,* his fourth volume of poetry, was published in 1921, and contained many "imagist" poems such as "Queen-Ann's-Lace" and the poignant "Widow's Lament in Springtime," another poem in which woman and white flower are the central images.

Until the final years of strokes leading to his death, Williams's artistic output was prodigious: more than fifty volumes of poetry, novels, short stories, plays, essays, autobiographies, and translations, besides countless magazine articles and reviews. In between patients, Dr. Williams wrote lines of poems on prescription pads or typed in short bursts, using the time and materials at hand. An urgent house call might drive him away temporarily from a poem and out into a blizzard, but his devotion to the human body and the body of language were not distinct, in his way of living. Speaking of his patients, Williams said, "We begin to see that the underlying meaning of all they want to tell us and have always failed to communicate is the poem, the poem which their lives are being lived to realize." The beauty of person and poem is never "so remote a thing."

Poem Text

Her body is not so white as
anemone petals nor so smooth—nor
so remote a thing. It is a field
of the wild carrot taking
the field by force; the grass   5
does not raise above it.
Here is no question of whiteness,
white as can be, with a purple mole
at the center of each flower.
Each flower is a hand's span   10
of her whiteness. Wherever

his hand has lain there is
a tiny purple blemish. Each part
is a blossom under his touch
to which the fibres of her being   15
stem one by one, each to its end,
until the whole field is a
white desire, empty, a single stem,
a cluster, flower by flower,
a pious wish to whiteness gone over—   20
or nothing.

Poem Summary

Lines 1-3:

The title of this poem is the name of a common wildflower, but the first words of the poem, "her body," immediately give it a human dimension. The comparison of woman to nature is common to every time and culture, but these lines particularly recall Shakespeare's "Sonnet 130," his famous parody of Petrarchan love poems: "My mistress' eyes are nothing like the sun / Coral is far more red than her lips' red ...." The Renaissance Italian sonneteer Petrarch used exaggerated metaphors to express the beauty of his beloved and of his suffering in love. In elaborate images he might express, for example, how her eyes shine brighter than the sun and her cheeks outbloom the rose. Shakespeare's poem exposes the "false compare" of those images and depicts instead a woman whose beauty lies in the truth of her love. Both Shakespeare and Williams establish from the beginning that their love is real, not ideal, and the beloved is quite human and imperfect, not an abstraction of beauty. In both poems, the loved one is described in terms of what she is "not"; here, she is neither as white nor as smooth as the anemone, and the lover knows this through sight and touch, the two dominant senses of the poem.

In line 2, because "nor" is placed at the end of the line and is set off by a dash, it is given great emphasis: this woman-flower is clearly *not* "so remote a thing." These lines are a kind of signature for Williams's art in its passion for the "here and now." He writes not about "remote" things, but what he can actually see and touch. The "white" of this flower is approachable in its impurity. Williams's great love and knowledge of painting emerges in his attention to color, and in this poem, white dominates the palette.

Lines 3-6:

Line 3 contains a cacsura, a pause or break in the line determined by the meaning and natural

Media Adaptations

- A four-CD set titled "In Their Own Voices: A Century of Recorded Poetry" (1996) features more than one hundred British and American poets reading their own work, including Williams reading "The Red Wheelbarrow" and "To Elsie." The set is available from Rhino Records, Word Beat.

- Well-written information about Williams, including an audio link, picture, and bibliography can be found in The Academy of American Poets' website: http://www.poets.org/LIT/POET.

- Williams reads selected poems in 1954 for a Caedmon audio recording. According to the Poet's Audio Center, from whom it can be ordered (www.writer.org/pac), the recording was made not long after Williams suffered from a stroke, "and it shows."

- The Watershed Archive Series has compiled several recordings of Williams reading poems that range from his first work to his last, selected to reveal his major themes and images. *The People & the Stones: Selected Poems* is available through the Poet's Audio Center (www.writer. org/pac).

- A comprehensive 15-tape set of every existing recording of Williams, *The Collected Recordings,* is available through the Poet's Audio Center, who says that the project is not complete, and more tapes will be forthcoming.

- The Voices and Visions series of videos has produced *William Carlos Williams* in Volume 1, available from Mystic Fire Video.

rhythms of speech. Here, one sentence ends and the next begins, and the poem expands suddenly from the exotic flower that it isn't to the whole field of flowers that it is. The feminine presence is now vast, wild, and fierce in her fertility, "taking / the field by force." This image, too, turns upside down the one-dimensional idea of a woman as a fragile flower in a glass vase. The diction, or word choice, is both formal and colloquial just as the flower at hand is both "Queen Ann's lace," refined and delicate, and the "wild carrot," dynamic, earthy, and strong. Its stalks are sturdy and tall, dominating the grasses that share the field.

Lines 7-13:

These lines continue that fluid shifting back and forth between the language of "lace" and "carrot," between "is" and "is not," and between flower and woman. The result is dynamic description, not static definition. We learn that each flower on the multifoliate stalk has a purple "mole" at its center, and thus prevents absolute "whiteness, / white as can be." Furthermore, it is a "mole," not a "star" or "jewel"—Williams's diction reinforces the sense that the beloved's imperfections are essential to her erotic attraction. Like a double exposure, the lover's touch comes into play as a way of "seeing" the flower's dimension: A "hand's span," not inches, is the unit of measure, implying that her body has been measured by his touch. There has been direct contact, not just dreamy imagining, and the proof is in the "tiny purple blemish" that remains "Wherever / his hand has lain." One can just as easily imagine the sun caressing the flower with its warmth as the poet-lover caressing the beloved. But whether Williams was first inspired by a woman and reminded of a flower, or vice versa, is irrelevant. It is important to see that neither flower nor woman is reduced to a tool of comparison for the other, but that, instead, the poem expresses a kind of erotic contact with both. For Williams, the erotic was an integrating force.

Lines 13-19:

Here the poem becomes intense and breathless in this long sentence with its vibrant verbs and words that run "enjambed," or without break, from one line to the next. Williams seamlessly blends his observation of the "erotic" growth of Queen Ann's lace—each tiny flower in the cluster emerging from its raised stem, white and open to the sun's rays—with human desire at its height. But the "white" of this desire is a paradox. White reflects the entire color spectrum and is thus a symbol of presence. It is also the color of silence and absence. At its height, the caressed field of flowers is a "white desire" perfectly full, but also completely "empty."

Lines 20-21:

Any attempt to sum up this poem as a lyric "about" sex or flowers is forestalled by the last two lines. If anything, "Queen-Ann's-Lace" is "about" desire in many dimensions and contexts—not only the mutual desire of flower for sun, or woman for man, but of poet for poem. There is no creation, in nature or art, without a "white desire": this is the fundamental eroticism that runs beneath all of Williams's work. The passion and awakening he observes in a field of Queen Ann's lace is "a pious wish to whiteness gone over," that is, completely "given over" to life in its fertile possibilities. (In this context, "pious" does not mean "hypocritical," but instead reflects its older sense of "holy observance" or "reverence.") In the last line, "nothing" is as paradoxical as "white," and the poem therefore rejects any attempts at a tidy interpretation. If the "or" of the last line is read as a contrast to what comes before, then "nothing" implies defeat and absence. In a word, it is life or death, all or nothing. On the other hand, the poem also supports "nothing" as simply another name for that "pious wish." As such, this "nothing" is not the defeated self. It is desire, fully surrendered, emptied, and waiting for possibility and plenitude. It is the letting go that invites life to begin.

Themes

Language and Meaning

The metaphor is one of the most important tools of language. It enables us to describe one thing in terms of another, when "straight" description is neither sufficient nor desirable. In the original Greek roots of the word, "metaphor" means "change-bearer": it transforms perception by means of language. It reimagines the world in words. When "like" or "as" is used to draw attention to the comparison, it is called a simile, as in Robert Burns's famous lines, "My luve is like a red, red rose." "Queen-Ann's-Lace" begins with a personification, a kind of metaphor in which a nonhuman thing is given human attributes. At first glance, Williams seems to be engaged in a rather commonplace poetic activity, saying on some level that a woman is like a flower and a flower is like a woman.

However, Williams was not content to use language and metaphors in traditional ways. And he was especially aware of the sentimental, worn-out expressions for flowers, women, and love. He even parodies Burns's image, because the rose produces such automatic associations. With tongue in cheek he wrote, "My luv / is like / a / greenglass insulator / on / a blue sky." When metaphors become worn out and all the freshness of the comparison

Topics for Further Study

- Look closely at three different "still life" paintings. Observe the artist's use of color, perspective, and composition. What do they say about the artists' relationship to those objects? What emotions are suggested? Write an imaginative description or dialogue between each artist and one or more objects in the painting.

- Write a poem about an ordinary object in the style of William Carlos Williams. Engage not only "straight looking," but also feeling.

- Williams was a doctor as well as a poet, and some critics have suggested his flower poems are "medicinal." How so? Flowers and herbs have been part of healing practices since ancient times. Trace the history of two or three common flowers in their medicinal use. If you are so inclined, accompany the writing with botanical illustrations.

- Investigate the work and life of two or more of the following writers: William Carlos Williams, Ernest Hemingway, James Joyce, T. S. Eliot, William Butler Yeats, and Ezra Pound. Then, write a one-act play for stage or screen revealing their character and basic artistic stance, as well the contrasts between (or among) them.

- Read numerous poems in *The Collected Poems of William Carlos Williams* and create a visual collage or montage of Williams images.

dissipates, they become "cliches" and can only numb or manipulate human feeling.

Williams was interested in freeing language from the burdens imposed by centuries of poetic formulas for rhyme, meter, and subject. After all, not many have made a common weed the subject of a love poem. To liberate language in poems meant restoring the rhythms of ordinary speech, the direct contact with things and, not least, the rich dimensions of human feeling. In the process, Williams questioned the traditional hierarchies and distinctions between the metaphor's tenor (the thing being compared, e.g."luve") and its vehicle (the term of comparison, e.g. "red rose"). He would not reduce one thing to serve another. Flower and woman are so fused in "Queen-Ann's-Lace" that neither can be said to be the "vehicle" of the other. "No ideas but in things," Williams insisted. And, because he followed his own maxim in this poem, there is no choice—both flower and woman either emerge from this poetic lovemaking whole, "or nothing." Williams removes both flower and woman from the confining "still life" of traditional language and plants the interpenetrating images in a field, where language can explore its own growth organically, taking the field "by force" of its own necessities, not those imposed by custom or rule.

Love and Passion

By every account, William Carlos Williams was just as impassioned a doctor as he was a poet. Love of the human body and love for the "body" of language were never distinct in Williams's life. Both engaged him in the art of healing, of "making whole." The healing power of art is illuminated in poems that mend the split between art and experience, body and spirit, self and world, ideas and things, sex and love—all of those either-or "dualisms" that separate, compartmentalize, and fracture perception and experience. The poem can be a healing force, bringing what was fractured back into a relationship of wholeness.

In "Queen-Ann's-Lace," that healing force is love. The poet's love of the flower brings his entire attention to bear on that single thing of nature, so that no detail is overlooked, neither in the flower's color and growing form, nor in its movement. This absorbed focus is no different from what passes between two lovers in their attention to every "hand's span" of the other's body. Being near the beloved is crucial and involves all of the senses. In this and countless other poems, Williams bridges that very short gap between sensory and sensual. The world we can apprehend through sight, sound, touch, and taste is also a world we can love. Love is a matter of "contact," an important word in the vocabulary of Williams's art. There can be no such thing as love in the abstract, "nor / so remote a thing." The flower's folk name, "wild carrot," gets its name from the carrot-like odor of its root, a fact known only through contact, from being near. In the second half of the poem, love is heightened to erotic passion, until all that was separate in the field, "one by one," becomes "a single stem." Such love involves surrender, letting go, until the entire field and its intertwined images of woman, flower, and poem, is a "white desire."

Art and Experience

William Carlos Williams loved art, and many readers have noticed the "painterly" aspects of Williams's writing, especially in his poems' close observation, careful use of color, and visual arrangement of words and lines. Williams said that he thought of "Queen-Ann's-Lace" and the other flower poems in *Sour Grapes* as "still lifes," but if so, they are "still lifes" in the lively style of Cezanne, with his sensual, vibrant colors and dancing contours. Williams closely followed the work of modern artists such as Duchamp, Demuth, Dada, Picasso, and Cezanne. The painters he admired were those who took great risks to move art out of textbooks and into the realm of immediate experience.

Cezanne rebelled against the style of art that represents objects on the canvas as though they are merely painted reproductions of the thing. He wanted to go back to the "beginning" of perception and explore the basic form of the object—cone, cylinder, or sphere—as well as the colors as they are actually seen, not as they "ought" to be thought of, according to aesthetic rules or theories. Williams liked the fact that Cezanne really *looked* at things, as though the painter were the very first to see the object or scene. That was being truly "original," Williams said of Cezanne, to be able to toss off all the layers of perceptions and prejudices maintained by certain "schools" of art with their theories and rules. Williams believed Cezanne painted as though he were Adam, naming first things, and he believed poets must do no less. They must really see, wide-awake and impassioned, and utter "first words." Art must not be remote from the pulse of life.

Williams's insistence on the unity of art and experience is born out in "Queen-Ann's-Lace." The poem takes the flower out of the "museum frame" in the first two lines by mixing the white in his palette with the colors of a common field and giving it an impasto, not a smooth surface. White and whiteness dominate the palette of this poem, but it is not a hothouse white, "white as can be." This perennial beauty is wild and its lacy white open to weather, set off against the earthen browns and greens of field grasses, and "blemished" by a "purple mole" at each blossom's center. Williams has "composed" this portrait of the wild carrot not only with color and form, but with verb and feeling, as the form, the very "fibres of her being," "stem by stem" respond to the impassioned caress of the sun, of the lover's touch, of the poet's gaze. The poem fuses noun and verb, art and experience, giving new definition to "still life."

Style

Since "Queen-Ann's-Lace" is written in free verse and lacks the ordering patterns of formal meter or rhyme, Williams has to depend on other elements of sound and sense to shape the poem and give it "music."

The first half of the poem is a series of descriptive statements—five sentences that tell what this flower-body both is and is not. Clauses are punctuated both in the middle of lines (caesura) and at the end of lines. The verbs in this part of the poem are largely verbs of being, not action, and together with the punctuation, they tend to slow the pace of the poem. But the picture is far from being "still." Amidst the facts of whiteness are planted verbs of "force," preparing the reader for the powerful awakening that occurs in the second half of the poem.

The long sentence that comprises line 13 to the end of the poem builds its breathless, erotic strength on the short phrases set off by commas, as well as by the unifying force of the word "stem," which doubles both as the main verb in line 16 and the climactic noun in line 18.

Williams also uses trochaic rhythm to great advantage. The trochee is the poetic "foot" or stress pattern called "falling," "running," or "dancing," since it consists of an accented, followed by an unaccented, syllable and sonically mimics those movements (as in "over" in line 20). The trochaic accent thus "falls," whereas the "iambic" foot characteristic of the traditional sonnet "rises" in its pattern of unaccented-accented syllables (as in "today"). The words "empty," "single," "cluster," "pious," "whiteness," and "over" are each trochees that carry the rhythm headlong toward the precipice of passion in the last two lines. Trochaic rhythm came naturally to Williams; he loved the dance and avoided the closure of formal poetic rules. In 1948 he said, "We do not live in a sonnet world; we do not live even in an iambic world; certainly not in a world of iambic pentameters."

Historical Context

America in the 1920s—both time and place—seems an unlikely context for a pastoral love poem such as "Queen-Ann's-Lace." The years between World Wars I and II were characterized on many fronts by disillusionment, despair, and upheaval. The "War to End All Wars," while officially over in 1918, had left its own dark legacy of violence, poverty, and social disruption across Europe. In the United States, amidst breathless advances in technology and transportation, there was also an atmosphere of anxiety, fear, and uncertainty. Ezra Pound's cry at the turn of the century to "Make it new!" could not have foreseen the challenges to the human spirit in the wake of The Great War's mass carnage and psychic disturbances. But by 1920, in his poem "Hugh Selwyn Mauberly," Pound was admitting "disillusionments as never told in the old days, / hysterias, trench confessions, / laughter out of dead bellies." For the artist, "making it new" must call now upon resources of language, color, and image capable of expressing the chaos and fragmentation of modern life.

In that regard, one of the most important poems not only of the 1920s, but of our century, is T. S. Eliot's *The Waste Land.* Eliot explained that it began as "the relief of a personal ... grouse against life," but the poem goes beyond the nightmarish images of personal dissipation to a bigger critique of a civilization in decay. The poem's form tells much: it is a ragged collage of unconnected conversations, scraps of quotations, broken images, Babel-language, and meaningless allusions. If a centerless poem can be said to have a center, it is paradoxically a self unselved and scattered across a meaningless universe.

William Carlos Williams was nothing short of enraged by *The Waste Land.* Its publication in *The Dial* in 1922 was at the stormy center of one of the most dramatic and divisive artistic quarrels of the 1920s. In his *Autobiography,* Williams said that "Eliot's poem ... wiped out our world as if an atom bomb had been dropped upon it and our brave sallies into the unknown were turned to dust.... Critically Eliot returned us to the classroom just at the moment when I felt that we were on the point of an escape to matters much closer to the essence of a new art form itself—rooted in the locality which should give it fruit." What Williams refers to in his accusation is rooted in their crucial aesthetic and philosophical differences. Simply put, Eliot traveled; Williams stayed home. When Eliot heard "Make it new," he held a broken mirror up to Western civilization. When Williams heard "Make it new," he held a lamp up close to the faces of patients in Rutherford. To read Eliot well and penetrate his complex webs of allusion requires a vast,

Compare & Contrast

- **1920:** Warren G. Harding was elected president of the United States, and Calvin Coolidge, vice-president. In 1923, while still serving his term, Harding died of an embolism amidst rumors of corruption and scandal.

  1963: On November 22, President John F. Kennedy becomes the fourth U. S. President to die by assassination. Kennedy's death shocked and grieved the nation.

  1999: In February, the U. S. Senate acquitted President Bill Clinton on charges of perjury and obstruction of justice relative to Clinton's rumored sexual affair with White House aide Monica Lewinsky.

- **1921-1922:** In hopes of reducing the chance of another multinational war, nine treaties were signed at the Conference for Limitation of Armaments among the United States, France, Japan, and Great Britain to reduce weapons proliferation.

  Today: The United States, in concert with the United Nations, is using military force against Iraq for its continued defiance of weapons inspection.

- **1922:** Dr. Alexis Carrel discovers leukocytes, also known as white corpuscles or "white cells," the agents present in blood that help protect the body from infection.

  1961: *The Journal of the American Medical Association* reports the first statistical evidence linking smoking and heart disease.

  1995: In a risky cross-species experiment, a 38-year-old man infected with the AIDS virus receives an injection of cells from the bone marrow of a baboon. The cells are thought to be AIDS-resistant and would therefore boost his failing immune system.

---

almost encyclopedic knowledge of history and literature. The foreground of Eliot's *Waste Land* is the "unreal city" of London, but its backdrop is dense with the ghosts of European history, far-flung times, places, and voices. Williams thoroughly resisted a poetics that either required an elite knowledge or took its images and forms from "museums." For him, the modernist revolution lay in fresh attention to the givens of American life and speech—"plain American," he said, "which cats and dogs can read."

Thus, while many of America's writers drifted among the major cities of Europe, Williams chose to be "at home," shaping an imagist poetics into a voice and line distinctly American. The time was ripe for such a voice, for at the same time Williams was writing "Overture to a Dance of Locomotives," the United States was "making new" a national identity that had just emerged from international conflict and was flexing its economic muscles, even while its psyche grew more complex and disturbed in the face of accelerated change. A production economy turned into a consumer economy, as crucial progress and inventions in transportation and communication increased America's mobility. By 1923, 15 million cars were registered, the number of household radios had jumped from 5,000 in 1920 to more than 2.5 million by 1924, and transatlantic telephone service was opened in 1927 between New York and London. Before the war, the United States owed European nations more than four billion dollars. By war's end, other nations owed the United States a debt in excess of ten billion dollars.

With newfound confidence in this prosperity, unprecedented numbers of Americans began to take risks and invest in the stock market, many on credit. Within a few short years, share prices had soared above their real value, and investors sold their stocks in panic. The resulting stock market crash in October of 1929 began the period known as the Great Depression. Vast stockades of personal and institutional wealth were reduced to rubble, and by 1932, 25 percent of the nation was unemployed.

The effects were felt disastrously in Europe, where Americans had heavily invested. The economic suffering left over from World War I was only exacerbated by troubles across the Atlantic. Many historians believe that the combined social and economic woes across Western Europe and the United States made the field fertile for leaders who promised a new order. That would take the form of Adolf Hitler in Germany, of Mussolini in Italy, Churchill in England, and Franklin D. Roosevelt in the United States.

Meanwhile, Williams, Eliot, and Pound continued to practice their conviction that poetry matters in a world full of chaos, cruelty, and rapid change. The body of the world in those years was far from ideal: "not so white as / anemone petals nor so smooth." Well into the first half of the century, they continued "making it new" in their own, often disparate ways. "Queen-Ann's-Lace" is therefore quite at home in a world that must either allow what is real and present to take "the field by force" or be reckoned "nothing."

Critical Overview

Many years after the publication of *Sour Grapes* in 1921, Williams recalled that "to me, at that time, a poem was an image, the picture was the important thing." "The picture" so perceptively and sensually composed in "Queen-Ann's-Lace" has stimulated many discussions about the relationship between the images of a field of wild carrot and the feminine body. Is one a metaphor for the other? Can an imagist poem support metaphoric language? Does it reject it? Does it redefine it?

Some readers discuss the poem's images in the traditional terms of metaphor, tenor, and vehicle. In Arthur Glowka's view, as he wrote in *The Explicator,* the flower serves as the vehicle for the sexual encounter: "The field of Queen Ann's lace becomes the metaphor for the touching of the woman's body as the poet unfolds a set of one-to-one correspondences between a species of foreplay and a field of flowers." In this way, Glowka has "privileged" the reality of the sexual encounter over that of the flower. Similarly, in *The Explicator,* Douglas Verdier reads the poem as a "Petrarchan conceit," an extended metaphor characteristic of Petrarch's love sonnets in which comparisons with the beloved are usually fanciful or exaggerated. But others have suggested that Williams has done just the opposite, as the opening lines suggest: "Her body is not so white as / anemone petals nor so smooth ...," thereby echoing Shakespeare's parody of Petrarch in "Sonnet 130," which begins, "My mistress' eyes are nothing like the sun."

Other critics believe that an imagist poem such as "Queen-Ann's-Lace" cannot even support the idea of metaphor, because the very act of making the flower a "vehicle" of the woman's body (or vice versa) dissipates its presence as a real, observed thing and renders it an abstraction or "idea" of something else. Thus, J. Hillis Miller's reading, in *William Carlos Williams: A Collection of Critical Essays,* closely follows Williams's dictum, "No ideas but in things," when he says Williams "experiences a woman and a field of the white flower not as metaphors of one another, but as interpenetrating realities."

In *The Visual Text of William Carlos Williams,* Henry Sayre suggests that rather than eliminating the "idea" of metaphor altogether, "Queen-Ann's-Lace" represents Williams's ability to "reconceive" the metaphor and liberate its function in the poem: where metaphor is generally considered to be a means of evoking and defining the image (pinning down the flower, in this case), the image now becomes at once the nexus and generator of a whole range of metaphors. Brian Bremen echoes this perception in his *William Carlos Williams and the Diagnostics of Culture* when he insists that "Queen-Ann's-Lace" "generates analogous situations without reducing one—flower or wife—to the terrain of the other." Those like Sayre and Bremen, who understand Williams's "generative" use of the metaphor, are able to honor the poem's immediate images and then go beyond— to Williams's broader engagement with the processes of creation. In *William Carlos Williams and Autobiography: The Woods of His Own Nature,* Ann Fisher-Wirth extends Williams's passionate observation of flower-woman to his greater love for the world, "whatever her earthly form ... the other is 'Beautiful Thing,' in every moment broken and most whole." These interpretations have taken in the greater context of Williams's work, which was powerfully influenced by early-century revolutions in art, and which, in turn, set new directions for poetry. A poem such as "Queen-Ann's-Lace" is both a passionate observation of a natural phenomenon and also an image for the processes of creation. The poem itself becomes a "field" of ordinary flowers, fertile and open to possibility, stemming to a "white desire" for birthing art through what is at hand.

Criticism

Kristina Zarlengo

Kristina Zarlengo, who received her doctorate in English from Columbia University in 1997, taught literature and writing for five years at Columbia University. A scholar of modern American literature, her articles have appeared in academic journals and various periodicals. In the following essay, Zarlengo describes Williams's philosophy of poetic creation as it relates to "Queen-Ann's-Lace."

Plato, Biblical scribes, and other lovers of the idea that the contents of our world are the pale copies of some more perfect world of heaven or truth have often measured the virtues of art with a yardstick of verisimilitude—the more a depiction resembles its subject matter, the better it is. William Carlos Williams moved against such ideas. For him, the world is complete and real in itself. For him, art depicting the world should not be measured by its capacity to copy:

> It is NOT to hold the mirror up to nature that the artist performs his work. It is to make, out of the imagination, something not at all a copy of nature but something different, a new thing, unlike any thing else in nature, a thing advanced and apart from it.... To copy is merely to reflect something already there, inertly.... But by imitation we enlarge nature itself, we become nature or we discover in ourselves nature's active part. This is enticing to our minds, it enlarges the concept of art, dignifies it to a place not yet fully realized.

Just so, "Queen-Ann's-Lace" gives us not flowers as symbols, nor flowers so intricately described that they are recognizable as some species that we pass on a stroll, but flowers described in strikingly spare language, described in conjunction with a woman's body and a man's touch. Above all, they are described.

Williams abhorred ideas in art. Yet his focus on the simple, the local, and the rhythms of American speech was deeply ideological insofar as he heralded and embraced the idea of no ideas. "No ideas but in things," he declared in his long poem *Paterson,* coining a motto for the poetic tradition of Objectivism, which rejects symbolism—wanting the words themselves to stand more boldly than some secret they might be supposed to suggest, demanding a description of concrete objects not because they represent any larger idea or greater power, but for their own sake. The resulting austerity, evident in "Queen-Ann's-Lace," is even more so found in Williams' notorious "The Red Wheelbarrow," which reads, in full:

> so much depends
> upon
>
> a red wheel
> barrow
>
> glazed with rain
> water
>
> beside the white
> chickens.

This extreme simplicity—this opacity to interpretation, the finality of the words, the meek subject matter—are Williams's trademark means for transmitting his things without ideas. Such a pure presentation of object is not so free of ideology as Williams seems to insist. With his poetry, we are thrown back on the words as much as on the objects from which they remain emphatically remote. We are thus left with words that are objects in themselves—glimpses of language extending itself like a tree. Yet, the worth of his poems stems importantly from the words being unhinged from observed reality—operating not as mirrors but as a reality of their own. In poetry, and indeed in any language, operating without ideas is, ironically, a powerful idea in itself.

As well as having palpable words, "Queen-Ann's-Lace" is a vision: "Each flower is a hand's span / of her whiteness. Wherever / his hand has lain there is / a tiny purple blemish." The emphases in these phrases are not tactile, but visual—the purple of the blemish, the measure of the flower. The body of the woman described is tactile only insofar as it is not smooth. What it does feel like, we do not learn. If this field of flowers has a smell, we are not told of it; here is no taste, here is silence. But we are drawn, in words, a vivid picture: a field so flowery it has been taken like a battlefield—conquered by blooms, the white and purple flowers, the woman's body that seems empty except for the flower stems of desire. "Queen-Ann's-Lace" is like a *trompe l'oeil* painting; it is a verbal optical illusion in which flowers and this white body's flesh are the same. The body does not symbolize the flowers, nor the flowers the body—they are themselves, as well as each other; they are identical.

"I thought of them as still-lifes," Williams said of "Queen-Ann's-Lace" and the three other flower poems in his volume titled *Sour Grapes.* It is easy to understand his comparison of this verbal vision to a painting of flowers. But unlike an image, his poem unfolds in time, on the space of the printed page. No time actually passes in the poem; it is suspended. But the poem's description in words hap-

What Do I Read Next?

- It is important to view "Queen-Ann's-Lace" in the context of other poems written during the first half of Williams's career. Volume one of the two-volume *Collected Poems,* edited by A. Walton Litz and Christopher MacGowan, provides this perspective. From the earliest poems in 1909 to "The Last Words of My English Grandmother" in 1939, it contains all of Williams's poems published both in volumes of poetry and singly in magazines and journals. With the exception of *Paterson,* volume two covers poems published between 1939 and 1962.

- Those interested in what Williams has to say about his own life will enjoy his *Autobiography* (1951) and its many amusing, dramatic, and poignant stories. The book's lively anecdotes contradict the poet's opening comment that he had "served sixty-eight years of a more or less uneventful life." A more specifically literary "autobiography" called *I Wanted to Write a Poem* is actually Williams's half of a serial conversation with Edith Heal about the circumstances surrounding the writing and publication of his major works.

- Williams was an unofficial but powerful "mentor" to many younger poets, including British-born Denise Levertov, who met an aging but still productive Williams in New York when she was in her early thirties. From him she learned invaluable ways of hearing American speech, seeing the world, and persisting in her work. This led, ultimately, to her own emergence as a major voice in American poetry. Their correspondence has been collected and edited by Williams scholar Christopher MacGowan in *The Letters of Denise Levertov and William Carlos Williams* (1998).

- T. S. Eliot's *The Waste Land,* a landmark poem of the twentieth century, was published just one year after *Sour Grapes* and provides a startling contrast to Williams's imagist poems in form, language, imagery, and essential worldview. Where "Queen-Ann's-Lace" reveals images of generativity and love, *The Waste Land* pronounces April "the cruellest month, breeding / Lilacs out of the dead land."

- Many young American-born writers and artists set up residence in Europe during the 1920s, between World Wars I and II. Of them, Gertrude Stein said, "You are all a lost generation." Ernest Hemingway was one of the most famous of that "Lost Generation," and his novel *The Sun Also Rises* (1926) embodies the lives of those drifting expatriates in the character of Jake Barnes. William Carlos Williams and his wife visited Paris and many of those writers—including Pound, Hemingway, Joyce, and Stein—in 1924, but returned to Rutherford with the commitment to writing as an American, in America.

- While in Europe, Williams worked on a collection of essays called *In the American Grain* (1925). Each essay deals with a figure, well-known or obscure, whom Williams believed played a role in shaping the character and conscience of America. Unlike most history texts, Williams supplies stories that revel in the ordinariness of figures such as Ben Franklin or George Washington, or which risk revealing their dark, less-than-heroic character. Williams's idea of "how to be American," says poet Denise Levertov, is bound up in the book's essential "respect for otherness ... essential to poets." By most accounts, it is Williams's most notable work of nonfiction.

---

pens in time, creating motion in the present tense while creating the space the poem takes up. Thirty-five years after writing "Queen-Ann's-Lace," he described his flower poems book as

a mood book, all of it impromptu. When the mood possessed me, I wrote. Whether it was a tree or a woman or a bird, the mood had to be translated into form.... To me, at that time ... the poem was an im-

> *Williams's achievement is often in merging what others have insisted is distinct. Refusing ideas seen through words, his poetry is a collage of ideas and images ...."*

age, the picture was the important thing. As far as I could, with the material I had, I was lyrical, but I was determined to use the material I knew and much of it did not lend itself to lyricism.

Even lyricism, or the sound of the words, in this poem is secondary to the poet's urge and to the picture.

The line breaks of "Queen-Ann's-Lace" are also regulated by the demands of images and words. Line breaks are an extraordinarily important dimension of poetry. Traditionally, in verse written in English and most Romance Languages, these breaks are governed by sometimes strict metrical forms that specify how many beats—conceived sometimes as syllables, sometimes as accents—are to compose each line. The lines are further defined by their sound relations with other lines—in rhyme. The line breaks of "Queen-Ann's-Lace" do not hinge on feet or syllable counts (although they are not irrelevant: all lines up to the dramatic last line have between six and ten syllables; most lines have three or four accented beats [trimeter or tetrameter]). The poem does not rely on rhyme. It is images and ideas—nearly all of which are split by the line breaks—that really regulate line breaks. Already, at the end of the poem's first lines, we are left dangling with "as" and "nor." We are pushed by a suspense, a desire to finish the idea or image, to the next lines. Or, as with "Here is no question of whiteness, / white as can be," we are jolted from being told there is no whiteness, to learning there is total whiteness. The contradiction is crushed between the two lines. The final line is shocking—equal parts bravado and humility. "Either this field, and this body are as I say here, or they are not at all," the poet seems to boast, but boast simply.

The accentuated sense of time in the poem is not any easier to decipher for its apparent importance to Williams. On one hand, he joined Imagist poets such as Ezra Pound in casting out metrical conventions for the kind of pure word economy and density of impression we get in Pound's poem "In a Station of the Metro," which reads—in full:

The apparition of these faces in a crowd;
Petals on a wet, black bough.

Associated with the Imagists during the early part of his career, Williams later reviled their eschewal of emphasis on the poetic foot: "There is no such thing as 'free verse,'" he claimed, no freedom from strict form. "Imagism was not structural: that was the reason for its disappearance," he complained. At the same time, Williams detested traditional metrical forms—he begged and labored for verse stripped of all stodginess. "I propose sweeping changes from top to bottom of the poetic structure. I said structure.... I say we are through with the iambic pentameter ... through with the measured quatrain, the staid concatenations of sounds in the usual stanza, the sonnet."

Calling free verse a contradiction on terms, the form-conscious Williams proposed in its place a variable foot, also called a relative foot—that is, a unit of beat less strict than the traditional iamb (ta-TA, as in the word "eclipse"), for instance. But a relative foot is no less a contradiction in terms than free verse. It seems at times that the strictness of form Williams espoused was a reflection of the great care he took in his poems' form, a meter he embraced because it insists that his verse was rightly regulated and was serious. Despite his meter's idiosyncrasy and occasional opacity, Williams was consistently adamant with regard to its magnitude: "Imagination creates an image point by point, piece by piece, segment by segment—into a whole, living. But each part as it plays into its neighbor, each segment to its neighbor segment and every part into every other, causing the whole—exists naturally in rhythm. And as there are waves there are tides and as there are ridges in the sand there are bars after bars."

Williams's fervent dedication to verse and writing—for he wrote not only poems, including the epic *Paterson*, but an autobiography, plays, historical studies, and novels—was not his only passion. A life-long physician, he practiced obstetrics in his native New Jersey, often producing poems from his desktop typewriter between delivering babies. Far from viewing his small-town home and profession as contrary to his poetic ambition,

Williams insisted that it was locally, in the speech patterns of American English, and in contact with what he liked to call the American Grain, that a revolution in poetry similar to the early century's revolutions in the visual arts and in science would take place. Literary critic Hugh Kenner summed up Williams's accomplishment in a way that should have pleased the poet: "That words set in New Jersey mean less but mean it with greater finality, is Williams' great technical perception."

Williams's achievement is often in merging what others have insisted is distinct. Refusing ideas seen through words, his poetry is a collage of ideas and images—in "Queen-Ann's-Lace," the body as touched field of flowers, or nothing; not so white, no question of whiteness, and white as can be. In his unfiltered focus on objects, Williams also merges the perceiver and the perceived; both the poet and the reader are alone with their perceptions, confronted not with naturalistic flowers, but with verbal flowers. "Queen-Ann's-Lace" is like a painting for the blind. Voyeurs of Williams's touch in entangling a woman's body and a field of flowers—or perceiver and perceived, object and subject, American idiom and a certain strictness of time meeting space on the printed page—we discover that Williams plants the page with a desire for the world, among whose strange natural growths language flourishes simply. "As birds' wings beat the solid air without which none could fly," he promises, "so words freed by the imagination affirm reality by their flight."

Source: Kristina Zarlengo, in an essay for *Poetry for Students,* The Gale Group, 1999.

Douglas L. Verdier

In the following essay, Verdier praises Williams for the visual achievement of "Queen-Ann's-Lace."

William Carlos Williams' poem "Queen Anne's Lace" (1921) illustrates most effectively the influence of the visual arts—particularly, in this case, the Imagist school—on his poetry, and it emphasizes his credo "No ideas but in things." Williams' goal in this poem, like that of the Imagist painters, is to create a single impression by freeze-framing his subject at a critical moment and then selectively highlighting certain details of the scene, building them up layer upon layer, compressing them, intensifying them, until finally, the "thing" emerges in one's consciousness as a single, unified experience in which the perceived whole is greater than the sum of its parts. "Queen Anne's Lace" is just such a poetic canvas.

Taking as his subject a field of wild carrot blossoms, Williams creates for the reader a fusion of color and detail which fills the imagination with vivid sensations that merge to become, at once, both a portrait of pastoral beauty and a celebration of physical love, expressed through the tension between the delicate blossoms and the overpowering force that excites them.

He begins the poem with a personification ("Her body"), which refers to "a field / of the wild carrot" (11.3–4), but at the same time introduces a feminine presence which will be sustained throughout the poem through a Petrarchan conceit. The whiteness of the wild carrot is emphasized by contrasting it with another flower ("anemone") that is a bit whiter and smoother in texture, but not markedly different in color. The flower's whiteness is also contrasted with the grass, which provides a background above which the carrot blossom stretches. Williams uses these initial images in the opening lines to describe precisely the whiteness of the "thing" for the reader, since even white can come in varying shades.

Once the whiteness of the central image has been established, another contrast is introduced— the "purple mole / at the center of each flower" (11.8–9). The image suggested is that of a beauty mark, so fashionable in the eighteenth century (particularly during the time of Queen Anne, who is alluded to in the title) that aristocratic ladies routinely helped nature by pasting artificial beauty marks wherever they were needed. Ladies of Queen Anne's day were supposed to have skin as white as the finest alabaster, and the use of these artificial marks served to emphasize their fairness by contrast. The suggestion of a beauty mark, coupled with the repeated emphasis of "whiteness," serves to expand Williams' conceit.

At the same time, the presence of the "purple mole" creates in the reader's mind the connotation of an imperfection, albeit one which is often considered desirable. This interpretation is given some support when the poet uses the word "blemish" (1.13) to describe the purple center of the flower, but in this case the blemish results "Wherever / his hand has lain ..." (11.11–12). Now the "purple blemish" takes on a new meaning, amplifying the poem's sensuousness by introducing a male hand that touches the white female body. This sensuous quality continues with the next line: "Each part / is a blossom under his touch ..." (11.13–14). At this point, one is tempted to believe that Williams is writing a seduction poem, with the whiteness of the flower symbolizing the purity of the female, and "his hand," which injects an unidentified male presence into the poem, suggesting a violation or a loss of that purity. But to dismiss the poem thusly is to miss the subtle effect of the artist's skillful blending of images and moods—it is to view the painting without "seeing" it.

Although the tone of the poem is quite sensual, and it is, in essence, a love poem, it is nevertheless a mature one. The "force" which takes over the field is not simply a one-sided display of carnal lust, but rather a mutual, shared desire which passes through the stages of arousal and climax until mutual fulfillment is achieved.

As "his touch" (1.14) gently caresses, the excitement builds. The increasing tension is apparent as the very "fibres of her being" (1.15) respond. Individual stems become nerves which are stimulated "one by one" (1.16) until the intensity of the sensations reach a peak, and "the whole field is a / white desire ..." (11.17–18). This is the climax toward which Williams has been building, and as it is reached, the images become fused in a unity suggestive of the culmination of an act of love. With this fulfillment, the excitement gradually subsides, slowly, part by part, "flower by flower," (1.19)— the "wish" has been realized.

In the energy of the poem's focal point, one is apt to forget that the subject of the poem is, after all, a field of common wild carrot flowers. But Williams does not forget. The field of blossoms has been there all along; only the focus has changed. As the intensity decreases, the field is gradually brought back into perspective, and one becomes aware once again of the "thing"—a field blanketed by thousands of tiny white flowers clustered so closely together that the impression is one of a single, large flower. But whiteness continues to permeate Williams' canvas, suggesting perhaps that the kind of purity which dominates his pastoral scene is also essential in the sort of love such a scene brings to mind.

Source: Douglas L. Verdier, "Williams' 'Queen Anne's Lace,'" in *The Explicator,* Vol. 40, No. 1, Fall 1981, pp. 46-7.

Sources

Bremen, Brian A., *William Carlos Williams and the Diagnostics of Culture,* New York: Oxford University Press, 1993.

Cooper, John Xiros, "William Carlos Williams," *Dictionary of Literary Biography* Vol. 54: *American Poets, 1880-1945,* third series, part 2, Detroit: Gale Research Inc., 1987, pp. 533-75.

Fisher-Wirth, Ann W., *William Carlos Williams and Autobiography: The Woods of His Own Nature,* University Park, PA: The Pennsylvania State University Press, 1989.

Glowka, Arthur, "Williams' 'Queen Ann's Lace,'" *The Explicator,* Vol. 39, No. 4, summer 1981, pp. 25-6.

Halter, Peter, *The Revolution in the Visual Arts and the Poetry of William Carlos Williams,* Cambridge, England: Cambridge University Press, 1994.

Hirsch, Edward, "Helmet of Fire: American Poetry in the 1920s," *A Profile of Twentieth-Century American Poetry,* edited by Jack Myers and David Wojahn, Carbondale: Southern Illinois University Press, 1991, pp. 54-83.

Mariani, Paul, *William Carlos Williams: A New World Naked,* New York: McGraw-Hill, 1982.

Marling, William, *William Carlos Williams and the Painters, 1909-1923,* Athens, OH: Ohio University Press, 1982.

Miller, J. Hillis, ed., *William Carlos Williams: A Collection of Critical Essays,* Englewood Cliffs, NJ: Prentice-Hall, Inc., 1966.

Sayre, Henry M., *The Visual Text of William Carlos Williams,* Urbana: University of Illinois Press, 1983.

Verdier, Douglas L., "Williams' 'Queen Ann's Lace,'" *The Explicator,* Vol. 40, No. 1, fall 1981, pp. 46-7.

Williams, William Carlos, *The Autobiography of William Carlos Williams,* New York: Random House, 1951.

Williams, William Carlos, *Selected Essays,* New York: Random House, 1954.

Williams, William Carlos, *Selected Poems,* edited and with an introduction by Charles Tomlinson, New York: New Directions, 1985.

For Further Study

Bartlett, Jeffrey, "'Many Loves': William Carlos Williams and the Difficult Erotics of Poetry," *The Green American Tradition: Essays and Poems for Sherman Paul,* edited by H. Daniel Peck, Baton Rouge: Louisiana State University Press, 1989, pp. 134-154.

This essay develops from the conviction that Williams has brought poetry "back to its senses," both literally and figuratively, in the way he restores authentic human feeling with its grounding in eyes, ears, and hands. There is nothing easy or sentimental about the work of love in Williams's writing, says Bartlett. The healing force of love, an "erotic" relationship with the world, is not something that a poem can prescribe or legislate, for Williams's poems are revelations, not representations, of love. Bartlett's essay makes a major contribution to our understanding of love in Williams's work, a crucial "force" both in his poetry and prose.

Bloom, Harold, ed., *Modern Critical Views: William Carlos Williams,* New York: Chelsea House Publishers, 1986.
This collection of essays by some of the foremost critics of the last half-century represents an important range of viewpoints and concerns. With the exception of two essays about *Paterson,* most of these readings look at a number of works in order to discuss a particular theme, image, or stylistic issue unique to Williams's art. Cushman, for instance, identifies Williams's use of the trochaic measure as a metaphor: the poem as "dance." Poet Donald Hall's brief essay convinces us that part of the Williams legacy is "a visual method for capturing speech."

Mariani, Paul, *William Carlos Williams: A New World Naked,* New York: McGraw-Hill, 1981.
In the process of chronicling the poet's life, this enormous, but quite readable biography of Williams also traces the many paths of artistic and social change in the first half of the century. Considered a tour de force of literary biography, Mariani's work is important for anyone interested in Williams's life or in a successful example of how a biographer composes the "thousand thousand" pieces of a person's life into a complex, human whole.

Whitaker, Thomas R., *William Carlos Williams,* revised edition, Twayne's United States Author Series 139, Boston: G. K. Hall, & Co., 1989.
In this perceptive overview of Williams's work, Whitaker builds his discussion of the poet's development and themes on the metaphor of "conversation as design." All of Williams's work can be understood, Whitaker suggests, as a manifold "conversation" between his time and place and the landscape of his own feelings and consciousness. Chronologically and work by work, this book combines an awareness of criticism with brief, lucid readings of selected poems or prose passages. In the helpful style of all Twayne studies, it provides a compact chronology of the author's life and publications as well as a selected bibliography of primary and secondary works.

Theme for English B

Langston Hughes
1951

"Theme for English B" appeared in print relatively late in Langston Hughes's career, and it both reenacts and complicates the ideas and poetic rhythms with which he had always been concerned. Published in 1951 in *Montage of a Dream Deferred*, Hughes's thirteenth book of poetry, "Theme for English B" contributes to the book's collection of African-American voices living in Harlem by questioning whether any voice—and any of our American voices in particular—can exist in isolation, distinct from those surrounding it. Stylistically, the piece is a dramatic monologue (in the voice of an African-American student at Columbia University, where Hughes himself spent a dissatisfying period during the early 1920s), and it utilizes the superficially simplistic rhymes for which Hughes had become famous. How he uses these techniques in this poem, however, differs somewhat from the way he winds the jazzy tunes of his first collection, *The Weary Blues* (1926), a book the established Harlem Renaissance poet Countee Cullen claimed could not be "dismissed as merely *promising*." Rather than use his poetic form to consolidate a distinctive sense of African-American identity, in "Theme for English B" Hughes flips and spins his rhymes in order to leave his reader wondering what actually distinguishes and divides the young black student in the poem from his socially established white professor.

Langston Hughes came to artistic prominence during the Harlem Renaissance, an explosive period of innovative creative expression in the New

York African-American community in the early-twentieth century. In his poetry, plays, and fiction, Hughes attempted to blend a variety of forms of African-American cultural expression, and in his poetry, in particular, Hughes pioneered the reinscription of jazz and blues tunes in written verse, paving the way for future writers to incorporate their own spoken folk vernacular in their own poems. While his contemporary critics often dismissed his work as simplistic or naive, Hughes's position as one of the twentieth-century's most important American poets is now openly recognized and celebrated.

Author Biography

Langston Hughes's writing career stretched from the Harlem Renaissance of the 1920s to the Black Arts movement of the 1960s. The most prolific African-American writer of his time, Hughes published sixteen collections of poetry, two novels, seven collections of short stories, two autobiographical works, five nonfictional texts, and nine books for children during his lifetime. He wrote thirty plays and either edited or translated numerous other collections. Not only was Hughes prolific, he was extremely well liked by a wide range of readers and, because of his popularity, was the first African American to make a living from his writing and lecturing alone. By the time his first book of poems was published, when he was just twenty-four years old, Hughes had already worked in a number of venues—from driving trucks, to waiting tables, to working on board the SS *Malone* as a seaman. He had also traveled extensively, visiting such places as Mexico, West Africa, Europe, and the Canary Islands.

Hughes was born in Joplin, Missouri, in 1902 to James Nathaniel, a businessman, lawyer, and rancher, and Carrie Mercer Langston, a schoolteacher. After graduating from high school in Cleveland, Ohio, he spent a little over a year in Mexico with his father before attending Columbia University. Quickly dissatisfied with the kind of formal education he was receiving there, Hughes left the university after a year. He went on to write, travel, lecture, and perform his poetry across this country and throughout the world. Hughes died on May 22, 1967, of congestive heart failure in New York City.

Even before his first book of poems appeared, Hughes had already established himself within the

Langston Hughes

artistic circle of the Harlem Renaissance with the 1921 publication of his poem "The Negro Speaks of Rivers" in *Crisis,* the key literary publication of the African-American arts community in New York. "I've known rivers," he wrote in the poem, "I bathed in the Euphrates when dawns were young. / I build my hut near the Congo and it lulled me to sleep. / … I heard the singing of the Mississippi when Abe Lincoln went down to New Orleans…." Indeed, the driving force behind all of Hughes's work seems to be a desire to articulate the experience and culture of the so-called "common man" and, more specifically, the laboring African American. As he noted in his famous description of race's influence on artistic production, "The Negro Artist and the Racial Mountain," "we younger Negro artists who create now intend to express our individual dark-skinned selves without fear or shame."

The Weary Blues signaled Hughes's drive to capture the style and patterns of African-American musical traditions in his writing. Blending written verse with "a drowsy syncopated tune," Hughes's title poem in that first collection describes the voice of a man Hughes hears in Harlem, "down on Lennox Avenue the other night," a man who plays a "sad raggy tune like a musical fool. / Sweet Blues! / Coming from a black man's soul. / O Blues!" While always staying close to the vernacular of the people and the working class, Hughes experimented with a range of forms and expressions throughout his career, publishing, for example, more overtly socialist pieces in the 1930s and a collection of poems lauding the natural world in *Fields of Wonder* in 1947.

Poem Text

The instructor said,

> go home and write
> a page tonight.
> And let that page come out of you—
> Then, it will be true.   5

I wonder if it's that simple?
I am twenty-two, colored, born in Winston-Salem.
I went to school there, then Durham, then here
to this college on the hill above Harlem.
I am the only colored student in class.   10
The steps from the hill lead down into Harlem,
through the park, then I cross St. Nicholas,
Eighth Avenue, Seventh, and I come to the Y,
the Harlem Branch Y, where I take the elevator
up to my room, sit down, and write this page: 15

It's not easy to know what's true for you or me
at twenty-two, my age. But I guess I'm what
I feel and see and hear, Harlem, I hear you:
hear you, hear me—we two—you, me, talk on this
      page.
(I hear New York, too.) Me—who?   20

Well, I like to eat, sleep, drink, and be in love.
I like to work, read, learn, and understand life.
I like a pipe for a Christmas present,
or record—Besie, bop, or Bach.
I guess being colored doesn't make me not like   25
the same things other folks like who are other
      races.
So will my page be colored that I write?
Being me, it will not be white.
But it will be
a part of you, instructor.   30
You are white—
yet a part of me, as I am part of you.
That's American.
Sometimes perhaps you don't want to be a part of
      me.
Nor do I often want to be a part of you.   35
But we are, that's true!
As I learn from you,
I guess you learn from me—
although you're older—and white—
and somewhat more free.   40

This is my page for English B.

Poem Summary

Title:

Hughes's title categorizes the poem for us, generically. This is going to be an assignment, a "theme" composed for "English B," a piece whose audience is essentially the speaker's teacher. But the title also plays on several words here: what else, for instance, might Hughes be referring to when he introduces the concept of the "theme?" Could this poem, in part, comprise a "theme" for his book of poems or for whatever else "English B" might refer to—a black English? A discourse centered on and emanating from the African-American community? Or perhaps an English that is not recognized as being as first—as English "A"? The "B" that follows English certainly raises these questions even as it directs the reader to a central understanding of the piece's generic classification—as an assignment for a class labeled "English B."

Lines 1-6:

This first stanza sets the scene for the poem, introduces its primary characters, and elaborates on the information already provided for us in the poem's title. Here, Hughes tells us what the occasion for the "theme" and the poem will be—an apparently simple assignment, just a page to be written that somehow characterizes the writer. "Let that page come out of you," the instructor commands, a necessity, he explains, if what is written is to be "true." The equation here is that if one writes out of the self, then it will be a sincere and accurate representation of that self. But the speaker of the poem, after quoting the teacher's description of the assignment, complicates this equation: "I wonder if it's that simple?" Hughes therefore, at once, introduces the situation for this expression as well as the problem of its very existence. Is telling who we imagine ourselves to be enough to adequately represent the self? Can we possibly be "true" simply by expressing who we believe ourselves to be?

Lines 7-10:

In these four lines, Hughes's student speaker actually seems to begin the assignment (although it could easily be argued that in fact the assignment begins right away, when the speaker names this occasion for writing and qualifies its possible problems) by informing the reader of the most basic autobiographical details of the writer's life. After explaining how old he is (we can infer that the speaker is male because we find out later that he lives at the YMCA rather than the YWCA), where he was born, and his educational history, the speaker adds one final, yet crucial, detail: "I am the only colored student in my class." This detail "colors" the description in line 9 of Columbia University as "this college on the hill above Harlem";

while this is certainly accurate geographically, it acquires additional significance once we learn that the speaker is black and an inhabitant of Harlem. The location of Columbia "above Harlem" mirrors its social, political, and economic position within the larger culture as a university composed primarily of white students and faculty, citizens socially considered "above" the inhabitants of Harlem.

Lines 11-15:

Here the speaker takes the reader on a tour of his own path home where the "page" will be written. The speaker descends from the university sitting high on its hill into Harlem in the way the gods of classical mythology descended into the world of mortal men from their elevated posts on Mount Olympus. He crosses a park and several streets to arrive at his home at the Y, short for YMCA, itself short for the Young Men's Christian Association, where rooms are cheaply rented. This information adds to our sketch of the student writer by showing us that he lives by himself, away from home, and probably doesn't have much extra money. It is ironic that the speaker tells us that we have finally arrived at the "place" where the page will be written, since we are already deep into that writing.

Lines 16-20:

In lines 16 and 17, the student speaker directly questions the nature of the assignment and its seeming simplicity: "It's not easy to know what is true for you or me / at twenty-two, my age." He then attempts to explain, in his own deceptively simplistic way, what he believes composes himself or any self: "I guess I'm what / I feel and see and hear." The line break between lines 17 and 18 emphasizes, in line 18, the fact that the speaker is a repository of sensual experience, feeling, seeing, and hearing such as any human with those sensual capabilities would be. But this expression is itself complicated by the speaker's pronouncement that part of what he hears is Harlem. In line 19, Hughes uses commands to further develop this "theme," commands that, despite their simple rhymes, encapsulate far from simple ideas: "hear you, hear me—we two—you, me talk on this page." To whom "you" refers in line 19 becomes muddled: is "you" Harlem, as line 18 suggests, or New York (as he parenthetically adds he also hears in line 20), or perhaps the reader who, given what we've been told about the poem thus far, must be the speaker's white professor? But if the speaker "is" what—and, one would presume, "who"—he feels, sees, and hears, then "who" he might be is hardly a simple

Media Adaptations

- Two recent audio releases feature Langston Hughes reading and discussing his poetry: *Langston Hughes Reads: "One Way Ticket," "The Negro Speaks of Rivers," "The Ku Klux Klan" and Other Of His Poems* was released in 1992 by Caedmon, and *Langston Hughes Reads and Talks About His Poems* appeared in 1987 from Spoken Arts.

thing. The complication of the "you, me" coupling who "talk on this page" sets us up for the final question the speaker asks in this section: "Me—who?"

Lines 21-26:

In lines 21 through 24, the speaker attempts to return to more solid, identity-determining ground by defining himself in terms of his likes: "I like to eat, sleep, drink, and be in love. / I like to work, read, learn, and understand life," etc. The records he likes "for a Christmas present" signify a range of tastes, from bebop to blues to classical music, and the speaker somewhat tentatively concludes in lines 25 and 26 that "being colored" doesn't make him "not like / the same things" others do, whether "colored" or not. The line break for line 25 also allows Hughes to playfully mislead his reader; we expect, perhaps, that the speaker will say that being colored doesn't make him unlike those of other races, but that of course would be saying something very different, and something Hughes's student-speaker would most probably see as overly simplistic and inaccurate. Being "colored" doesn't make the student "not like" those things others from other races might like, but it doesn't mean he is "like" them either, simply because they might "like" the same things. The way in which Hughes plays with the multiple meanings of words such as "like" and "you" clearly indicates that a writer doesn't need a highly academic vocabulary to deal with difficult concepts.

Lines 27-33:

In these lines, Hughes further indicates the centrality of difference in establishing identity and particularly racial difference in America. Will "my page be colored that I write?" asks the student in line 27, and his answer indicates that it certainly will be: "being me, it will not be white," he says, just as he indicates that it will also be in part something "like" white, given that it is necessarily a part of "you, instructor." In lines 31 through 33, Hughes opens the "page" up to signify something more than simply this one student's identity; here, we understand that in fact being "colored" is understandable only in terms of being "white," just as the reverse is also true—the instructor is as much "a part of me, as I am a part of you," and this is, as the student declares, "American."

Lines 34-41:

In lines 34 and 35, the student concedes that both he and his instructor may have wished to be more separate from one another than is possible: "Sometimes perhaps you don't want to be a part of me. / Nor do I often want to be a part of you." But the two are indivisible, nevertheless—"But we are, that's true!" Here, the student has basically turned the assignment upside down. Rather than writing a page from himself that will be himself because he alone supposedly writes it, the student declares that no self is separable from the selves around it. No one white can exist as white without his/her "colored" counterpart, and vice versa. And so the student finally declares that, as much as the student can learn from his instructor, the instructor can learn from the student, although, as he says, "you're older—and white— / and somewhat more free." The student asserts his ability to teach figures in his American community who still maintain the positions of greatest authority in it. In line 40, the student avows that the free man can still learn something from those "less" free—the descendent of slaves and the still politically, economically, and socially marginalized member of American society. The final line, then, is full of irony. "This is my page for English B" re-situates the student—from whom we now understand the teacher himself can learn—in his student role, completing his assignment, while it also stresses the word "my" which, given how the speaker has complicated the whole issue of identity and self-determination, seems finally both simplistic and ironic.

Themes

Identity

The central questions Hughes poses in "Theme for English B" seem simple: who are we and how is it that we know who we are? Such questions, he suggests, must be simple because an instructor in a basic English class—"English B"—uses them as the basis for an almost offhand assignment: "Go home and write / a page tonight. / And let that page come out of you— / Then, it will be true." But of course it is exactly this idea—that knowing who we are is never simple—that Hughes plays with throughout the duration of the poem. In it, he illustrates the various ways in which we come to understand our identities by having the student list the most basic autobiographical details about himself (how old he is, where he was born, where he now lives, etc.) and, later, by indicating the ways in which he likes to spend his time and the things he enjoys. But as is evident from the student's initial autobiographical details—"I am the only colored student in my class," he says in line 10—identity contains, or references, or "means" much, much more than this.

For Hughes's student, identity is as much a product of racial distinction and difference as it isn't a product of that. This idea—that we know who we are by virtue of who we are not ("You are white," he says to the instructor, "yet a part of me, as I am a part of you")—directly contradicts the Romantic, Emersonian idea that the self is an organic entity, internally and autonomously generated and sustained. Hughes makes clear that this student knows who he is in contradistinction to the white students who surround him and the instructor who tells him to "let that page come out of you." But his sense of self is perhaps most importantly or positively linked to the Harlem he hears and celebrates throughout *Montage of a Dream Deferred,* the book in which "Theme for English B" appears. In "Theme for English B," identity is something a community creates, whether that community be racially homogeneous (as Harlem is largely for the student and Columbia University is for his white professor) or racially heterogeneous and divided, as is the nation for both the student and his teacher. As the student explains, despite our differences and even our desires to pull apart and see ourselves as independent, autonomous, and not in relation to one another, we remain connected; "That's American," he says in line 33, indicating Hughes's belief in a nationally influenced identity and how big this page would necessarily have to be in order to adequately represent any of us.

Race and Racism

Although the poem builds on the individual themes of identity and race or racism, in some sense

Topics for Further Study

- Write your own version of "Theme for English B," listing all those things that you believe make you uniquely you. What would you have to do to accurately write a page that "came out of you"?

- Go through "Theme for English B" and note all the possible referents that exist for the pronouns in the poem. How does such an exercise help you to understand what Hughes is saying about identity in the poem itself?

- Write a dramatic monologue (a poem spoken from the voice of someone other than yourself) from the perspective of a person living in an area distinctly different from where you live. Imagine yourself living in that area and describe what you would see on your way to school and how it might make you feel to live there.

---

it is both unrealistic and disingenuous to separate these issues given that Hughes's poem seems so poignantly to argue for their interconnectedness. Nevertheless, it is clear that Hughes would not want his reader to see "Theme for English B" as a poem only about the complications of identity and understanding who we are, but to also be made aware of the role race plays in the life of this young student at this time in America. This is the voice of the "only colored student in the class" at Columbia, a detail that highlights for the reader just who in New York City are receiving the best educations. The poem also introduces the reader to the dilemma of this student attempting to understand what sets him apart from his white peers: surely, he is not different in any essential way; he is human, he has likes, he wants to "work, read, learn, and understand life" just like anyone else. Yet, as lines 38 through 40 indicate, something divides him from his white professor, who is "somewhat more free" than he. Published in 1951, "Theme for English B" appears on the brink of the Civil Rights Movement when students like the one in the poem will begin to take direct action against the segregation that still

divided (and to some extent still divides) America's white and black communities. In this way, Hughes's poem is prophetic. In just a couple of years, students like the one in "Theme for English B" will be using nonviolent techniques to open lunch counters and the fronts of buses to African Americans; they will also be using them to register African-Americans voters so that they can take their rightful places in a national political community.

Style

"Theme for English B" is a lyric poem, which means that it is fairly brief, that it contains the thoughts of one speaker who speaks in the first person throughout the poem, and, rather than relying on action and plot to convey its point as a narrative poem would do, it largely reflects on the speaker's experiences and feelings about those experiences. The lyric is the most common and popular form of poetic writing today.

"Theme for English B" is also a dramatic monologue insofar as it adopts the voice of a character and allows Hughes to speak in that character's voice. In some ways, the fact that Hughes writes this as a dramatic monologue in and of itself indicates the slipperiness of identity that the poem's speaker addresses; such a poem allows the poet to wear a mask of sorts and speak in someone else's voice (a point that may or may not have particular relevance here given that Hughes certainly is relying on some autobiographical experience in the piece). Using the form of the lyric also allows us, the readers, to get as close to this experience as language can permit. In form, "Theme for English B" reveals the "self" of the speaker even as that speaker explains the complications of the very idea of a "self."

In terms of Hughes's use of sound in the poem, "Theme for English B" stands out from the rest of the poems in *Montage of a Dream Deferred* because it does not rely on the bebop boogie beat Hughes employed for most of the other poems. Hughes introduced the entire collection by saying: "In terms of current Afro-American popular music and the sources from which it has progressed— jazz, ragtime, swing, blues, boogie-woogie, and bebop—this poem on contemporary Harlem, like bebop, is marked by conflicting changes, sudden nuances, sharp and impudent interjections, broken rhythms, and passages sometimes in the manner of the jam session, sometimes the popular song, punctuated by the riffs, runs, breaks, and disc-tortions of the music of a community in transition." "Theme for English B" is certainly a "sharp and impudent interjection" in the collection, if only because it adopts a voice not marked by a African-American folk vernacular. Its rhythms are fairly straightforward; it sounds like a letter someone might write, or an account you might receive from a friend over dinner. But despite this apparently simple exterior, the poem does use rhyme and rhythm in interesting ways in order to stress some of its central points.

In the first stanza, Hughes's speaker quotes the instructor's directions for this assignment. Lines 2 through 5 embody that quote and each of these lines holds to a basic iambic pattern—one unstressed syllable followed by a stressed syllable. "Home" and "write" are stressed in line 2, "page" and "-night" in line 3, "let," "page," "out," and "you" in line 4, and, save for the single stress of "Then" at the beginning of the line, "will" and "true" in line 5. However, after this fairly reliable rhythmic opening, Hughes sheds this pattern and follows no strict form whatsoever for the rest of the poem, until the final line when he returns—ironically, given what he's illustrated within the piece—to the nursery rhyme-sounding pattern with which he began: "This is my page for English B," he concludes, stressing "is," "page," the first syllable of "English," and "B." This format alone signifies the complexities Hughes will address within the piece, but of which the professor appears unaware. The rhythms' complexities mirror those of the subjects covered.

Hughes uses internal rhyme in a similar way here. In stanza 3, lines 16 through 20, the student explores the interconnectedness of his sensual experiences (out of which he argues his identity is in part composed) with the things that spur those experiences, all of which indicate how layered his identity must be. Hughes underscores this idea by internally rhyming many of these words—"you," "me," "two," "we," "too," and "who." The rhymes mix these words up until it becomes difficult to clearly separate them, an effect Hughes also creates by employing tricky repetition. "Harlem, I hear you: / hear you, hear me—we two—you, me talk on this page. / (I hear New York, too.) Me—who?" the student finally asks, interweaving these pronouns to the point that no one can be sure to whom—or what—they refer; this is precisely the point Hughes seems to be trying to make elsewhere in the poem. By rhyming these key pronouns—and doing so very simply—Hughes indicates their inseparability on the level of sound. All of these

words—and others, such as "white," "write," "true," and "free"—are fundamental to the poem's larger argument regarding identity and American racial awareness.

Historical Context

Langston Hughes "arrived" as a literary figure in American culture with the 1921 publication of "The Negro Speaks of Rivers" in *The Crisis,* the literary journal of the National Association for the Advancement of Colored People (NAACP), which itself had been formed out of The Niagra Movement in 1910. *The Crisis* was under the general editorship of W. E. B. Du Bois, perhaps the most prominent and vital spokesperson for African Americans at that time. It is significant that Hughes appeared on the literary scene at this time and in the pages of this magazine because both facts firmly establish him as one of the key figures in what has been called the Harlem Renaissance or the New Negro Renaissance. While "Theme for English B" did not actually appear in print until 1951, it is necessary to look at where Hughes's career began and the conditions in which his writings were first grounded in order to understand how and why Hughes was doing what he was doing later on.

As critics have shown, an exact start date for the Harlem Renaissance is difficult, if not impossible, to discern. Scholars seem to agree that this phase of literary, artistic, and cultural development ended during the Great Depression, and certainly the 1920s saw its greatest achievements and events. But this explosion of artistic endeavor was prompted by a range of factors linked to World War I. While industrial production in northern cities increased, the pool of unskilled laborers decreased due to the war effort and the slowdown in foreign immigration brought about by the war. In 1914, the number of foreign immigrants was 1,218,480; in just one year, that figure dropped to 326,700, dropping again to just 110,618 only three years after that. At the same time, some four million citizens were drafted for military service. This situation propelled northern factory owners to solicit southern blacks for employment in their factories. According to David Levering Lewis, from 1915 on, "the South was full of agents recruiting labor for northern industry. Railroad tickets were dispensed gratis or advanced against forthcoming wages; trains backed into small towns and steamed away with most of the young and the fit; and the Chicago *De-*

Compare & Contrast

- **1917:** 2,132 African Americans attend American universities and colleges.

- **1927:** 13,580 African Americans attend American universities and colleges.

- **1950:** 180,830 African Americans hold an undergraduate or graduate degree from a four-year university or college in America.

- **1980:** 1,163,000 African Americans are enrolled in American universities and colleges.

- **1990:** 1,393,000 African Americans are enrolled in American universities and colleges.

- **1915:** As many as 1,300,000 African Americans are either reading or having read to them the weekly national edition of the Chicago *Defender*. The impact of the newspaper on migration trends of African American to the North is, without doubt, immense.

- **1953:** The Chicago *Defender* moves to a daily edition.

- **1998:** Circulation for what is now the local, daily edition of the Chicago *Defender* is somewhere between 20,000 and 25,000. Due to falling subscriptions and a general decrease in readership, the historic newspaper is put up for sale by its current owners.

---

fender ballyhooed the milk and honey up North." These factors, combined with the rising tide of Ku Klux Klan activity and lynchings in the South, led to what historians now refer to as the Great Migration of 1915. From Chicago to New York, northern cities saw a vast increase in African-American populations in the years just before the 1920s.

This migration led to the development of significant black communities in these cities. Harlem was not the only such area, but for the development of African-American culture and art, it was clearly the most influential. Outside of the *Defender*, Chicago's leading national African-American newspaper, most key African-American publications came out of New York. The two most important of these were the *Crisis* and Charles S. Johnson's *Opportunity*, published under the auspices of the National Urban League as, initially, a sociological journal intended to discuss issues of race; it quickly became a literary and arts magazine. Music and entertainment in Harlem were also rapidly growing and changing during this period, and, as historians have noted, it was during this time that the blues and ragtime played in Harlem's night clubs contributed to the fusion of musical forms that led to the development of what we now call modern jazz. Ragtime had already taken over

as one of the most popular kinds of music nationwide, and musicians such as James Reese Europe, Duke Ellington, and Fats Waller further developed and expanded the music of African-American New York and Harlem.

Hughes, of course, was just one writer in a diverse and rich community of writers. Other poets, such as Countee Cullen and Claude McKay, were more interested in appropriating and redefining traditional poetic forms—the sonnet, for instance—to reflect their experience rather than expanding and incorporating the musical rhythms of jazz as were Hughes and poet Sterling Brown. Other key writers include Jean Toomer (whose *Cane* defies clear generic categorization, moving between poetry, prose, and drama in its pages), poets Gwendolyn Bennett and Arna Bontemps, novelist Nella Larsen, and Zora Neale Hurston, the anthropologist-folklorist with whom Hughes traveled in the deep South in the late 1920s. Hughes collaborated on a range of projects with most of these figures and many others who were key to the development of African-American cultural and artistic identity during the early part of the twentieth century.

The Depression of the 1930s brought an end to the time when, as historians put it, "Harlem was in vogue." As Gerald Early notes, "the Harlem Renaissance is the story of the creation of a national black community but ... blacks did not control or influence loans for mortgages, rent policies, small businesses, banking practices in general; in short, they did not control nearly any economic aspect of the community they wished to create. This is why the Harlem Renaissance failed and Harlem became a ghetto." Certainly, the years following the Depression became increasingly politically and economically difficult for African Americans who suffered under segregation—both its legalized version in the South in the form of the notorious Jim Crow laws, and its informal, but no less powerful social dictates in the North. It was during this later period of increased political disenfranchisement that Hughes wrote "Theme for English B," in which he questions American identity and race's part in its inscription. And it was this period as well that spurred the events of the Civil Rights Movement in the late 1950s and 1960s, when the question of racial discrimination gained long overdue national attention.

Critical Overview

Scholars and critics today generally agree that the work of Langston Hughes exhibits a tremendous experimental force, one that derives its importance not simply from the influence it has had on other writers (particularly those working to integrate poetic discourse with more generally popular forms of expression, such as jazz or vernacular speech), but from the firm foundation it has provided later twentieth-century, African-American literary and artistic cultures. But the initial reception Hughes received as a writer was much less clearly positive. Countee Cullen reviewed Hughes's *The Weary Blues* in the journal *Opportunity* when it came out, and his opening statement indicates the kind of mixed response Cullen himself had to the work— a response that was nonetheless admiring: "Here is a poet with whom to reckon," Cullen says, "to experience, and here and there, with that apologetic feeling of presumption that should companion all criticism, to quarrel." While excited by the possibilities inherent in Hughes's melding of poetry with musical and folk forms, Cullen also believed that the poems were "one-sided" and tended to "hurl this poet into the gaping pit that lies before all Negro writers, in the confines of which they become racial artists instead of artists pure and simple." "There is too much emphasis here on strictly Negro themes," Cullen asserts, "and this is probably

an added reason for my coldness toward the jazz poems—they seem to set a too definite limit upon an already limited field."

Babette Deutsch reviewed *Montage of a Dream Deferred* for the *New York Times Book Review* when the book appeared, and she writes that "sometimes the verse invites approval, but again it lapses into a facile sentimentality that stifles real feeling as with cheap scent ....The book as a whole leaves one less responsive to the poet's achievement than conscious of the limitations of folk art." Many critics and writers responded to Hughes's work in this vein, but even these acknowledged the expansiveness of Hughes's experimentation in *Montage*. In another *New York Times Book Review* assessment of the collection, Saunders Redding claims that Hughes requires of his readers a "sophisticated ear" in order to appreciate the often jarring twists and turns of his rhythms and that, while Redding believes it's time for Hughes to get on with saying the things he's been seeking a proper form to say, these are things that Hughes, "alone of American poets, was born to say." In another article published not long after the collection appeared, Arthur P. Davis claims that *Montage* offers the most mature and complete picture of Harlem that Hughes had attempted up to that time. As was the case with many of Hughes's critics, even those that found him problematic, Davis concedes that when Hughes depicts "the hopes, the aspirations, the frustrations, and the deep-seated discontent of the New York ghetto," he speaks for all African Americans living in urban ghettoized communities. Despite their own disgruntlement with his individual texts then, even Hughes's most dissenting critics acknowledge and respect his attempts to give voice to the passions and opinions of a largely unheard community.

"Theme for English B" seems to be a poem of greater interest to critics of the latter half of the twentieth century—an observation that makes certain sense given the increased interest among literary scholars with the overall question of identity in general. Critics often refer to the voice in the poem as one particularly aware of the difficulties of understanding racial identity in twentieth-century America. According to Onwuchekwa Jemie, who published one of the first full-length studies of Hughes's poetry, "Theme for English B" speaks to the biracial nature of American identity and how the experiences of Anglo and African Americans "interpenetrate, are defined one by the other, even though neither group relishes the idea." In one of the most recent treatments of the collection and the poem in particular, David R. Jarraway calls "Theme for English B" "arguably the most important poem in the *Montage* sequence" because it "explodes the notion of a racially pure self." In it, "the writer eventually realizes that neither his self nor the words that form the social and cultural extension of that self exist in a vacuum.... The call for intuitive self-expression, derived from a rigid separation between self and other, writing and reality, black and white, comes completely unraveled by the end."

In a different vein, Gayle Pemberton returns to Hughes's poem in order to understand what has been lost in the black—and white—communities of the late 1990s in her autobiographical and critical reflection, "Another 'Theme for English B.'" She sees the central point in the poem to be the speaker's ability to claim for himself, despite rampant racial inequality, "an equal share of the possibilities of imagination." Pemberton goes on to ask "what about the *imagination* today?" and ironically surmises that at least one point of equality between blacks and whites is a significant loss of imagination due to an increased and increasingly dangerous materialist impulse in the culture. "Under such circumstances," she says, "the guarded hope of mutual discovery, imagination, and life—of the mind, soul, and heart—found in Hughes's 'Theme for English B' is an indecipherable hieroglyph from a long lost age." Pemberton's piece makes clear that, whatever it is we find there, there remains much for the contemporary reader to find in Hughes's poem.

Criticism

Kristina Zarlengo

Kristina Zarlengo, who received her doctorate in English from Columbia University in 1997, taught literature and writing for five years at Columbia University. A scholar of modern American literature, her articles have appeared in academic journals and various periodicals. In the following essay, Zarlengo examines "Theme for English B" in its relationship as one part of the larger cultural statement of Montage of a Dream Deferred.

A poem that is both a college student's tale of being asked to write an essay for his English class and the "true" essay he therefore writes, "Theme for English B" is also one piece of the long poem

Montage of a Dream Deferred. Written in Harlem in 1948, and published in 1951, it is Hughes's sustained effort at crafting a thoroughly modern, thoroughly relevant poem.

Appearing near its center is the brief "Theme for English B," whose familar vocabulary and speech ryhthms make it read like something we might hear every day. The narrator, who wonders if his homework assignment is really simple, poses his question in a poem that seems to answer it— the question comes from the midst of an uncomplicated bunch of words. This poetry is free of the strange phrases and the forced language and rhythm that inspire many readers of poetry to revile the genre. On closer inspection, we realize that the poem's themes are challenging, its patterns of rhythm, rhyme and sound refined. These marks of effort will never, however, remove from the poem its accessibility.

"Theme for English B" is written in free verse—it stays the track of no one rhythmic pattern; it has no regular rhyme scheme. It does, however, establish patterns. The instructor's homework assignment, for instance, is in an *aabb* rhyme pattern. Then, "Salem" and "Harlem" begin to establish one rhyme every other line, while "class" and "Nicholas" briefly establish another. By the end of the first stanza, however, both end-rhyme patterns have disappeared. Brief, catchy rhymes will reappear—the rhymes "white," "write," and later "me," "free," and "B" are conspicuous. A rhyming poem, "Theme for English B" is, however, ready to abandon its rhymes.

Also repeating—also unpredictably—are the hill in Harlem; "a part of me" and" a part of you"; the important word "true"; and, clumped at the center of the poem, "hear"—five times. If we thus feel urged to hear this poem as much as we read it silently off the page, it's no wonder: with "Theme for English B," as for the whole of *Montage of a Dream Deferred,* Hughes wrote poetry closely tied to music—especially bebop. Rather than observing strict beat or sound patterns, Hughes favors musical phrases that use pattern as a springboard, rather than a limit: he prefers the melody to the metronome. Borrowing bebop's skill with establishing assorted sound patterns only to break them, with making of tempo and beat an ornate cage, then flying the coop with improvisation, Hughes emulates jazz.

Always a jazz enthusiast, Hughes was, in 1948, particularly inspired by bcbop, the kind of jazz developed by saxophonist Charlie Parker, trumpeter

> *Rather than observing strict beat or sound patterns, Hughes favors musical phrases that use pattern as a springboard, rather than a limit: he prefers the melody to the metronome.*"

Dizzie Gillespie, and pianist Thelonious Sphere Monk—all black Americans who cultivated their musical innovations in New York City between 1942 and 1950. At first playing in Harlem, bop musicians eventually attracted large white audiences that joined its longer-standing black audiences, signalling their "popular" success. Around 1944, bop albums were profitably produced, and the New York City jazz scene moved downtown to 52nd Street.

Bebop was an outgrowth of swing and big band music, whose catchy melodies and smooth rhythms had long attracted large audiences, even as the tunes' simplicity had made them easy to learn by musicians with no special affiliation to the gospels, blues, and early jazz of black American musical tradition. Relative to these earlier traditions, bebop is a difficult style of music—difficult to master as a musician, difficult to dance or hum along with, and difficult to listen to. It was, therefore, in its way, all the more rewarding: while other musical forms do well as background music or as prompts for dancing, humming along, or imitating, bebop's turbulent tempos, virtuoso improvisational solos, and intricate melodies made it an art form that accentuated the evanescence of the present and seemed to demand of audience and practitioners alike a careful attention to the tunes, which, if improvised, would never again be played in that form.

Around the time Hughes wrote "Theme for English B," bebop was changing jazz's status. Long considered a disreputable form of music, jazz in the form of bebop was beginning to be seen as a form of high art. Indeed, jazz has since been widely recognized as one of America's most revered cultural products—a whole artistic form that could not have arisen elsewhere and that has forever reshaped the course of world music. In its day, however, it never shook its notoriety, even after bebop. Jazz recordings were often used to suggest an urban underworld where things fall apart. Jazz was regular background music for gangster films and television detective shows; for many audiences—especially those outside of the cities where jazz boomed—it was the soundtrack to seedy clubs and secret downtown back rooms.

For Hughes, however—a self-appointed, publicly applauded bard of black America—jazz was like what he wished his poetry to be: part of his people's history—the extension of folk tradition, yet always fresh and thoroughly modern; approachable enough to draw crowds, yet capable of standing up well when measured by high art standards. Eventually, Hughes became something of a jazz performer himself, reading poems to the accompaniment of bassist Charles Mingus to packed audiences at the Village Vanguard, then later with a quintet, and with blues musicians at the Newport Jazz Festival. With *Montage of a Dream Deferred,* Hughes was at the height of applying bebop to poetry on the page. Alongside "Theme for English B" are sections titled "Flatted Fifths" (a term for the diminished fifth note on a scale—a "blue note" favored in bebop); "Jam Session" (the term for a session in which musicians play together with little predetermined structure); and "Be-Bop Boys." The latter poem is laced with syllables from "scat singing," the nonsense syllables sung by some jazz vocalists; the poem's second section ends with "Oop-pop-a-da! / Skee! Daddle-de-do! / Be-bop! / Salt'peanuts! / De-dop!"

Montage of a Dream Deferred as a whole reads like scenes from a dream. Some sections contain the first-person anecdotes of Harlem residents: a Harlem old-timer who reflects on the area's growth; a man who shudders at the news that his wife is pregnant again; someone who wants to crown his lover with the neon lights of Harlem. Other pieces are preacherly: the narrator tells the reader, "If you're not alive and kicking, / shame on you!" In still other sections, slices of life are narrated by an undefined voice omniscient in the ways of Harlem:

Mellow
Into the laps
of black celebrities
white girls fall
like pale plums from a tree
beyond a high tension wall
wired for killing
which makes it
more thrilling.

"The mood of the blues is almost always despondency," Hughes wrote, "but when they are sung people laugh." A similar mood of intermixed sadness and laughter unites the disparate sections of *Montage of a Dream Deferred.* But the poem's greatest cohesion is its motif of the deferred dream. Hughes is riveted by the question, "What happens to a dream deferred?": What happens in the gulf between America's promise and what it delivers? A place of sweet relations, dancing, and smiles, Hughes's Harlem is never just cheery: he tells of homes lost to greedy landlords, lives lost to drunk oblivion, youths lost in bleak labor, dreams that yield to world.

In "Harlem," one of the poem's final pieces, in lines that have since become their own kind of gospel, Hughes asks his question, then tries out some answers:

> What happens to a dream deferred?
> Does it dry up
> like a raisin in the sun?
> Or fester like a sore—
> and then run?
> Or crust up and sugar over—
> like a syrupy sweet?
> Maybe it sags
> like a heavy load.
> Or does it explode?

This passage—a distillate of *Montage of a Dream Deferred*—delivers not answers but urgency. What happens to that dream is a question that burns, that involves us. Highly accessible, easily readable, catchy in its diction, *Montage of a Dream Deferred* also borrows its title from a pictorial technique developed by avant-garde painters in which cutout illustrations, or their fragments, are arranged together. In a montage, ready-made images—sometimes called found art—are collected together into an assembly in which each fragment changes the appearance of each other, and, united, they point to a subject and a message no fragment could illustrate alone. For Hughes, high art and the quotidian—such as social and aesthetic aims—were always and everywhere the same. In urging us, Hughes also asserts the high relevance of questions of everyday social conditions. His normalcy is cultivated.

In the context of the montage of which it is a fragment, "Theme for English B" is in some ways incongruous. Its first person narrator, a twenty-two-year-old student at the "college on the hill above Harlem" (Columbia University) has moved to New York from the South, where he was raised and schooled. The move itself is suggestive of the mi-

What Do I Read Next?

- Langston Hughes was not only the writer, but the editor of a significant body of fiction. *The Best of Simple,* a "greatest hits" collection of Hughes's stories featuring his popular folk character, Simple, appeared in 1990. Also of interest is the collection of African-American short stories Hughes edited in 1969—*The Best Short Stories by Black Writers: The Classic Anthology from 1899 to 1967.*

- Hughes published two autobiographies in his lifetime, both of which were recently reissued in 1993 by Hill and Wang Press. *The Big Sea: An Autobiography* originally appeared in 1940 and *I Wonder as I Wander: An Autobiographical Journey* first came out in 1956.

- The Harlem Renaissance saw the emergence of many central women writers of the century; Zora Neale Hurston is one of these, and her *Their Eyes Were Watching God* (1937) tells the story of a woman struggling to find love and happiness in Hurston's native Florida.

- Produced by the Center of Black Music, Columbia College, Chicago and edited by Samuel A. Floyd, *Black Music in the Harlem Renaissance: A Collection of Essays* (1994) establishes that the musical developments of the Harlem Renaissance—forms that Hughes played with in all of his writing—were indeed central to a more global development of black culture.

grations north of blacks who sought a better social world than that of the oppressive South, but our narrator is also living another black—and indeed universal—American dream: going to college. It seems, then, that he has realized his dreams; he is living an unfolding promise.

His geography is more complicated, though, than one dividing North and South. A college student, he is, however, the only colored student in his class. The college on a hill over Harlem therefore experiences little traffic between Harlem and itself.

> *As 'Theme for English B' indicates, Hughes, from the beginning of his career, consistently explored the idea of an American voice, and he repeatedly insisted that what we define as "American" must include the experiences, language, and visions of both its black and white citizens."*

What's more, our narrator supposes, "I'm what / I feel and see, Harlem, I hear you: / hear you, hear me." When his English instructor in college, who knows nothing of the world he lives in, asks of him a true page, he knows he will be writing about Harlem. That is, he knows himself to be a portion of the world where he lives. This insight—this "guess"—transforms his assignment into a lesson for the teacher. He asks:

So will my page be colored that I write?
Being me, it will not be white
But it will be
a part of you, instructor.
You are white—
yet a part of me, as I am a part of you.

Our narrator is a witness to how his dream must affect other colored people and the place where he lives before it will have been realized. We are all of a part, he insists. "Sometimes," he says, "perhaps you don't want to be a part of me," (and indeed, the instructor's college seems to want to be on a hill above Harlem without being in Harlem or educating its residents). "Nor do I often want to be a part of you," he rejoins, then delivers the truth that has been asked of him: "But we are, that's true!" what's more, "That's American." America, our narrator claims, is all of its parts. All of its parts are its people—you and I are America, the Harlem slum lord and the Harlem girl on the stoop are America. And the American dream is a dream of all people; no one can have it when others are refused it.

It is tempting to identify the voice of "Theme for English B" as Hughes's own. Raised poor, he, too, attended Columbia University. Hughes, too, was a favored American dreamer—he was educated, well travelled, and eventually widely hailed. He wrote novels, poems, operettas, autobiographies, biographies, newspaper columns, children's books, and histories of blacks in America. Indeed, he wrote *Montage of a Dream Deferred* after having realized his long dream of owning a home—in Harlem. And like the narrator of "Theme for English B," Hughes wanted to participate in not just his own prosperity, but that of the people and places that made him; Hughes made of his own successes an amplified demand that they be better shared by his people.

But the poem's narrator is not Hughes. Hughes hailed not from the South, but from the Midwest. Also, Hughes's race was mixed. Of black, white, and Indian ancestry, he alone was part white, part black—as the poem's narrator says all of America is. The differences between Hughes and the narrator of "Theme for English B" may be of a part with Hughes's career-long ideal of focusing on the archetypal black man—a man similar to, but also distinct from, Hughes himself. In the estimate of his biographer, Arnold Rampersand, Hughes's "surge of art" resulting in *Montage of a Dream Deferred* came out of his feeling "the depth of his emotional dependency on the black masses, as well as his painful detachment from them both as an artist endowed with second sight and, suddenly, as a bourgeois property owner." Whether or not his alliance with all blacks, everywhere, was produced out of such a reverse identification and sense of longing, Hughes himself clung always to the concerns of the black working-class American. In doing so, he produced what is sometimes called social art:

Most of my own poems are racial in theme and treatment, derived from the life I know. In many of them I try to grasp and hold some of the meanings and rhythms of jazz. I am as sincere as I know how to be in these poems and yet, after every reading, I answer questions like these from my own people: Do you think Negroes should always write about Negroes? … Why do you write about black people? You aren't black. What makes you do so much Jazz poems?

One of Hughes's books features a wise but simple, brash poor black man, a character named Simple, who declares that the term bebop comes from police brutality against blacks: "Every time a cop hits a Negro with his billy club that old club says Bop! Bop! ... BE -BOP! ... MOP! ... BOP!" As tragicomic an explanation as this is for the birth of bebop, it is also a serious example of Hughes's understanding of the relationship between social circumstance and art: neither is identifiable without the other. And in the prolific writing that at once realized his own American Dream of social acclaim and trumpeted the urgent beauties and damned the persistent oppression of American black people, Hughes manages to capture despondency without romanticizing it—indeed, he demands that we overcome it. In managing this approach, Hughes did not, in the end, work in a poetic form much like that of complexly stunning bebop composition: Hughes's work, such as "Theme for English B," is always accessible, right away. He therefore did not prevent imitators, but inspired them—opening up audiences, earning international acclaim, and changing American literary history. "The realistic position assumed by Hughes has become the dominant outlook of all those Negro writers who have something to say," wrote Richard Wright. "Hughes's role has become," he added, "that of a cultural ambassador."

Source: Kristina Zarlengo, in an essay for *Poetry for Students,* The Gale Group, 1999.

Jeannine Johnson

Jeannine Johnson received her Ph.D. from Yale University and is currently a visiting assistant professor of English at Wake Forest University. In the following essay, Johnson reveals the ways in which the short poem "Theme for English B" encapsulates Hughes's larger poetic projects.

"Theme for English B" is the forty-ninth of eighty-seven lyrics in Langston Hughes's long poetic sequence titled *Montage of a Dream Deferred* (1951). Even though Hughes assigns titles to each of the shorter poems included in *Montage,* he imagined this work as a single, unified poem. The whole gives coherence to the parts, and it may be best to think of *Montage of a Dream Deferred* as a mosaic of lyrics that vary in voice, theme, imagery, vocabulary, and structure. Having no single subject, speaker, or setting, there is a sense of transience in the poem, and it is therefore appropriate that there are no lengthy poems or sustained meditations. *Montage of a Dream Deferred* moves relentlessly forward, capturing the irregular rhythms of ordinary life, demonstrating how art and beauty can be made from the artless and ugly. There is also a musical strain throughout the poem, as the rhythms of jazz and bebop drive the text. Hughes,

in a prefatory note to *Montage of a Dream Deferred,* describes his poetic design this way:

> In terms of current Afro-American popular music and the sources from which it has progressed—jazz, ragtime, swing, blues, boogie-woogie, and be-bop—this poem on contemporary Harlem, like be-bop, is marked by conflicting changes, sudden nuances, sharp and impudent interjections, broken rhythms, and passages sometimes in the manner of a jam session, sometimes the popular song, punctuated by the riffs, runs, breaks, and distortions of the music of a community in transition.

The "community in transition" of which Hughes speaks is, first, Harlem in particular and, second, African-American culture in general. For Hughes, as for many other African-American artists who lived during the 1920s and 1930s and witnessed its renaissance, Harlem is a symbol of excellence in black creative production in America. As Hughes argues, its music accommodates the various, irregular, and sometimes conflicting rhythms, ideas, and experiences of black life and expression. Of course, when he speaks of Harlem's music, he is also referring to its poetry and to the ideals toward which his own poetry strives. "Theme for English B" exemplifies the style Hughes details in his preface to *Montage of a Dream Deferred,* as it contains conflicts within sound and meter as well as within the personality of the poem's speaker. This brief poem encapsulates Hughes's theories of poetry as well as any of his single lyrics and demonstrates that the identity of the poet is inevitably influenced by nonpoetic factors.

There is a strong autobiographical element in this poem, but like all good poems, "Theme for English B" is not a transparent reproduction of the poet's actual past. Hughes did not grow up in North Carolina, as his poetic persona did, but in the Midwest. Nevertheless, Hughes did attend Columbia University in the early 1920s, and Columbia appears in the poem as the "college on the hill above Harlem." The situation he describes comes generally from his personal experience, consolidated and modified to create this specific incident. At the core of the poem is Hughes's concern with the relationship between race and literature. The poet is both flippant and serious when he asks, "So will my page be colored that I write? / Being me, it will not be white." When he was a student at Columbia, Hughes intended one day to become a professional writer, but even then he recognized that as a black man aspiring to join a largely white vocation, he faced potential difficulties that ranged from the personal to the artistic to the professional. Hughes left Columbia after that first year and, within a relatively short time, began to publish some of his writing. Still, he was not making enough money to support himself, and even after modest success with the publication of two poetry collections and *Not Without Laughter* (1930), his first novel, Hughes still wondered whether he, "a *Negro,* could make a living in America from writing." He recalls in his autobiography, *I Wonder as I Wander* (1956), that he could not imagine compromising his literary vision, despite the racial barriers that existed in this country: "There was one other dilemma—how to make a living from the kind of *writing I wanted to do.* I did not want to write for the pulps, or turn out fake 'true' stories to sell under anonymous names as Wallace Thurman did. I did not want to bat out slick non-Negro short stories in competition with a thousand other commercial writers trying to make *The Saturday Evening Post.* I wanted to write seriously and as well as I knew how about the Negro people, and make that kind of writing earn for me a living."

These same sentiments inform "Theme for English B" which, like *I Wonder as I Wander,* is a retrospective account, written many years after his early days as a writer. As "Theme for English B" indicates, Hughes, from the beginning of his career, consistently explored the idea of an American voice, and he repeatedly insisted that what we define as "American" must include the experiences, language, and visions of both its black and white citizens. In his poem, he puts it simply: "You are white— / yet a part of me, as I am a part of you. / That's American." Hughes recognizes that this ideal view is not without its challenges and admits, "Sometimes perhaps you don't want to be a part of me. / Nor do I often want to be a part of you. / But we are, that's true!" And though he is certain that there must be mutual respect and reciprocity, the poet ends with an acknowledgement of the inequalities of present circumstances: "As I learn from you, / I guess you learn from me— / although you're older—and white— / and somewhat more free."

Though Hughes accepted and welcomed the critical praise his writing received from professional, mostly white readers, he wrote with a popular, African-American audience in mind. The divisions between the educated and the uneducated, between black and white, between the varying uses of poetry, are evident in "Theme for English B." Is poetry for personal use, as a vehicle for self-expression? Or is there a communal component to poems? Is poetry a space of privilege or an egalitarian realm? How do race and class influence poetic language? Is poetry to be composed out of

obligation (such as to fulfill a class requirement)? Or are there other, more valuable motivations for writing poetry? The poem opens with his instructor's voice: *"Go home and write / a page tonight. / And let that page come out of you— / Then it will be true."* Throughout the rest of the poem, Hughes both ridicules and confirms this philosophy of poetry. The poet asks, "I wonder if it's that simple?" And he shows that, in fact, there is nothing simple about establishing and then writing from a particular identity. Hughes wonders who he is: "Me—who? / Well, I like to eat, sleep, drink, and be in love. / I like to work, read, learn, and understand life. / I like a pipe for a Christmas present, / or records—Bessie, bop, or Bach." As he inspects his individuality, he discovers a conflation of white and black cultural influences and is confronted again with questions of ethnicity.

For Hughes, poetry is to some degree about self-expression and self-exploration, especially when the "self" is understood to mark the identity of an individual who is always affected by and affecting a larger culture. More than that, the goal of Hughes's poetry is communication—creating and employing language and forms that can authentically convey the visions of African-American artists. "But I guess I'm what / I feel and see and hear, Harlem, I hear you: / hear you, hear me—we two—you, me, talk on this page." Though Hughes imagines an intimate conversation between himself and other African Americans, he adds "(I hear New York, too.)" He acknowledges that white Manhattan also inhabits his poem. The parentheses diminish the importance of white influence, but they do not altogether eliminate it. Nevertheless, the presence of white New York is not as significant as that of Harlem's, and even though the poet adopts the fictional pose of writing for a white English professor, his true aim is to reach black readers.

In *I Wonder as I Wander,* Hughes writes of his motives for embarking on a speaking tour of the South in the early 1930s and also of his fears that his poetry will not be received by his intended audience. "I did not want a job. I wanted to continue to be a poet. Yet sometimes I wondered if I was barking up the wrong tree. I determined to find out by taking poetry, *my* poetry, to *my* people. After all, I wrote about Negroes, and primarily *for* Negroes. Would they have me? Did they want me?" As Hughes discovered, many blacks—from North and South—did want him and embraced his poetry. Over the next few decades, Hughes became very well known and was generally well respected as a major figure in black letters. However, by the time that *Montage of a Dream Deferred* was published, Hughes's reputation had changed from that of a voice for his people to that of a spokesman for outdated ideas. Some intellectuals, both black and white, had begun to criticize Hughes's poetry as too conservative and even as old-fashioned.

Throughout his life, some small piece of Hughes's early concern about his work's reception remained with him. Yet he never wavered in his rather grand conception of the nature and purpose of poetry itself. In his biography of Hughes, literary critic Arnold Rampersad quotes Hughes's definition of poetry, as offered in a 1951 lecture: "Poetry is rhythm—and, through rhythm, has its roots deep in the nature of the universe; the rhythms of the stars, the rhythm of the earth moving around the sun, of day, night, of the seasons, of the sowing and the harvest, of fecundity and birth. The rhythms of poetry give continuity and pattern to words, to thoughts, strengthening them, adding the qualities of permanence, and relating the written word to the vast rhythms of life."

Source: Jeannine Johnson, in an essay for *Poetry for Students,* The Gale Group, 1999.

Chris Semansky

Chris Semansky's fiction, poetry, and essays appear regularly in literary journals and magazines such as Mississippi Review, College English, *and* American Letters & Commentary. *In the following essay, Semansky argues that "Theme for English B" complicates the idea that lyric poems can truthfully represent a coherent, stable self.*

One of the primary features of a lyric poem is that it expresses the thoughts and feelings of its speaker. The assumption of such poems is that by describing what is inside of them, narrators of lyrics are able to articulate the truth about themselves. Expression, then, assumes that the speaker has a coherent identity that is accessible and only needs to be retrieved and described in order to manifest the truth.

In his poem "Theme for English B," Langston Hughes complicates the idea that the lyric "I" is a reflection of a coherent, stable identity by calling into question the notion that one can reveal the truth simply by expressing oneself. Instead, Hughes suggests that the self, rather than being coherent and autonomous, is actually the effect of relationships. These relationships inevitably involve power and, in Hughes's case, include race, age, national, and professional identity.

Hughes frames the idea that expression can get at the truth by exploring what we can only take to

> " *... Hughes suggests that the self, rather than being coherent and autonomous, is actually the effect of relationships.* "

be an autobiographical encounter between himself and one of his college teachers. After introducing his teacher's assignment instructions for an essay, Hughes spends the rest of the poem responding to them and exposing their faulty assumptions. He answers his instructor's directive to go home and write by first questioning the directive's apparent simplicity and then by providing a brief history of his home. He tells us that he is a black man who was born in the South (Winston-Salem, North Carolina) and is now attending a white school in the North (Columbia University in New York City). These differences alone complicate the assignment, as they highlight Hughes's feeling of alienation and the difficulty of "going home." Underscoring this difficulty is the speaker's description of the long route he takes to his current home, a room at the Harlem YMCA, and his description of Harlem—a predominantly black community—as literally down the hill from the university. By characterizing his "home" in terms of distance and difficulty, Hughes emphasizes how "un-simple" description is; how, regardless of what we say or write about something, we are always taking a position because we are saying one thing instead of another. If, for example, he had described himself in terms of gender (male) and sexuality instead of age and race, and if he had described Columbia University in terms of how it appeared rather than where it was in relation to Harlem, we would have a completely different image of Hughes and his dilemma.

In the second stanza, Hughes moves from description to meditation, as he continues to ponder the very possibility of fulfilling his white instructor's assignment.

> It's not easy to know what is true for you or me
> At twenty-two, my age. But I guess I'm what
> I feel and see and hear, Harlem, I hear you:
> Hear you, hear me—we two—you, me, talk on this
>   page.
> (I hear New York, too.) Me—who?

Here the speaker underlines the fact that what is true for him might not be true for his instructor. But he isn't quite sure of what is true for himself. Even the outside world that he sees, feels, and hears isn't enough to provide a definition of his identity. Though he identifies with Harlem (presumably because of its black population), he also recognizes that Harlem itself is a part of a larger entity, New York City. Hughes then moves from answering his instructor to answering himself, as he ruminates on what makes him different from others. His search for difference, in this case, instead yields both similarities and differences, as he first lists relatively common human desires—"Well, I like to eat, sleep, drink, and be in love. / I like to work, read, learn, and understand life."—then more personal preferences—"I like a pipe for a Christmas present, / or records—Bessie, bop, or Bach." This recognition of commonality and separateness returns him once again to the assignment, as he asks, "So will my page be colored that I write?"

Hughes provides the answer in the rest of the poem. But it is not a simple answer. His meditation on the assignment has led him to conclude that he is not one thing or another, but rather one thing and another. His black identity rests on the fact that there is also a white identity; his identity as a Southerner rests on the fact that there is a North; his identity as a student rests on the fact that there is a teacher; and his youth rests on the fact that there are those older than him. All of these relationships, Hughes suggests, not only help constitute the way that he thinks of himself, the image of himself that he carries around, but also the way that his teacher (and by implication, all human beings) thinks of himself.

For Hughes, this idea that the many are contained in the one is a common denominator of the American national identity. In this way he echoes the ideas of Walt Whitman, the nineteenth-century American poet who regarded each individual as a microcosm of society and the universe. But rather than singing the praises of American democracy and equality as Whitman did, Hughes points out that although Americans' differences help form what they take to be their own "individual" identities, these differences also help to make some of these identities less equal than others: students are subordinate to teachers; whites are more privileged than blacks, etc. After acknowledging the ways in which his own identity informs his teacher's identity and vice versa, Hughes addresses his teacher, saying:

As I learn from you, I guess you learn from me—
although you're older—and white—
and somewhat more free.

His hesitancy ("I guess you learn from me") and his claim that because his teacher is older and white, he is "somewhat more free" than him underscore the role that power plays in all of the relationships the poem explores. That Hughes (as student) feels "free" to write these things to his instructor demonstrates that to a certain extent he has managed to overcome (or at least challenge) the limitations of his various identities. In so doing, he has fulfilled the directions of the assignment to "let the page come out of you." Or has he?

By questioning his instructor's very directions, the student-speaker is questioning his instructor's authority. While some instructors might think this action shows independent thinking and reward the student for such an action, it isn't clear that this will be the case in this poem. Hughes's description of the situation and of the instructor suggest that the instructor is most likely fairly conventional in his thinking (consider the generic nature of the assignment and the fact that the student isn't certain that the instructor can learn anything from him). Rather than seeing this poem as an example of creative independent thinking, the instructor might very well punish the student both for challenging him and for writing a poem instead of an essay. Seen in this light the poem, then, becomes an act of rebellion—of questioning the instructor's very identity as teacher. Such a response would be ironic if we consider that the very act of writing the poem is a result of the power relationships that make the student who he is. More ironic still would be the teacher's blindness to the very relationships that also form him.

Source: Chris Semansky, in an essay for *Poetry for Students,* The Gale Group, 1999.

Sources

Early, Gerald, "Three Notes Toward a Cultural Definition of the Harlem Renaissance," in *Callaloo,* Vol. 14, No. 1, 1991, pp. 136-49.

Gates, Henry Louis, Jr., and K. A. Appiah, *Langston Hughes: Critical Perspectives Past and Present,* New York: Amistad Press, 1993.

Hughes, Langston, *Fine Clothes to the Jew,* New York: Alfred A. Knopf, 1927.

Hughes, Langston, *I Wonder as I Wander,* New York: Hill and Wang, 1956.

Hughes, Langston, *Montage of a Dream Deferred,* in *Collected Poems,* Vintage, 1994.

Hughes, Langston, "The Negro Artist and the Racial Mountain," *Nation,* 1926, reprinted in *The Black Aesthetic,* edited by Addison Gayle, Jr., New York: Doubleday, 1971.

Hughes, Langston, *Selected Poems of Langston Hughes,* New York: Vintage Classics, 1990.

Hughes, Langston, *Simple Takes a Wife,* New York: Simon and Schuster, 1953.

Hutchinson, George, *The Harlem Renaissance in Black and White,* Cambridge, MA: Belknap Press of Harvard University Press, 1995.

Jarraway, David R., "Montage of an Otherness Deferred: Dreaming Subjectivity in Langston Hughes," *American Literature,* Vol. 68, No. 4, 1996, pp. 819-47.

Lauter, Paul, ed., *The Heath Anthology of American Literature,* Vol. 2, second edition, Lexington, MA: D. C. Heath, 1994.

Martin, Henry, *Enjoying Jazz,* New York: Macmillan Books, 1986.

Mullen, Edward J., ed., *Critical Essays on Langston Hughes,* Boston: G.K. Hall, 1986.

Rampersad, Arnold, *The Life of Langston Hughes,* two volumes, New York: Oxford University Press, 1988.

Wright, Richard, "The Big Sea," *A Journal of Opinion,* October 28, 1940.

For Further Study

Gates, Henry Louis, Jr., and K. A. Appiah, eds., *Langston Hughes: Critical Perspectives Past and Present,* New York: Amistad Press, 1993.

Gates and Appiah present a range of critical texts regarding Hughes's work in this collection, including contemporary reviews of Hughes's publications and scholarly essays on those same collections. The reviews are particularly interesting, given that they provide the best portrait of Hughes's critical reception at the time he was actively writing and publishing.

Jemie, Onwuchekwa, *Langston Hughes: An Introduction to the Poetry,* New York: Columbia University Press, 1976.

Jemie's text is the first full-length treatment of Hughes's poetry. In it, Jemie carefully works his way through the breadth of Hughes's work, making connections between the different kinds of experimentation Hughes attempted and the themes that run throughout all the poems.

Lewis, David Levering, *When Harlem Was in Vogue,* New York: Knopf, 1981.

Lewis provides a clear and lively depiction of Harlem during the period to which we now refer as the Harlem Renaissance, moving easily between general descriptions of this community and what affected its growth and development and individual portraits of the people who figured prominently in it.

Pemberton, Gayle, "Another 'Theme for English B,'" in *The Ethnic Moment: The Search for Equality in the American Experience,* edited by Philip L. Fetzer, New York: M.E. Sharpe, Inc., 1997, pp. 137-50.

In this autobiographical essay, Pemberton first talks about what she finds interesting to her personally about Hughes's "Theme for English B," even reprinting the poem to completely orient her reader. She then goes on to talk about her own experience with her father in order to demonstrate what she sees as a decline in imagination in all late twentieth-century American readers, both black and white, in particular a decline in the ability to imagine ourselves free from the psychological and economic constraints of a highly materialistic society.

There's a Certain Slant of Light

Emily Dickinson

1861

Written in 1861 at the beginning of Emily Dickinson's most prolific period as a poet, "There's a Certain Slant of Light" was first published in 1890 by Thomas Higginson in an edited version. It was not available in its original form until Thomas H. Johnson's 1955 edition of Dickinson's *Collected Works*. In stark contrast to Emerson's Romantic spiritualization of nature, this poem portrays nature as a distant, alien, and indifferent force fraught with reminders of death's universal presence. Dickinson's poem lays open the dialectic between outer nature and the inner self and places the source of meaning firmly within the interpretive self. In other words, all of the physical and psychological impressions that natural phenomena exert upon human consciousness only receive significance within the individual mind, "Where the Meanings, are."

"There's a Certain Slant of Light" also exemplifies Dickinson's poetic treatment of grief and loss present in so many of her works. On the surface, the poem explores the depression that light deprivation may inflict upon the mind during winter. And yet it also opens out to a cluster of associations that are specific to Dickinson herself. Indirectly, for example, the poem reveals Dickinson's ambivalence toward God, the force behind this winter light as well as the rest of nature. But overall, this work discloses the feelings of isolation and alienation all grieving people suffer "After great pain." In brilliantly "cut" gem-like language, "There's a Certain Slant of Light" casts light upon the quiet desperation that misery knows. This poem

tells all the truth about pain but tells it "slant," or indirectly

Author Biography

Emily Elizabeth Dickinson was born on December 10, 1830, in Amherst, Massachusetts, the second of three children to respectable, upper-middle-class Puritan parents. She would later describe her father as domineering and her mother as emotionally distant. Early on, she was a great admirer of and a great rival to her brother, Austin, born nearly two years previously. She was active, precocious, and strong-willed as a child. But in time, she would become increasingly sensitive, shy, and retiring.

After two years at Amherst Academy, Dickinson entered the Mount Holyoke Female Seminary (now Mount Holyoke College), where she studied for one year until homesickness drove her home. Although only seventeen at the time, Dickinson quietly defied both official and peer pressure to experience a conversion to Christianity. Dickinson later admitted in a letter that she secretly worried that somehow she had willfully put herself beyond God's grace by her rebellion.

Despite the brevity of her formal education, Dickinson voraciously read all of her father's books and subscribed to the great literary journals of her time. In fact, her struggle with social Christendom may have actually propelled her into a quest for the sublime in literature. (This Romantic transference from orthodox Christianity to a worship of nature and the powers of the imagination has been described by M. H. Abrams in *The Mirror and the Lamp*.) By the late 1850s, Dickinson had begun to take herself seriously as a poet, inspired by the successes of George Eliot, George Sand, and Elizabeth Barrett Browning, the great women writers of her time.

Many speculate that a tragic end to a love affair caused Dickinson's prodigious poetic output in the early 1860s. The story goes that Dickinson's heart was broken when clergyman Charles Wadsworth told her, in 1860, that he was journeying to California. There are, in fact, many poems from this period that accurately describe the processes of a severe mental breakdown. Nevertheless, all such speculations are just that—speculations. What is more interesting is that Dickinson so successfully portrayed various life experiences and mental states considering that, by the early

Emily Dickinson

1860s, she had chosen to live in almost total physical isolation from the outside world.

In 1862, Dickinson sent Thomas Higginson, editor of *The Atlantic Monthly,* a letter and included some of her poems. She internalized his observation that she was not ready for publication in a way he never would have suspected. She resolved to continue writing in her own unique style and await future readers that would appreciate her voice, while still sending Higginson poetry for advice she never followed. She lived out the remainder of her life in relative obscurity, caring for her invalid mother until her death in 1882. Emily Dickinson's own death—from a kidney ailment called Bright's Disease—followed nearly four years later, in 1886.

Poem Text

There's a Certain Slant of Light,
Winter Afternoons—
That oppresses, like the Heft
Of cathedral Tunes—

Heavenly Hurt it gives us—   5
We can find no scar,
But internal difference,
Where the Meanings, are—

None may teach it—Any—
'Tis the Seal Despair—   10
An imperial affliction
Sent us of the Air—

When it comes, the Landscape listens—
Shadows—hold their breath—
When it goes, 'tis like the Distance   15
On the look of Death—

Poem Summary

Lines 1-2:

The opening lines of "There's a Certain Slant of Light" speak of the declination of southern sunlight one always sees on bright winter afternoons. But the unusual syntax of these lines is uniquely Dickinsonian. The comma separating "Slant of light" from "Winter Afternoons" causes "Afternoons" to stand in apposition to "Slant." In grammar, an appositive is a noun or a noun phrase, set off by commas, that further explains or defines the noun or phrase that immediately precedes it, as in "Celeste, president of our club." In this particular sentence, we would normally expect a preposition like "on" to govern the phrase "Winter Afternoons" and connect it to "Slant of light" as a temporal adverb telling exactly "when" this "Slant of light" occurs (in fact, this is precisely how Dickinson's "mentor," Thomas Higginson, edited the poem for its first publication in 1890). But by making the second line an appositive of "Slant," Dickinson compresses the two events together to emphasize that the angle of light she is describing can only be seen on winter afternoons.

Lines 3-4:

"Heft," a word in common use in the New English dialect of Dickinson's time, means "weight, heaviness, and ponderousness," according to the *Oxford English Dictionary*. It can even signify the force of falling blows or the pressure of circumstances. Given this semantic environment, then, the word "oppresses" reinforces the sense of stress and torment arising from the depression brought on by winter's southwestern light. But note how Dickinson relates this sense of heaviness to "Cathedral Tunes." We can actually imagine the sensation of the light in terms of sonic "blows" of an organ blasting out a hymn in full voice into vast, reverberating space. Describing light in terms of weight and sound is an example of synesthesia, that is, a fusion of different sensations. But linking light and sound with weight is also an example of metonymy,

Media Adaptations

- Produced in 1988 by Jill Jannows for the *Voices & Visions* public television series of the New York Center for Visual History, *Voices & Visions: Emily Dickinson* has recently been released in VHS by Mystic Fire Video.

- Reissued in November of 1997 by the University of Missouri, *Emily Dickinson: A Certain Slant of Light* is a thirty-minute-long VHS documentary of the poet's life and work.

- Twelve of Emily Dickinson's poems were set to music by American composer Aaron Copland between 1948 and 1950. In 1992, Music Masters Classics formatted a compact disc of eight of the songs Copland orchestrated in the late 1960s along with other works.

- Dove Books Audio has published three volumes of *Fifty Poems,* read by Cheryl Ladd, Amy Irving, Glenda Jackson, Meryl Streep, and others. These readings are available on both cassette and CD.

- Meryl Streep also lent her vocal talents to Time-Warner's Audio Books cassette *Into the Beautiful: Selected Poems of Emily Dickinson,* published in July of 1998.

- Internet Multicasting Service has created an "Internet Town Hall" web-site where you can download "This is my letter to the world," a 1961 recording of British actress Julie Harris reading assorted poems and letters by Dickinson, by Harper Audio (a division of Harper Books) in three parts. The URL is http://town.hall.org/radio/Harper Audio/012794_harp_ITH.html.

a figure of speech in which the name of one object or concept is used for another of which it is a part or to which it is related. Logically speaking, it is difficult to see how the elements of such a synesthetic experience are metonymically related. But on an intuitive level, the meaning of the image strikes the reader as profoundly revealing of the speaker's attitude not only toward the "Slant of light" but also toward her experience with the Church.

Lines 5-6:

Besides forming an oxymoron (an image that is incongruous or self-contradictory), the expression "Heavenly Hurt" suggests that the oppression the psyche suffers from winter sunlight has a transcendental source as does "the Heft / Of Cathedral Tunes." But there is also a play on words here because "Heavenly" can refer to either the abode of God, the "Heavenly Father," or the sun's place in the sky. But whatever its cause, this resultant injury leaves "no scar." Its wounds are not obvious to an external observer because of their location within the self.

Lines 7-8:

The wound wrought by the southern light of a winter's afternoon creates an "internal difference, / Where the Meanings, are—." These two lines epitomize not only the crux of this particular poem but also Dickinson's entire approach to writing poetry. "Where the Meanings, are" is the self's interpretive faculty that ascribes signification to sensuous experience. Not only do all the scars of psychic abuse form there, but all interactions with the external world have also left their marks there. Conversely, this discriminative sense projects meaning upon events and things outside of the individual. The cognitive process therefore primarily consists of assigning meaning to phenomena as they relate to the self.

Lines 9-10:

But this depressing light resists all "instruction" and cannot be changed, no matter how urgently wished for by the sufferer. The word "Any" of line 9 is another example of Dickinson's challenging syntactical compression. When Higginson first edited this poem, he changed the word to "anything," which is perhaps the best reading. It could also conceivably act to emphasize "None," as in "[not] Any," but this is unlikely.

The word "Seal" in line 10 could mean that the feeling of "Despair" has completely enclosed and locked off the speaker from any hope of finding consolation. But it could also carry various Christian connotations, such as the seal of the Spirit that comes with conversion or the various "seals" broken to open scrolls in St. John's Book of Revelation. If either of these apply, then "Seal Despair" creates an even greater sense of spiritual emptiness and apocalyptic terror.

Lines 11-12:

Yet another incongruity, "imperial affliction" joins "Heavenly Hurt" and "Seal Despair" to describe the devastating effect of the light. "Imperial" also has a special meaning in Dickinson's vocabulary. In her letters and poetry, it often refers to the royalty of Deity, to which she attaches negative associations. In other words, what is normally thought of as good is actually quite the opposite. Furthermore, the phrase "Sent us of the Air" presents the same ambiguity as "Heavenly Hurt": the source of the "imperial affliction" is at once atmospheric and divine.

Lines 13-14:

Employing Romantic poetics, Dickinson utilizes personification (dealing with inanimate objects as though they were human) to emphasize the disastrous enormity winter light represents. The silent "Landscape listens," and even the "Shadows—hold their breath" as the oppressive light sinks in the West and darkness spreads across the land. The response of the landscape could embody the speaker's sense of dread. But does suspending the breath and listening intently as the sun sets portend fear or respect? And what does the "Landscape" expect to hear?

Lines 15-16:

At the final setting of the sun and the coming of darkness, the reason for the desolation brought by winter's "Certain Slant of Light" in the late afternoon becomes clear. In its "Distance" (or, its separation from the normal life-giving qualities of light) caused by its low position in the sky, this winter sun afflicts the speaker's consciousness with the realization of death's universal presence in the natural world.

Themes

Nature and Its Meaning

From her correspondence, we know that Emily Dickinson was first exposed to Ralph Waldo Emerson's Transcendental philosophy in the early 1850s. A pantheistic reaction to the materialism then usurping traditional Christian belief, Emerson's thought drew on German Idealism and Hindu Vedanta to support the idea that all of nature was essentially divine. This was actually a compromise between Christian dogmas and the prevailing scientific assumptions about the nature of reality. With

Topics for Further Study

- Dickinson does not directly describe the winter landscape in her poem or even the "Slant of Light" playing across it. She only provides information about their effects upon the speaker's mind. Write your own prose description or paint a picture that "fills in the gaps." What colors, shapes, or patterns should this scene have to produce such dire psychological effects? Share your "vision" of despair with others in a general class discussion.

- What images drawn from nature evoke the sense of desolate despair Dickinson sees in that afternoon winter light? Write a poem that uses concrete imagery to tell it "slant." Share your work for discussion.

- Two of Dickinson's more famous poems about death, "Because I Could Not Stop for Death" and "I Heard a Fly Buzz—When I Died—" have appeared in previous volumes of *Poetry for Students*. Referring to the texts and commentary of these two poems, along with "There's a Certain Slant of Light," compare and contrast Dickinson's attitudes toward death in all three. How are they similar and/or different? Does Dickinson present a consistent view of death in them? Which poem of the three do you prefer and why?

---

materialism, his philosophy shared a "monist" perspective (that is, the belief that all phenomena ultimately derive from only one source); with Christianity, it agreed that a single Supreme Being is the source of all beings.

Early on, Dickinson was taken with Emerson's teachings and the general Romantic view that Nature and God were harmoniously one. But in "There's a Certain Slant of Light" we encounter a very different sentiment. Nature appears as an alien force entirely separate from and opposed to the human self. Emerson had posited a great "Unity," a transcendent "Over-Soul," behind the masks of divergent phenomena and personalities. However, Dickinson implicitly presents the self as a subsis-

tent individual identity, much in the tradition of conventional Christianity. Furthermore, this self is wounded by the cold, loveless indifference of a material world utterly divorced from human desires and wishes. Dickinson explodes Emerson's unity of God, Nature, and Humanity into disaffected fragments of loneliness and despair.

God and Religion

But as much as Dickinson's poem rejects the Emersonian idea of Nature, it also implicitly attacks the Christian concept of a "good and loving" Father. The fact that the hurt from "Winter Afternoons" is "Heavenly," its affliction "imperial," and its oppressiveness "like the Heft / Of Cathedral Tunes" suggests that the deathly quality of winter light has a spiritual as well as a physical origin. The poem not only seems to imply the existence of a Creator utterly "other" than and separate from His creation, but also tacitly blames Him for reality's shortcomings. Still, Dickinson's letters betray the fact that she was no theologian, that her understanding of Christian doctrines remained rather childlike even to the end of her life. In fact, many critics see her ambivalence towards the Christian God as symptomatic of her ambivalence toward her emotionally distant father. But this is not to suggest that such was her intended meaning here.

Alienation and Loneliness

Without directly describing the slanted light illuminating a winter afternoon, Dickinson metonymically recounts the results that angle of light brings about in the mind. It oppresses, hurts, scars, creates despair in, and afflicts the viewer. When the sun sets, the light is "like the Distance / On the look of Death." Without any concrete description whatsoever, Dickinson succeeds in conveying the sense of utter emptiness that the light produces in the speaker. One can imagine the silence in the land and the gathering shadows lengthening as the oppressive light disappears below the rim of the world. It is a landscape of utter desolation and despair. The physical light, both engendering and reflecting the speaker's own inner estrangement and isolation, stands for that unbridgeable chasm of mutual alienation that tears nature and humanity apart.

Death

A review of Dickinson's many other death poems demonstrates that winter, afternoon, and sunset often represent death iconographically. Nevertheless, this poem does not focus so much upon death as much as it does upon reality's "broken-ness," which mirrors death's omnipresence. The signs of death in natural phenomena assault the inward self ("Where the Meanings, are") with the realization that death and loss ultimately rule all existence. The depression resulting from this realization is organically joined to and inseparable from winter sunlight itself.

Consciousness

The physical phenomena of nature, nevertheless, take on significance only within the "internal difference, / Where the Meanings are." Consciousness itself therefore informs these phenomena with meaning by noting the "difference" between one event and another. In fact, the use of metonymy as a poetic device establishes the meaning of sensuous experience by "naming" phenomena after their impressions upon the mind. In many ways, then, Dickinson actually anticipates structuralist and poststructuralist theories about language and meaning. These theories contend that words (or "signs") have no meaning in themselves but that meaning exists only in the mind, which establishes connections between words and the things they represent.

Style

Composed of four quatrains, "There's a Certain Slant of Light," as does the rest of Dickinson's poetry, follows one of many variations of hymn meter. Growing up with volumes of Isaac Watt's hymns in her home, Dickinson, ever the folk artist, adapted hymnody's lyric conventions to her own uses. By and large, this particular poem employs alternating lines of seven and five syllables in a trochaic pattern of four stresses followed by three stresses (that is, tetrameters followed by trimeters). Trochees are metric units of two syllables, the first stressed and the second unstressed. If we look at the first two lines of this poem, we can see how this works:

There's a **Cer**tain **Slant** of **Light,** / **Win**ter **After-noons—**

The odd foot (metric unit) of each line ends in a monometer (a metric unit with only one stressed syllable). Of course, this pattern doesn't persist through the whole poem, or the poetry would definitely fall into a singsong rhythm. In the second stanza, for example, there's a question as to whether "Heavenly" and "difference" should be pronounced with two or three syllables (if three, then these form anapests, feet of one stressed followed by two un-

stressed syllables) and whether "imperial" has three or four syllables. If it does, then line nine joins lines thirteen and fifteen to scan with eight syllables to form true trochaic tetrameter.

Another oddity readers encounter in Dickinson's poetry is her unusual punctuation. Critics are divided over the exact significance of her dashes and strangely placed punctuation marks. It's safe to say, however, that the dashes are usually intended to make the reader pause between words. Commas, like those between "oppresses" and "like" on line three and between "Meanings" and "are" on line eight, also serve to slow down the reading of the line but with shorter pauses than dashes represent. In other words, these marks are intentionally placed to control the rhythm of the poem and act as a kind of musical notation. For example, "Heavenly Hurt" in line five, linked to "Heft" two lines above by a shared alliteration (the use of repeated consonants to convey musicality and meaning), stands isolated from the more bland assertion, "it gives us," by the intervening comma. In line thirteen, breath is literally held because the reader is directed by hyphens to pause.

Historical Context

Emily Dickinson was born six years before Ralph Waldo Emerson published *Nature,* the essay that became the manifesto of the Transcendentalist movement. Although from Germany by way of Great Britain, Emerson's Transcendentalism is a uniquely American phenomenon because it evolved organically from the very Puritan culture it rejected. It is no wonder, then, that Emily Dickinson, herself a rebel from an even more traditionally Calvinist environment, would have been drawn to Emerson's thought. In fact, two generations of American writers—from romantics to realists and idealists to pragmatists—worked under or against Transcendentalism's allure. Transcendentalism fostered a brief release of creative energy during the New England Renaissance, a time of great visionary hopes that would soon be dashed by war and capitalistic greed. To appreciate Transcendentalism's actual significance both in Dickinson's work and in American culture, however, we must locate it within its full philosophical and religious contexts.

The various revolutions that have jolted European and, now, world culture for the last five hundred years have a common source in the dyad (a unity of two parts) of the Renaissance-Reformation.

Compare & Contrast

- **1861:** On July 21, roughly equal forces from the North and South met near Manassas, Virginia, in an engagement now known as the Battle of Bull Run, the first major battle of the American Civil War, also called by historians the first modern industrialized war. Although at first successful, federal troops were nearly routed by day's end. The fratricide between North and South would continue for another four years. More Americans died in the Civil War than in World Wars I and II and the Korean and the Vietnam Wars combined.

  1936: Beginning on July 17, with a military uprising in Spanish Morocco led by General Francisco Franco, the Spanish Civil War would continue until the fall of the Spanish Republic to fascist forces on March 28, 1939. Even at the start, the war took on international political and ideological importance. Fascist Italy sent thousands of ground troops and Nazi Germany provided planes, pilots, arms, and technicians to aid the nationalists, while the U.S.S.R. sent weapons and advisors to help the republicans. Europe was given a preview of all the horrors of blitzkrieg and total war they were soon to experience themselves.

  1994: On February 10, after exactly two years of intense fighting and genocidal mass murder and rape (known as "ethnic cleansing"), NATO finally issued a ten-day ultimatum to the Bosnian Serb forces besieging Sarajevo, declaring that their heavy weapons must be withdrawn 20 kilometers (12 miles) from the city or risk attack by NATO aircraft. This began the process that would eventually lead to a brokered "peace" and an official end to the Bosnian Civil War. NATO troops still occupy and police a fragile peace in Bosnia and Hercegovina.

  1994: After years of ethnic hatred and rivalry between Hutu and Tutsi tribal peoples in Rwanda, President Habyarimana was killed in a suspicious plane crash on April 3. Almost immediately, a wave of planned and orchestrated ethnic violence released a blood bath that took the lives of an estimated 200,000 to 500,000 Tutsi and moderate Hutu. After the Rwandan Patriotic Front gradually gained control of the country and installed a new government of national unity headed by a moderate Hutu president and prime minister on July 19, more than one million Rwandans, mostly Hutu, crossed the border into a remote area of neighboring Zaire in the greatest mass flight of refugees in modern times. Before long, there were four million displaced Rwandans in various countries of the region.

  Today: NATO has again entered the Balkans to prevent a genocidal civil war, this time in the former Serbian autonomous region of Kosovo. Problems began when the Serb government revoked Kosovo's self-rule in 1990 and again in 1992 when the Kosovars, mostly ethnic Albanians, voted in favor of union with Albania. With the ensuing liberation struggle, Serbs once again began to apply "ethnic cleansing" to regain control of the province.

- **1886:** Austrian physicist Ernst Mach (1838-1916), a thorough-going positivist and strict empiricist, wrote his essay, *The Analysis of Sensations,* in which he challenged the Newtonian model of absolute space and time as a "metaphysical" notion not in keeping with strict empiricism. By admitting that models of reality intrude upon our apprehension of reality (a Kantian, not an empiricist idea), Mach opened the way for non-Newtonian physical models of the universe.

  1900: During his studies of blackbody radiation in 1897, Max Planck (1858-1947) discovered that at long wavelengths it did not obey the distribution laws previously given by Wilhelm Wien. This discovery led him to yet another, that an oscillator could emit energy only in discrete quanta, contrary to classical physical theory. Planck's constant and this inchoate quantum theory was used by Albert Einstein to explain

(Continued on next page)

the photoelectric effect and later by Niels Bohr to propose a model of the atom with quantized electronic states; the rudimentary theory later developed into quantum mechanics.

- **1905:** While working in a patent office without scientific research texts or colleagues with whom to discuss his ideas, Albert Einstein (1879-1955), inspired by Mach's ideas and Planck's discoveries, developed his Special Theory of Relativity and brought about the beginning of the end of the Newtonian model of a universe of absolute time and motion.

1927: After extended conversations with Einstein and Niels Bohr, Werner Heisenberg (1901-1976), Bohr's student and protégé, advanced his uncertainty principle that holds that the accurate measurement of one of two related observable quantities produces uncertainties in the mea-

surement of the other. In other words, physical phenomena, at least on a quantum level, are not susceptible to completely accurate "empirical" measurement.

Today: Cosmologists and physicists continue to seek a unified theory to explain both quantum mechanics and general relativity. Hawking's theory of "unbounded boundary conditions" incorporates quantum mechanics into the general theory of relativity and postulates that there is no need to define the beginning and end of the universe. Super String Theory and other cosmological theories prepare us to enter the twenty-first century on a quest to understand (if that is at all possible) how the infinitesimal meets the infinite. But in all these theories, human consciousness is always factored into the matrix of observation. In the end, human consciousness is science's only limiting horizon.

Many writers treat these two events of modern European history as separate entities, but this is to ignore the fact that the Reformation is itself a child of the Renaissance and that each cultural stream fed and reinforced the other until the scientism of the Renaissance turned to materialist atheism during the Enlightenment period. Even the social and political revolutions of the eighteenth, nineteenth, and twentieth centuries could never have occurred without the Protestant revolutions of the sixteenth and seventeenth centuries. Because of their common origin in rationalism, the Reformation and Renaissance cultures have seen many attempts to harmonize them since they first began to drift apart.

After René Descartes (1596-1650) changed the thrust of Western metaphysics from the study of being as such to a study of epistemology (how the mind knows), Western philosophy began to distrust humanity's ability to discern "absolute truth." Beginning with Francis Bacon's (1561-1626) scientific method, British skeptics maintained that one could really only trust empirical results from carefully constructed and repeatable experiments to create conjectural models to explain observable phenomena. Any question of a transcendent reality or a Supreme Being was, for them, a proposition that could never adequately be scientifically tested. But philosopher John Locke (1632-1704) had previously taught that, at the time of birth, the human mind is a *tabula rasa,* a "blank slate," entirely de-

pendent on sensuous experience for its concepts. Human understanding must correspond, in his opinion, to an exterior and consistent reality. So, given an ordered and perceivable universe of absolute time and space, whose existence Sir Isaac Newton's (1642-1727) physics had demonstrated, the existence of some sort of Deity could be inferred. Seizing upon this shred of hope that God could rationally be said to exist, the Deists arose, proclaiming a scientifically observable God whose existence could be inductively proven but whom one could never personally experience. The formal denominational expression of this idea was the new belief system called Unitarianism.

For obvious reasons, such a dry, rationalist faith excluded the affective sensibilities of the human heart. At the same time, German philosopher Immanuel Kant (1724-1804) took Locke's epistemological theory to task. Drawing on concepts from Platonic philosophy, Kant opposed Locke's *tabula rasa* with what he called transcendental forms, innate ideas that structure the mind's experience of the world. Kant maintained that our understanding actually prescribes laws to nature instead of just inferring them from sensuous experience. Kant's intellectual counterrevolution to materialism inspired a generation of German philosophers to propound philosophical Idealism. These ideas converted British poet Samuel Taylor Coleridge from Unitarianism, and through his direct influence, Emerson, himself a Unitarian minister, sought an immediate perception of God's presence in the human mind as well as in nature.

Still, Emerson's Transcendentalism was not so much formal philosophy as it was a philosophical religion. In many ways Transcendentalism retained Unitarianism's basic critique of Calvinism. Where Calvinism taught that humanity was integrally and irredeemably flawed by Original Sin without an infusion of irresistible grace, both movements countered that the world and humanity are essentially good and that "grace" is a natural, not a supernatural, endowment. The two also withstood Calvinism's theology of Predestination which so denigrated the freedom of the individual will as to conceive of people as puppets at the end of God's strings. The major difference that separated Transcendentalism from Unitarianism was its belief that intuition, not reason, was the place where God could be known, where God's essential oneness with creation could be perceived.

However, changing material circumstances and intellectual opinions in America doomed Emerson's philosophical faith to history's curiosity shop. During Dickinson's relatively short lifetime, America finally succumbed to the forces of industrialism. In fact, the Civil War demarcates the turning of the tide from rural agrarian society to urban industrialism. With the triumph of capitalism's materialism, the power elite of America largely turned away from both Puritan Christianity and Emerson's idealist religion, though both survive as cultural forces in America to this day in the various Protestant churches and theologies and in the so-called "New Age" movement. In many ways, "There's a Certain Slant of Light," written at the beginning of the Civil War, mirrors America's movement away from idealism and toward realism. Admittedly, Dickinson's poem operates from Emerson's assumption that subjective consciousness is the arbiter, if not creator, of meaning, but it rejects his belief in the fundamental goodness of nature.

Critical Overview

In critic Charles Anderson's opinion, "There's a Certain Slant of Light" is Dickinson's "finest poem on despair." Anderson's 1960 interpretive study of one hundred of her poems, *Emily Dickinson's Poetry: Stairway of Surprise,* the first truly extensive critical examination of her poetry, provides a thorough and thought-provoking explication of this poem. He

notes that the speaker's "internal experience is not talked about but is realized in a web of images that constitutes the poem's statement, beginning with one drawn from nature, or rather from the firmament above it, and returning to it in the end with significant change of meaning." This change consists of a movement from the physical to the spiritual. The speaker's despair "comes from the sudden instinctive awareness of man's lot since the Fall, doomed to mortality and irremediable suffering…. When the psyche is once stricken with the pain of such knowledge it can never be the same again." In other words, it is "sealed" by despair. Despite such an encompassing despair, however, Anderson does not rule out Dickinson's belief in possible redemption, although he admits it isn't present here.

Even though he calls "There's a Certain Slant of Light" Dickinson's "best poem on the winter season," Ernest Sandeen, in his essay, "Delight Deterred by Retrospect: Emily Dickinson's Late-Summer Poems," sees this poem as another example of Dickinson's method of presenting "a highly internalized experience which is at the same time submitted to a detailed analytical examination." Beyond the first line, none of the poem's similes and metaphors really have anything to do with winter but form "figures of the inner life, analyzing and defining an introspective, not a physical reality."

In his 1974 study, *The Landscape of Absence: Emily Dickinson's Poetry,* Inder Nath Kher interprets this poem from the perspective of "archetypal criticism" in the tradition of Northrop Frye, who viewed literary motifs in terms of universal mythic forms. Extolling "There's a Certain Slant of Light" as one of Dickinson's finest works and a perfect expression of what he calls "the spirit of absence-presence," Kher says this poem "makes concrete the experience of despair and death," but he sees the slant of light's "spiritual significance" in positive terms: the psychic wound from the light is actually "providential" and "creates the internal difference or the psychological metamorphosis." For Kher, "absence-presence" represents the "inner-outer movement" between the poet's consciousness and the surrounding world. It is an intense moment of present insight into what is ever fleetingly absent. The "landscape of absence" (Kher's name for Dickinson's poetry) "is paradoxical and suggests something tangibly intangible, concrete yet vanishing, near and remote, apprehensible and elusive." With this in mind, he maintains that "to read the poem for negative despair, depression, and desolation is to read it incorrectly."

Criticism

George Monteiro

In the following essay, Monteiro argues that the light in this poem corresponds to divinity, not despair.

Readings of Emily Dickinson's "There's a Certain Slant of Light" agree on two main points: (1) the conceit that light has the effect upon the poet of a great physical weight is indicative of the poet's characteristic originality; and (2) the poet's theme is one of despair and darkness. The tone of current interpretations can be illustrated by Clark Griffith's remarks in *The Long Shadow: Emily Dickinson's Tragic Poetry* (1964). He finds the poem to be marked by naturalized romanticism: "Seeing Nature in a way that Emerson never would—as the source of pain rather than of benevolent tidings—Miss Dickinson still manages to stay well within the Transcendentalist tradition.... Nature acts, while the human observer is acted upon.... The light *gives* her an injury, and the air has *sent* her the *Seal Despair*. Furthermore, both light and air are portrayed as symbolic of God, so that they become agents through whom God imposes His *Heavenly Hurt* upon the speaker, or maims her with His *imperial affliction*."

There is no question that Emily Dickinson wrote anti-Emersonian poems, just as we can no longer deny that she wrote Emersonian poems as well. The point is, however, that it distorts this poem to read it as either pro- or anti-Emerson. To do either, in fact, one must ignore the poet's traditional use of the historical idea which is at the center of the poem. Griffith's reading of the symbolism of the poem misleads us precisely because it does not allow for historical and biographical context. It is as if the poem were totally modern, even though by some miracle written over a hundred years ago. But the contextual evidence points us to something else: the poet's commitment to certain Puritan and Pauline ideas concerning the ways of divine Grace. Precise interpretation of the central "light" symbolism in context indicates that the poem is less existential, written less out of anguish and the concomitant desire to express anguish—in short, that it is less "modern" in every way—than current readings have made it out to be. There are, of course, many Dickinson poems that look ahead to the poetry of the twentieth century; this one does not.

Though the poet has been widely commended, as noted, for the conceit of "light" that has physical weight—for her ingenious crossing of the senses of sight and touch—this figure is not original to Emily Dickinson. In conceiving of the "heft" of "Cathedral Tunes" and the weight of "light" on "Winter Afternoons," the poet draws upon the Biblical idea of glory ("light") which has the literal meaning of *weight*. To her Puritan ancestors, steeped in the Bible, the idea was commonplace. As Cotton Mather put it [in *Right Thoughts in Sad Hours*], "the hebrew word for glory signifies the same that your own sense of affliction feels—a weighty thing. Well, from one weight you shall pass to the other. Your crown of thorns will shortly be exchanged for a crown of glory; a weighty, a massy, a never-fading crown." The Puritans had derived this idea, at least in part, from *Second Corinthians,* a book which was among Emily Dickinson's cherished favorites. As Saint Paul promises, "For our light affliction, which is but for a moment, worketh for us a far more exceeding and eternal weight of glory" (*II Corinthians,* IV, 17). We are fortunate in knowing just how the poet herself interpreted this passage. At the time of her mother's death she explained that "The sunshine almost speaks, this morning, resembling the division, and Paul's remark grows graphic, 'the *weight* of glory'" (*The Letters of Emily Dickinson,* ed. Thomas H. Johnson, 1958, III, 771). The emphasis here—the poet's own—reveals her acceptance of the idea that the experience of glory is literally one of physical *weight*. Here she narrows in on the Puritan concept of a divine grace that is both violent and a violation of the self. Grace is "a holy kind of violence," wrote one Puritan divine; it does not come through "morall perswasion" but through God's "powerfull operation, an omnipotent hand put forth for such a purpose" (quoted in Richard Chase, *Emily Dickinson,* 1951, p. 148).

Thus it is clear that when Emily Dickinson talks about an "affliction" that results from "light" she refers to that "affliction" which is part of the experience of "glory." This traditional equation resolves the seeming paradox which emerges when the poet characterizes the "Hurt" that is inflicted as "Heavenly" and the overall "affliction" as "imperial." Such characterizations are fully consonant with Paul's remark made "graphic" by sunlight, as the poet notes, just as the "internal difference" caused by this experience of "light" is one of renewal, recalling Paul's promise that "though our outward man perish, yet the inward man is renewed day by day" (*II Corinthians,* IV, 16).

The remainder of the poem rounds out this fundamental idea. In the line "'Tis the Seal Despair," for instance, "Despair" is itself a divine "Seal"—

What Do I Read Next?

- To get at the core of Transcendentalism and to judge for yourself how Dickinson's thought converges with and diverges from Emerson's, read the work that started the American Renaissance. Shambala Books published Emerson's *Nature and Other Writings,* edited by Peter Turner, in 1994.

- Japanese Dickinsonian scholarship has traditionally viewed her as a Transcendentalist mystic poet similar to William Blake. Shoei Ando, Professor of American literature from Okayama University, gave a series of lectures comparing American Transcendentalism with Zen Buddhism at San Jose State College in the 1962-63 school year. In 1970, he published his notes in book form as *Zen and American Transcendentalism: An Investigation of One's Self,* still available from the Hokuseido Press.

- In her 1984 study, *An American Triptych: Anne Bradstreet, Emily Dickinson, Adrienne Rich* (published by the University of North Carolina Press), Professor Wendy Martin of the Claremont Colleges' Graduate School demonstrates with thorough historical and critical detail that Puritanism and the women's movement are organically linked. This work shows Dickinson's pivotal place at America's transit from Puritanism to post-modernism.

- Sharon Cameron's fascinating book, *Choosing, Not Choosing: Dickinson's Fascicles* (published in 1993 by the University of Chicago Press), allows the student into the hidden world of literary editing. Dickinson actually published her own work by sewing her poems into packets called fascicles. Editors since Thomas Higginson have had to choose which readings to accept or to reject and in which order to present her work. This book lets the reader decide.

---

the "White Sustenance" she names in a related poem. The divine "Seal" forced upon the poet is honorific and desirable; but "Despair" is its human price, for "Despair's *advantage* is achieved / By suffering—Despair." In the last stanza the poet makes the simple and direct point that the disappearance of winter's afternoon light has the same effect upon her that she experiences whenever she encounters "the Distance / On the look of Death." The Dickinson canon abundantly documents the importance the poet attached to that distant look in the eyes of the near-dying and the just-dead. To Emily Dickinson that look signaled man's contact with eternity.

Sunlight on a winter afternoon provided the poet with one of her direct experiences of Divinity: "Glory is that bright tragic thing," runs another poem, "That for an instant / Means Dominion." Experiences like the one behind "There's a Certain Slant of Light" were piers to sustain those moments when she could genuinely believe in a "long Paradise of Light."

Source: George Monteiro, "Dickinson's *There's a Certain Slant of Light," The Explicator,* Vol. 31, No. 2, October 1972.

Michael Lake

Michael Lake is a published poet who holds a master's in English from Eastern Illinois University. In the following essay, Lake explains why "There's a Certain Slant of Light" "makes for an excellent example of Dickinson's esthetic sensibility and poetic technique."

First-time readers of Emily Dickinson's poetry are often confused or put off by her unusual vocabulary and word usage, her oftentimes disjunctive sentence structure, and her compressed language and distorted imagery. But the more of her poems one reads, the more understandable her style becomes and the more impressed one grows with her self-taught genius. A consummate folk artist, she pressed Isaac Watts's hymn meters into service to create lyric meditations very much in the tradition of seventeenth-century Puritanism. For this reason, she has often been compared with seventeenth-century Metaphysical poets, such as John Donne or George Herbert. Despite their extreme differences in language and style, the poems of all three poets, in fact, often reflect upon the evanescence, or the fleeting quality, of life. For as Dickinson once wrote, "All we secure of Beauty is its Evanescences" (Letter 781), a statement that distills both her esthetics and her poetics.

The evanescent, or fleeting, perception of beauty cannot be captured or made fast. It exists in a flash of intense insight, a moment of recognition that can only be savored within the reflective soul. But as soon as the perception of beauty comes, the moment that brought it forth is gone. The poet's job, for Dickinson, is to compress and concentrate imagery and language so that the moment of recognition can be re-created in an almost crystalline form for the apprehension of the reader. In other words, the reader participates in the poet's recognition of beauty's truth, but, as Roland Hagenbüchle said in his essay, "Precision and Indeterminacy in the Poetry of Emily Dickinson," "what previously could be experienced as a sustained mood is now compressed into a single moment; the myth is reduced to an act of pure consciousness."

"There's a Certain Slant of Light," although its subject is despair before death's ubiquitous presence in nature, makes for an excellent example of Dickinson's esthetic sensibility and poetic technique. Following Hagenbüchle's statement above, we could say that this poem "reduces" the Greek myth of Pluto's rape of Persephone to the "pure consciousness" of death's haunting habitation within the heart of winter. But the poem imparts this awareness indirectly. In fact, Dickinson prefers an indirect path to communicate the perception of beauty and truth, for, in this way, the reader truly participates in the meditative discovery of the poem's meaning. Ironically, one of Dickinson's terms for indirect communication is "slantness," as in her poem, "Tell all the truth but tell it slant" (Poem 1129 in Johnson's edition). As line two of her poem says, "Success in Circuit lies." Dickinson's poetry seldom "tells it straight" because she prefers the gnomic quality of proverbs, riddles, and hymns for their evocative powers to elicit an intuitive comprehension to the "mere prose" of straightforward exposition. "Circuit," like "circumference," another of her favorite expressions for indirectness, "goes round" the periphery of the

subject to encompass its truth without stating it explicitly. The indirect light of this "certain Slant of light" succeeds in exposing "all the truth" about nature from Dickinson's point of view. Where in traditional Christian symbolism light stands for grace and the kingdom of God, it represents, when viewed in its "Slant" or indirect aspect, a state of affliction. "There's a Certain Slant of Light" uses the poetic tools of "slantness" to bring about the evanescent realization that both nature and the God of nature are flawed because death, loneliness, and isolation predominate within the natural world and afflict the human soul.

To communicate this perception indirectly, Dickinson uses metonymy (literally Greek for "a change of name"), one of her preferred rhetorical devices. However, Dickinson's metonymy itself is "slant" when compared with that of classical Greek orators. When, in the first stanza, the speaker compares that "Certain Slant of Light" with "the Heft / Of cathedral Tunes," the resulting imbalance produces a synesthetic effect. The metonymy is unbalanced because in no way is a "Heft" or weight logically a part of or related to sound. This componential or relational aspect of metonymy is violated by Dickinson's choice of words. But bringing these unrelated elements together conjoins two different sensuous experiences into one and jolts the reader into an entirely new apprehension of both the winter light and church music. Twentieth-century poet T. S. Eliot used a similar technique, which he dubbed the "objective correlative." In Dickinson's practice, the correlation with the metonymically objectified sensibility can only be inferred from the evanescent impressions left in the reader's mind.

Although she was a poet and not a philosopher, Dickinson was far ahead of her time in her depth of understanding of how language and consciousness work. For example, in his basic text on language and logic, the *Categories,* Aristotle wrote, "Those things are called relative, which, being either said to be of something else or related to something else, are explained by reference to that other thing." Accordingly, correlatives relate objects to their attributes or qualities with external reference to or comparison with something else. In other words, "double" implies that a quantity is twice as much as some other quantity. Similarly, metonymy, originally a rhetorical device, not a "logical category," applies the name of one thing to another with which it shares connected experience or close association. But as Dickinson has proven, there does not have to be any relational symmetry between the

> *Dickinson prefers an indirect path to communicate the perception of beauty and truth, for, in this way, the reader truly participates in the meditative discovery of the poem's meaning."*

two objects sharing a name if what relates them together does not exist in any "objective" sense but lies solely in the personal associations of the perceiver. Dickinson thereby reverses a long-held Western philosophical tradition that maintains that language is a reflection of reality. She thereby embraces an implicitly Kantian position that language is a reflection of our thought about reality. At the moment of evanescent insight, the so-called "real" object disappears altogether.

The "Slant of Light," then, inflicts a "Heavenly Hurt" that leaves "no scar" but instead creates an "internal difference / Where the Meanings, are—." In other words, the wound wrought by the southern light of a winter's afternoon creates an inward transformation where consciousness ascribes signification to the phenomena of the outer world. Meaning therefore lies within the "signifier," not in either the "sign" or the "signified." As a maker of meaning, the poet wrestles "signs" (words) into new relationships with the objects "signified." This, in fact, explains how "Heft" and "cathedral Tunes" are metonymically related. Their associational connection exists entirely in the speaker's mind and now the reader's consciousness, "Where the Meanings, are." But once expressed, the objective correlative (in this case, the "Heft" of church music) disappears as an objective phenomenon that can be symmetrically related to another experience or object, as in the case of a true metaphor (Greek for "a transfer") or a simile (Latin for "a likeness"). Or as Hagenbüchle said of Dickinson's method, an object's "ideal presence in the mind presupposes absence in actuality." And as Dickinson herself wrote in Poem 1071 of Johnson's edition, "Perception of an object costs / Precise the Object's loss—."

But Dickinson uses other "slant" poetic tools than just metonymy to effect this "Perception" and "loss." Notice how alliteration binds "Heft" with "Heavenly Hurt." Repeating the initial "H" sound creates a phonic—and thus an associational—link to cleave these images together. The connection between them is further extended through parallelism with "Heavenly Hurt" to include "Seal Despair" and "imperial affliction." The metonym, "Heft / Of cathedral Tunes," thus finds reinforcement in these three oxymorons to produce an "internal difference" in the mind of the reader. The overall effect is "apocalyptic" in its desolation. The word "Seal," after all, carries Christian baggage, as do "Heavenly" and, in Dickinson's private lexicon, "imperial." A person is sealed for glory in the Calvinist tradition by God's irresistible grace in an intense moment of transformation. If we take "Seal" in this sense, to be sealed *with* "Despair" then amounts to a reversal of the confirming seal of the Spirit at conversion. If, however, we take "Seal" to refer to the various seals opened in the Book of Revelation, then the "Seal Despair" assumes an even greater cosmic implication: this dying light mirrors the death inherent in all created beings, and there is no hope of escape from it.

In keeping with such a cosmic catastrophe, the setting winter sun draws forth a response from the landscape. Dickinson uses personification to project the awareness of the light's—and therefore of life's—transient passing into nature itself. Here again, the real object disappears, and all that remains are its effects upon consciousness. But the setting of the winter sun is even more explicitly catastrophic, for "'tis like the Distance / On the look of Death—." Having witnessed so many deaths in her lifetime, Dickinson knew only too well the faraway look the dead often get in their glazed, open eyes. However, all kinds of distance are reminiscent of death, such as separation from the beloved, inward isolation even in the midst of friends and family, and, indeed, alienation from one's own life. All of these little deaths are comprehended in that "Certain Slant of Light," because just as within the seeming fullness of life lurks the emptiness of death, so too the rending sorrow of loss resides potentially within the joy of love.

Through its poetic "slantness," Dickinson's "There's a Certain Slant of Light" illuminates more than a desolate winter landscape; it reflects in that pale, cold light the broken nature of the world and the transcendental failure of the world's Creator because of the death, loneliness, and alienation that devastate both creation and the soul. And yet, instead of seeing this conclusion as an indictment of God and reality, we should perhaps view the whole poem more as an insight into the lonely heart itself. After all, what Kher calls "absence-presence" works at once both outwardly and inwardly. While critic Sharon Cameron in her book, *Lyric Time: Dickinson and the Limits of Genre,* may be right in saying the light in this poem is a *"figura"* of death, it may also be true to say that both the "Slant of Light" and "Death" itself are really *figurae* of heartwrenching loneliness. To paraphrase Dickinson, then, we can say that all we secure of alienation is its "Evanescences" within our minds.

Source: Michael Lake, in an essay for *Poetry for Students,* The Gale Group, 1999.

Donald Eulert

In the following essay, Eulert suggests that readings of "There's a Certain Slant of Light" should focus on emotion rather than philosophy.

Careful attention to the emotional movement of one of Emily Dickinson's best poems is informative not only of her methods in general, but also of the Procrustean stretching and lopping to which she was subjected by her critics of the last decade. Dickinson scholars, notably Charles R. Anderson [in his *Emily Dickinson's Poetry: Stairway of Surprise*] and Clark Griffith, have seen "There's a certain Slant of light" as a philosophical-theological treatise variously treating nature, the Fall, Redemption, God, and man's role in the world. To Griffith [as noted in his *The Long Shadow: Emily Dickinson's Tragic Poetry*], the poem demonstrates Dickinson's anti-Emersonian view that nature acts as an extension of God in a deliberate plot to injure and oppress the human.

Dickinson does sometimes use poetry to illuminate her sense of universal ideas, but generally she is not writing philosophy in poetry, and should not be explicated as if she were writing an Emersonian (Melvillian?) poetry in which phenomenological images unfailingly reflect a transcendent reality. As with much of her best work, we are not justified in making this poem an intellectual cipher, to discover either a judgment of Nature of the nature of the Judge in a simple "Slant of light." In this poem, a real, physical "Slant of light" comes and goes. Meanwhile, an elusive mutation that is emotional, not philosophical, occurs. Thus we must read the poem in terms of how it works to inform us emotionally: *how* the experience is. *What* happens is unsayable. It leaves no scar, only an internal difference that "None may teach."

In this poem, the reader, shaped by Dickinson's conditioning language, may come to understand an "affliction" of despair. Whether we can follow Dickinson to the brink of her emotional crisis, and beyond it to and through the experience itself, depends critically on our use of the first four lines where Dickinson colors her "Slant of light" to bring us into her emotional condition.

Her "imperial affliction" took place on a winter afternoon; the moment crowning it was connected to her observation of "a certain Slant of light." In common-sense terms, we don't believe slanting light caused all the "internal difference." But the slant of light was evidently a focal event in the causal chain. More important, perhaps, the poet can use it as an emotional touchstone, can shape it to contain all the emotional elements of cause. For example, besides that slant of light, other elements must have been focusing on that despair: memories of other afternoons, a prior emotional set, even the fact that she was tired. But the poet takes a single focus and colors it with the other factors. Thus a single communicable image can be true to the total emotional condition in which she saw the light. On this winter afternoon, the other unnamed emotional sets added to this focus are best called up by saying that the light oppresses like "Cathedral Tunes." Of course Dickinson has a habit of substituting one sense for another, perhaps because the technique "Distills amazing sense / From ordinary Meanings" (#448). For instance, this technique is bright and playful in "Resonance of Emerald" (#1463) and "Pianos in the Woods" (#348). But here in making her slant of light oppress "like Cathedral Tunes" she manages to integrate sight and sound in a suggestive conceit that involves the reader's senses and channels his emotions to Dickinson's own emotional set. The "Slant of light" becomes not only a definitive emotional focus of depression but a surrounding tonal matrix of despair.

In order to be explicit about the winter afternoon, then, she first presents its emotional focus—the slanted light. In order to control how we are to feel about this, she compares it to something that communicates her sense of setting the mood—the sound of organ music. The choice is a masterful integration of sight and sound that together produce the psyiological-psychological effects she wants to define. To get this effect, she manages a kind of metaphysical conceit that makes the sight and sound fused already in cause.

This sense of complementing mood is only one reason why I hear an organ rather than carillon bells of Charles R. Anderson. Since the light is slanted, it must be partly blocked somewhere, and has length; it is a "bar" of indefinite length, held in this setting like a solemn organ chord. The experience even seems to be set in an atmosphere of closeness, suggestive of a surrounding and oppressing organ chording. A "Slant of light" in this context even suggests the slanting light inside high cathedral windows. Moreover, Miss Dickinson plays the organ notes for us; we cannot overlook the "Heft," the weight that oppresses. In terms of sound, a constant press of heavy sound has more weight than fragmented bell sounds. The press of organ chording is heard in "Aftern*oo*ns … *o*ppresses … of Cath*edra*l T*u*nes." They are dark long sounds, not bright round ones.

Anyone giving the first stanza a careful reading must notice that the last three syllables call for accents, but each one less and therefore slightly further down the scale. He must also notice that the "oo" of "noons" is the longest sound in the stanza, and that its pitch is crossed by the descending sounds of "…èdràl Tunes." Because of its length and the emphasis of rhyme, "noons" is still echoing when I read the last sound, "Tunes." What results is an emotionally depressing minor chord, since that lowest pitch, "Tunes," strikes discordantly and darkly with the held-and-waiting sound of "noons." I hear that discordant, oppressing cord throughout the poem; since "it goes" in a faded sight/sound in line 15, there is structural evidence that we should hear it all the while. As a conceit, the auditory light is not much used in the middle stanzas, but it echoes until it is integrated again in the last stanza when "the Landscape listens."

I do not want to belabor the point of the music in the first stanza, nor do I mean to overlook the connotative senses of "Winter Afternoons" and "oppresses." The point is that with the sense and the sound, and their mixture in metaphor, a careful reader should be ready to come to the brink of Emily's emotional crisis of despair.

Moving to the middle stanzas, descriptive of *what* happens, we are likely to find them as inadequate and unclear as the "internal difference" itself is inherently ambiguous and unclear. At any rate, the "difference" is not well defined by such phrases as "Heavenly Hurt," "Seal Despair," and "imperial affliction." These semi-playful phrases take the reader out of the poem to do intellectual analyses of meaning. For participation in the poem's mystic experience (of which it is at least a minor sort) I am better informed by the emotional matrix of the experiences in the first and last stanzas. The middle two serve mostly to indicate the height of the experience; they do not, I think, indicate her philosophical position or allow a rational determination of this irrational experience.

But to give "meaning" its due, "Heavenly Hurt" I would take minimally to indicate that the "Hurt" is not of an earthly (ordinary) sort, but strikes instead at the spirit. Realizing Dickinson's habitual use of biblical language for metaphors of the simplest moments, I see no justification in saying that she is charging God with visiting pain to man. The rest of the stanza is consistent to my reading; it emphasizes simply the internal nature of the "Hurt." Dickinson likely chose "Heavenly" because it also allows her to continue the metaphor of oppression caused by the slant of light. The light comes from above, but to insist it shines from theological heavens strains textual evidence.

The next four lines again name the despairing mood, noting that the chorded slant-of-light is the "Seal" of despair—another indication that this natural phenomenon is only one among others, but is their "sealing" emotional focus. It is not a metaphor of God's visitation, *the* agency sent by air; so that it does not stand singularly as symbol. Also in this stanza occurs another phrase which critics use to bring a personal God into her fit of depression: "imperial affliction." I read simply a statement that the "affliction" of this mood has her as a subject in its "ruling" grip.

We cannot find out explicitly *what* Emily Dickinson saw or felt, then, from these static stanzas. She goes back to the linear experience and working conceit in the last stanza. Now the chorded slant-of-light serves to stand not only for stimulus, but comes to stand for the experience as well. When it comes, "the Landscape listens— / Shadows— hold their breath." All sentient nature is involved in a revelation. In terms of communicating the awesomeness of her experience, this metaphorical expansion not only gives us a renewed sense of the "affliction," but also allows conjecture about what she experienced. At its most general, despair involves loss of optimism and a questioning of purpose; when even nature holds its breath, the question of purpose seems directed to existence itself. And if there is a question of the meaninglessness of life, its corollary is a glimpse of death. We do not know explicitly, of course, that Dickinson had an unveiled look at the face of death, but, if not, her experience was somehow like that; when the "chorded" mood passes into the distance, it has the same look as the distance on the look of death.

Three interrelated things are working in "like the Distance / On the look of Death." First of all, the experience passes. It began in the first stanza with (a) the logical movement of cause-to-effect, and with (b) the emotional movement of the chorded slant-of-light. Both of them now move away. Growing from this fact is a second consideration. Perhaps she can now give her best description of what happened to her, as she looks at the experience receding. That it is *like* the "Distance / On the look of Death" seems a straight-forward description. But the reader does not know how literally to understand the use of "like." But I take "like the Distance" to indicate a third facet of these lines: that once the experience is past, it is not possible to know it. It is impenetrable, like glimpsing death and then trying to remember how it looked. To recast these lines: "In passing, this despair already has the look that death has, namely, a look of distance." In making a comparison for clarification, any writer compares the unfamiliar with something he assumes the reader knows more familiarly. In this case, Dickinson must assume that we recognize this distance on the look of death, a distance provided by the interposing intellect—at all times save moments like this one just past. Afterward, the intellect can look only at the outside countenance of such an internal affliction, the way it sees death.

What really happened inside her cannot be attested by a scar, cannot be taught, and cannot be explicated. That is why a reader must read the poem from first to last in terms of emotion and sense, or he misses the poem and only plays with it from the distance of intellect. The last stanza gives an expansion of the emotional conceit begun in line one, and adds a glimpse of *what* she saw as well, before closing off the experience. Even then the relief we expect from the passing of a traumatic experience does not take place. For one thing, we do not believe life can be resumed quite the way it was before (there has been an internal change "Where the Meanings, are"). And that the mood has receded is not much relief because it still has the "look of Death." And finally there is our subjective response to the way description of the mood begins with the word "oppresses" and ends with the final word "Death."

Source: Donald Eulert, "Emily Dickinson's Certain Slant of Light," in *American Transcendental Quarterly,* Vol. 14, No. 4, Spring 1972, pp. 164-66.

Sources

Anderson, Charles, *Emily Dickinson's Poetry: Stairway of Surprise,* New York: Holt, Rinehart, and Winston, 1960.

Cameron, Sharon, *Lyric Time: Dickinson and the Limits of Genre,* Baltimore: Johns Hopkins University Press, 1979.

Chase, Richard, *Emily Dickinson,* New York: William Sloan Associates, 1951.

Donoghue, Denis, "Emily Dickinson" in *Six American Poets from Emily Dickinson to the Present: An Introduction,* edited by Allen Tate, Minneapolis: University of Minnesota Press, 1969, pp. 9-44.

Griffith, Clark, *The Long Shadow: Emily Dickinson's Tragic Poetry,* Princeton, NJ: Princeton University Press, 1964.

Ford, Thomas W., *Heaven Beguiles the Tired: Death in the Poetry of Emily Dickinson,* University: University of Alabama Press, 1968.

Hagenbüchle, Roland, "Precision and Indeterminacy in the Poetry of Emily Dickinson," in *ESQ: A Journal of the American Renaissance,* Vol. 20, No. 1, 1974, pp. 33-56.

Kher, Inder Nath, *The Landscape of Absence: Emily Dickinson's Poetry,* New Haven, CT: Yale University Press, 1974.

Lindberg-Seyersted, Brita, *The Voice of the Poet: Aspects of Style in the Poetry of Emily Dickinson,* Cambridge, MA: Harvard University Press, 1968.

Porter, David T., *The Art of Emily Dickinson's Early Poetry,* Cambridge, MA: Harvard University Press, 1966.

Sandeen, Ernest, "Delight Deferred by Retrospect: Emily Dickinson's Late-Summer Poetry" in *New England Quarterly,* Vol. 40, 1967, pp. 483-500.

Tate, Allen, "New England Culture and Emily Dickinson" in *Collected Essays,* Denver: Swallow Press, 1959, pp. 197-211.

For Further Study

Diehl, Joanne Feit, *Dickinson and the Romantic Imagination,* Princeton: Princeton University Press, 1981.

> For those interested in discovering how Emily Dickinson evolved from and transcended her roots in Romanticism, Joanne Diehl's study is rich in literary and cultural history and makes its arguments firmly from within the body of Dickinson's work. In Diehl's opinion, Dickinson's gender determined her relationship with the Anglo-American Romantic tradition. As a woman and a poet, Dickinson was truly a revolutionary.

Miller, Cristanne, *Emily Dickinson: A Poet's Grammar,* Cambridge, MA: Harvard University Press, 1987.

> Cristanne Miller's study takes the student deep into the magic of Dickinson's unique use of the English language. Miller's book elucidates some of Dickinson's most challenging passages, but it also provides the linguistic tools necessary for an intelligent explication of Dickinson's poetry.

Patterson, Rebecca, *Emily Dickinson's Imagery,* Amherst: University of Massachusetts Press, 1979.

Although controversial for its interpretive examination of Dickinson's possible sexual orientation, Rebecca Patterson's study does a great job of penetrating into the archetypal deeps of Dickinson's imagery. Patterson collates the whole of Dickinson's corpus to establish Dickinson's symbolic lexicon.

St. Armand, Barton Levi, *Emily Dickinson and Her Culture: The Soul's Society,* London: Cambridge University Press, 1984.

Drawing upon all of the gilded culture of America's gilded age, Barton St. Armand, as an expert in American studies, has sought to explain Dickinson's art as well as her concerns and obsessions from within the artistic and cultural milieu of her time. St. Armand's work is always interesting and full of little-known facts, even if one does not always share his conclusions.

To My Dear and Loving Husband

Anne Bradstreet
1678

"To My Dear and Loving Husband" was written between 1641 and 1643 by Anne Bradstreet, America's first published poet. This poem offers modern readers insights into Puritan attitudes toward love, marriage, and God. In the poem, Bradstreet proclaims her great love for her husband and his for her. She values their love more than any earthly riches, and she hopes that their physical union on earth signifies the continuation of their spiritual union in heaven. In this poem, Bradstreet views earthly love as a sign of spiritual salvation. This poem presents a central question in Puritan thought: how do one's earthly and immortal lives connect?

This poem was first published in 1678, six years after Bradstreet's death, in an edition of her poems entitled *Several Poems Compiled with Great Variety of Wit and Learning, Full of Delight*. During Bradstreet's lifetime, there were almost no women writers, because education was rarely wasted on daughters. Over half of the women in colonial America were illiterate. Bradstreet was very privileged, she but also courageous and dedicated to her art. Despite her culture's biases, Bradstreet wrote poetry that was widely acclaimed and remains relevant today for its emotional honesty and wisdom.

Author Biography

Bradstreet was born Anne Dudley around 1612 in England to a Puritan family. Her father, Thomas

Anne Bradstreet

Dudley, was steward to the Earl of Lincoln. Because of Dudley's high position, his daughter received an excellent education. In 1630, she moved with her parents and husband, Simon Bradstreet, to the Massachusetts Bay Colony, where her husband and father served as governors of the settlement. As a New England colonist, Bradstreet encountered a life of hardship to which she was unaccustomed. Despite illness and the difficulties of raising her eight children in the American wilderness, she found time to write. By the age of thirty she had composed most of her poetry. When her brother-in-law John Woodbridge returned to England in 1647, he took with him the manuscript of Bradstreet's poems. Without her knowledge, he published them, titling the collection *The Tenth Muse Lately Sprung Up in America*. The volume met with immediate success in London. Surprised by the work's reception, but disturbed by its unpolished state, Bradstreet began to revise the poems. Some of these alterations were lost, however, when her home burned in 1666. Bradstreet died in 1672, and six years afterward, the revisions, along with a number of new pieces, were published under the title *Several Poems Compiled with Great Variety of Wit and Learning, Full of Delight.*

Poem Text

If ever two were one, then surely we.
If ever man were lov'd by wife, then thee.
If ever wife was happy in a man,
Compare with me, ye women, if you can.
I prize thy love more than whole Mines of gold,   5
Or all the riches that the East doth hold.
My love is such that Rivers cannot quench,
Nor ought but love from thee give recompence.
Thy love is such I can no way repay;
The heavens reward thee manifold I pray.   10
Then while we live, in love let's so persevere,
That when we live no more, we may live ever.

Poem Summary

Line 1:

The first line establishes the couple's complete union. The speaker's confident use of the words "surely" and "we" implies that she can speak for her husband about his feelings because they exactly match her own. In lines 1 and 2, the poet omits an implied last word: "are." Bradstreet may omit this word to make her rhymes and meter work, to stress the couple in the end words "we" and "thee" (you), or because the lines' meanings are clear without it.

Line 2:

Line 2 repeats the syntax of line 1. This repetition of structure serves to emphasize the poet's point: this union in marriage is more harmonious and passionate than all others across all of time. The repetition of "ever" points the reader toward a key theme in this poem: the passage of time. The repetition of the phrase "If … then" highlights the poet's intent to persuade her audience of the truth of her claims. Rather than exclaiming "Honey, I love you so much!" the poet conveys her message in a phrase usually reserved for arguing philosophical truths. Bradstreet reinforces the authority of these two lines through punctuation. Whereas all of the subsequent couplets form one sentence, ending with the second line, lines 1 and 2 are each complete sentences with periods at the end. In other words, Bradstreet begins her poem with two bold, independent, declarative statements in order to underscore her confidence in this union of two strong, independent spirits.

Lines 3-4:

In these lines, Bradstreet turns from addressing her husband ("thee") to address other women with "ye women." She dares other women to even try to compare their marital happiness with hers. Like the end words of the first two lines, the end words of these lines rhyme to form a couplet. Unlike the first couplet, lines 3 and 4 form just one sentence.

Lines 5-6:

Having compared her love to other people's relationships, the speaker now addresses her husband again ("thy love") and compares how much she values his love to the most valued goods on earth: gold and riches. It is common for poets and lovers to place greater value on love than money. While boasting of the extraordinary value of their love, she humbly restricts its value to a human scale of worth so as not to insult her Lord. Gold is only valuable in human society; it has no value after death. Bradstreet may capitalize "Mines" simply to emphasize vast wealth. Until almost the early nineteenth century, rules for capitalization were not standardized, and writers often capitalized nouns for emphasis.

Line 7:

Shifting from how much she values this earthly love, the speaker expresses the scope and insatiability of her desire. By arguing that "Rivers cannot quench" her love, the speaker implies that her love is an ongoing thirst that no amount of water can slake. The metaphors of thirst and rivers introduce the idea that the speaker's desire can be neither stopped nor quantified (as riches can). These "natural," earthly images of never-ending desire prepare the way for the speaker's wish for eternal, heavenly love later in the poem.

Line 8:

This line can be paraphrased as "the only thing on earth that equals or compensates my love for you is yours for me." By choosing the word "recompence," Bradstreet returns to the metaphor of monetary exchange. This couplet is the only one in the poem that uses a slant rhyme. The words "quench" and "recompence" do not rhyme exactly as the other end words do. Bradstreet may have paired these slightly ill-fitting sounds to parallel the mismatch of ideas, since comparing love to thirst and then money in the same sentence creates a mixed metaphor.

Lines 9-10:

Line 9 expands the idea in line 8: the speaker cannot "repay" her husband's love; only heaven can. The first four words of this line rhyme with

Media Adaptations

- An audio cassette titled *Anne Bradstreet* was released by Everett/Edwards in 1976.

- *The Courage to Write III: Pioneering American Poets* was released as audio cassettes by the University of Wisconsin Board of Regents in 1996.

- *Three Hundred Years of Great American Poetry, from Anne Bradstreet Through Stephen Crane,* a sound tape reel, is part of the Caedmon's "Great American Poetry" series.

those of line 7, "My love is such," and thereby link the previous couplet to this one through sound. Bradstreet connects the couplets because both develop the metaphor of love as riches. This rhyme reminds the reader of the spouses' mirrored, reciprocated love. That mirror, however, implies an exact exchange that lines 7 though 10 contradict. That is, the speaker implies she cannot repay her husband's love exactly, perhaps because she is a woman and therefore unequal to men. The only greater source of love is God, so the speaker prays in line 10 that "the heavens" will reward her husband's love "manifold," or in multiple and diverse ways. Note that the word "reward" continues the metaphor of monetary exchange. Bradstreet also invokes the phrase, "our heavenly reward," which means that one will be rewarded for good works in life with eternal life in heaven.

Lines 11-12:

The closing couplet of this almost-sonnet has stirred much controversy among scholars. Though in line 11 the speaker merely urges the lovers to "persevere," or persist in loving while they live, in line 12 she dares to wish that their love live on forever. Bradstreet's wish that love outlive death follows from the poem's argument that "holy matrimony" on earth is spiritual and may be the vehicle of salvation. In *Critical Essays on Anne Bradstreet,* Robert Richardson sees earthly and heavenly love as continuous: "As the poem expresses it, the transition from this world to the next involves not re-nunciation, not a change even, but an expansion." Many critics observe that Bradstreet's poems detail great love for the creatures and experiences of this world, but then reassert a Puritan devotion to spiritual existence in their final lines and images. Some critics view these endings as insincere attempts to reconcile wayward feelings with Puritan dogma. Other critics regard these dualistic poems as prayers, in which the speaker explores the limits of her faith in order to reaffirm it more truthfully in the end. However one interprets the last lines of " To My Dear and Loving Husband," this poem closes on a heartfelt note. In one sense, as you read the poem's lines, Bradstreet's wish for immortality is granted.

Themes

Wealth

The speaker of this poem discusses her love in terms of income and wealth for two different reasons. Sometimes, she uses the wealth that is valued on earth to show how insignificant material possessions are when compared to her feelings. She also uses financial imagery to compare her love with that of her husband's. The first use appears in lines 5 and 6, with her mention of "mines of gold" and "the riches that the East doth hold." She brings up these extreme examples of wealth in order to belittle them and show that, even though they represent shocking excesses of material fortune in worldly terms, they are worth less to her than the love of her husband. The next set of images from the world of commerce takes money a little more seriously. The poem makes frequent use of nouns that are usually associated with financial transactions: "recompence," "repay," and "reward" all suggest resources passing from one party to another, usually to balance out something equally worthy passing in the other direction. This technique is effective for Bradstreet's purpose, which is to measure the quantity of her love against the quantity of her husband's. Money, after all, is just a way to measure the material possessions of one person against the possessions of everyone else: if everyone on earth owned the same amount, then exchanging money would be pointless. According to the financial balance sheet that is presented here, the speaker of this poem feels quite satisfied that the love she gives out to her husband is paid back to her, but she fears that he is not being given a fair

Topics for Further Study

- This poem uses rhyming couplets to steadily emphasize the speaker's love for her husband. But what if he feels exactly the opposite? Write a poem in this style about a husband who hates his wife. Try to use the same iambic pentameter rhythm.

- Study Puritan life in America during the 1600s. Not much is written about personal relationships, but find out what you can and make some assumptions. Based on the available evidence, explain whether you think Bradstreet's relationship with her husband was typical for a Puritan of her time.

- Over the years, the power has been lost from familiar associations like "Mines of gold," "riches of the East," and love that "Rivers cannot quench." What fresh, new expressions could be used in their place to make readers realize how extreme the speaker's love is?

repayment for all that he does for her. The balance of their transaction is off because, as she humbly admits, her ability is limited. Her hope is that the love he gives her will receive an equal return when he dies, goes to heaven, and receives the reward that she sees herself as being too weak to provide.

Time

The concept of time introduces several points of contradiction into this poem, and it is these contradictions that make "To My Dear and Loving Husband" as interesting as it is. The first two couplets, with their heavy reliance on the phrase "If ever …," imply the concept of eternity, which is an idea that is often associated with the romantic conception of love. Eternity is often used to show, as this poem is attempting to show, the supernatural power that love has. But these lines do not actually say anything about the speaker's love lasting forever, only that the love between her and her husband are better than *other* loves throughout eternity. "Ever" here says nothing about how long their love will last, only that there has not been another to match it throughout history. To claim a love that lasts beyond death would contradict the principles of Bradstreet's strong Puritan faith, which held that personal relations were supposed to end with death, along with all other things of the earth. The spirit would then be able to proceed to heaven unencumbered. As a matter of fact, line 11 does put a time limit on love, saying that it lasts only "while we live" and implying that love will therefore expire when life ends. The last line, though, contradicts this, by saying that love does not end with death but that it can overpower death, causing life to last for eternity. Critics who are familiar with Anne Bradstreet's strongly held religious beliefs doubt that she would contradict the teachings of her faith by saying that love lasts eternally, or, even worse, that it would be love of others, and not God's grace, that creates eternal life. These critics soften the meaning of the word "that" in the last line, making worldly love and eternal love two separate things, with no real connection. If that were Bradstreet's point, a clearer way to say it might have been, "in love let's so persever, / And when we live no more, we will live forever."

Sex Roles

It is clear that the speaker of this poem relies on her husband for her sense of who she is; this idea is present in the first line, which tells readers that these two are one. The identity that the speaker willingly assigns to herself is "wife." In lines 2 and 3, using parallel phrasings, she expresses both her love and then her contentedness with the relationship in terms of being a wife. Both times, however, she using the word "man," not the corresponding term "husband"; this grants him a degree of independence from the relationship that she does not give herself. The imbalance in this marriage, with her unquenchable thirst for his love, has been called an indicator of the unevenness of gender roles in Puritan culture, in which the wife is vulnerable and subservient to the husband. A similar type of vulnerability, though, has been expressed by men throughout the centuries; it is the identifying trait of romantic love, a tradition handed down from the chivalrous code of King Arthur and the Knights of the Round Table since the sixth century. In a sense, the fact that the speaker of this poem sacrifices her will for love is a claim for the mental and emotional abilities of women. At a time when women were dismissed lightly by men as being ignorant and shallow, Bradstreet demonstrates, through her poem, a depth and profundity that challenges the stereotypes assigned to her gender.

Style

"To My Dear and Loving Husband" is written in iambic pentameter, which means that five iambs occur in a row in most lines of the poem. A few variations in this rhythmic pattern keep the meter from sounding monotonous. If we mark iambs as unstressed, then stressed syllables, here is how the syllables in the first line are stressed:

If **e** / ver **two** / were **one**, / then **sure** / ly **we.**

In addition to regular rhythms, each pair of lines rhymes. These rhymed pairs are called couplets. In this poem, the couplets reinforce the theme of love between two people. There are twelve lines in the poem. It is just two lines short of being a sonnet. A traditional form, the sonnet has 14 lines, follows a regular rhyme scheme and rhythm—usually iambic pentameter—and often discusses love or mortality. This poem is also written in first person point of view, using "I." Although speakers in poems and stories often represent fictional characters or personas, critics agree that Bradstreet speaks as herself in this and many other poems.

To emphasize the wife and husband's mutual love, Bradstreet uses internal rhyme, rhymes within the lines, and parallelism, phrases with parallel or repeated syntax. The rhymed and repeated phrases reinforce two ideas: one, that each spouse's love mirrors the other's, and two, that this earthly love mirrors eternal love. The first two lines employ a parallel phrase, "If ever ... were / then...." The third word in each line signals key themes: "two, man, wife." The phrase, "If ... then" is also a rhetorical tool used to persuade an audience of an argument's truth. Through such repetition of parallel, persuasive phrases, Bradstreet tries to convince both the reader and her husband that their great love may signify salvation. Bradstreet uses additional parallel, rhymed phrases in lines 7 and 9: "My love is such" and "Thy love is such"; and lines 11 and 12: "Then while we live" and "That when we live."

Historical Context

Anne Bradstreet was the first significant poet living in New England, which developed into the United States. She came from England to the Massachusetts Bay Colony in 1630 as part of the Great Migration of Puritans. Many brief histories of America refer to the fact that the Puritans who left

Compare & Contrast

- **1678:** Only eleven of the original thirteen colonies had been established: Virginia, Massachusetts, New York, Maryland, Rhode Island, Connecticut, Delaware, New Hampshire, North Carolina, South Carolina and New Jersey. William Penn purchased Pennsylvania from the Indians in 1682, and Georgia was added in 1732.

  Today: No new states have been added since Alaska and Hawaii in 1959, although Puerto Rico is always considered a possible candidate.

- **1678:** England was alive with talk about a "Popish Plot," which supposedly was a plan by the Catholic Church to massacre Protestants, burn London, and assassinate Charles II. Historians doubt that such a thing existed, but the Papists' Disabling Act that was passed kept Roman Catholics out of Parliament until 1829.

  Today: The Roman Catholic Pope is recognized as a statesman and welcomed with enthusiasm throughout the world.

- **1678:** Dutch traders sold approximately 15,000 slaves from Angola in the American colonies each year. It would be almost two hundred years until the Civil War was fought to free the descendants of these slaves.

  Today: Racial divisions in America reflect the fact that American society has included slavery for nearly twice as long as it has been without it.

England did so to avoid religious persecution, leaving the impression that they were a small band with unusual religious practices that the government decided suddenly to hunt down and destroy. Actually, the roots of Puritanism run deep within the Church of England and far back into English history. The defining characteristic of the Church of England, also referred to as the Anglican church, is its opposition to the Catholic rules that require obedience to the pope. Back before 597 A.D., ancient Celtic religious practices were followed in England, but in that year Catholic missionaries from Rome arrived. As Catholicism grew, it created, as any idea brought into a new environment will, a unique blend with the religious notions that preceded it. By the sixteenth century, Catholicism was clearly the single most dominating religion in Western civilization (a term used to indicate the societies of western Europe), but many people were unhappy. They felt that Roman Catholic ceremonies placed too much emphasis on the officers of the church, inserting levels of cardinals, bishops, and even the pope between ordinary people and God. In Germany, Martin Luther led the Protestant Reformation when he published his Ninety-five Theses in 1517, objecting to the Church's practices—especially the way that it collected money. In France, John Calvin's *Institutes of the Christian Religion,* which emphasized the virtues of hard work and supported a doctrine of predestination, became the most influential work of the Protestant movement. In England, King Henry VIII tried to have his marriage to Catherine of Aragon annulled by the Catholic Church, and when his request was refused, he created the separate Church of England, making the ruler of England the head of the church. When his daughter by Catherine, Mary Tudor, became queen in 1553, she tried to restore Catholicism in England, executing many Protestants and forcing hundreds more to leave the country. She died in 1558, and her sister, Elizabeth, took the throne. Queen Elizabeth restored the Church of England that Mary had, for the most part, dismantled. About a sixth of the Protestants returning from exile, though, did not agree with Elizabeth's policies, feeling that she was giving too many concessions to the Catholic Church. They felt that the Church of Rome was corrupting the purity of human relations with God, and so they gained the name Puritans.

The Puritans' doctrine emphasized the belief that all humans are sinners and that man cannot understand God. Their beliefs were unpopular, and the ideas of religious tolerance that we are familiar with, mostly because of the influence of their experience, were unknown then. The fortune of English politics shifted between Catholics and Protestants, but neither side liked Puritans, who were tortured and jailed. With the development of New England, Puritans saw a chance to get away from the persecution they suffered at home. In 1606, the Virginia Company was organized as a functional corporation to develop the resources of the new land; they settled Jamestown, the first European settlement in New England, in 1607. In 1623, the Reverend John White of Dorchester arrived in America with about fifty Puritans, but the land where they arrived was too hard to cultivate, so most went back to England, leaving a few who, with the help of the Indians, settled Salem, Massachusetts. In 1628, White founded a new corporation, the New England Company, which he later renamed the Massachusetts Bay Company for legal reasons. They received permission from the government to establish the territory of Massachusetts, and, most important, to run the government of the colony from Massachusetts, not from England. The Massachusetts Territory ranged for about sixty miles north and south of Salem (a western boundary was not set, because they believed America only extended a few miles past the Atlantic ocean anyway). In 1630, eleven ships owned by the Massachusetts Bay Company carried Puritans to America. On the flagship, the *Arabella,* were seventeen-year-old Anne Bradstreet, her husband, and her parents.

The Puritans saw America as a broad, empty wilderness that was open for development. They did not see the indigenous people, the Indians, as being fully human, but as "savages," and therefore it did not bother them to encroach upon the Indians' land. The Puritans, who had gotten used to unfamiliar, sometimes deadly, experiences since the first moments of their sea voyage, were for the most part disappointed when they arrived in the New World. They had concentrated on the rich fertility and open spaces of the land and found themselves, cultured and educated urban people for the most part, faced with clearing trees, plowing soil, and building houses. Thomas Dudly, the first deputy governor of the colony in Massachusetts and the father of Anne Bradstreet, explained in a letter back to England that accounts of wealth and easy living in the colony were often exaggerated: "In a word, we yet enjoy little to be envied, but endure much to be pitied in the sickness and mortality of our people." Before farms were developed, Puritans went hungry; when the first winter came, the weather was harsher than they could have guessed,

and sicknesses that they did not recognize infected the colony. Even common illnesses were deadly because of a shortage of medication. Faith kept many working along, and even more stayed because they feared that the ocean voyage back would be just as bad as the one that had brought them. Eventually, cities sprung up and a culture arose, although it was still more than a hundred years until the colonies fought the Revolutionary War and formed their own independent country.

Critical Overview

Most critics observe a distinct split between Anne Bradstreet's early and later poetry. The early poetry, published in the 1650 volume, *The Tenth Muse, Lately Sprung Up in America,* concerns public, formal themes. This poetry demonstrates Bradstreet's considerable knowledge and poetic skill, but critics prefer her later poetry, published after her death in the 1678 edition, *Several Poems.* The 1678 volume includes more "private" or personal poems than the earlier volume, including " To My Dear and Loving Husband." In these poems, Bradstreet records her personal experiences as a Puritan woman, wife, and mother. Through these experiences, the poet analyzes her religious faith and draws lessons for living.

Critics agree that "To My Dear and Loving Husband," along with Bradstreet's other private poems, offers a unique glimpse into the mind-set of both the Puritans and Anne Bradstreet. The Puritans were not quite the dour, religious fanatics that many people once believed they were. They gratefully celebrated physical love, food, nature, and other worldly pleasures as gifts from God. "To My Dear and Loving Husband" demonstrates that a Puritan woman's physical passion could be proclaimed as the nearest thing on earth to heaven. However, the speaker's love for her husband almost seems to outweigh her devotion to God. Devout Puritans tried not to love any earthly thing more than God. The poet wishes for the union to continue after death, even though Christians then and now believe that earthly unions dissolve at death. Critic Robert Richardson, writing in the collection *Critical Essays on Anne Bradstreet,* argues that "In this poem, this world and the next validate one another. Love is the way to heaven and the best image of heaven is a realm of eternal love." Critics disagree over how conventional Bradstreet's religious beliefs were. Most agree, however, that the poet powerfully dramatizes tensions between "the flesh and the spirit" in her struggle to interpret earthly signs of God's will.

Criticism

Ann Stanford

In the following essay, Stafford summarizes Bradstreet's poetic achievements.

The poetry of Anne Bradstreet has two claims upon the reader of American literature. The first grows out of her place as the earliest poet to produce a large body of original work in America; the second, by far the more important, comes from the high quality of the poetry itself. Hers is a voice which overleaps the limits of an age and speaks in fresh and vibrant tones of human concerns. In recognition of such timelessness at least one edition of her poems has been published or reprinted in each century of our history.

Given its place and merit, the poetry of Anne Bradstreet deserves the scrutiny of a full-length study, for her accomplishment becomes clearer in the light of the circumstances, both literary and ideological, under which she wrote. Her work is influenced, first of all, by the ideas circulated generally among all educated people of the late sixteenth and early seventeenth centuries, ideas of the nature of man and the universe and of politics that differ markedly from those we hold today. Beyond these, her work reflects the Puritan religious concepts with which she was thoroughly indoctrinated; it shows, too, a remarkable sensitivity to the forms and genres which she inherited from the Elizabethans and which were being developed by other seventeenth-century writers.

But above all, Anne Bradstreet's entire canon represents the struggle between the visible and the invisible worlds. Earth and the things of earth had on her a solid grasp. Though the spirit might point out the virtues of the unseen, Anne Bradstreet was always most conscious of the pleasures and rewards of earth—love, family, comfort, learning, fame. Even the harsh realities of the new world, this wilderness in which she made her home, were preferable to the gold and jewels of the invisible kingdom. Her argument was a constant one, conducted life-long; the voice of the world was never quite overwhelmed even in her most religious poems. In keeping with her long inner dialogue, most of her poetry takes the form of argument—in the early poems, between characters; in the later, between the two parts of herself. During the first half of her career, the world is clearly supreme; during the latter part, the invisible wins, but never a clear victory.

The poet's involvement in the world is symbolized by the wide range of forms in which she cast her writing and the influences we can see in them. Her range included the encyclopedic quaternions, rhymed history, metrical prayers, formal memorial eulogies, elegies of personal grief, political broadsides, Biblical paraphrases, love poems, meditative poems, and in prose, a personal journal and meditations. All these she wrote in "a few hours snatched from sleep and other refreshment," and all these she wrote in styles varied according to the purpose of each, as dictated by the literary decorum of her day. But though she was familiar with the general current of ideas and with the work of many of the then popular writers, she did not slavishly follow any master. She rearranged and synthesized the literary forms she encountered to serve her own purposes. Despite its roots in the baroque, her work is essentially pragmatic and realistic as befits a writer so admiring of the world. In part these qualities grew out of the poet's character. But they may also have come from her experience of the American wilderness, where, severed from the full impact of changing literary fashions, she developed her own responses to those events which touched her most.

Like other true poets, she enlivened the conventions she received, transforming them into a unique and vigorous instrument. But she did not use that instrument for small or temporary ends. Her work is very much a whole.

Source: Ann Stanford, preface to *Anne Bradstreet: The Worldly Puritan,* New York: Burt Franklin & Co., 1974.

David Kelly

David Kelly is an instructor of creative writing and literature at Oakton Community College and College of Lake County in Illinois. In this essay, Kelly explains the reasons we want to believe that a poet like Bradstreet, unlike modern poets, is entirely open, but then he raises doubts about whether this poem really is as simple as it seems.

What draws me to Anne Bradstreet's poem "To My Dear and Loving Husband" is the directness of the poet's expression of her love. We don't see that in literature, especially not in twentieth-century literature, where authors have learned to tell about a thing by talking about anything but the thing. By modern standards, a poem that claims to be about a woman's love for her husband would really intend to suggest her childhood traumas, or the husband's personality, or just about anything except what it seems to be about. Not that complexity, though sometimes frustrating, is bad. Overall, I'm glad when a work of literature tries to keep a few steps ahead of its readers, dodging and hiding behind whatever camouflage it can muster and leaving us wondering where it is going and where it has been. Life would be a lot less interesting if poems said things flat out, such as, "This is a tree, and I like it." The human mind will wander anyway—twentieth-century authors prepare for that curiosity and write their poems mindful of the fact that people are going to want to know more about what a poem is telling them than just what it says. They program clues into the blank spaces to indicate who is telling us this and why they like the tree. Some of this comes from the rise of psychoanalysis at the beginning of the century and its theory that the subconscious creates events that we cannot see; some of it is the result of stratospheric jumps in the numbers of educated people, especially in the college-educated since World War II, which has given us a huge army of literary critics trying to gouge even the tiniest clues out of a poem. Once in a while, after pondering poetry for a long time, it is nice to just sit down with a poem like "To My Dear And Loving Husband" that has a thing to say and says it, then lets its readers go off to new pursuits.

I should say, it would be nice, but unfortunately a good poem never releases its grasp, and any good poem deserves study. The basic questions are answered within this poem—the person speaking is Mistress Bradstreet herself, and the "why" for her writing is that she loves her husband very much and wants him to know about it. Even these simple answers, though, raise further issues. Who is this Bradstreet woman? The normal, dismissive answer is that she is a Puritan, followed by a long essay about who the Puritans were and what they stood for. Why is she so bent on telling her husband how much she loves him, especially since Puritans were a notoriously tight-lipped and unemotional bunch who generally are not considered the type to pour out their emotions? The conventional answer is that she was a poet, and this is what poets do—pour out their feelings on the page for all to see.

In her book *Anne Bradstreet Revisited*, Rosamond Rosenmeier raises the question of whether

What Do I Read Next?

- Bradstreet was a fan of one of England's greatest poets, John Milton, who wrote during her lifetime. Milton's most stunning achievement in a full career was the book-length poem *Paradise Lost,* which was published in 1667.

- Andrew Marvell was an English metaphysical poet who wrote at the same time as Bradstreet. He frequently wrote satirical works, including his most famous poem, "To His Coy Mistress," which takes the opposite position from the one that Bradstreet took toward love. This poem and others are in *The Essential Marvell,* published in 1991 by Ecco Press.

- Bradstreet's poetry has been in print continuously since its first printing in 1678. The 1967 Harvard University Press edition of *The Works of Anne Bradstreet,* edited by Jeannine Hensley, has a good introduction by respected poet and critic Adrienne Rich.

- *An American Triptych: Anne Bradstreet, Emily Dickinson, Adrienne Rich,* by Wendy Martin, examines the continuity in styles and themes of female writers from the seventeenth, nineteenth and twentieth centuries. This book was published by the University of North Carolina Press in 1984.

- A postmodern look at the world Anne Bradstreet faced came from one of the century's greatest poets, John Berryman, who first gained national attention with his long poem *Homage to Mistress Bradstreet.* It was published in 1956, first in *The Partisan Review* and then as a book by Farrar Straus.

"To My Dear and Loving Husband," or any of the other four that make up the group we refer to as "The Marriage Poems," was actually meant for the public to see. The Marriage Poems were added to the 1678 edition of her poetry after Bradstreet's death; there is no way of determining what her wishes were about their publication—whether she meant them only for her husband (but he felt they were so good he had to share them with the world), or if she meant all along to use them as part of her overall message to the world (addressing them to him as a literary device). On the one hand, there seems to be no reason to question the poem's sincerity when it speaks to Bradstreet's husband, Simon: as mentioned before, the demand for irony and complexity that has intensified over the past hundred years had not come to bear on Bradstreet in the seventeenth century, and, besides, her staunch religious beliefs would make her unlikely to bend the truth too far in the name of "art for art's sake." On the other hand, as Rosenmeier points out, there are signs within the Marriage Poems, such as Biblical allusions and recurring imagery from Renaissance science, that make it seem clear that these poems weren't just pleasant, colorful little gifts for Simon Bradstreet—they were written with the public in mind.

At this point, the question seems entirely academic (which is to say that it's the sort of thing that only a college professor with too much time to kill and an itch to stir up controversy might raise). It is a sweet poem, and a lot of readers would probably like to leave it at that. But once the question is raised about whether what we see in this poem is Anne Bradstreet talking to her husband or a character named "Anne Bradstreet" talking to us readers, then there is no way to read the poem well without feeling confident about one answer or the other.

Since historians and Anne Bradstreet's biographers have never been able to settle on a satisfactory answer—there is neither a journal entry saying, "Am working on a poem about marriage, but I'll address it as a letter to Simon," nor a note on the original poem telling her husband, "Don't show this to anyone!"—the best place to look is at the five Marriage Poems. These poems were probably written within a close time frame, and they address events in the author's life, ranging from the birth of one of her children (she had eight) to her husband's travels on political business (he was a governor of Massachusetts and had to leave their home in Ipswich to spend time 200 miles away in Boston).

The first poem in the set is titled, plainly enough, "Before the Birth of One Of Her Children" and is addressed directly to her husband. Of the group, this one seems most likely to have been meant for his eyes only and not for public display.

I say this because it contains orders about what he should do if she should die during childbirth, which was a likely enough possibility in those days. She asks to remain in his memory, while, at the same time, encouraging him to go on with his life "when the knot's untied." She tells him to watch after their children, but then adds that he is not to let a new wife have them ("These O protect from step-dame's injury"), presenting him with a complex mixture of permission and threat. The mixed emotions throughout suggest—though of course there is no way to prove it—that this is a personal poem, or is at least spun from emotions that Bradstreet herself experienced, with no tradition to defend it.

By contrast, "To My Dear and Loving Husband" seems stiff and formal. The imagery—mines of gold, riches of the East—is standard and unoriginal, the kind of stuff that can be appreciated equally by a great number of people. Perhaps Simon Bradstreet was an unoriginal thinker, and his wife knew that the way to praise him in a poem was to address him in the broadest terms possible, but the evidence leans toward her having at least one eye on her literary reputation here.

"A Letter To Her Husband, Absent Upon Public Employment" takes a personal situation—it even mentions that she is at Ipswich, rather than vaguely defining the situation with two unnamed places—and uses a more universal condition, the winter sun's absence, to broaden it. Is this a letter? As with "Before the Birth of One Of Her Children," the references seem to be personal and even sexual ("His warmth such frigid colds did cause to melt / My chilled limbs now numbed lie forlorn"). Of all the marriage poems, this one seems the most careful balance of public and private, describing a situation that lovers everywhere cope with and also Anne Bradstreet's situation in particular. If "To My Dear and Loving Husband" is pure poetry, the kind of thing a wife might use to engrave a clock or raise a glass to toast with, "A Letter To Her Husband" offers the kind of personal expansion on her husband's life that we have come to expect of poetry.

The last two Marriage Poems are both called "Another" in the authoritative version of Bradstreet's collected works, although the first of them is sometimes known as "Phoebus," which is its initial word. This one is addressed to Phoebus, the Middle English name for the Greek sun god Apollo, asking the sun to carry her love to her husband, far away, conveying to him the darkness she lives in while they are apart. It is the only one of the Marriage Poems that is not addressed to her husband, yet there is a vulnerability to it that is missing from "To My Dear and Loving Husband," as in the quatrain before last: "Tell him I would say more, but cannot well / Oppressed minds abruptest tales do tell." The second "Another" seems like a creative writing exercise in the device of the simile, comparing her marriage to two deer, some mullet, and turtles. The comparisons are more developed than "mines of gold" and "riches of the East," but that could merely be because more time is spent in them.

The older a poem is, the less credit we give its writer for cleverness and diversity. In Anne Bradstreet's case, the historical facts help to scatter readers' expectations: often, more attention is given to the social circumstances that limited a woman in colonial Massachusetts, and not enough is paid to what her overall plan was. I do not think she had a hidden agenda in writing "To My Dear and Loving Husband," and I do think that too much time can be wasted in treating this poem as an archeological artifact, a signifier, rather than taking her at her word. It wouldn't bother me, though, to know if her audience was the wide world of readers, as I think the polish of the poem implies, or if it really was meant just for her husband.

Source: David Kelly, in an essay for *Poetry for Students,* The Gale Group, 1999.

Ann Stanford

In the following excerpt, Stafford discerns Bradstreet's views on love and marriage as evidenced in her poems to her husband.

Anne Bradstreet had small patience with the Petrarchan convention in which a poet adores his lady from afar....

For Anne Bradstreet, the ideal love finds its consummation and continuation in marriage.

The importance of marriage for her as for all Puritans, was increased by the belief in the family as the basic unit of government in both the state and the congregation. Especially in New England the state was considered to be made up of families, who were expected to exercise control over their members. Thus marriage was important to the state, but essential to marriage was love. God had commanded man and wife to love one another; hence the duty to love was a part of the marriage contract. Though marriages were usually arranged by Puritan families on the basis of social rank, young people were not forced to marry where they felt love would be impossible. That a tender relationship was achieved among many Puritan couples is attested by such writings as the letters of John Winthrop to his wife, Thomas Shepard's references to his wife in his *Autobiography,* and the poems Anne Bradstreet wrote to her husband. Four of these are love poems. The first, twelve lines titled "To my Dear and loving Husband," comes as close to being a sonnet as anything Anne Bradstreet wrote. But it rhymes in couplets and the syntax is simple and direct, without the involution of phrase or meaning to be found in most sonnets. The other three are letters "to my husband, absent upon Public Employment." Since they bear the same title, I shall distinguish them by terms prominent in them, as the "Ipswich," the "Phoebus," and the "Loving-hind" poems.

Just as, thematically, the poems express a love exactly opposite to the Petrarchan ideal, so the methods, characters, and imagery differ. Here is no oxymoron, no freezing while burning, as in the Petrarchan conceits, but a straightforward analogy—the author is cold when her husband is away and warm when he is there, regardless of the season. Neither lady or love is idealized or distant; rather the marriage is happy in its consummation....

The Petrarchan love poem tended to blend with Neo-Platonism, and the final outcome of Petrarchan love was the approach to heavenly or ideal beauty through a series of steps beginning with physical love. For the Puritan, such an approach to heavenly beauty was not possible. Love was not used for the purpose of striving for ideal beauty, since the ideal was to be achieved by other means—the regenerate heart was given the power to see the "beauty of holiness" and the world as an expression of God's glory. The Puritan attitude toward love was more utilitarian. Married union was a near necessity. Love, both for Puritans and many other Elizabethans, when consummated by marriage, was to issue, not in aesthetic appreciation, but in the procreation of children. From the *Epithalamion* of Spenser, which closes with several references to fertility and procreation as the hoped-for outcome of the joys of the wedding night, to Milton, who couples marriage and procreation in the lines "Hail wedded Love, true source / Of human offspring," the theme recurs. Nor does Anne Bradstreet divorce her love for her husband from a consciousness of love's utilitarian functions. In the Ipswich poem she says "In this dead time, alas, what can I more / Then view those fruits which through thy heat I bore?" Here married love, while treated metaphorically, is nevertheless approached in a straight-forward, almost sensuous manner.

The four lyrics are bound together around a central idea—the union of husband and wife and the insistence on that unity despite physical separation. The first poem states the theme: "If ever two were one, then surely we." The Ipswich poem continues, inquiring "If two be one, as surely thou and I, / How stayest thou there, whilst I at *Ipswich* lye?" The poet addresses her husband as Sol and begs him to return northward; while he is in the south, the day is too long. In the Phoebus poem she reflects this idea in the first line ("*Phoebus* make haste, the day's too long, be gone") before proceeding to ask the sun to carry a message to her husband. The Loving-hind poem, which compares the poet to a hind, a dove, and a mullet, repeats the idea which concludes the second poem of the series ("I here, thou there, yet both but one") by stating "I here, he there, alas, both kept by force" and ends by asking him to return so they may browse at one tree, roost in one house, glide in one river. Its last line echoes the first line of the first poem by "Let's still remain but one, till death divide." Thematically, then, the poems are closely knit. The expression of sorrow over separation controls them as each moves toward the conclusion that the division should be ended by the reunion of the spouses.

The linking of the love poems by reiteration of a common theme illustrates a practice Bradstreet followed in several genres. The early elegies, for example, though written at different times, coalesced around the theme of fame, heightened in each case by the central technique of showing the subject outdoing other great figures. Later, "Contemplations" and the personal elegies, written as successive pieces of a long work or as single poems, were to be connected by central themes. Bradstreet's poetic canon shows a remarkable wholeness. Themes and images recur, often controlling the structure of all the poems in a single genre, or like the concept of the four elements, being repeated as motifs throughout her work. The four poetic letters to her husband, are the most conspicuous example of Bradstreet's ability to unify separate pieces of her work, but the tendency persists throughout.

Within the letters themselves, movement occurs by a method characteristic of other lyrics of the late sixteenth and early seventeenth centuries, when poetry was considered a branch of rhetoric.... The three letters of Anne Bradstreet were all written with the ostensible purpose of persuasion. Their method is not to describe realistically the state of her mind, but to move her husband by a series of arguments. Puttenham in his discussion of "that form of Poesie in which amorous affections and allurements were uttered" comments on the appropriate language for love poetry: "it requireth a forme of Poesie variable, inconstant, affected, curious and most witty of any others." Anne Bradstreet's language and metaphors in general conform to the rules of poetic decorum described by Puttenham. Certainly these love poems are the most "curious and witty" of her work.

The three love letters may have been written between 1641 and 1643, a period of high poetic excitement for Anne Bradstreet. Possibly she wrote them soon after the re-reading of Du Bartas in 1641, for they represent her closest approach to the use of exaggerated comparisons. By the time she wrote another poem to her husband a few years later, she had completely abandoned the "witty" style and adopted the more direct manner of her later poetry.

The language of "Before the Birth of one of her Children" is completely straightforward. Writing with great seriousness, the poet suggests that she may die in the coming childbirth. She asks her husband to forget her faults and remember what virtues she may have had, and to protect her little children from "step Dames injury." She is aware that life is fleeting but she also says

> love bids me
> These farewell lines to recommend to thee,
> That when that knot's unty'd that made us one,
> I may seem thine, who in effect am none.

It was the Puritan belief that a marriage was dissolved at death. Marriage was for the earthly life only, and in any after life any union between spirits was no longer in effect. Perhaps partly for this reason the regenerate spirits in Wigglesworth's poem *The Day of Doom* (stanzas 195–201) could watch without a quiver while their spouses, children, or parents went down to everlasting hell. God had said that a person must not love any earthly thing inordinately, and even excessive grief for a departed spouse was contrary to God's command. Anne Bradstreet voiced the Puritan view when she spoke of untying the knot "that made us one," just as she expressed it in the last line of the Loving-hind poem, "Let's still remain but one till death divide." But she tries to get around the idea of the complete severance of death by writing lines so that "I may seem thine, who in effect am none." She wants to be remembered. Admitting that her husband will probably marry again, she still hopes that

> if chance to thine eyes shall bring this verse,
> With some sad sighs honour my absent Herse;
> And kiss this paper for thy loves dear sake.

Further, she requests him

when thou feel'st no grief, as I no harms,
Yet love thy dead, who long lay in thine arms.

In its emotional content, the poem—one of Bradstreet's several farewells to the world—tries to gain for its author earthly continuance in the memory of the living. In the earlier love poems, also, the poet attempted to circumvent the finality of death. Throughout, they reflect a love that goes beyond the merely rational and dutiful. "To my Dear and loving Husband" ends:

Then while we live, in love lets so persevere,
That when we live no more, we may live ever.

The turn of phrase here reminds us of Cavalier poetry, though the lines themselves are ambiguous. They may mean that the loving couple will produce descendants, so that they may live on in their line. Or the couplet may mean that the two will become famous as lovers and live on in that fame. And the fame will come in part through the exertions of Anne Bradstreet's muse.

Such might be the whole import of these lines had they been based completely on the commonplaces of Renaissance sonneteers. But the intensity with which the Puritans focussed on grace and divine love adds religious overtones to this poem. The word love is played upon. As Saints, the lovers must persevere in the consciousness of the divine love within the covenant of grace in order to live ever. The love between husband and wife in the ideal state of marriage may be considered an analogy for the love between Christ and the soul or Christ and his Church. So the "Argument" preceding the Song of Solomon in the Geneva Bible explains: "In this Song, Salomon by moste swete and comfortable allegories and parables describeth the perfite love of Jesus Christ, the true Salomon and King of peace, and the faithful soule or his Church, which he hath sanctified and appointed to be his spouse, holy, chast and without reprehension." Even so, the ardor with which Bradstreet addresses her husband in this "sonnet" and the three love poems threatens to overshadow a proper love of God by placing so high a value on one who is a mere creature.

Source: Ann Stanford, "The Poems to Her Husband," *Anne Bradstreet: The Worldly Puritan,* New York: Burt Franklin & Co., 1974.

Sources

Bremer, Francis J., *The Puritan Experiment: New England Society from Bradford to Edwards,* New York: St. Martin's Press, 1976.

Carroll, Peter N., *Puritanism and The Wilderness: The Intellectual Significance of the New England Frontier, 1629-1700,* New York: Columbia University Press, 1969.

Kenyon, J. P., *Stuart England,* New York: St. Martin's Press, 1978.

Morison, Samuel Eliot, *Builders of the Bay Colony,* Boston: Houghton Mifflin Co., 1930.

Richardson, Robert D., "The Puritan Poetry of Anne Bradstreet," in *Critical Essays on Anne Bradstreet,* edited by Pattie Cowell and Ann Stanford, G.K. Hall & Co., 1983, pp. 101-15.

Rosenmeier, Rosamond, *Anne Bradstreet Revisited,* Boston: Twayne Publishers, Inc., 1991.

Stanford, Ann, *Anne Bradstreet, The Worldly Puritan: An Introduction to Her Poetry,* Burt Franklin & Co., 1974.

For Further Study

Douglas, Emily Taft, *Remember the Ladies: The Story of Great Women Who Helped Shape America,* New York: Putnam, 1966.

As the title indicates, the tone of this book is quite more patronizing toward female authors than is generally seen in more contemporary studies; still, the sheer range of women covered here, putting Bradstreet in a category with Eleanor Roosevelt and Isadora Duncan, makes this source worthwhile.

Dudley, Thomas, "Problems of Settlement," *The Puritan Tradition in America, 1620-1730,* edited by Alden T. Vaughan, Columbia: University of South Carolina Press, 1972. pp. 59-63.

This brief excerpt, written by Anne Bradstreet's father (who came from England with her) describes the starvation and freezing faced by the Puritans on their arrival. This whole book consists of first-person accounts of America's early days.

Dunham, Montrew, *Anne Bradstreet: Young Puritan Poet,* Indianapolis: Bobbs-Merrill, 1969.

Although this book is actually written for children in primary school, it is one of the few sources to concentrate on the poet's childhood before she left England.

Hammond, Jeffrey, *Sinful Self, Saintly Self: The Puritan Experience of Poetry,* Athens: University of Georgia Press, 1993.

Hammond's book explores the religious determinism that shaped Bradstreet's thought and defined her experience.

Miller, Perry, *Orthodoxy in Massachusetts, 1630-1650,* Evanston, IL: Harper Torchbook, 1933.

The interesting thing about this history is the way that it treats religion as a political tool, showing how the Puritan way of thought evolved into the American way of social interaction.

Piercy, Josephine K., *Anne Bradstreet,* New York: Twayne Publishers, Inc., 1965.

This is a very thorough and basic overview of Bradstreet's life and the critical reception of her oeuvre.

Rosenmeier, Rosamond, *Anne Bradstreet Revisited,* Boston: Twayne Publishers, Inc., 1991.
 A companion piece to Piercy's book, this corrects some historical inaccuracies and takes a more psy-

chological approach to Bradstreet, using newer materials.

Stanford, Ann, *Anne Bradstreet, The Worldly Puritan: An Introduction to Her Poetry,* New York: B. Franklin, 1975.
 A respected survey of the poet and her work that is written at a level appropriate for readers who are not familiar with Bradstreet.

We Real Cool

Gwendolyn Brooks
1960

Gwendolyn Brooks's "We Real Cool" first appeared in *Poetry* magazine in September of 1958 and was later published in her fourth volume of poetry, *The Bean Eaters* (1960). This short, poignant poem is perhaps Brooks's most famous and is characterized by its use of vernacular and the way its short, staccato lines and internal rhyming pattern quickly carry the work to a crisp, startling ending. The locale of "We Real Cool" is a pool hall called The Golden Shovel. The poem's action is recounted by the collective voice of seven pool players who, although their race is unspecified, are generally thought to be black because of their language and because the poet, herself, is African American. While "We Real Cool" could be read as a boast, the distinctive way that Brooks breaks the lines transforms egotistical display into momentary candor as the players realize the struggle of being outsiders or misfits. Neither moralizing nor maudlin, the pool players reflect on their situation but give no indication that they will change their behavior in any way. In this way, the poem is realistic and avoids a quick and easy fix. "We Real Cool" ends on an unsettling note, as the players' predict their own fate.

Author Biography

Gwendolyn Brooks was born in Topeka, Kansas, in 1917. Her father, David Anderson Brooks, the son of a runaway slave, was the only child of twelve

Gwendolyn Brooks

to finish high school. He wanted to be a doctor, but after a year of college, he was forced to become a janitor at a music publishing company because of money problems. Before Gwendolyn was born, her mother, Keziah Wims Brooks, was a schoolteacher and was studying to be a concert pianist. She would, however, settle in to become a Methodist Sunday-school teacher, a wife, and mother. Mrs. Brooks encouraged her daughter to continue with the rhymes she began writing at age seven. Later, Brooks's mother took her to see poets James Weldon Johnson and Langston Hughes. Hughes read the poems the teenager had brought to the reading and encouraged her to pursue her literary aspirations. By age thirteen, Brooks published her first poem in *American Childhood* magazine, and by the time she was twenty, several of her poems had appeared in the *Chicago Defender* and her work was represented in two poetry anthologies.

Graduating from junior college and unable to land a job at the *Chicago Defender,* Brooks took a job as a maid; later, she worked as a secretary. At age twenty-one, Brooks joined the NAACP Youth Council and there met a man named Henry Lowington Blakely II, who was also a writer. The couple married in 1939 and their first child, Henry Lowington Blakely III, was born a year later. While Brooks and her husband were living in Chicago,

she attended a workshop taught by Inez Cunningham Stark. Taking Stark's advice to avoid cliché and make every word work, Brooks won first prize in a workshop contest and the 1944 and 1945 Midwestern Writers Conference prize for poems that would be included in her first book, *A Street in Bronzeville* (1945). In 1950, her volume of poetry *Annie Allen* (1949) won the Pulitzer Prize, marking the first time the prize was awarded to an African American. After a productive period in which she wrote several books, Brooks attended Fisk University's Black Writer's Conference and was simultaneously shocked and electrified by poets such as Don L. Lee and Amiri Baraka, who proclaimed black revolt, nationhood, and power. The fruits of her awakening first appeared in *In the Mecca* (1968), in which she untied herself from traditional poetic forms associated with whites and counseled her readers to leap into the whirlwind of righteous black anger and action. Among Brooks's many volumes of poems, she also published one novel, *Maud Martha* (1953). Brooks has been awarded more than fifty honorary doctorates, and her awards and distinctions are numerous. In 1968, she became Poet Laureate of Illinois, and, from 1985 to 1986, she served as poetry consultant to the Library of Congress. Honored by fans, peers, and presidents, Brooks is one of America's most distinguished writers.

Poem Text

The Pool Players.

Seven at the Golden Shovel.

> We real cool. We
> Left school. We
>
> Lurk late. We
> Strike straight. We
>
> Sing sin. We   5
> Thin gin. We
>
> Jazz June. We
> Die soon.

Poem Summary

Subtitle:

Brooks breaks the subtitle into two parts, both of which are subjects without predicates. She does not, for instance, write what would be a more economic alternative, *Seven Pool Players at the*

Golden Shovel, even though economy is a hallmark of this poem. A possible explanation is that Brooks's fragments allow a reading of the word "seven" as both "seven pool players" and as a lucky number. With the latter possibility, the number is ironic since, by the end of this poem, the pool players reveal that they are not lucky at all. The players are at a pool parlor called the Golden Shovel. The name initially suggests good fortune ("digging for gold"), but by the end of the poem, it implies a negative connotation as an implement used for digging graves.

Lines 1-2:

The first line is the only one with "We" at the beginning and the end. Contrast this with the last line, which contains no pronoun. Perhaps with the poem's opening, then, the pool players' identity is at its strongest, but wanes until its weakest point—the end. "Real cool" and "left school" are more sonically dissimilar within each pair than the other paired words of the poem, such as "thin gin," except for the last line's "die soon." Still, "real cool" and "left school" do link up with the use of the recurring "l" sound. "Die" and "soon," however, have only one similarity: as is true for all of the words in the poem, they are monosyllabic. With one exception, the word "We" is enjambed, or placed at the end of the previous line with which it does not semantically belong, instead of being placed with the line it does belong with, the one that follows. The technique forces the reader to hesitate after each "We." Brooks has remarked that the hesitation, coupled with her choice of a quiet uttering of "We," signals a weak sense of the pool players' identity. In fact, so weak is this identity that these pool players, while almost always thought to be black males—perhaps because the poet is black and it is boys who usually hang out in pool parlors—could be white males or even females.

Lines 3-4:

Alliteration of "l" and "str" sounds mark these two lines. The words "Lurk" and "Strike" both have sinister connotations; lurking involves hiding and watching, possibly with an evil intent, while strike suggests an assault. But "Lurk" might mean little more than to hide out in the pool parlor, and "Strike straight" may refer to playing pool well or to "telling it like it is."

Lines 5-6:

To "Sing sin" probably means to proclaim sin as morally fitting or good—or at least pleasurable.

Media Adaptations

- A cassette titled *Broadside on Broadway: Seven Poets Read* was released in 1970 by Broadside Voices. Dudley Randall, Jerry Whittington, Frenchy Hodges, Sonia Sanchez, Don L. Lee, Margaret Walker, and Gwendolyn Brooks read.

- A sound recording titled *Gwendolyn Brooks Reading Her Poetry,* with an introduction by Don L. Lee, is available from Caedmon.

- A cassette titled *Gwendolyn Brooks and Lucille Clifton* was released in 1993 through the American Academy of Poets on Tape Program.

"Thin gin" refers to drinking gin with a mixer such as ginger ale or tonic water, the point simply being that these pool players drink hard liquor. "Sing" and "sin" alliterate but "Thin" and "gin" rhyme.

Lines 7-8:

"Jazz June" can have several readings. "Jazz" here is a verb and could mean to have sex, or a good time, with a woman named June. "Jazz June" could also mean have a good time in the month of June. Finally, these pool players might listen to or play jazz. During the 1950s, the time this poem was written, cool was the prevalent form of jazz, a music of intricate harmonies and subdued dynamics. By the last line of the poem, it is not exactly certain whether the players are bragging or noticing a profound problem with their way of life.

Themes

Appearance vs. Reality

Most assessments about the pool players in "We Real Cool" fall somewhere between the following two extremes: the players are cool or they are worthy of pity. The players are arguably cool because they had the nerve to drop out of school, perhaps have refused to work, because they drink (and might be underage), and because they engage

Topics for Further Study

- Conduct a research project on school desegregation in the 1950s, either by state or part of the country.

- Analyze the game of pool in terms of its history and sociology. Explain how pool came to be associated with the urban underclass and underbelly.

- Research the life expectancies of black youths versus white youths. Account for differences with research, or, in lieu of research, hypotheses.

in activities that are frowned upon or forbidden. In addition, and perhaps most important, the players are cool because they are fearless—unafraid of telling the truth (they are "straight shooters") and facing the dangers that those who "sing sin" could encounter. If we accept this evaluation, the poem functions as a boast all the way through its last line, making the players cooler still. Conversely, these players can be viewed as deserving pity because they seem to be trying to boost their self-esteem by placing high value on meaningless activities. There is the sense that they are trying to forget their socioeconomic circumstances by drinking and playing games. In this way, they embrace the attitudes and activities that will only compound their plight. They have given up on means of advancement, such as education. Dying soon would not so much be tragic, but a way of escaping a harsh reality.

These are the extremes of perception—of appearance—that the pool players would have to struggle with and could not help but internalize. Their response might be to "shoot straight": to those to whom they appear romantically rebellious, they might say that theirs is actually a life of confusion, fear, anger, and alienation. "We Real Cool," then, is a cautionary tale for those who would think them cool. But to those who would condemn them, the players' response might again be to shoot straight: "At least we haven't been suckered into buying into a system that may not even reward us

if we work hard and follow the rules." In this case, "We Real Cool" is a defiant response to those who would condemn them out of hand and who unthinkingly accept the status quo.

Free Will and Chance

The last statement of this poem, "We / Die soon," raises the question of whether these pool players have any control over their lives or if they are simply characters who will succumb to a predetermined fate. People often refer to "the luck of the draw" to describe a situation that is the result of chance; in this case, the pool players were born into a set of circumstances over which they had no control. Because they are not adults, they have no way of affecting their socioeconomic status. The players, however, show free will in that they choose to skip school, "Lurk late," and "Sing sin." Free will involves taking responsibility for one's own action, and by making what many would see as negative choices—foregoing education and instead playing—they effectively have decided give up on their future and risk their safety by hanging around dangerous people and areas. Someone with a fatalistic viewpoint, though, would argue that it wouldn't matter what choices the players made—any path they took would lead to the same place. This, then, is the difficult problem this poem tries to solve: to keep the reader from simply pronouncing the pool players either guilty (with free will) or innocent (subject to fate or chance).

Style

The monosyllabic words and quick lines of "We Real Cool" suggest the jabbing of pool cues and the short, fast life of the pool players. The poem is made up of four, two-line stanzas, each of which is end-rhymed. The lines also internally rhyme ("Thin gin") or alliterate ("Strike straight"). The "We" at the end of each line is not for the purpose of rhyme, but rhythm. Normally, the voice continues on or falls at the end of a line. In this poem, however, the voice falls just before the end and then rises, yielding an unusual accented syllable at the end of each line—except for the last. This is due to the repeated foot throughout the poem, the rather unusual dactyl, a three-syllable foot with the first syllable accented and the following two unaccented. A dactyl yields a falling rhythm that is evident in the poem's first three syllables: "**We** real cool." Afterward, however, the dactyl foot is bro-

Compare & Contrast

- **1955:** Emmett Till, a black fourteen-year-old, is killed by white men while visiting relatives in Money, Mississippi, because he called a white woman, "Baby."

  1998: James Byrd, a forty-nine-year-old African American, is murdered in Jasper, Texas by several whites associated with the Aryan Brotherhood and Ku Klux Klan.

- **1957:** A desegregation crisis occurs in Little Rock, Arkansas. President Eisenhower sends in the 101st Airborne to stop whites from keeping black high school students away from a formerly segregated high school

  1996: Proposition 209 passed in California, ending affirmative action at all campuses of the University of California.

  1998: At the University of California at Berkeley enrollment drops for African-American, Hispanic, and Native-American freshmen combined, from 23.1 percent in 1997 to 10.4 percent in 1998.

- **1957:** Samuel Beckett publishes *Endgame,* a bleak farce situated in a postapocalyptic landscape decimated by, presumably, nuclear weapons.

  1998: India blows up several nuclear bombs as part of what is called a "test." Pakistan answers with the same. The shows of force are part of a long-standing rivalry between India and Pakistan about territory and religion.

---

ken between the two lines of each stanza, with the accented "We" being placed on the line before. This unusual distribution suggests waltz rhythm or, if one pauses after "We," jazz syncopation—a shifting of accents to unusual positions. The rhythm of the poem suggests a burst of bravado that quickly peters out, as if the pool players boldly proclaim who they are but cannot maintain that elevated status.

Historical Context

Brooks wrote "We Real Cool" at the end of the 1950s. To many, this decade, especially the period of eight years that contained the presidential administration of Dwight Eisenhower, is remembered as being a time of bland harmony. When popular culture looks back on the 1950s, it shows us a time of prosperity and innocence that was ignorant of the explosive, independence-minded "freedom culture" that was to emerge in the 1960s. To some extent, the 1950s were a socially peaceful time. On the other hand, the 1950s brought about unprecedented forward motion in the cause of civil rights,

as local laws that had been used to keep blacks out of white social institutions were opposed by the federal government, and, in turn, the federal government was opposed by the supporters of segregation.

Although slavery had been abolished for nearly a hundred years, various laws had been enacted, particularly in the southern states, that made it impossible for African Americans to achieve equal social footing with whites. Late in the nineteenth century, a number of laws referred to as "Jim Crow" laws (after a silly, childlike Negro in an 1832 minstrel show) made it illegal for blacks and whites to ride the same trains, eat in the same restaurants, swim at the same beaches, and so on. These laws were upheld by the U.S. Supreme Court, most memorably in the case of *Plessy vs. Ferguson* in 1896, when the court ruled that it was not the federal government's place to overrule states' segregationist laws, as long as black facilities were "equal." In practice, the facilities provided to blacks were seldom very equal, since businessmen had no motivation to duplicate their best offerings for society's poorest members. In the mid-1950s, African-American resistance to the "separate but equal" doctrine began to have results.

In December of 1955, after a secretary named Rosa Parks refused to give up her seat to a white person on a bus in Montgomery, Alabama, the city's African Americans boycotted the transit system for a year, eventually winning integration and elevating local minister Martin Luther King Jr. to international attention. In 1953 *Plessy vs. Ferguson* was overturned by a new Supreme Court ruling, *Brown vs. the Board of Education of Topeka, Kansas,* which recognized that " 'separate but equal' facilities are inherently unequal." In another historic case, the president had to send army troops to Central High School in Little Rock, Arkansas, to protect nine blacks who were entering the school because the state's governor, Orval Faubus, tried using national guard troops to keep them out. Among the reasons why integration was finally able to achieve these gains were the hard work and peaceful protest methods of black organizations such as the Southern Christian Leadership Council, the National Association for the Advancement of Colored People, and the Congress of Racial Equality. Peaceful organized protests had been held before, but in the 1950s television sets became common in most American households, and people could see for themselves the passivity of the protesters and the violence that was being used against them.

Critical Overview

"We Real Cool," one of Gwendolyn Brooks's best-known poems, was written in the late 1950s and was included in her fifth book, *The Bean Eaters* (1960). In 1972, Houston Baker called the attitude of "We Real Cool" "sympathetic irony." In Brooks's autobiography, *Report from Part One,* the poet remarked that the pool players "have no pretensions to any glamor. They are supposedly dropouts, or at least they're in the poolroom when they should be possibly in school.... These are people who are essentially saying, 'Kilroy is here. We *are.*' But they're a little uncertain of the strength of their identity. The 'We'—you're supposed to stop after the 'We' and think about *validity;* of course, there's no way for you to tell whether it should be said softly or not, I suppose, but I say it rather softly because I want to represent their basic uncertainty, which they don't bother to question every day, of course." In 1976, Barbara B. Sims wrote that the lines of "We Real Cool" are short to suggest the shortness of the lives of the

pool players, and that the words "lurk," "strike," and "sin" suggest pool players who, outside the pool hall, thieve, rape, and kill. In a 1979 analysis of the work, Hortense Spillers stressed that, down to the very last line, it is the pool players who speak, implying that the poet does not actively intervene with commentary, especially in the last line. In *Gwendolyn Brooks,* the first critical volume on the poet's work, Harry B. Shaw commented, not on the shortness of lines but on the monosyllables of dialogue, which indicate to him that the youths suffer from "aborted mental growth," and are, in fact, "pitiable" and not cool at all. In an article in *The Explicator,* Gary Smith asserted that Brooks is ambivalent about the players: "To be sure, she dramatizes the tragic pathos in their lives, but she also stresses their existential freedom ...." The most extensive reading of the poem appears to by D. H. Melhem in his *Gwendolyn Brooks: Poetry and the Heroic Voice.* After detailed formal analysis, Melhem, like Smith, also remarked on the poet's ambivalence, but an ambivalence of a different sort: "... this is a maternal poem, gently scolding yet deeply sorrowing for the hopelessness of the boys."

Criticism

Joe Sarnowski

Joe Sarnowski is a doctoral candidate in English at the University of Toledo. He has written articles for The Kentucky Review *and the* Encyclopedia of American War Literature. *In the following essay, Sarnowski demonstrates how the poem can be read in two different ways—one way according to the dominant culture, another way according to the counterculture—and explains the social implications of this circumstance.*

A poem can be interpreted in many different ways—a different way for each reader. But with some poems, particularly those dealing with contentious social issues, readers tend to align themselves with one of two sides. In these cases, the poem serves as a kind of door. That is, one door has two sides: you can be on one side or the other but not both. And yet, doors are points of access through which people can move in and out. Such a poem is Gwendolyn Brooks's "We Real Cool." While there is one poem, we can see it has two opposing sides: that of the dominant culture and that of the counterculture. As with a door, the poem can be used as the dividing point between these two sides. But also like a door, the poem can be an access point whereby one side can gain some understanding of the other. So ultimately, the challenge in the poem is not to understand what it means or even to determine on which side you stand; the real challenge here is what you will do with the viewpoints the poem conveys.

In one reading, the poem functions as a subtle, ironic indictment by the dominant culture upon anyone who deviates from its norms. This viewpoint is established in the poem's epigraph: "The Pool Players. / Seven at the Golden Shovel." Such a statement isolates these seven individuals for examination, making the body of the poem the findings of this examination. And what we find, then, are people flaunting the conventions of the dominant culture, thus bringing destruction upon themselves. Or, as George E. Kent remarked in *A Life of Gwendolyn Brooks,* "the naive confrontations of youth with the ills of life will lead to their doom." Notice, for example, how the seven "Left school." This act is a violation of one of the dominant culture's primary commandments: one must complete one's formal education (how many times have we all heard, "Stay in school!"?). From here, the seven are seen to be caught in a downward spiral that leads to death.

By saying that the seven "Lurk late," the poem suggests that they are sneaking around at night, which leads to the possibility that they are engaged in criminal activities. Thus, it comes as no surprise that they also "Strike straight"—that is, that they attack people or pick fights with others. Also, by saying that they "Sing sin," the poem intimates that not only do they commit indiscretions but that they revel in their acts. This interpretation, in turn, leads members of the dominant culture to conclude that the seven have neither a sense of propriety nor a sense of shame. That they "Thin gin" reflects their abuse of alcohol—which is even more troubling when we consider that they may be underage. Just as troubling is the contention by Gary Smith, in his article for the *Explicator,* that "Jazz June" can be interpreted as a veiled reference to sexual activity or even rape ("jazz," at one time, was a common euphemism for sex, while "June" is a female name).

Thus, says the dominant culture, this behavior will result in death; the seven will "Die soon." Here, the inevitable deaths of these young people are tragedies that could have been averted if only they would have stayed in school and stayed out of trouble. Additionally, the fact that the seven always

What Do I Read Next?

- *The World of Gwendolyn Brooks* is a collection of five works: four volumes of poetry and her one novel, *Maud Martha,* all of which were written between 1945 and 1968. *Maud Martha* is about the coming of age of a black girl.

- *Soul on Ice* (1968) was written by Eldridge Cleaver, the former Black Panther minister of information and U.S. presidential candidate on the Peace and Freedom Party. Cleaver writes about the forces that shaped his life during the 1950s and 1960s.

- A seminal work in African-American literature is W. E. B. Dubois's *The Souls of Black Folk* (1969), a series of essays on what it means to be a black American.

- Frantz Fanon's *The Wretched of the Earth* (1963) was written in anger, but the book is no mere diatribe. Fanon was a black psychiatrist and leading spokesman for Algerian independence and, in this important work, he details the role of violence in one of Africa's many independence movements.

- Dudley Randall's anthology *The Black Poets* (1971) covers poetry from the 1850s to the 1960s and includes such poets as James Weldon Johnson, Langston Hughes, Amiri Baraka as well as Brooks herself.

- *Malcolm X Speaks* (1965) is a collection of the great leader's speeches and statements from 1962 to 1965, before he was killed at the age of forty.

identify themselves as "We" indicates that each one has sacrificed his or her individual identity for the sake of being part of the group. As a result, each individual has lost his or her ability to think independently or to save him- or herself. Consequently, with all of these elements considered together, when we hear the phrase, "We real cool," we hear it in a sneering or mocking way: none of these activities can be "cool" if they lead to death.

> *... [I]t is a sense of pride—of group pride— that prompts the constant use of 'We' rather than the loss of individuality, as the dominant culture maintains.*"

Of course, members of the counterculture would not view the poem in this way at all. These seven are people who, as Gary Smith says, live "in defiance of moral and social conformity and their own fate." And it is the act of defiance that gives members of the counterculture their sense of identity. That is, whatever the dominant culture says not to do, the counterculture does in order to differentiate themselves from the dominant culture. So when the seven say "We real cool" at the beginning of the poem, they are confirming their sense of identity as being separate from the dominant, uncool culture. The rest of the poem, therefore, becomes a catalogue of the acts that demonstrate their coolness—the very same acts that the dominant culture so deplores.

When the seven say they have "Left school," they have effectively expressed their rejection of the dominant culture by rejecting its formal education—the primary way by which the dominant culture recruits its members. The assumption is that people will obtain good educations, seek gainful employment, and thereby become respectable citizens. But members of the counterculture do not want to be respectable citizens (or at least not "respectable" as the dominant culture defines the term). The seven have rejected the dominant society's formal education in favor of the informal education of the pool hall and the streets. Thus, the seven confirm their counterculture status by maintaining that they "Lurk late"; as everyone knows, to have a good job and to be a respectable citizen, one cannot stay out late every night. But this is precisely what member of the counterculture chooses to do—again, in direct defiance of the dominant culture's norms. In such a reading, this act of staying out late need not be indicative of criminal activity, so neither does the phrase, "Strike straight."

Taken literally, the phrase may mean that the seven do not shrink back when threatened but react directly. Or taken metaphorically, the phrase may mean that the seven take immediately to whatever pleasures present themselves. Such pleasures of course are intimated in the phrase "Sing sin." Here, the seven do not repress the pleasures of life (as do, presumedly, members of the dominant society) but revel in them. Along these lines, that they "Thin gin" certainly indicates seeking pleasure in alcohol. Yet, by virtue of the fact that they "Thin" the beverage, it seems less likely that they are abusing it and more of an indication of playful mischief. When reading from this point of view, the meaning of "Jazz June" is not likely to refer to something as stark as rape; rather, as D. H. Melhem contends in *Gwendolyn Brooks: Poetry and the Heroic Voice,* the "usage pertains to 'having fun.'" And when we consider together all of these phrases made by the seven, it is this idea of "having fun" that comes to mind.

With this notion of "having fun" as the prime concern of the counterculture, it is difficult to read the final sentence, "We / Die soon," as being a tragic declaration (as the dominant culture does). Instead, the seven seem to say that life is too short: that we all die too soon, so why not enjoy life while one has it? And even if the phrase does refer to the deaths of the young, this statement represents the ultimate defiance, the ultimate fearlessness. To face death without fear or regret is indicative of great pride—an admirable pride rather a vain pride. Additionally, it is a sense of pride—of group pride— that prompts the constant use of "We" rather than the loss of individuality, as the dominant culture maintains. (In any event, the counterculture would state, there is no greater loss of individuality than in compliance with the dominant culture.) Consequently, with all of these elements of this viewpoint considered together, we can perceive a different impression of the counterculture than the dominant culture offers. Instead of posing a threat to the dominant culture, the poem seems to contend, the counterculture merely regards a different set of values.

So, what can we conclude from this poem with its two, diametrically opposed points of view? Of course, the easy thing to do is to take one side or the other and, like a door, use the poem as a marker of division ("I'm not like those people!"). Yet, to do so is to contribute to the divisiveness that ultimately strangles us all. Instead, are you able— again, like a door—to use the poem as a point of access to understanding something about the opposing point of view? That is, if you find yourself agreeing with the dominant culture, can you begin to understand how some people can live for the moment? Or if you find yourself agreeing with the counterculture, can you begin to understand how there are limitations in living for the moment and advantages to becoming a respectable member of society? This is not to say that you must agree with what the other side thinks, but it does mean you have to be willing to make the effort to understand why other people value what they do. For only if people on both sides are willing to try to understand each other will communication between these sides be possible. And then maybe, just maybe, some barriers can be broken down. Gwendolyn Brooks has given you this poem, this door: you can either close it and walk away, or you can open it and walk through. What will you do now?

Source: Joe Sarnowski, in an essay for *Poetry for Students,* The Gale Group, 1999.

Sources

Donaldson, Gary, *Abundance and Anxiety: America, 1945-1960,* Westport, CT: Praeger, 1997.

Kent, George, E., *A Life of Gwendolyn Brooks,* Lexington: University Press of Kentucky, 1990.

Melhem, D. H., *Gwendolyn Brooks: Poetry and the Heroic Voice,* Lexington: University Press of Kentucky, 1987.

Mootry, Maria K., and Gary Smith, eds., *A Life Distilled: Gwendolyn Brooks, Her Poetry and Fiction,* Urbana: University of Illinois Press, 1987.

O'Neill, William O., *American High: The Years of Confidence, 1945-1960,* New York: The Free Press, 1986.

Shaw, Harry B., *Gwendolyn Brooks,* Boston: Twayne Publishers, 1980.

Smith, Gary, "Brooks's 'We Real Cool,'" *The Explicator* Vol. 43, No. 2, Winter 1985, pp. 49-50.

Wright, Stephen Caldwell, *On Gwendolyn Brooks: Reliant Contemplation,* Ann Arbor: University of Michigan Press, 1996.

For Further Study

Adams, Olive Arnold, *Mississippi Exposed and the Full Story of Emmett Till,* The Mississippi Regional Council of Negro Leadership, 1956.

> The story of Emmett Till, a black fourteen-year-old who was killed by whites for calling a white woman, "Baby," is an important one in civil rights history. It is said that the story had a profound effect on Gwendolyn Brooks.

Albert, Judith Clavir, and Stewart Edward Albert, eds., *The Sixties Papers: Documents of a Rebellious Decade,* New York: Praeger, 1984.

> This anthology consists of essays by the leading lights (Mills, Ginsburg, Malcolm X, etc.,) and on the leading struggles (antiwar, counterculture, feminist) of the 1960s. The volume is introduced by an overview of the 1950s.

Burk, Robert Fredrick, *The Eisenhower Administration and Black Civil Rights,* Knoxville: University of Tennessee Press, 1984.

> Burk exposes the government's failures regarding civil rights.

Goldman, Eric F., *The Crucial Decade: America, 1945-55,* New York: Alfred A. Knopf, 1956.

> Goldman's history includes material on Truman's presidency, the end of World War II, the onset of the Cold War, the Korean War, and the Eisenhower Era of Equilibrium.

Williams, Juan, *Eyes on the Prize: America's Civil Rights Years, 1954-65,* New York: Penguin, 1987.

> For a history heavily informed by those who participated in the civil rights struggle, this anthology can't be beat. Not only does the volume include time lines, quotes, and photos, but there is an excellent PBS companion video series.

The Wood-Pile

Robert Frost

1914

"The Wood-Pile" was originally published in 1914 in *North of Boston,* which was Robert Frost's second book of verse and the one that developed the author's distinctive character—that of a New England country gentleman. The poem is probably not one of the top five most-discussed poems of Robert Frost, but it surely is in the top ten, and out of the hundreds of poems produced during a career that spanned fifty years, that is a distinction. It was written, according to Frost, in Derry, New Hampshire, where he lived as a farmer and schoolteacher before any of his poems were published. Like his other poems written during this period, "The Wood-Pile" deals with nature and loneliness, and it implies a greater overall purpose in the world that cannot be directly explained, only felt. What is distinct about Frost's early poems is the eerie sense of life's isolation. In "The Wood-Pile" the speaker is out in the cold wooded country, with nature, represented by the small bird, being wary of the speaker, and the speaker uneasy to suddenly realize himself to be far from home, with his feet falling through the hard snow.

Author Biography

Robert Frost was born in 1874 and lived in New England for practically his entire life. He was co-valedictorian of his high-school class along with Elinor White, whom he married three years later (their marriage lasting until her death fifty-three years later). Frost attended Dartmouth College in 1892, but dropped out after two months; he also attended Harvard between 1897 and 1899, but he never graduated from there, either. From 1900 to 1912, he lived on a farm on Derry, New Hampshire, that his grandfather had brought for him, raising chickens and sometimes teaching at the local secondary school. In 1912, at the age of thirty-eight, he committed one of legendary acts in the annals of American poetry: he sold the farm and moved with his wife and four children to Beaconsfield, Buckinghamshire, near London, in order to pursue a literary career. The move turned out to be a wise one. In England he made the acquaintances of a number of writers, including Edward Thomas, Lascelles Abercrombie, and Ezra Pound. He also presented the poems he had written in New Hampshire to David Nutt and Company in London; the company agreed to print them, and in 1913 *A Boy's Will* was published to favorable reviews. *North of Boston,* which includes "The Wood-Pile," was published in England in 1914 and in the United States in 1915. It was this book that established Frost as a New England poet and introduced him to American audiences.

When World War I broke out in England, Frost and his family returned to the United States, where he was received by publishers and magazine editors who had previously rejected his work. He was invited to speak to literary clubs and was introduced to influential poets and critics. The publication of *Mountain Interval* in 1916 and *New Hampshire* in 1923 helped to solidify Frost's reputation as one of the most original and important poets of his era. *New Hampshire* won the Pulitzer Prize, as did *Collected Poems* (1930) and *A Witness Tree* (1943). Frost received numerous other awards during his long and productive career. Among the most notable were the Congressional Gold Medal and a mountain in Ripton, Vermont, that was named "Robert Frost Mountain" by a state legislative act. He read a famous poem at the inaugural of President John F. Kennedy in 1961, and Kennedy later sent him on a goodwill mission to meet with Nikita Khrushchev, the leader of the Soviet Union, at a time when diplomatic relations between the two countries were at their worst. Frost was eighty-seven at the time of the trip. Soon after returning from Russia, Frost was operated on for prostrate problems. He died in January of 1963.

Robert Frost

Poem Text

Out walking in the frozen swamp one gray day,
I paused and said, 'I will turn back from here.
No, I will go on farther—and we shall see.'
The hard snow held me, save where now and then
One foot went down. The view was all in lines   5
Straight up and down of tall slim trees
Too much alike to mark or name a place by
So as to say for certain I was here
Or somewhere else: I was just far from home.
A small bird flew before me. He was careful   10
To put a tree between us when he lighted,
And say no word to tell me who he was
Who was so foolish as to think what *he* thought.
He thought that I was after him for a feather—
The white one in his tail; like one who takes   15
Everything said as personal to himself.
One flight out sideways would have undeceived
    him.
And then there was a pile of wood for which
I forgot him and let his little fear
Carry him off the way I might have gone,   20
Without so much as wishing him good-night.
He went behind it to make his last stand.
It was a cord of maple, cut and split
And piled—and measured, four by four by eight.
And not another like it could I see.   25
No runner tracks in this year's snow looped near it.
And it was older sure than this year's cutting,
Or even last year's or the year's before.
The wood was gray and the bark warping off it
And the pile somewhat sunken. Clematis   30

Had wound strings round and round it like a
   bundle.
What held it though on one side was a tree
Still growing, and on one a stake and prop,
These latter about to fall. I thought that only   35
Someone who lived in turning to fresh tasks
Could so forget his handiwork on which
He spent himself, the labour of his axe,
And leave it there far from a useful fireplace
To warm the frozen swamp as best it could
With the slow smokeless burning of decay.   40

Poem Summary

Lines 1-3:

The opening lines of "The Wood-Pile" establish the speaker as a person who is taking a walk through a frozen swamp. Although it is not explicitly said, there are a few things about this person that are evident from the situation. For instance, this seems to be a contemplative person, the sort of person who would take a walk without having a clear goal in mind. He decides to stop, but then changes his mind; clearly, where he ends up is not so important to this stroll as the act of walking itself. It is not clear whether this is a person who is so lost in thought that his surroundings do not matter, or if he is the sort of person who can appreciate the sublime beauty of a frozen swamp on a gray day, but the setting is certainly not one of traditional beauty. An interesting facet of his personality is revealed by his use of the plural pronoun in the third line. "We shall see" is a common twist of language for a simple, plainspoken person, but in this poem it implies that the speaker, though he walks alone, thinks of himself as being bound to some greater being—perhaps nature or God.

Lines 4-9:

There is a sense of danger implied within these lines, starting with just a small hint that all is not well and growing into an irrational fear that is barely mentioned, yet present. This section starts with a declaration of faith, that the speaker is secure walking on top of the hard snow, but it immediately brings up exceptions to that rule. The phrase "now and then" in line 4 indicates both some degree of frequency—it has happened several times—and also that the speaker is trying to minimize the importance of falling through the snow by mentioning it in casual terms. It may not be a dangerous situation, but the idea of instability, of the ground not holding beneath one's feet, adds a touch

of insecurity to the mood of the poem. This section goes on to say that the speaker is not sure where he is because the terrain lacks character. The trees all look alike and stand similarly, tall and in rows, facing him with cold and impersonal efficiency. The only thing he says about the situation defines it negatively: this environment is not friendly enough for him to feel at home, and he is quite aware that the place where he does feel at home is far away. "Home" is a continuing theme in Frost's poetry, especially in the poems of *North of Boston*. One of his most famous lines, from "The Death of The Hired Man," is, "Home is the place where, when you have to go there, they have to take you in." Nothing more is said about home in this poem, but the fact that it is on the speaker's mind explains the cautious tone that is used throughout.

Lines 10-13:

The bird is introduced in these lines, and its character is defined. Line 10 says that the bird was "careful"; this is an example of anthropomorphism, of seeing human qualities in nonhuman things. After calling the bird "careful," the speaker goes on to ascribe a complex thought process to it, making it secretive and self-conscious. After the straightforward simplicity of the rows of identical trees, the bird's entry adds some confusion to the poem, especially in lines 11 to 13, where the abundance of prepositions twists the language into knots, forcing the reader to think carefully about who is doing what. Considering that the flow of the thought changes direction with every "to," "when," "who," and "what," and that these four words appear a total of seven times in three lines, it is almost impossible to understand the basic meaning of this part of the poem after reading it through only once. What it says is that the bird is foolish for distrusting the man (he was "so foolish as to think what he thought"), but, being that distrustful, he would not let the man hear the bird song that might identify him (he would "say no word to tell me who he was"). The bird probably thinks that the man is a hunter, if it thinks at all. More likely, it is a bird that has survived by staying away from people, and the author is just projecting this whole thought process onto it.

Lines 14-17:

Having already identified the threat that the bird perceives from him, the speaker then proceeds to minimize the danger that he might pose. Rather than supposing that the bird might fear being shot, he phrases the hunter's attack as the stealing of a tail-feather. With good humor, but somewhat patronizingly and, ironically, very blind to the way the bird would see such a fearful situation, he gently mocks it for being too self-centered, for thinking that the whole world would be interested in its feathers. The irony is that it is the man who is thinking these thoughts who deems the bird paranoid for thinking about him so much. Part of the beauty of the understated psychology in Frost's work is that it allows his poems to be vain while thinking about vanity, but even in their vanity they still fit into the vast natural world.

Lines 18-22:

This section brings an end to the brief drama with the bird: it flies off "the way I might have gone," indicating that the speaker might have gone on thinking about the psychological struggle between them if he had not had his attention drawn instead to the wood-pile. As indicated by the change of plan in line 3, this speaker is a person who has the leisure and the curiosity to follow whatever path his imagination may lead him down. His imagination is impartial enough to be drawn to the mundane as much as to the exotic, to focus on a pile of rotting wood over a quirky white-feathered bird. He still sees the bird as being motivated by fear, and it is fear that carries it out of the poem, although it does show an inkling of courage by going behind the wood-pile "to make his last stand." Here again the little bird plays a comic foil to the narrator; it prepares for some mortal confrontation while the man has moved on in his thoughts and forgotten about it. While the bird braces itself, the man points out, in line 21, that their rivalry was all a game in his mind—that he would have wished the bird a good night if he had not been thinking about the pile of wood.

Lines 23-26:

These four lines give the reader a visual impression of the scene, showing what the poem's speaker saw before his imagination had a chance to dig into the details and start wondering what it all meant. At first, the information in line 24 seems redundant—a mere repetition of what has already been told: a cord of wood is a pile that measures four feet by four feet by eight. Not until later in the poem, when readers find out that the wood is lying on the ground and propped against a tree, does it becomes apparent that repetition was important because it emphasized that the person who left the wood followed the standards for measuring an official cord. A cord is not a small amount of wood,

Media Adaptations

- *An Introduction to Robert Frost's Poetry,* a video cassette narrated by Helen Vendler, is available from Omnigraphics.

- Susan Anspach and Carl Reiner perform on an audio cassette titled *Poetry of Robert Frost,* released by Dove Audio in 1996.

- As part of their Poetry America Series, AIMS Media offers a video cassette titled *Robert Frost.*

- *Robert Frost—1958 Interview* is available on video cassette from Zenger Video.

but neither is it a large amount—at least not the kind of cache that one would travel far to reach. This is why the narrator takes a moment to note that there is not another pile near it. Its relative uselessness is confirmed by the evidence that no one has come out for the wood this winter.

Lines 27-31:

In his enthusiasm about figuring out how old the wood-pile is and what it is doing in the woods, the speaker slips from his bland, emotionless tone into a New England rural dialect in line 27. "It was older sure" is not proper grammar, but the speaker is too preoccupied to be concerned about that. This is someone who can tell the age of cut wood by sight, as many country people in cold climates (where firewood was crucial) probably could. The fact that the narrator and the culture in which he lives take firewood so seriously is not just an interesting fact; it underscores how strange it is— what an infraction it is—that someone would bundle perfectly good wood in a place and then never use it. "Clematis," mentioned in line 30, is a creeping vine that grows flowers. By using the simile "wound strings round ... it like a bundle," the poem is furthering the theme of cooperation between man and nature. Some anonymous person has cut, measured, and stacked the wood, and the vines do their part by binding it together.

Lines 32-40:

In this last section, the speaker reveals what made this experience memorable enough to be recorded in verse. This section starts with the image of the old wood being propped between a clumsy stake on one side and a live tree on the other, indicating that it is a work both of man and of nature. Line 33 makes a point of mentioning that the tree is "still growing," which, coming after the detailed description of the cut wood's decay in lines 27 to 29, implies the wastefulness of the dead wood. Lines 33 through 37, however, turn that wastefulness into a virtue; they shift the emphasis away from the time and energy squandered on the task and turn the reader's attention to the fact that the anonymous stranger must have had a full and busy life if he was distracted after doing all of this work. In one sense, the conclusion seems a bit optimistic: after all, why assume that he is "turning to fresh tasks" when there could be more ominous reasons for his failure to return to the site? On the other hand, this assumption fits in perfectly with the rest of the poem, ascribing to the stranger the curiosity and lack of concentration that have already been seen in both the speaker and the bird. In the end, the effort is not presented as having been wasted at all, since the decaying wood is expending its energy back into the frozen swamp—into the tree at whose base it sits. Thus, the axeman's effort does not result in personal gain, but it benefits nature.

Themes

Cycle of Life

The image that ends this poem, that of the wood-pile warming the swamp "with the slow smokeless burning of decay," brings to mind the idea that life is, on a basic biological level, cyclical, with the decaying remains of those that die going back into the cycle and feeding new life with their spent nutrients. To farmers, there is nothing deep or revolutionary about this idea. Decaying animal and plant matter has been put on crops as fertilizer for as long as people have been farming, roughly 10,000 years. The idea has wider implications, however, when it is taken out of the narrow scope of organic chemistry and applied to poetic concepts. If, for instance, it were actions and thoughts, instead of molecules, that transferred to the living from the dead, then life would be meaningful even when no evidence of success or failure

existed. Many works of literature use this concept to make the meaningless seem meaningful by showing a life that is affected through indirect means by another that is unrelated. In this poem, the apparent futility of someone having taken the time to cut and stack wood out in the middle of a swamp is given meaning when it is explained that the swamp will benefit from it. The phrase "far from a useful fireplace" can be seen as ironic, because the wood does have a use and, since decay is called "burning," it is in a fireplace. Before the image of the wood-pile is introduced into the poem, though, life for the narrator seems to be linear, not cyclical. Early on, he has the idea to circle around and go back where he came from, but he decides to push ahead, to go where he has not gone before. He is not even sure what he is looking for, but he is looking for something; this is implied when he says "We shall see." It is the speaker's realization of the cycle of life at poem's end—of the fact that dead and discarded things are still serving a purpose—that gives him a sense of meaning that is missing from the beginning.

Return to Nature

Nature is not presented as a welcoming environment in the beginning of "The Wood-Pile." It is impassive at first, cold and undistinguished, with rows of trees that all look like one another to the observer. With the introduction of the small bird, the narrator feels himself to be observed, judged as a threat, and feared. The poem is fairly clear about the fact that the thoughts attributed to the bird are actually thoughts that the speaker dares not see in himself, especially in lines 14 through 16, which supply the bird with the following thought: "He thought I was after him … like one who takes everything said as personal to himself." The bird would have no interest in the man except for wanting to know how the man will affect his life, and animals do not have the ego to take things "personal"—that is strictly a human psychological trait. If the phrase is actually meant to reflect back upon the man, this extreme self-consciousness might indicate his uneasiness in a natural environment and his awareness that he is, as line 9 points out, far from home. He learns something within the course of this poem about the coexistence of man and nature. It might be that the cooperation of the woodchopper's neat stacking with the Clematis vine's wrapping has helped him bridge the gap between man and nature in his mind, or that his realization, in line 36, about the laborer's "forgetfulness" helps him forget about his human concerns and accept his place in the natural world. Whatever the reason, by the end of the poem the frozen swamp seems like a big open fireplace to him, and the fireplace, the hearth, is a universal symbol of home.

Fear

When, at the midpoint of the "The Wood-Pile," the bird is carried off by "his little fear," the narrator loses his own uncertainty. From the very start he has been uneasy about his trip; no sooner does he mention (in line 4) that he was able to walk across the hard snow than he adds that it is not entirely sturdy—that a foot fell through now and then. He refers to being not just away from home, but "far from home." The bird itself does not seem like a friendly companion, because it approaches him like an adversary. Something in the way that they relate either makes the bird prepare for his "last stand" or makes the poem's speaker feel that he should prepare for his own. Whatever the cause of his fear—whether it is an uneasiness about nature's callousness, loneliness, or suspicion that he is a fool for what he thinks—it seems to lessen when he decides that the person who left the wood must be "Someone who lived in turning to fresh tasks." This poem speaks with Robert Frost's customary dry, factual, slightly bemused voice, but there is an un-

easiness about it—an uncertainty that borders on fear—that needs the example of someone with a purpose to calm it.

Style

Like much of Frost's poetry, "The Wood-Pile" is written in blank verse, or unrhymed iambic pentameter. Each line has five feet of one unstressed and one stressed syllable each, although the order of the stresses and the number of feet occasionally vary. (For instance, line 14 in "The Wood-Pile" has six feet.) Frost used blank verse in his poetry because he was trying to capture what he called "the sound of sense," or the natural rhythms of actual speaking voices. The blank verse in "The Wood-Pile" reflects Frost's character and setting: a solitary figure in a rural landscape. The narrator's voice does not sound traditionally "poetic" but is more homely and vernacular.

Historical Context

Although Frost said that "The Wood-Pile," or at least part of it, was written before he left the United States for England in 1912, the book that it was published in and that built his reputation—*North of Boston*—was published in America in 1914. Frost's stay in England was fruitful in that it marked the birth of the poet's career, but a global crisis prompted him to leave the country and return to the United States.

World War I started in 1914, ushering in a new era of modern warfare of a greater scale and with more savage weaponry than had ever been known before. Like many previous wars, the war started as a localized territorial dispute, but its scope blossomed to global proportions due to alliances between countries: as one nation was dragged into the conflict, its allies were obliged to join too, and the allies of each one of them were then required to join along. At the center of the conflict were two main alliances: the Triple Entente of Germany, Italy, and Austria-Hungary, and the Triple Alliance of France, Great Britain, and Russia. Trouble had been brewing for decades in the area along the Adriatic Sea, where the Austro-Hungarian Empire, the Ottoman Empire, and Russia each had some influence, which they wanted to expand into control. Serbia, which was under the rule of Austria-Hun-

Compare & Contrast

- **1914:** Advertising writer W. B. Laughhead, designing pamphlets to promote the Red River Lumber Co. of Minneapolis, invents the legend of Paul Bunyan and his blue ox named Babe.

  Today: Many people think that the legend of Paul Bunyan is a folk story that grew up among lumberjacks.

- **1914:** The term "birth control" was introduced by feminist Margaret Higgins Sanger, who had to leave the country to avoid federal prosecution for publishing and mailing *Family Limitation,* a brochure dealing with contraception.

  Today: After records show rising birthrates, especially among teenagers, birth control is taught in schools and promoted in public advertising.

- **1914:** After Archduke Franz Ferdinand, heir to the Austria-Hungarian throne, was assassinated in Sarajevo, the nations of Europe lined up in a war that eventually involved almost all civilized countries on the planet.

  1996: The Dayton Peace Accord ends four years of open warfare in the former Yugoslavia. Sarajevo, which withstood a 1,395-day siege, becomes the united capital of Bosnia and Herzegovina. During the conflict, more than 10,000 people were killed in Sarajevo.

- **1914:** President Woodrow Wilson signed the declaration that established the second Sunday of each May as national Mother's Day.

  Today: For businesses such as florists and interstate telephone services, Mother's Day is the busiest day of the year.

- **1914:** Threatened by the prospect of strikes, Ford Motor Company raised the minimum wage of their workers to $5 per day—a rate more than twice the average U.S. wage.

  1998: According to a UAW report, Ford Motor Company paid union members an average of $22.97 an hour in wages in 1997.

---

gary, had many separatists who wanted to align with one of the other empires and still more who wanted the country to be a free, independent state. On June 28, 1914, the heir to the throne of the Austria-Hungary empire, Archduke Franz Ferdinand, made a ceremonial visit to the Serbian capital of Sarajevo: his car was stopped, and he and his wife were shot to death.

The Serbian government's official explanation was that the assassination was the work of renegade terrorists, but the Austro-Hungarian Empire claimed that the Serbs had supported the killing in a bid for independence. It is not clear even today whether the Serbian government actually did support the separatist movement (called the Black Hand) that had provided the gun for the assassins. Nor is it known if the Austro-Hungarians actually believed that the Serbian government was in any way involved in the killing, or if they just used this charge as an excuse to assert their control over the country—to intimidate both separatists and the other federations that were interested in having Ser-

bia join them. The Austro-Hungarians issued a list of demands to Serbia, saying that they were needed for security purposes. The Serbs, however, balked at the order to let Austro-Hungarian troops search their houses for suspected terrorists. The Austro-Hungarian empire declared war against Serbia on July 28th. Within a few months, most of the 32 nations that would eventually join the conflict were already involved. Russia had an agreement to help Serbia, and so they joined the fight against Austria-Hungary immediately; Germany had a deal with the Austro-Hungarians, and they wanted to weaken Russia, so they attacked Russia and her ally France; Germany's invasion of Belgium brought Great Britain into the war. Countries off of the European continent, such as Egypt, Japan, and Canada became involved too. One country that initially stayed out of the conflict was the United States. Many Americans considered it a European problem, and few wanted their sons and brothers to die for something so abstract. President Woodrow Wilson won reelection in 1916 by promoting himself as the man who had kept America out of the war. Nonetheless, the United States was drawn into the war in April of 1917. In the end, it was the boost provided by U.S. troops and armaments that helped the Allies claim victory; World War I ended a year later, in 1918.

Critical Overview

From the very start of his literary career, Frost enjoyed that rare combination that all writers strive for: popularity and critical success. (The fact that he was a charming and likable person did not hurt his cause either.) His first collection of poetry, *A Boy's Will,* was received with delight and wonder that a poet with such talent could suddenly appear on the horizon. An unsigned review in *Academy and Literature* concluded with, "We have not the slightest idea who Mr. Robert Frost may be, but we welcome him unhesitatingly to the ranks of the poets born, and are convinced that if this is a true sample of his parts he should presently give us work far worthier of honour than much which passes for front-rank poetry at the present time." Having made his entry into "the ranks of the poets born," Frost was able to have his second book, *North of Boston* (in which "The Wood-Pile" appears), taken seriously on both sides of the Atlantic Ocean. Ezra Pound, with whom Frost had developed a friendship in England, reviewed the book in *Poetry,* explaining what was so good about this unfamiliar style: "Mr. Frost's work is not 'accomplished,' but it is the work of a man who will make neither concessions nor pretenses. He will perform no money-tricks. His stuff sticks in your head—not his words, nor his phrases, nor his cadences, but his subject matter." Amy Lowell, who was an acquaintance of Pound's but who did not meet Frost until after he visited to thank her for her glowing review, wrote in *The New Republic* that he "tells you what he has seen *exactly* as he has seen it. And in the word *exactly* lies the half of his talent. The other half is a great and beautiful simplicity of phrase ...." Lowell added, "He goes his own way, regardless of anyone else's rules, and the result is a book of unusual power and sincerity."

Having quickly established his place in the realm of American poetry, Frost was, amazingly, able to hold onto it for the next fifty years. One reason was that after 1938, when he was widowed after his wife's death, he did not produce much poetry, although he did remain active in the field, giving lectures and eventually acting as a goodwill am-

bassador for the U.S. government. With no new works to consider, and with his obvious social prestige, critics focused their attention on the *idea* of Robert Frost more than his works. Many of the subsequent articles written about him were favorable, wondering why poets were not taking chances and developing original styles like he did. One notable exception came from renowned critic Malcolm Cowley, who printed a piece in *The New Republic* in 1944 titled "The Case Against Mr. Frost." Despite the wording of his title, his case was a minor one—that Frost's philosophical range was too narrow, and that homey little tales of rustic Yankees are limited in their usefulness. "In spite of his achievements as a narrative and lyric poet ... there is a case against Robert Frost as a social philosopher in verse and as a representative of the New England Tradition," Cowley wrote. "He is too much walled in by the past." This assessment is representative of the type of minor complaints that critics labored to dredge up during the poet's long and distinguished career.

Criticism

Bruce Meyer

Bruce Meyer is the director of the creative writing program at the University of Toronto. He has taught at several Canadian universities and is the author of three collections of poetry. In the following essay, Meyer describes "The Wood-Pile" as "a study in the relationship between art and nature."

Like many of the poems in Robert Frost's 1914 collection, *North of Boston,* "The Wood-Pile" is set in winter and deals with the narration of a mind as it goes through the process of decision and indecision. Frost sees that the processes of the mind are a binary system where even the slightest choice or determination is weighed and balanced. "I will turn back from here. / No, I will go on farther," is suggestive not of hesitancy but of understanding. The persona is on a journey not simply through the woods but through his own epistemology. The journey itself, even the insignificant act of walking through the woods on "hard snow" that "held me," is a metaphor for the discovery of the unexpected and the ways in which that discovery is comprehended.

As a poem, "The Wood-Pile" is structured like many of Frost's narrative poems. It tells a story that appears simple on the surface yet belies some com-

"… [T]he final lines of Frost's poem do embrace the type of paradox of both comprehension and apprehension that is characteristic of the elegiac voice."

plex observations and ideas beneath the gauze of seemingly insignificant events. Frost loves this kind of deception. For him, the poem is a mask for truths, a way in which commonplace events of life contain elements of much larger themes and issues. "The Wood-Pile" depicts someone walking through the woods on a winter evening and discovering a pile of maple cords somebody else has chopped and left in the middle of nowhere. The ambiguousness of this gesture—of leaving a record of labor abandoned both in space and time—presents an anomaly that triggers a whole range of speculations. The goal of the poem is not to tell a story for the reader's edification, but to show the reader how the process of mental discovery works in the mind of a persona who details and chronicles every motion of thought and observation within the experience.

In some respects, "The Wood-Pile" is a "stream-of-consciousness" narrative. In such a story, the structural intent of the descriptions is to portray the way in which thoughts are connected and to show a mind at work. In the case of this poem, the narrative is not carried through physical action but through the mental dynamics of the persona/narrator who records the processes of comprehension and apprehension. Along the way, there are various markers of observation noted by the persona. The first is the arrangement of the trees. "The view," he notes, "was all in lines / Straight up and down of tall slim trees / Too much alike to mark or name a place by / So as to say for certain I was here / Or somewhere else …" The very placelessness of the location, the indistinctiveness of the setting, shifts the reader's attention to the inner world of the poem—to the landscape of the persona's mind. This sense of both an inner narration and an inner world is further enhanced by the presence of the small bird who becomes, momentarily,

an external distraction. But as often happens in Frost's poems, the external observation gives way to the speculations of inner narrative; the persona starts "to think what he [the bird] thought," so that—quite literally—"Everything" is "said as personal to himself." What is often a key element in a stream-of-consciousness narrative is the assimilation of the outer world to the inner, a place where events, ideas, and perceptions blend to form not just a story but the process behind the making of a story. The problem is that the actual wood pile the persona discovers is an ambiguity, an anomaly in the landscape that cannot be explained.

The "cord of maple, cut and split / And piled" has no plausible explanation. Its discovery is the result of the bird darting behind it for protection from the observer, and in a moment, after a brief period of detailed observation, it is suddenly recognized as an absurdity. The persona questions why someone would leave it there "far from a useful fireplace." The relationship between the labor-intensive act of chopping a tree and cording it for firewood and its pointless location, seemingly forgotten, troubles the narrator. The utilitarian-minded Frost is struck by the artifice and effort that went into the act of creating the wood pile, yet is confronted by the paradox of the "slow smokeless burning of decay" and the waste of both effort and fuel.

Jeffrey Meyers, in his *Robert Frost: A Biography* (1996), draws a parallel between the final two lines of "The Wood-Pile" and the final line of Thomas Gray's "Elegy" ("They kept the noiseless tenor of their way"). Although "The Wood-Pile" is far from being an elegy (there is no serious sense of loss, grief, or lamentation), the final lines of Frost's poem do embrace the type of paradox of both comprehension and apprehension that is characteristic of the elegiac voice. The wood warms "the frozen swamp as best it could." The contradiction at the heart of this perception is not simply wastefulness but the realization that the world can present one with moments of purposelessness where an object or a situation suggests a lack of fulfillment, a turning-away from intent. This, Frost finds troubling. So what does it mean?

The setting seems to be the key to the answer. The poem, like one Frost would write nine years later, "Stopping by Woods on a Snowy Evening," locates the persona in the waste landscape of winter. For Frost, the winter landscape is nature's own anomaly, a contradiction of the driving life force that lies behind the seasons, a time when the absence of life is both a troubling sign of seasonal death and a signal of mortality for the beholder. In "After Apple-Picking" (1914), another poem from *North of Boston,* Frost concludes the poem with the realization that after the labor of life there is the disconcerting prospect of "This sleep of mine, what sleep it is." Like Hamlet in the famous "To be or not to be" speech of Act II, Scene ii, death contains the prospect of misapprehension—"To sleep—perchance to dream: ay there's the rub." For Frost in "The Wood-Pile," the abandoned artifice and effort that went into the cutting of the tree, the chopping of the cords, and the building of the pile is a signal of how happenstance, death, and the unexpected can enter the world and make a folly of human endeavor. "I thought that only / Someone who lived in turning to fresh tasks / Could so forget his handiwork on which / He spent himself, the labor of his ax," is a supposition that the hand that built the pile has turned his efforts to other endeavors. But the narrator has no proof of that, and the speculation of the life behind the work being redirected to other ends is a wish for some sign of poetic justice in a world where death is the ultimate distraction from both concentration and purpose.

What underlies "The Wood-Pile" is the problem of distractions. The trees are a distraction because they signal a lack of a defined place. The bird is a distraction from the trees, and the wood pile a distraction from the bird. The final distraction is the purposelessness of the pile itself, and, "knowing how way leads on to way" (as Frost says in "The Road Not Taken"), the lack of resolution either to thought or to action is, in itself, a problematic condition imposed upon the human experience. Art, poetry, and even wood cutting suggest an inherent desire for resolution; yet that resolution is missing from "The Wood-Pile," and if the purpose of art and poetry is to improve or reform the world as we know it, then that resolution must be present not only in narrative but in nature. The poet in Frost hopes this is so—that the power of the mind can impose purpose where there is none. But if that mind is distracted, the net result is a failure of art, and failure in art is tantamount to tragedy. Much like Hamlet's struggle to make up his mind or resolve himself to a purpose, the inner debate of the persona in the opening lines of "The Wood-Pile" shows how fragile intent, purpose, and resolution can be. The line between poetic justice (the desired resolution of a narrative or an extended action) and tragedy (the failure to achieve a reasonable resolution to the narrative) is a fine one indeed. The winding "Clematis" that ties the pile into a neat bundle

What Do I Read Next?

- The collection in which "The Wood-Pile" originally appeared, *North of Boston,* was released in an expanded edition in 1977, with illustrations and the addition of thirteen more of his poems that had appeared in other books during Frost's lifetime.

- The main purpose of a literary biography is to draw connections between the writer's life and the elements that are on display in his work. Biography and criticism are brought together smoothly and comprehensively in William H. Pritchard's 1984 study, *Frost: A Literary Life Reconsidered.*

- Essays about Frost and interviews with him constitute a large section of John Ciardi's collection of magazine pieces called *Dialogue with an Audience.* Ciardi was poetry editor of the *Saturday Review* for a long time, and his articles, even when they are not about Frost, are worth reading for their insight and compassion.

- The authorized biography of Robert Frost was written by his lifelong friend Lawrence Thompson and issued in three parts: *Robert Frost: The Early Years, 1874-1915, Robert Frost: The Years of Triumph, 1915-1938* and *Robert Frost: The Later Years, 1938-1963.*

- A very interesting study of the way that the human mind processes poetry used Robert Frost's works as an example. Norman M. Holland's *The Brain of Robert Frost,* published in 1988 by Routledge Press, uses its science-fiction-like title to draw readers into a discussion of the deeper mysteries of the psychology of creativity.

is a metaphor for nature's indifference to the human need for resolution and suggests that what we perceive as organic design is merely happenstance. Nature, Frosts suggests, is not a binary system of either/or, but an endless cycle of life and death. The conflict between man and nature that recurs so often in Frost's poetry is really the battle between the human desire for purpose, resolution, and enduring, life-sustaining poetic justice and nature's own agenda of cyclical life, death, and decay. "The Wood-Pile," therefore, is a study in the relationship between art and nature.

Source: Bruce Meyer, in an essay for *Poetry for Students,* The Gale Group, 1999.

David Kelly

David Kelly is an instructor of creative writing and literature at several community colleges in Illinois. In the following essay, Kelly argues that the core of Frost's appeal is his ability to equally respect both sides of an issue: in the case of "The Wood-Pile," this means recognizing both the desire to have more leisure time and the fear of being too free.

I think that the appeal of "The Wood-Pile," and of many of Robert Frost's most popular works, is that he manages to stay poised between action and inaction, and in an uncertain world of increasingly unforeseeable consequences, that is not a bad place to be. Consider, for instance, one of his most popular and heavily anthologized works, "The Road Not Taken." Somewhere, probably in the antiauthoritarian 1960s, the poem developed a reputation for being in favor of individualism—for telling readers to forget about popularity, to not be afraid, and to follow their instincts, wherever that may lead them. These are fine sentiments that I would like to believe, but, unfortunately, there is nothing about any sort of inner voice in the poem. In fact, the poem never tells us, even after the intense pondering that goes on at the crossroads, what the outcome of its speaker's choice is going to be: it only says that things turn out differently if you go down one road than they will if you go down another. There is something in Frost's elegant, quiet language that drives readers to identify with the narrator and confirm, without evidence, that the choice made is *the* right one, as if the phrase "I took the one less traveled by, / And that has made all the difference" were proof that this is the road we all ought to follow (which, if you think about it, would make for a pretty crowded less-traveled road). I would almost want to accuse Frost of dithering, but that implies a state of hyperactive indecision—of someone who can neither sit still nor make a move in any direction—and he is too sedate for that.

In another of Frost's famous poems, "Fire and Ice," he says, in effect, that given a choice between passion and apathy, he would choose the world to end in passion, but that, having seen the passion of hatred, apathy would also be okay. The poem's message isn't such a profound declaration when I phrase it this way; the beauty, of course, is in the way that he says it. It's quite the nonissue, since we won't have much choice in the way the world will end and, besides, the two finales are fairly equal in appeal. Still, Frost makes us walk away from this nine-line piece feeling that we have accomplished something.

One of the most touching, truly human characters in Frost's works must be the speaker of "The Wood-Pile," a person who is so uncomfortable about the consolations of philosophy that he can immerse himself in a rich situation of fear, nature, suspicion, rebirth, futility, intrusion, and harmony, and walk away envious of that unknown someone else who was able to leave these rampant ideas and focus on something else. This is a pensive man who, when he sees a little bird flitting about in the forest, imagines a whole drama about the bird's wants and fears; a man who knows the significance of mentioning the contrast between a manmade prop and a still-living tree; a man who has time to walk in the woods.

The speaker also seems to yearn for more important and compelling duties to carry out that would preclude him from musing about birds or wood-piles. The phrase "fresh tasks" has a positive connotation; it seems clear that he wishes they were his. While his mind is so open to suggestion that it skips from one item to the next, one plan to another, he also knows that there is someone out there who can spend time and grueling labor chopping and stacking wood and not even keep track of the results. We all have the same envy. Think of how, if Bill Gates let a thousand-dollar bill slip down the back of the couch, he would not even notice its absence; now, think of what that thousand dollars would mean to you. The commodity here isn't money, and it isn't even time, which this speaker has plenty of. What he lacks is a purpose so important that an afternoon of labor would seem meaningless in comparison.

A few years after composing "The Wood-Pile," Frost wrote "Stopping By Woods on a Snowy Evening." In this poem, after the narrator briefly contemplates the forest and snow, he decides that it is time to move on, because "I have promises to keep / And miles to go before I sleep." Missing here is a sense of self-recrimination—that feeling that he does not deserve to treat himself to quiet time in the forest. If the speaker in "Stopping by Woods on a Snowy Evening" feels that he deserves it, though, he also has responsibilities that set off an alarm clock within him, telling him that he must leave. This character's relationship to the narrator of "The Wood-Pile" is clear—they are both people who can appreciate a good quiet forest—but his relationship with himself is a little calmer, less self-accusing. It is interesting to compare Frost's positions in life when he wrote the two poems. When he wrote "The Wood-Pile," he was a poet who ran a chicken farm. It was an occupation that he, understandably, had little interest in but accepted because his grandfather, tired of his poet-like idleness, had bought it and made him promise to run it for at least ten years. Who could blame him if he had trouble keeping on task? When he wrote "Stopping by Woods on a Snowy Evening" in 1923, he was a successful poet—not only published but also praised for the depth of his thoughts. He wrote it after staying up one sleepless but productive night, working out the problems in another poem, and he could be assured that there would be another challenge presented to his talent coming up soon. He was, in other words, in a position to appreciate the sweetness of a few minutes' rest without fear of losing himself to indolence.

Philosophers have suggested that too much freedom is frightening for humans—that the heaviest of responsibilities is being accountable for deciding what to do with ourselves. This is the burden that the narrator of this poem imagines the woodchopper to be free of, and he wishes his mind could take on such ballast. At first reading, "The Wood-Pile" seems to offer a fantasy to those of us who feel over-occupied and would like to be able to take a stroll and then even prolong it a little just to see what we can see. True to Frost's fashion, though, at the same time the poem offers its opposite, a fantasy for the under-occupied who would rather not have so much time for strolling. The genius of it is that both groups—meaning just about everyone—come away from the poem happy.

Source: David Kelly, in an essay for *Poetry for Students,* The Gale Group, 1999.

William Doreski

In the following excerpt, Doreski focuses on the allegorical landscape in "The Wood-Pile."

In "Education by Poetry," published in *The Amherst Graduates' Quarterly* in 1931, Robert Frost invoked the intricacies, including the limits, of metaphor as knowledge. "All metaphor breaks down somewhere," he argued. "That is the beauty of it. It is touch and go with the metaphor, and un-til you have lived with it long enough you don't know when it is going." By that time, Frost had "lived with" metaphor through many books. His early poems, which he had collected and published sixteen years before, had displayed a sophisticated sense of the limits of metaphor, a careful testing of allegorical possibilities, and an inclination to expand narrative models through rhetorical motifs other than those already enshrined in lyric conventions. The best of the poems Frost would write in the next two decades would go further by making rhetorical self-critique an intrinsic structural and thematic element of their poetics.

"The Wood-Pile" and "After Apple-Picking," both from *North of Boston* (1914), illustrate the two poles of a language of meditation drawn, respectively, from Dante and the tradition of allegorical landscape, and from Wordsworth and the romantic acknowledgement of the otherness of landscape. Each poem confronts comparable problems in signification: the limits of allegory (a walk in winter woods, a journey over a rutted country road), the unruly complexity of the symbol (the wood-pile, the Grail), and the loss of religious faith and iconography and the difficulty of finding a comparably significant but secular language. These problems signal an apparent exhaustion of lyric conventions and encourage Frost to use his characteristic irony to deconstruct the meditative voice, expose it as a fiction, and renew the lyric sense of wonder and discovery by invoking a speech-oriented language (a dialogic, rather than monologic, voice) more informal, less conventionally poetic, more intimate than the language it displaces. That is, the renewal proceeds by visibly displacing one language-model for another. Frost, unlike Williams, for example, does not refuse established lyric models, but escapes the conventional language of meditation, monologue, and lyric ecstasy without entirely abandoning established formal paradigms....

"The Wood-Pile" opens by invoking Dante's motif of the lost soul, the wanderer in the dark wood. The speaker warns us that like many other allegorical landscapes this one is no place in particular and cannot be readily named, too formal with its "view ... all in lines / Straight up and down of tall slim trees / Too much alike to mark or name a place by...." Such places, lacking adequately differentiated signifiers, typically entrap the traveller, and the reader might well expect this speaker to fall prey to self-doubts, misgivings of the sort that suggest that inner and outer landscapes are actually one. Frost's wood is frozen, grey, and snowy, and by lacking clear definition it threatens the absorption or erasure of the self.

The speaker is neither passive nor desperate. He offers no particular moral dilemma, displays no fear, and asserts a role in his own salvation by positing the choice between turning back and going on. Also, no leopard—a figure clearly not of the waking world—leads him on, though another natural emblem, an otherwise undistinguished "small bird," flies before him, neither leading him nor quite fleeing from him, as if it toyed with its own allegorical role which it cannot quite fulfil. The speaker implies, in his playful, uncommitted personification of the bird, that its reluctance to name itself derives from its reluctance to expose its inner life, which centres, for the moment, on fear. The speaker assumes that the bird believes he is being chased for his feather, his metonymic self, "like one who takes / Everything said as personal to himself." One can conceive of someone foolish enough to take all landscapes, allegorical or otherwise, as personal to himself; but this Wordsworthian stance is not Frost's, and his refusal of this relatively simple link between being and nature redirects the poem from allegory to a less conventionally predicated mode.

By invoking the convention of the allegorical landscape, Frost suggests the possibility of constructing his poem entirely within a structural certainty in which every motif, every emblem finds a place and contributes towards the reconciliation of self and other. But Frost has a delicate sense of scale. Dante's immensely complex poem accomplishes its task only by invoking the entire structure of medieval Catholic theology and shaping it to the even more inclusive convention of landscape allegory. Frost, who always insists that the play of language is central to poetry, loves to tease the reader by setting up expectations of grandeur that if actually attempted in so brief and colloquial a poem would surely fail.

"The Wood-Pile" turns abruptly, takes "One flight out side-ways," as it were, and forgets its allegorical beginnings as the speaker forgets the bird and lets "his little fear / Carry him off the way I might have gone." The bird, that is, delves further into the allegorical landscape, but the speaker, alerted by his discovery, enters a new mode.

As some versions of literary history would have it, poetry altered its course in the romantic era by positing the symbol as a logocentric repository of meaning outside of language. "The Wood-Pile" somewhat wryly critiques that version of literary history, and critiques as well both the convention the poem first invokes then abandons and the newer convention it turns to and gently mocks. [In *The Rhetoric of Romanticsm*] Paul de Man notes that the earlier romantics resisted the temptation to collapse being and the natural object into a single entity or sign. Wordsworth toyed with the idea that in place of a firm grounding of faith, imagination, by means of a self-reflexive poetic language, might empower the sign with the presence of nature. But he well understood the paradoxical quality of his endeavour, and the *Prelude* displays his awareness of the negating power as well as the nostalgia of the imagination.

In "The Wood-Pile," at the very moment of empowerment, Frost undercuts the utility of the wood-pile as a symbol of human presence by recalling that, like all signifiers, it has something of allegory in it—in this instance, the bird, which "went behind it [the wood-pile] to make his last stand." He also reminds us that the symbol, unlike the allegorical emblem, embodies, rather than merely suggesting metonymically, its own history. Though isolated in its human import, the wood-pile is the monolith that represents all history, all endeavour, all made things, and is, therefore, "older sure than this year's cutting, / Or even last year's or the year's before." Yet isolate, human-made, and symbolic though it is, the wood-pile lacks stability, and is losing its own sense of origin by returning to nature and surrendering its logocentric status. Already "Clematis / Had wound strings round and round it like a bundle," reclaiming it as the bark warps off it and it deconstructs into its natural status. This disintegrative process generates the tropes of impoverishment Richard Poirier [in his *Robert Frost: The Work of Knowing*] finds in this poem. The woodpile, claimed from nature and therefore claimed by Being, is slowly reverting to a simpler form of sign, returning to the world of allegory, in de Man's sense, in which the primal and ethical distinction between the mind and the world is relatively clearly defined, but in which metaphor, deprived of a central shaping role, seems impoverished.

Frost's paradoxical moralism—which argues that "only / someone who lived in turning to fresh tasks / Could so forget his handiwork on which / He spent himself, the labour of his axe"—both conceals and reveals the gap between being and nature by calling into question the very process of making and naming. What is the use of doing tasks at all if one spends oneself only to abandon and forget the results of one's labour? The answer is the poem's critique of its own process of hacking a symbol—the wood-pile—from conventional allegorical motifs. In concealing its refusal to cross the gulf between sign and nature, this symbolic decaying wood-pile exposes its—and the poem's—self-deconstruction. The wood-pile completes the failure of signification by refusing to warm its author and instead warming, "as best it could," the original allegorical landscape it seemed, momentarily, to endow with a human presence.

The consequence of this shift from allegory to symbol is to suggest that neither language-mode is sufficient to engender a poetic sufficient to overcome the nostalgia for the human world, the primacy of the external object. "The Wood-Pile" is a poem about the search for origins and the limitations of the most obvious attempts to reconcile nature and the mind. It is also a poem about the power of language to invoke the very idea of presence, an idea that if not realized in fact is capable of generating imagery that is so evocative as to demonstrate that metaphor-generated illusion can as generously engage the sensuous being as the actual presence of the evoked object. The opening line—"Out walking in the frozen swamp one gray day"—signals a pattern of open vowel sounds that corresponds to the open view through the leafless trees. The imagery, including the closing picture of the wood-pile decaying in the middle of the swamp, corresponds to a sense of expanding possibilities. The forgetfulness of the woodcutter corresponds, the speaker believes, to a larger sense of purpose. Renewal through language, then, is not the property of particular language-models (allegory or symbol) but a larger argument shaped by and around their limitations. By exploiting and conflating lyric conventions rather than attempting to abandon them, Frost argues from their relationship; in miniaturizing a literary-historical model (the displacement of allegory by symbolism), he replicates the expansive history of the attempt to resolve through language and imagination the isolation of the mind. In doing so, he implicitly argues that the positing of fictional modes of representation affirms the practical utility of the language of imagery to engage the senses and sustain at least a momentary illusion of natural or human presence.

Source: William Doreski, "Meta-Meditation in Robert Frost's 'The Wood-Pile,' 'After Apple-Picking,' and 'Directive,'" in *Ariel: A Review of International English Literature,* Vol. 23, No. 4, October 1992, pp. 35-40.

Sources

Cowley, Malcolm, "The Case Against Mr. Frost," *The New Republic,* September 15, 1944, pp. 345-47.

Cramer, Jeffrey S., *Robert Frost Among His Poems: A Literary Companion to the Poet's Own Biographical Contexts and Associations,* Jefferson, NC: McFarland & Co., 1996.

Lowell, Amy, "North of Boston," *New Republic,* Vol. 2, February 20, 1915, pp. 81-2.

Pound, Ezra, "Modern Georgics," *Poetry,* Vol. 5, December 1914, pp. 27-130.

Pritchard, William, "Robert Frost: Elevated Play," *Lives of the Modern Poets,* New York: Oxford University Press, 1980.

"The Procession of the Muse," *Academy and Literature,* September 20, 1913, pp, 359-60.

"Summer 1998 Report: How the Union Advantage Helps Workers," http://www.uaw.org/publications/jobs_pay/unionpay2.html, accessed May 3, 1999.

For Further Study

Barry, Elaine, *Robert Frost,* New York: Frederick Ungar Publishing Co., 1978.
> Barry's book is a concise rendering of the poet's voice, themes, and narrative technique.

Frost, Robert, *Robert Frost: Farm-Poultryman,* edited by Edward Connery Lathem and Lawrence Thompson, Hanover, NH: Dartmouth Publications, 1963.
> This is a compilation of eleven articles about farming by Frost that were published in poultry journals between 1903 and 1905, while the poet was raising chickens in New Hampshire. As a look at Frost's development, this is as useful as most biographies.

Nitchie, George W., *Human Values in the Poetry of Robert Frost,* Durham, NC: Duke University Press, 1960.
> Surprisingly, this book does not mention "The Wood-Pile," not even in the chapter entitled "A Momentary Stay Against Confusion." Still, it is excessively well-researched, weaving together Frost's major themes with just about every intellectual strain imaginable.

Potter, James L., *Robert Frost Handbook,* University Park, PA: The Pennsylvania State University Press, 1982.
> Designed for the general student, not necessarily for literary scholars, this book provides a neat and readable overview of Frost's life and techniques.

Winter, Yvor, "Robert Frost: Or, the Spiritual Drifter as Poet," *Robert Frost: A Collection of Critical Essays,* edited by James M. Cox, Englewood Cliffs, NJ: Prentice-Hall, Inc., 1962.
> This famous essay, by a respected literary critic, examines the question of whether Frost's poetry has a solid moral or philosophical base.

Glossary of Literary Terms

A

Abstract: Used as a noun, the term refers to a short summary or outline of a longer work. As an adjective applied to writing or literary works, abstract refers to words or phrases that name things not knowable through the five senses.

Accent: The emphasis or stress placed on a syllable in poetry. Traditional poetry commonly uses patterns of accented and unaccented syllables (known as feet) that create distinct rhythms. Much modern poetry uses less formal arrangements that create a sense of freedom and spontaneity.

Aestheticism: A literary and artistic movement of the nineteenth century. Followers of the movement believed that art should not be mixed with social, political, or moral teaching. The statement "art for art's sake" is a good summary of aestheticism. The movement had its roots in France, but it gained widespread importance in England in the last half of the nineteenth century, where it helped change the Victorian practice of including moral lessons in literature.

Affective Fallacy: An error in judging the merits or faults of a work of literature. The "error" results from stressing the importance of the work's effect upon the reader—that is, how it makes a reader "feel" emotionally, what it does as a literary work—instead of stressing its inner qualities as a created object, or what it "is."

Age of Johnson: The period in English literature between 1750 and 1798, named after the most prominent literary figure of the age, Samuel Johnson. Works written during this time are noted for their emphasis on "sensibility," or emotional quality. These works formed a transition between the rational works of the Age of Reason, or Neoclassical period, and the emphasis on individual feelings and responses of the Romantic period.

Age of Reason: See *Neoclassicism*

Age of Sensibility: See *Age of Johnson*

Agrarians: A group of Southern American writers of the 1930s and 1940s who fostered an economic and cultural program for the South based on agriculture, in opposition to the industrial society of the North. The term can refer to any group that promotes the value of farm life and agricultural society.

Alexandrine Meter: See *Meter*

Allegory: A narrative technique in which characters representing things or abstract ideas are used to convey a message or teach a lesson. Allegory is typically used to teach moral, ethical, or religious lessons but is sometimes used for satiric or political purposes.

Alliteration: A poetic device where the first consonant sounds or any vowel sounds in words or syllables are repeated.

Allusion: A reference to a familiar literary or historical person or event, used to make an idea more easily understood.

Amerind Literature: The writing and oral traditions of Native Americans. Native American literature was originally passed on by word of mouth, so it consisted largely of stories and events that were easily memorized. Amerind prose is often rhythmic like poetry because it was recited to the beat of a ceremonial drum.

Analogy: A comparison of two things made to explain something unfamiliar through its similarities to something familiar, or to prove one point based on the acceptedness of another. Similes and metaphors are types of analogies.

Anapest: See *Foot*

Angry Young Men: A group of British writers of the 1950s whose work expressed bitterness and disillusionment with society. Common to their work is an anti-hero who rebels against a corrupt social order and strives for personal integrity.

Anthropomorphism: The presentation of animals or objects in human shape or with human characteristics. The term is derived from the Greek word for "human form."

Antimasque: See *Masque*

Antithesis: The antithesis of something is its direct opposite. In literature, the use of antithesis as a figure of speech results in two statements that show a contrast through the balancing of two opposite ideas. Technically, it is the second portion of the statement that is defined as the "antithesis"; the first portion is the "thesis."

Apocrypha: Writings tentatively attributed to an author but not proven or universally accepted to be their works. The term was originally applied to certain books of the Bible that were not considered inspired and so were not included in the "sacred canon."

Apollonian and Dionysian: The two impulses believed to guide authors of dramatic tragedy. The Apollonian impulse is named after Apollo, the Greek god of light and beauty and the symbol of intellectual order. The Dionysian impulse is named after Dionysus, the Greek god of wine and the symbol of the unrestrained forces of nature. The Apollonian impulse is to create a rational, harmonious world, while the Dionysian is to express the irrational forces of personality.

Apostrophe: A statement, question, or request addressed to an inanimate object or concept or to a nonexistent or absent person.

Archetype: The word archetype is commonly used to describe an original pattern or model from which all other things of the same kind are made. This term was introduced to literary criticism from the psychology of Carl Jung. It expresses Jung's theory that behind every person's "unconscious," or repressed memories of the past, lies the "collective unconscious" of the human race: memories of the countless typical experiences of our ancestors. These memories are said to prompt illogical associations that trigger powerful emotions in the reader. Often, the emotional process is primitive, even primordial. Archetypes are the literary images that grow out of the "collective unconscious." They appear in literature as incidents and plots that repeat basic patterns of life. They may also appear as stereotyped characters.

Argument: The argument of a work is the author's subject matter or principal idea.

Art for Art's Sake: See *Aestheticism*

Assonance: The repetition of similar vowel sounds in poetry.

Audience: The people for whom a piece of literature is written. Authors usually write with a certain audience in mind, for example, children, members of a religious or ethnic group, or colleagues in a professional field. The term "audience" also applies to the people who gather to see or hear any performance, including plays, poetry readings, speeches, and concerts.

Automatic Writing: Writing carried out without a preconceived plan in an effort to capture every random thought. Authors who engage in automatic writing typically do not revise their work, preferring instead to preserve the revealed truth and beauty of spontaneous expression.

Avant-garde: A French term meaning "vanguard." It is used in literary criticism to describe new writing that rejects traditional approaches to literature in favor of innovations in style or content.

B

Ballad: A short poem that tells a simple story and has a repeated refrain. Ballads were originally intended to be sung. Early ballads, known as folk ballads, were passed down through generations, so their authors are often unknown. Later ballads composed by known authors are called literary ballads.

Baroque: A term used in literary criticism to describe literature that is complex or ornate in style or diction. Baroque works typically express tension, anxiety, and violent emotion. The term "Baroque Age" designates a period in Western European literature beginning in the late sixteenth century and ending about one hundred years later.

Works of this period often mirror the qualities of works more generally associated with the label "baroque" and sometimes feature elaborate conceits.

Baroque Age: See *Baroque*

Baroque Period: See *Baroque*

Beat Generation: See *Beat Movement*

Beat Movement: A period featuring a group of American poets and novelists of the 1950s and 1960s—including Jack Kerouac, Allen Ginsberg, Gregory Corso, William S. Burroughs, and Lawrence Ferlinghetti—who rejected established social and literary values. Using such techniques as stream of consciousness writing and jazz-influenced free verse and focusing on unusual or abnormal states of mind—generated by religious ecstasy or the use of drugs—the Beat writers aimed to create works that were unconventional in both form and subject matter.

Beat Poets: See *Beat Movement*

Beats, The: See *Beat Movement*

Belles-lettres: A French term meaning "fine letters" or "beautiful writing." It is often used as a synonym for literature, typically referring to imaginative and artistic rather than scientific or expository writing. Current usage sometimes restricts the meaning to light or humorous writing and appreciative essays about literature.

Black Aesthetic Movement: A period of artistic and literary development among African Americans in the 1960s and early 1970s. This was the first major African-American artistic movement since the Harlem Renaissance and was closely paralleled by the civil rights and black power movements. The black aesthetic writers attempted to produce works of art that would be meaningful to the black masses. Key figures in black aesthetics included one of its founders, poet and playwright Amiri Baraka, formerly known as LeRoi Jones; poet and essayist Haki R. Madhubuti, formerly Don L. Lee; poet and playwright Sonia Sanchez; and dramatist Ed Bullins.

Black Arts Movement: See *Black Aesthetic Movement*

Black Comedy: See *Black Humor*

Black Humor: Writing that places grotesque elements side by side with humorous ones in an attempt to shock the reader, forcing him or her to laugh at the horrifying reality of a disordered world.

Black Mountain School: Black Mountain College and three of its instructors—Robert Creeley, Robert Duncan, and Charles Olson— were all influential in projective verse, so poets working in projective verse are now referred to as members of the Black Mountain school.

Blank Verse: Loosely, any unrhymed poetry, but more generally, unrhymed iambic pentameter verse (composed of lines of five two-syllable feet with the first syllable accented, the second unaccented). Blank verse has been used by poets since the Renaissance for its flexibility and its graceful, dignified tone.

Bloomsbury Group: A group of English writers, artists, and intellectuals who held informal artistic and philosophical discussions in Bloomsbury, a district of London, from around 1907 to the early 1930s. The Bloomsbury Group held no uniform philosophical beliefs but did commonly express an aversion to moral prudery and a desire for greater social tolerance.

Bon Mot: A French term meaning "good word." A *bon mot* is a witty remark or clever observation.

Breath Verse: See *Projective Verse*

Burlesque: Any literary work that uses exaggeration to make its subject appear ridiculous, either by treating a trivial subject with profound seriousness or by treating a dignified subject frivolously. The word "burlesque" may also be used as an adjective, as in "burlesque show," to mean "striptease act."

C

Cadence: The natural rhythm of language caused by the alternation of accented and unaccented syllables. Much modern poetry—notably free verse—deliberately manipulates cadence to create complex rhythmic effects.

Caesura: A pause in a line of poetry, usually occurring near the middle. It typically corresponds to a break in the natural rhythm or sense of the line but is sometimes shifted to create special meanings or rhythmic effects.

Canzone: A short Italian or Provencal lyric poem, commonly about love and often set to music. The *canzone* has no set form but typically contains five or six stanzas made up of seven to twenty lines of eleven syllables each. A shorter, five- to ten-line "envoy," or concluding stanza, completes the poem.

Carpe Diem: A Latin term meaning "seize the day." This is a traditional theme of poetry, especially lyrics. A *carpe diem* poem advises the reader or the person it addresses to live for today and enjoy the pleasures of the moment.

Catharsis: The release or purging of unwanted emotions—specifically fear and pity—brought about by exposure to art. The term was first used by the Greek philosopher Aristotle in his *Poetics* to refer to the desired effect of tragedy on spectators.

Celtic Renaissance: A period of Irish literary and cultural history at the end of the nineteenth century. Followers of the movement aimed to create a romantic vision of Celtic myth and legend. The most significant works of the Celtic Renaissance typically present a dreamy, unreal world, usually in reaction against the reality of contemporary problems.

Celtic Twilight: See *Celtic Renaissance*

Character: Broadly speaking, a person in a literary work. The actions of characters are what constitute the plot of a story, novel, or poem. There are numerous types of characters, ranging from simple, stereotypical figures to intricate, multifaceted ones. In the techniques of anthropomorphism and personification, animals—and even places or things—can assume aspects of character. "Characterization" is the process by which an author creates vivid, believable characters in a work of art. This may be done in a variety of ways, including (1) direct description of the character by the narrator; (2) the direct presentation of the speech, thoughts, or actions of the character; and (3) the responses of other characters to the character. The term "character" also refers to a form originated by the ancient Greek writer Theophrastus that later became popular in the seventeenth and eighteenth centuries. It is a short essay or sketch of a person who prominently displays a specific attribute or quality, such as miserliness or ambition.

Characterization: See *Character*

Classical: In its strictest definition in literary criticism, classicism refers to works of ancient Greek or Roman literature. The term may also be used to describe a literary work of recognized importance (a "classic") from any time period or literature that exhibits the traits of classicism.

Classicism: A term used in literary criticism to describe critical doctrines that have their roots in ancient Greek and Roman literature, philosophy, and art. Works associated with classicism typically exhibit restraint on the part of the author, unity of design and purpose, clarity, simplicity, logical organization, and respect for tradition.

Colloquialism: A word, phrase, or form of pronunciation that is acceptable in casual conversation but not in formal, written communication. It is considered more acceptable than slang.

Complaint: A lyric poem, popular in the Renaissance, in which the speaker expresses sorrow about his or her condition. Typically, the speaker's sadness is caused by an unresponsive lover, but some complaints cite other sources of unhappiness, such as poverty or fate.

Conceit: A clever and fanciful metaphor, usually expressed through elaborate and extended comparison, that presents a striking parallel between two seemingly dissimilar things—for example, elaborately comparing a beautiful woman to an object like a garden or the sun. The conceit was a popular device throughout the Elizabethan Age and Baroque Age and was the principal technique of the seventeenth-century English metaphysical poets. This usage of the word conceit is unrelated to the best-known definition of conceit as an arrogant attitude or behavior.

Concrete: Concrete is the opposite of abstract, and refers to a thing that actually exists or a description that allows the reader to experience an object or concept with the senses.

Concrete Poetry: Poetry in which visual elements play a large part in the poetic effect. Punctuation marks, letters, or words are arranged on a page to form a visual design: a cross, for example, or a bumblebee.

Confessional Poetry: A form of poetry in which the poet reveals very personal, intimate, sometimes shocking information about himself or herself.

Connotation: The impression that a word gives beyond its defined meaning. Connotations may be universally understood or may be significant only to a certain group.

Consonance: Consonance occurs in poetry when words appearing at the ends of two or more verses have similar final consonant sounds but have final vowel sounds that differ, as with "stuff" and "off."

Convention: Any widely accepted literary device, style, or form.

Corrido: A Mexican ballad.

Couplet: Two lines of poetry with the same rhyme and meter, often expressing a complete and self-contained thought.

Criticism: The systematic study and evaluation of literary works, usually based on a specific method or set of principles. An important part of literary studies since ancient times, the practice of criticism has given rise to numerous theories, methods, and "schools," sometimes producing conflicting, even contradictory, interpretations of literature in general as well as of individual works. Even such basic issues as what constitutes a poem or a novel have been the subject of much criticism over the centuries.

D

Dactyl: See *Foot*

Dadaism: A protest movement in art and literature founded by Tristan Tzara in 1916. Followers of the movement expressed their outrage at the destruction brought about by World War I by revolting against numerous forms of social convention. The Dadaists presented works marked by calculated madness and flamboyant nonsense. They stressed total freedom of expression, commonly through primitive displays of emotion and illogical, often senseless, poetry. The movement ended shortly after the war, when it was replaced by surrealism.

Decadent: See *Decadents*

Decadents: The followers of a nineteenth-century literary movement that had its beginnings in French aestheticism. Decadent literature displays a fascination with perverse and morbid states; a search for novelty and sensation—the "new thrill"; a preoccupation with mysticism; and a belief in the senselessness of human existence. The movement is closely associated with the doctrine Art for Art's Sake. The term "decadence" is sometimes used to denote a decline in the quality of art or literature following a period of greatness.

Deconstruction: A method of literary criticism developed by Jacques Derrida and characterized by multiple conflicting interpretations of a given work. Deconstructionists consider the impact of the language of a work and suggest that the true meaning of the work is not necessarily the meaning that the author intended.

Deduction: The process of reaching a conclusion through reasoning from general premises to a specific premise.

Denotation: The definition of a word, apart from the impressions or feelings it creates in the reader.

Diction: The selection and arrangement of words in a literary work. Either or both may vary depending on the desired effect. There are four general types of diction: "formal," used in scholarly or lofty writing; "informal," used in relaxed but educated conversation; "colloquial," used in everyday speech; and "slang," containing newly coined words and other terms not accepted in formal usage.

Didactic: A term used to describe works of literature that aim to teach some moral, religious, political, or practical lesson. Although didactic elements are often found in artistically pleasing works, the term "didactic" usually refers to literature in which the message is more important than the form. The term may also be used to criticize a work that the critic finds "overly didactic," that is, heavy-handed in its delivery of a lesson.

Dimeter: See *Meter*

Dionysian: See *Apollonian and Dionysian*

Discordia concours: A Latin phrase meaning "discord in harmony." The term was coined by the eighteenth-century English writer Samuel Johnson to describe "a combination of dissimilar images or discovery of occult resemblances in things apparently unlike." Johnson created the expression by reversing a phrase by the Latin poet Horace.

Dissonance: A combination of harsh or jarring sounds, especially in poetry. Although such combinations may be accidental, poets sometimes intentionally make them to achieve particular effects. Dissonance is also sometimes used to refer to close but not identical rhymes. When this is the case, the word functions as a synonym for consonance.

Double Entendre: A corruption of a French phrase meaning "double meaning." The term is used to indicate a word or phrase that is deliberately ambiguous, especially when one of the meanings is risque or improper.

Draft: Any preliminary version of a written work. An author may write dozens of drafts which are revised to form the final work, or he or she may write only one, with few or no revisions.

Dramatic Monologue: See *Monologue*

Dramatic Poetry: Any lyric work that employs elements of drama such as dialogue, conflict, or characterization, but excluding works that are intended for stage presentation.

Dream Allegory: See *Dream Vision*

Dream Vision: A literary convention, chiefly of the Middle Ages. In a dream vision a story is presented as a literal dream of the narrator. This device was commonly used to teach moral and religious lessons.

E

Eclogue: In classical literature, a poem featuring rural themes and structured as a dialogue among shepherds. Eclogues often took specific poetic forms, such as elegies or love poems. Some were written as the soliloquy of a shepherd. In later centuries, "eclogue" came to refer to any poem that was in the pastoral tradition or that had a dialogue or monologue structure.

Edwardian: Describes cultural conventions identified with the period of the reign of Edward VII of England (1901-1910). Writers of the Edwardian Age typically displayed a strong reaction against the propriety and conservatism of the Victorian Age. Their work often exhibits distrust of authority in religion, politics, and art and expresses strong doubts about the soundness of conventional values.

Edwardian Age: See *Edwardian*

Electra Complex: A daughter's amorous obsession with her father.

Elegy: A lyric poem that laments the death of a person or the eventual death of all people. In a conventional elegy, set in a classical world, the poet and subject are spoken of as shepherds. In modern criticism, the word elegy is often used to refer to a poem that is melancholy or mournfully contemplative.

Elizabethan Age: A period of great economic growth, religious controversy, and nationalism closely associated with the reign of Elizabeth I of England (1558-1603). The Elizabethan Age is considered a part of the general renaissance—that is, the flowering of arts and literature—that took place in Europe during the fourteenth through sixteenth centuries. The era is considered the golden age of English literature. The most important dramas in English and a great deal of lyric poetry were produced during this period, and modern English criticism began around this time.

Empathy: A sense of shared experience, including emotional and physical feelings, with someone or something other than oneself. Empathy is often used to describe the response of a reader to a literary character.

English Sonnet: See *Sonnet*

Enjambment: The running over of the sense and structure of a line of verse or a couplet into the following verse or couplet.

Enlightenment, The: An eighteenth-century philosophical movement. It began in France but had a wide impact throughout Europe and America. Thinkers of the Enlightenment valued reason and believed that both the individual and society could achieve a state of perfection. Corresponding to this essentially humanist vision was a resistance to religious authority.

Epic: A long narrative poem about the adventures of a hero of great historic or legendary importance. The setting is vast and the action is often given cosmic significance through the intervention of supernatural forces such as gods, angels, or demons. Epics are typically written in a classical style of grand simplicity with elaborate metaphors and allusions that enhance the symbolic importance of a hero's adventures.

Epic Simile: See *Homeric Simile*

Epigram: A saying that makes the speaker's point quickly and concisely.

Epilogue: A concluding statement or section of a literary work. In dramas, particularly those of the seventeenth and eighteenth centuries, the epilogue is a closing speech, often in verse, delivered by an actor at the end of a play and spoken directly to the audience.

Epiphany: A sudden revelation of truth inspired by a seemingly trivial incident.

Epitaph: An inscription on a tomb or tombstone, or a verse written on the occasion of a person's death. Epitaphs may be serious or humorous.

Epithalamion: A song or poem written to honor and commemorate a marriage ceremony.

Epithalamium: See *Epithalamion*

Epithet: A word or phrase, often disparaging or abusive, that expresses a character trait of someone or something.

Erziehungsroman: See *Bildungsroman*

Essay: A prose composition with a focused subject of discussion. The term was coined by Michel de Montaigne to describe his 1580 collection of brief, informal reflections on himself and on various topics relating to human nature. An essay can also be a long, systematic discourse.

Existentialism: A predominantly twentieth-century philosophy concerned with the nature and perception of human existence. There are two major strains of existentialist thought: atheistic and Christian. Followers of atheistic existentialism believe that the individual is alone in a godless universe and that the basic human condition is one of suffering and loneliness. Nevertheless, because there are no fixed values, individuals can create their own characters—indeed, they can shape themselves—through the exercise of free will. The atheistic strain culminates in and is popularly associated with the works of Jean-Paul Sartre. The Christian existentialists, on the other hand, believe that only in God may people find freedom from life's anguish. The two strains hold certain beliefs in common: that existence cannot be fully understood or described through empirical effort; that anguish is a universal element of life; that individuals must bear responsibility for their actions; and that there is no common standard of behavior or perception for religious and ethical matters.

Expatriates: See *Expatriatism*

Expatriatism: The practice of leaving one's country to live for an extended period in another country.

Exposition: Writing intended to explain the nature of an idea, thing, or theme. Expository writing is often combined with description, narration, or argument. In dramatic writing, the exposition is the introductory material which presents the characters, setting, and tone of the play.

Expressionism: An indistinct literary term, originally used to describe an early twentieth-century school of German painting. The term applies to almost any mode of unconventional, highly subjective writing that distorts reality in some way.

Extended Monologue: See *Monologue*

F

Feet: See *Foot*

Feminine Rhyme: See *Rhyme*

Fiction: Any story that is the product of imagination rather than a documentation of fact. Characters and events in such narratives may be based in real life but their ultimate form and configuration is a creation of the author.

Figurative Language: A technique in writing in which the author temporarily interrupts the order, construction, or meaning of the writing for a particular effect. This interruption takes the form of one or more figures of speech such as hyperbole, irony, or simile. Figurative language is the opposite of literal language, in which every word is truthful, accurate, and free of exaggeration or embellishment.

Figures of Speech: Writing that differs from customary conventions for construction, meaning, order, or significance for the purpose of a special meaning or effect. There are two major types of figures of speech: rhetorical figures, which do not make changes in the meaning of the words, and tropes, which do.

Fin de siecle: A French term meaning "end of the century." The term is used to denote the last decade of the nineteenth century, a transition period when writers and other artists abandoned old conventions and looked for new techniques and objectives.

First Person: See *Point of View*

Folk Ballad: See *Ballad*

Folklore: Traditions and myths preserved in a culture or group of people. Typically, these are passed on by word of mouth in various forms—such as legends, songs, and proverbs—or preserved in customs and ceremonies. This term was first used by W. J. Thoms in 1846.

Folktale: A story originating in oral tradition. Folktales fall into a variety of categories, including legends, ghost stories, fairy tales, fables, and anecdotes based on historical figures and events.

Foot: The smallest unit of rhythm in a line of poetry. In English-language poetry, a foot is typically one accented syllable combined with one or two unaccented syllables.

Form: The pattern or construction of a work which identifies its genre and distinguishes it from other genres.

Formalism: In literary criticism, the belief that literature should follow prescribed rules of construction, such as those that govern the sonnet form.

Fourteener Meter: See *Meter*

Free Verse: Poetry that lacks regular metrical and rhyme patterns but that tries to capture the cadences of everyday speech. The form allows a poet to exploit a variety of rhythmical effects within a single poem.

Futurism: A flamboyant literary and artistic movement that developed in France, Italy, and Russia from 1908 through the 1920s. Futurist theater and poetry abandoned traditional literary forms. In their place, followers of the movement attempted to achieve total freedom of expression through bizarre imagery and deformed or newly invented words. The Futurists were self-consciously modern artists who attempted to incorporate the appearances and sounds of modern life into their work.

G

Genre: A category of literary work. In critical theory, genre may refer to both the content of a given work—tragedy, comedy, pastoral—and to its form, such as poetry, novel, or drama.

Genteel Tradition: A term coined by critic George Santayana to describe the literary practice of certain late nineteenth-century American writers, especially New Englanders. Followers of the Genteel

Tradition emphasized conventionality in social, religious, moral, and literary standards.

Georgian Age: See *Georgian Poets*

Georgian Period: See *Georgian Poets*

Georgian Poets: A loose grouping of English poets during the years 1912-1922. The Georgians reacted against certain literary schools and practices, especially Victorian wordiness, turn-of-the-century aestheticism, and contemporary urban realism. In their place, the Georgians embraced the nineteenth-century poetic practices of William Wordsworth and the other Lake Poets.

Georgic: A poem about farming and the farmer's way of life, named from Virgil's *Georgics.*

Gilded Age: A period in American history during the 1870s characterized by political corruption and materialism. A number of important novels of social and political criticism were written during this time.

Gothic: See *Gothicism*

Gothicism: In literary criticism, works characterized by a taste for the medieval or morbidly attractive. A gothic novel prominently features elements of horror, the supernatural, gloom, and violence: clanking chains, terror, charnel houses, ghosts, medieval castles, and mysteriously slamming doors. The term "gothic novel" is also applied to novels that lack elements of the traditional Gothic setting but that create a similar atmosphere of terror or dread.

Graveyard School: A group of eighteenth-century English poets who wrote long, picturesque meditations on death. Their works were designed to cause the reader to ponder immortality.

Great Chain of Being: The belief that all things and creatures in nature are organized in a hierarchy from inanimate objects at the bottom to God at the top. This system of belief was popular in the seventeenth and eighteenth centuries.

Grotesque: In literary criticism, the subject matter of a work or a style of expression characterized by exaggeration, deformity, freakishness, and disorder. The grotesque often includes an element of comic absurdity.

H

Haiku: The shortest form of Japanese poetry, constructed in three lines of five, seven, and five syllables respectively. The message of a *haiku* poem usually centers on some aspect of spirituality and provokes an emotional response in the reader.

Half Rhyme: See *Consonance*

Harlem Renaissance: The Harlem Renaissance of the 1920s is generally considered the first significant movement of black writers and artists in the United States. During this period, new and established black writers published more fiction and poetry than ever before, the first influential black literary journals were established, and black authors and artists received their first widespread recognition and serious critical appraisal. Among the major writers associated with this period are Claude McKay, Jean Toomer, Countee Cullen, Langston Hughes, Arna Bontemps, Nella Larsen, and Zora Neale Hurston.

Hellenism: Imitation of ancient Greek thought or styles. Also, an approach to life that focuses on the growth and development of the intellect. "Hellenism" is sometimes used to refer to the belief that reason can be applied to examine all human experience.

Heptameter: See *Meter*

Hero/Heroine: The principal sympathetic character (male or female) in a literary work. Heroes and heroines typically exhibit admirable traits: idealism, courage, and integrity, for example.

Heroic Couplet: A rhyming couplet written in iambic pentameter (a verse with five iambic feet).

Heroic Line: The meter and length of a line of verse in epic or heroic poetry. This varies by language and time period.

Heroine: See *Hero/Heroine*

Hexameter: See *Meter*

Historical Criticism: The study of a work based on its impact on the world of the time period in which it was written.

Hokku: See *Haiku*

Holocaust: See *Holocaust Literature*

Holocaust Literature: Literature influenced by or written about the Holocaust of World War II. Such literature includes true stories of survival in concentration camps, escape, and life after the war, as well as fictional works and poetry.

Homeric Simile: An elaborate, detailed comparison written as a simile many lines in length.

Horatian Satire: See *Satire*

Humanism: A philosophy that places faith in the dignity of humankind and rejects the medieval perception of the individual as a weak, fallen creature. "Humanists" typically believe in the perfectibility of human nature and view reason and education as the means to that end.

Humors: Mentions of the humors refer to the ancient Greek theory that a person's health and personality were determined by the balance of four basic fluids in the body: blood, phlegm, yellow bile, and black bile. A dominance of any fluid would cause extremes in behavior. An excess of blood created a sanguine person who was joyful, aggressive, and passionate; a phlegmatic person was shy, fearful, and sluggish; too much yellow bile led to a choleric temperament characterized by impatience, anger, bitterness, and stubbornness; and excessive black bile created melancholy, a state of laziness, gluttony, and lack of motivation.

Humours: See *Humors*

Hyperbole: In literary criticism, deliberate exaggeration used to achieve an effect.

I

Iamb: See *Foot*

Idiom: A word construction or verbal expression closely associated with a given language.

Image: A concrete representation of an object or sensory experience. Typically, such a representation helps evoke the feelings associated with the object or experience itself. Images are either "literal" or "figurative." Literal images are especially concrete and involve little or no extension of the obvious meaning of the words used to express them. Figurative images do not follow the literal meaning of the words exactly. Images in literature are usually visual, but the term "image" can also refer to the representation of any sensory experience.

Imagery: The array of images in a literary work. Also, figurative language.

Imagism: An English and American poetry movement that flourished between 1908 and 1917. The Imagists used precise, clearly presented images in their works. They also used common, everyday speech and aimed for conciseness, concrete imagery, and the creation of new rhythms.

In medias res: A Latin term meaning "in the middle of things." It refers to the technique of beginning a story at its midpoint and then using various flashback devices to reveal previous action.

Induction: The process of reaching a conclusion by reasoning from specific premises to form a general premise. Also, an introductory portion of a work of literature, especially a play.

Intentional Fallacy: The belief that judgments of a literary work based solely on an author's stated or implied intentions are false and misleading. Critics who believe in the concept of the intentional fallacy typically argue that the work itself is sufficient matter for interpretation, even though they may concede that an author's statement of purpose can be useful.

Interior Monologue: A narrative technique in which characters' thoughts are revealed in a way that appears to be uncontrolled by the author. The interior monologue typically aims to reveal the inner self of a character. It portrays emotional experiences as they occur at both a conscious and unconscious level. Images are often used to represent sensations or emotions.

Internal Rhyme: Rhyme that occurs within a single line of verse.

Irish Literary Renaissance: A late nineteenth- and early twentieth-century movement in Irish literature. Members of the movement aimed to reduce the influence of British culture in Ireland and create an Irish national literature.

Irony: In literary criticism, the effect of language in which the intended meaning is the opposite of what is stated.

Italian Sonnet: See *Sonnet*

J

Jacobean Age: The period of the reign of James I of England (1603-1625). The early literature of this period reflected the worldview of the Elizabethan Age, but a darker, more cynical attitude steadily grew in the art and literature of the Jacobean Age. This was an important time for English drama and poetry.

Jargon: Language that is used or understood only by a select group of people. Jargon may refer to terminology used in a certain profession, such as computer jargon, or it may refer to any nonsensical language that is not understood by most people.

Journalism: Writing intended for publication in a newspaper or magazine, or for broadcast on a radio or television program featuring news, sports, entertainment, or other timely material.

K

Knickerbocker Group: A somewhat indistinct group of New York writers of the first half of the nineteenth century. Members of the group were linked only by location and a common theme: New York life.

Kunstlerroman: See *Bildungsroman*

L

Lais: See *Lay*

Lake Poets: See *Lake School*

Lake School: These poets all lived in the Lake District of England at the turn of the nineteenth century. As a group, they followed no single "school" of thought or literary practice, although their works were uniformly disparaged by the *Edinburgh Review*.

Lay: A song or simple narrative poem. The form originated in medieval France. Early French *lais* were often based on the Celtic legends and other tales sung by Breton minstrels—thus the name of the "Breton lay." In fourteenth-century England, the term "lay" was used to describe short narratives written in imitation of the Breton lays.

Leitmotiv: See *Motif*

Literal Language: An author uses literal language when he or she writes without exaggerating or embellishing the subject matter and without any tools of figurative language.

Literary Ballad: See *Ballad*

Literature: Literature is broadly defined as any written or spoken material, but the term most often refers to creative works.

Lost Generation: A term first used by Gertrude Stein to describe the post-World War I generation of American writers: men and women haunted by a sense of betrayal and emptiness brought about by the destructiveness of the war.

Lyric Poetry: A poem expressing the subjective feelings and personal emotions of the poet. Such poetry is melodic, since it was originally accompanied by a lyre in recitals. Most Western poetry in the twentieth century may be classified as lyrical.

M

Mannerism: Exaggerated, artificial adherence to a literary manner or style. Also, a popular style of the visual arts of late sixteenth-century Europe that was marked by elongation of the human form and by intentional spatial distortion. Literary works that are self-consciously high-toned and artistic are often said to be "mannered."

Masculine Rhyme: See *Rhyme*

Measure: The foot, verse, or time sequence used in a literary work, especially a poem. Measure is often used somewhat incorrectly as a synonym for meter.

Metaphor: A figure of speech that expresses an idea through the image of another object. Metaphors suggest the essence of the first object by identifying it with certain qualities of the second object.

Metaphysical Conceit: See *Conceit*

Metaphysical Poetry: The body of poetry produced by a group of seventeenth-century English writers called the "Metaphysical Poets." The group includes John Donne and Andrew Marvell. The Metaphysical Poets made use of everyday speech, intellectual analysis, and unique imagery. They aimed to portray the ordinary conflicts and contradictions of life. Their poems often took the form of an argument, and many of them emphasize physical and religious love as well as the fleeting nature of life. Elaborate conceits are typical in metaphysical poetry.

Metaphysical Poets: See *Metaphysical Poetry*

Meter: In literary criticism, the repetition of sound patterns that creates a rhythm in poetry. The patterns are based on the number of syllables and the presence and absence of accents. The unit of rhythm in a line is called a foot. Types of meter are classified according to the number of feet in a line. These are the standard English lines: Monometer, one foot; Dimeter, two feet; Trimeter, three feet; Tetrameter, four feet; Pentameter, five feet; Hexameter, six feet (also called the Alexandrine); Heptameter, seven feet (also called the "Fourteener" when the feet are iambic).

Modernism: Modern literary practices. Also, the principles of a literary school that lasted from roughly the beginning of the twentieth century until the end of World War II. Modernism is defined by its rejection of the literary conventions of the nineteenth century and by its opposition to conventional morality, taste, traditions, and economic values.

Monologue: A composition, written or oral, by a single individual. More specifically, a speech given by a single individual in a drama or other public entertainment. It has no set length, although it is usually several or more lines long.

Monometer: See *Meter*

Mood: The prevailing emotions of a work or of the author in his or her creation of the work. The mood of a work is not always what might be expected based on its subject matter.

Motif: A theme, character type, image, metaphor, or other verbal element that recurs throughout a single work of literature or occurs in a number of different works over a period of time.

Motiv: See *Motif*

Muckrakers: An early twentieth-century group of American writers. Typically, their works exposed the wrongdoings of big business and government in the United States.

Muses: Nine Greek mythological goddesses, the daughters of Zeus and Mnemosyne (Memory). Each muse patronized a specific area of the liberal arts and sciences. Calliope presided over epic poetry, Clio over history, Erato over love poetry, Euterpe over music or lyric poetry, Melpomene over tragedy, Polyhymnia over hymns to the gods, Terpsichore over dance, Thalia over comedy, and Urania over astronomy. Poets and writers traditionally made appeals to the Muses for inspiration in their work.

Myth: An anonymous tale emerging from the traditional beliefs of a culture or social unit. Myths use supernatural explanations for natural phenomena. They may also explain cosmic issues like creation and death. Collections of myths, known as mythologies, are common to all cultures and nations, but the best-known myths belong to the Norse, Roman, and Greek mythologies.

N

Narration: The telling of a series of events, real or invented. A narration may be either a simple narrative, in which the events are recounted chronologically, or a narrative with a plot, in which the account is given in a style reflecting the author's artistic concept of the story. Narration is sometimes used as a synonym for "storyline."

Narrative: A verse or prose accounting of an event or sequence of events, real or invented. The term is also used as an adjective in the sense "method of narration." For example, in literary criticism, the expression "narrative technique" usually refers to the way the author structures and presents his or her story.

Narrative Poetry: A nondramatic poem in which the author tells a story. Such poems may be of any length or level of complexity.

Narrator: The teller of a story. The narrator may be the author or a character in the story through whom the author speaks.

Naturalism: A literary movement of the late nineteenth and early twentieth centuries. The movement's major theorist, French novelist Emile Zola, envisioned a type of fiction that would examine human life with the objectivity of scientific inquiry. The Naturalists typically viewed human beings as either the products of "biological determinism," ruled by hereditary instincts and engaged in an endless struggle for survival, or as the products of "socioeconomic determinism," ruled by social and economic forces beyond their control. In their works, the Naturalists generally ignored the highest levels of society and focused on degradation: poverty, alcoholism, prostitution, insanity, and disease.

Negritude: A literary movement based on the concept of a shared cultural bond on the part of black Africans, wherever they may be in the world. It traces its origins to the former French colonies of Africa and the Caribbean. Negritude poets, novelists, and essayists generally stress four points in their writings: One, black alienation from traditional African culture can lead to feelings of inferiority. Two, European colonialism and Western education should be resisted. Three, black Africans should seek to affirm and define their own identity. Four, African culture can and should be reclaimed. Many Negritude writers also claim that blacks can make unique contributions to the world, based on a heightened appreciation of nature, rhythm, and human emotions—aspects of life they say are not so highly valued in the materialistic and rationalistic West.

Negro Renaissance: See *Harlem Renaissance*

Neoclassical Period: See *Neoclassicism*

Neoclassicism: In literary criticism, this term refers to the revival of the attitudes and styles of expression of classical literature. It is generally used to describe a period in European history beginning in the late seventeenth century and lasting until about 1800. In its purest form, Neoclassicism marked a return to order, proportion, restraint, logic, accuracy, and decorum. In England, where Neoclassicism perhaps was most popular, it reflected the influence of seventeenth-century French writers, especially dramatists. Neoclassical writers typically reacted against the intensity and enthusiasm of the Renaissance period. They wrote works that appealed to the intellect, using elevated language and classical literary forms such as satire and the ode. Neoclassical works were often governed by the classical goal of instruction.

Neoclassicists: See *Neoclassicism*

New Criticism: A movement in literary criticism, dating from the late 1920s, that stressed close textual analysis in the interpretation of works of literature. The New Critics saw little merit in historical and biographical analysis. Rather, they aimed to examine the text alone, free from the question of how external events—biographical or otherwise—may have helped shape it.

New Journalism: A type of writing in which the journalist presents factual information in a form usually used in fiction. New journalism emphasizes description, narration, and character development to bring readers closer to the human element of the story, and is often used in personality profiles and in-depth feature articles. It is not compatible with "straight" or "hard" newswriting, which is generally composed in a brief, fact-based style.

New Journalists: See *New Journalism*

New Negro Movement: See *Harlem Renaissance*

Noble Savage: The idea that primitive man is noble and good but becomes evil and corrupted as he becomes civilized. The concept of the noble savage originated in the Renaissance period but is more closely identified with such later writers as Jean-Jacques Rousseau and Aphra Behn.

O

Objective Correlative: An outward set of objects, a situation, or a chain of events corresponding to an inward experience and evoking this experience in the reader. The term frequently appears in modern criticism in discussions of authors' intended effects on the emotional responses of readers.

Objectivity: A quality in writing characterized by the absence of the author's opinion or feeling about the subject matter. Objectivity is an important factor in criticism.

Occasional Verse: poetry written on the occasion of a significant historical or personal event. *Vers de societe* is sometimes called occasional verse although it is of a less serious nature.

Octave: A poem or stanza composed of eight lines. The term octave most often represents the first eight lines of a Petrarchan sonnet.

Ode: Name given to an extended lyric poem characterized by exalted emotion and dignified style. An ode usually concerns a single, serious theme. Most odes, but not all, are addressed to an object or individual. Odes are distinguished from other lyric poetic forms by their complex rhythmic and stanzaic patterns.

Oedipus Complex: A son's amorous obsession with his mother. The phrase is derived from the story of the ancient Theban hero Oedipus, who un-

knowingly killed his father and married his mother.

Omniscience: See *Point of View*

Onomatopoeia: The use of words whose sounds express or suggest their meaning. In its simplest sense, onomatopoeia may be represented by words that mimic the sounds they denote such as "hiss" or "meow." At a more subtle level, the pattern and rhythm of sounds and rhymes of a line or poem may be onomatopoeic.

Oral Tradition: See *Oral Transmission*

Oral Transmission: A process by which songs, ballads, folklore, and other material are transmitted by word of mouth. The tradition of oral transmission predates the written record systems of literate society. Oral transmission preserves material sometimes over generations, although often with variations. Memory plays a large part in the recitation and preservation of orally transmitted material.

Ottava Rima: An eight-line stanza of poetry composed in iambic pentameter (a five-foot line in which each foot consists of an unaccented syllable followed by an accented syllable), following the abababcc rhyme scheme.

Oxymoron: A phrase combining two contradictory terms. Oxymorons may be intentional or unintentional.

P

Pantheism: The idea that all things are both a manifestation or revelation of God and a part of God at the same time. Pantheism was a common attitude in the early societies of Egypt, India, and Greece—the term derives from the Greek *pan* meaning "all" and *theos* meaning "deity." It later became a significant part of the Christian faith.

Parable: A story intended to teach a moral lesson or answer an ethical question.

Paradox: A statement that appears illogical or contradictory at first, but may actually point to an underlying truth.

Parallelism: A method of comparison of two ideas in which each is developed in the same grammatical structure.

Parnassianism: A mid nineteenth-century movement in French literature. Followers of the movement stressed adherence to well-defined artistic forms as a reaction against the often chaotic expression of the artist's ego that dominated the work of the Romantics. The Parnassians also rejected the moral, ethical, and social themes exhibited in the works of French Romantics such as Victor Hugo. The aesthetic doctrines of the Parnassians strongly influenced the later symbolist and decadent movements.

Parody: In literary criticism, this term refers to an imitation of a serious literary work or the signature style of a particular author in a ridiculous manner. A typical parody adopts the style of the original and applies it to an inappropriate subject for humorous effect. Parody is a form of satire and could be considered the literary equivalent of a caricature or cartoon.

Pastoral: A term derived from the Latin word "pastor," meaning shepherd. A pastoral is a literary composition on a rural theme. The conventions of the pastoral were originated by the third-century Greek poet Theocritus, who wrote about the experiences, love affairs, and pastimes of Sicilian shepherds. In a pastoral, characters and language of a courtly nature are often placed in a simple setting. The term pastoral is also used to classify dramas, elegies, and lyrics that exhibit the use of country settings and shepherd characters.

Pathetic Fallacy: A term coined by English critic John Ruskin to identify writing that falsely endows nonhuman things with human intentions and feelings, such as "angry clouds" and "sad trees."

Pen Name: See *Pseudonym*

Pentameter: See *Meter*

Persona: A Latin term meaning "mask." *Personae* are the characters in a fictional work of literature. The *persona* generally functions as a mask through which the author tells a story in a voice other than his or her own. A *persona* is usually either a character in a story who acts as a narrator or an "implied author," a voice created by the author to act as the narrator for himself or herself.

Personae: See *Persona*

Personal Point of View: See *Point of View*

Personification: A figure of speech that gives human qualities to abstract ideas, animals, and inanimate objects.

Petrarchan Sonnet: See *Sonnet*

Phenomenology: A method of literary criticism based on the belief that things have no existence outside of human consciousness or awareness. Proponents of this theory believe that art is a process that takes place in the mind of the observer as he or she contemplates an object rather than a quality of the object itself.

Plagiarism: Claiming another person's written material as one's own. Plagiarism can take the form of direct, word-for-word copying or the theft of the substance or idea of the work.

Platonic Criticism: A form of criticism that stresses an artistic work's usefulness as an agent of social engineering rather than any quality or value of the work itself.

Platonism: The embracing of the doctrines of the philosopher Plato, popular among the poets of the Renaissance and the Romantic period. Platonism is more flexible than Aristotelian Criticism and places more emphasis on the supernatural and unknown aspects of life.

Plot: In literary criticism, this term refers to the pattern of events in a narrative or drama. In its simplest sense, the plot guides the author in composing the work and helps the reader follow the work. Typically, plots exhibit causality and unity and have a beginning, a middle, and an end. Sometimes, however, a plot may consist of a series of disconnected events, in which case it is known as an "episodic plot."

Poem: In its broadest sense, a composition utilizing rhyme, meter, concrete detail, and expressive language to create a literary experience with emotional and aesthetic appeal.

Poet: An author who writes poetry or verse. The term is also used to refer to an artist or writer who has an exceptional gift for expression, imagination, and energy in the making of art in any form.

Poete maudit: A term derived from Paul Verlaine's *Les poetes maudits* (*The Accursed Poets*), a collection of essays on the French symbolist writers Stephane Mallarme, Arthur Rimbaud, and Tristan Corbiere. In the sense intended by Verlaine, the poet is "accursed" for choosing to explore extremes of human experience outside of middle-class society.

Poetic Fallacy: See *Pathetic Fallacy*

Poetic Justice: An outcome in a literary work, not necessarily a poem, in which the good are rewarded and the evil are punished, especially in ways that particularly fit their virtues or crimes.

Poetic License: Distortions of fact and literary convention made by a writer—not always a poet—for the sake of the effect gained. Poetic license is closely related to the concept of "artistic freedom."

Poetics: This term has two closely related meanings. It denotes (1) an aesthetic theory in literary criticism about the essence of poetry or (2) rules prescribing the proper methods, content, style, or diction of poetry. The term poetics may also refer to theories about literature in general, not just poetry.

Poetry: In its broadest sense, writing that aims to present ideas and evoke an emotional experience in the reader through the use of meter, imagery, connotative and concrete words, and a carefully constructed structure based on rhythmic patterns. Poetry typically relies on words and expressions that have several layers of meaning. It also makes use of the effects of regular rhythm on the ear and may make a strong appeal to the senses through the use of imagery.

Point of View: The narrative perspective from which a literary work is presented to the reader. There are four traditional points of view. The "third person omniscient" gives the reader a "godlike" perspective, unrestricted by time or place, from which to see actions and look into the minds of characters. This allows the author to comment openly on characters and events in the work. The "third person" point of view presents the events of the story from outside of any single character's perception, much like the omniscient point of view, but the reader must understand the action as it takes place and without any special insight into characters' minds or motivations. The "first person" or "personal" point of view relates events as they are perceived by a single character. The main character "tells" the story and may offer opinions about the action and characters which differ from those of the author. Much less common than omniscient, third person, and first person is the "second person" point of view, wherein the author tells the story as if it is happening to the reader.

Polemic: A work in which the author takes a stand on a controversial subject, such as abortion or religion. Such works are often extremely argumentative or provocative.

Pornography: Writing intended to provoke feelings of lust in the reader. Such works are often condemned by critics and teachers, but those which can be shown to have literary value are viewed less harshly.

Post-Aesthetic Movement: An artistic response made by African Americans to the black aesthetic movement of the 1960s and early '70s. Writers since that time have adopted a somewhat different tone in their work, with less emphasis placed on the disparity between black and white in the United States. In the words of post-aesthetic authors such as Toni Morrison, John Edgar Wideman, and Kristin Hunter, African Americans are portrayed as looking inward for answers to their own questions, rather than always looking to the outside world.

Postmodernism: Writing from the 1960s forward characterized by experimentation and continuing to apply some of the fundamentals of modernism, which included existentialism and alienation. Postmodernists have gone a step further in the rejection of tradition begun with the modernists by also rejecting traditional forms, preferring the anti-novel over the novel and the anti-hero over the hero.

Pre-Raphaelites: A circle of writers and artists in mid nineteenth-century England. Valuing the pre-Renaissance artistic qualities of religious symbolism, lavish pictorialism, and natural sensuousness, the Pre-Raphaelites cultivated a sense of mystery and melancholy that influenced later writers associated with the Symbolist and Decadent movements.

Primitivism: The belief that primitive peoples were nobler and less flawed than civilized peoples because they had not been subjected to the tainting influence of society.

Projective Verse: A form of free verse in which the poet's breathing pattern determines the lines of the poem. Poets who advocate projective verse are against all formal structures in writing, including meter and form.

Prologue: An introductory section of a literary work. It often contains information establishing the situation of the characters or presents information about the setting, time period, or action. In drama, the prologue is spoken by a chorus or by one of the principal characters.

Prose: A literary medium that attempts to mirror the language of everyday speech. It is distinguished from poetry by its use of unmetered, unrhymed language consisting of logically related sentences. Prose is usually grouped into paragraphs that form a cohesive whole such as an essay or a novel.

Prosopopoeia: See *Personification*

Protagonist: The central character of a story who serves as a focus for its themes and incidents and as the principal rationale for its development. The protagonist is sometimes referred to in discussions of modern literature as the hero or anti-hero.

Proverb: A brief, sage saying that expresses a truth about life in a striking manner.

Pseudonym: A name assumed by a writer, most often intended to prevent his or her identification as the author of a work. Two or more authors may work together under one pseudonym, or an author may use a different name for each genre he or she publishes in. Some publishing companies maintain "house pseudonyms," under which any number of authors may write installations in a series. Some authors also choose a pseudonym over their real names the way an actor may use a stage name.

Pun: A play on words that have similar sounds but different meanings.

Pure Poetry: poetry written without instructional intent or moral purpose that aims only to please a reader by its imagery or musical flow. The term pure poetry is used as the antonym of the term "didacticism."

Q

Quatrain: A four-line stanza of a poem or an entire poem consisting of four lines.

R

Realism: A nineteenth-century European literary movement that sought to portray familiar characters, situations, and settings in a realistic manner. This was done primarily by using an objective narrative point of view and through the buildup of accurate detail. The standard for success of any realistic work depends on how faithfully it transfers common experience into fictional forms. The realistic method may be altered or extended, as in stream of consciousness writing, to record highly subjective experience.

Refrain: A phrase repeated at intervals throughout a poem. A refrain may appear at the end of each stanza or at less regular intervals. It may be altered slightly at each appearance.

Renaissance: The period in European history that marked the end of the Middle Ages. It began in Italy in the late fourteenth century. In broad terms, it is usually seen as spanning the fourteenth, fifteenth, and sixteenth centuries, although it did not reach Great Britain, for example, until the 1480s or so. The Renaissance saw an awakening in almost every sphere of human activity, especially science, philosophy, and the arts. The period is best defined by the emergence of a general philosophy that emphasized the importance of the intellect, the individual, and world affairs. It contrasts strongly with the medieval worldview, characterized by the dominant concerns of faith, the social collective, and spiritual salvation.

Repartee: Conversation featuring snappy retorts and witticisms.

Restoration: See *Restoration Age*

Restoration Age: A period in English literature beginning with the crowning of Charles II in 1660 and running to about 1700. The era, which was characterized by a reaction against Puritanism, was the first great age of the comedy of manners. The finest literature of the era is typically witty and urbane, and often lewd.

Rhetoric: In literary criticism, this term denotes the art of ethical persuasion. In its strictest sense, rhetoric adheres to various principles developed since classical times for arranging facts and ideas in a clear, persuasive, appealing manner. The term is also used to refer to effective prose in general and theories of or methods for composing effective prose.

Rhetorical Question: A question intended to provoke thought, but not an expressed answer, in the reader. It is most commonly used in oratory and other persuasive genres.

Rhyme: When used as a noun in literary criticism, this term generally refers to a poem in which words sound identical or very similar and appear in parallel positions in two or more lines. Rhymes are classified into different types according to where they fall in a line or stanza or according to the degree of similarity they exhibit in their spellings and sounds. Some major types of rhyme are "masculine" rhyme, "feminine" rhyme, and "triple" rhyme. In a masculine rhyme, the rhyming sound falls in a single accented syllable, as with "heat" and "eat." Feminine rhyme is a rhyme of two syllables, one stressed and one unstressed, as with "merry" and "tarry." Triple rhyme matches the sound of the accented syllable and the two unaccented syllables that follow: "narrative" and "declarative."

Rhyme Royal: A stanza of seven lines composed in iambic pentameter and rhymed *ababbcc*. The name is said to be a tribute to King James I of Scotland, who made much use of the form in his poetry.

Rhyme Scheme: See *Rhyme*

Rhythm: A regular pattern of sound, time intervals, or events occurring in writing, most often and most discernably in poetry. Regular, reliable rhythm is known to be soothing to humans, while interrupted, unpredictable, or rapidly changing rhythm is disturbing. These effects are known to authors, who use them to produce a desired reaction in the reader.

Rococo: A style of European architecture that flourished in the eighteenth century, especially in

France. The most notable features of *rococo* are its extensive use of ornamentation and its themes of lightness, gaiety, and intimacy. In literary criticism, the term is often used disparagingly to refer to a decadent or over-ornamental style.

Romance:

Romantic Age: See *Romanticism*

Romanticism: This term has two widely accepted meanings. In historical criticism, it refers to a European intellectual and artistic movement of the late eighteenth and early nineteenth centuries that sought greater freedom of personal expression than that allowed by the strict rules of literary form and logic of the eighteenth-century neoclassicists. The Romantics preferred emotional and imaginative expression to rational analysis. They considered the individual to be at the center of all experience and so placed him or her at the center of their art. The Romantics believed that the creative imagination reveals nobler truths—unique feelings and attitudes—than those that could be discovered by logic or by scientific examination. Both the natural world and the state of childhood were important sources for revelations of "eternal truths." "Romanticism" is also used as a general term to refer to a type of sensibility found in all periods of literary history and usually considered to be in opposition to the principles of classicism. In this sense, Romanticism signifies any work or philosophy in which the exotic or dreamlike figure strongly, or that is devoted to individualistic expression, self-analysis, or a pursuit of a higher realm of knowledge than can be discovered by human reason.

Romantics: See *Romanticism*

Russian Symbolism: A Russian poetic movement, derived from French symbolism, that flourished between 1894 and 1910. While some Russian Symbolists continued in the French tradition, stressing aestheticism and the importance of suggestion above didactic intent, others saw their craft as a form of mystical worship, and themselves as mediators between the supernatural and the mundane.

S

Satire: A work that uses ridicule, humor, and wit to criticize and provoke change in human nature and institutions. There are two major types of satire: "formal" or "direct" satire speaks directly to the reader or to a character in the work; "indirect" satire relies upon the ridiculous behavior of its characters to make its point. Formal satire is further divided into two manners: the "Horatian," which

ridicules gently, and the "Juvenalian," which derides its subjects harshly and bitterly.

Scansion: The analysis or "scanning" of a poem to determine its meter and often its rhyme scheme. The most common system of scansion uses accents (slanted lines drawn above syllables) to show stressed syllables, breves (curved lines drawn above syllables) to show unstressed syllables, and vertical lines to separate each foot.

Second Person: See *Point of View*

Semiotics: The study of how literary forms and conventions affect the meaning of language.

Sestet: Any six-line poem or stanza.

Setting: The time, place, and culture in which the action of a narrative takes place. The elements of setting may include geographic location, characters' physical and mental environments, prevailing cultural attitudes, or the historical time in which the action takes place.

Shakespearean Sonnet: See *Sonnet*

Signifying Monkey: A popular trickster figure in black folklore, with hundreds of tales about this character documented since the 19th century.

Simile: A comparison, usually using "like" or "as", of two essentially dissimilar things, as in "coffee as cold as ice" or "He sounded like a broken record."

Slang: A type of informal verbal communication that is generally unacceptable for formal writing. Slang words and phrases are often colorful exaggerations used to emphasize the speaker's point; they may also be shortened versions of an often-used word or phrase.

Slant Rhyme: See *Consonance*

Slave Narrative: Autobiographical accounts of American slave life as told by escaped slaves. These works first appeared during the abolition movement of the 1830s through the 1850s.

Social Realism: See *Socialist Realism*

Socialist Realism: The Socialist Realism school of literary theory was proposed by Maxim Gorky and established as a dogma by the first Soviet Congress of Writers. It demanded adherence to a communist worldview in works of literature. Its doctrines required an objective viewpoint comprehensible to the working classes and themes of social struggle featuring strong proletarian heroes.

Soliloquy: A monologue in a drama used to give the audience information and to develop the speaker's character. It is typically a projection of the speaker's innermost thoughts. Usually delivered while the speaker is alone on stage, a soliloquy is intended to present an illusion of unspoken reflection.

Sonnet: A fourteen-line poem, usually composed in iambic pentameter, employing one of several rhyme schemes. There are three major types of sonnets, upon which all other variations of the form are based: the "Petrarchan" or "Italian" sonnet, the "Shakespearean" or "English" sonnet, and the "Spenserian" sonnet. A Petrarchan sonnet consists of an octave rhymed *abbaabba* and a "sestet" rhymed either *cdecde, cdccdc,* or *cdedce.* The octave poses a question or problem, relates a narrative, or puts forth a proposition; the sestet presents a solution to the problem, comments upon the narrative, or applies the proposition put forth in the octave. The Shakespearean sonnet is divided into three quatrains and a couplet rhymed *abab cdcd efef gg.* The couplet provides an epigrammatic comment on the narrative or problem put forth in the quatrains. The Spenserian sonnet uses three quatrains and a couplet like the Shakespearean, but links their three rhyme schemes in this way: *abab bcbc cdcd ee.* The Spenserian sonnet develops its theme in two parts like the Petrarchan, its final six lines resolving a problem, analyzing a narrative, or applying a proposition put forth in its first eight lines.

Spenserian Sonnet: See *Sonnet*

Spenserian Stanza: A nine-line stanza having eight verses in iambic pentameter, its ninth verse in iambic hexameter, and the rhyme scheme ababbcbcc.

Spondee: In poetry meter, a foot consisting of two long or stressed syllables occurring together. This form is quite rare in English verse, and is usually composed of two monosyllabic words.

Sprung Rhythm: Versification using a specific number of accented syllables per line but disregarding the number of unaccented syllables that fall in each line, producing an irregular rhythm in the poem.

Stanza: A subdivision of a poem consisting of lines grouped together, often in recurring patterns of rhyme, line length, and meter. Stanzas may also serve as units of thought in a poem much like paragraphs in prose.

Stereotype: A stereotype was originally the name for a duplication made during the printing process; this led to its modern definition as a person or thing that is (or is assumed to be) the same as all others of its type.

Stream of Consciousness: A narrative technique for rendering the inward experience of a character. This technique is designed to give the impression of an ever-changing series of thoughts, emotions, images, and memories in the spontaneous and seemingly illogical order that they occur in life.

Structuralism: A twentieth-century movement in literary criticism that examines how literary texts arrive at their meanings, rather than the meanings themselves. There are two major types of structuralist analysis: one examines the way patterns of linguistic structures unify a specific text and emphasize certain elements of that text, and the other interprets the way literary forms and conventions affect the meaning of language itself.

Structure: The form taken by a piece of literature. The structure may be made obvious for ease of understanding, as in nonfiction works, or may be obscured for artistic purposes, as in some poetry or seemingly "unstructured" prose.

Sturm und Drang: A German term meaning "storm and stress." It refers to a German literary movement of the 1770s and 1780s that reacted against the order and rationalism of the enlightenment, focusing instead on the intense experience of extraordinary individuals.

Style: A writer's distinctive manner of arranging words to suit his or her ideas and purpose in writing. The unique imprint of the author's personality upon his or her writing, style is the product of an author's way of arranging ideas and his or her use of diction, different sentence structures, rhythm, figures of speech, rhetorical principles, and other elements of composition.

Subject: The person, event, or theme at the center of a work of literature. A work may have one or more subjects of each type, with shorter works tending to have fewer and longer works tending to have more.

Subjectivity: Writing that expresses the author's personal feelings about his subject, and which may or may not include factual information about the subject.

Surrealism: A term introduced to criticism by Guillaume Apollinaire and later adopted by Andre Breton. It refers to a French literary and artistic movement founded in the 1920s. The Surrealists sought to express unconscious thoughts and feelings in their works. The best-known technique used for achieving this aim was automatic writing—transcriptions of spontaneous outpourings from the unconscious. The Surrealists proposed to unify the contrary levels of conscious and unconscious, dream and reality, objectivity and subjectivity into a new level of "super-realism."

Suspense: A literary device in which the author maintains the audience's attention through the buildup of events, the outcome of which will soon be revealed.

Syllogism: A method of presenting a logical argument. In its most basic form, the syllogism consists of a major premise, a minor premise, and a conclusion.

Symbol: Something that suggests or stands for something else without losing its original identity. In literature, symbols combine their literal meaning with the suggestion of an abstract concept. Literary symbols are of two types: those that carry complex associations of meaning no matter what their contexts, and those that derive their suggestive meaning from their functions in specific literary works.

Symbolism: This term has two widely accepted meanings. In historical criticism, it denotes an early modernist literary movement initiated in France during the nineteenth century that reacted against the prevailing standards of realism. Writers in this movement aimed to evoke, indirectly and symbolically, an order of being beyond the material world of the five senses. Poetic expression of personal emotion figured strongly in the movement, typically by means of a private set of symbols uniquely identifiable with the individual poet. The principal aim of the Symbolists was to express in words the highly complex feelings that grew out of everyday contact with the world. In a broader sense, the term "symbolism" refers to the use of one object to represent another.

Symbolist: See *Symbolism*

Symbolist Movement: See *Symbolism*

Sympathetic Fallacy: See *Affective Fallacy*

T

Tanka: A form of Japanese poetry similar to *haiku*. A *tanka* is five lines long, with the lines containing five, seven, five, seven, and seven syllables respectively.

Terza Rima: A three-line stanza form in poetry in which the rhymes are made on the last word of each line in the following manner: the first and third lines of the first stanza, then the second line of the first stanza and the first and third lines of the second stanza, and so on with the middle line of any

stanza rhyming with the first and third lines of the following stanza.

Tetrameter: See *Meter*

Textual Criticism: A branch of literary criticism that seeks to establish the authoritative text of a literary work. Textual critics typically compare all known manuscripts or printings of a single work in order to assess the meanings of differences and revisions. This procedure allows them to arrive at a definitive version that (supposedly) corresponds to the author's original intention.

Theme: The main point of a work of literature. The term is used interchangeably with thesis.

Thesis: A thesis is both an essay and the point argued in the essay. Thesis novels and thesis plays share the quality of containing a thesis which is supported through the action of the story.

Third Person: See *Point of View*

Tone: The author's attitude toward his or her audience may be deduced from the tone of the work. A formal tone may create distance or convey politeness, while an informal tone may encourage a friendly, intimate, or intrusive feeling in the reader. The author's attitude toward his or her subject matter may also be deduced from the tone of the words he or she uses in discussing it.

Tragedy: A drama in prose or poetry about a noble, courageous hero of excellent character who, because of some tragic character flaw or *hamartia*, brings ruin upon him- or herself. Tragedy treats its subjects in a dignified and serious manner, using poetic language to help evoke pity and fear and bring about catharsis, a purging of these emotions. The tragic form was practiced extensively by the ancient Greeks. In the Middle Ages, when classical works were virtually unknown, tragedy came to denote any works about the fall of persons from exalted to low conditions due to any reason: fate, vice, weakness, etc. According to the classical definition of tragedy, such works present the "pathetic"—that which evokes pity—rather than the tragic. The classical form of tragedy was revived in the sixteenth century; it flourished especially on the Elizabethan stage. In modern times, dramatists have attempted to adapt the form to the needs of modern society by drawing their heroes from the ranks of ordinary men and women and defining the nobility of these heroes in terms of spirit rather than exalted social standing.

Tragic Flaw: In a tragedy, the quality within the hero or heroine which leads to his or her downfall.

Transcendentalism: An American philosophical and religious movement, based in New England from around 1835 until the Civil War. Transcendentalism was a form of American romanticism that had its roots abroad in the works of Thomas Carlyle, Samuel Coleridge, and Johann Wolfgang von Goethe. The Transcendentalists stressed the importance of intuition and subjective experience in communication with God. They rejected religious dogma and texts in favor of mysticism and scientific naturalism. They pursued truths that lie beyond the "colorless" realms perceived by reason and the senses and were active social reformers in public education, women's rights, and the abolition of slavery.

Trickster: A character or figure common in Native American and African literature who uses his ingenuity to defeat enemies and escape difficult situations. Tricksters are most often animals, such as the spider, hare, or coyote, although they may take the form of humans as well.

Trimeter: See *Meter*

Triple Rhyme: See *Rhyme*

Trochee: See *Foot*

U

Understatement: See *Irony*

Unities: Strict rules of dramatic structure, formulated by Italian and French critics of the Renaissance and based loosely on the principles of drama discussed by Aristotle in his *Poetics*. Foremost among these rules were the three unities of action, time, and place that compelled a dramatist to: (1) construct a single plot with a beginning, middle, and end that details the causal relationships of action and character; (2) restrict the action to the events of a single day; and (3) limit the scene to a single place or city. The unities were observed faithfully by continental European writers until the Romantic Age, but they were never regularly observed in English drama. Modern dramatists are typically more concerned with a unity of impression or emotional effect than with any of the classical unities.

Urban Realism: A branch of realist writing that attempts to accurately reflect the often harsh facts of modern urban existence.

Utopia: A fictional perfect place, such as "paradise" or "heaven."

Utopian: See *Utopia*

Utopianism: See *Utopia*

V

Verisimilitude: Literally, the appearance of truth. In literary criticism, the term refers to aspects of a work of literature that seem true to the reader.

Vers de societe: See *Occasional Verse*

Vers libre: See *Free Verse*

Verse: A line of metered language, a line of a poem, or any work written in verse.

Versification: The writing of verse. Versification may also refer to the meter, rhyme, and other mechanical components of a poem.

Victorian: Refers broadly to the reign of Queen Victoria of England (1837-1901) and to anything with qualities typical of that era. For example, the qualities of smug narrowmindedness, bourgeois materialism, faith in social progress, and priggish morality are often considered Victorian. This stereotype is contradicted by such dramatic intellectual developments as the theories of Charles Darwin, Karl Marx, and Sigmund Freud (which stirred strong debates in England) and the critical attitudes of serious Victorian writers like Charles Dickens and George Eliot. In literature, the Victorian Period was the great age of the English novel, and the latter part of the era saw the rise of movements such as decadence and symbolism.

Victorian Age: See *Victorian*

Victorian Period: See *Victorian*

W

Weltanschauung: A German term referring to a person's worldview or philosophy.

Weltschmerz: A German term meaning "world pain." It describes a sense of anguish about the nature of existence, usually associated with a melancholy, pessimistic attitude.

Z

Zarzuela: A type of Spanish operetta.

Zeitgeist: A German term meaning "spirit of the time." It refers to the moral and intellectual trends of a given era.

Cumulative Author/Title Index

Cumulative Author/Title Index

Cumulative
Nationality/Ethnicity Index

Shine, Perishing Republic: V4
Johnson, James Weldon
  The Creation: V1
Komunyakaa, Yusef
  Facing It: V5
Longfellow, Henry Wadsworth
  Paul Revere's Ride: V2
Lowell, Robert
  *The Quaker Graveyard in
    Nantucket*: V6
MacLeish, Archibald
  Ars Poetica: V5
McElroy, Colleen
  A Pièd: V3
McKay, Claude
  The Tropics in New York: V4
Merriam, Eve
  Onomatopoeia: V6
Merwin, W. S.
  Leviathan: V5
Millay, Edna St. Vincent
  *The Courage that My Mother
    Had*: V3
Momaday, N. Scott
  Angle of Geese: V2
Ortiz, Simon
  Hunger in New York City: V4
Plath, Sylvia
  Mirror: V1
Poe, Edgar Allan
  The Bells: V3
  The Raven: V1
Pound, Ezra
  In a Station of the Metro: V2
Randall, Dudley
  Ballad of Birmingham: V5
Reed, Ishmael
  Beware: Do Not Read This Poem:
    V6
Revard, Carter
  Birch Canoe: V5
Robinson, E. A.
  Richard Cory: V4
Roethke, Theodore
  My Papa's Waltz: V3
Sandburg, Carl
  Chicago: V3
  Cool Tombs: V6
Sexton, Anne
  Oysters: V4
Shapiro, Karl
  Auto Wreck: V3
Song, Cathy
  Lost Sister: V5
Stafford, William
  Fifteen: V2
Thayer, Ernest Lawrence
  Casey at the Bat: V5
Whitman, Walt
  I Hear America Singing: V3
  O Captain! My Captain!: V2
Williams, William Carlos
  Queen-Ann's-Lace: V6
  The Red Wheelbarrow: V1

Canadian

McCrae, John
  In Flanders Fields: V5
Purdy, Al
  Lament for the Dorsets: V5

Cherokee

Momaday, N. Scott
  Angle of Geese: V2

English

Arnold, Matthew
  Dover Beach: V2
Auden, W. H.
  As I Walked Out One Evening: V4
  Musée des Beaux Arts: V1
  The Unknown Citizen: V3
Blake, William
  The Tyger: V2
Bradstreet, Anne
  To My Dear and Loving Husband:
    V6
Browning, Elizabeth Barrett
  Sonnet 43: V2
Browning, Robert
  My Last Duchess: V1
Byron, Lord
  *The Destruction of
    Sennacherib*: V1
Coleridge, Samuel Taylor
  Kubla Khan: V5
  The Rime of the Ancient Mariner:
    V4
Donne, John
  Holy Sonnet 10: V2
Eliot, T. S.
  *The Love Song of J. Alfred
    Prufrock*: V1
Hardy, Thomas
  *Ah, Are You Digging on My
    Grave?*: V4
  The Man He Killed: V3
Housman, A. E.
  When I Was One-and-Twenty: V4
Hughes, Ted
  Hawk Roosting: V4
Keats, John
  Ode on a Grecian Urn: V1
  Ode to a Nightingale: V3
  *When I Have Fears that I May
    Cease to Be*: V2
Larkin, Philip
  High Windows: V3
  Toads: V4
Lawrence, D. H.
  Piano: V6
Marvell, Andrew
  To His Coy Mistress: V5
Masefield, John
  Cargoes: V5
Milton, John
  [On His Blindness] Sonnet 16: V3

Noyes, Alfred
  The Highwayman: V4
Shakespeare, William
  Sonnet 18: V2
  Sonnet 30: V4
  Sonnet 55: V5
  Sonnet 116: V3
  Sonnet 130: V1
Shelley, Percy Bysshe
  Ode to the West Wind: V2
Smith, Stevie
  Not Waving but Drowning: V3
Tennyson, Alfred, Lord
  *The Charge of the Light
    Brigade*: V1
  Tears, Idle Tears: V4
  Ulysses: V2
Williams, William Carlos
  Queen-Ann's-Lace: V6
  The Red Wheelbarrow: V1
Wordsworth, William
  *Lines Composed a Few Miles
    above Tintern Abbey*: V2
Yeats, W. B.
  Easter 1916: V5
  *An Irish Airman Forsees His
    Death*: V1
  Sailing to Byzantium: V2

German

Roethke, Theodore
  My Papa's Waltz: V3

Irish

Heaney, Seamus
  Digging: V5
  Midnight: V2
Yeats, William Butler
  Easter 1916: V5
  *An Irish Airman Foresees His
    Death*: V1
  Sailing to Byzantium: V2

Jamaican

McKay, Claude
  The Tropics in New York: V4

Japanese

Bashō, Matsuo
  Falling Upon Earth: V2

Jewish

Shapiro, Karl
  Auto Wreck: V3

Kiowa

Momaday, N. Scott
  Angle of Geese: V2

Native American

Momaday, N. Scott
Angle of Geese: V2
Ortiz, Simon
Hunger in New York City: V4
Revard, Carter
Birch Canoe: V5

Osage

Revard, Carter
Birch Canoe: V5

Russian

Merriam, Eve
Onomatopoeia: V6

Shapiro, Karl
Auto Wreck: V3

Scottish

Byron, Lord
*The Destruction of
Sennacherib*: V1

Spanish

Williams, William Carlos
The Red Wheelbarrow: V1

Swedish

Sandburg, Carl
Chicago: V3

Welsh

Thomas, Dylan
*Do Not Go Gentle into that Good
Night*: V1
Fern Hill: V3

West Indian

Walcott, Derek
A Far Cry from Africa: V6

Subject/Theme Index